Legal Guidebook in Mental Health

Ronald Jay Cohen
William E. Mariano

THE FREE PRESS
A Division of Macmillan Publishing Co., Inc.
NEW YORK

Collier Macmillan Publishers
LONDON

The Free Press
A Division of Macmillan Publishing Co., Inc.
866 Third Avenue, New York, N.Y. 10022

Collier Macmillan Canada, Inc.

Library of Congress Catalog Card Number: 81-71323

Printed in the United States of America

printing number

1 2 3 4 5 6 7 8 9 10

Library of Congress Cataloging in Publication Data

Cohen, Ronald Jay.
Legal guidebook in mental health.

Bibliography: p.
Includes index.
1. Psychotherapists—Malpractice—United States.
2. Psychotherapists—Legal status, laws, etc.—United States. I. Mariano, William E. II. Title. [DNLM: 1. Mental health—Legislation. WM 33.1 C678L]
KF2910.P753C629 346.7303'32 81-71323
ISBN 0-02-905740-X 347.306332 AACR2

Contents

Foreword

THIS IS a valuable book. It will prove its value to the reader in the following three ways:

1. by its comprehensive coverage of the legal concepts and supporting materials which are important to mental health professionals, law students, and practicing attorneys;
2. by its timeliness in being available when the courses followed by litigation-minded mental health service consumers and liability-vulnerable mental health service providers are colliding in courtrooms in all jurisdictions; and
3. by its literal money value to each service provider who avoids a law suit and its expense, as a benefit of familiarity with the contents of this *Guidebook*.

We cannot put a dollar sign on the cost of psychological and physical stress engendered by receipt of a summons and complaint alleging one or more of the causes of action fully described and defined in these pages by Cohen and Mariano. Let each prospective defendant—and today that includes every practicing mental health professional—make his or her own estimate of that price; then, read on and learn a sorely needed new skill regarding potential legal actions: how to practice prevention.

This *Guidebook* was designed by Cohen and Mariano to provide an all-in-one reference work for professionals in every discipline related to mental health and mental health law. It succeeds admirably, in that it is a guide to proper practice, a hornbook of applicable legal principles, a treatise on the pertinent laws, and a compendium of both classical and current landmark cases with full citations and transcripts of the relevant judicial opinions—all enriched by a goldmine of bibliographical references and resource documents. These commendable characteristics create a valuable text for teachers and students of mental health law, professional ethics, and principles of practice, as well as a useful desk book for practicing attorneys. The authors, however, have exceeded these specifications on behalf of a much broader additional audience for their presentation: psychiatrists, psychologists, social workers, psychiatric nurses, persons from other specialties working in the mental health field, and, of course, mental health administrators.

Professionals in the practice of mental health are laymen in the law. With the needs of these readers in mind, Cohen and Mariano have augmented their legal scholarship with original commentary and interpretative annotations which are written in a style characterized by flowing logic and engaging readability. This welcome (and rare) dual virtue is amplified by the authors' selection of engrossing examples to vividly illuminate their analysis of legal principles and case law. If you start by browsing in this book, you will stay to read, and we suggest that you don't skip the sometimes fascinating and usually important footnotes.

Ron Cohen is a psychologist; Bill Mariano is an attorney. Both have extensive experience in the specialized field where psychotherapy, law, and regulations interact. Each has written earlier works on this subject (e.g., Cohen, 1979; Jurow and Mariano, 1972), and the *Guidebook* is their current joint capstone endeavor. All of us in mental health have needed this very book; now, we have it.

It seems likely to me that, as one of its many values, Cohen and Mariano's book will stimulate systematic discussion and action on issues of ethics and practice, by state and national associations in all the mental health professions. I expect that it will also be found in the hands of legislators and regulatory agency officials as well. And, I venture still another prediction that, after they have read the *Guidebook,* better than 90 percent of today's practitioners in mental health will find cause for change in the procedures which structure their practice.

The *Legal Guidebook in Mental Health* is not a substitute for a lawyer. But Cohen and Mariano can help mental health professionals to know when they need the services of an attorney and, even better, make it less likely for that need to arise. It is indeed a valuable book.

JUSTIN P. CAREY, Ph.D., J.D.

REFERENCES

COHEN, R. J. *Malpractice: A guide for mental health professionals*. New York: The Free Press, 1979.

JUROW, G. L., & MARIANO, W. E. Law and private practice. In G. D. Goldman & G. Stricker (Eds.), *Practical problems for a private psychotherapy practice*. Springfield, Ill.: Charles C. Thomas, 1972.

Preface

THIS VOLUME IS a compendium of case law, legislation, and other materials that impact on practitioners in the mental health field. The product of the joint efforts of a psychologist and an attorney, this book is designed to provide students and practitioners in the legal and mental health professions with a firm foundation in the law as it relates to the practice and malpractice of psychology, psychiatry, social work, psychiatric nursing, occupational therapy, and allied professions. This work complements existing works in the area (e.g., Cohen, 1979) by providing original source material and detailed discussion of the more universal legal principles. Law students and practicing attorneys may find this book to be a particularly valuable resource; here, in one volume, are all of the landmark cases in the mental health field complete with notes, related materials, and a comprehensive bibliography.

Our study begins with some introductory observations regarding the factors that have contributed to the growing number of claims against psychotherapists. Chapter I contains an overview of how the mental health profession is regulated by statute, by the courts, and by nongovernmental agencies. In Chapter II, a definition of "malpractice" is derived with the aid of various source materials. The range of causes of action that have been, or could be brought, against mental health professionals is explored in Chapter III and in Chapter IV. In Chapter V, we examine the countersuit as a remedy for unjust, frivolous litigation. In the final chapter we survey existing theories of liability as they might be applied with respect to the growing number of self-proclaimed psychotherapists who are neither licensed nor credentialed. Throughout this book, the cases reprinted were selected on the basis of the significance of the legal principles set forth in the decisions, not necessarily on the basis of the fact situations. Our intention was to include study materials to serve as a guide in new or novel situations in addition to serving as a guide in everyday practice. The present paucity of court decisions involving mental health professionals per se necessitated the inclusion of some illustrative case material involving other practitioners in the health field.

Because this book was designed for working professionals and students in disciplines as diverse as psychology, medicine, and law, certain stylistic problems arose regarding the citation of references to the medical/psychological literature and to the law. Our solution to these problems was to employ two styles. References to books, journal articles, and related sources have been cited in accordance with the style of the *Publication Manual* of the American Psychological Association (1977). Citations of cases, statutes, and other legal materials appear in the usual manner used in the legal literature. Psychologists, psychiatrists, social workers, nurses, occupational therapists, and others unfamiliar with the legal style of citation are referred to the "Note on Retrieving Legal Information" in Cohen, 1979, p. xiii.

For their assistance in various phases of the development of this casebook the authors wish to express their gratitude to Lawrence A. Brenner, Esq., Edgar A. Dunn, Esq., Sharon Marie Allen, Caroline B. Kneessy, Arlene L. Ramphul, and Karen Myers.

REFERENCES

American Psychological Association. *Publication manual.* Washington, D.C.: Author, 1977.

COHEN, R. J. *Malpractice: A guide for mental health professionals.* New York: The Free Press, 1979.

About the Authors

RONALD JAY COHEN, Ph.D., is a licensed psychologist who received his doctorate in clinical psychology from the State University of New York at Albany. A former Senior Psychologist at New York University-Bellevue Medical Center, Dr. Cohen is currently Adjunct Associate Professor of Psychology at St. John's University. He is the author of numerous articles in the professional literature, and his book credits include *Malpractice: A Guide for Mental Health Professionals* (The Free Press, 1979) and *Psychological Testing and Assessment* (forthcoming). Dr. Cohen has offices in Manhattan, where he maintains a private clinical and consulting practice.

WILLIAM E. MARIANO, Esq., received his law degree from Columbia Law School. Mr. Mariano serves as legal counsel to the New York State Psychological Association, Inc., as well as many other professional associations. A lecturer, writer, and consultant on issues of mental health and the law, Mr. Mariano is also an Adjunct Professor at Pace University, where he teaches a graduate course in forensic psychology. He has served as counsel with both houses of the New York State legislature for over twenty years and presently serves as counsel to the New York State Senate Majority Whip. Mr. Mariano is engaged in the private practice of law with offices in New York City. In 1977, Mr. Mariano was selected for listing in *Who's Who in American Law*.

Introduction

IN THE PAST, a lawsuit against a mental health professional was a relatively rare occurrence. Whereas the average neurosurgeon could expect to be sued approximately once for every two years of practice, the average psychiatrist could expect to be sued once for every 50 to 100 years of practice (Trent & Muhl, 1975). For psychologists, social workers, and other mental health professionals who do not administer medication, the risk of incurring professional liability was even lower than that of the psychiatrist. In recent years, however, the relative immunity from litigation enjoyed by mental health professionals has begun to erode. The erosion has occurred as a consequence of a number of interacting factors, including the following:

Declining Respect for Authority in General

In the wake of Watergate, "Koreagate," "Lancegate," "Billygate," Abscam, and countless other national and local "gates" and "scams," general respect for authority has significantly dropped. Professionals whose authority was once revered and virtually unquestioned are reluctantly becoming accustomed to the threat of skeptical scrutiny and legal challenge. No member of the professional community, not even clergymen, are immune. A recent law suit alleging "clergy malpractice" has prompted Insurance Company of North America, Aetna Life and Casualty, and other insurance companies to begin offering pastoral professional liability policies to a clientele that apparently believes that the Lord helps those who help themselves (Freedman, 1982). Reverend John MacArthur, the first clergyman to be sued on the grounds of clergy malpractice, observed that an increasing number of clergymen are seeking professional liability coverage and that "This is a very litigious society; the clergy know it and want to cover their bases" (Freedman, 1982, p. 8).

Health professionals, particularly physicians, have emerged as particularly vulnerable to the negative consequences of the general public's attitude reversal. As noted by Smith (1975, p. 295), "citizens and lawyers, who only 30 years ago regarded with respect their local hospitals, doctors, dentists, and nurses, are suddenly getting the urge to consider them only as bonded mechanics contractually guaranteeing health in the Hammurabic tradition." With specific reference to the mental health professional, Atthowe (1975, p. 36) has observed that the "days of the autocratic, all-wise therapist and the humble all-accepting patient are numbered."

The Changing Nature of What Is Done in Psychotherapy

Psychotherapy is no longer the "talking cure" it traditionally used to be. Today, that which occurs in the name of "psychotherapy" may involve various modes of therapist-patient and patient-patient touching as well as violently cathartic methods of treatment. In addition, some forms of "treatment" flirt with sexual involvement on the part of the participants (e.g., nude marathon therapy) or actually prescribe such contact (patient-surrogate sex therapy). As mental health professionals stray from therapy that relies primarily on the use of words, so their potential for legal liability will also rise.

The New Candor with Which Mental Health Problems Are Discussed

In a bygone era psychotherapy patients made deliberate efforts to obscure from public knowledge the fact that they were undergoing such treatment. At that time the prospect of having to reveal in open court the intimate, personal details relating to material discussed in psychotherapy sessions discouraged bringing suit against a psychotherapist. Today, conversations about sessions with psychotherapists are commonplace in a variety of settings from cocktail parties to business lunches. With the lessening of the stigma attendant to consulting a mental health professional, there has come about a new willingness—indeed eagerness—on the part of patients to discuss the happenings in their therapy sessions with others. Few people in contemporary America are deterred from bringing suit by the prospect of revealing that they have been in treatment with a psychologist, psychiatrist, or other mental health professional.

Increasing Reliance on Psychotropic Medication

Surveys have indicated that psychotropic drug use in America is widespread. For example, a survey of surgical and medical wards in Boston area hospitals indicated that 20 percent of the patients on those wards had a history of psychotropic drug use, the majority of these medical and surgical patients having taken such medication for a year or more (Greenblatt, Shader & Koch-Weber, 1975). Gottlieb, Nappi, and Strain (1978) reported that more than 20 percent of all adult Americans who are not confined to institutions receive at least one prescription for a psychotropic drug annually. It has even been said that the apparent attempt by pharmaceutical houses to promote their products by advertisements that confuse medical problems with problems in living (see Lennard et al., 1979; Carstairs, 1969) may contribute to the public demand and to physicians' willingness to write prescriptions for such drugs. However, the psychiatrist's potential for legal liability increases as the number of pills prescribed increases.

The Rise of the "Psychosomatic Society"

Widespread public acceptance of theories and notions relating to possible psychosomatic causes of disease has brought with it a rise in the popularity of so-called holistic medicine—and a greater burden on the mental health practitioner. Cohen (1979, pp. 28–29) explained why this is so:

> The medical establishment and the public at large have long acknowledged the well-documented importance of psychological factors in causing and/or aggravating most varieties of diseases. At the same time, however, there may be an unwholesome trend on the part of physicians to "write off" too many of their patients' complaints as "psychological." For example, this author is personally acquainted with a dermatologist who, almost as a matter of course, diagnoses many of the cases of dermatitis that he sees in his daily office practice as psychogenic. This doctor will routinely (mis)inform his patients about the advantages of psychotherapy with respect to the treatment of dermatological problems. Perhaps all of these cases are psychogenic and perhaps they are not. Perhaps this doctor is merely "passing the buck" to the mental health professional when he cannot effect a cure himself and perhaps he is not. Regardless, what does the patient come away from the dermatologist's office believing? How many dermatologists or other medical specialists say to their patients: "I'm sorry, but the state of medical technology today does not allow me to tell you what is causing your problem. We simply lack the medical sophistication necessary to detect the pathogen." The point here is that an unwarranted expectancy of therapeutic gain has been set up in the medical patient who is referred for psychotherapeutic treatment. When a belief and expectancy that a certain course of therapy will ameliorate a condition exists in the absence of a technology for effecting such cures, the result is dissatisfaction and a sense of being "wronged." Such feelings are the "royal road to the courtroom."

The Rise of Consumerism

Consumer advocates in print and electronic media have encouraged consumers to ask probing questions about the goods and services they purchase. Although mental health professionals can applaud the consumer movement for its mobilization of what might be termed "group assertiveness," questions remain concerning exactly how the consequences of this movement will affect the conduct of psychotherapy. For example, one tenet of the consumer movement is a demand for a written contract specifying exactly what services are to be supplied for the fee paid. Experienced psychotherapists are aware that the goal in therapy will frequently change during the course of the therapy. Is a new contract to be written every time the goal in therapy changes? There are other logistical problems attendant to psychotherapy contracts. While behavioral therapists can explain to clients what behaviors they intend to attack and what behaviors they intend to enhance, the dynamically oriented therapist is not so lucky. The dynamic therapist who believes that agoraphobia (fear of going out into the street) is actually a fear of becoming a streetwalker, for example, would be forced to explain his theory to his prospective client right at the outset of therapy, but the client may not be ready for such an interpretation. As Freud (1913/1959) pointed out:

> Even in later stages of analysis one must be careful not to communicate the meaning of a symptom or the interpretation of a wish until the patient is already close upon it, so that he has only a short step to take in order to grasp the explanation himself. In former years I often found that premature communication of interpretations brought the treatment to an untimely end, both on account of the resistances suddenly aroused thereby and also because of the relief resulting from the insight so obtained. (p. 361)

One can only speculate that the net effect of the consumer movement on the frequency with which suit is brought against mental health practitioners will be an increase of such suits.

The Changing Nature of Judicial Interpretations of Negligence

The ambit of what is regarded as a compensable injury and what amounts to negligence is widening. In particular, there is a strong trend toward broadening potential liability for the unintentional infliction of emotional distress.

The Changing Nature of Statutory and Judicial Interpretations of Patients' Rights

Statutes and court decisions that impact on patients' constitutionally guaranteed rights and privileges such as the right to treatment, the right to refuse treatment, and the right to give fully informed consent before treatment may have the effect of increasing health professionals' exposure to legal liability. While such laws successfully provide patients with more control over the treatment process, it is still only the professional who can be sued for malpractice if the treatment is deficient. Particularly in the mental health field, the patient's judgment of the best course of treatment is not necessarily preferable to the doctor's judgment.

The "Sunsetting" of Credentialing Laws Affecting the Practice of Psychology

In recent years many states have begun "sunsetting," in effect nullifying, existing laws affecting the credentialing of psychologists. During the time that the psychology licensing law was sunset in the state of Florida, a psychologist was able to purchase state registration forms for his entire family, thus allowing all of his family members—including the family's pet hamster—to call themselves state-sanctioned psychologists (Foltz, 1979). As a result of the repeal of licensing laws, the number of dubiously trained persons of questionable ethics may be expected to increase, and the ability of the consumer to determine the qualifications of the practitioner will therefore be further eroded. While the ire of the general public may be raised by such "therapists," it very well may be the professionals who will bear the brunt of this anger in the courtroom. The nonprofessional therapist has no license that can be revoked—nor can he or she be called to account for his or her activities before any regulatory body.

The Nonexistence of Regulations Concerning Various Titles

Like the problem of sunset legislation, the problem of nonexistence of regulations concerning various titles related to the practice of mental health work may ultimately cause legal difficulties for the duly qualified practitioner in the field. Titles such as "psychotherapist," "therapist," and "hypnotist" remain unregulated in most jurisdictions. The potential consequence of this state of affairs has been discussed elsewhere:

> Anyone can use any one (or more) of these sundry other titles that imply some psychotherapeutic expertise and act totally within the law in doing so. Members of the public who find their way to these "therapists"—who are, by and large, uneducated, uncredentialed, and unethical—may be very displeased with the results. It is, of course, bad enough when a client is displeased with the services of a properly credentialed therapist and the entire profession receives a bad name as a result. Unfortunately, the good name of professional therapists is as likely to be sullied by an incompetent, noncredentialed "therapist" as by a fellow professional. (Cohen, 1979, p. 21)

These ten factors bring us to the inescapable conclusion that there are many reasons besides lack of ordinary competence that may contribute to a practitioner's being sued for malpractice. It is therefore not enough for practitioners to be ethical and competent; they must also be familiar with the law. This book, when used in conjunction with more rudimentary discussions of the subject, can help to provide that familiarity. For the practicing attorney or law student, this book will be of value as a comprehensive reference to landmark cases and related materials.

REFERENCES

ATTHOWE, J. M., JR. Legal and ethical accountability in everyday practice. *Behavioral Engineering,* 1975 (3), 25-38.

CARSTAIRS, G. M. A land of lotus eaters? *American Journal of Psychiatry,* 1969, *125,* 1576-1580.

COHEN, R. J. *Malpractice: A guide for mental health professionals.* New York: The Free Press, 1979.

FOLTZ, D. Sun sets on psychology licensing boards in South Dakota and Florida. *APA Monitor,* September/October 1979, pp. 3; 14.

FREEDMAN, A. M. Malpractice approaches the pulpit. *The New York Times,* June 6, 1982, p. 8.

FREUD, S. Further recommendations in the technique of psycho-analysis. In E. Jones (Ed.) and J. Riviere (trans.), *Collected papers,* (Vol. 2). New York: Basic Books, 1959. (Originally published, 1913.)

GOTTLIEB, R. M., NAPPI, T., & STRAIN, J. J. The physician's knowledge of psychotropic drugs: Preliminary results. *American Journal of Psychiatry,* 1978, *135,* 29-32.

GREENBLATT, D. J., SHADER, R. I., & KOCH-WEBER, J. Psychotropic drug use in the Boston area. *Archives of General Psychiatry,* 1978, *32,* 518-521.

LENNARD, H. J., EPSTEIN, L. J., BERNSTEIN, A., & RANSOM, D. C. Hazards implicit in prescribing psychoactive drugs. *Science,* 1970, *169,* 438-441.

SMITH, S. M. Whose malpractice crisis? *The Journal of the Louisiana State Medical Society,* 1975, *127,* 293-297.

CHAPTER I

The Regulation of the Mental Health Profession

PURSUANT TO ITS constitutionally granted police powers, each state is free to regulate and control the professional conduct of practitioners of any profession that has been defined by law. The definition of the profession and the regulation and control of the professionals is accomplished by statute and by the courts; regulation of a profession is also effected by its professional organizations. In considering the "mental health profession," we are actually considering at least four distinctly different professions: medicine, psychology, social work, and nursing. While in some states other providers of mental health care are covered by some form of regulation, it is generally practitioners who are either board-certified psychiatrists, board-eligible psychiatrists, psychologists, social workers, or registered nurses who constitute the core of the mental health profession. In the future, other professionals such as occupational therapists may also commonly be regarded as professionals in the mental health field.

STATUTORY REGULATION OF MENTAL HEALTH PROFESSIONALS

As noted above, the regulation of a profession is carried out on many levels. The first and controlling level is statutory regulation; statutes define the profession and provide for an administrative agency to supervise the credentialing of practitioners of that profession. Along with that authority go the power to regulate the conduct of persons holding the professional credential and the power to revoke that credential. The degree of regulation and control the administrative agency is empowered to exert will vary with the type of statute that exists. Three types of statutes are applicable: licensure, certification, and registration.

Licensure. Under a licensing law the nature of the professional service to be provided is set forth and then restricted to licensed practitioners of the profession. Only those individuals meeting the criteria established to obtain the necessary license are allowed to practice the functions defined by the statute. Most licensing laws also contain restrictions on the use of certain titles in connection with the controlled function.

The provisions of the New York State Education Law regulating the practice of a profession and the licensing of physicians typify the licensing statutes found throughout the country. This law sets forth who is to be licensed, who will do the licensing, definitions of various professions, definitions of professional misconduct, and various other issues. Note that it also provides for the promulgation of additional rules and regulations by the administering body. Consequently, it is not the sole statutory reference for the professional practitioner.

New York Education Law §§6500–6547 (McKinney 1972 & Supp. 1979)

§ 6500. Introduction

This title provides for the regulation of the admission to and the practice of certain professions. This first article applies to all the professions included in this title, except that prehearing procedures and hearing procedures in connection with the regulation of professional conduct of the profession of medicine shall be conducted pursuant to the provisions of Title II-A of article two of the public health law. Each of the remaining articles applies to a particular profession.

§ 6501. Admission to a Profession (Licensing)

Admission to practice of a profession in this state is accomplished by a license being issued to a qualified applicant by the education department. To qualify for a license an applicant shall meet the requirements prescribed in the article for the particular profession.

§ 6502. Duration and Registration of a License

1. A license shall be valid during the life of the holder unless revoked, annulled or suspended by the board of regents. A licensee must register biennially with the department to practice in this state.

2. The department shall establish the beginning dates of the two-year registration for each profession and mail an application for registration to every licensee currently registered at least four months prior to the beginning of the registration period for the respective profession.

3. An application for registration and the required registration fee shall be submitted together with or as a part of the application for a license. A person initially licensed or a licensee resuming practice after a lapse of registration in the last four months of a two-year registration period shall be registered for the succeeding registration period without an additional registration fee. The department shall renew the registration of

each licensee upon receipt of a proper application, on a form prescribed by the department, and the registration fee. Any licensee who fails to register by the beginning of the appropriate registration period shall be required to pay an additional fee for late filing of five dollars for each month that registration has been delayed while such licensee continued to practice his profession. The licensee resuming practice after a lapse of registration shall be permitted to practice without actual possession of the registration certificate for not more than four months after mailing to the department the required application fee.

4. Any licensee who is not engaging in the practice of his profession in this state and does not desire to register shall so advise the department. Such licensee may subsequently register and resume practice without paying an additional fee for failure to register at the beginning of the registration period.

5. Licensees shall notify the department of any change of name or mailing address within thirty days of such change.

§ 6503. Practice of a Profession

Admission to the practice of a profession (1) entitles the licensee to practice the profession as defined in the article for the particular profession, (2) entitles the individual licensee to use the professional title as provided in the article for the particular profession, and (3) subjects the licensee to the procedures and penalties for professional misconduct as prescribed in this article (sections sixty-five hundred nine, sixty-five hundred ten, and sixty-five hundred eleven).

§ 6504. Regulation of the Professions

Admission to the practice of the professions (licensing) and regulation of such practice shall be supervised by the board of regents (section sixty-five hundred six) and administered by the education department (section sixty-five hundred seven), assisted by a state board for each profession (section sixty-five hundred eight).

. . . .

§ 6506. Supervision by the Board of Regents

The board of regents shall supervise the admission to and the practice of the professions. In supervising, the board of regents may:

1. Promulgate rules;
2. Establish by rule, high school, preprofessional, professional and other educational qualifications required for licensing in the professions regulated by this title;
3. Charter schools offering educational programs for the professions regulated by this title, and no such school shall operate in this state without such a charter, except Columbia University, any school chartered by special act of the legislature prior to September one, nineteen hundred seventy-one, and schools specifically authorized to conduct such programs by the regents;
4. Appoint such committees as it deems necessary and compensate members of such committees who are not members of the board of regents or the department up to one hundred dollars per day for each day devoted to committee functions together with their necessary expenses;

5. Waive education, experience and examination requirements for a professional license prescribed in the article relating to the profession, provided the board of regents shall be satisfied that the requirements of such article have been substantially met;
6. Indorse a license issued by a licensing board of another state or country upon the applicant fulfilling the following requirements:
   (a) Application: file an application with the department;
   (b) Education: meet educational requirements in accordance with the commissioner's regulations;
   (c) Experience: have experience satisfactory to the board and in accordance with the commissioner's regulations;
   (d) Examination: pass an examination satisfactory to the board and in accordance with the commissioner's regulations;
   (e) Age: be at least twenty-one years of age;
   (f) Citizenship: be a United States citizen, or file a declaration of intention to become a citizen, unless such requirement is waived, in accordance with the commissioner's regulations;
   (g) Character: be of good moral character as determined by the department; and
   (h) Fees: pay a fee to the department for indorsement of forty dollars.
7. Direct the department to remedy any error, omission, delay or other circumstances in the issuance or registration of a license;
8. Designate a professional conduct officer on recommendation of the commissioner in connection with professional licensing and misconduct proceedings and criminal matters, such officer to be empowered to issue subpoenas and administer oaths in connection with such proceedings;
9. Establish by rule, standards of conduct with respect to advertising, fee splitting, practicing under a name other than that of the individual licensee (when not specifically authorized), proper use of academic or professional degrees or titles tending to imply professional status, and such other ethical practices as such board shall deem necessary; and
10. Delegate to department officers the disposition of any licensing matters pursuant to rules.

§ 6507. Administration by the Education Department

1. The commissioner and the department shall administer the admission to and the practice of the professions.

2. In administering, the commissioner may:
   (a) Promulgate regulations;
   (b) Conduct investigations;
   (c) Issue subpoenas;
   (d) Grant immunity from prosecution in accordance with section 50.20 of the criminal procedure law to anyone subpoenaed in any investigation or hearing conducted pursuant to this title; and
   (e) Excuse, for cause acceptable to the commissioner, the failure to register biennially. Such excuse shall validate and authorize such practitioner's right to practice pending registration.

3. The department assisted by the board for each profession, shall:
   (a) Establish standards for preprofessional and professional education, experience and licensing examinations as required to implement the article for each profession;
   (b) Review qualifications in connection with licensing requirements; and
   (c) Provide for licensing examinations and reexaminations.
4. The department shall:
   (a) Register or approve educational programs designed for the purpose of providing professional preparation which meet standards established by the department.
   (b) Issue licenses, registrations, and limited permits to qualified applicants;
   (c) i. Issue a certificate of authority to a qualified professional service corporation being organized under section fifteen hundred three of the business corporation law on payment of a fee of twenty-five dollars, ii. file a certified copy of each certificate of incorporation and amendment thereto within thirty days after the filing of such certificate or amendment on payment of a fee of ten dollars, iii. file the annual statement required by section fifteen hundred fourteen of the business corporation law on payment of a fee of ten dollars.
   (d) Revoke limited permits on the recommendation of the committee on professional conduct for the profession concerned;
   (e) Maintain public records of licenses issued and retain in its files identifying data concerning each person to whom a license has been issued; and
   (f) Collect the fees prescribed by this title or otherwise provided by law.
5. The commissioner and the department shall perform any other functions necessary to implement this title.

§ 6508. Assistance by State Boards for the Professions

1. A board for each profession shall be appointed by the board of regents on the recommendation of the commissioner for the purpose of assisting the board of regents and the department on matters of professional licensing, practice, and conduct. The composition of each board shall be as prescribed in the article relating to each profession. Within each board a committee on licensing and one or more committees on professional conduct may be appointed by the board chairman.

   Except as provided in paragraph (a) of this subdivision, the membership of each professional licensing board shall be increased by one member, and each such board shall have at least one public representative who shall be selected by the board of regents from the general public.
   (a) The membership of the professional licensing boards created under sections sixty-five hundred twenty-three, sixty-eight hundred four, sixty-nine hundred three, and seventy-four hundred three of this chapter shall be increased by two members, and each such board shall have at least two public representatives, who shall be selected by the board of regents from the general public.
   (b) For the purposes of this title, a "public representative" shall be a person who is a consumer of services provided by those licensed or otherwise supervised or regulated by the boards created hereunder, and shall not be, nor within five years immediately preceding appointment have been:
      i. a licensee or person otherwise subject to the supervision or regulation of the board to which appointed; or

ii. a person maintaining a contractual relationship with a licensee of such board, which would constitute more than two percentum of the practice or business of any such licensee, or an officer, director, or representative of such person or group of persons.

2. Each board, or its committee on licensing, shall select or prepare examinations, may conduct oral and practical examinations and reexaminations, shall fix passing grades, and assist the department in other licensing matters as prescribed by the board of regents.
3. Each board, or its committee or committees on professional conduct, shall conduct disciplinary proceedings as prescribed in this article and shall assist in other professional conduct matters as prescribed by the board of regents. Former members of each board may be re-appointed by the board of regents, on the recommendation of the commissioner, to serve as members of the board and of its committee or committees on professional conduct for the sole purpose of conducting disciplinary proceedings pursuant to this article. Former board members so appointed may not comprise a majority of any hearing panel.
4. Members of each board shall be appointed by the board of regents for five-year terms except that the terms of those first appointed shall be arranged so that as nearly as possible an equal number shall terminate annually. A vacancy occurring during a term shall be filled by an appointment by the board of regents for the unexpired term. Each state professional association or society may nominate one or more candidates for each appointment to be made to the board for its profession, but the board of regents shall not be required to appoint candidates so nominated.
5. Each member of a board shall receive a certificate of appointment, shall before beginning his term of office file a constitutional oath of office with the secretary of state, shall receive up to one hundred dollars as prescribed by the board of regents for each day devoted to board work, and shall be reimbursed for his necessary expenses. No member shall serve beyond the age of seventy. Any member may be removed from a board by the board of regents for misconduct, incapacity or neglect of duty.
6. Each board shall elect from its members a chairman and vice-chairman annually, shall meet upon call of the chairman or the department, and may adopt bylaws consistent with this title and approved by the board of regents. A quorum for the transaction of business by the board shall be a majority of members but not less than five members.
7. An executive secretary to each board shall be appointed by the board of regents on recommendation of the commissioner. Such executive secretary shall not be a member of the board, shall hold office at the pleasure of, and shall have the powers, duties and annual salary prescribed by the board of regents.

§ 6509. Definitions of Professional Misconduct

Each of the following is professional misconduct, and any licensee found guilty of such misconduct under the procedures prescribed in section sixty-five hundred ten shall be subject to the penalties prescribed in section sixty-five hundred eleven:

1. Obtaining the license fraudulently,
2. Practicing the profession fraudulently, beyond its authorized scope, with gross

incompetence, with gross negligence on a particular occasion or negligence or incompetence on more than one occasion,

3. Practicing the profession while the ability to practice is impaired by alcohol, drugs, physical disability, or mental disability,
4. Being habitually drunk or being dependent on, or a habitual user of narcotics, barbiturates, amphetamines, hallucinogens, or other drugs having similar effects,
5. Being convicted of committing an act constituting a crime under;
   (a) New York State law or,
   (b) Federal law or,
   (c) The law of another jurisdiction and which, if committed within this state, would have constituted a crime under New York state law.
6. Refusing to provide professional service to a person because of such person's race, creed, color, or national origin,
7. Permitting, aiding or abetting an unlicensed person to perform activities requiring a license,
8. Practicing the profession while the license is suspended, or wilfully failing to register or notify the department of any change of name or mailing address, or, if a professional service corporation wilfully failing to comply with sections fifteen hundred three and fifteen hundred fourteen of the business corporation law, or
9. Committing unprofessional conduct, as defined by the board of regents in its rules or by the commissioner in regulations approved by the board of regents.
10. A willful violation by a licensed physician of subdivision eleven of section two hundred thirty of the public health law.

. . . .

§ 6512. Unauthorized Practice a Crime

1. Anyone not authorized to practice under this title who practices or offers to practice or holds himself out as being able to practice in any profession in which a license is a prerequisite to the practice of the acts, or who practices any profession as an exempt person during the time when his professional license is suspended, revoked or annulled, or who aids or abets an unlicensed person to practice a profession, or who fraudulently sells, files, furnishes, obtains, or who attempts fraudulently to sell, file, furnish or obtain any diploma, license, record or permit purporting to authorize the practice of a profession, shall be guilty of a class E felony.
2. Anyone who knowingly aids or abets three or more unlicensed persons to practice a profession or employs or holds such unlicensed persons out as being able to practice in any profession in which a license is a prerequisite to the practice of the acts, or who knowingly aids or abets three or more persons to practice any profession as exempt persons during the time when the professional licenses of such persons are suspended, revoked or annulled, shall be guilty of a class E felony.

§ 6513. Unauthorized Use of a Professional Title a Crime

1. Anyone not authorized to use a professional title regulated by this title, and who uses such professional title, shall be guilty of a class A misdemeanor.
2. Anyone who knowingly aids or abets three or more persons not authorized to use a

professional title regulated by this title, to use such professional title, or knowingly employs three or more persons not authorized to use a professional title regulated by this title, who use such professional title in the course of such employment, shall be guilty of a class E felony.

. . . .

§ 6521. Definition of Practice of Medicine

The practice of the profession of medicine is defined as diagnosing, treating, operating or prescribing for any human disease, pain, injury, deformity or physical condition.

§ 6522. Practice of Medicine and Use of title "Physician"

Only a person licensed or otherwise authorized under this article shall practice medicine or use the title "physician."

§ 6523. State Board for Medicine

A state board for medicine shall be appointed by the board of regents on recommendation of the commissioner for the purpose of assisting the board of regents and the department on matters of professional licensing in accordance with section sixty-five hundred eight of this title. The board shall be composed of not less than twenty physicians licensed in this state for at least five years, two of whom shall be doctors of osteopathy. An executive secretary to the board shall be appointed by the board of regents on recommendation of the commissioner and shall be a physician licensed in this state.

. . . .

§ 6524. Requirements for a Professional License

To qualify for a license as a physician, an applicant shall fulfill the following requirements:

1. Application: file an application with the department;
2. Education: have received an education, including a degree of doctor of medicine, "M.D.", or doctor or osteopathy, "D.O.", or equivalent degree in accordance with the commissioner's regulations;
3. Experience: have experience satisfactory to the board and in accordance with the commissioner's regulations;
4. Examination: pass an examination satisfactory to the board and in accordance with the commissioner's regulations;
5. Age: be at least twenty-one years of age;
6. Citizenship: be a United States citizen, or file a declaration of intention to become a citizen, unless such requirement is waived in accordance with the commissioner's regulations;
7. Character: be of good moral character as determined by the department . . . .

§ 6525. Limited Permits

Permits limited as to eligibility, practice and duration, shall be issued by the department to eligible applicants, as follows:

1. Eligibility: The following persons shall be eligible for a limited permit:
   (a) A person who fulfills all except the examination and citizenship requirements for a license as a physician;
   (b) A foreign physician who holds a standard certificate from the educational council for foreign medical graduates or who has passed an examination satisfactory to the state board for medicine and in accordance with the commissioner's regulations; or
   (c) A foreign physician or a foreign intern who is in this country on a non-immigration visa for the continuation of medical study, pursuant to the exchange student program of the United States department of state.
2. Limit of practice. A permittee shall be authorized to practice medicine only under the supervision of a licensed physician and only in a public, voluntary, or proprietary hospital.
3. Duration. A limited permit shall be valid for two years. It may be renewed biennially at the discretion of the department.

§ 6526. Exempt Persons

The following persons under the following limitations may practice medicine within the state without a license:

1. Any physician who is employed as a resident in a public hospital, provided such practice is limited to such hospital and is under the supervision of a licensed physician;
2. Any physician who is licensed in a bordering state and who resides near a border of this state, provided such practice is limited in this state to the vicinity of such border and provided such physician does not maintain an office or place to meet patients or receive calls within this state;
3. Any physician who is licensed in another state or country and who is meeting a physician licensed in this state, for purposes of consultation, provided such practice is limited to such consultation;
4. Any physician who is licensed in another state or country, who is visiting a medical school or teaching hospital in this state to receive medical instruction for a period not to exceed six months or to conduct medical instruction, provided such practice is limited to such instruction and is under the supervision of a licensed physician;
5. Any physician who is authorized by a foreign government to practice in relation to its diplomatic, consular or maritime staffs, provided such practice is limited to such staffs;
6. Any commissioned medical officer who is serving in the United States armed forces or public health service or any physician who is employed in the United States Veterans Administration, provided such practice is limited to such service or employment;
7. Any intern who is employed by a hospital and who is a graduate of a medical school in the United States or Canada, provided such practice is limited to such hospital and is under the supervision of a licensed physician; or

8. Any medical student who is performing a clinical clerkship or similar function in a hospital and who is matriculated in a medical school which meets standards satisfactory to the department, provided such practice is limited to such clerkship or similar function in such hospital.

§ 6527. Special Provisions

1. A not-for-profit medical or dental expense indemnity corporation or a hospital service corporation organized under the insurance law may employ licensed physicians and enter into contracts with partnerships or medical corporations organized under article forty-four of the public health law, health maintenance organizations possessing a certificate of authority pursuant to article forty-four of the public health law, professional corporations organized under article fifteen of the business corporation law or other groups of physicians to practice medicine on its behalf for persons insured under its contracts or policies.
2. Notwithstanding any inconsistent provision of any general, special or local law, any licensed physician who voluntarily and without the expectation of monetary compensation renders first aid or emergency treatment at the scene of an accident or other emergency, outside a hospital, doctor's office or any other place having proper and necessary medical equipment, to a person who is unconscious, ill or injured, shall not be liable for damages for injuries alleged to have been sustained by such person or for damages for the death of such person alleged to have occurred by reason of an act or omission in the rendering of such first aid or emergency treatment unless it is established that such injuries were or such death was caused by gross negligence on the part of such physician. Nothing in this subdivision shall be deemed or construed to relieve a licensed physician from liability for damages for injuries or death caused by an act or omission on the part of a physician while rendering professional services in the normal and ordinary course of his practice.
3. No individual who serves as a member of (a) a committee established to administer a utilization review plan of a hospital, including a hospital as defined in article twenty-eight of the public health law or (b) a committee having the responsibility of evaluation and improvement of the quality of care rendered in a hospital as defined in article twenty-eight of the public health law, or (c) any medical review committee or subcommittee thereof of a local, county or state medical, dental, podiatry or optometrical society, any such society itself, a professional standards review organization or an individual when such committee, subcommittee, society, organization or individual is performing any medical review function either described in clauses (a) and (b) of this subdivision, required by law, or involving any controversy or dispute between (i) a physician, dentist, podiatrist or optometrist or hospital administrator and a patient concerning the diagnosis, treatment or care of such patient or the fees or charges therefor or (ii) a physician, dentist, podiatrist or optometrist or hospital administrator and a provider of medical, dental, podiatric or optometrical services concerning any medical or health charges or fees of such physician, dentist, podiatrist or optometrist, shall be liable in damages to any person for any action taken or recommendations made, by him within the scope of his function in such capacity provided that (a) such individual has taken action or made recommendations within the scope of his function and without malice, and (b) in the reasonable belief after reasonable investigation that the act or recommendation was warranted, based upon the facts disclosed.

   Neither the proceedings nor the records relating to performance of a medical review function described herein shall be subject to disclosure under article thirty-one of the civil practice law and rules except as hereinafter provided or as provided by any other provision of law. No person in attendance at a meeting when a medical review function described herein was performed shall be required to testify as to what transpired thereat. The prohibition relating to discovery of testimony shall not apply to the statements made by any person in attendance at such a meeting who is a party to an action or proceeding the subject matter of which was reviewed at such meeting.

4. This article shall not be construed to affect or prevent the following:
   (a) The furnishing of medical assistance in an emergency;
   (b) The practice of the religious tenets of any church;
   (c) A physician from refusing to perform an act constituting the practice of medicine to which he is conscientiously opposed by reason of religious training and belief.
   (d) The organization of a medical corporation under article forty-four of the public health law or the organization of a professional service corporation under article fifteen of the business corporation law.
5. There shall be no monetary liability on the part of, and no cause of action for damages shall arise against, any person, partnership, corporation, firm, society, or other entity on account of the communication of information in the possession of such person or entity, or on account of any recommendation or evaluation, regarding the qualifications, fitness, or professional conduct or practices of a physician, to any governmental agency, medical or specialists society, or hospital as defined in article twenty-eight of the public health law. The foregoing shall not apply to information which is untrue and communicated with malicious intent.

. . . .

§ 6540. Definitions

As used in this article:

1. Physician's assistant. The term "physician's assistant" means a person who is registered as a physician's assistant pursuant to this article.
2. Specialist's assistant. The term "specialist's assistant" means a person who is registered pursuant to this article as a specialist's assistant for a particular medical specialty as defined by regulations promulgated by the commissioner of health pursuant to section thirty-seven hundred one of the public health law.
3. Physician. The term "physician" means a practitioner of medicine licensed to practice medicine pursuant to article one hundred thirty-one of this chapter.
4. Approved program. The term "approved program" means a program for the education of physician's assistants or specialist's assistants which has been formerly approved by the department.
5. Hospital. The term "hospital" means an institution or facility possessing a valid operating certificate issued pursuant to article twenty-eight of the public health law and authorized to employ physician's assistants and specialist's assistants in accordance with rules and regulations of the state hospital review and planning council.

§ 6541. Registration

1. The department shall register each person as a physician's assistant or specialist's assistant who shall pay a fee of fifty dollars to the department for admission to a

department conducted examination and for an initial license, a fee of twenty dollars for each reexamination and a fee of thirty dollars for an initial license for persons not requiring admission to a department conducted examination. Each person shall also submit satisfactory evidence, verified by oath or affirmation, that he:

(a) at the time of application is at least twenty-one years of age;
(b) is of good moral character;
(c) has successfully completed a four-year course of study in a secondary school approved by the board of regents or has passed an equivalency test;
(d) has satisfactorily completed an approved program for the training of physician's assistants or specialist's assistants. The approved program for the training of physician's assistants shall include not less than forty weeks of supervised clinical training and thirty-two credit hours of classroom work. The commissioner is empowered to determine whether an applicant possesses equivalent education and training, such as experience as a nurse or military corpsman, which may be accepted in lieu of all or part of an approved program.

2. The department shall furnish to each person applying for registration hereunder an application form calling for such information as the department deems necessary and shall issue to each applicant who satisfies the requirements of subdivision one of this section a certificate of registration as a physician's assistant or specialist's assistant in a particular medical specialty for the period expiring December thirty-first of the first odd-numbered year terminating subsequent to such registration.
3. Every registrant shall prior to the first day of each even-numbered year apply to the department for a certificate of biennial registration. On or before the first day of November of each odd-numbered year, the department shall mail to every registered physician's assistant and specialist's assistant an application form for registration, addressed to the registrant's post office address on file with the department. Upon receipt of such application properly executed and a fee of ten dollars, together with evidence of satisfactory completion of such continuing education requirements as may be established by the commissioner of health pursuant to section thirty-seven hundred one of the public health law, the department shall issue a certificate of biennial registration for the ensuing two calendar years.

§ 6542. Performance of Medical Services

1. Notwithstanding any other provision of law, a physician's assistant may perform medical services, but only when under the supervision of a physician and only when such acts and duties as are assigned to him are within the scope of practice of such supervising physician.
2. Notwithstanding any other provision of law, a specialist's assistant may perform medical services, but only when under the supervision of a physician and only when such acts and duties as are assigned to him are related to the designated medical specialty for which he is registered and are within the scope of practice of his supervising physician.
3. Supervision shall be continuous but shall not be construed as necessarily requiring the physical presence of the supervising physician at the time and place where such services are preformed.
4. No physician shall employ or supervise more than two physician's assistants and two specialist's assistants in his private practice.
5. Nothing in this article shall prohibit a hospital from employing physician's assistants or specialist's assistants provided they work under the supervision of a physi-

cian designated by the hospital and not beyond the scope of practice of such physician. The numerical limitation of subdivision four of this section shall not apply to services performed in a hospital.

6. Notwithstanding any other provision of law, a trainee in an approved program may perform medical services when such services are performed within the scope of such program.
7. Nothing in this article, or in article thirty-seven of the public health law, shall be construed to authorize physician's assistants or specialist's assistants to perform those specific functions and duties specifically delegated by law to those persons licensed as allied health professionals under the public health law or the education law.

§ 6543. Filing Requirements

Every physician shall file a notice with the department upon the employment or discharge of a physician's assistant or specialist's assistant in accordance with such regulations as may be prescribed by the commissioner.

§ 6544. Disciplinary Proceedings

1. The registration of a registered physician's assistant or a specialist's assistant may be suspended or revoked upon decision after due hearing that he:
   (a) has been guilty of fraud or deceit while acting as a physician's assistant or a specialist's assistant or in procuring his registration; or
   (b) has been convicted in a court of competent jurisdiction, either within or without this state, of a crime involving moral turpitude; or
   (c) is an alcohol abuser or is or has been addicted to the use of narcotic or depressant or stimulant drugs, or has become mentally ill; or
   (d) has violated any of the regulations promulgated by the commissioner of health pursuant to section thirty-seven hundred one of the public health law; or
   (e) is incompetent or has been grossly negligent or has been guilty of unprofessional conduct.
2. Disciplinary proceedings shall be conducted in accordance with the provisions of article one hundred thirty-one of the education law relating to similar proceedings against physicians.
3. The commissioner may promulgate regulations defining unprofessional conduct, which regulations shall not be inconsistent with such regulations as may be promulgated by the commissioner of health pursuant to section thirty-seven hundred one of the public health law.

§ 6545. Construction

1. Only a person registered as a physician's assistant by the department may use the title "registered physician's assistant" or the letters "R.P.A." after his name.
2. Only a person registered as a specialist's assistant by the department may use the title "registered specialist's assistant" or the letters "R.S.A." after his name.

§ 6546. Regulations

The commissioner may promulgate such other regulations as are necessary to carry out the purposes of this article.

Certification. Under a certification law only certain titles related to the practice of a profession are regulated. However, the law need not contain a definition of the profession. Thus, for example, in states having certification laws controlling the professional practice of psychology, uncertified persons are prohibited from using the title "psychologist" and holding themselves out to the public as psychologists. Depending on the wording of the statute, they may further be prohibited from using the word "psychological" or any derivative of the word "psychology" to describe the services offered. Note that, although a certification law may regulate the use of specified titles, it does not control the practice of a profession and need not control all possible titles related to the practice of the profession. Thus uncertified persons may legally practice psychology in states with certification laws provided they do not hold themselves out to the public as "psychologists" or describe their services as "psychological." Uncertified practitioners frequently use titles that are not controlled by the certification statute, such as "psychotherapist," "therapist," "marriage counselor," "counselor," "hypnotist," and so forth. Exactly which titles are and are not regulated by statute will vary from state to state. The New York statute regarding psychologists and social workers that follows is a typical certification law.

New York Education Law §§7601–7705 (McKinney 1972 & Supp. 1979)

§ 7601. Use of Title "Psychologist"

Only a person licensed under this article shall be authorized to use the title "psychologist" or to describe his services by use of the words "psychologist", "psychology" or "psychological" in connection with his practice.

§ 7602. State Board for Psychology

A state board for psychology shall be appointed by the board of regents on recommendation of the commissioner for the purpose of assisting the board of regents and the department on matters of professional licensing and professional conduct in accordance with section sixty-five hundred eight of this title. The board shall be composed of not less than eleven psychologists licensed in this state. An executive secretary to the board shall be appointed by the board of regents upon the recommendation of the commissioner and shall be a psychologist, licensed in this state.

§ 7603. Requirements for a Professional License

To qualify for a license as a psychologist, an applicant shall fulfill the following requirements:

1. Application: file an application with the department;
2. Education: have received an education, including a doctoral degree in psychology, granted on the basis of completion of a program of psychology registered with the department or the substantial equivalent thereof, in accordance with the commissioner's regulations;

3. Experience: have two years of supervised employment or engagement in appropriate psychology activities satisfactory to the board and in accordance with the commissioner's regulations;
4. Examination: pass an examination satisfactory to the board and in accordance with the commissioner's regulations;
5. Age: be at least twenty-one years of age;
6. Citizenship: meet no requirement as to United States citizenship;
7. Character: be of good moral character as determined by the department; and
8. Fees: pay a fee to the department for admission to the examination and for initial license of forty dollars, for each reexamination fifteen dollars and for each biennial registration fifteen dollars.

§ 7604. Limited Permits

1. On recommendation of the board, the department may issue a limited permit to practice as psychologist to an applicant holding a certificate or license to practice psychology issued by another state or country, and whose qualifications have been approved for admission to the examination for a license as psychologist and who has resided in this state for a period of not more than six months prior to the filing of such application. The limited permit shall be valid for a period of not more than eighteen months, or until the results of a licensing examination have been received from the department, whichever comes first.
2. Fees. The fee for each limited permit shall be ten dollars.

§ 7605. Exempt Persons

Nothing in this article shall be construed to affect or prevent:

1. The activities, services, and use of the title of psychologist, or any derivation thereof, on the part of a person in the employ of a federal, state, county or municipal agency, or other political subdivision, or a chartered elementary or secondary school or degree-granting educational institution insofar as such activities and services are a part of the duties of his salaried position.
2. The activities and services required of a student, intern, or resident in psychology, pursuing a course of study leading to a doctoral degree in psychology in an institution approved by the department, provided that such activities and services constitute a part of his supervised course of study in psychology. Such persons shall be designated by title as "psychological intern", "psychological trainee" or other such title which clearly indicates his training status.
3. The activities and services on the part of a person who has fulfilled requirements of paragraphs (2), (5), (6) and (7) of section seventy-six hundred three of this article, and is fulfilling requirements of paragraph (3) of such section, provided that the period of the experience of such person in carrying on such activities and services does not exceed an aggregate of thirty-six months subsequent to the attainment of the doctoral degree and provided that the title used by such person is "assistant psychologist".
4. The representation as a psychologist and the rendering of services as such in this state for a temporary period of a person who resides outside the state of New York and who engages in practice as a psychologist and conducts the major part of his practice as such outside this state, provided such person has filed with the depart-

ment evidence that he has been licensed or certified in another state or has been admitted to the examination in this state pursuant to section seventy-six hundred three of this article. Such temporary period shall not exceed ten consecutive business days in any period of ninety consecutive days or in the aggregate exceed more than fifteen business days in any such ninety-day period.

§ 7701. Definition of Practice as a "Certified Social Worker"

The practice of social work as a "certified social worker" is defined as engaging, under such title, in social casework, social group work, community organization, administration of a social work program, social work education, social work research, or any combination of these in accordance with social work principles and methods. The practice of social work is for the purpose of helping individuals, families, groups and communities to prevent or to resolve problems caused by social or emotional stress.

§ 7702. Use of the Title "Certified Social Worker"

Only a person licensed under this article shall be authorized to use the title "certified social worker".

§ 7703. State Board for Social Work

A state board for social work shall be appointed by the board of regents on recommendation of the commissioner for the purpose of assisting the board of regents and the department on matters of professional licensing and professional conduct in accordance with section sixty-five hundred eight of this title. The board shall be composed of not less than seven certified social workers licensed in this state. An executive secretary to the board shall be appointed by the board of regents on recommendation of the commissioner and shall be a certified social worker licensed in this state.

§ 7704. Requirements for a Professional License

To qualify for a license as a "certified social worker" an applicant shall fulfill the following requirements:

1. Application: file an application with the department;
2. Education: have received an education, including a master's or equivalent degree in social work, in accordance with the commissioner's regulations;
3. Experience: meet no requirement as to experience;
4. Examination: pass an examination satisfactory to the board and in accordance with the commissioner's regulations;
5. Age: be at least twenty-one years of age;
6. Citizenship: meet no requirement as to United States citizenship;
7. Character: be of good moral character as determined by the department; and
8. Fees: pay a fee of eighty dollars to the department for admission to a department conducted examination and for an initial license, a fee of forty dollars for each reexamination, a fee of fifty dollars for an initial license for persons not requiring admission to a department conducted examination, a fee of thirty dollars for each

biennial registration, and for additional authorization for the purposes of subdivision sixteen of section one hundred sixty-two and subdivision eight of section two hundred fifty-three of the insurance law, fifty dollars.

§ 7705. Limited Permits

1. On recommendation of the board, the department may issue a limited permit to practice social work as a certified social worker to an applicant whose qualifications have been approved for admission to the examination. This limited permit shall be valid for a period of not more than eighteen months or until the results of the next licensing examination for which the person is eligible are officially available, whichever comes first.
2. Fees: The fee for each limited permit shall be ten dollars.

Professional conduct. Professionals, whether licensed, certified, or registered, become subject to the control of an administrative body authorized to establish standards of care, conduct, and discipline. The administrative body typically establishes a code of professional conduct that impacts on the manner in which professional services are to be provided and the quality of same. The practitioner's failure to adhere to this code of professional/ethical conduct may lead to charges of unprofessional conduct and hearings conducted by the administrative body. That body is empowered to suspend or revoke the credential that authorizes the practitioner to engage in professional practice.

In New York State mental health professionals, as well as other professionals, are governed by the Education Law. As provided in that law, the administrative body authorized to establish standards of care and conduct for the professionals is the Board of Regents. The Regents have promulgated rules and regulations for professionals which have the force of law by virtue of the statutory authority given the Regents. Below we see how the Regents have defined "unprofessional conduct."

Regulations of the Board of Regents of the University of New York §29 (1977)

Section 29.1 General Provisions for All Professions

(a) Unprofessional conduct shall be the conduct prohibited by this section. The provisions of these rules applicable to a particular profession may define additional acts or omissions as unprofessional conduct and may establish exceptions to these general prohibitions.

(b) Unprofessional conduct in the practice of any profession licensed or certified pursuant to title 8 of the Education Law shall include:

   (1) willful or grossly negligent failure to comply with substantial provisions of Federal, State or local laws, rules of regulations governing the practice of the profession;

   (2) exercising undue influence on the patient or client, including the promotion of

the sale of services, goods, applicances or drugs in such manner as to exploit the patient or client for the financial gain of the practitioner or of a third party;

(3) directly or indirectly offering, giving, soliciting, or receiving or agreeing to receive, any fee or other consideration to or from a third party for the referral of a patient or client or in connection with the performance of professional services;

(4) permitting any person to share in the fees for professional services, other than: a partner, employee, associate in a professional firm or corporation, professional subcontractor or consultant authorized to practice the same profession, or a legally authorized trainee practicing under the supervision of alicensed practitioner. This prohibition shall include any arrangement or agreement whereby the amount received in payment for furnishing space, facilities, equipment or personnel services used by a professional license constitutes a percentage of, or is otherwise provided by law with respect to a facility licensed pursuant to article 28 of the Public Health Law or article 13 of the Mental Hygiene Law;

(5) conduct in the practice of a profession which evidences moral unfitness to practice the profession;

(6) willfully making or filing a false report, or failing to file a report required by law or by the Education Department, or willfully impeding or obstructing wuch filing, or inducing another person to do so;

(7) failing to make available to a patient or client, upon request, copies of documents in the possession or under the control of the licensee which have been prepared for and paid for by the patient or client;

(8) revealing of personally identifiable facts, data or information obtained in a professional capacity without the prior consent of the patient or client, except as authorized or required by law;

(9) practicing or offering to practice beyond the scope permitted by law, or accepting and performing responsibilities which the licensee knows or has reason to know that he or shw is not competent to perform, or performing without adequate supervision professional services which the licensee is authorized to perform only under the supervision of a licensed professional, except in an emergency situation where a person's life or health is in danger;

(10) delegating professional responsibilities to a person when the licensee delegating such responsibilities knows or has reason to know that such person is not qualified by training, by experience or by licensure, to perform them;

(11) performing professional services which have not been duly authorized by the patient client or his or her legal representatives;

(12) advertising or soliciting for patronage that is not in the public interest:

(i) Advertising or soliciting not in the public interest shall include but not be limited to advertising that:

(*a*) is false, fraudulent, deceptive, misleading, sensational or flamboyant;

(*b*) represents intimidation or undue pressure;

(*c*) uses testimonials;

(*d*) guarantees any service;

(*e*) offers gratuitous services or discounts in connection with professional services; but this clause shall not be construed to relate to the negotiation of fees between professionals and patients or clients, or to prohibit the rendering of professional services for which no fee is charged;

(*f*) makes claims of professional superiority which cannot be substantiated by the licensee, who shall have the burden of proof; or

(*g*) states or includes prices for professional services, except as provided for in clause (*b*) of subparagraph (ii) of this paragraph;

(ii) The following shall be deemed appropriate means of informing the public of the availability of professional services:

(*a*) informational advertising not contrary to the foregoing prohibitions; and

(*b*) the advertising in a newspaper, periodical or professional directory or on radio or television of fixed prices, or a stated range of prices, for specified routine professional services, provided that if there is an additional charge for related services which are an integral part of the overall service being provided by the licensee, the advertisement shall so state, and provided further that the advertisement indicates the period of time for which the advertised prices shall be in effect;

(iii) (*a*) all licensees placing advertisements shall maintain, or cause to be maintained, an exact copy of each advertisement, transcript, tape or videotape thereof as appropriate for the medium used, for a period of one year after its last appearance. This copy shall be made available for inspection upon demand of the Education Department or in the case of physicians, physician's and specialist's assistants, the Department of Health;

(*b*) A licensee shall not compensate or give anything of value to representatives of the press, radio, television or other communications media in anticipation of or in return for professional publicity in a news item;

(iv) No demonstrations, dramatizations or other portrayals of professional practice shall be permitted in advertising on radio or television;

(13) failing to respond within 30 days to written communications from the Education Department and to make available any relevant records with respect to an inquiry or complaint about the licensee's unprofessional conduct. The period of 30 days shall commence on the date when such communication was sent from the department by registered or certified mail, with return receipt requested, to the address appearing in the last registration.

(14) violating any term of probation or condition or limitation imposed on the licensee by the Board of Regents pursuant to Education Law section 6511.

29.2 General Provisions for Health Professions

(a) Unprofessional conduct shall also include, in the professions of:

medicine	ophthalmic dispensing
acupuncture	psychology
physical therapy	social work
physician's assistant	massage
specialist's assistant	occupational therapy
chiropractic	speech pathology
dentistry	audiology
dental hygiene	nursing
pharmacy	(registered professional nurse,
podiatry	licensed practical nurse):
optometry	

(1) abandoning or neglecting a patient or client under and in need of immediate professional care, without making reasonable arrangements for the continuation of such care, or abandoning a professional employment by a group practice, hospital, clinic or other health care facility, without reasonable notice and under circumstances which seriously impair the delivery of professional care to patients or clients;
(2) willfully harassing, abusing or intimidating a patient either physically or verbally;
(3) failing to maintain a record for each patient which accurately reflects the evaluation and treatment of the patient. Unless otherwise provided by law, all patient records must be retained for at least six years. Obstetrical records and records of minor patients must be retained for at least six years, and until one year after the minor patient reaches the age of 21 years;
(4) using the word ''Doctor'' in offering to perform professional services without also indicating the profession in which the licensee holds a doctorate;
(5) failing to exercise appropriate supervision over persons who are authorized to practice only under the supervision of the licensed professional;
(6) upon a patient's written request, failing to make available to a patient, or, to another licensed health practitioner consistent with that practitioner's authorized scope of practice, copies of the record required by paragraph (3) of this subdivision and copies of reports, test records, evaluation or X rays relating to the patient which are in the possession or under the control of the licensee, or failing to complete forms or reports required for the reimbursement of a patient by a third party. Reasonable fees may be charged for such copies, forms or reports, but prior payment for the professional services to which such records relate may not be required as a condition for making such records available. A practitioner may, however, withhold information from a patient if, in the reasonable exercise of his or her professional judgment, he or she believes release of such information would adversely affect the patient's health, and this section shall not require release, to the parent or guardian of a minor, of records or information relating to venereal disease or abortion except with the minor's consent. This provision shall apply in lieu of section 29.1 (b) (7) of this Part;
(7) guaranteeing that satisfaction or a cure will result from the performance of professional services;
(8) ordering of excessive tests, treatment, or use of treatment facilities not warranted by the condition of the patient;
(9) claiming or using any secret or special method of treatment which the licensee refuses to divulge to the State Board for the profession;
(10) failing to wear an identifying badge, which shall be conspicuously displayed and legible, indicating the practitioner's name and professional title authorized pursuant to the Education Law, while practicing as an employee or operator of a hospital, clinic, group practice or multiprofessional facility, or at a commercial establishment offering health services to the public;
(11) entering into an arrangement or agreement with a pharmacy for the compounding and/or dispensing of coded or specially marked prescriptions;
(12) with respect to all professional practices conducted under an assumed name, other than facilities licensed pursuant to article 28 of the Public Health Law or article 13 of the Mental Hygiene Law, failing to post conspicuously at the site

of such practice the names and the licensure field of all of the principal professional licensees engaged in practice at that site (i.e., principal partners, officers or principal shareholders.)

29.4 Special Provisions for the Profession of Medicine

(a) Unprofessional conduct in the practice of medicine shall include all conduct prohibited by sections 29.1 and 29.2 of this Part except as provided in this section, and shall also include the following:
  (1) knowingly or willfully performing a complete or partial autopsy on a deceased person without lawful authority;
  (2) failing to comply with a signed agreement to practice medicine in New York State in an area designated by the Commissioner of Education as having a shortage of physicians or refusing to repay medical education costs in lieu of such required service, or failing to comply with any provision of a written agreement with the State or any municipality within which the licensee has agreed to provide medical service or refusing to repay funds in lieu of such service as consideration of awards made by the State or any municipality thereof for his or her professional education in medicine, or failing to comply with any agreement entered into to aid his or her medical education;
  (3) a physician who prescribes or dispenses lenses or frames for the correction of vision shall be subject to the provisions of sections 29.8 and 29.9 of this Part relating to unprofessional conduct in optometry and/or ophthalmic dispensing;
  (4) in the conduct of psychological research, failing to undertake reasonable efforts to remove the possible harmful aftereffects of emotional stress as soon as the design of the research permits, or failing to inform prospective research subjects or their authorized representatives fully of the danger or serious aftereffects, if such danger exists, before they are utilized as research subjects;
  (5) in the interpretation of the provisions of section 29.1 (b) (5) of this Part and in the treatment of sexual dysfunction as well as in other areas of the practice of psychiatry:
    (i) immoral conduct shall include any physical contact of a sexual nature between physician and patient; but immoral conduct shall not include the use of films and/or other audiovisual aids with individuals or groups in the development of appropriate responses to overcome sexual dysfunction;
    (ii) in therapy groups, immoral conduct shall include activities which promote explicit physical sexual contact between group members during sessions.

29.12 Special Provisions for the Profession of Psychology

(a) Unprofessional conduct in the practice of psychology shall include conduct prohibited by sections 29.1 and 29.2 of this Part, except as provided in this section, and shall also include the following:
  (1) in the conduct of psychological research, failing to undertake reasonable efforts to remove the possible harmful aftereffects of emotional stress as soon as the design of the research permits, or failing to inform prospective research subjects or their authorized representatives fully of the danger of serious aftereffects, if such danger exists, before they are utilized as research subjects;
  (2) in the interpretation of the provisions of section 29.1 (b) (5) of this Part and in

the treatment of sexual dysfunction, as well as in other areas of the practice of psychology:

(i) immoral conduct shall include any physical contact of a sexual nature between psychologist and client; but immoral conduct shall not include the use of films and/or other audiovisual aids with individuals or groups in the development of appropriate responses to overcome sexual dysfunction;

(ii) in therapy groups, immoral conduct shall include activities which promote or allow explicit physical sexual contact between group members during sessions;

(3) the provisions of section 29.2(a)(5) of this Part shall apply to psychologists, who may also list in directories and on professional stationery areas of specialization and subspecialties recognized by the Board of Regents.

Sunset legislation. Sunset legislation is legislation that calls for the review of the necessity for the state to intervene in the regulation of a profession. The rationale for and the far-reaching influence of such legislation is illustrated in the Florida Regulatory Reform Act of 1976.

Florida Regulatory Reform Act §11.61 (1976)

11.61 Legislative Review of Regulatory Functions

(1) This act shall be known as the "Regulatory Reform Act of 1976."

(2) It is the intent of the legislature:

(a) That no profession, occupation, business, industry, or other endeavor shall be subject to the state's regulatory power unless the exercise of such power is necessary to protect the public health, safety, or welfare from significant and discernible harm or damage. The exercise of the state's police power shall be done only to the extent necessary for that purpose.

(b) That the state shall not regulate a profession, occupation, industry, business, or other endeavor in a manner which will unreasonably adversely affect the competitive market.

(c) To provide systematic legislative review of the need for, and the public benefits derived from, a program or function which licenses or otherwise regulates the initial entry into a profession, occupation, business, industry, or other endeavor by a periodic review and termination, modification, or reestablishment of such programs and functions.

(3) Legislative committee review of licensing and regulatory functions shall begin 2 years prior to the repeal date of the respective sections and chapters enumerated in subsections (2), (3), and (4) of s. 3, chapter 76-168, Laws of Florida, and shall conclude with a recommendation, on or before January 1 prior to the repeal date, for continuation, modification, or repeal.

(4) In determining whether to reestablish a program or function, the Legislature shall consider the following criteria:

(a) Would the absence of regulation significantly harm or endanger the public health, safety, or welfare?

(b) Is there a reasonable relationship between the exercise of the state's police power and the protection of the public health, safety, or welfare?

(c) Is there another, less restrictive method of regulation available which could adequately protect the public?

(d) Does the regulation have the effect of directly or indirectly increasing the costs of any goods or services involved, and, if so, to what degree?
(e) Is the increase in cost more harmful to the public than the harm which could result from the absence of regulation?
(f) Are all facets of the regulatory process designed solely for the purpose of, and have as their primary effect, the protection of the public?

(5) One year from the date of repeal of any section or chapter enumerated in s. 3, chapter 76–168, Laws of Florida, the unit of government or subunit thereof and the personnel positions responsible for carrying out the powers, duties, and functions created by such section or chapter shall be abolished, and all unexpended balances of appropriations, allocations, or other funds shall revert to the fund from which they were appropriated or, if that fund is abolished, to the General Revenue Fund.
(6) Any program or function scheduled for termination under this act or any subsequent act may be reestablished by the Legislature for any period of time specified by law, not to exceed 6 years, at the end of which time the Legislature shall again review such program or function pursuant to s. 3, chapter 76–168, Laws of Florida, and may again reestablish, modify, or allow the termination of such program or function pursuant to this section.
(7) Any program or function created in part to regulate the entry into any profession, occupation, business, industry or other endeavor by law enacted after the effective date of this act shall be reviewed by the Legislature, as required in s. 3, chapter 76–168, Laws of Florida, beginning not later than 48 months after the law authorizing the regulation becomes law, and such review shall be completed not later than January 1 of the next odd-numbered year following the commencement of review. Any such law is repealed on July 1 of such odd-numbered year unless reestablished by the Legislature.
(8) The Speaker of the House and the President of the Senate shall act to appoint a select joint committee to be named no later than January 1, 1977. Said select joint committee shall be charged with the duty of assisting in the implementation of the provisions of this act and shall be charged with the duty of establishing administrative procedures which shall facilitate the review and evaluation required in this act. The appropriate substantive committees of both the House and Senate, upon assignment by the Speaker and the President, respectively, and sitting jointly, shall be responsible for completing the review and evaluation required in this act. A report of their recommendations and a proposed bill shall be completed pursuant to subsection 3 and shall be submitted to the offices of the Speaker and the President for distribution to legislators prior to the ensuing legislative session.
(9) This act shall not affect the right to institute or prosecute any cause of action by or against a unit or subunit of government terminated pursuant to this act if the cause of action accrued prior to the date the unit or subunit was terminated. Any cause of action pending on the date the unit or subunit is terminated, or instituted thereafter, shall be prosecuted or defended in the name of the state by the Department of Legal Affairs.

JUDICIAL REGULATION

All laws and administrative regulations are subject to review by the courts. Laws and administrative regulations affecting professional practice in the mental health field have been challenged in the courts on a variety of grounds; it has been charged, for example, that such laws and regulations constitute an abuse of the police power. Claims of void for vagueness of language have also been common. Generally, the claims have reached the courts as the result of (1) litigants contesting some aspect of the law or regulation governing entry to the profession or (2) litigants who are professionals contesting some disciplinary action taken against them.

Entry-level professional practice. Statutes designed to give status to a profession and to protect the health and welfare of the public at large frequently impinge on the pre-existing rights and privileges of persons practicing that profession before the statute was passed. Shortly after a law regulating the profession of psychology went into effect in New York State, a private organization called the National Psychological Association for Psychoanalysis, Inc. (NPAP), brought suit against the University of the State of New York charging (1) that the law was an improper exercise of the state's police power, (2) that empowering the state university to implement the statute was an invalid delegation of legislative power, and (3) that the statute was void by reason of the fact that it contained no formal definition of "psychologist" or its proscribed derivatives. NPAP had brought suit when the state university had found that the training program offered by NPAP was not equivalent to that prescribed by statute. In *National Psychological Association for Psychoanalysis, Inc.* v. *University of the State of New York,* 8 N.Y.2d 197, 168 N.E.2d 649 (1960), we see how the court argued against NPAP's claims.

Statutes regulating a profession always contain some provision for practitioners who had been earning their livings in that profession prior to the enactment of the statute. This provision is referred to as a "grandfather clause." As stated in *State ex rel. Krausmann* v. *Streeter,* 226 Minn. 458, 33 N.W.2d 56:

> The purpose of an exception or grandfather clause is to exempt from the statutory regulations imposed for the first time on a trade or profession those members thereof who are then engaged in the newly regulated field on the theory that they who have acceptably followed such profession or trade for a period of years, or who are engaged therein on a certain date, may be presumed to have the qualifications which subsequent entrants to the field must demonstrate by examination. *Watson* v. *Maryland,* 218 U.S. 173, 30 S.Ct. 644, 54 L.Ed. 987; *Hart* v. *Folsom,* 70 N.H. 213, 47 A. 603; Annotation, 136 A.L.R. 219.

As illustrated in the cases of *Berger* v. *Board of Psychologist Examiners,* 521 F.2d 1056 (1975), and *Whittle* v. *State Board of Examiners of Psychologists,* Okl., 483 P.2d 328 (below), the courts tend to view the practice of a professional engaged in that practice before the enactment of a licensing statute as a vested property right, subject only to such regulation as might be reasonably and rationally related to safeguarding public health and welfare. In general, the courts have been sympathetic to "grandfathers" and "grandmothers" and have encouraged—indeed compelled—state boards to develop alternative and less restrictive methods to assess such practitioners' suitability for credentialing.

Numerous other questions pertaining to entry into professional practice find their way to the courtroom. "Is a doctorate in pupil placement services equivalent to a doctorate in psychology?" was the question before the court in *Carroll* v. *State,* Fla.App. 355 So.2d 495 (below). In *Jackson* v. *Sargent,* 394 F.Supp. 162 (D.C.D.Mass. 1975), the issue of whether any degree requirement is inherently racially discriminatory is dealt with by the court. When questions such as these are raised, the tendency of the courts has been to support the administrative actions and regulations if they can be shown to have a modicum of justification.

National Psychological Association for Psychoanalysis, Inc. v. *University of State of New York,* 8 N.Y.2d 197, 168 N.E.2d 649 (1960)

FROESSEL, J. The constitutionality of article 153 (§§ 7601–7614) of the Education Law (L. 1956, ch. 737), which deals with the certification of psychologists, was unsuccessfully challenged by plaintiff membership corporation, dedicated to the advancement of psychoanalysis (herein called NPAP), and four of its members, each of whom has since been certified under the statute. Since the question involved is of important public interest and one likely to arise again, we deem it appropriate to entertain the appeal on the merits (*Matter of United Press Assns.* v. *Valente,* 308 N.Y. 71, 76).

Drafted by State agencies and interested professional groups, and widely approved by the psychological fraternity (see Governor's Message, Public Papers of Governor Harriman, 1956, pp. 416–417; Memoranda of Education Department, N.Y. Legis. Ann., 1956, pp. 214–215, and Mental Hygiene Department, McKinney's 1956 Session Laws, pp. 1928–1929), article 153 is a certification rather than a licensing law, i.e., it does not prohibit anyone from rendering psychological services, but proscribes the professional use by noncertificants of the title "psychologist" and its derivatives, for remuneration. Section 7602 prohibits noncertified individuals from representing themselves as psychologists, and section 7601 defines a person who "represents himself to be a 'psychologist' " as one who "holds himself out to the public by any title or description of services incorporating the words 'psychological,' 'psychologist' or 'psychology,' *and under such title or description offers to render or renders services to individuals, corporations, or the public for remuneration.*" (Emphasis supplied.)

Section 7605 empowers the Department of Education to issue "a certificate as psychologist" to a citizen (or one who has declared his intention), of good moral character, at least 21 years of age, who pays a $40 fee, "passes a satisfactory examination in psychology," has "received the doctoral degree based on a program of studies whose content was primarily psychological from an educational institution having a graduate program registered by the department, *or its substantial equivalent in both subject matter and extent of training*" (emphasis supplied), and has had "at least two years of satisfactory supervised experience in rendering psychological services." For a specified period, the board is empowered to waive examination for those meeting prescribed standards of academic achievement and professional experience.

The statute further provides for biennial registration of certified psychologists (§ 7606); nondisclosure of privileged communications (§ 7611); and revocation or suspension of certificates, after notice and hearing before the Commissioner of Education, with the right of judicial review by way of an article 78 proceeding of the suspension, revocation, "or refusing to issue or renew a certificate" (§ 7607). Employees of governmental agencies and chartered educational institutions are exempt from the operation of the statute (§ 7609); the practice of medicine is not authorized (§ 7610); and violation of the statute is made a misdemeanor (§ 7608).

Article 153 was designed to accomplish a two-fold purpose. On the one hand, it "recognizes and gives status to the profession of psychology" (Governor's Message, *supra*) by "giving qualified psychologists official recognition" (Memo., Mental Hygiene Dept., *supra*), and by placing the "confidential relations and communications" between a registered psychologist and his client "on the same basis as those provided by law between attorney and client" (§ 7611). In this aspect, its sponsors felt that the statute would encourage bona fide psychologists with university training and professionally supervised experience to offer their needed professional services to the public in increasing numbers.

On the other hand, it was "apparent to all who are concerned with the field of public health that the public [was] entitled to protection in the form of state supervision" over the increasingly important field of psychology (Memo., Education Dept., *supra*). By prohibiting the use of the word "psychologist" and its variants in connection with the rendition of professional services for pay, it was felt that the statute would "make it possible to eliminate unqualified persons who are presently able to hold themselves out to the public as psychologists" (Memo., Education Dept., *supra*), and help to protect the public against charlatans and quacks who, despite inadequate training and professional experience, guarantee easy solutions to psychological problems.[1]

Aside from the presumption of constitutionality which must be accorded a legislative enactment (*Lincoln Bldg. Associates* v. *Barr,* 1 NY 2d 413, 415), it cannot be gainsaid that the statute is reasonably related to the public health and welfare, and thus constitutes a proper exercise of the State's police power under the due process clause of the State and Federal Constitutions. Through the medium of official certification of qualifications, it helps the public to identify those who have appropriate training and background in the profession of psychology. At the same time, it affords protection against the incompetent practitioner by providing a yardstick by which the public can judge the competence of persons offering psychological services.

We have upheld the certification as opposed to the complete licensing approach in the fields of accountancy (*Berkowitz* v. *Wilson,* 307 N.Y. 851), and plumbing (*People ex rel. Nechamcus* v. *Warden of City Prison,* 144 N.Y. 529), and, as stated in the latter case (pp. 538–539), "if the act is a step in the direction of something which will enure to the public health and comfort, that it does not go as far as it might, is not a reason for invalidating it"[2]. Since "we may not, of course, substitute our judgment for that of the Legislature as to the wisdom or expediency of the legislation" (*Thompson* v. *Wallin* [and two companion cases], 301 N.Y. 476, 488, affd. 342 U.S. 485, 801, 951), the strong convictions expressed by plaintiffs against the soundness and efficacy of the statute have no bearing on its constitutionality (see *Beauharnais* v. *Illinois*, 343 U.S.

[1]See note, 51 Col. L. Rev. (1951) 474, which points up "The selling power of the term 'psychologist' and its variants" and the importance, in terms of practical protection to the public, of proscribing "the professional use by noncertificants of the very terms which have apparently captured the popular imagination" (pp. 484–485).

[2]See, also, former article 56 of the Education Law (§§ 1475, 1476, added by L. 1927, ch. 85, and derived from former §§ 77, 77-a of the General Business Law), which, as noted in *Roth* v. *Hoster Realty Co.* (119 Misc. 686), was "directed solely against the assumption of the title *architect or registered architect*" (emphasis supplied), and did "not forbid the practice of the profession or occupation generally."

250, 262; *People* v. *Schweinler Press,* 214 N.Y. 395, 406–407, appeal dismissed 242 U.S. 618).

The constitutional arguments pressed on this appeal revolve around the fact that the statute does not contain a formal definition of "psychologist" or its proscribed derivatives. Plaintiffs contend that the absence of such a definition renders the statute violative of due process in two respects: (1) it arbitrarily restricts the carrying on of a lawful occupation in that it prohibits a noncertified psychologist from truthfully describing his professional services, and (2) the statute's qualifying standards are meaningless without a definition to which they can attach, and hence the statute unlawfully delegates legislative power without accompanying standards to guide the exercise of administrative discretion.

The omission of a formal definition of "psychology" or its variants was no legislative oversight. Attempts to draft a definition that would sufficiently delineate the nature and scope of psychology had failed (Memos., Mental Hygiene and Education Depts., *supra*), and, as noted by Special Term, "the law was enacted in a form that was acceptable to interested groups and that requires no interpretation of that term for its enforcement." The standards of fitness established by the Legislature imbue the title "psychologist" with meaningful content, and a person with a bona fide claim to that title will meet those qualifications and be accorded official recognition, as were the individual plaintiffs herein. To "assure adequate representation of the diverse fields of psychology" on the State Board of Examiners, the Legislature specifically provided that "the board shall at all times, except for vacancies, have two members representing the training institutions in psychology, three members who engage in rendering service in psychology and two members who devote a majority of their time to rendering service in psychology" (§ 7603). The membership of the Advisory Council established by the Legislature to "aid in the formulation of policy" was likewise apportioned among professional practitioners and "representatives of the professional training centers" to insure that it would be "broadly representative of psychology" (§ 7604).

That the Legislature assigned to respondent the task of implementing the statute—by recognizing accredited psychology courses in the graduate curriculum of chartered institutions, by determining the scope of the qualifying examination, by fixing the "substantial equivalent" of a doctoral degree, and by deciding what constitutes "satisfactory supervised experience"—does not constitute an invalid delegation of legislative power (*Matter of Marburg* v. *Cole,* 286 N.Y. 202, 211–212; *Matter of City of Utica* v. *Water Pollution Control Bd.,* 5 NY 2d 164). The statute prescribes clearly discernible standards to govern the exercise of the power of certification, and it was "proper and fitting for the Legislature to assign broad functions to the Board, particularly when it was contemplated and understood that its members were to bring to their work a familiarity with conditions which the individual legislators could not be expected to possess" (*Matter of City of Utica* v. *Water Pollution Control Bd., supra,* p. 170).

While plaintiffs maintain, on the one hand, that there is as yet "no unified concept of what psychology is," nor a "generally accepted definition of psychology, psychologists or psychological services," they nonetheless contend, on the other hand, that the constitutional infirmity in the statute lies in its failure to define those very terms. They recognize that the profession of psychology is affected with a public interest, and hence subject to regulation under the police power. Yet the end result of their argument is that the Legislature may not constitutionally regulate psychologists, since the title and the field are incapable of precise definition, and a statute without such definition is invalid.

The short answer to this thoroughly untenable argument is that section 7605, in practical effect, defines a psychologist as an individual who meets prescribed standards of fitness, and since the statute merely proscribes *the use of specific words* to *describe* the rendition of services, without making it criminal for noncertificants to render such services, no further definition of that term is constitutionally required or necessary (see *Pitts* v. *State Bd. of Examiners of Psychologists,* 222 Md. 224, 227). The statute is easily complied with by the nonuse of particular words, and hence it completely ''satisfies the requirement that a criminal statute must be sufficiently definite, 'clear and positive' to give 'unequivocal warning' to citizens of the rule which is to be obeyed'' (*People* v. *Firth,* 3 NY 2d 472, 474).

Plaintiffs' real quarrel with the statute is not that it lacks a formal definition of ''psychologist'', but that the definition adopted—by way of qualifying standards—does not meet with their approval. NPAP conducts a training program for members in training, and respondent has refused to accept that program as satisfying the academic requirements of the statute, contrary to NPAP's expectation at the time it supported the statute. The major portion of plaintiffs' affidavits, as well as their complaint, is devoted to the merits of NPAP's training program, and why it should qualify as a ''substantial equivalent'' of ''the specialized advanced courses in psychological theory and professional skills in a typical graduate psychology program given by degree-granting institutions leading to a degree of Doctor of Philosophy in psychology.'' However, a disagreement with the judgment of the Legislature as to the proper standards of fitness for persons wishing to be certified in their craft cannot rise to the level of a constitutional argument by couching that disagreement in the language of due process or equal protection of the laws. If certification is denied to one of NPAP's members, and he can establish that respondent's refusal to accept his training as a ''substantial equivalent'' of formal university training was an arbitrary abuse of administrative discretion, then he may obtain the necessary relief in the courts by way of an article 78 proceeding (§ 7607, subd. 3; see *Matter of Marburg* v. *Cole, supra*).

As to plaintiffs' contention that ''the issue of constitutionality cannot be determined without a trial''—which is inconsistent with their motion for summary judgment—the issues of fact which assertedly exist all go to the wisdom and efficacy of the statute, and have no bearing on its constitutionality.

The judgment should be affirmed, with costs.

Chief Judge DESMOND and Judges DYE, FULD, BURKE and FOSTER concur with Judge FROESSEL; Judge VAN VOORHIS concurs on the assumption that this statute affects the use of the title ''psychologist'' only in conjunction with services rendered to individuals in the solution of personal problems or treatment of illness.

Judgment affirmed.

Berger v. *Board of Psychologist Examiners,* 521 F.2d 1056 (1975)

Before MACKINNON and WILKEY, Circuit Judges, and VAN PELT*, United States Senior District Judge for the District of Nebraska.

Opinion for the court filed by Circuit Judge MACKINNON.

MACKINNON, Circuit Judge:

Appellant Joseph R. Berger, a practitioner of psychology in the District of Columbia since 1961, challenges the constitutionality of a 1971 law requiring that all psy-

*Sitting by designation pursuant to 28 U.S.C. § 294(d).

chologists practicing in the District be licensed and specifying that licenses shall be issued only to applicants possessed of certain academic credentials. Berger contends that the Due Process Clause of the Constitution guarantees him some alternative means of demonstrating his professional competence, in the nature of a "grandfather" concession to psychologists practicing at the time the licensure requirement was enacted. We agree, and remand to the licensing board for action consistent with this opinion.

I

In 1971 Congress passed the District of Columbia Practice of Psychology Act, P.L. 91-657, D.C.Code § 2-481 *et seq.*, a licensing statute designed to impose minimum educational requirements upon all psychologists practicing in the District.[1] Section 7 of the Act, § 2-486, directs an appointed Commissioner to grant a license to anyone who

[1]The Act provides:

§ **2-486. Qualification requirements—Written examination—Application fee**

The Commissioner shall grant a license to practice psychology to each applicant who submits satisfactory proof that—

(A) he is of good moral character;

(B) he holds either (1) a doctoral degree in psychology from an accredited college or university and has completed two years of postgraduate experience acceptable to the Commissioner, such two years not to include terms of internship, or (2) a doctoral degree from an accredited college or university in a field determined by the Commissioner to be related to psychology and has completed two years of postgraduate experience: *Provided,* That his experience and training are considered by the Commissioner to be comparable to the requirements set forth in (B)(1) of this subsection;

(C) he has passed an examination, written or oral or both, the scope and form of which shall be determined by the Commissioner: *Provided,* That at any given examination session all examinations shall be uniform; and

(D) his application has been accompanied by the fees required by the Commissioner.

§ **2-487. License without examination**

(a) Notwithstanding any other provision of this subchapter, a license shall be issued without examination to any applicant who is of good moral character, who, at any time during the twelve-month period preceding the effective date of this subchapter, maintained a residence or office, or participated in psychological practice acceptable to the Commissioners, in the District of Columbia, and who, within one year after the effective date of this subchapter, submitted an application for license accompanied by the required fee, and who—

(1) holds a doctoral degree in psychology or forty-five credit hours taken subsequent to a bachelor's degree in courses related to psychology, from accredited colleges or universities, and has engaged in psychological practice acceptable to the Commissioner for at least two years prior to the filing of such application pursuant to this subchapter;

(2) holds a master's degree in psychology or twenty-four credit hours taken subsequent to a bachelor's degree in courses related to psychology, from accredited colleges or universities, and has engaged in psychological practice acceptable to the Commissioner for at least seven years prior to the filing of such application pursuant to this subchapter; or

(3) presents evidence of completion of a curriculum of study acceptable to the Commissioner, taken subsequent to a bachelor's degree in psychology, in courses related to psychology from an institution outside the United States acceptable to the Commissioner, and has engaged in psychological practice acceptable to the Commissioner for at least seven years prior to the filing of such application pursuant to this subchapter.

(b) For purposes of subsection (a) of this section, the term—

(1) "courses related to psychology" means any combination of the following behavioral science courses not necessarily in one department of one school: human development, education, educational psychology, guidance, counseling, guidance and counseling, vocational counseling, school psychology, school guidance, family counseling, counseling and psychotherapy, special education, learning disabilities, anthropology, sociology, human ecology, social ecology, rehabilitation counseling, group counseling and psychotherapy, or any substantially similar field of study acceptable to the Commissioner, and

(2) "psychological practice acceptable to the Commissioner" includes any job in which the job title or description contains any term acceptable to the Commissioner, or any of the following terms: psychologists, psychotherapy, group therapy, family therapy, art therapy, activity therapy, psychometry, measurement and evaluation, psychodiagnosis, pupil personnel services, counseling and guidance, special education, rehabilitation, or any job in which the person or organization was recognized or reimbursed under public or private health insurance programs by reason of being engaged in psychological practice.

(a) submits "satisfactory proof" of good moral character, (b) possesses a doctoral degree in psychology or in some other discipline deemed by the Commissioner to be sufficiently closely related, and (c) passes a written or oral examination. Section 8 of the Act is a limited "grandfather" clause which provides less stringent requirements for licensure for an applicant engaged in the practice of psychology in the District at the time the statute was enacted. The pertinent distinction is that section 8 permits substitution of a master's degree or "twenty-four credit hours taken subsequent to a bachelor's degree in courses related to psychology" and seven years' practice for possession of a doctorate and passage of an examination. Section 14 prescribes a misdemeanor penalty of up to $500 and/or six months in jail for failure to comply with the Act's licensing requirements.[2]

Appellant Berger was awarded a BCS degree in accounting from Southeastern University in 1943. He received training in the field of psychology from several psychiatrists and was given credit for numerous courses in various areas of psychology which he took at American University, the United States Department of Agriculture Graduate School, and the Washington School of Psychiatry. Although he has never been certified or licensed to practice in any other jurisdiction and is not a member of any professional psychological association, he has practiced psychology in the District of Columbia for approximately 14 years, co-authored a book on hypnosis published by Prentice-Hall, and lectured and written on clinical topics. The licensing board established by the Act ignored these facts and letters written by some of Berger's colleagues testifying to his competency, and denied his application because of his failure to make the threshold showing required by the Act. The board concluded:

> Inasmuch as it is conceded by the applicant that he possesses neither a doctor's degree nor a master's degree in psychology, it is clear that he is not qualified for a license under Section 8 of the Act.

Appellee's Brief at 9.

In 1971 Berger moved the District Court for a Temporary Restraining Order and Preliminary and Permanent Injunction to prevent enforcement of the Act and the denial of his right to practice psychology. He alleged that the absence of a proper grandfather clause and of discernible standards for licensure rendered the Act unconstitutional on its face. Judge Pratt granted Berger's request for a temporary restraining order but denied further relief without prejudice to reinstitution of the action after the licensing system had been established and Berger had exhausted his administrative remedies. In 1972 the Board rejected Berger's application for a license, and he immediately appealed to the District of Columbia Court of Appeals, attacking the statute as unconstitutional. In December 1973 the Court of Appeals ruled that because it sat as a reviewing board it could not pass on the constitutionality of the statute under which it proceeded, and consequently affirmed the Board's decision.[3] Proceeding under the express terms

[2]Section 14 provides:

§ 2–493. Penalties

Any person who shall practice psychology, as defined in this subchapter, without having a valid, unexpired, unrevoked, and unsuspended license or certificate of registration issued as provided in this subchapter, shall be deemed guilty of a misdemeanor and, upon conviction, shall be fined not more than $500, or confined in jail for not more than six months, or both. Prosecutions shall be in the name of the District of Columbia by the Corporation Counsel or one of his assistants.

[3]A majority of the District of Columbia Court of Appeals also concluded that they lacked jurisdiction to entertain any review proceeding: since Berger had admitted that the Board possessed no power under the Act to grant his request, the denial of a license was not "for any cause" under D.C.Code 1973, § 2-492(B). Judge Nebeker, in a concurring opinion, insisted that "failure to have the requisite academic degree is a

of the Act, which provides that "review [by the District of Columbia Court of Appeals] shall be subject to appeal to the United States Court of Appeals for the District of Columbia Circuit" Act, § 2-492, Berger brought his challenge here.

While Berger's appeal was pending in this court, Congress amended the Practice of Psychology Act, P.L. 93-515, passed December 7, 1974, to effect two modifications relevant to this controversy. Subsection (C) of section 13 was modified to remove all federal court jurisdiction to entertain appeals of D.C. Court of Appeals decisions, but only "with respect to petitions filed after the date of enactment of [these amendments]." Although this change lends support to appellee's argument that this court had appellate jurisdiction only through legislative oversight, it does not undercut our power to entertain an appeal in this case. Second, the statute's limited concession to current practitioners was expanded to accord an applicant with 24 post-graduate credit hours the same right as one holding a master's degree: either the degree or the course credits, plus seven years' practice prior to the filing of an application, entitled an individual to licensure. For one who has studied outside the United States, any "acceptable curriculum" taken upon completion of a bachelor's degree program is sufficient. Appellant Berger does not qualify even under these amendments.

Berger attacks the Act on four grounds: (1) that it fails to prescribe standards for licensure; (2) that the absence of meaningful grandfather rights or an equivalency provision constitutes invidious discrimination and a denial of due process; (3) that a classification which excludes from the profession a successful practitioner of 14 years is arbitrary and capricious; and (4) that a review board comprised of professional psychologists with apparent or actual qualifications under the Act is not a properly impartial adjudicatory body. Arguing for the licensing board, Corporation Counsel for the District of Columbia defends the statute as a rational exercise of congressional police power over the District and insists that this court cannot pass on constitutional issues in what is in essence an administrative proceeding.

II

The Corporation Counsel raises a threshold objection of Berger's appeal which we must consider before we reach the merits of this dispute. The argument is that Berger is precluded from challenging the constitutionality of a statute under which he has sought licensure. Corporation Counsel insists that Berger may not avail himself of the statutory review procedure outlined in the Act in order to prosecute that constitutional challenge, but must instead attend the institution of criminal proceedings against him for violating the licensure requirement, at which point his constitutional claim may be interposed as a defense. Because Corporation Counsel has both misapprehended the scope of Berger's constitutional attack on the Act and sought support from inapposite precedent, we conclude that this preliminary contention is insubstantial.

Corporation Counsel persuaded the District of Columbia Court of Appeals below that Berger should not be allowed to challenge the validity of the Act in a proceeding instituted under its review procedures. That court concluded that since Berger was aware the Board of Psychologist Examiners lacked the power to waive the academic requirements for licensure at the time of his administrative hearing, he

'cause' for refusing a license and such may be reviewed by this court." *Berger* v. *Board of Psychologist Examiners*, 313 A.2d 602, 607 (D.C.App.1973).

> expected no relief from the Board. As far as he was concerned, the proceeding before the Board was a formality, used merely as a step to come to this court. Having gotten here by that procedure, in effect he seeks to institute an original action to have this court declare the Act invalid and unconstitutional. Does he have a right to institute such action and do we have a right to entertain it? We think not.[4]

Two interpretations of this determination are possible. Corporation Counsel argues that the Court of Appeals found applicants for licensure proceeding under the review provisions of the Act to be utterly without an avenue of constitutional attack, and urges us to concur in that judgment. Alternatively, we might conclude that the Court of Appeals declined to pass on the constitutional claim because the Act specifically gave it the more limited function of *reviewing* Board decisions, in contradistinction to this court's jurisdiction to entertain *appeals* of rulings by the District of Columbia Court of Appeals. That court had no occasion to decide the breadth of our appellate jurisdiction, and the Corporation Counsel is in error in arguing that its decision foreclosed our scrutiny of the constitutionality of the Act.

In fact we need not define the difference between our jurisdiction on appeal and that of the D.C. Court of Appeals in review proceedings. In our opinion either tribunal has the power to pass on the particular constitutional claim Berger advanced. He sought not an erosion of the statutory scheme by which this court assumes appellate jurisdiction, but rather a simple declaration, consistent with the major provisions of the Act, that the Board's refusal to test his professional competence by some standard other than his academic credentials constituted a violation of fundamental due process. We might append to the statute an appropriate proviso designed to rectify this constitutional infirmity, without substantial modification of the statutory plan by which we are called to review Berger's administrative odyssey.

A judicial declaration that the Act must include an alternative criterion of Berger's professional skill is quite distinct from the results sought in the cases to which Corporation Counsel attempts to draw an analogy—for example, the invalidation of a trademark registration statute at the behest of one who had long profited by such registration,[5] or the voiding of a law allowing the federal government to acquire an appellant's land, when the prospect of condemnation had yielded the appellant substantial proceeds.[6] These cases involve the concept of equitable estoppel, and would be apposite to the instant controversy if Berger attacked the validity of the licensing statute after he had enjoyed the benefits of licensure. But they do not limit the scope of his challenge to the Act in an initial application for a license.

We thus reject the Corporation Counsel's challenge to the jurisdiction of this court over Berger's constitutional claim. We do not risk cutting off the limb upon which we sit by entertaining his limited challenge to the validity of the Act's licensure qualifications.

III

Our opportunity and obligation to pass on Berger's claim to meaningful grandfather treatment under the District's licensing scheme is in a sense unique. Whether our

[4] *Berger* v. *Board of Psychologist Examiners*, 313 A.2d 602, 604 (D.C.App.1973).

[5] *Fulton Waterworks* v. *Bear Lithia Springs Co.*, 47 App.D.C. 437 (1918).

[6] *Young* v. *Anderson*, 81 U.S.App.D.C. 379, 160 F.2d 225, *cert. denied*, 331 U.S. 824, 67 S.Ct. 1316, 91 L.Ed. 1840 (1947).

short-lived appellate jurisdiction under the Act was the product of legislative oversight, it was surely anomalous.[7] Because the power to license the practice of psychology belongs generally to the states and is the subject of congressional enactment only in the District of Columbia, state courts will in almost every instance pass on the validity of specific licensure qualifications. But the question we confront is no less important for its rarity: appellant, and perhaps many other psychologists in the District of Columbia who have acquired their skills through apprenticeship, may lose the right to practice their profession because the Congress has suddenly decided the field needs regulating. But the very reason psychology has not been regulated before is that it has been and remains an amorphous, inexact and even mysterious discipline. Possession of a graduate degree in psychology does not signify the absorption of a corpus of knowledge as does a medical, engineering, or law degree; rather it is simply a convenient line for legislatures to draw, on the brave assumption that whatever is taught in the varied graduate curricula of university psychology departments must make one a competent psychologist, or at least competent enough to be allowed to take a licensing examination. While it may not be irrational to assume that this academic background should in the future be a prerequisite to the practice of psychology, it is of questionable rationality to insist that current practitioners, who may have studied and practiced at a time when graduate courses in psychology were even less meaningful, are conclusively incapable of meeting today's new standards because they did not take those courses.[8] Supporting this view are several decisions by the United States Supreme Court upholding state licensing statutes which presumed *competence* on the part of professionals who had practical experience but no degree.[9]

The limited nature of Berger's challenge to the D.C. statute bears reemphasis. He does not argue that anyone has an absolute right to practice a profession. The logic of his argument allows that a legislature might ban the practice of psychology altogether, on a conclusion that the discipline was not beneficial or that it should be subsumed by traditional medical practice. Appellant maintains only that current practitioners should not be denied the opportunity to continue their chosen profession, without prior notice of the licensing requirement and without some occasion to demonstrate their adequacy to the task. In short, in order to protect his "liberty" and "property" interests in his

[7]The D.C. Court of Appeals below was "puzzled" that the Act's grant of appellate jurisdiction to this court was contemporaneous with enactment of the District of Columbia Court Reform and Criminal Procedure Act of 1970, effective February 1, 1971, rendering the D.C. Court of Appeals the "highest court of the District of Columbia," D.C.Code 1973, § 11-102, with jurisdiction to review orders and decisions of any agency of the District of Columbia, D.C.Code 1973, § 11-722. Congress simultaneously withdrew this court's previous power to review decisions of the D.C. Court of Appeals, with limited exceptions. *See M.A.P.* v. *Ryan,* 285 A.2d 310, 312 (D.C.App.1971).

[8]As Berger notes, the D.C. statute would deny a license and even a hearing to Erik Erickson, perhaps the most eminent psychologist of our time, for his failure to glean his considerable insights from an academic regimen.

[9]In both *Dent* v. *West Virginia,* 129 U.S. 114, 9 S.Ct. 231, 32 L.Ed. 623 (1889), and *Watson* v. *Maryland,* 218 U.S. 173, 30 S.Ct. 644, 54 L.Ed. 987 (1910), the Court upheld state physician licensing statutes against charges that without due process of law they deprived practicing physicians (who did not meet the requirements of the grandfather clause) of a vested right to practice their profession. The West Virginia statute allowed to practice medicine only those who were (a) graduates of reputable medical schools, (b) doctors who had practiced continuously for ten years in the state, or (c) doctors who had passed the examination given by the state Board of Health. Under the Maryland law all doctors were blanketed in who had been practicing four years before the enactment of the licensing statute and who could show that they had treated at least twelve persons within one year of that date. It is to be noted that in the case of physicians the risk to the individual patient from an unqualified practitioner is even greater than it is in the present case.

profession,[10] appellant seeks an opportunity to rebut the statutory presumption of his incompetence.

The Supreme Court has long held irrebuttable statutory presumptions to be disfavored. *See, e.g., Bell* v. *Burson,* 402 U.S. 535, 91 S.Ct. 1586, 29 L.Ed.2d 90 (1971); *Tot* v. *United States,* 319 U.S. 463, 468-96, 63 S.Ct. 1241, 87 L.Ed. 1519 (1943); *Schlesinger* v. *Wisconsin,* 270 U.S. 230, 46 S.Ct. 260, 70 L.Ed. 557 (1926). Recently the Court has struck down irrebuttable presumptions that unmarried fathers are unqualified to raise children, *Stanley* v. *Illinois,* 405 U.S. 645, 92 S.Ct. 1208, 31 L.Ed. 551 (1972); that women more than four months pregnant cannot teach school, *Cleveland Board* v. *Lafleur,* 414 U.S. 632, 94 S.Ct. 791, 39 L.Ed.2d 52 (1974); and that those who apply to the Connecticut State University system as non-residents can never become residents for the purpose of paying lower in-state tuition, *Vlandis* v. *Kline,* 412 U.S. 441, 446-53, 93 S.Ct. 2230, 37 L.Ed.2d 63 (1974). *See also U.S. Department of Agriculture* v. *Murry,* 413 U.S. 508, 93 S.Ct. 2832, 37 L.Ed.2d 767 (1973); *Boddie* v. *Connecticut,* 401 U.S. 371, 91 S.Ct. 780, 28 L.Ed.2d 113 (1971); *cf. Morrisey* v. *Brewer,* 408 U.S. 471, 92 S.Ct. 2593, 33 L.Ed.2d 484 (1972). In *Vlandis,* in response to the argument that the presumption of non-residency provided "a degree of administrative certainty," Justice Stewart noted that "the Constitution recognizes higher values than speed and efficiency," 412 U.S. at 451, 93 S.Ct. 2236, citing *Stanley* v. *Illinois,* 405 U.S. at 656, 92 S.Ct. 1208. Justice Stewart continued:

> The State's interest in administrative ease and certainty cannot, in and of itself, save the conclusive presumption from invalidity under the Due Process Clause where there are other reasonable and practicable means of establishing the pertinent facts on which the State's objective is premised.

412 U.S. at 451, 93 S.Ct. at 2236.

The principle of *Vlandis* is applicable to the facts of the instant case. A part, and presumably a significant part, of the D.C. licensing process is the administration pursuant to D.C.Code § 2-481 of an examination devised by the licensing board to applicants holding a doctoral degree. No reason has been suggested why the Board could not fashion a similar examination and substitute passage of that test for the current requirement of passing an examination plus holding a degree. As an administrative body the Board cannot ignore or reinterpret parts of the statute under which it operates. But on remand, following a declaration by this court that the statute's irrebuttable presumption does not accord with principles clearly set forth in the case law, the Board could proceed to determine whether Berger's extensive clinical experience, coupled with his limited academic training and apprenticeship, have afforded him a professional competence equivalent to that of a doctor of psychology who has only two years of acceptable postgraduate experience.

We conclude that the Act's irrefutable presumption arbitrarily and unreasonably deprives Berger of his constitutionally recognized interest in the practice of psychology[11] in violation of the Due Process Clause of the Fifth Amendment. Our decision cannot be wholly founded in any single opinion of the Supreme Court cited above, for those cases have involved statutory presumptions invalid as to all individuals covered by the respective acts. Here the irrebuttable presumption of professional incompetence

[10] *See Fitzgerald* v. *Hampton,* 152 U.S.App. D.C. 1, 7 and n.21, 467 F.2d 755, 761 and n.21 (1972), and cases cited therein.

[11] *Id.*

absent a graduate degree is not invalid with respect to future psychologists, but only with respect to current practitioners who have no meaningful grandfather rights. But this distinction actually cuts in favor of applying the doctrine of *Vlandis* to this case: the *Vlandis* rule is based on due process notions, on the right to notice and hearing before final agency action, and it is precisely the inadequacy of the notice afforded current practitioners by the new D.C. licensing statute which makes the denial of grandfather rights unfair. Certainly a graduate degree may be required of a practicing psychologist, just as it is required of doctors and lawyers. The inequity of the statute is that it fails to account for those competent psychologists who embarked upon their profession when no degree was required and who thus are denied a fair opportunity to come within the statute's licensing requirements at this point.

The federal courts have apparently not considered the issue we confront in this case, but at least one state court has entertained a similar claim and has reached a virtually identical conclusion. In *Taylor* v. *Hayes,* 131 Ill.App.2d 305, 264 N.E.2d 814 (1970), a panel of the Illinois Appellate Court found that state's Psychologist Registration Act to be unconstitutional as applied to a psychologist who had practiced for nine years before the statute's enactment and who had *not* been awarded a master's degree for his considerable post-graduate studies. The court held:

> In the instant case the right of the plaintiff to pursue his profession was fixed during the pre-regulatory period and any subsequent legislation affecting his profession must be reasonable as it affects his special situation. We find that the requirement that plaintiff, as a practicing psychologist at the time of the enactment of the Act, possess a master's or doctoral degree to qualify for registration is unreasonable and arbitrary and denied him due process of law since it effectively excludes him from continuing to practice without providing an alternative method for evaluating his ability.

264 N.E.2d at 818. The Illinois court declined, as we must, to compel its licensing board to grant the applicant licensure, but insisted that some method be devised to determine if the level of his professional skills warranted the granting of a license to him. The fact that the applicant in *Taylor* v. *Hayes* fell just short of the academic credentials the Illinois statute required does not undermine the reasoning of the case or make it less analogous to this litigation. Lest the *Taylor* decision be erroneously distinguished as an attempt by judicial fiat to weaken Illinois' licensure requirements in order to admit to practice a marginal case, we emphasize that the Illinois court voiced its concern in that case, as we do here, not with the specific duration of the graduate education required by the legislature, but with the absence of some non-academic criteria available on a grandfather basis to current practitioners. Whether an applicant previously engaged in the practice of psychology misses the statutory standard by an inch or a country mile, he must be accorded a fair opportunity to demonstrate his professional skill according to reasonable standards before he is denied the right to continue his practice.

Although the Supreme Court has stated that administrative efficiency alone does not justify violations of procedural due process through the use of unjustifiable presumptions, efficiency must always be a consideration. In that context it is significant that invalidating the Psychology Act's conclusive presumption *only with respect to individuals practicing at the time the Act was passed* imposes on the licensing board a definable burden of finite duration. As Berger's situation will probably not be common, and as the examination he and others similarly situated will have to pass will be administered by academically qualified psychologists with genuine concern for the quality of their profession in the District, affording this opportunity to rebut the statutory presumption hardly threatens to frustrate the Act and flood the city with charlatans.[12]

Accordingly, we remand the case to the D.C. Court of Appeals for further remand to the licensing board to administer to appellant Berger an examination designed to determine whether his professional skill is commensurate with that of new psychologists being currently licensed under the Act. In so doing, we do not act as a legislature to add this requirement to the statute, but rather strike down as unconstitutional that part of the statute which requires an applicant to have an academic credential as well as a certain number of years experience in order to qualify to take a license examination. Only by this action can we remedy the constitutional defect of the statute as it is applied to Berger and to other psychologists without the requisite academic credentials but possibly possessed of the necessary skills.

Judgment accordingly.

Whittle v. *State Board of Examiners of Psychologists*, Okl., 483 P.2d 328 (1971)

McINERNEY, Justice.

Plaintiff-in-Error is a psychological consultant to commerce and industry who has been practicing his profession in Oklahoma since the early 1950's. He has both a bachelor's and a master's degree in psychology from Southern Methodist University, and was later enrolled in the doctoral program in psychology at the University of Oklahoma—leaving to go into full-time practice. For the most part, he has always been a sole practitioner.

In 1965 the Legislature enacted the Oklahoma Psychologists Licensing Act, 59 O.S. Supp.1970, § 1351 et seq., which for the first time made licensing a prerequisite to the practice of psychology in this State. Generally speaking, the doctorate was made the prime prerequisite for licensing, but two exceptions, commonly known as "grandfather clauses," were allowed to persons already practicing as psychologists with only master's degrees in psychology. Under one, contained in Section 1362(b) of Title 59, a master's holder could take a qualifying examination provided he had had five years of practice under supervision; and under the other exception, Section 1366(b)(2), such an applicant could be licensed without examination if he had had eight years of practice "satisfactory to the Board."

Because of the solitary nature of Plaintiff-in Error's practice, he could not assert the five years' practice "under supervision" required for admission to take the examination under Section 1362, supra. He therefore filed, on the basis of his more than eight years of practice, for licensing under the non-examination provisions of Section 1366.

[12]Recognizing that the Board he must face at a hearing on his application may not be favorably disposed toward him, Berger attacks the composition of the Board, alleging that a panel of statutorily qualified psychologists cannot assess his qualifications with impartiality, particularly in an area as small as the city of Washington. Though this claim is facially appealing, it ignores the realities of the situation: no one but a qualified psychologist can possibly assess his equivalency, just as admissions to the bar cannot be passed on by accountants.

We note at the outset that the filing periods under both "grandfather" clauses referred to above terminated one year from the effective date (June 28, 1965) of the Act, or on June 28, 1966; and since almost five years have passed since the closing deadline for these "grandfather" filings, no one now seeking licensing can be eligible thereunder. All persons applying for licensing within Oklahoma since 1966 have been required to possess the doctorate and take an examination, Section 1362(a) (except persons applying under the reciprocity provision of § 1366(c)). The rule announced here, therefore, has no application to present licensing.

In the applicant's Section 1366 proceedings before the Board, there appears to have been no dispute as to his academic qualifications, nor as to the length (or successful nature) of his practice (i.e., in excess of eight years). However, in emphasizing the requirement of eight years' practice "satisfactory to the Board," the Board apparently took the position, possibly under the broad language of Section 1364, that it could become "satisfied" of the character of an applicant's practice only by the testimonial letters of three to five licensed (or eligible for licensing) psychologists personally familiar with the character of the applicant's practice. Since Plaintiff-in-Error had been a sole practitioner for virtually all of his career, and dealing with industrial clients rather than with other professionals, it was naturally impossible for him to comply with this administrative requirement (although he did produce a number of favorable letters from his former professors, plus one from a former associate who did vouch for the character of his practice); and solely for lack of these three-to-five letters of other psychologists familiar with his actual practice, the Board denied licensing.

That order of denial was affirmed on appeal to the District Court of Oklahoma County, from which this appeal has been taken. The District Court, however, did stay execution of the Board's order, without bond, pending this appeal. We reverse the denial of licensing.

Since Plaintiff-in-Error had established a successful practice of psychology in Oklahoma at a time when it was lawful to do so in this State without licensing, that practice must be viewed as a vested property right, subject only to such subsequent regulation as might be reasonably and rationally related to safeguarding the public health and welfare. State *ex rel. Whetsel* v. *Wood,* 207 Okl. 193, 248 P.2d 612, 34 A.L.R.2d 1321 (1952). And given the proprietary nature of an already established practice, we feel that the Board was unduly restrictive in insisting that the nature of the applicant's lengthy and successful practice could be established as "satisfactory to the Board" *only* by three-to-five letters of other psychologists familiar with the applicant's practice. We feel that under the circumstances, the Board should have established some reasonable alternative procedure for allowing the applicant to demonstrate his competence. See *Taylor* v. *Hayes,* Ill.App., 264 N.E.2d 814 (1970). We hold that since the applicant was not statutorily entitled to take the examination to demonstrate his competence, the administrative rule herein resulting in the denial of a license without a suitable alternative procedure to demonstrate such competence was unreasonable. This Court feels confident that on remand the Board's expertise will easily enable it to promulgate and apply some reasonable and acceptable means for determining whether or not the character of the applicant's practice, or his competence, is sufficiently satisfactory so as to allow him to continue his profession.

Upon the District Court's own remand to the Board for further proceedings in accordance with his opinion, the District Court should also, in the interests of justice, retain supervisory jurisdiction and continue its previous stay order allowing applicant in the interim to continue, without bond, his industrial consultation practice.

Reversed and remanded with directions.

BERRY, C. J., DAVISON, V. C. J., and WILLIAMS, BLACKBIRD, JACKSON, HODGES and LAVENDER, JJ., concur.

Carroll v. *State*, Fla.App., 355 So.2d 495

PER CURIAM.

Petitioner brings for review the final agency action of the Board of Examiners of Psychology in declining to permit her to take the Florida examination pursuant to the provisions of Section 490.19, Florida Statutes.

The hearing officer heard and considered conflicting evidence concerning the question of whether the university from which the petitioner had received a doctoral degree in pupil placement services maintained in such doctoral program a standard of training comparable to those universities having programs approved by the American Psychological Association for the granting of a doctoral degree in psychology.

The hearing officer concluded that such a training was not the equivalent of that required by Section 490.19, and, therefore, upheld the order of the Board of Examiners of Psychology. The Board of Examiners of Psychology considered and approved the report of the hearing officer.

This matter is before this court upon conflicting testimony. It is not for this court to substitute its judgment for that of the hearing officer or the Board of Examiners of Psychology. Therefore, the order entered by the Board of Examiners of Psychology denying to Halcyon H. Carroll the right to take such examination is hereby

AFFIRMED.

SMITH, Acting C. J., and ERVIN and MELVIN, JJ., concur.

Disciplinary proceedings. The court reluctantly accepts its obligation to arbitrate disciplinary proceedings instituted against individual practitioners by regulatory bodies. This reluctance is illustrated below in *Napolitani* v. *Board of Regents,* 31 App.Div. 685, 295 N.Y.S.2d 781 (1968). The court's concern with protecting individual practitioners' right to develop new methods and technique of treatment is illustrated below in *Sherman* v. *Board of Regents of University of State of New York,* 24 App.Div.2d 315, 266 N.Y.S.2d 39 (1966). In the latter case, the Board of Regents of the University of the State of New York had determined that Dr. Sherman, a physician specializing in the treatment of obesity, had been guilty of fraud and deceit. Dr. Sherman appealed this determination and won a reversal of the determination. As stated in the court's opinion, "in medicine there are honest and positive differences of opinion as to the method of examination and the type of prescription in the care and treatment of a patient. . . . If the advancement of medicine is to continue, the avenues of differences must be left open, and, under circumstances such as here, not be the basis of a charge of fraud and deceit. . . . It is not fraud or deceit for one already skilled in the medical art, with the consent of the patient, to attempt new methods." The application of this principle to new methods in psychotherapy will be an issue raised in the following chapter.

Napolitani v. *Board of Regents of State of New York,* 31 App.Div.2d 685, 295 N.Y.S.2d 781 (1968)

MEMORANDUM BY THE COURT. Proceeding under CPLR article 78 to review and annul a determination of the Board of Regents suspending petitioner's license to practice medicine for three months. Petitioner has been found guilty of a charge of unprofessional conduct within the meaning of paragraph [g] of subdivision 2 of section 6514 of the Education Law as well as the charge of having been convicted of a crime within the meaning of paragraph [b] of subdivision 2 of the same section. He does not dispute his guilt but argues that the three months' suspension is unduly severe. Interference should not be had with the discipline imposed by the Board of Regents unless it "is so disproportionate to the offense, in the light of all the circumstances, as to be shocking to one's sense of fairness". (*Matter of Stolz* v. *Board of Regents*, 4 A D 2d 361, 364). Upon the record before us, which does not here require the recitation and delineation of the well-founded charges, we do not find the imposed punishment to be disproportionate to the offenses nor can we say it is shocking to one's sense of fairness and, in such case, we find no reason to disturb the board's action. (*Matter of Scire* v. *Board of Regents,* 23 A D 2d 943.) Determination confirmed, and petition dismissed, without costs. GIBSON, P. J., HERLIHY, REYNOLDS, STALEY, JR., and GABRIELLI, JJ., concur in memorandum by the court.

Sherman v. *Board of Regents of State of New York,* 24 App.Div.2d 315, 266 N.Y.S.2d 39 (1966)

PROCEEDING under article 78 of CPLR (transferred to the Appellate Division of the Supreme Court in the Third Judicial Department by an order of the Supreme Court at Special Term, entered in Albany County) to review a determination of the Board of Regents which censured and reprimanded petitioner for fraud and deceit in the practice of medicine.

HERLIHY, J. P. This proceeding, pursuant to article 78 of the CPLR, is brought to review and annul a determination of the Board of Regents which censured and reprimanded the petitioner upon a finding of guilt of fraud and deceit in the practice of medicine within the purview of paragraph (a) of subdivision 2 of section 6514 of the Education Law.

The first specification of the charges, designated Third (a) in the petition, stated: "In or about or between the 1st day of August, 1958 and the 30th day of September, 1962 the respondent and/or his employees or associates under his direction, did prescribe or cause to be prescribed and did deliver or cause to be delivered certain medication in the nature of pills to various persons without any physical examination or without proper or adequate physical examination, to determine whether the condition of each of the said persons was such that the said medication could be taken without injury or harm to the said persons or without aggravation of any pre-existing physical condition; and that the said persons relying on the holding out by the respondent and/or his employees and associates under his direction, that they were physicians and skilled and competent in the practice of such profession, were led to the belief that such medication was proper and safe and would not cause any injury or harm to them or aggravate any existing condition or preexisting condition that they might have; whereas in truth and in fact, the examination conducted by the respondent and/or his employees and associates was insufficient to determine whether there was a condition or predisposition to a condition of any of the said persons to harm or injury from the said medication and in some instances, no examination was conducted.''

The petitioner has been a doctor for 27 years and is a member of the staff of two reputable Long Island hospitals.

Following a number of years as a general practitioner, he directed his attention to the study of obesity which eventually resulted in his practice being confined to the treatment of this particular condition. He testified, without dispute, that since he began specializing he had been consulted by over 48,000 people; that he had never been sued for malpractice nor had any consequential complaints been lodged against him by patients or other doctors with reference to his prescribed treatment.

Five of the witnesses who testified at the hearing were special investigators for the Education Department and the testimony, in some instances, was indefinite, based upon recollections of investigations made three years earlier. In sum, it showed that they had visited different offices of the doctor on one or more occasions; that their blood pressure had been taken by a doctor or some other office personnel and they were questioned concerning their prior health; that thereafter they had been given a lecture as to their diet and the use of the pills and instructed that if there were any reaction, to call the doctor's office and that, in any event, to return within a period of one or two weeks. Some of the investigators stated that they were suffering from a cardiac condition and in another instance, asthma, but the method of treatment was not altered.

A patient of the doctor testified that one of the attendants had taken her blood pressure; that she was asked if she had any illnesses or diseases, to which she replied that she had a thyroid condition. She thereafter attended a lecture as to the diet and the taking of the medication.

The last witness was the complainant, Dr. Elmer A. Kleefield. He stated that a patient, whose name he refused to reveal—whose husband was a pharmacist—came to him complaining of aches and pains, fatigue, nervousness, insomnia, itching, increased thirst and frequent urination. The doctor stated that as a result of his examination, the details of which are not in the record, he made a diagnosis that the patient was suffering from ''diabetes mellitus, mild overweight, and possible addiction to possibly amphetamine and barbiturates.'' He stated with reference to some of the symptoms that ''I would describe possibly some relation to the amphetamine and phenobarbital.'' The doctor testified that the patient informed him that she was advised by Dr. Sherman's staff to ''eat what you want'' but the witness stated ''It's very possible that those are not the instructions which he gave her.'' The statement by the patient was in contradiction of the other witnesses who testified that they had attended a lecture concerned with diet. It is apparent that this patient did not follow instructions given her and what she did or did not do during the interim between her last visit to the petitioner and her visit to Dr. Kleefield is a matter of speculation. How many times the patient saw Dr. Kleefield is not shown in the record, but apparently only on one occasion. He was asked a general hypothetical question with reference to the composition of pills and the type of examination and as to whether or not this would be sufficient and he stated ''No, it is not sufficient.'' The doctor testified he resented the fact that Dr. Sherman had not answered his letter of inquiry and that when he did receive a reply, it was disappointing. The probative value of the testimony of this witness, when considered in its entirety, is minimal.

Dr. Sherman testified in detail concerning his study and research as to obesity, the compounding of medications for the purpose of aiding in weight reduction which, in his opinion, would not interfere with any prior condition from which a patient might be suffering, the necessity of explaining by way of lectures to patients the relationship between the recommended diet and the medication and the instruction to call him if there were any reaction from the pills but in any event to report to his office on a designated date for further treatment. He readily advised the members of the committee as to the contents of the medication and outlined the directives which he had given to the members of his staff and testified that if there were any violations of these directives, it was without his knowledge or consent.

He was subject to repeated examination by the members of the Grievance Committee and answered forthrightly.

The Subcommittee found him guilty of fraud and deceit as outlined in the specification.

The board stated:

"In our opinion, a patient consulting the respondent, consults him on the basis that he is a physician and holds himself out to be such and that the patient relies entirely on the professional skill of the respondent and thereby assumes that all proper medical precautions will be taken by the respondent and all proper medical examinations will be made and that all medication received will be safe and all supervisions thereafter will be adequate. As stated above, we find that the respondent's present procedures fail satisfactorily to meet these tests.

"We unanimously conclude and find respondent guilty of that portion of the charge of fraud and deceit to the extent stated above as contained in Paragraph Third, Subdivision 1(a) of the charges herein."

From an examination of the decisional law, it appears that charges of fraud and deceit in the practice of medicine have been sustained in four general categories:

(1) Narcotics. (See *Matter of Tompkins* v. *Board of Regents,* 299 N. Y. 469.)

(2) Fraudulent or excessive statements for services rendered. (See *Matter of Wassermann* v. *Board of Regents,* 11 N Y 2d 173)

(3) Aiding or abetting an unlicensed person to practice. (See *Matter of O'Neill* v. *Board of Regents,* 272 App. Div. 1086.)

(4) Concealment of material facts. (See *Matter of Hutschnecker* v. *Board of Regents*, 269 App. Div. 891; *Matter of Gilbert* [*Cole*], 266 App. Div. 894.)

That the courts have intentionally limited the scope of such charges is demonstrated where fraud and deceit were not sustained. (See *Matter of Stammer* v. *Board of Regents,* 262 App. Div. 372, affd. 287 N. Y. 359; *Matter of Cowles* v. *Board of Regents,* 266 App. Div. 629, affd. 292 N. Y. 650.)

On this appeal the issue is whether the manner and method of the doctor's practice were such as to constitute a basis for fraud or deceit or whether it constituted the proper exercise of his professional judgment.

There is no charge, intimation or proof that Dr. Sherman was a charlatan or a quack or that he did anything illegal or immoral. In his judgment, his method of examination and prescription for obesity were proper, based upon his experience, observation, study and research, and more particularly the accomplished results. The Grievance Committee found his procedures not satisfactory and concluded therefrom that he was guilty of fraud and deceit.

It would be possible to find such a difference of opinion in any branch of medicine.

An internist from his examination diagnosed diabetes mellitus and prescribed therefor, the result being that the patient's condition worsened. An examination by another internist produced an entirely different diagnosis, the result of his examination and prescription being helpful to the condition.

A general practitioner advised his patient to start putting weight on his fractured leg, which direction was premature and caused the development of osteomyelitis. An orthopedic surgeon from his examination determined that the doctor's judgment was wrong and that an X ray would have revealed that the fracture had not sufficiently mended.

A doctor, following an examination, diagnosed indigestion and prescribed therefor, as the result of which the patient's condition worsened. A subsequent examination by a cardiologist revealed a serious heart condition and with proper medication the condition was considerably improved.

It is commonplace in the courts to find testimony by a physician that trauma causes or aggravates carcinoma and to the contrary that trauma is not the cause of carcinoma or aggravative of such condition.

These, and many other instances which could be cited, are mistakes in medical judgment and prescription and to affirm here would be, in our opinion, a matter of grave concern to the general practitioner, and particularly the specialist, and might tend to seriously limit medical research.

Through the medium of the press, considerable publicity is being directed to experiments with "memory pills," apparently premised on a statement in 1884 by a brain chemist who said "Behind every twisted mind is a twisted molecule." According to the article, until the chemical "RNA" was discovered, there were no means to improve memory defects. The said medication, when administered, has a side effect of inducing abdominal pains and nausea.

In a recent newspaper article a leading medical scientist in the study of leukemia referred to a slogan which stated: "Reasoned heresy versus unreasoned orthodoxy—the scientific challenge." To the doctor it meant that in research, you really go where the road leads you and it is impossible to draw the route in advance.

It may be readily conceded that these examples are not necessarily pertinent to the present facts, but they do make clear the point that in medicine there are honest and positive differences of opinion as to the method of examination and the type of prescription in the care and treatment of a patient, which is precisely the issue before this court. If the advancement of medicine is to continue, the avenues of differences must be left open, and, under circumstances such as here, not be the basis of a charge of fraud and deceit.

We would further note that the statement in the findings to the effect that an examination by the members of the committee of the boxes of medication in evidence with the daily dosages stated on the same *makes it extremely doubtful* that the phenobarbital was present in sufficient amounts to offset the effects of the amphetamine, standing alone, is neither binding nor controlling on the courts and is not of such evidentiary value as to be substantial. Dr. Kleefield was asked the following: "Q. Assuming a person had received in one day, 45 mgs of amphetamine sulfate, 3 grains of the desiccated whole thyroid, and a sixth of a grain and a quarter of a grain of phenobarbital in one day, of a period of a couple of weeks. Would you say that would be sufficient phenobarbital to offset the amount of amphetamine sulfate and the other drugs? A. I can't say because this is a variable thing with each individual patient. Nobody can give a specific answer to that."

Paragraph (a) of subdivision 2 of section 6514 [fraud and deceit] does not expressly consider the meaning of the terms but it may be characterized as intentional misrepresentation or concealment of fact. The statute shall not be construed to require that anyone actually be misled so long as the intent is present. (See *Matter of Tompkins* v. *Board of Regents,* 299 N. Y. 469, 476, *supra.*)

It is not fraud or deceit for one already skilled in the medical art, with the consent of the patient, to attempt new methods.

The Medical Grievance Committee has the duty to conduct hearings and weigh testimony in a quasi-judicial manner. The board's findings are general and equivocal attempts to establish a professional classification for fraud and deceit which the present record does not sustain. There is no evidence of any intentional misrepresentation or concealment of facts from the patient. Dr. Sherman's methods may not have been as orthodox as some members of the profession might desire but that is not the test for a finding of fraud and deceit.

Finally, it appears to be sufficiently demonstrated that, while only Dr. Sherman is here involved, an affirmance of the charges of fraud and deceit on the present record has the possibilities of reaching far beyond the present facts and having serious consequences upon the practice of medicine. Proper remedies and safeguards for the protection of the profession and particularly the public are already a hundredfold.

We hold in high regard the medical expertise of the Grievance Committee in its application of the facts to the law, but the courts are mandated to intervene when, as here, there is a misapplication of the law to the facts.

In view of our decision, we do not reach the procedural questions raised by the appellant.

The determination should be annulled and the charges dismissed.

Reynolds, Taylor, Aulisi and Hamm, JJ., concur.

Determination annulled and charges dismissed, without costs.

NONGOVERNMENTAL REGULATION

In addition to governmental definition and regulation of the field, professionals themselves have, in some instances, created competency, specialty, and ethical standards. To the extent that these standards are recognized and accepted by members of the profession, they have become rules of conduct that govern and control the practice of the mental health care practitioner. They therefore define the standard of care expected. Failure to act in accordance with the promulgated standards can subject the practitioner to civil liability and disciplinary action such as suspension or revocation of license.

Ethical codes. A code of ethics is no more than a compendium of rules governing the conduct by which members of a professional association agree to abide. While governmental regulations can be applied to every person holding a credential, ethical codes apply only to members of the particular profession whose professional organization is promulgating that code. Note that ethical codes generally do not deal with standards of quality or care. Rather they address the relationship of the professional both to the patient and to the general public. To the extent that any professional regulation or code of ethics establishes a standard of conduct, it becomes a benchmark against which the acceptability of a professional's actions may be measured. On the ground that a proper standard of care and treatment was not provided, the violation of a professional code of ethics furnishes the basis for liability in malpractice; the patient has not received the degree of competence that could reasonably be expected from a practitioner of that profession.

Most if not all professional organizations promulgate their own codes of ethics. Reprinted below are the *Ethical Standards of Psychologists* promulgated by the American Psychological Association, the "principles of medical ethics, with annotations especially applicable to psychiatry" promulgated by the American Psychiatric Association, and the *Code of Ethics* promulgated by the National Association of Social Workers.

Ethical Principles of Psychologists (1981 Revision)*

This version of the Ethical Principles of Psychologists (formerly entitled: Ethical Standards of Psychologists) was adopted by the American Psychological Assocation's Council of Representatives on January 24, 1981. The Ethical Principles of Psychologists (1981 Revision) contains both substantive and grammatical changes in each of the nine ethical principles which comprised the Ethical Standards of Psychologists previously adopted by the Council of Representatives in 1979, plus a new tenth principle entitled: Care and Use of Animals. Inquiries concerning the Ethical Principles of Psychologists should be addressed to the Administrative Officer for Ethics; American Psychological Association; 1200 Seventeenth Street, N.W.; Washington, D.C. 20036.

Ethical Principles of Psychologists[1,2]

Preamble

Psychologists respect the dignity and worth of the individual and strive for the preservation and protection of fundamental human rights. They are committed to increasing knowledge of human behavior and of people's understanding of themselves and others and to the utilization of such knowledge for the promotion of human welfare. While pursuing these objectives, they make every effort to protect the welfare of those who seek their services and of the research participants that may be the object of study. They use their skills only for purposes consistent with these values and do not knowingly permit their misuse by others. While demanding for themselves freedom of inquiry and communication, psychologists accept the responsibility this freedom requires: competence, objectivity in the application of skills, and concern for the best interests of clients, colleagues, students, research participants and society. In the pursuit of these ideals, psychologists subscribe to principles in the following areas: 1. Responsibility, 2. Competence, 3. Moral and Legal Standards, 4. Public Statements,

[1]Approved by the Council of Representatives (January 1981).

[2]These Ethical Principles apply to psychologists, to students of psychology and others who do work of a psychological nature under the supervision of a psychologist. They are also intended for the guidance of non-members of the Association who are engaged in psychological research or practice.

5. Confidentiality, 6. Welfare of the Consumer, 7. Professional Relationships, 8. Assessment Techniques, 9. Research with Human Participants, and 10. Care and Use of Animals.

Acceptance of membership in the American Psychological Association commits the member to adherence to these principles.

Psychologists cooperate with duly constituted committees of the American Psychological Association, in particular, the Committee on Scientific and Professional Ethics and Conduct, by responding to inquiries promptly and completely. Members also respond promptly and completely to inquiries from duly constituted state association ethics committees and professional standards review committees.

Principle 1
Responsibility

In providing services, psychologists maintain the highest standards of their profession. They accept responsibility for the consequences of their acts and make every effort to insure that their services are used appropriately.

a. As scientists, psychologists accept responsibility for the selection of their research topics and the methods used in investigation, analysis, and reporting. They plan their research in ways to minimize the possibility that their findings will be misleading. They provide thorough discussion of the limitations of their data, especially where their work touches on social policy or might be construed to the detriment of persons in specific age, sex, ethnic, socioeconomic or other social groups. In publishing reports of their work, they never suppress disconfirming data, and they acknowledge the existence of alternative hypotheses and explanations of their findings. Psychologists take credit only for work they have actually done.

b. Psychologists clarify in advance with all appropriate persons and agencies the expectations for sharing and utilizing research data. They avoid relationships which may limit their objectivity or create a conflict of interest. Interference with the milieu in which the data are collected is kept to a minimum.

c. Psychologists have the responsibility to attempt to prevent distortion, misuse, or suppression of psychological findings by the institution or agency of which they are employees.

d. As members of governmental or other organizational bodies, psychologists remain accountable as individuals to the highest standards of their profession.

e. As teachers, psychologists recognize their primary obligation to help others acquire knowledge and skill. They maintain high standards of scholarship by presenting psychological information objectively, fully, and accurately.

f. As practitioners, psychologists know that they bear a heavy social responsibility because their recommendations and professional actions may alter the lives of others. They are alert to personal, social, organizational, financial, or political situations and pressures that might lead to misuse of their influence.

Principle 2
Competence

The maintenance of high standards of competence is a responsibility shared by all psychologists in the interest of the public and the profession as a whole. Psychologists recognize the boundaries of their competence and the limitations of their techniques.

They only provide services and only use techniques for which they are qualified by training and experience. In those areas in which recognized standards do not yet exist, psychologists take whatever precautions are necessary to protect the welfare of their clients. They maintain knowledge of current scientific and professional information related to the services they render.

a. Psychologists accurately represent their competence, education, training, and experience. They claim as evidence of educational qualifications only those degrees obtained from institutions acceptable under the Bylaws and Rules of Council of the American Psychological Association.

b. As teachers, psychologists perform their duties on the basis of careful preparation so that their instruction is accurate, current, and scholarly.

c. Psychologists recognize the need for continuing education and are open to new procedures and changes in expectations and values over time.

d. Psychologists recognize differences among people, such as those that may be associated with age, sex, socioeconomic, and ethnic backgrounds. When necessary, they obtain training, experience, or counsel to assure competent service or research relating to such persons.

e. Psychologists responsible for decisions involving individuals or policies based on test results have an understanding of psychological or educational measurement, validation problems, and test research.

f. Psychologists recognize that personal problems and conflicts may interfere with professional effectiveness. Accordingly, they refrain from undertaking any activity in which their personal problems are likely to lead to inadequate performance or harm to a client, colleague, student, or research participant. If engaged in such activity when they become aware of their personal problems, they seek competent professional assistance to determine whether they should suspend, terminate, or limit the scope of their professional and/or scientific activities.

Principle 3
Moral and Legal Standards

Psychologists' moral and ethical standards of behavior are a personal matter to the same degree as they are for any other citizen, except as these may compromise the fulfillment of their professional responsibilities, or reduce the public trust in psychology and psychologists. Regarding their own behavior, psychologists are sensitive to prevailing community standards and to the possible impact that conformity to or deviation from these standards may have upon the quality of their performance as psychologists. Psychologists are also aware of the possible impact of their public behavior upon the ability of colleagues to perform their professional duties.

a. As teachers, psychologists are aware of the fact that their personal values may affect the selection and presentation of instructional materials. When dealing with topics that may give offense, they recognize and respect the diverse attitudes that students may have toward such materials.

b. As employees or employers, psychologists do not engage in or condone practices that are inhumane or that result in illegal or unjustifiable actions. Such practices include but are not limited to those based on considerations of race, handicap, age, gender, sexual preference, religion, or national origin in hiring, promotion, or training.

c. In their professional roles, psychologists avoid any action that will violate or diminish the legal and civil rights of clients or of others who may be affected by their actions.

d. As practitioners and researchers, psychologists act in accord with Association standards and guidelines related to the practice and to the conduct of research with human beings and animals. In the ordinary course of events psychologists adhere to relevant governmental laws and institutional regulations. When federal, state, provincial, organizational, or institutional laws, regulations, or practices are in conflict with Association standards and guidelines, psychologists make known their commitment to Association standards and guidelines, and wherever possible work toward a resolution of the conflict. Both practitioners and researchers are concerned with the development of such legal and quasi-legal regulations as best serve the public interest, and they work toward changing existing regulations that are not beneficial to the public interest.

Principle 4
Public Statements

Public statements, announcements of services, advertising, and promotional activities of psychologists serve the purpose of helping the public make informed judgments and choices. Psychologists represent accurately and objectively their professional qualifications, affiliations, and functions, as well as those of the institutions or organizations with which they or the statements may be associated. In public statements providing psychological information or professional opinions or providing information about the availability of psychological products, publications, and services, psychologists base their statements on scientifically acceptable psychological findings and techniques with full recognition of the limits and uncertainties of such evidence.

a. When announcing or advertising professional services, psychologists may list the following information to describe the provider and services provided: name, highest relevant academic degree earned from a regionally accredited institution, date, type and level of certification or licensure, diplomate status, APA membership status, address, telephone number, office hours, a brief listing of the type of psychological services offered, an appropriate presentation of fee information, foreign languages spoken, and policy with regard to third-party payments. Additional relevant or important consumer information may be included if not prohibited by other sections of these Ethical Principles.

b. In announcing or advertising the availability of psychological products, publications, or services, psychologists do not present their affiliation with any organization in a manner that falsely implies sponsorship or certification by that organization. In particular and for example, psychologists do not state APA membership or fellow status in a way to suggest that such status implies specialized professional competence or qualifications. Public statements include, but are not limited to, communication by means of periodical, book, list, directory, television, radio, or motion picture. They do not contain: (i) a false, fraudulent, misleading, deceptive, or unfair statement; (ii) a misinterpretation of fact, or a statement likely to mislead or deceive because in context it makes only a partial disclosure of relevant facts; (iii) a testimonial from a patient regarding the quality of a psychologist's services or products; (iv) a statement intended or likely to create false or unjustified expectations of favorable results; (v) a statement implying unusual, unique, or one-of-a-kind abilities; (vi) a statement intended or likely to appeal to a client's fears, anxieties, or emotions concerning the possible results of a failure to obtain the offered services; (vii) a statement concerning the comparative desirability of offered service; (viii) a statement of direct solicitation of individual clients.

c. Psychologists do not compensate or give anything of value to a representative of the press, radio, television, or other communication medium in anticipation of or in return for professional publicity in a news item. A paid advertisement must be identified as such, unless it is apparent from the context that it is a paid advertisement. If communicated to the public by use of radio or television, an advertisement shall be prerecorded and approved for broadcast by the psychologist, and a recording of the actual transmission shall be retained by the psychologist.

d. Announcements or advertisements of "personal growth groups," clinics, and agencies give a clear statement of purpose and a clear description of the experiences to be provided. The education, training, and experience of the staff members are appropriately specified.

e. Psychologists associated with the development or promotion of psychological devices, books, or other products offered for commercial sale make reasonable efforts to insure that announcements and advertisements are presented in a professional, scientifically acceptable, and factually informative manner.

f. Psychologists do not participate for personal gain in commercial announcements or advertisements recommending to the public the purchase or use of proprietary or single-source products or services when that participation is based solely upon their identification as psychologists.

g. Psychologists present the science of psychology and offer their services, products, and publications fairly and accurately, avoiding misrepresentation through sensationalism, exaggeration, or superficiality. Psychologists are guided by the primary obligation to aid the public in developing informed judgments, opinions, and choices.

h. As teachers, psychologists insure that statements in catalogs and course outlines are accurate and not misleading, particularly in terms of subject matter to be covered, bases for evaluating progress, and the nature of course experiences. Announcements, brochures, or advertisements describing workshops, seminars, or other educational programs accurately describe the audience for which the program is intended as well as eligibility requirements, educational objectives, and nature of the materials to be covered. These announcements also accurately represent the education, training, and experience of the psychologists presenting the programs, and any fees involved.

i. Public announcements or advertisements soliciting research participants in which clinical services or other professional services are offered as an inducement, make clear the nature of the services as well as the costs and other obligations to be accepted by the participants of the research.

j. Psychologists accept the obligation to correct others who represent that psychologist's professional qualifications, or associations with products or services, in a manner incompatible with these guidelines.

k. Individual diagnostic and therapeutic services are provided only in the context of a professional psychological relationship. When personal advice is given by means of public lecture or demonstration, newspaper or magazine articles, radio or television programs, mail, or similar media, the psychologist utilizes the most current relevant data and exercises the highest level of professional judgment.

l. Products that are described or presented by means of public lectures or demonstrations, newspaper or magazine articles, radio or television programs, or similar media meet the same recognized standards as exist for use in the context of a professional relationship.

Principle 5
Confidentiality

Psychologists have a primary obligation to respect the confidentiality of information obtained from persons in the course of their work as psychologists. They reveal such information to others only with the consent of the person or the person's legal representative, except in those unusual circumstances in which not to do so would result in clear danger to the person or to others. Where appropriate, psychologists inform their clients of the legal limits of confidentiality.

a. Information obtained in clinical or consulting relationships, or evaluative data concerning children, students, employees, and others, are discussed only for professional purposes and only with persons clearly concerned with the case. Written and oral reports present only data germane to the purposes of the evaluation and every effort is made to avoid undue invasion of privacy.

b. Psychologists who present personal information obtained during the course of professional work in writings, lectures, or other public forums either obtain adequate prior consent to do so or adequately disguise all identifying information.

c. Psychologists make provisions for maintaining confidentiality in the storage and disposal of records.

d. When working with minors or other persons who are unable to give voluntary, informed consent, psychologists take special care to protect these persons' best interests.

Principle 6
Welfare of the Consumer

Psychologists respect the integrity and protect the welfare of the people and groups with whom they work. When there is a conflict of interest between a client and the psychologist's employing institution, psychologists clarify the nature and direction of their loyalties and responsibilities and keep all parties informed of their commitments. Psychologists fully inform consumers as to the purpose and nature of an evaluative, treatment, educational or training procedure, and they freely acknowledge that clients, students, or participants in research have freedom of choice with regard to participation.

a. Psychologists are continually cognizant of their own needs and of their potentially influential position vis-a-vis persons such as clients, students, and subordinates. They avoid exploiting the trust and dependency of such persons. Psychologists make every effort to avoid dual relationships which could impair their professional judgment or increase the risk of exploitation. Examples of such dual relationships include but are not limited to research with and treatment of employees, students, supervisees, close friends, or relatives. Sexual intimacies with clients are unethical.

b. When a psychologist agrees to provide services to a client at the request of a third party, the psychologist assumes the responsibility of clarifying the nature of the relationships to all parties concerned.

c. Where the demands of an organization require psychologists to violate these Ethical Principles, psychologists clarify the nature of the conflict between the demand and these principles. They inform all parties of psychologists' ethical responsibilities, and take appropriate action.

d. Psychologists make advance financial arrangements that safeguard the best interests of and are clearly understood by their clients. They neither give nor receive any remuneration for referring clients for professional services. They contribute a portion of their services to work for which they receive little or no financial return.

e. Psychologists terminate a clinical or consulting relationship when it is reasonably clear that the consumer is not benefiting from it. They offer to help the consumer locate alternative sources of assistance.

Principle 7
Professional Relationships

Psychologists act with due regard for the needs, special competencies, and obligations of their colleagues in psychology and other professions. They respect the prerogatives and obligations of the institutions or organizations with which these other colleagues are associated.

a. Psychologists understand the areas of competence of related professions. They make full use of all the professional, technical, and administrative resources that serve the best interests of consumers. The absence of formal relationships with other professional workers does not relieve psychologists of the responsibility of securing for their clients the best possible professional service nor does it relieve them of the obligation to exercise foresight, diligence, and tact in obtaining the complementary or alternative assistance needed by clients.

b. Psychologists know and take into account the traditions and practices of other professional groups with whom they work and cooperate fully with such groups. If a person is receiving similar services from another professional, psychologists do not offer their own services directly to such a person. If a psychologist is contacted by a person who is already receiving similar services from another professional, the psychologist carefully considers that professional relationship and proceeds with caution and sensitivity to the therapeutic issues as well as the client's welfare. The psychologist discusses these issues with the client so as to minimize the risk of confusion and conflict.

c. Psychologists who employ or supervise other professionals or professionals in training accept the obligation to facilitate the further professional development of these individuals. They provide appropriate working conditions, timely evaluations, constructive consultation and experience opportunities.

d. Psychologists do not exploit their professional relationships with clients, supervisees, students, employees, or research participants sexually or otherwise. Psychologists do not condone nor engage in sexual harassment. Sexual harassment is defined as deliberate or repeated comments, gestures, or physical contacts of a sexual nature that are unwanted by the recipient.

e. In conducting research in institutions or organizations, psychologists secure appropriate authorization to conduct such research. They are aware of their obligation to future research workers and insure that host institutions receive adequate information about the research and proper acknowledgement of their contributions.

f. Publication credit is assigned to those who have contributed to a publication in proportion to their professional contribution. Major contributions of a professional character made by several persons to a common project are recognized by joint authorship, with the individual who made the principal contribution listed first. Minor contributions of a professional character and extensive clerical or similar nonprofessional assistance may be acknowledged in footnotes or in an introductory statement. Acknowledgement through specific citations is made for unpublished as well as published material that has directly influenced the research or writing. A psychologist who compiles and edits material of others for publication publishes the material in the name of the originating group, if appropriate, with his/her own name appearing as chairperson or editor. All contributors are to be acknowledged and named.

g. When psychologists know of an ethical violation by another psychologist, and it seems appropriate, they informally attempt to resolve the issue by bringing the behavior to the attention of the psychologist. If the misconduct is of a minor nature and/or appears to be due to lack of sensitivity, knowledge, or experience, such an informal solution is usually appropriate. Such informal corrective efforts are sensitive to any rights to confidentiality involved. If the violation does not seem amenable to an informal solution, or is of a more serious nature, psychologists bring it to the attention of the appropriate local, state, and/or national committee on professional ethics and conduct.

Principle 8
Assessment Techniques

In the development, publication, and utilization of psychological assessment techniques, psychologists make every effort to promote the welfare and best interests of the client. They guard against the misuse of assessment results. They respect the client's right to know the results, the interpretations made and the bases for their conclusions and recommendations. Psychologists make every effort to maintain the security of tests and other assessment techniques within limits of legal mandates. They strive to assure the appropriate use of assessment techniques by others.

a. In using assessment techniques, psychologists respect the right of clients to have a full explanation of the nature and purpose of the techniques in language that the client can understand, unless an explicit exception to this right has been agreed upon in advance. When the explanations are to be provided by others, the psychologist establishes procedures for insuring the adequacy of these explanations.

b. Psychologists responsible for the development and standardization of psychological tests and other assessment techniques utilize established scientific procedures and observe the relevant APA standards.

c. In reporting assessment results, psychologists indicate any reservations that exist regarding validity or reliability because of the circumstances of the assessment or the inappropriateness of the norms for the person tested. Psychologists strive to insure that the results of assessments and their interpretation are not misused by others.

d. Psychologists recognize that assessment results may become obsolete. They make every effort to avoid and prevent the misuse of obsolete measures.

e. Psychologists offering scoring and interpretation services are able to produce appropriate evidence for the validity of the programs and procedures used in arriving at interpretations. The public offering of an automated interpretation service is considered as a professional-to-professional consultation. The psychologist makes every effort to avoid misuse of assessment reports.

f. Psychologists do not encourage or promote the use of psychological assessment techniques by inappropriately trained or otherwise unqualified persons through teaching, sponsorship, or supervision.

Principle 9
Research with Human Participants

The decision to undertake research rests upon a considered judgment by the individual psychologist about how best to contribute to psychological science and human welfare. Having made the decision to conduct research, the psychologist considers alternative directions in which research energies and resources might be invested. On the basis of this consideration, the psychologist carries out the investigation with respect and concern for the dignity and welfare of the people who participate, and with cognizance of federal and state regulations and professional standards governing the conduct of research with human participants.

a. In planning a study, the investigator has the responsibility to make a careful evaluation of its ethical acceptability. To the extent that the weighing of scientific and human values suggests a compromise of any principle, the investigator incurs a correspondingly serious obligation to seek ethical advice and to observe stringent safeguards to protect the rights of human participants.

b. Considering whether a participant in a planned study will be a "subject at risk" or a "subject at minimal risk," according to recognized standards, is of primary ethical concern to the investigator.

c. The investigator always retains the responsibility for insuring ethical practice in research. The investigator is also responsible for the ethical treatment of research participants by collaborators, assistants, students, and employees, all of whom, however, incur similar obligations.

d. Except for minimal risk research, the investigator establishes a clear and fair agreement with the research participants, prior to their participation, that clarifies the obligations and responsibilities of each. The investigator has the obligation to honor all promises and commitments included in that agreement. The investigator informs the participant of all aspects of the research that might reasonably be expected to influence willingness to participate, and explains all other aspects of the research about which the participant inquires. Failure to make full disclosure prior to obtaining informed consent requires additional safeguards to protect the welfare and dignity of the research participant. Research with children or participants who have impairments which would limit understanding and/or communication, requires special safeguard procedures.

e. Methodological requirements of a study may make the use of concealment or deception necessary. Before conducting such a study, the investigator has a special responsibility to: (i) determine whether the use of such techniques is justified by the study's prospective scientific, educational, or applied value; (ii) determine whether alternative procedures are available that do not utilize concealment or deception; and (iii) insure that the participants are provided with sufficient explanation as soon as possible.

f. The investigator respects the individual's freedom to decline to participate in or to withdraw from the research at any time. The obligation to protect this freedom requires careful thought and consideration when the investigator is in a position of authority or influence over the participant. Such positions of authority include but are not limited to situations when research participation is required as part of employment or when the participant is a student, client, or employee of the investigator.

g. The investigator protects the participants from physical and mental discomfort, harm, and danger that may arise from research procedures. If risks of such consequences exist, the investigator informs the participant of that fact. Research procedures likely to cause serious or lasting harm to a participant are not used unless the failure to use these procedures might expose the participant to risk of greater harm, or unless the research has great potential benefit and fully informed and voluntary consent is obtained from each participant. The participant should be informed of procedures for contacting the investigator within a reasonable time period following participation should stress, potential harm, or related questions or concerns arise.

h. After the data are collected, the investigator provides the participant with information about the nature of the study and attempts to remove any misconceptions that may have arisen. Where scientific or humane values justify delaying or withholding information, the investigator incurs a special responsibility to monitor the research and to assure that there are no damaging consequences for the participant.

i. Where research procedures result in undesirable consequences for the individual participant, the investigator has the responsibility to detect and remove or correct these consequences, including long-term effects.

j. Information obtained about the research participant during the courses of an investigation is confidential unless otherwise agreed upon in advance. When the possibility exists that others may obtain access to such information, this possibility, together with the plans for protecting confidentiality, is explained to the participant as part of the procedure for obtaining informed consent.

Principle 10
Care and Use of Animals

An investigator of animal behavior strives to advance our understanding of basic behavioral principles and/or to contribute to the improvement of human health and welfare. In seeking these ends, the investigator insures the welfare of the animals and treats them humanely. Laws and regulations notwithstanding, the animal's immediate protection depends upon the scientist's own conscience.

a. The acquisition, care, use, and disposal of all animals is in compliance with current federal, state or provincial, and local laws and regulations.

b. A psychologist trained in research methods and experienced in the care of laboratory animals closely supervises all procedures involving animals and is responsible for insuring appropriate consideration of their comfort, health, and humane treatment.

c. Psychologists insure that all individuals using animals under their supervision have received explicit instruction in experimental methods and in the care, maintenance, and handling of the species being used. Responsibilities and activities of individuals participating in a research project are consistent with their respective competencies.

d. Psychologists make every effort to minimize discomfort, illness, and pain to the animals. A procedure subjecting animals to pain, stress, or privation is used only when an alternative procedure is unavailable and the goal is justified by its prospective scientific, educational, or applied value. Surgical procedures are performed under appropriate anesthesia; techniques to avoid infection and minimize pain are followed during and after surgery.

e. When it is appropriate that the animal's life be terminated, it is done rapidly and painlessly.

The Principles of Medical Ethics with Annotations Especially Applicable to Psychiatry (APA)*

In 1973, the American Psychiatric Association published the first edition of *The Principles of Medical Ethics with Annotations Especially Applicable to Psychiatry*. Subsequently, revisions were published as the board of trustees and the assembly approved additional annotations. In July 1980 the American Medical Association approved a new version of the *Principles of Medical Ethics* (the first revision since 1957) and the APA Ethics Committee incorporated many of its annotations into the new principles, which resulted in the 1981 edition.

Foreword

All physicians should practice in accordance with the medical code of ethics set forth in the Principles of Medical Ethics of the American Medical Association. An up-to-date expression and elaboration of these statements is found in the *Opinions and Reports of the Judicial Council* of the American Medical Association.[1] Psychiatrists are strongly advised to be familiar with these documents.[2]

However, these general guidelines have sometimes been difficult to interpret for psychiatry, so further annotations to the basic principles are offered in this document. While psychiatrists have the same goals as all physicians, there are special ethical problems in psychiatric practice that differ in coloring and degree from ethical problems in other branches of medical practice, even though the basic principles are the same. The annotations are not designed as absolutes and will be revised from time to time so as to be applicable to current practices and problems.

Following are the AMA Principles of Medical Ethics, printed in their entirety, and then each principle printed separately along with an annotation especially applicable to psychiatry.

Principles of Medical Ethics, American Medical Association

Preamble

The medical profession has long subscribed to a body of ethical statements developed primarily for the benefit of the patient. As a member of this profession, a

*From the *American Journal of Psychiatry*, 1973, *130* (9), 1058-1064. Copyright 1973, the American Psychiatric Association. Reprinted by permission.

[1] *Opinions and Reports of the Judicial Council* (Chicago: American Medical Association, 1981).

[2] Chapter 8, Section 1 of the By-Laws of the American Psychiatric Association states, "All members of the American Psychiatric Association shall be bound by the ethical code of the medical profession, specifically defined in the *Principles of Medical Ethics* of the American Medical Association." In interpreting the APA Constitution and By-Laws, it is the opinion of the Board of Trustees that inactive status in no way removes a physician member from responsibility to abide by the *Principles of Medical Ethics*.

physician must recognize responsibility not only to patients, but also to society, to other health professionals, and to self. The following Principles, adopted by the American Medical Association, are not laws, but standards of conduct which define the essentials of honorable behavior for the physician.

Section 1

A physician shall be dedicated to providing competent medical service with compassion and respect for human dignity.

Section 2

A physician shall deal honestly with patients and colleagues, and strive to expose those physicians deficient in character or competence, or who engage in fraud or deception.

Section 3

A physician shall respect the law and also recognize a responsibility to seek changes in those requirements which are contrary to the best interests of the patient.

Section 4

A physician shall respect the rights of patients, of colleagues, and of other health professionals, and shall safeguard patient confidences within the constraints of the law.

Section 5

A physician shall continue to study, apply, and advance scientific knowledge, make relevant information available to patients, colleagues, and the public, obtain consultation, and use the talents of other health professionals when indicated.

Section 6

A physician shall, in the provision of appropriate patient care, except in emergencies, be free to choose whom to serve, with whom to associate, and the environment in which to provide medical services.

Section 7

A physician shall recognize a responsibility to participate in activities contributing to an improved community.

Principles with Annotations

Following are each of the AMA Principles of Medical Ethics printed separately along with annotations especially applicable to psychiatry.

Preamble

The medical profession has long subscribed to a body of ethical statements developed primarily for the benefit of the patient. As a member of this profession, a physician must recognize responsibility not only to patients, but also to society, to other health professionals, and to self. The following Principles, adopted by the American Medical Association, are not laws, but standards of conduct which define the essentials of honorable behavior for the physician.[3]

Section 1

A physician shall be dedicated to providing competent medical service with compassion and respect for human dignity.

1. The patient may place his/her trust in his/her psychiatrist knowing that the psychiatrist's ethics and professional responsibilities preclude him/her gratifying his/her own needs by exploiting the patient. This becomes particularly important because of the essentially private, highly personal, and sometimes intensely emotional nature of the relationship established with the psychiatrist.

2. A psychiatrist should not be a party to any type of policy that excludes, segregates, or demeans the dignity of any patient because of ethnic origin, race, sex, creed, age, socioeconomic status, or sexual orientation.

3. In accord with the requirements of law and accepted medical practice, it is ethical for a physician to submit his/her work to peer review and to the ultimate authority of the medical staff executive body and the hospital administration and its governing body. In case of dispute, the ethical psychiatrist has the following steps available:

a. Seek appeal from the medical staff decision to a joint conference committee, including members of the medical staff executive committee and the executive committee of the governing board. At this appeal, the ethical psychiatrist could request that outside opinions be considered.
b. Appeal to the governing body itself.
c. Appeal to state agencies regulating licensure of hospitals if, in the particular state, they concern themselves with matters of professional competency and quality of care.
d. Attempts to educate colleagues through development of research projects and data and presentations at professional meetings and in professional journals.
e. Seek redress in local courts, perhaps through an enjoining injunction against the governing body.
f. Public education as carried out by an ethical psychiatrist would not utilize appeals based solely upon emotion, but would be presented in a professional way and without any potential exploitation of patients through testimonials.

Section 2

A physician shall deal honestly with patients and colleagues, and strive to expose those physicians deficient in character or competence, or who engage in fraud or deception.

[3]*Statements in italics are taken directly from the American Medical Association's Principles of Medical Ethics* or annotations thereto (Chicago: American Medical Association, 1981).

1. The requirement that the physician conduct himself with propriety in his/her profession and in all the actions of his/her life is especially important in the case of the psychiatrist because the patient tends to model his/her behavior after that of his/her therapist by identification. Further, the necessary intensity of the therapeutic relationship may tend to activate sexual and other needs and fantasies on the part of both patient and therapist, while weakening the objectivity necessary for control. Sexual activity with a patient is unethical.

2. The psychiatrist should diligently guard against exploiting information furnished by the patient and should not use the unique position of power afforded him/her by the psychotherapeutic situation to influence the patient in any way not directly relevant to the treatment goals.

3. A psychiatrist who regularly practices outside his/her area of professional competence should be considered unethical. Determination of professional competence should be made by peer review boards or other appropriate bodies.

4. Special consideration should be given to those psychiatrists who, because of mental illness, jeopardize the welfare of their patients and their own reputations and practices. It is ethical, even encouraged, for another psychiatrist to intercede in such situations.

5. Psychiatric services, like all medical services, are dispensed in the context of a contractual arrangement between the patient and the treating physician. The provisions of the contractual arrangement, which are binding on the physician as well as on the patient, should be explicitly established.

6. It is ethical for the psychiatrist to make a charge for a missed appointment when this falls within the terms of the specific contractual agreement with the patient. Charging for a missed appointment or for one not cancelled 24 hours in advance need not, in itself, be considered unethical if a patient is fully advised that the physician will make such a charge. The practice, however, should be resorted to infrequently and always with the utmost consideration of the patient and his/her circumstances.

7. An arrangement in which a psychiatrist provides supervision or administration to other physicians or nonmedical persons for a percentage of their fees or gross income is not acceptable; this would constitute fee-splitting. In a team of practitioners, or a multidisciplinary term, it is ethical for the psychiatrist to receive income for administration, research, education, or consultation. This should be based upon a mutually agreed upon and set fee or salary, open to renegotiation when a change in the time demand occurs. (See also Section 5, Annotations 2, 3, and 4.)

8. When a member has been found to have behaved unethically by the American Psychiatric Association or one of its constituent district branches, there should not be automatic reporting to the local authorities responsible for medical licensure, but the decision to report should be decided upon the merits of the case.

Section 3

A physician shall respect the law and also recognize a responsibility to seek changes in those requirements which are contrary to the best interests of the patient.

1. It would seem self-evident that a psychiatrist who is a lawbreaker might be ethically unsuited to practice his/her profession. When such illegal activities bear directly upon his/her practice, this would obviously be the case. However, in other instances, illegal activities such as those concerning the right to protest social injustices

might not bear on either the image of the psychiatrist or the ability of the specific psychiatrist to treat his/her patient ethically and well. While no committee or board could offer prior assurance that any illegal activity would not be considered unethical, it is conceivable that an individual could violate a law without being guilty of professionally unethical behavior. Physicians lose no right of citizenship on entry into the profession of medicine.

2. Where not specifically prohibited by local laws governing medical practice, the practice of acupuncture by a psychiatrist is not unethical per se. The psychiatrist should have professional competence in the use of acupuncture. Or, if he/she is supervising the use of acupuncture by nonmedical individuals, he/she should provide proper medical supervision. (See also Section 5, Annotations 3 and 4.)

Section 4

A physician shall respect the rights of patients, of colleagues, and of other health professionals, and shall safeguard patient confidences within the constraints of the law.

1. Psychiatric records, including even the identification of a person as a patient, must be protected with extreme care. Confidentiality is essential to psychiatric treatment. This is based in part on the special nature of psychiatric therapy as well as on the traditional ethical relationship between physician and patient. Growing concern regarding the civil rights of patients and the possible adverse effects of computerization, duplication equipment, and data banks makes the dissemination of confidential information an increasing hazard. Because of the sensitive and private nature of the information with which the psychiatrist deals, he/she must be circumspect in the information that he/she chooses to disclose to others about a patient. The welfare of the patient must be a continuing consideration.

2. A psychiatrist may release confidential information only with the authorization of the patient or under proper legal compulsion. The continuing duty of the psychiatrist to protect the patient includes fully apprising him/her of the connotations of waiving the privilege of privacy. This may become an issue when the patient is being investigated by a government agency, is applying for a position, or is involved in legal action. The same principles apply to the release of information concerning treatment to medical departments of government agencies; business organizations, labor unions, and insurance companies. Information gained in confidence about patients seen in student health services should not be released without the student's explicit permission.

3. Clinical and other materials used in teaching and writing must be adequately disguised in order to preserve the anonymity of the individuals involved.

4. The ethical responsibility of maintaining confidentiality holds equally for the consultations in which the patient may not have been present and in which the consultee was not a physician. In such instances, the physician consultant should alert the consultee to his/her duty of confidentiality.

5. Ethically the psychiatrist may disclose only that information which is relevant to a given situation. He/she should avoid offering speculation as fact. Sensitive information such as an individual's sexual orientation or fantasy material is usually unnecessary.

6. Psychiatrists are often asked to examine individuals for security purposes, to determine suitability for various jobs, and to determine legal competence. The psychia-

trist must fully describe the nature and purpose and lack of confidentiality of the examination to the examinee at the beginning of the examination.

7. Careful judgment must be exercised by the psychiatrist in order to include, when appropriate, the parents or guardian in the treatment of a minor. At the same time the psychiatrist must assure the minor proper confidentiality.

8. Psychiatrists at times may find it necessary, in order to protect the patient or the community from imminent danger, to reveal confidential information disclosed by the patient.

9. When the psychiatrist is ordered by the court to reveal the confidences entrusted to him/her by patients he/she may comply or he/she may ethically hold the right to dissent within the framework of the law. When the psychiatrist is in doubt, the right of the patient to confidentiality and, by extension, to unimpaired treatment, should be given priority. The psychiatrist should reserve the right to raise the question of adequate need for disclosure. In the event that the necessity for legal disclosure is demonstrated by the court, the psychiatrist may request the right to disclosure of only that information which is relevant to the legal question at hand.

10. With regard for the person's dignity and privacy and with truly informed consent, it is ethical to present a patient to a scientific gathering, if the confidentiality of the presentation is understood and accepted by the audience.

11. It is ethical to present a patient or former patient to a public gathering or to the news media only if that patient is fully informed of enduring loss of confidentiality, is competent, and consents in writing without coercion.

12. When involved in funded research, the ethical psychiatrist will advise human subjects of the funding source, retain his/her freedom to reveal data and results, and follow all appropriate and current guidelines relative to human subject protection.

13. Ethical considerations in medical practice preclude the psychiatric evaluation of any adult charged with criminal acts prior to access to, or availability of, legal counsel. The only exception is the rendering of care to the person for the sole purpose of medical treatment.

Section 5

A physician shall continue to study, apply, and advance scientific knowledge, make relevant information available to patients, colleagues, and the public, obtain consultation, and use the talents of other health professionals when indicated.

1. Psychiatrists are responsible for their own continuing education and should be mindful of the fact that theirs must be a lifetime of learning.

2. In the practice of his/her speciality, the psychiatrist consults, associates, collaborates, or integrates his/her work with that of many professionals, including psychologists, psychometricians, social workers, alcoholism counselors, marriage counselors, public health nurses, etc. Furthermore, the nature of modern psychiatric practice extends his/her contacts to such people as teachers, juvenile and adult probation officers, attorneys, welfare workers, agency volunteers, and neighborhood aides. In referring patients for treatment, counseling, or rehabilitation to any of these practitioners, the psychiatrist should ensure that the allied professional or paraprofessional with whom he/she is dealing is a recognized member of his/her own discipline and is competent to carry out the therapeutic task required. The psychiatrist should have the same attitude toward members of the medical profession to whom he/she refers patients. Whenever

he/she has reason to doubt the training, skill, or ethical qualifications of the allied professional, the psychiatrist should not refer cases to him/her.

3. When the psychiatrist assumes a collaborative or supervisory role with another mental health worker, he/she must expend sufficient time to assure that proper care is given. It is contrary to the interests of the patient and to patient care if he/she allows himself/herself to be used as a figurehead.

4. In relationships between psychiatrists and practicing licensed psychologists, the physician should not delegate to the psychologist or, in fact, to any nonmedical person any matter requiring the exercise of professional medical judgment.

5. The psychiatrist should agree to the request of a patient for consultation or to such a request from the family of an incompetent or minor patient. The psychiatrist may suggest possible consultants, but the patient or family should be given free choice of the consultant. If the psychiatrist disapproves of the professional qualifications of the consultant or if there is a difference of opinion that the primary therapist cannot resolve, he/she may, after suitable notice, withdraw from the case. If this disagreement occurs within an institution or agency framework, the differences should be resolved by the mediation or arbitration of higher professional authority within the institution or agency.

Section 6

A physician shall, in the provision of appropriate care, except in emergencies, be free to choose whom to serve, with whom to associate, and the environment in which to provide medical services.

1. Physicians generally agree that the doctor-patient relationship is such a vital factor in effective treatment of the patient that preservation of optimal conditions for development of a sound working relationship between a doctor and his/her patient should take precedence over all other considerations. Professional courtesy may lead to poor psychiatric care for physicians and their families because of embarrassment over the lack of a complete give-and-take contract.

Section 7

A physician shall recognize a responsibility to participate in activities contributing to an improved community.

1. Psychiatrists should foster the cooperation of those legitimately concerned with the medical, psychological, social, and legal aspects of mental health and illness. Psychiatrists are encouraged to serve society by advising and consulting with the executive, legislative, and judiciary branches of the government. A psychiatrist should clarify whether he/she speaks as an individual or as a representative of an organization. Furthermore, psychiatrists should avoid cloaking their public statements with the authority of the profession (e.g., "Psychiatrists know that . . .").

2. Psychiatrists may interpret and share with the public their expertise in the various psychosocial issues that may affect mental health and illness. Psychiatrists should always be mindful of their separate roles as dedicated citizens and as experts in psychological medicine.

3. On occasion psychiatrists are asked for an opinion about an individual who is in the light of public attention, or who has disclosed information about himself/herself

through public media. It is unethical for a psychiatrist to offer a professional opinion unless he/she has conducted an examination and has been granted proper authorization for such a statement.

4. The psychiatrist may permit his/her certification to be used for the involuntary treatment of any person only following his/her personal examination of that person. To do so, he/she must find that the person, because of mental illness, cannot form a judgment as to what is in his/her own best interests and without which treatment substantial impairment is likely to occur to the person or others.

Code of Ethics, National Association of Social Workers (1979)*

Preamble

This code is intended to serve as a guide to the everyday conduct of members of the social work profession and as a basis for the adjudication of issues in ethics when the conduct of social workers is alleged to deviate from the standards expressed or implied in this code. It represents standards of ethical behavior for social workers in professional relationships with those served, with colleagues, with employers, with other individuals and professions, and with the community and society as a whole. It also embodies standards of ethical behavior governing individual conduct to the extent that such conduct is associated with an individual's status and identity as a social worker.

This code is based on the fundamental values of the social work profession that include the worth, dignity, and uniqueness of all persons as well as their rights and opportunities. It is also based on the nature of social work, which fosters conditions that promote these values.

In subscribing to and abiding by this code, the social worker is expected to view ethical responsibility in as inclusive a context as each situation demands and within which ethical judgement is required. The social worker is expected to take into consideration all the principles in this code that have a bearing upon any situation in which ethical judgement is to be exercised and professional intervention or conduct is planned. The course of action that the social worker chooses is expected to be consistent with the spirit as well as the letter of this code.

In itself, this code does not represent a set of rules that will prescribe all the behaviors of social workers in all the complexities of professional life. Rather, it offers general principles to guide conduct, and the judicious appraisal of conduct, in situations that have ethical implications. It provides the basis for making judgements about ethical actions before and after they occur. Frequently, the particular situation determines the ethical principles that apply and the manner of their application. In such cases, not only the particular ethical principles are taken into immediate consideration, but also the entire code and its spirit. Specific applications of ethical principles must be judged within the context in which they are being considered. Ethical behavior in a given situation must satisfy not only the judgement of the individual social worker, but also the judgement of an unbiased jury of professional peers.

This code should not be used as an instrument to deprive any social worker of the opportunity or freedom to practice with complete professional integrity; nor should any disciplinary action be taken on the basis of this code without maximum provision for safeguarding the rights of the social worker affected.

*Published 1979, National Association of Social Workers, Inc. Reprinted with permission.

The ethical behavior of social workers results not from edict, but from a personal commitment of the individual. This code is offered to affirm the will and zeal of all social workers to be ethical and to act ethically in all that they do as social workers.

The following codified ethical principles should guide social workers in the various roles and relationships and at the various levels of responsibility in which they function professionally. These principles also serve as a basis for the adjudication by the National Association of Social Workers of issues in ethics.

In subscribing to this code, social workers are required to cooperate in its implementation and abide by any disciplinary rulings based on it. They should also take adequate measures to discourage, prevent, expose, and correct the unethical conduct of colleagues. Finally, social workers should be equally ready to defend and assist colleagues unjustly charged with unethical conduct.

I. The Social Worker's Conduct and Comportment as a Social Worker

A. *Propriety-The social worker should maintain high standards of personal conduct in the capacity or identity as social worker.*
   1. The private conduct of the social worker is a personal matter to the same degree as is any other person's, except when such conduct compromises the fulfillment of professional responsibilities.
   2. The social worker should not participate in, condone, or be associated with dishonesty, fraud, deceit, or misrepresentation.
   3. The social worker should distinguish clearly between statements and actions made as a private individual and as a representative of the social work profession or an organization or group.

B. *Competence and Professional Development—The social worker should strive to become and remain proficient in professional practice and the performance of professional functions.*
   1. The social worker should accept responsibility or employment only on the basis of existing competence or the intention to acquire the necessary competence.
   2. The social worker should not misrepresent professional qualifications, education, experience, or affiliations.

C. *Service—The social worker should regard as primary the service obligation of the social work profession.*
   1. The social worker should retain ultimate responsibility for the quality and extent of the service that individual assumes, assigns, or performs.
   2. The social worker should act to prevent practices that are inhumane or discriminatory against any person or group of persons.

D. *Integrity—The social worker should act in accordance with the highest standards of professional integrity and impartiality.*
   1. The social worker should be alert to an resist the influences and pressures that interfere with the exercise of professional discretion and impartial judgement required for the performance of professional functions.
   2. The social worker should not exploit professional relationships for personal gain.

E. *Scholarship and Research—The social worker engaged in study and research should be guided by the conventions of scholarly inquiry.*
   1. The social worker engaged in research should consider carefully its possible consequences for human beings.

2. The social worker engaged in research should ascertain that the consent of participants in the research is voluntary and informed, without any implied deprivation or penalty for refusal to participate, and with due regard for participants' privacy and dignity.
3. The social worker engaged in research should protect participants from unwarranted physical or mental discomfort, distress, harm, danger, or deprivation.
4. The social worker who engages in the evaluation of services or cases should discuss them only for the professional purposes and only with persons directly and professionally concerned with them.
5. Information obtained about participants in research should be treated as confidential.
6. The social worker should take credit only for work actually done in connection with scholarly and research endeavors and credit contributions made by others.

II. The Social Worker's Ethical Responsibility to Clients

F. *Primacy of Clients' Interests—The social worker's primary responsibility is to clients.*

1. The social worker should serve clients with devotion, loyalty, determination, and the maximum application of professional skill and competence.
2. The social worker should not exploit relationships with clients for personal advantage, or solicit the clients of one's agency for private practice.
3. The social worker should not practice, condone, facilitate or collaborate with any form of discrimination on the basis of race, color, sex, sexual orientation, age, religion, national origin, marital status, political belief, mental or physical handicap, or any other preference or personal characteristic, condition or status.
4. The social worker should avoid relationships or commitments that conflict with the interests of clients.
5. The social worker should under no circumstances engage in sexual activities with clients.
6. The social worker should provide clients with accurate and complete information regarding the extent and nature of the services available to them.
7. The social worker should apprise clients of their risks, rights, opportunities, and obligations associated with social service to them.
8. The social worker should seek advice and counsel of colleagues and supervisors whenever such consultation is in the best interest of clients.
9. The social worker should terminate service to clients, and professional relationships with them, when such service and relationships are no longer required or no longer serve the clients' needs or interests.
10. The social worker should withdraw services precipitously only under unusual circumstances, giving careful consideration to all factors in the situation and taking care to minimize possible adverse effects.
11. The social worker who anticipates the termination or interruption of service to clients should notify clients promptly and seek the transfer, referral, or continuation of service in relation to the clients' needs and preferences.

G. *Rights and Prerogatives of Clients—The social worker should make every effort to foster maximum self-determination on the part of clients.*

1. When the social worker must act on behalf of a client who has been adjudged

legally incompetent, the social worker should safeguard the interests and rights of that client.

2. When another individual has been legally authorized to act in behalf of a client, the social worker should deal with that person always with the client's best interest in mind.
3. The social worker should not engage in any action that violates or diminishes the civil or legal rights of clients.

H. *Confidentiality and Privacy—The social worker should respect the privacy of clients and hold in confidence all information obtained in the course of professional service.*

1. The social worker should share with others confidences revealed by clients, without their consent, only for compelling professional reasons.
2. The social worker should inform clients fully about the limits of confidentiality in a given situation, the purposes for which information is obtained, and how it may be used.
3. The social worker should afford clients reasonable access to any official social work records concerning them.
4. When providing clients with access to records, the social worker should take due care to protect the confidences of others contained in those records.
5. The social worker should obtain informed consent of clients before taping, recording, or permitting third party observation of their activities.

I. *Fees-When setting fees, the social worker should ensure that they are fair, reasonable, considerate, and commensurate with the service performed and with due regard for the clients' ability to pay.*

1. The social worker should not divide a fee or accept or give anything of value for receiving or making a referral.

III. The Social Worker's Ethical Responsibility to Colleagues

J. *Respect, Fairness, and Courtesy—The social worker should treat colleagues with respect, courtesy, fairness, and good faith.*

1. The social worker should cooperate with colleagues to promote professional interests and concerns.
2. The social worker should respect confidences shared by colleagues in the course of their professional relationships and transactions.
3. The social worker should create and maintain conditions of practice that facilitate ethical and competent professional performance by colleagues.
4. The social worker should treat with respect, and represent accurately and fairly, the qualifications, views, and findings of colleagues and use appropriate channels to express judgements on these matters.
5. The social worker who replaces or is replaced by a colleague in professional practice should act with consideration for the interest, character, and reputation of that colleague.
6. The social worker should not exploit a dispute between a colleague and employers to obtain a position or otherwise advance the social worker's interest.
7. The social worker should seek arbitration or mediation when conflicts with colleagues require resolution for compelling professional reasons.
8. The social worker should extend to colleagues of other professions the same respect and cooperation that is extended to social work colleagues.

9. The social worker who serves as an employer, supervisor, or mentor to colleagues should make orderly and explicit arrangements regarding the conditions of their continuing professional relationship.
10. The social worker who has the responsibility for employing and evaluating the performance of other staff members, should fulfill such responsibility in a fair, considerate, and equitable manner, on the basis of clearly enunciated criteria.
11. The social worker who has the responsibility for evaluating the performance of employees, supervisees, or students should share evaluations with them.

K. *Dealing with Colleagues' Clients—The social worker has the responsibility to relate to the clients of colleagues with full professional consideration.*
1. The social worker should not solicit the clients of colleagues.
2. The social worker should not assume professional responsibility for the clients of another agency or a colleague without appropriate communication with that agency or colleague.
3. The social worker who serves the clients of colleagues, during a temporary absence or emergency, should serve those clients with the same consideration as that afforded any client.

IV. The Social Worker's Ethical Responsibility to Employers and Employing Organizations

L. *Commitments to Employing Organization—The social worker should adhere to commitments made to the employing organization.*
1. The social worker should work to improve the employing agency's policies and procedures, and the efficiency and effectiveness of its services.
2. The social worker should not accept employment or arrange student field placements in an organization which is currently under public sanction by NASW for violating personnel standards, or imposing limitations on or penalties for professional actions on behalf of clients.
3. The social worker should act to prevent and eliminate discrimination in the employing organization's work assignments and in its employment policies and practices.
4. The social worker should use with scrupulous regard, and only for the purpose for which they are intended, the resources of the employing organization.

V. The Social Worker's Ethical Responsibility to the Social Work Profession

M. *Maintaining the Integrity of the Profession—The social worker should uphold and advance the values, ethics, knowledge, and mission of the profession.*
1. The social worker should protect and enhance the dignity and integrity of the profession and should be responsible and vigorous in discussion and criticism of the profession.
2. The social worker should take action through appropriate channels against unethical conduct by any other member of the profession.
3. The social worker should act to prevent the unauthorized and unqualified practice of social work.
4. The social worker should make no misrepresentation in advertising as to qualifications, competence, service, or results to be achieved.

N. *Community Service—The social worker should assist the profession in making social services available to the general public.*
   1. The social worker should contribute time and professional expertise to activities that promote respect for the utility, the integrity, and the competence of the social work profession.
   2. The social worker should critically examine, and keep current with emerging implementation of social policies of concern to the profession.

O. *Development of Knowledge—The social worker should take responsibility for identifying, developing, and fully utilizing knowledge for professional practice.*
   1. The social worker should base practice upon recognized knowledge relevant to social work.
   2. The social worker should critically examine, and keep current with emerging knowledge relevant to social work.
   3. The social worker should contribute to the knowledge base of social work and share research knowledge and practice wisdom with colleagues.

VI. The Social Worker's Ethical Responsibility to Society

P. *Promoting the General Welfare—The social worker should promote the general welfare of society.*
   1. The social worker should act to prevent and eliminate discrimination against any person or group on the basis of race, color, sex, sexual orientation, age, religion, national origin, marital status, political belief, mental or physical handicap, or any other preference or personal characteristic, condition, or status.
   2. The social worker should act to ensure that all persons have access to the resources, services, and opportunities which they require.
   3. The social worker should act to expand choice and opportunity for all persons, with special regard for disadvantaged or oppressed groups and persons.
   4. The social worker should promote conditions that encourage respect for the diversity of cultures which constitute American society.
   5. The social worker should provide appropriate professional services in public emergencies.
   6. The social worker should advocate changes in policy and legislation to improve social conditions and to promote social justice.
   7. The social worker should encourage informed participation by the public in shaping social policies and institutions.

Standards for provision of professional services. Generally, statutes prescribe only minimal entrance requirements to the profession. Some professional organizations have developed their own internal structures for crediting those practitioners who have achieved higher levels of training and/or skill. The American Nursing Association, for example, has established an internal standard for psychiatric nurses. The American Psychological Association (APA) has developed its Standards for Providers of Psychological Services, and that professional organization is currently in the process of developing specialty standards that will apply to practitioners of the various psychological specialties (e.g., clinical psychology, industrial/organizational psychology, school psychology). Through its affiliated organization, the American Board of Professional Psychology (ABPP), the American Psychological Association has gone beyond defining minimal standards of competence and has endeavored to define standards of excellence. Upon the successful completion of the ABPP examination, the practitioner is awarded an ABPP diploma in one of four professional specialties: clinical psychology, counseling psychology, industrial and organizational psychology, or school psychology. Below we have reprinted the APA's Standards for Providers of Psychological Services and ABPP's Policies and Procedures for the Creation of Diplomates in Professional Psychology.

Although it is commonly believed that a psychiatrist holds a specific license to practice psychiatry, the term "psychiatrist" is generally not protected by statute. Rather, psychiatrists are regulated internally by professional medical associations. In theory, then, any physician is legally entitled to hold himself out to the public as a psychiatrist (i.e., any physician may legally limit his practice to psychiatry should he choose to do so, just as he may choose to limit his practice to any other specialty of medical practice). Although physicians must uniformly obtain some form of governmental authorization to practice medicine in every state of the union, it is the profession and not the government that sets the standard of practice for the various medical specialties. It is possible, therefore, that a consumer may find his way to a "psychiatrist" who has in fact had little or no training in psychology or psychiatry. This point has been made by O'Keefe and McCullough:

> Physicians, although well-trained in a broad spectrum of physical sciences, have few academic or training requirements specifically in the area of human behavior. While most medical schools include some training in psychiatry, the exposure for the individual student may be quite minimal.
>
> . . . [T]he average mental health consumer not only has little access to information concerning the qualifications of psychiatrists but often must use their services in lieu of those of psychologists. Recent research discovered, for example, that there are more than 2,000 persons in the state of Ohio who are licensed to practice psychology. The AMA *Directory* lists more than 800 physicians in that state whose practices are limited to psychiatry. The Ohio Psychiatric Association includes approximately 500 members. The *Directory of Medical Specialists,* however, lists only 229 Ohio physicians who have been certified by the American Specialty Boards in psychiatry. (O'Keefe & McCullough, 1979, pp. 615-616)

Standards for Providers of Psychological Services, American Psychological Association (1977)*

The Standards that follow are the first revision of the national Standards for Providers of Psychological Services originally adopted by the American Psychological Association (APA) on September 4, 1974.[1] The intent of these Standards is to improve

[1]Members of the Task Force on Standards for Service Facilities that submitted the original Standards in September 1974 were Milton L. Blum, Jacqueline C. Bouhoutsos, Jerry H. Clark, Harold A. Edgerton,

the quality, effectiveness, and accessibility of psychological services to all who require them.[2]

These Standards represent the attainment of a goal for which the Association has striven for over 20 years, namely, to codify a uniform set of standards for psychological practice that would serve the respective needs of users, providers, and third-party purchasers and sanctioners of psychological services. In addition, the Association has established a standing committee charged with keeping the Standards responsive to the needs of these groups and with upgrading and extending them progressively as the profession and science of psychology continue to develop new knowledge, improved methods, and additional modes of psychological service. These Standards have been established by organized psychology as a means of self-regulation to protect the public interest.

While these revised Standards contain a number of important changes, they differ from the original Standards in two major respects:

1. They uniformly specify the *minimally acceptable levels* of quality assurance and performance that providers of those psychological services covered by the Standards must reach or exceed. Care has been taken to assure that each standard is clearly stated, readily measurable, realistic, and implementable.

2. The revised Standards apply to a more limited range of services than the original Standards. The present Standards have been restricted to applications in "human services" with the goal of facilitating more effective human functioning. The kinds of psychological services covered by the present Standards are those ordinarily involved in the practice of specialists in clinical, counseling, industrial-organizational, and school psychology. However, it is important to note that these Standards cover psychological *functions* and not classes of practitioners.

Any persons representing themselves as psychologists, when providing any of the covered psychological service functions at any time and in any setting, whether public or private, profit or nonprofit, are required to observe these standards of practice in order to promote the best interests and welfare of the users of such services. It is to be understood that fulfillment of the requirements to meet these Standards shall be judged by peers in relation to the capabilities for evaluation and the circumstances that prevail in the setting at the time the program or service is evaluated.

Standards covering other psychological service functions may be added from time to time to those already listed. However, functions and activities related to the teaching of psychology, the writing or editing of scholarly or scientific manuscripts, and the conduct of scientific research do not fall within the purview of the present Standards.

Historical Background

Early in 1970, acting at the direction of the Association's Council of Representatives, the Board of Professional Affairs appointed a Task Force composed of practicing psychologists with specialized knowledge in at least one of every major class of human

---

Marian D. Hall, Durand F. Jacobs (Chair, 1972–1974), Floyd H. Martinez, John E. Muthard, Asher R. Pacht, William D. Pierce, Sue A. Warren, and Alfred M. Wellner (Chair, 1970–1971). Staff liaisons from the APA Office of Professional Affairs were John J. McMillan (1970–1971), Gottlieb C. Simon (1971–1973), and Arthur Centor (1973–1974).

[2]The footnotes appended to these Standards represent an attempt to provide a coherent context of other policy statements of the Association regarding professional practice. The Standards extend these previous policy statements where necessary to reflect current concerns of the public and the profession.

service facility and with experience relevant to the setting of standards. Its charge was to develop a set of standards for psychological practice. Soon thereafter, partial support for this activity was obtained through a grant from the National Institute of Mental Health.[3]

First, the Task Force established liaison with national groups already active in standard setting and accreditation. It was therefore able to influence the adoption of certain basic principles and wording contained in standards for psychological services published by the Joint Commission on Accreditation of Hospitals (JCAH) Accreditation Council for Facilities for the Mentally Retarded (1971) and by the Accreditation Council for Psychiatric Facilities (JCAH, 1972). It also contributed substantially to the "constitutionally required minimum standards for adequate treatment of the mentally ill" ordered by the U.S. District Court in Alabama (*Wyatt* v. *Stickney,* 1972). In concert with other APA committees, the Task Force also represented the Association in national-level deliberations with governmental groups and insurance carriers that defined the qualifications necessary for psychologists involved in providing health services.

These interim outcomes involved influence by the Association on actions by groups of nonpsychologists that directly affected the manner in which psychological services were employed, particularly in health and rehabilitation settings. However, these measures did not relieve the Association from exercising its responsibility to speak out directly and authoritatively on what standards for psychological practice should be throughout a broad range of human service settings. It was also the responsibility of the Association to determine how psychologists would be held accountable should their practice fail to meet quality standards.

In September 1974, after more than 4 years of study and broad consultations, the Task Force proposed a set of standards, which the Association's Council of Representatives adopted and voted to publish in order to meet urgent needs of the public and the profession. Members of Council had various reservations about the scope and wording of the Standards as initially adopted. By establishing a continuing Committee on Standards, Council took the first step in what would be an ongoing process of review and revision.

The task of collecting, analyzing, and synthesizing reactions to the original Standards fell to two successive committees. They were charged similarly to review and revise the Standards and to suggest means to implement them, including their acceptance by relevant governmental and private accreditation groups. The dedicated work of the psychologists who served on both those committees is gratefully acknowledged. Also recognized with thanks are the several hundred comments received from scores of interested persons representing professional, academic, and scientific psychology, consumer groups, administrators of facilities, and others. This input from those directly affected by the original Standards provided the major stimulus and much of the content for the changes that appear in this revision.

Principles and Implications of Standards

A few basic principles have guided the development of these Standards:

1. There should be a single set of standards that governs psychological service functions offered by psychologists, regardless of their specialty, setting, or form of

[3]NIMH Grant MH 21696.

remuneration. All psychologists in professional practice should be guided by a uniform set of standards just as they are guided by a common code of ethics.

2. Standards should clearly establish minimally acceptable levels of quality for covered psychological service functions, regardless of the character of the users, purchasers, or sanctioners of such covered services.

3. All persons providing psychological services shall meet minimally acceptable levels of training and experience, which are consistent and appropriate with the functions they perform. However, final responsibility and accountability for services provided must rest with psychologists who have earned a doctoral degree in a program that is primarily psychological at a regionally accredited university or professional school. Those providing psychological services who have lesser (or other) levels of training shall be supervised by a psychologist with the above training. This level of qualification is necessary to assure that the public receives services of high quality.

4. There should be a uniform set of standards governing the quality of services to all users of psychological services in both the private and public sectors. There is no justification for maintaining the double standard presently embedded in most state legislation whereby providers of private fee-based psychological services are subject to statutory regulation, while those providing similar psychological services under governmental auspices are usually exempt from such regulations. This circumstance tends to afford greater protection under the law for those receiving privately delivered psychological services. On the other hand, those receiving privately delivered psychological services currently lack many of the safeguards that are available in governmental settings; these include peer review, consultation, record review, and staff supervision.

5. While assuring the user of the psychologist's accountability for the nature and quality of services rendered, standards must not constrain the psychologist from employing new methods or making flexible use of support personnel in staffing the delivery of services.

The Standards here presented have broad implications both for the public who use psychological services and for providers of such services:

1. Standards provide a firmer basis for a mutual understanding between provider and user and facilitate more effective evaluation of services provided and outcomes achieved.

2. Standards are an important step toward greater uniformity in legislative and regulatory actions involving providers of psychological services, and Standards provide the basis for the development of accreditation procedures for service facilities.

3. Standards give specific content to the profession's concept of ethical practice.

4. Standards have significant impact on tomorrow's training models for both professional and support personnel in psychology.

5. Standards for the provision of psychological services in human service facilities influence what is considered acceptable structure, budgeting, and staffing patterns in these facilities.

6. Standards are living documents that require continual review and revision.

The Standards illuminate weaknesses in the delivery of psychological services and point to their correction. Some settings are known to require additional and/or higher standards for specific areas of service delivery than those herein proposed. There is no intent to diminish the scope or quality of psychological services that exceed these Standards.

Systematically applied, these Standards serve to establish uniformly the *minimally acceptable levels* of psychological services. They serve to establish a more effective and consistent basis for evaluating the performance of individual service providers, and they serve to guide the organizing of psychological service units in human service settings.

Definitions

Providers of psychological services refers to the following persons:

A. Professional psychologists.[4] Professional psychologists have a doctoral degree from a regionally accredited university or professional school in a program that is primarily psychological[5] and appropriate training and experience in the area of service offered.[6]

B. All other persons who offer psychological services under the supervision of a professional psychologist.

Psychological services refers to one or more of the following:[7]

A. Evaluation, diagnosis, and assessment of the functioning of individuals and groups in a variety of settings and activities.

B. Interventions to facilitate the functioning of individuals and groups. Such interventions may include psychological counseling, psychotherapy, and process consultation.

C. Consultation relating to A and B above.

[4]For the purpose of transition, persons who met the following criteria on or before the date of adoption of the original Standards on September 4, 1974, shall also be considered professional psychologists: (a) a master's degree from a program primarily psychological in content from a regionally accredited university or professional school; (b) appropriate education, training, and experience in the area of service offered; (c) a license or certificate in the state in which they practice, conferred by a state board of psychological examiners, or the endorsement of the state psychological association through voluntary certification, or, for practice in primary and secondary schools, a state department of education certificate as a school psychologist provided that the certificate required at least two graduate years.

[5]Minutes of the Board of Professional Affairs meeting, Washington, D.C., March 8-9, 1974.

[6]This definition is less restrictive than Recommendation 4 of the APA (1967) policy statement setting forth model state legislation affecting the practice of psychology (hereinafter referred to as State Guidelines), proposing one level for state license or certificate and "requiring the doctoral degree from an accredited university or college in a program that is primarily psychological, and no less than 2 years of supervised experience, one of which is subsequent to the granting of the doctoral degree. This level should be designated by the title of 'psychologist' " (p. 1099).

The 1972 APA "Guidelines for Conditions of Employment of Psychologists" (hereinafter referred to as CEP Guidelines) introduces slightly different shadings of meaning in its section on "Standards for Entry into the Profession" as follows:

> Persons are properly identified as psychologists when they have completed the training and experience recognized as necessary to perform functions consistent with one of the several levels in a career in psychology. This training includes possession of a degree earned in a program primarily psychological in content. In the case of psychological practice, it involves services for a fee, appropriate registration, certification, or licensing as provided by laws of the state in which the practices will apply. (APA, 1972, p. 331)

In some situations, specialty designations and standards may be relevant. *The National Register of Health Service Providers in Psychology,* which based its criteria on this standard, identifies qualified psychologists in the health services field.

[7]As noted in the opening section of these Standards, functions and activities of psychologists relating to the teaching of psychology, the writing or editing of scholarly or scientific manuscripts, and the conduct of scientific research do not fall within the purview of these Standards.

D. Program development services in the areas of A, B, and C above.[8]

E. Supervision of psychological services.

A *psychological service unit* is the functional unit through which psychological services are provided:

A. A psychological service unit is a unit that provides predominantly psychological services and is composed of one or more professional psychologists and supporting staff.

B. A psychological service unit may operate as a professional service or as a functional or geographic component of a larger governmental, educational, correction, health, training, industrial, or commercial organizational unit.[9]

C. A psychologist providing professional services in a multioccupational setting is regarded as a psychological service unit.

D. A psychological service unit also may be an individual or group of individuals in a private practice or a psychological consulting firm.

User includes:

A. Direct users or recipients of psychological services.

B. Public and private institutions, facilities, or organizations receiving psychological services.

C. Third-party purchasers—those who pay for the delivery of services but who are not the recipients of services.

Sanctioners refers to those users and nonusers who have a legitimate concern with the accessibility, timeliness, efficacy, and standards of quality attending the provision of psychological services. In addition to the users, sanctioners may include members of the user's family, the court, the probation officer, the school administrator, the employer, the union representative, the facility director, etc. Another class of sanctioners is represented by various governmental, peer review, and accreditation bodies concerned with the assurance of quality.

[8]These definitions should be compared to the State Guidelines, which include definitions of *psychologist* and the *practice of psychology* as follows:

> A person represents himself to be a psychologist when he holds himself out to the public by any title or description of services incorporating the words "psychology," "psychological," "psychologist," and/or offers to render services as defined below to individuals, groups, organizations, or the public for a fee, monetary or otherwise.
>
> The practice of psychology within the meaning of this act is defined as rendering to individuals, groups or organizations, or the public any psychological service involving the application of principles, methods, and procedures of understanding, predicting, and influencing behavior, such as the principles pertaining to learning, perception, motivation, thinking, emotions, and interpersonal relationships; the methods and procedures of interviewing, counseling, and psychotherapy; of constructing, administering, and interpreting tests of mental abilities, aptitudes, interests, attitudes, personality characteristics, emotion, and motivation, and of assessing public opinion.
>
> The application of said principles and methods includes but is not restricted to: diagnosis, prevention, and amelioration of adjustment problems and emotional and mental disorders of individuals and groups; hypnosis; educational and vocational counseling; personnel selection and management; the evaluation and planning for effective work and learning situations; advertising and market research; and the resolution of interpersonal and social conflicts.
>
> Psychotherapy within the meaning of this act means the use of learning, conditioning methods, and emotional reactions, in a professional relationship, to assist a person or persons to modify feelings, attitudes, and behavior which are intellectually, socially, or emotionally maladjustive or ineffectual.
>
> The practice of psychology shall be as defined above, any existing statute in the state of ____________ to the contrary notwithstanding. (APA, 1967, pp. 1098–1099)

[9]The relation of a psychological service unit to a larger facility or institution is also addressed indirectly in the CEP Guidelines, which emphasize the roles, responsibilities, and prerogatives of the psychologist when he or she is employed by or provides services for another agency, institution, or business.

Standard 1. Providers

1.1 *Each psychological service unit offering psychological services shall have available at least one professional psychologist and as many more professional psychologists as are necessary to assure the quality of services offered.*

INTERPRETATION: The intent of this Standard is that one or more providers of psychological services in any psychological service unit shall meet the levels of training and experience of the professional psychologist as specified in the preceding definitions.[10]

When a professional psychologist is not available on a full-time basis, the facility shall retain the services of one or more professional psychologists on a regular part-time basis to supervise the psychological services provided. The psychologist(s) so retained shall have authority and participate sufficiently to enable him or her to assess the needs for services, review the content of services provided, and assume professional responsibility and accountability for them.

1.2 *Providers of psychological services who do not meet the requirements for the professional psychologist shall be supervised by a professional psychologist who shall assume professional responsibility and accountability for the services provided. The level and extent of supervision may vary from task to task so long as the supervising psychologist retains a sufficiently close supervisory relationship to meet this standard.*

1.3 *Wherever a psychological service unit exists, a professional psychologist shall be responsible for planning, directing, and reviewing the provision of psychological services.*

INTERPRETATION: This psychologist shall coordinate the activities of the psychological service unit with other professional, administrative, and technical groups, both within and outside the facility. This psychologist, who may be the director, chief, or coordinator of the psychological service unit, has related responsibilities including, but

[10]This Standard replaces earlier recommendations in the 1967 State Guidelines concerning exemption of psychologists from licensure. Recommendations 8 and 9 of those Guidelines read as follows:

> 8. Persons employed as psychologists by accredited academic institutions, governmental agencies, research laboratories, and business corporations should be exempted, provided such employees are performing those duties for which they are employed by such organizations, and within the confines of such organizations.
>
> 9. Persons employed as psychologists by accredited academic institutions, governmental agencies, research laboratories, and business corporations consulting or offering their research findings or providing scientific information to like organizations for a fee should be exempted. (APA, 1967, p. 1100)

On the other hand, the 1967 State Guidelines specifically denied exemptions under certain conditions, as noted in Recommendations 10 and 11.

> 10. Persons employed as psychologists who offer or provide psychological services to the public for a fee, over and above the salary that they receive for the performance of their regular duties, should not be exempted.
>
> 11. Persons employed as psychologists by organizations that sell psychological services to the public should not be exempted. (APA, 1967, pp. 1100–1101)

The present APA policy, as reflected in this Standard, establishes a single code of practice for psychologists providing covered services to users in any setting. The present minimum requirement is that a psychologist providing any covered service must meet local statutory requirements for licensure or certification. See the section Principles and Implications of the Standards for an elaboration of this position.

not limited to, recruiting qualified staff, directing training and research activities of the service, maintaining a high level of professional and ethical practice, and assuring that staff members function only within the areas of their competency.

In order to facilitate the effectiveness of services by increasing the level of staff sensitivity and professional skills, the psychologist designated as director shall be responsible for participating in the selection of the staff and supporting personnel whose qualifications and skills (e.g., language, cultural and experiential background, race, and sex) are directly relevant to the needs and characteristics of the users served.

1.4 *When functioning as part of an organizational setting, professional psychologists shall bring their background and skills to bear whenever appropriate upon the goals of the organization by participating in the planning and development of overall services.*[11]

INTERPRETATION: Professional psychologists shall participate in the maintenance of high professional standards by representation on committees concerned with service delivery.

As appropriate to the setting, these activities may include active participation, as voting and as office-holding members on the facility's executive, planning, and evaluation boards and committees.

1.5 *Psychologists shall maintain current knowledge of scientific and professional developments that are directly related to the services they render.*

INTERPRETATION: Methods through which knowledge of scientific and professional development may be gained include, but are not limited to, continuing education, attendance at workshops, participation in staff development, and reading scientific publications.[12]

The psychologist shall have ready access to reference material related to the provision of psychological services.

Psychologists must be prepared to show evidence periodically that they are staying abreast of current knowledge and practices through continuing education.

1.6 *Psychologists shall limit their practice to their demonstrated areas of professional competence.*

INTERPRETATION: Psychological services will be offered in accordance with the provider's areas of competence as defined by verifiable training and experience. When extending services beyond the range of their usual practice, psychologists shall obtain pertinent training or appropriate professional supervision.

[11]A closely related principle is found in the APA (1972) CEP Guidelines:

> It is the policy of APA that psychology as an independent profession is entitled to parity with other health and human service professions in institutional practices and before the law. Psychologists in interdisciplinary settings such as colleges and universities, medical schools, clinics, private practice groups, and other agencies expect parity with other professions in such matters as academic rank, board status, salaries, fringe benefits, fees, participation in administrative decisions, and all other conditions of employment, private contractual arrangements, and status before the law and legal institutions. (APA, 1972, p. 333)

[12]See CEP Guidelines (section entitled "Career Development") for a closely related statement:

> Psychologists are expected to encourage institutions and agencies which employ them to sponsor or conduct career development programs. The purpose of these programs would be to enable psychologists to engage in study for professional advancement and to keep abreast of developments in their field. (APA, 1972, p. 332)

1.7 *Psychologists who wish to change their service specialty or to add an additional area of applied specialization must meet the same requirements with respect to subject matter and professional skills that apply to doctoral training in the new specialty.*[13]

INTERPRETATION: Training of doctoral-level psychologists to qualify them for change in specialty will be under the auspices of accredited university departments or professional schools that offer the doctoral degree in that specialty. Such training should be individualized, due credit being given for relevant coursework or requirements that have previously been satisfied. Merely taking an internship or acquiring experience in a practicum setting is not considered adequate preparation for becoming a clinical, counseling, industrial-organizational, or school psychologist when prior training has not been in the relevant area. Fulfillment of such an individualized training program is attested to by the award of a certificate by the supervising department or professional school indicating the successful completion of preparation in the particular specialty.

Standard 2. Programs

2.1 *Composition and organization of a psychological service unit:*

2.1.1 *The composition and programs of a psychological service unit shall be responsive to the needs of the persons or settings served.*

INTERPRETATION: A psychological service unit shall be so structured as to facilitate effective and economical delivery of services. For example, a psychological service unit serving a predominantly low-income, ethnic, or racial minority group should have a staffing pattern and service program that is adapted to the linguistic, experiential, and attitudinal characteristics of the users.

2.1.2 *A description of the organization of the psychological service unit and its lines of responsibility and accountability for the delivery of psychological services shall be available in written form o staff of the unit and to users and sanctioners upon request.*

INTERPRETATION: The description should include lines of responsibility, supervisory relationships, and the level and extent of accountability for each person who provides psychological services.

2.1.3 *A psychological service unit shall include sufficient numbers of professional and support personnel to achieve its goals, objectives, and purposes.*

INTERPRETATION: The workload and diversity of psychological services required and the specific goals and objectives of the setting will determine the numbers and qualifications of professional and support personnel in the psychological service unit. Where shortages in personnel exist so that psychological services cannot be rendered in

[13]This Standard follows closely the statement regarding "Policy on Training for Psychologists Wishing to Change Their Specialty" adopted by the APA Council of Representatives in January 1976. Included therein was the implementing provision that "this policy statement shall be incorporated in the guidelines of the Committee on Accreditation so that appropriate sanctions can be brought to bear on university and internship training programs which violate [it]."

a professional manner, the director of the psychological service unit shall initiate action to modify appropriately the specific goals and objectives of the service.

2.2 *Policies:*

2.2.1 *When the psychological service unit is composed of more than one person wherein a supervisory relationship exists or is a component of a larger organization, a written statement of its objectives and scope of services shall be developed and maintained.*

INTERPRETATION: The psychological service unit shall review its objectives and scope of services annually and revise them as necessary to insure that the psychological services offered are consistent with staff compentencies and current psychological knowledge and practice. This statement should be distributed to staff and, where appropriate, to users and sanctioners upon request.

2.2.2 *All providers within a psychological service unit shall support the legal and civil rights of the user.*[14]

INTERPRETATION: Providers of psychological services shall safeguard the interests of the user with regard to personal, legal, and civil rights. They shall continually be sensitive to the issue of confidentiality of information, the short-term and long-term impact of their decisions and recommendations, and other matters pertaining to individual, legal, and civil rights. Concerns regarding the safeguarding of individual rights of users include, but are not limited to, problems of self-incrimination in judicial proceedings, involuntary commitment to hospitals, protection of minors or legal incompetents, discriminatory practices in employment selection procedures, recommendations for special education provisions, information relative to adverse personnel actions in the armed services, and the adjudication of domestic relations disputes in divorce and custodial proceedings. Providers of psychological services should take affirmative action by making themselves available for local committees, review boards, and similar advisory groups established to safeguard the human, civil, and legal rights of service users.

2.2.3 *All providers within a psychological service unit shall be familiar with and adhere to the American Psychological Association's* Ethical Standards of Psychologists, Psychology as a Profession, Standards for Educational and Psychological Tests, *and other official policy statements relevant to standards for professional services issued by the Association.*

INTERPRETATION: Providers of psychological services, users, and sanctioners may order copies of these documents from the American Psychological Association.

2.2.4 *All providers within a psychological service unit shall conform to relevant statutes established by federal, state, and local governments.*

INTERPRETATION: All providers of psychological services shall be familiar with appropriate statutes regulating the practice of psychology. They shall also be informed about agency regulations that have the force of law and that relate to the delivery of

[14]See also APA's (1977) *Ethical Standards of Psychologists,* especially Principles 5 (Confidentiality), 6 (Welfare of the Consumer), and 9 (Pursuit of Research Activities); and see *Ethical Principles in the Conduct of Research with Human Participants* (APA, 1973a).

psychological services (e.g., evaluation for disability retirement and special education placements). In addition, all providers shall be cognizant that federal agencies such as the Veterans Administration and the Department of Health, Education, and Welfare have policy statements regarding psychological services. Providers of psychological services shall be familiar with other statutes and regulations, including those addressed to the civil and legal rights of users (e.g., those promulgated by the federal Equal Employment Opportunity Commission) that are pertinent to their scope of practice.

It shall be the responsibility of the American Psychological Association to publish periodically those federal policies, statutes, and regulations relating to this section. The state psychological associations are similarly urged to publish and distribute periodically appropriate state statutes and regulations.

2.2.5 *All providers within a psychological service unit shall, where appropriate, inform themselves about and use the network of human services in their communities in order to link users with relevant services and resources.*

INTERPRETATION: It is incumbent upon psychologists and supporting staff to be sensitive to the broader context of human needs. In recognizing the matrix of personal and societal problems, providers shall, where appropriate, make available information regarding human services such as legal aid societies, social services, employment agencies, health resources, and educational and recreational facilities. The provider of psychological services shall refer to such community resources and, when indicated, actively intervene on behalf of the user.

2.2.6 *In the delivery of psychological services, the providers shall maintain a continuing cooperative relationship with colleagues and co-workers whenever in the best interest of the user.*[15]

INTERPRETATION: It shall be the responsibility of the psychologist to recognize the areas of special competence of other psychologists and of other professionals for either consultation or referral purposes. Providers of psychological services shall make appropriate use of other professional, technical, and administrative resources whenever these serve the best interests of the user, and shall establish and maintain cooperative arrangements with such other resources as required to meet the needs of users.

2.3 *Procedures:*

2.3.1 *Where appropriate, each psychological service unit shall be guided by a set of procedural guidelines for the delivery of psychological services. If appropriate to the setting, these guidelines shall be in written form.*

INTERPRETATION: Depending on the nature of the setting, and whenever feasible, providers should be prepared to provide a statement of procedural guidelines in either oral or written form that can be understood by users as well as sanctioners. This statement may describe the current methods, forms, procedures, and techniques being used to achieve the objectives and goals for psychological services.

[15]Support for this position is found in the section in *Psychology as a Profession* on relations with other professions:

> Professional persons have an obligation to know and take into account the traditions and practices of other professional groups with whom they work and to cooperate fully with members of such groups with whom research, service, and other functions are shared. (APA, 1968, p. 5)

This statement shall be communicated to staff and, when appropriate, to users and sanctioners. The psychological service unit shall provide for the annual review of its procedures for the delivery of psychological services.

2.3.2. *Providers shall develop a plan appropriate to the provider's professional strategy of practice and to the problems presented by the user.*

INTERPRETATION: Whenever appropriate or mandated in the setting, this plan shall be in written form as a means of providing a basis for establishing accountability, obtaining informed consent, and providing a mechanism for subsequent peer review. Regardless of the type of setting or users involved, it is desirable that a plan be developed that describes the psychological services indicated and the manner in which they will be provided.[16]

A psychologist who provides services as one member of a collaborative effort shall participate in the development and implementation of the overall service plan and provide for its periodic review.

2.3.3 *There shall be a mutually acceptable understanding between the provider and user or responsible agent regarding the delivery of service.*

INTERPRETATION: Varying service settings call for understandings differing in explicitness and formality. For instance, a psychologist providing services within a user organization may operate within a broad framework of understanding with this organization as a condition of employment. As another example, psychologists providing professional services to individuals in clinical, counseling, or school settings require an open-ended agreement, which specifies procedures and their known risks (if any), costs, and respective responsibilities of provider and user for achieving the agreed-upon objectives.

2.3.4 *Accurate, current, and pertinent documentation shall be made of essential psychological services provided.*

INTERPRETATION: Records kept of psychological services may include, but not be limited to, identifying data, dates of services, types of services, and significant actions taken. Providers of psychological services shall insure that essential information concerning services rendered is appropriately recorded within a reasonable time of their completion.

[16]One example of a specific application of this principle is found in Guidelines 2 in APA's (1973b) "Guidelines for Psychologists Conducting Growth Groups":

The following information should be made available *in writing* [italics added] to all prospective participants:

- *(a)* An explicit statement of the purpose of the group;
- *(b)* Types of techniques that may be employed;
- *(c)* The education, training, and experience of the leader or leaders;
- *(d)* The fee and any additional expense that may be incurred;
- *(e)* A statement as to whether or not a follow-up service is included in the fee.
- *(f)* Goals of the group experience and techniques to be used;
- *(g)* Amounts and kinds of responsibility to be assumed by the leader and by the participants. For example, *(i)* the degree to which a participant is free not to follow suggestions and prescriptions of the group leader and other group members; *(ii)* any restrictions on a participant's freedom to leave the group at any time; and,
- *(h)* Issues of confidentiality. (p. 933)

2.3.5 *Providers of psychological services shall establish a system to protect confidentiality of their records.*[17]

INTERPRETATION: Psychologists are responsible for maintaining the confidentiality of information about users of services whether obtained by themselves or by those they supervise. All persons supervised by psychologists, including nonprofessional personnel and students, who have access to records of psychological services shall be required to maintain this confidentiality as a condition of employment.

The psychologist shall not release confidential information, except with the written consent of the user directly involved or his or her legal representative. Even after the consent has been obtained for release, the psychologist should clearly identify such information as confidential to the recipient of the information.[18] If directed otherwise by statute or regulations with the force of law or by court order, the psychologist shall seek a resolution to the conflict that is both ethically and legally feasible and appropriate.

Users shall be informed in advance of any limits in the setting for maintenance of confidentiality of psychological information. For instance, psychologists in hospital settings shall inform their patients that psychological information in a patient's clinical record may be available without the patient's written consent to other members of the professional staff associated with the patient's treatment or rehabilitation. Similar limitations on confidentiality of psychological information may be present in certain school, industrial, or military settings, or in instances where the user has waived confidentiality for purposes of third-party payment.

When the user intends to waive confidentiality, the psychologist should discuss the implications of releasing psychological information, and assist the user in limiting disclosure only to information required by the present circumstance.

Raw psychological data (e.g., test protocols, therapy or interview notes, or questionnaire returns) in which a user is identified shall be released only with the written consent of the user or legal representative and released only to a person recognized by the psychologist as competent to use the data.

Any use made of psychological reports, records, or data for research or training purposes shall be consistent with this Standard. Additionally, providers of psychological services shall comply with statutory confidentiality requirements and those embodied in the American Psychological Association's *Ethical Standards of Psychologists* (APA, 1977).

Providers of psychological services should remain sensitive to both the benefits and the possible misuse of information regarding individuals that is stored in large computerized data banks. Providers should use their influence to ensure that such information is used in a socially responsible manner.

[17]See again Principle 5 (Confidentiality) in *Ethical Standards of Psychologists* (APA, 1977).

[18]Support for the principle of privileged communication is found in at least two policy statements of the Association:

> In the interest of both the public and the client and in accordance with the requirements of good professional practice, the profession of psychology seeks recognition of the privileged nature of confiden tial communications with clients, preferably through statutory enactment or by administrative policy where more appropriate. (APA, 1968, p. 8)
>
> 25. Wherever possible, a clause protecting the privileged nature of the psychologist—client relationship be included.
>
> 26. When appropriate, psychologists assist in obtaining general "across the board" legislation for such privileged communications. (APA, 1967, p. 1103)

Standard 3. Accountability

3.1 *Psychologists' professional activity shall be primarily guided by the principle of promoting human welfare.*

INTERPRETATION: Psychologists shall provide services to users in a manner that is considerate, effective, and economical.

Psychologists are responsible for making their services readily accessible to users in a manner that facilitates the user's freedom of choice.

Psychologists shall be mindful of their accountability to the sanctioners of psychological services and to the general public, provided that appropriate steps are taken to protect the confidentiality of the service relationship. In the pursuit of their professional activities they shall aid in the conservation of human, material, and financial resources.

The psychological service unit will not withhold services to a potential client on the basis of that user's race, color, religion, sex, age, or national origin. Recognition is given, however, to the following considerations: The professional right of psychologists to limit their practice to a specific category of user (e.g., children, adolescents, women); the right and responsibility of psychologists to withhold an assessment procedure when not validly applicable; the right and responsibility of psychologists to withhold evaluative, psychotherapeutic, counseling, or other services in specific instances where considerations of race, religion, color, sex, or any other difference between psychologist and client might impair the effectiveness of the relationship.[19]

Psychologists who find that psychological services are being provided in a manner that is discriminatory or exploitative to users and/or contrary to these Standards or to state or federal statutes shall take appropriate corrective action, which may include the refusal to provide services. When conflicts of interest arise, the psychologist shall be guided in the resolution of differences by the principles set forth in the *Ethical Standards of Psychologists* of the American Psychological Association and by the Guidelines for Conditions of Employment of Psychologists (1972).[20]

3.2 *Psychologists shall pursue their activities as members of an independent, autonomous profession.*[21]

INTERPRETATION: Psychologists shall be aware of the implications of their activities for the profession as a whole. They shall seek to eliminate discriminatory practices

[19]This paragraph is drawn directly from the CEP Guidelines (APA, 1972, p. 333).

[20]"It is recognized that under certain circumstances, the interests and goals of a particular community or segment of interest in the population may be in conflict with the general welfare. Under such circumstances, the psychologist's professional activity must be primarily guided by the principle of promoting human welfare." (APA, 1972, p. 334)

[21]Support for the principle of the independence of psychology as a profession is found in the following:

> As a member of an autonomous profession, a psychologist rejects limitations upon his freedom of thought and action other than those imposed by his moral, legal, and social responsibilities. The Association is always prepared to provide appropriate assistance to any responsible member who becomes subjected to unreasonable limitations upon his opportunity to function as a practitioner, teacher, researcher, administrator, or consultant. The Association is always prepared to cooperate with any responsible professional organization in opposing any unreasonable limitations on the professional functions of the members of that organization.
>
> This insistence upon professional autonomy has been upheld over the years by the affirmative actions of the courts and other public and private bodies in support of the right of the psychologist—and other

instituted for self-serving purposes that are not in the interest of the user (e.g., arbitrary requirements for referral and supervision by another profession). They shall be cognizant of their responsibilities for the development of the profession, participate where possible in the training and career development of students and other providers, participate as appropriate in the training of paraprofessionals, and integrate and supervise their contributions within the structure established for delivering psychological services. Where appropriate, they shall facilitate the development of, and participate in, professional standards review mechanisms.[22]

Psychologists shall seek to work with other professionals in a cooperative manner for the good of the user and the benefit of the general public. Psychologists associated with multidisciplinary settings shall support the principle that members of each participating profession shall have equal rights and opportunities to share all privileges and responsibilities of full membership in the human service facility, and to administer service programs in their respective areas of competence.

3.3 *There shall be periodic, systematic, and effective evaluations of psychological services.*[23]

INTERPRETATION: When the psychological service unit is a component of a larger organization, regular assessment of progress in achieving goals shall be provided in the service delivery plan, including consideration of the effectiveness of psychological services relative to costs in terms of time, money, and the availability of professional and support personnel.

---

professionals—to pursue those functions for which he is trained and qualified to perform. (APA, 1968, p. 9)

Organized psychology has the responsibility to define and develop its own profession, consistent with the general canons of science and with the public welfare.

Psychologists recognize that other professions and other groups will, from time to time, seek to define the roles and responsibilities of psychologists. The APA opposes such developments on the same principles that it is opposed to the psychological profession taking positions which would define the work and scope of responsibility of other duly recognized professions. (APA, 1972, p. 333)

[22]APA support for peer review is detailed in the following excerpt from the APA (1971) statement entitled "Psychology and National Health Care":

All professions participating in a national health plan should be directed to establish review mechanisms (or performance evaluations) that include not only peer review but active participation by persons representing the consumer. In situations where there are fiscal agents, they should also have representation when appropriate. (p. 1026)

[23]This Standard on program evaluation is based directly on the following excerpts of two APA position papers:

The quality and availability of health services should be evaluated continuously by both consumers and health professionals. Research into the efficiency and effectiveness of the system should be conducted both internally and under independent auspices. (APA, 1971, p. 1025)

The comprehensive community mental health center should devote an explicit portion of its budget to program evaluation. All centers should inculcate in their staff attention to and respect for research findings; the larger centers have an obligation to set a high priority on basic research and to give formal recognition to research as a legitimate part of the duties of staff members.

. . . Only through explicit appraisal of program effects can worthy approaches be retained and refined, ineffective ones dropped. Evaluative monitoring of program achievements may vary, of course, from the relatively informal to the systematic and quantitative, depending on the importance of the issue, the availability of resources, and the willingness of those responsible to take the risks of substituting informed judgment for evidence. (Smith & Hobbs, 1966, pp. 21–22)

Evaluation of the efficiency and effectiveness of the psychological service delivery system should be conducted internally and, when possible, under independent auspices.

It is highly desirable that there be a periodic reexamination of review mechanisms to ensure that these attempts at public safeguards are effective and cost efficient and do not place unnecessary encumbrances on the provider or unnecessary additional expense to users or sanctioners for services rendered.

3.4 *Psychologists are accountable for all aspects of the services they provide and shall be responsive to those concerned with these services.*[24]

INTERPRETATION: In recognizing their responsibilities to users, sanctioners, third-party purchasers, and other providers, wherever appropriate and consistent with the user's legal rights and privileged communications, psychologists shall make available information about, and opportunity to participate in, decisions concerning such issues as initiation, termination, continuation, modification, and evaluation of psychological services. Additional copies of these *Standards for Providers of Psychological Services* can be ordered from the American Psychological Association.

Depending upon the settings, accurate and full information shall be made available to prospective individual or organization users regarding the qualifications of providers, the nature and extent of services offered, and, where appropriate, financial and social costs.

Where appropriate, psychologists shall inform users of their payment policies and their willingness to assist in obtaining reimbursement. Those who accept reimbursement from a third party should be acquainted with the appropriate statutes and regulations and should instruct their users on proper procedures for submitting claims and limits on confidentiality of claims information, in accordance with pertinent statutes.

Standard 4. Environment

4.1 *Providers of psychological services shall promote the development in the service setting of a physical, organizational, and social environment that facilitates optimal human functioning.*

INTERPRETATION: Federal, state, and local requirements for safety, health, and sanitation must be observed. Attention shall be given to the comfort and, where relevant, to the privacy of providers and users.

As providers of services, psychologists have the responsibility to be concerned with the environment of their service unit, especially as it affects the quality of service, but also as it impinges of human functioning in the larger unit or organization when the service unit is included in such a larger context. Physical arrangements and organizational policies and procedures should be conducive to the human dignity, self-respect, and optimal functioning of users, and to the effective delivery of service. The atmosphere in which psychological services are rendered should be appropriate to the service and to the users, whether in office, clinic, school, or industrial organization.

[24]See also the CEP Guidelines for the following statement: "A psychologist recognizes that . . . he alone is accountable for the consequences and effects of his services, whether as teacher, researcher, or practitioner. This responsibility cannot be shared, delegated, or reduced" (APA, 1972, p. 334).

References

ACCREDITATION COUNCIL for FACILITIES for the MENTALLY RETARDED. *Standards for residential facilities for the mentally retarded*. Chicago, Ill.: Joint Commission on Accreditation of Hospitals, 1971.

AMERICAN PSYCHOLOGICAL ASSOCIATION, COMMITTEE on LEGISLATION. A model for state legislation affecting the practice of psychology 1967. *American Psychologist,* 1967, *22,* 1095–1103.

AMERICAN PSYCHOLOGICAL ASSOCIATION. *Psychology as a profession*. Washington, D.C.: Author, 1968.

AMERICAN PSYCHOLOGICAL ASSOCIATION. Psychology and national health care. *American Psychologist,* 1971, *26,* 1025–1026.

AMERICAN PSYCHOLOGICAL ASSOCIATION. Guidelines for conditions of employment of psychologists. *American Psychologist,* 1972, *27,* 331–334.

AMERICAN PSYCHOLOGICAL ASSOCIATION. *Ethical principles in the conduct of research with human participants*. Washington, D.C.: Author, 1973. (a)

AMERICAN PSYCHOLOGICAL ASSOCIATION. Guidelines for psychologists conducting growth groups. *American Psychologist,* 1973, *28,* 933. (b)

AMERICAN PSYCHOLOGICAL ASSOCIATION. *Standards for educational and psychological tests*. Washington, D.C.: Author, 1974.

AMERICAN PSYCHOLOGICAL ASSOCIATION. *Ethical standards of psychologists* (Rev. ed.). Washington, D.C.: Author, 1977.

JOINT COMMISSION on ACCREDITATION of HOSPITALS. *Accreditation manual for psychiatric facilities 1972*. Chicago, Ill.: Author, 1972.

SMITH, M. B., & HOBBS, N. *The community and the community mental health center*. Washington, D.C.: American Psychological Association, 1966.

Policies and Procedures for the Creation of Diplomates in Professional Psychology, American Board of Professional Psychology (1978)*

Purposes and Aims

The American Board of Professional Psychology, Inc., originally incorporated as the American Board of Examiners in Professional Psychology, was established in 1947 in order (1) to grant, issue, and control the use of its diploma of special competence in fields of professional psychology and (2) to arrange, conduct, and control investigations and examinations to determine the qualifications of individuals who make voluntary application for such diplomas.

The Board now awards diplomas in four professional specialties: Clinical Psychology, Counseling Psychology, Industrial and Organizational Psychology, and School Psychology.

The Board encourages the pursuit of excellence via its program of certification at an advanced professional level. The ABPP diploma signifies, to the public and to the profession, the highest recognition of competence as judged by one's professional peers.

*Used with permission.

Basic Requirements for Application

A. Psychologists are eligible to apply for candidacy if they successfully meet the following requirements:

1. A doctoral degree in psychology from a college or university, which, at the time the degree was awarded, met the existing standards of the American Psychological Association for doctoral training in the specialty of the applicant.

   a. Beginning on July 1, 1978, all candidates for the diplomate examination must fulfill the following criteria defining a Psychology Program

      (1) Training in professional psychology is doctoral training offered in a regionally accredited institution of higher education.

      (2) The program, wherever it may be administratively housed, must be clearly identified and labeled as a psychology program. Such a program must specify in pertinent institutional catalogues and brochures its intent to educate and train professional psychologists.

      (3) The psychology program must stand as a recognizable, coherent organizational entity within the institution.

      (4) There must be a clear authority and primary responsibility for the core and specialty areas whether or not the program cuts across administrative lines.

      (5) The program must be an integrated, organized sequence of study.

      (6) There must be an identifiable psychology faculty and a psychologist responsible for the program.

      (7) The program must have an identifiable body of students who are matriculated in that program for a degree.

      (8) The program must include supervised practicum, internship, field, or laboratory training appropriate to the practice of psychology.

      (9) The curriculum shall encompass a minimum of three academic years of full time graduate study. In addition to instruction in scientific and professional ETHICS and STANDARDS, RESEARCH DESIGN and METHODOLOGY, STATISTICS, and PSYCHOMETRICS, the core program shall require each student to demonstrate competence in each of the following substantive content areas. This typically will be met by including a minimum of three or more graduate semester hours (five or more graduate quarter hours) in each of these four substantive content areas:

         (a) BIOLOGICAL BASES OF BEHAVIOR: physiological psychology, comparative psychology, neuropsychology, sensation and perception, psychopharmacology.

         (b) COGNITIVE-AFFECTIVE BASES OF BEHAVIOR: learning, thinking, motivation, emotion.

         (c) SOCIAL BASES OF BEHAVIOR: social psychology, group processes, organizational and systems theory.

         (d) INDIVIDUAL DIFFERENCES: personality theory, human development, abnormal psychology.

      (10) One or more faculty members or internship supervisors should show evidence of distinction as a psychologist. Such evidence may include, but is not limited to, Fellow status in APA, diplomate status (ABPP), national reputation as a psychologist, etc.

NOTE: Item 9 identified the core psychology curriculum. In addition to these criteria, all professional education programs in psychology will include course requirements in specialty areas. The above curriculum requirements then, represent the necessary core but not the sufficient number of graduate hours for a degree in professional psychology.

2. Beginning on July 1, 1978 candidates will be required to take their examination in the specialty in which they received their doctoral degree. Exceptions can be made for those individuals who have been formally retrained in another specialty within an APA accredited program or within a program that meets the definition of a psychology program as detailed above. The Director of the training program must certify that retraining has taken place. (See Appendix.)
3. For candidates in clinical, counseling, and school psychology an internship is required. It should be from an APA approved internship facility. For candidates in industrial psychology, one year of supervised field training experience will be required in lieu of internship.
4. Internship or field experience is defined as a minimum of 1800 hours of training experience in an organized psychological service setting and must be completed within a period of two years.
5. Five years of acceptable qualifying experience. Four years of this experience shall be post-doctoral.

   The Board recognizes that a candidate may not have been engaged full time in the actual practice of his or her specialty. Part time activities may include teaching, research, and administration. Such experience counts as qualifying if these activities are in the field of specialization in which the candidate seeks the diploma and provided the candidate devotes a significant amount of time to professional practice in this specialty.

   Experience in independent private practice will be accepted only if preceded by three years of experience under professional supervision. The requirements are that the first year of supervision should have been under the direction of a psychologist. It is preferred that psychologists participate in the supervision of the second and third years as well.

   Appropriate pre-private practice experience is defined as work in a setting where systematic direct supervision is provided by a qualified person and the candidate's total work is subject to review. Group practice in which the members band together merely to share a suite of offices does not satisfy this experience requirement.
6. Present engagement in professional work in the field of specialization.
7. Evidence of continuing education in the profession of psychology during the years of post-doctoral experience.
8. Membership in the American Psychological Association, or where appropriate, in the Canadian Psychological Association.

B. For candidates whose doctoral degree is not from an institution of higher learning which met APA standards for doctoral training, the following requirements must be met for eligibility to candidacy:

1. EDUCATION
   a. The institution awarding the doctoral degree must be accredited by one of the regional accrediting associations or be a recognized candidate for accreditation within three years of the time the degree was conferred.
   b. The doctoral degree must be awarded by a department of psychology. The

locus of that department may be in a college or school of Education, Theology, Business, etc., but the department must be clearly identified as a department of psychology in the official catalogue of the institution and must be so identified in written statements by the chief administrative officers of the institution. The department must clearly indicate that it is offering education and training in the specialty for which the applicant applies.

c. The doctoral program in psychology must be an integrated, organized program in psychology as opposed to an accumulation of credits or courses.
d. Over half of the courses must be psychology courses, psychological in content, and taught by psychologists.
e. The basic core of psychology courses must be comparable to those required for APA accreditation.
f. The program must have appropriate practicum and internship (supervised field experiences) in applied, professional areas.

C. Internship requirements for candidates whose internship was not APA approved:
1. Candidates in clinical psychology
Internship consists of a minimum of 1800 hours of supervised experience (supervision must be de facto and face to face and must include substantial supervision by psychologists) in an organized psychological service setting. It must be completed within a two year span.
2. Candidates in counseling psychology
Internship consists of a minimum of 1800 hours of supervised experience (supervision must be de facto and face to face and must include substantial supervision by psychologists). The experience may be in a health service setting or other appropriate organized setting. It must be completed within a two year span.
3. Candidates in school and industrial psychology
Supervised experience consists of a minimum of 1800 hours of field experience supervised by psychologists and found acceptable to the applicant's doctoral committee and to the BOARD.

Application and Admission to Candidacy

When a psychologist meets the basic requirements listed above he or she is eligible to apply for candidacy.

After the application has been submitted the applicant will be sent the appropriate forms to be forwarded to each of the listed endorsers and will be asked to arrange for transcripts of credits to be sent to the Executive Office.

When all the necessary documents have been received, the Executive Office conducts whatever investigation seems necessary to provide appropriate information for review and appraisal. This includes sending inquiries to the State Psychological Association and the State Board of Examiners of Psychologists. When all credentials have been assembled the Board will seek, on the basis of the record, clear evidence that the applicant meets its standards in accordance with the following four criteria:

1. Adequacy and extent of basic training
2. Amount, breadth, and quality of professional experience
3. Special competence
4. Reputation among professional colleagues for standards of personal integrity which

are irreproachable as a representative of the profession of psychology in the community

When the Board determines that the applicant has met its qualifying standards, he or she will be considered an applicant, will be notified of admission to candidacy and will then be eligible to register for examination. The registration consists of the submission of the Professional Work Sample(s) and other such supplementary information and materials as may be requested. The registration privilege extends for one year from the date the applicant is admitted to candidacy.

Work Samples

To provide substantive content for the examination, the candidate must present one or more work samples of his or her typical practice as a professional psychologist. The samples usually will consist of a verbatim or summarized report of interactions and may be accompanied by audiotape, videotape, motion picture, or other in-depth depiction of the candidate's activity.

The candidate prepares four copies of this written work sample, of which *three* copies are sent to a Regional Board and *one* copy to ABPP's Executive Office. If the submissions include audio or visual tape or similar materials, no copy of these need be sent to the Executive Office.

In all cases, the samples shall provide the examining committee with data representative of the candidate's professional practice, including assessment of individual(s), group(s), or situation(s), and professional efforts to effect or influence change.

The work samples will be used as a springboard for discussion of the candidate's functioning. Committee chairs will have the right to request more extensive work samples if they feel that further information will be needed to effectively evaluate candidate's competence.

Arrangements for the Examination

A Regional Board is assigned responsibility for reviewing candidacy material and establishing examining committees. A Regional Board representative will communicate with each candidate concerning the nature and site of the examination.

If it should be determined that the examination will be held in a distant city, the candidate will bear personal travel costs. Similarly, in cases where it is impossible to find appropriate examiners locally, the candidate will be expected to share in the expenses of ABPP examiners who must travel significant distances to participate in the evaluation. The candidate will be expected to pay the examiners' out of pockets expenses up to a maximum of $100 plus the round trip transportation from their homes to the nearest possible testing site. Ordinarily the examination will be scheduled within six months after the candidate registers and submits his or her work sample.

The Examination Committee

The ABPP Examination is conducted by a committee of Diplomate examiners. The chair is an experienced senior examiner, and the examination committee should include examiners whose orientation and approach in professional practice is similar to that of the candidate. The candidate may expect to spend approximately four hours in the examination session.

The ABPP Examination

The ABPP Examination is designed to judge competence at the Diplomate level in the candidate's professional practice. It will cover the following interrelated areas:

The Effectiveness of the Candidate's Efforts Toward Constructive Intervention Based on Realistic Assessment of the Problem Presented

The Board recognizes that professional psychologists use a variety of approaches, techniques, and theoretical orientations. The examiners will seek to establish the candidate's level of competence within his or her own frame of reference. A field examination, in addition to the submitted work sample, will ordinarily be required, in which the candidate demonstrates to the examiners what he or she does and how it is done. This is an actual "on the job" demonstration of the candidate's work. It is understood that assessment can take a variety of forms, ranging from the administration of standardized tests to observations and interviews. Similarly, intervention may take the form of counseling, psychotherapy, consultation, or environmental manipulation. The Board recognizes that in some legitimate forms of professional practice, assessment and intervention are integral parts of the same process. Nothing in these policies shall be construed as ascribing greater value or importance to any of these over any other.

Awareness of the Relevance of Research and Theory

It is assumed that a professional psychologist at the Diplomate level is continually aware of scientific and scholarly developments in order to infuse his or her practice with the most valid and reliable data that the science provides.

It is the purpose of this aspect of the examination procedure, therefore, to ascertain whether the candidate can present and discuss critically the implications and applications of contemporary psychological knowledge in his or her specialty.

Sensitivity to the Ethical Implications of Professional Practice

A professional psychologist at the Diplomate level is expected to be aware of 1) the ethical standards and principles adopted by the profession and 2) the implications of these in practice, including the responsibility of practicing in the best interest of the clients and of society. Further, it is anticipated that a Diplomate will be identified with the profession by appropriate memberships and activities and will be aware of current issues and problems involved in the development of a creative and responsible profession.

Notification and Award of the Diploma

Each candidate will receive formal notification of the Board's judgment within one month of the examination. Diplomas will either be conferred on successful candidates at a convocation held during the annual convention of the American Psychological Association or will be sent to the new diplomate by mail within a reasonable time after the examination. An explanation of reasons for failure will be supplied to each unsuccessful candidate in order to guide further professional development. If the examination has been twice failed, (not including nullified examination), the candidate must wait for 3 years before reapplying for examination. Evidence of continuing education in the specialty area may be required before a third examination can be scheduled.

Policies Concerning Candidacy and Examination

1. The privilege of an ABPP examination begins with admission to candidacy.

2. Candidates who are not awarded the diploma may request re-examination. A completely new examining committee will be appointed. A fee of $150 is charged for re-examination.

3. The Board expects that the conditions of each examination will be consistent with the principles and standards stated in this manual. Recognizing that exceptions may occur, the Board permits the privilege of appeal. If a candidate believes that the examination was not conducted in an appropriate and fair manner, he or she may request a review. Such request should be submitted within 30 days of the notice of failure. It shall include a definitive statement of factors and conditions considered by the candidate as interfering with or inconsistent with an adequate evaluation. Such a Board review may have two possible outcomes: 1) nullification of the examination; or 2) a confirmation of the No Award decision. A candidate cannot be awarded the diploma as a result of the review.

Professional Affiliation and Standards of Practice

The Board will suspend action on any candidate in whose case allegations are being investigated by the Committee on Scientific and Professional Ethics and Conduct of the American Psychological Association, by a state psychological association, and/or by a state board of examiners of psychologists.

In order to protect the significance of the diploma, the Board reserves the right to revoke the diploma of an individual whenever it judges that the recipient no longer represents the standards of practice which were the basis of the original award, or which are currently endorsed by the profession. Specifically this provision shall be construed as including failure of the individual to maintain a reputation among professional colleagues for standards of personal integrity which are irreproachable as a representative of the profession of psychology in the community or failure to maintain affiliation with the American Psychological Association or, where applicable, the Canadian Psychological Association. As leaders in psychology, Diplomates are expected to continue to support the profession and the Board. Encouraging deserving colleagues to apply for Diplomate status, serving as examiners for future candidates, participation in local professional groups and continuing educational activities are some appropriate types of life-long Diplomate participation in professional affairs.

Appendix

ABPP Policy on Training for Psychologists Wishing to Change Their Specialty

Inasmuch as it is to the advantage of psychology and society to provide for a change of specialty or the development of dual specialties so as to encourage unique contributions that might be made by psychologists with broadly diversified backgrounds, ABPP adopts the following as official policy:

1. We strongly urge Psychology Departments currently engaged in doctoral training to offer training for individuals already holding the doctoral degree in psychology, who wish to change their specialty. Such programs should be individualized, since background and career objectives vary greatly. It is desirable that financial assistance be made available to students in such programs.
2. Programs engaging in such training should declare so publicly and include a statement to that effect as a formal part of their program description and/or their application for accreditation.
3. Psychologists seeking to change their specialty should take training in a program of the highest quality, and, where appropriate, exemplified by the doctoral training programs and internships accredited by the APA.
4. With respect to subject matter and professional skills, psychologists taking such training must meet all requirements of doctoral training in the new psychological specialty, being given due credit for relevant course work or requirements they have previously satisfied.
5. It must be stressed, however, that merely taking an internship or acquiring experience in a practicum setting is not, for example, considered adequate preparation for becoming a clinical, counseling, or school psychologist when prior training had not been in the relevant area.
6. Upon fulfillment of all formal requirements of such training program, the students should be awarded a certificate indicating the successful completion of preparation in the particular specialty, thus according them due recognition for their additional education and experience.

REFERENCES FOR CHAPTER I

FOLTZ, D. Sun sets on psychology licensing boards in South Dakota and Florida. *APA Monitor,* September/October 1979, pp. 3; 14.

O'KEEFE, A. M. & MCCULLOUGH, S. J. Physician domination in the health care industry: The pursuit of antitrust redress. *Professional Psychology,* 1979, *10,* 605-618.

CHAPTER II

Malpractice Defined

UNDER THE LAW, all persons owe to each other a duty of care that can reasonably be expected from ordinary, reasonable, and prudent persons. This means, for example, that even if you are late for the commuter train, you are not entitled to push and shove and harm others in hurrying to the gate; if you unintentionally hurt people in this process and it can be shown that you failed to act in the way that any reasonable and prudent person might have acted in the same or similar circumstances, you are said to be *negligent*. Malpractice is a form of negligence that is applied to professionals. Professionals—like all other persons—owe to their fellow humans this duty of care. However, in rendering professional services, professionals owe more; they are obliged to perform in a manner consistent with the way an ordinary, reasonable, and prudent *professional* would act under the same or similar circumstances in their profession. If it can be shown that a professional unintentionally failed to meet this standard (i.e., failed to fulfill this obligation to the patient or client) then malpractice is said to have occurred.

The place of malpractice within the law is illustrated in Figure 1. In brief, all law (statutory, common, criminal, civil, tort) derives from constitutional law. Tort law is subsumed under civil law, and there are three broad bases for liability in tort: intentional torts, negligent or unintentional torts, and torts based on strict or absolute liability. Intentional torts may involve torts to person (e.g., assault, battery, false imprisonment), torts to property (e.g., trespass), or other torts (e.g., deceit, intentional invasion of privacy, intentional causing of emotional distress). Negligent torts involve the breach of a duty of care and other negligent actions such as negligent misrepresentation, negligent causing of emotional distress, negligent invasion of privacy, and negligent failure to act. Torts based on strict liability are neither intentional nor the result of negligent acts (e.g., trespass by livestock). In this last category someone

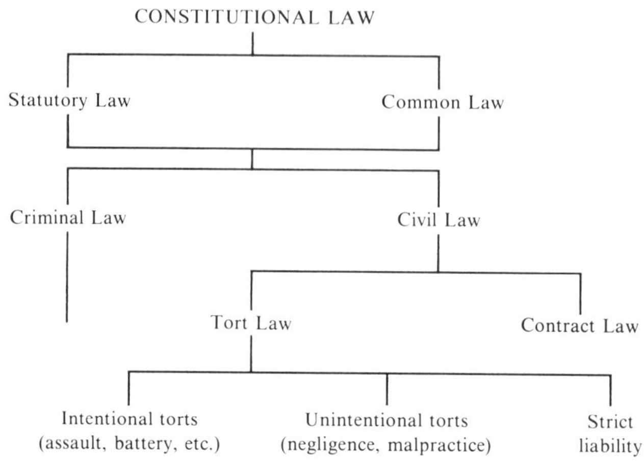

FIGURE 1. The Place of Malpractice Within the Law

deemed legally responsible is liable, regardless of intention or inadvertance. (N.B.: most insurance companies have stopped referring to the policies they offer practitioners as "malpractice insurance" and have substituted the broader term "professional liability" insurance.)

The basic elements needed to support a malpractice action are the same as those needed to support a negligence action. The plaintiff must prove by the preponderance of the evidence that

- the professional owed a duty of care to the patient or client
- The professional breached that duty
- some harm or injury befell the patient or client
- the harm or injury was factually and proximately the result of the professional's breach of duty

THE DOCTOR–PATIENT RELATIONSHIP

A physician or other health professional owes a duty of due care to a person once the two form a doctor–patient (or "professional–client") relationship. This relationship traditionally arises when the patient contracts with the practitioner, either expressly or by implication, for treatment. In extraordinary situations, such as the case in which the patient is unconscious, an "undertaking" theory rather than a contract theory is the applicable legal basis for the creation of the professional relationship. Simply stated, the "undertaking" theory holds that the physician who undertakes to treat a patient engenders a duty of due care to that patient (see Restatement 2d, Torts §323 [1965]). The undertaking theory may also be applicable in situations involving laboratory and x-ray analyses done by physicians and other medical personnel who may never have seen, let alone contracted with, the patient.

Below in *O'Neill* v. *Montefiore Hospital,* 11 App.Div.2d 132. 203

N.Y.S.2d 436 (1960), and in *Rainer* v. *Grossman,* 31 Cal.App.3d 539, 107 Cal.Rptr. 469 (1973), we see rather extreme attempts to stretch the undertaking theory to its limits. In *O'Neill* the court deals with the issues surrounding a claim that a doctor-patient relationship arose as the result of a telephone conversation. In *Rainer* the court deals with the issue of whether remarks made at a professional conference by a medical school professor can give rise to a doctor-patient relationship that can serve as the basis for a malpractice action.

In litigation involving mental health professionals, the issue of whether the practitioner was or was not in a professional relationship is seldom, if ever, the primary question. Rather, proving that the practitioner's care did not meet the required standard and proving that harm or injury was proximately caused by the practitioner's breach or derelection of duty are the issues of primary importance in proceedings involving mental health professionals. These two issues are more closely examined in the following two sections of this chapter.

O'Neill v. *Montefiore Hospital,* 11 App.Div.2d 132, 203 N.Y.S.2d 436 (1960)

APPEAL from a judgment of the Supreme Court, entered November 14, 1956, in Bronx County upon a dismissal of the complaint as against defendant Montefiore Hospital at the end of plaintiff's case and against defendant Craig at the end of the entire case upon a trial at a Trial Term (SAUL S. STREIT, J.).

Per Curiam. In this action for the wrongful death of John J. O'Neill, who died of a heart attack on the morning of June 29, 1952, the widow sought recovery against a hospital for failure to render necessary emergency treatment, and against a physician for his failure and refusal to treat the deceased. Since the complaint against the hospital was dismissed at the trial at the close of plaintiff's case and the complaint against the doctor was dismissed at the conclusion of all of the evidence, the question posed on this appeal is whether plaintiff made out a prima facie case sufficient for submission to the jury. In other words, the issue presented is whether, under the circumstances hereinafter described, there was a duty owing respectively by the hospital and the doctor to examine and treat plaintiff's deceased husband.

We need not emphasize that since this case is one to recover for wrongful death, the plaintiff is not held to the degree of proof required from a plaintiff seeking recovery in his own right (*Noseworthy* v. *City of New York*, 298 N. Y. 76; *Swensson* v. *New York, Albany Desp. Co.*, 309 N. Y. 497). Moreover, upon the dismissal of the complaint, the plaintiff is entitled to the benefit of every inference favorable to her (*De Wald* v. *Seidenberg,* 297 N. Y. 335), and, if negligence may be reasonably inferred from the evidence proffered by the plaintiff, the question should be submitted to the jury (*Betzag* v. *Gulf Oil Corp.*, 298 N. Y. 358; *Cornbrooks* v. *Terminal Barber Shops,* 282 N. Y. 217).

Briefly, the facts, as they appear in the record, are that the plaintiff awoke shortly before 5:00 A.M., and saw her husband standing at the window, rubbing his arms and chest. His mouth was open "and he was trying to get as much air as he possibly could." He was perspiring, his face was white as contrasted with his normally ruddy complexion, and he complained of severe pains in his chest and arms. With the assistance of the plaintiff, O'Neill dressed and walked to the hospital, which was three blocks away. He stopped frequently on the way in order to rest and to find a taxicab, but none was available.

It appears that the hospital maintained an emergency room or clinic. When Mr. and Mrs. O'Neill arrived at the hospital, the doorman conducted them to the nurse in charge of the emergency room. The plaintiff told the nurse that the deceased was very ill, was suffering chest and arm pains, and she thought he was having a heart attack, and she requested the services of a doctor. At that point, Mr. O'Neill mentioned that they were members of the Hospital Insurance Plan (hereinafter referred to as HIP). Thereupon the nurse stated that the hospital had no connection with HIP and did not take care of HIP patients. After reflecting for a minute or two, the nurse stated, "I'll try and get you a HIP doctor," and then telephoned the defendant Craig, telling him that the deceased was in the emergency room of the hospital, complaining of the pains hereinbefore described. She then handed the telephone to Mr. O'Neill who described his pains to Dr. Craig, and then, after a pause, stated, "Dr. Kirstein." After another pause Mr. O'Neill said, "Well I could be dead by 8 o'clock." When the deceased concluded the telephone conversation, he informed the nurse that Dr. Craig had told him to go home and come back when HIP was open. Mrs. O'Neill, however, asked the nurse to have a doctor examine her husband since it was an emergency. Disregarding the request, the nurse told her that their family doctor would see Mr. O'Neill at 8 o'clock, to which he again replied, "I could be dead by 8 o'clock."

When examination or treatment at the hospital was refused, the plaintiff and the deceased left and returned home on foot, pausing occasionally to permit him to catch his breath. After they arrived at their apartment, and as the plaintiff was helping her husband to disrobe, he fell to the floor and died before any medical attention could be obtained.

Insofar as the cause of action against Dr. Craig is concerned, the proof indicates and the court found that the plaintiff and her husband were members of the Montefiore Group of HIP. Two of the doctors composing that group, and under contract with HIP to treat its members, were Doctors Kirstein and Craig, the former being the physician ordinarily consulted by the O'Neills, while the latter was the doctor on call on the morning in question.

Dr. Craig confirmed Mrs. O'Neill's testimony that he received a phone call from the Montefiore Hospital emergency room and spoke to the deceased. Dr. Craig testified in some detail concerning that conversation, and related the inquiries he made concerning symptoms, prior episodes, electrocardiograms, and other items of the patient's medical history. He then went on to state that he offered to come to the emergency room and make an examination, but Mr. O'Neill declined, stating that he felt better and would prefer to wait to see Dr. Kirstein who would be available at 8 o'clock.

We are not called upon to decide whether, by his contract with HIP, Dr. Craig assumed to examine and treat the deceased and failed to do so as distinguished from whether he, defendant Craig, independently undertook or assumed to examine and treat and failed to exercise due care in so doing. Perhaps a more complete development of the facts in that regard might have been desirable. Thus whether, as the plaintiff claimed, there was an abandonment of the patient by the doctor, or as the defendant claimed there was a refusal to accept a proffered examination presents a question of fact which should have been submitted to the jury.

However, from the proof in the record, we must hold that the jury could have concluded that Dr. Craig undertook to diagnose the ailments of the deceased and could have decided whether he abandoned the patient, inadequately or improperly advised him, or, conversely, made a proper diagnosis fully appropriate under the circumstances, or offered an examination which was rejected.

The law is settled that a physician who undertakes to examine or treat a patient and then abandons him, may be held liable for malpractice (*Meiselman* v. *Crown Heights Hosp.,* 285 N. Y. 389; see Ann. 57 A. L. R. 2d 432–464).

With respect to the action against the hospital, there is also a question of fact presented which should have been submitted to the jury. That question is whether the conduct of the nurse in relation to the deceased was in the nature of a personal favor to him or whether her conduct was that of an attaché of the hospital trying to discharge her duty, and if so, whether what she did was inadequate. So, too, whether the alleged request of the nurse for an examination of Mr. O'Neill, following the telephone conversation with Dr. Craig, and the nurse's refusal to have Mr. O'Neill examined at the hospital constituted negligent conduct, would also be a question for the jury. In this posture it matters not, insofar as the liability of the hospital is concerned, whether any act of the nurse was a medical or administrative one (*Bing* v. *Thunig,* 2 N Y 2d 656).

In this case the plaintiff's proof was prima facie sufficient to permit, but not to mandate, the inference that the nurse in charge of the emergency ward undertook to provide medical attention for the deceased. In sum, this was a question of fact for the jury. It was error, therefore, to dismiss the case against the hospital at the close of the plaintiff's case. Whether there was a reasonable fulfillment of any obligation undertaken is a matter of defense and a determination of that issue is for the jury.

The judgment should, therefore, be reversed on the law and a new trial ordered, with costs to abide the event.

McNALLY, J. (concurring and dissenting). I concur in the order for reversal and for a new trial as against defendant Frank Craig. I dissent and vote to affirm the dismissal of the complaint against defendant Montefiore Hospital. Through the efforts of the hospital's nurse, the decedent had been enabled to communicate by telephone with Dr. Craig who had knowledge of the decedent's presence at the hospital. Dr. Craig did not indicate in any manner that emergency treatment was required nor did he direct or request the admittance of the decedent as a patient to the hospital. Any action by the nurse contrariwise would not have been in keeping with her position. It is my view that the conduct of the nurse was by way of favor and I fail to see any legal basis for liability on the part of the hospital.

BREITEL, J. P., RABIN and VALENTE, JJ., concur in *Per Curiam* opinion; Mcœ NALLY and STEVENS, JJ., dissent in part and vote to affirm as to defendant Montefiore Hospital in dissenting opinion by McNALLY, J.

Judgment reversed on the law and a new trial ordered, with costs to abide the event.

Rainer v. *Grossman,* 31 Cal.App.3d 539, 107 Cal.Rptr. 469 (1973)

Opinion

COMPTON, J.—Plaintiff appeals from a summary judgment entered in favor of Dr. Morton I. Grossman, one of several doctors joined as defendants in a complaint alleging medical malpractice in connection with a surgical operation performed on plaintiff on June 20, 1960, and seven subsequent operations from February 28, 1962, and including September 4, 1962.

Prior to instituting this action, plaintiff on February 27, 1963, commenced a malpractice action in the Superior Court of Ventura County (hereafter Ventura case) against the Buena Memorial Hospital where the surgery was performed and a number of doctors, most of whom are also named as defendants in this action. Dr. Grossman, however, was not a defendant in that action.

With one relatively minor exception, a jury in that case found in favor of all defendants on each of the various theories of recovery. Judgment was entered April 5, 1968, and plaintiff appealed. (See *Rainer* v. *Community Memorial Hosp.*, 18 Cal.App.3d 240 [95 Cal.Rptr. 901], filed June 21, 1971, for a description of the facts surrounding the surgery which was performed on plaintiff.)

In the Ventura case one of plaintiff's theories of recovery was that Dr. David Rainer (named as defendant in both cases) negligently advised plaintiff as to the need for surgery. At the trial Dr. Grossman appeared as an expert witness and opined that under the circumstances of plaintiff's condition surgery was properly recommended. As noted, judgment was in favor of Dr. Rainer.

The present action, based on additional theories of recovery, was filed in the Superior Court of Los Angeles County on July 9, 1968, the complaint alleging in essence that Dr. Grossman (hereafter defendant) was a specialist who served as a "consultant" with Dr. Rainer prior to plaintiff's surgery and that he negligently recommended surgery which was in fact unnecessary. The claimed negligence rests on his failure to examine plaintiff and amass sufficient information prior to making his recommendation.

In an apparent effort to avoid the application of the doctrine of res judicata or collateral estoppel, plaintiff has embellished her complaint with allegations that defendant knew that Dr. Rainer would rely on his recommendations and that Dr. Rainer did in fact rely on them.

(1) Of course, the procedure for summary judgment is to permit the court to pierce the allegations in the pleadings to ascertain whether a genuine cause of action exists or whether the complaint is simply the product of artful pleading, (*Property Controllers, Inc.* v. *Shewfelt*, 245 Cal.App.2d 755 [54 Cal.Rptr. 218].)

Thus we examine the papers offered in connection with the motion for summary judgment to determine if the facts would support a judgment for defendant and negate the existence of a triable issue. (*Leggett* v. *Di Giorgio Corp.*, 276 Cal.App.2d 306 [80 Cal.Rptr. 697].)

Here the defendant's moving papers consisted principally of (1) the opinion of the Court of Appeal in the Ventura case; (2) a deposition of defendant taken in connection with the Ventura case; (3) a transcript of defendant's testimony in the Ventura case; (4) a transcript of Dr. Rainer's testimony in the Ventura case; and (5) an affidavit by defendant. Plaintiff's opposition consists of a declaration by her counsel which is nothing more than an argument based on her interpretation of the evidence and presents no factual material.

Defendant, in his affidavit, states flatly that he never at any time met, saw or treated plaintiff for any condition and that he had not been called in "consultation" by any doctor concerning the care or treatment of plaintiff.

The uncontroverted testimony of defendant and Dr. Rainer in the Ventura case in summary is as follows:

Defendant is a physician and surgeon specializing in gastroenterology. He is a professor of medicine teaching in his specialty at the U.C.L.A. Medical School. Sometime in 1960, he was invited to lecture to a group of some 20 to 50 physicians at a medical education meeting at the Ventura General Hospital. The session lasted approximately an hour, during which various cases and X-rays were presented for discussion.

Dr. Rainer, who at the time was treating plaintiff for a condition described as ulcerative colitis, without mentioning her name, presented the facts of plaintiff's history together with X-rays. Defendant gave an opinion that in such a case surgery was indicated. This opinion was shared by most of the physicians present at the meeting. Subsequently, Dr. Rainer made his recommendation to plaintiff and surgery followed.

(2) A necessary element of any cause of action for negligence is, of course, the existence of a duty of care which defendant owed to the plaintiff. (*Routh* v. *Quinn,* 20 Cal.2d 488 [127 P.2d 1, 149 A.L.R. 215].) The existence of such a duty is a question of law. (*Amaya* v. *Home Ice, Fuel & Supply Co.,* 59 Cal.2d 295 [29 Cal.Rptr. 33, 379 P.2d 513]; *Starr* v. *Mooslin,* 14 Cal.App.3d 988 [92 Cal.Rptr. 583].)

In the usual case of medical malpractice the duty of care springs from the physician-patient relationship which is basically one of contract. (*Agnew* v. *Parks,* 172 Cal.App.2d 756, 764 [343 P.2d 118].) It is clear that the imposition on defendant of a duty of care to plaintiff here cannot rest on the physician-patient relationship. There was none.

However, as was observed in *McGarvey* v. *Pacific Gas & Elec. Co.,* 18 Cal.App.3d 555, 561-562 [95 Cal.Rptr. 894]: "Our Supreme Court, . . . has on a 'case-by-case basis' [citation] blazed new trails in fields in which new or rediscovered duties of care have been asserted—e.g., in *Greenman* v. *Yuba Power Products, Inc.* (1963) 59 Cal.2d 57 [27 Cal.Rptr. 697, 377 P.2d 897, 13 A.L.R.3d 1049] (liability of manufacturers for defective design of products); *Dillon* v. *Legg, supra* [68 Cal.2d 728 (69 Cal.Rptr. 72, 441 P.2d 912, 29 A.L.R.3d 1316)] (extension of liability of a tort-feasor who injures a child to encompass limited liability for its parent's resultant mental-physical illness); *Rowland* v. *Christian, supra,* 69 Cal.2d 108 [70 Cal.Rptr. 97, 443 P.2d 561, 32 A.L.R.3d 496] (abolishing rigid and illogical distinctions relating to a land occupant's liability based upon plaintiff's status as trespasser, invitee or licensee)."

(3a) However, the facts before us bearing on the connection between defendant's conduct and plaintiff's alleged injury, which are not in dispute, do not call for "blazing a new trail."

As a teacher of doctors, defendant used as a teaching vehicle cases presented to him by his pupils. It is conceded that his opinion became part of the total information upon which one of those pupils, Dr. Rainer, drew in giving advice to his patient.

Presumably every professor or instructor in a professional school hopes, expects or foresees that his students will absorb and apply in their own careers at least some of the information he imparts. Does he thereby assume a duty of care and potential liability to those persons who may ultimately become the clients or patients of those students? We think not.

(4) The following oft-quoted language from *Biakanja* v. *Irving,* 49 Cal.2d 647, 650 [320 P.2d 16, 65 A.L.R.2d 1358], provides the yardstick for resolving the case at bench: "The determination whether in a specific case the defendant will be held liable to a third person not in privity is a matter of policy and involves the balancing of various factors, among which are the extent to which the transaction was intended to affect the plaintiff, the foreseeability of harm to him, the degree of certainty that the plaintiff suffered injury, the closeness of the connection between the defendant's conduct and the injury suffered, the mortal blame attached to the defendant's conduct,

and the policy of preventing future harm.'' (Also see *Merrill* v. *Buck*, 58 Cal.2d 552 [25 Cal.Rptr. 456, 375 P.2d 304]; *Amaya* v. *Home Ice, Fuel & Supply Co., supra*, 59 Cal.2d 295.) *Raymond* v. *Paradise Unified School Dist.*, 218 Cal.App.2d 1 [31 Cal.Rptr. 847], suggested some additional considerations, i.e., (1) the social utility of the activity causing the injury compared with the risks involved in its conduct; (2) the kind of a person with whom the actor is dealing; (3) the workability of a rule of care especially in terms of the parties' relative ability to adopt practical means of preventing injury; (4) the prophylactic effect of a rule of liability.

(3b) This case fails on all counts to call for the imposition on defendant of a duty to plaintiff. There is no suggestion that defendant's conduct was morally blameworthy. The continuing education of its members by the medical profession and the exchange of information between doctors is of great social benefit. The so-called ''case method'' of instruction is an excellent vehicle for such purposes, a method which would become unwieldy if the expert were required to personally examine the patient and in effect accept the patient as his own prior to embarking on any discussion of the case.

Defendant here was dealing with medical doctors who were not under his direction or control. He was entitled to assume that these doctors were cognizant of the circumstances under which the various cases were discussed, i.e., without defendant having personally examined the patient, and would themselves in dealing directly with their patients rely on their own ultimate opinions following proper medical procedures. Imposition of liability under these circumstances would not be prophylactic but instead counter-productive by stifling efforts at improving medical knowledge.

Plaintiff claims that support for her position is to be found in *Vesely* v. *Sager*, 5 Cal.3d 153 [95 Cal.Rptr. 623, 486 P.2d 151], where a vendor of alcoholic beverages whose intoxicated customer injured a third party was held to owe a duty to that third party as a member of the public and *Heyer* v. *Flaig*, 70 Cal.2d 223 [74 Cal.Rptr. 225, 449 P.2d 161], where a lawyer who negligently drafted a will for a client was held to owe a duty to a beneficiary who thereby suffered damage. Neither case is of comfort to plaintiff.

The duty in *Vesely* was based upon a penal statute enacted for the protection of the public. In *Heyer*, at page 228, the court simply applied the *Biakanja* criteria and reiterated the rule that ''liability *may* flow from relationships which are not expressed by contract between the parties, not in 'privity' with each other, and that such duty *could* emanate from the policy considerations [set forth in *Biakanja*].'' (Italics added.)

In balancing the various factors it is our conclusion that public policy considerations militate against establishing any duty in this case.

The judgment is affirmed.

ROTH, P. J., and FLEMING, J., concurred.

A petition for a hearing was denied May 9, 1973, and appellant's petition for a hearing by the Supreme Court was denied June 7, 1973.

THE STANDARD OF CARE

Those who consult with professionals have a right to expect that the services received are equal in quality to those that could be expected from any other comparable professional in the field. Thus, for example, an individual has a right to expect that the services rendered by a given clinical psychologist will be at least as competently and skillfully rendered as those rendered by any ordinary clinical psychologist. The individual does not have the right to expect that the services will be as competently and skillfully rendered as those rendered by a psychiatrist, a social worker, a developmental psychologist, and so forth. As mental health professionals well know, even if you compare the therapeutic approaches of two clinical psychologists—even two clinical psychologists trained in the same school of psychotherapy (e.g., psychoanalysis)—it would not be unusual to find vast differences of opinion as to the proper method of treatment. One can readily appreciate the complex problems attendant on defining an applicable standard by which to judge a professional's action in any field, and particularly the mental health field.

Only by establishing a fair and just standard by which to gauge the actions of the defendant can the court determine that services of acceptable quality were or were not rendered. The problem of defining a standard and applying it to the facts in cases involving mental health professionals is accentuated by the lack of tangible elements; unlike physical injuries, which can be seen and documented, alleged mental injuries can easily become a matter of contrasting professional opinions. As regards treatment, there are upwards of two hundred different approaches to psychotherapy, and two practitioners who profess to adopt the same approach may well disagree as to how the therapy should be undertaken. For example, in the treatment of phobias, systematic desensitization and implosion are two vastly different techniques that appear in textbooks on the subject of behavior therapy. The former technique involves muscle relaxation and a gradual imaginal exposure to the feared object, while the latter technique involves exaggerated imaginal exposure to the feared object, which is supposed to raise anxiety to a point where the patient spontaneously "implodes." One behavior therapist may advocate the use of systematic desensitization in the treatment of most phobias while another might advocate the use of implosion. Where does this leave the court? Where does this leave the injured patient?

The law does not prefer one form of treatment over another. The judiciary has traditionally judged practitioners against the standards of the practitioner's own school of treatment (see for example, *Nelson* v. *Dahl,* 174 Minn. 574, 219 N.W. 941 [1928]). In the past any form of treatment would be considered by the courts to be legitimate provided that it was an approach supported by at least a "respectable minority of the profession." However as Harris (1973, p. 419) has pointed out, "'respected minorities' are legion in psychotherapy" and "in several cases courts have shifted the burden to the doctor to justify the use of unorthodox methods."

As we have noted, the courts generally look to the profession for the definition of the applicable standard of care. However, there are exceptional situations. One such situation is when the mere fact that an injury occurred suggests that there probably was negligence on the part of the defendant. Here the doctrine of *res ipsa loquitur* ("the act speaks for itself") is invoked by the court. This doctrine has frequently been applied in medical malpractice situations in which some foreign object has been left inside a patient. However, it has also found applicability in situations involving mental health professionals and institutions. In *Rodriguez* v. *State,* 78 Misc.2d 174, 355 N.Y.S.2d 912 (Ct.Cl. 1974), a profoundly retarded, institutionalized five-year-old girl who could not sit, crawl or move her legs because of medical complications was found by her mother to have a fractured leg. The mother brought suit against the hospital claiming that since the child was unable to move when placed on a flat surface the hospital must have been responsible for the injury. The court found for the plaintiff invoking the doctrine of *res ipsa loquitur*.

Another exception to the court's custom of looking to the profession to define the applicable standard occurs in the relatively rare situation in which the applicable standard is prescribed by statute. Still another exception—even more rare—is when the court takes it upon itself to define the applicable standard. In *Helling* v. *Carey,* 83 Wash.2d 514, 519 P.2d 981 (1974), supra, an ophthalmologist was sued for damages relating to his failure to perform a routine pressure test for glaucoma on a thirty-two-year-old patient. Expert testimony at the trial unanimously agreed that because of the low incidence of glaucoma in the under-forty population, the pressure test was not routinely performed. The court rejected the standard set by the profession as being too low and found for the plaintiff. In *Tarasoff* v. *Regents of University of California,* 13 Cal.3d 425, 551 P.2d 334, 131 Cal.Rptr. 14 (1976), supra, the court rejected the standard of the mental health profession with respect to the need for confidentiality of patient–therapist communications and ruled that "protective privilege ends where the public peril begins."

The following cases are illustrative of the problem of defining the applicable standard of care as a basic statement of the law of negligence or malpractice.

Baker v. *United States*, 343 F.2d222 (8th Cir. 1965)

STEPHENSON, Chief Judge.

This action was brought by Mrs. Kenneth Baker as legal guardian for Kenneth Baker, an incompetent, against the United States of America under the provisions of the Federal Tort Claims Act, Title 28 U.S.C.A., § 1346(b) and §§ 2671–2680. Plaintiff seeks to recover damages in the sum of $100,000 for injuries allegedly sustained by her ward in atempting to commit suicide by jumping into a concrete window well on the grounds of the Veterans Administration Hospital at Iowa City, Iowa, where said ward was under psychiatric treatment. In addition plaintiff, individually, seeks damages in the sum of $25,000 for loss of consortium. Plaintiff charges the V.A. Hospital staff with specific acts of negligence in failing to: (1) maintain sufficient physical restriction over said patient; (2) maintain proper supervision over said patient; (3) exercise ordinary and due care for said patient in his existing mental and physical condition; (4) properly diagnose the patient's illness and mental condition and to reasonably determine that he was in such condition that he might be reasonably expected to commit suicide if not properly supervised and restrained; (5) heed the information and warning from the patient's attending physician and family regarding his condition; and in (6) maintaining a deep pit or window well uncovered in close proximity to the area provided for mental patients and freely accessible to them. Plaintiff also charges negligence under the doctrine of res ipsa loquitur. The government denied its hospital staff or employees were negligent as charged.

Counsel for both parties presented this matter vigorously and furnished the Court with excellent briefs.

In considering the various allegations of negligence it should first be observed that there is no evidence indicating that hospital employees failed to carry out the orders of Dr. Kennedy or any other physicians in the care of the patient. Failure on the part of hospital employees to carry out the instructions of a patient's physician may constitute a violation of the standard of care required of hospitals. *Shover* v. *Iowa Lutheran Hospital,* 252 Iowa 706, 107 N.W.2d 85 (1961). Neither is there evidence indicating any appreciable change in the patient's condition from the time of his admission to the time of the suicidal attempt which might require action on the part of hospital employees not covered by Dr. Kennedy's instructions. *Bradshaw* v. *Iowa Methodist Hospital,* 251 Iowa 375, 101 N.W.2d 167 (1960). It should also now be observed that the window well into which the patient leaped was enclosed by a heavy mesh wire fence which was at least three feet high. This was not a case of the patient falling into the window well but the injury was caused by a deliberate leap of the patient over the fence into the window well.

Although it may have been better practice to cover the window well[1] the Court finds that under the evidence in this case the defendant was not negligent in failing to close the window well with a suitable covering.

The negligence, if any, which was the proximate cause of the patient's injuries arises out of the failure of Dr. Kennedy to properly diagnose the patient as a sufficient suicide risk so as to require closer supervision than was furnished by the immediate assignment of the patient to an open ward. A closed ward on the 9th floor was available to which patients were assigned when close supervision was deemed advisable. The issues are: What standard of care was required of the hospital and its staff? Was that standard of care violated in assigning the patient to an open ward?

There appear to be no Iowa cases involving the standard of care required of mental hospitals toward their patients. But it appears generally, that the care required of a hospital includes giving such care to a patient as the hospital knew or in the exercise of reasonable care should have known was required. This duty is measured by the degree of care, skill and diligence customarily exercised by hospitals generally in the community. A hospital is not an insurer of a patient's safety and is not required to guard against that which a reasonable person under the circumstances would not anticipate. *Shover* v. *Iowa Lutheran Hospital,* supra, 252 Iowa 712, 107 N.W.2d 85; *Bradshaw* v. *Iowa Methodist Hospital,* supra, 251 Iowa 384–385, 101 N.W.2d 167; 41 C.J.S. Hospitals § 8c(3), pp. 349–350.

The standard of care required of mental hospitals in other jurisdictions follow these same general standards. *Mounds Park Hospital* v. *Von Eye,* 245 F.2d 756, 70 A.L.R.2d 335 (8 Cir. 1957). It is particularly recognized in the treatment of mental patients that diagnosis is not an exact science. Diagnosis with absolute precision and certainty is impossible. Further the objective is treatment not merely incarceration. Treatment requires the restoration of confidence in the patient. This in turn requires

[1]The investigating board appointed to investigate the suicide attempt by the patient recommended that a suitable covering be placed over all window wells as an added precaution and this was done.

that restrictions be kept at a minimum. Risks must be taken or the case left as hopeless. See *Fahey* v. *United States,* 153 F.Supp. 878, 885 (S.D.N.Y.1957), reversed on other grounds, 2 Cir., 219 F.2d 445; *Mills* v. *Society of New York Hospital,* 242 App. Div. 245, 274 N.Y.S. 233, 270 N.Y. 594, 1 N.E.2d 346 (1936). The standard of care which stresses close observation, restriction and restraint has fallen in disrepute in modern hospitals and this policy is being reversed with excellent results. See, Perr, Suicide Responsibility of Hospital and Psychiatrist, 9 Cleveland-Marshall L.Rev. 427. This trend in the treatment and care of the mentally ill is reflected in regulations promulgated by the Administration of Veterans Affairs pursuant to the authority granted in 38 U.S.C.A. § 621.

> *Treatment and care of the Mentally Ill.* The policy of the V.A. is to allow each psychiatric patient the maximum independence that his condition permits and to administer the hospital so as to allow as normal a life as possible for the patient. All medically accepted therapeutic facilities will be available to each patient as required and if necessary such facilities will be made available by transfer to appropriate hospital. [Reg. M2-10 change at Par. 102]

The difficulty lies in the application of the foregoing policy. Each case must rest on its specific facts. The assignment of the patient to an open ward by Dr. Kennedy is the critical issue before this Court. Was the doctor negligent? In *Wilson* v. *Corbin,* 241 Iowa 593, 599, 41 N.W.2d 702, 705 (1950), the Iowa Supreme Court said:

> A physician is bound to use that degree of knowledge, skill, care, and attention ordinarily exercised by physicians under like circumstances and in like localities. He does not impliedly guarantee results. *Bartholomew* v. *Butts,* supra, 232 Iowa 776, 779, 5 N.W.2d 7, 9, and citations.
>
> Of course malpractice may consist in lack of skill or care in diagnosis as well as in treatment. *In re Estate of Johnson,* 145 Neb. 333, 16 N.W.2d 504, 511, and citation; *Kuechler* v. *Volgmann,* 180 Wis. 238, 192 N.W. 1015, 31 A.L.R. 826, 829, and citation; 41 Am.Jur., Physicians and Surgeons, section 92.
>
> A patient is entitled to a thorough and careful examination such as his condition and attending circumstances will permit, with such diligence and methods of diagnosis as are usually approved and practiced by physicians of ordinary learning, judgment and skill in the community or similar localities. A physician does not insure the correctness of his diagnosis. *Ramberg* v. *Morgan,* 209 Iowa 474, 477, 218 N.W.2d 504, 510, and citations; *Hill* v. *Boughton,* 146 Fla. 505, 1 So.2d 610, 134 A.L.R. 678, 682; 41 Am.Jur., Physicians and Surgeons, section 92.
>
> Ordinarily, evidence of the requisite skill and care exercised by a physician must come from experts. *Bartholomew* v. *Butts,* supra, and citations. But there are exceptions to this rule. *Whetstine* v. *Moravec,* 228 Iowa 352, 370 et seq., 291 N.W. 425 and citations, especially *Kopecky* v. *Hasek Bros.,* 180 Iowa 45, 49, 162 N.W. 828, 830, also cited with approval in *Wambold* v. *Brock,* 236 Iowa 758, 762, 19 N.W.2d 582, 584; *Peterson* v. *Hunt,* 197 Wash. 255, 84 P.2d 999, 1000, and citations.

See also, *Lagerpusch* v. *Lindley,* 253 Iowa 1033, 115 N.W.2d 207 (1962).

In the case at hand plaintiff offered evidence of practices followed at the State University of Iowa Psychopathic Hospital in the same city and during the same period of time as here involved. In this connection Dr. Paul Huston, Director of that hospital since 1956, testified as follows:

A. The first step would have been to establish the diagnosis and to determine if in fact this man was depressed, as the note from the referring physician had indicated. Since the referring physician had indicated that there was suicidal content to this man's thinking, we would have paid particular attention to this in order to determine what kind of precautions would be necessary in handling the case.
Q. And what kind of precautions would be used until it was found definitely he was subject to that suicidal content or was not?
A. Well, this varies some. It depends upon the presence or absence of the suicidal content. If present, this means certain precautions. If they are absent, then precautions aren't generally taken. If one is unsure, one is apt to be conservative and keep the patient under observation for a few days and try to determine whether there are suicidal thoughts in the patient's mind. Now as to the exact nature of precautions, this means generally that the patient is never let out of somebody's sight, out of sight of an employee of the hospital, a nurse or an attendant. It means that he does not have access to materials which he could readily destroy himself with—knives, razors, belts, and so on. If the suicidal intent is prominent, then an attendant even accompanies the patient to the bathroom. He isn't left alone, you see. So that it varies, depending upon the degree or judgment of the degree of the suicidal impulse and whether it's present or not.
Q. Doctor, would a patient such as referred to there in Exhibit 1 have been given free access to go and come from his quarters and freedom of the building and grounds at the Psychopathic Hospital during the month of August, 1960?
A. This would be very difficult to determine. The patient, when he arrived at the hospital, may not have been as depressed as was indicated by the referral note from Doctor Schrock. In Doctor Kennedy's report, he made a very definite attempt to determine the depth of the depression. He brought out that there had been history of it and that there were certain signs present now. But this comes, in the end, to a matter of judgment. It's entirely possible to miss a depression or suicidal thought on the first examination. On the other hand, if the referring physician has referred to this, then one is perhaps inclined to be more conservative and take extra precautions. So that, this is an extraordinarily difficult question to answer, you see.
Q. Well, ordinarily, doctor, what would be the practice in a case such as Mr. Baker where there is suicidal content indicated by the referring doctor?
A. We would have taken this very seriously.
Q. And what procedure would have been followed in regard to his care and treatment there at the Psychopathic Hospital during that time?
A. I think we would have been conservative in our approach to it.
Q. And what do you mean by that?
A. Well, I can't say for sure, I didn't see the patient, you see. But we possibly would have written in the note "suicidal precautions" at least for a few days until we got a chance to know this patient better, and this would have meant that he would have been under observation and that somebody would have watched him closely all the time.

. . . .

Q. To summarize your testimony then, doctor, in this particular case, such as Mr. Baker, you would have been on the conservative side as I understand your testimony. Is that correct?

A. Yes, I think so. If you are going to err, err on the conservative side, I feel. But again let me emphasize, I wasn't there, I didn't examine the patient. It's impossible to say what I would have done had I seen him, you see.

Dr. H. J. Madsen, Director of the 1540 bed Neuropsychiatric Veterans Hospital at Knoxville, Iowa, expressed the opinion that the patient received perfectly acceptable psychiatric care.

Judgement for the United States.

Hicks v. *United States,* 368 F.2d 626 (4th Cir. 1966)

Before SOBELOFF and BRYAN, Circuit Judges, and HEMPHILL, District Judge.

SOBELOFF, Circuit Judge:

This action was brought under the Federal Tort Claims Act, 28 U.S.C. § 1346, to recover damages for the death of Carol Greitens. The plaintiff, administrator of her estate, alleges that death was due to the negligence of the doctor on duty at the dispensary of the United States Naval Amphibious Base, Little Creek, Virginia, in diagnosing and treating her illness. The District Court, concluding that the evidence was insufficient to establish that the doctor was negligent, or that his concededly erroneous diagnosis and treatment was the proximate cause of her death, dismissed the complaint. From this action, the administrator appeals.

The decedent, 25 years of age, had been a diabetic since the age of 13, although the condition was under control. As the wife of a Navy enlisted man, she was entitled to medical care at the dispensary. Mrs. Greitens' husband brought her to the dispensary at about 4 A.M. on August 25, 1963, suffering from intense abdominal pain and continual vomiting which had begun suddenly an hour before. The corpsman on duty in the examining room procured her medical records, obtained a brief history, took her blood pressure, pulse, temperature, and respiration and summoned the doctor on duty, then asleep in his room at the dispensary. The doctor arrived 15 or 20 minutes later and after questioning the patient concerning her symptoms, felt her abdomen and listened to her bowel sounds with the aid of a stethoscope. Recording his diagnosis on the chart as gastroenteritis, he told Mrs. Greitens that she had a "bug" in her stomach, prescribed some drugs for the relief of pain, and released her with instructions to return in eight hours. The examination took approximately ten minutes.

The patient returned to her home, and after another episode of vomiting, took the prescribed medicine and lay down. At about noon, she arose and drank a glass of water, vomited immediately thereafter and fell to the floor unconscious. She was rushed to the dispensary, but efforts to revive her were unsuccessful. She was pronounced dead at 12:48 P.M. and an autopsy revealed that she had a high obstruction, diagnosed formally as an abnormal congenital peritoneal hiatus with internal herniation into this malformation of some of the loops of the small intestine. Death was due to a massive hemorrhagic infarction of the intestine resulting from its strangulation.

I

The plaintiff contends that the doctor at the dispensary did not meet the requisite standard of care and skill demanded of him by the law of Virginia. Compliance with this standard, the plaintiff maintains, would have required a more extended examination and immediate hospitalization. More specifically, plaintiff's expert witnesses, two general practitioners in the Norfolk-Virginia Beach area, testified that, according to prevailing practice in the community, the doctor should have inquired whether the patient had had diarrhea and should have made a rectal examination to determine whether the patient was suffering from an obstruction rather than from gastroenteritis. While the latter condition does not ordinarily require immediate radical treatment, a high obstruction is almost invariably lethal unless promptly operated upon. Plaintiff's experts further testified that on observing the symptoms manifested by Mrs. Greitens, the procedure of general practitioners in the community would have been to order immediate hospitalization. This the dispensary physician failed to do, although the Naval Hospital in Portsmouth was available to him.

The standard of care which Virginia law exacts from a physician, in this case a general practitioner, is stated in *Reed* v. *Church,* 175 Va. 284, 8 S.E.2d 285, 288 (1940), as follows:

A physician holds himself out as possessing the knowledge and ability necessary to the effective practice of medicine. . . . However, he is not an insurer, nor is he held to the highest degree of care known to his profession. . . . He must exhibit only that degree of skill and diligence employed by the ordinary, prudent practitioner in his field and community, or in similar communities, at the time.

Accord, *Alexander* v. *Hill,* 174 Va. 248, 6 S.E.2d 661 (1940); *Fox* v. *Mason,* 139 Va. 667, 124 S.E. 405 (1924). See Shepherd, The Law of Medical Malpractice in Virginia, 21 Wash. & Lee L.Rev. 212 (1964). Thus, if he uses ordinary care in reaching his diagnosis, and thereafter acts upon it, he incurs no liability, even if the diagnosis proves to be a mistake in judgment.

It is undisputed that the symptoms of high obstruction and of gastroenteritis are quite similar. The District Court placed great emphasis on this fact as an indication that the doctor's erroneous diagnosis was not negligent, but was merely an error of judgment. It would seem, however, that where the symptoms are consistent with either of two possible conditions, one lethal if not attended to promptly, due care demands that a doctor do more than make a cursory examination and then release the patient. See *Jenkins* v. *Charleston Gen. Hospital & Training School,* 90 W.Va. 230, 110 S.E. 560, 22 A.L.R. 323 (1922), holding that where a "partial and very hurried investigation" was made, the physician was liable for failure of his diagnosis to disclose an injury which caused detriment to the patient. The fact that an intestinal obstruction is a rare occurrence, and that some form of gastroenteritis is the more likely of the two conditions, does not excuse the failure to make inquiries and perform recognized additional tests that might have served to distinguish the one condition from the other. The dispensary doctor himself, as well as the experts for both sides, agreed that an inquiry as to diarrhea and a rectal examination were the "proper procedure" and "the accepted standard" in order to be able to rule out gastroenteritis and to make a definite diagnosis of high intestinal obstruction. If he had made the inquiry which he admits was the accepted standard, he would at least have been alerted to the fact that the case was one calling for close observation with a view to immediate surgical intervention if the graver diagnosis were confirmed. In these circumstances, failure to make this investigation constitutes a lack of due care on the part of the physician. It was stated in *Kelly* v. *Carroll,* 36 Wash.2d 482, 494, 219 P.2d 79, 86, 19 A.L.R.2d 1174 (1950), cert. denied, 340 U.S. 892, 71 S.Ct. 208, 95 L.Ed. 646 (1950), a case in which an erroneous diagnosis had led to improper treatment, that "if there was a possibility that it was appendicitis, he [defendant] had no right to gamble with [decedent's] life, on the theory that it might be something else." Only if a patient is adequately examined, is there no liability for an erroneous diagnosis.[1]

Our conclusion that the physician was negligent in his diagnosis and treatment of the patient is not inconsistent with Fed.R.Civ.P. 52(a), which declares that the trial judge's findings of fact are not to be disturbed unless clearly erroneous. This Rule comes into play primarily where the trial judge as fact finder has had to reconcile conflicting testimony. Where the veracity of witnesses is in issue, the decision is for the judge who has had the opportunity to see and evaluate the witnesses' demeanor. The trial court's findings of fact on conflicting evidence will not be disturbed by the appellate court unless clearly erroneous. *United States* v. *General Motors Corp.*, 384 U.S. 127, 141 n. 16, 86 S.Ct. 1321, 16 L.Ed.2d 415 (1966); *Walling* v. *Gen. Industries Co.*, 330 U.S. 545, 550, 67 S.Ct. 883, 91 L.Ed. 1088 (1947); *Nationwide Mutual Ins. Co.* v. *DeLoach*, 262 F.2d 775, 778 (4th Cir. 1959). But we are dealing here with the testimony of expert witnesses who are not in controversy as to the basic facts; thus, the opportunity of the trial court to observe the witnesses is of limited significance. It has often been held that where the trial court's conclusions are based on undisputed facts, they are not entitled to the finality customarily accorded basic factual findings under Rule 52(a). *United States* v. *General Motors Corp.*, supra; *United States* v. *Parke, Davis & Co.*, 362 U.S. 29, 44, 80 S.Ct. 503, 4 L.Ed.2d 505 (1960); *Shapiro, Bernstein & Co.* v. *H. L. Green Co.*, 316 F.2d 304, 306–307 (2d Cir. 1963); *St. Louis Union Trust Co.* v. *Finnegan*, 197 F.2d 565, 568 (8th Cir. 1952).

The question before us is not one of fact in the usual sense, but rather whether the undisputed facts manifest negligence. Although the absence of a factual dispute does not *always* mean that the conclusion is a question of law, it becomes so *here* since the ultimate conclusion to be drawn from the basic facts, i.e., the existence or absence of negligence, is actually a question of law. For this reason, the general rule has been that when a judge sitting without a jury makes a determination of negligence, his conclusion, as distinguished from the evidentiary findings leading to it, is freely reviewable on appeal. *Mamiye Bros.* v. *Barber Steamship Lines, Inc.*, 360 F.2d 774, 776 (2d Cir. 1966). The determination of negligence involves not only the formulation of the legal standard, but more particularly in this case, its application to the evidentiary facts as established; and since these are uncontested, there is no basis for applying the "clearly erroneous" rule. *United States* v. *Parke, Davis & Co.*, supra; *Kippen* v. *American Automatic Typewriter Co.*, 324 F.2d 742, 745 (9th Cir. 1963); *Romero* v. *Garcia &*

[1]Numerous cases have held that a physician has a duty to make proper use of all available diagnostic aids to establish a firm basis for the diagnosis and choice of treatment. See, e.g., *Price* v. *Neyland*, 115 U.S.App.D.C. 355, 320 F.2d 674, 99 A.L.R.2d 1391 (1963) (pediatrician negligent in stopping short of making all possible diagnostic tests which might have enabled him to distinguish physiologic from pathologic jaundice); *Kingston* v. *McGrath*, 232 F.2d 495, 54 A.L.R.2d 267 (9th Cir. 1956) (ordinary skill and care required further examination of patient and taking of additional X-ray pictures even though first X-rays did not disclose fracture); *Dowell* v. *Mossberg*, 226 Or. 173, 355 P.2d 624 (1960), rev'd on other grounds on rehearing, 359 P.2d 541 (1961) (failure to diagnose disease as diabetes negligent because blood sugar test not performed); *Harvey* v. *Silber*, 300 Mich. 510, 2 N.W.2d 483 (1942) (doctor's erroneous diagnosis of position of bullet in decedent's body negligent because of reliance on manual examination rather than X-rays); *Peterson* v. *Hunt*, 197 Wash. 255, 84 P.2d 999 (1938) (diagnosis of ovarian cyst as pregnancy negligent because of failure to employ standard "rabbit test"); *Ramberg* v. *Morgan*, 209 Iowa 474, 218 N.W. 492 (1929) (erroneous diagnosis of auto accident victim's condition as intoxication, rather than skull fracture, negligent because of failure to give more thorough examination, including X-rays); *Coleman* v. *Wilson*, 85 N.J.L. 203, 88 A. 1059 (1913) (negligent failure to analyze tissue of growth in decedent's nostril, leading to improper operation, when analysis would have revealed non-malignant character of growth); Note, Problems of Negligent Malpractice, 26 Va.L.Rev. 919, 922 (1940).

Diaz, Inc., 286 F.2d 347, 355 (2d Cir. 1960), cert. denied, 365 U.S. 869, 81 S.Ct. 905, 5 L.Ed.2d 860 (1961); *Galena Oaks Corp.* v. *Scofield,* 218 F.2d 217, 219 (5th Cir. 1954).

The government's expert opined that the dispensary physician exercised "average judgment," but analysis of his entire testimony points unavoidably to the opposite conclusion. Revealing are his statements that it was wrong not to inquire about diarrhea, conceding that "that is one question that one usually asks," and that given a patient with abdominal pain of one hour's duration, it is too soon "to expect anybody to come up with a proper diagnosis." Furthermore, his opinion was predicated upon a factual assumption not permissible in this case. His assumption was that the dispensary physician had made only a "working" or "tentative" diagnosis, which the expert felt to be appropriate in view of the fact that the symptoms had their onset such a short time before. However, the uncontradicted evidence indicates that this was not a "tentative" diagnosis.

The examining doctor himself testified that he had already considered and ruled out at the beginning of his examination the possibility of an obstruction without making the additional differentiating diagnostic tests. He said that his only reason for asking the patient to return eight hours later was because her diabetic condition could become complicated by a case of gastroenteritis. A further indication of the final nature of the diagnosis is his notation of gastroenteritis on the chart, made without further qualification. He also testified that he told the woman not to return for eight hours, regardless of the persistence of pain; yet even the government's expert testified that if abdominal pain were present for "*three or four* hours and wouldn't go away, you would probably have to operate." By releasing the patient, the dispensary physician made his diagnosis final, allowing no further opportunity for revision, and this prematurely determined final diagnosis was based on an investigation not even minimally adequate.

On careful scrutiny, therefore, the government's expert is seen to have demonstrated that the examiner did *not* conform to the required standard of care. Coupled with the explicit testimony of the plaintiff's experts, the government's testimony leads us inevitably to the conclusion that the doctor was negligent as a matter of law. We think that the District Court gave undue weight to the purely conclusory opinion of the government witness. The District Court is not bound by his statement that "average judgment" had been exercised, nor are we bound by it. Only the standard of care is to be established by the testimony of experts. If under the undisputed facts the defendant failed to meet that standard it is not for the expert but for the court to decide whether there was negligence.

II

The government further contends that even if negligence is established, there was no proof that the erroneous diagnosis and treatment was the proximate cause of the death, asserting that even if surgery had been performed immediately, it is mere speculation to say that it would have been successful. The government's contention, however, is unsupported by the record. Both of plaintiff's experts testified categorically that if operated on promptly, Mrs. Greitens would have survived, and this is nowhere contradicted by the government expert. *Price* v. *Neyland,* 115 U.S.App.D.C. 355, 320 F.2d 674, 99 A.L.R.2d 1391 (1963), decided under Virginia law, held that a doctor was liable for negligent diagnosis, although even when correctly diagnosed, the disease requires *immediate* treatment for success.

When a defendant's negligent action or inaction has effectively terminated a person's chance of survival, it does not lie in the defendant's mouth to raise conjectures as to the measure of the chances that he has put beyond the possibility of realization. If there was any substantial possibility of survival and the defendant has destroyed it, he is answerable. Rarely is it possible to demonstrate to an absolute certainty what would have happened in circumstances that the wrongdoer did not allow to come to pass. The law does not in the existing circumstances require the plaintiff to show to a *certainty* that the patient would have lived had she been hospitalized and operated on promptly. *Harvey* v. *Silber*, 300 Mich. 510, 2 N.W.2d 483 (1942).[2]

An apt analogy is found in a case which arose in this circuit.[3] In *Gardner* v. *National Bulk Carriers, Inc.*, 310 F.2d 284, 91 A.L.R.2d 1023 (4th Cir. 1962), cert. denied, 372 U.S. 913, 83 S.Ct. 728, 9 L.Ed.2d 721 (1963), a seaman, last seen on board at 6 P.M., was not discovered to be missing until 11:30 P.M. A search was then made of the ship, but the master did not alter the speed or course of the vessel or take other steps to find the missing seaman. It was contended that there was no causal connection between the failure to reverse the course of the ship to conduct a search and the seaman's death, since there was no definite showing that when it was discovered that he was missing, he was still alive and could have been saved. This court held, however, that the master's duty to attempt a rescue

> is of such a nature that its omission will contribute to cause the seaman's death. The duty arises when there is a reasonable possibility of rescue. Proximate cause is tested by the same standard, i.e., *causation is proved if the master's omission destroys the reasonable possibility of rescue*. [Citation omitted.] Therefore, proximate cause here is implicit in the breach of duty. Indeed, the duty would be empty if it did not itself embrace the loss as a consequence of its breach. *Once the evidence sustains the reasonable possibility of rescue, ample or narrow, according to the circumstances,* total disregard of the duty, refusal to make even a try, as was the case here, imposes liability. Id. at 287. [Emphasis supplied.]

In sum, the dispensary physician's negligence in failing to make a thorough examination and in omitting standard diagnostic tests, led to an erroneous diagnosis. Because of this, he sent the patient home with instructions not to return for eight hours, rather than immediately admitting her to a hospital. Since the uncontradicted testimony was that with prompt surgery she would have survived, the conclusion follows that the

[2]In *Harvey,* the defendant negligently diagnosed the decedent's wound as merely superficial, whereas a correct diagnosis would have indicated that the intestine had been pierced, and that an operation would be necessary to stop the hemorrhaging. As here, the expert witnesses in that case agreed that the decedent could not have survived without an operation. Since the negligent diagnosis was the proximate cause of the failure to operate, and there was testimony to the effect that there was a *probability* that an operation would have saved decedent's life, it was held that the negligent diagnosis was the proximate cause of death. The appellate court found that the jury had been properly charged when told that it was "not incumbent on the plaintiff to show that to a certainty surgical intervention would have saved his life." Id. 300 Mich. at 521, 2 N.W. 2d at 488.

[3]Other circuits have similarly held that if the victim *might* have been saved by a precaution which the defendant negligently omitted, the omission is deemed to have caused the harm, even though it is not possible to demonstrate conclusively that the precaution would in fact have saved the victim. See, e.g., *Kirincich* v. *Standard Dredging Co.*, 112 F.2d 163 (3d Cir. 1940) (seaman who could not swim was thrown inch heaving line rather than larger and more buoyant object); *Zinnel* v. *United States Shipping Board,* 10 F.2d 47 (2d Cir. 1925) (whether guard rope, absence of which constituted negligence of defendant, would have prevented plaintiff's intestate from being washed overboard). In the latter case, it was stated that although nobody could be sure intestate would have seized rope or that it would have stopped his body, the court was not "justified, where certainty is impossible, in insisting upon it."

dispensary doctor's negligence nullified whatever chance of recovery she might have had and was the proximate cause of the death.

Judgment reversed and cause remanded for the determination of damages.

Hicks v. *United States,* 511 F.2d 407 (D.C.Cir. 1975)

Before FAHY, Senior Circuit Judge, and MCGOWAN and TAMM, Circuit Judges.

Opinion for the Court filed by Senior Circuit Judge FAHY.

Concurring opinion filed by Circuit Judge TAMM, with whom Circuit Judge MCGOWAN joins.

FAHY, Senior Circuit Judge:

Plaintiffs in the District Court, appellees in this court, are co-administratrices of the estate of Corinne Morgan, deceased. They sued the United States under the Federal Tort Claims Act, 28 U.S.C. §§ 1346(b) and 2671,[1] and also under the District of Columbia survival statute, 12 D.C.Code § 101. The complaint attributed the death of Corinne Morgan to the negligence of St. Elizabeths Hospital (the Hospital) as agent of the United States. She was killed by her husband, Joseph Morgan, who had been a patient at the Hospital, and who shot her after he had been given his liberty in circumstances, allegedly, of negligence on the part of the Hospital which were a proximate cause of the homicide. The case was tried by Judge Curran of the District Court without a jury, and resulted in a judgment for plaintiffs of $90,000 under the Federal Tort Claims Act, and of $10,000 under the survival statute. Hicks v. United States, 357 F.Supp. 434 (D.D.C.1973). The amount of the judgment is not challenged. It is the liability of the United States that is in question. We affirm.

I
The Factual Situation

Morgan for many years had been a heavy drinker. Prior to the homicide he had been arrested for drunkenness, disorderly conduct or assault at least sixteen times between 1957 until the homicide in 1967. His wife had been the complainant on eight of these occasions. On July 11, 1966, she obtained a warrant for his arrest for assault upon her on July 7. In the affidavit which was the basis for the warrant she averred that she had been kicked, choked and beaten by him and that he had also threatened to murder her. According to her statement, Morgan was intoxicated at the time. He was arrested July 12 and arraigned the same day in the Court of General Sessions of the District of Columbia, superseded now by the Superior Court of the District of Columbia. The court committed him to the District of Columbia General Hospital to determine his competency. On August 11, that hospital reported to the Court of General Sessions in considerable detail.[2] The report stated that Morgan was suffering from "a moderately severe organic brain syndrome," and that "[t]his condition is due to actual brain

[1]28 U.S.C. § 1346(b) permits recovery against the United States for injury or death caused by the negligent act or omission "of any employee of the Government while acting within the scope of his office or employment, under circumstances where the United States, if a private person, would be liable to the claimant in accordance with the law of the place where the act or omission occurred." Section 2671 defines "employee of the Government" as used in section 1346(b) to include officers or employees of any federal agency.

[2]See, *Hicks, supra,* at 436.

damage, and is probably a result of prolonged, excessive drinking.'' 357 F.Supp. at 436. The report also stated:

> It is our opinion that the patient's mental impairment is such that he is not yet ready to function in society. This type of brain condition sometimes clears with the passage of time, good diet, and absolute abstinence from alcohol. We therefore think it would be important for him to receive further treatment and hospitalization, and recommend that he be committed to St. Elizabeths Hospital for the same. It is also our recommendation that he be given psychological tests in one month, and then again in six months (whether in the hospital or not) to see if there is any change in his mental condition.

Id.

The report nevertheless gave the opinion that the patient was able to understand the nature of the charge against him and ''despite his impaired mental functioning, probably able to assist counsel in his defense and competent to stand trial.'' *Id.* The court, however, found him incompetent to stand trial and on August 12, 1966, committed him again, this time to St. Elizabeths.

The Clinical Record of the Hospital contains a report of October 21, 1966, made by a Psychiatric Social Worker on the basis of an interview with Mrs. Morgan. It notes that among the number of previous charges against him six were,

drunk in house, disorderly and assault. Mrs. Morgan reports that although patient [Morgan] has been drinking heavily for the past 12–15 years, his behavior had become much more unbearable in the past few years.

> The informant [Mrs. Morgan] is contemplating separation or divorce as she does not wish to live again with the patient. . . .
>
> . . . patient's family can definitely not be used as a community resource as they are afraid of him and are not interested in having him back in the home.
>
> [The] relationship [between Morgan and Mrs. Morgan] is estimated to have been quite destructive for marital partners.

The Clinical Record shows also that a ''Psychological Summary'' was made October 25, 1966, by Dr. Borriello at the request apparently of the ward in which Morgan was living at the Hospital. It contains the following under the heading ''General Impression'':

> Outstanding in the test results is organic brain damage due to the effects of a long history of alcohol consumption. Inner resources for the effective and efficient solution of every day problems are lacking. Stressful situations can bring on emotionally labile acting out aggressive behavior.
>
> Women pose a threat to him and he does not have adequate understanding of his feelings, needs and desires in relation to them. He places insatiable demands upon them that they could never satisfy and which could result in him a violent rage that he could possibly act out.
>
> In general the projective test protocols are confirmatory of the general impression.

On October 26, 1966, the Clinical Record, moreover, contains a report of his ''Psychiatric Case Study.'' It states, *inter alia:*

> On July 7, 1966, the patient's wife called the police complaining that he was drunk and had been beating, choking and kicking her and had threatened to kill her. This was the eighth time Mrs. Morgan had him arrested for similar reasons.
>
> Mr. Morgan has had at least 16 arrests since 1957, at which time he was 31 years old, for being drunk and disorderly or assault. In eight of these his wife was the complainant.
>
> The marriage was fraught with problems almost from the start, with a couple relating to each other in a mutually destructive manner. The patient has been drinking excessively now for approximately 15 years.

This study, made by a Senior Psychiatric Resident, and signed by the Clinical Director of the West Side Division of the Hospital,[3] refers to the report of the District of Columbia General Hospital as revealing "psychologicals which evidenced organicity. He was described as lucid, friendly, and cooperative and was given a diagnosis of organic brain syndrome, moderately severe."

The study further states,

> There was no evidence of an underlying psychosis. . . . Psychological testing revealed marked evidence of organicity and personality factors consistent with alcoholism.
>
> [There was] no evidence of hallucinations or delusions. He remained oriented in all spheres, showed appropriate affect, and posed a problem only in the assessment of memory loss in the presence of such massive denial. He has a tendency to be impulsive and react quickly when angry.

On October 27, 1966, the same Senior Psychiatric Resident made a "Recommendation for Diagnosis and Discharge to Court." This report was a virtually verbatim recital of the previous day's study, except it concluded in the following language:

> . . . Those who know him best feel that he is ready soon to return to Court for trial.

Recommended Diagnosis:	02.1 Acute Brain Syndrome Associated with Alcohol Intoxication. (Recovered).
Recommendations:	In our Opinion, 1. He is mentally competent to stand trial. 2. On or around July 9, 1966, he was suffering from a mental disorder, acute brain syndrome due to alcohol intoxication, from which he has now recovered, and the alleged offense with which he is charged, if committed by him, was a product of his illness.
Condition on Discharge:	Recovered.

[3]He had also approved the Psychological Summary of October 25, 1966.

Shortly before Morgan was released from St. Elizabeths in January, 1967, he was visited by his wife, one of his sons, his daughter (one of the appellees) and her husband.

According to testimony given by the daughter at trial, Morgan began,

> "... yelling that he was going to kill her [Mrs. Morgan] when he got out because she was the reason for him being over there: it was her fault.... [W]e had to take my mother out of the visiting room."

The son's testimony at trial supported this account and added that he had accompanied his mother, immediately after the incident, when she sought assurances from an employee of the Hospital that she would be notified if her husband was released, or if she would have to go to court.

On January 30, 1967, Morgan was discharged by the Hospital as recovered, to appear in court. Mrs. Morgan did not appear and a nolle prosequi was entered. A copy of the case jacket of the Court of General Sessions which is before us—the original we are advised has been lost—bears a stamped legend, "Jan 30 1967 Nolle Prosequi in Open Court." A nolle prosequi did not require the court's approval and none is indicated.[4] The following in handwriting also appears on the jacket: "See Letter attached from St. Eliz. Hosp. Set for hearing 1-19-67," a stamped "Jan 19 1967" and a handwritten "C 1/26/67 Return to Hospital." These entries indicate that the case had been set for hearing January 19, was on that day continued to January 26, when Morgan was returned to the Hospital, followed on January 30 by the nolle prosequi. Morgan had been discharged to the court by the Hospital and went free when the charge against him was dismissed on the nolle prosequi.

The letter referred to as "from St. Eliz. Hosp." was from the then Superintendent of St. Elizabeths, dated December 19, 1966, addressed to the Clerk of the Criminal Division of the District of Columbia Court of General Sessions, and reads as follows:

> It is the opinion of the physicians that Mr. Morgan has recovered from his mental disorder, Acute Brain Syndrome Associated With Alcohol Intoxication, and that he is now mentally competent to stand trial in that he has a rational and reasonable understanding of the nature of the charge against him and can properly assist counsel in his defense. These determinations were made on the basis of psychiatric examinations which indicate that there is no evidence of delusions or hallucinations, that he is oriented in all spheres, shows appropriate affect and can discuss the charges rationally. Perception, comprehension and memory are within normal limits. Intellectual functions are in the borderline range. There is indication that he was suffering from a mental disorder on or around July 9, 1966, from which he has now recovered, and that the alleged crime, if committed by him, was the product of his illness. He is not receiving medication.

On February 3, 1967, four days after his release, the West Side Division Clinical Director of the Hospital wrote a letter to Mrs. Morgan as follows:

> This is to inform you that your husband, Mr. Joseph Morgan was officially discharged from St. Elizabeths Hospital on January 30, 1967.
>
> We trust he will make a good adjustment in the community.

[4] "The United States Attorney and the Corporation Counsel may file a dismissal or nolle prosequi of an information or complaint and the prosecution shall thereupon terminate...." Rule 48(a), D.C. Court of General Sessions Criminal Rules, January, 1970.

At trial of the present case a daughter of Mrs. Morgan testified that on January 30, 1967, she had received a phone call from, she thinks, the clerk at the court. He asked if Corinne Morgan was at home, was told she was not, that she was at work, and that it was her daughter talking, and he then said, "Well, didn't she know that she was supposed to be in court this morning?" She testified that upon learning her father was released that day she was so upset she ran across the street to her mother's best girlfriend and asked what should she do. They decided to call her mother because she (Mrs. Morgan) had been saying that she wanted to be away and hoped she could move before he got out. They called her mother (who apparently was approaching the house) from the friend's window and broke the news to her that he had been released. Mrs. Morgan was very upset.

Two days after his release, on February 1, Morgan was arrested for intoxication. On the 3rd of February he was committed by the Court of General Sessions to the Alcoholic Unit at Occoquan, Virginia. On February 23rd the court released him to the Director of the Clinic for outpatient treatment. On March 26, 1967, when he came to the family home[5] his wife told him he could not stay. He then shot and thus killed her.

He was indicted for second-degree murder and assault with a dangerous weapon on May 23, 1967. Following his commitment to the Hospital he was found incompetent to stand trial on August 26, 1967. On August 25, 1967, his Clinical Record there shows his condition to have been diagnosed as "Chronic Brain Syndrome, Associated with Alcohol Intoxication. . . ." The opinion recorded that this "Chronic Brain Syndrome existed on or about March 26, 1967" [the date of the homicide] and the homicide "was a product of that illness."

On September 23, 1968, he was acquitted of the murder at an uncontested trial before a judge who found him not guilty by reason of insanity. A staff doctor of the Hospital testified on this occasion that he and another doctor, as the result of a conference August 25, 1967, had concluded that Morgan had been suffering from chronic brain syndrome on March 26, 1967, when he killed his wife.

During this civil action trial there was admitted in evidence a transcript of the staff doctor's testimony during the homicide trial. This included a reference to a psychological summary made by another doctor at the Hospital in July, 1967, which appellees' counsel read as follows [apparently summarizing the most relevant substance of the summary]:

> "Previous testing: Mr. Morgan was tested in October 1966 and again in July of 1967. The test data reflected a deteriorative process consistent with the effects of prolonged alcoholism in an already profoundly inadequate individual. The most severe deterioration was in the area of emotional controls. There was an unusual ineptness in handling hostile feelings. Additional relevant findings will be incorporated in the report below. For a fuller discussion, see the previous reports."

Counsel then interposed:

> And for the record, the only previous psychological report was the one in October of 1966. (This was the report of Dr. Boriello.)

The examination of the staff doctor at the homicide trial then resumed as follows:

[5]He came home the day of his release and got his clothes, and returned for a time the day before the homicide.

QUESTION: Do you agree with that statement in your appraisal of the relationship of Mr. Morgan's condition to the offense against his wife?
ANSWER: Yes, that was our finding at the staff conference.

Dr. Borriello's statement of October 25, 1966, noted *supra*, had included the following:

> Outstanding in the test results is organic brain damage due to the effects of a long history of alcohol consumption.

As we have stated, the District Court concluded that the Hospital was negligent in not more fully advising the court as to Morgan's mental condition and that the negligence of the Hospital was in its failure to transmit adequate information to the court concerning that condition. Finding also that the Hospital's negligence was a proximate cause of the death of Mrs. Morgan, the court awarded judgment against the United States in favor of appellees.

II
A Question of Jurisdiction

The United States on appeal advances for the first time the position that the District Court lacked jurisdiction by reason of section 2680(h) of the Federal Tort Claims Act which excepts from its coverage "any claim arising out of . . . misrepresentation. . . ." The theory is that appellees base their claim upon a negligent misrepresentation, and that section 2680(h) excludes such a claim under the decision of United States v. Neustadt, 366 U.S. 696, 81 S.Ct. 1294, 6 L.Ed.2d 614 (1961). It is not clear that appellant's reliance upon section 2680(h) poses a jurisdictional issue or only an issue of fact concerning application of the Act. If the latter, it need not be considered, for it was not raised or litigated in the District Court.

That aside, we consider the contention not well founded. The trial court found liability because of the negligence of an agent of the United States in fulfilling an obligation grounded upon much more than the contents of the Hospital's report to the court. Judge Curran held:

> The hospital has a duty to make a full report to the court and the report rendered violated the hospital duty if there was knowledge of an underlying chronic condition. The negligent failure to disclose pertinent information has been well established as a violation of medical duty. (Footnote omitted.)

Hicks, supra, 357 F.Supp. at 438. Again:

> The psychiatrists at St. Elizabeths Hospital should realize that in submitting a competency report, they should include all information relative to the defendant's mental condition in order that the judge may make a proper determination.

Id. at 440. Moreover, the decision of the court states:

> This Court finds that the United States of America through St. Elizabeths Hospital negligently made a competency report. . . .

Id.

These bases of the decision contain the answer we must give to the contention that the case rests upon a negligent misrepresentation. The letter to the court—the asserted representation—manifests as we shall see not only its own contents but, in the context of the evidence, manifests also a negligent omission of information essential to fulfillment of the duty of the Hospital. The complaint is not based upon injury to appellees or to Mrs. Morgan, through whom they claim, due to a negligent misrepresentation to them which they relied upon to their injury. Compare *Neustadt, supra*. Moreover, to interpret what occurred as proving only a negligent diagnostic misrepresentation, rather than proof of negligent performance by the Hospital of a public responsibility with respect to the discharge of the patient to the court, would inaccurately describe the basis for the claim. Involved is the alleged lack of care required of a branch of the government in carrying out a responsibility, leading, allegedly, to injury to private persons. The Tort Claims Act was enacted to afford a remedy if such a case is proven. Section 2680(h) does not in our view grant an exception to a tortious failure of an agency of the United States to perform a duty imposed upon it by law, though proof of such failure rests in part upon a representation to a court in response to the agency's duty to the court.[6]

III
The Question of Negligence

1. By reason of its nature as a public institution St. Elizabeths Hospital owes a duty to the public in carrying out its difficult responsibilities. We have no occasion now to

[6]The cases primarily relied upon by the United States touching upon misrepresentation are: *Matthews* v. *United States,* 456 F.2d 395 (5th Cir. 1972); *De Lange* v. *United States,* 372 F.2d 134 (9th Cir. 1967); *Beech* v. *United States,* 345 F.2d 872 (5th Cir. 1965); and *Hungerford* v. *United States,* 307 F.2d 99 (9th Cir. 1962). These are now briefly reviewed. *Matthews* involved a claim by the wife of an Air Force officer injured in a collision of an automobile with a United States Army vehicle. The plaintiff and her husband sought the legal advice and assistance of Air Force personnel in connection with their claim for the injuries. The advice given was that the wife had done all she was required to do to protect her claim. In fact this was not correct. In the suit under the Tort Claims Act, the Court of Appeals said by way of dicta in reversing the dismissal of the complaint by the District Court, "[t]he medical malpractice cases hold that a communicated diagnosis, with nothing more, is within the § 2680(h) exception . . ." 456 F.2d at 398, citing in a footnote *De Lange* v. *United States, supra,* for the position that when a physician is under a duty to proceed further and treat a patient section 2680(h) does not apply. *De Lange* is a brief per curiam opinion stating:

> We affirm the judgment below; holding that the communicated diagnosis was a representation. (*Hall* v. *United States,* 274 F.2d 69 (10th Cir. 1959).) An incorrect representation is "misrepresentation" within the meaning of the statute (28 U.S.C.A. §§ 2674 and 2680(h)) . . . [citing *Neustadt* and referring to *Hungerford*.]

372 F.2d at 134. In *Beech* summary judgment had been granted by the District Court against a complaint alleging injury due to the negligence of an Army Hospital. In reversing and remanding the Court of Appeals said:

> . . . the Government had not only the duty to communicate to [the injured party] a diagnosis of her condition, but also to render proper care for her treatment. Under the allegations of the complaint there was a failure to perform this latter duty and such a failure is not covered by the 2680(h) exception. Hungerford v. United States (9 Cir., 1962), 307 F.2d 99.

345 F.2d at 874. In *Hungerford* it is stated that a communicated diagnosis of physical condition is a misrepresentation, citing *Hall* v. *United States, supra,* but held that,

> . . . where the Government, on the basis of facts which it is chargeable with ascertaining by a proper examination, has a duty to perform in addition to the duty of disclosing those facts, negligence in the conduct of such examination which results in a failure to perform the additional duty is not covered by the § 2680(h) exception.

307 F.2d at 103. The case turned on the allegation of failure to perform a duty of care with respect to an examination and diagnosis of the plaintiff's condition, and diagnostic tests, or because of failure to make tests which in the exercise of proper medical care should have been made. The exception was not applied. In *Hall, supra,* the representation held to come within the exception had resulted from alleged negligent testing of livestock for a disease. It had been incorrectly represented to claimant that some of the cattle were diseased, which led him to sell the cattle to his loss. The court applied the section 2680(h) exception.

decide, however, whether its public duty included an entirely separate duty to Mrs. Morgan. There was a particular duty to the Court of General Sessions, and in the circumstances of this case it was intertwined with a duty to her. See *infra,* note 12.

As to the Hospital's responsibility to the Court of General Sessions, considered in the context of a claim by private parties that the Hospital has been negligent in discharging a patient alleged to be suffering from a mental disease, the judiciary must recognize the difficulties confronting the Hospital. Generalizations must be avoided as much as possible in the area of psychiatry. Negligence cannot be imputed to the Hospital merely because of a mistake. A claim of negligence must be considered in light of the elusive qualities of mental disorders and the difficulty of analyzing and evaluating them. Exactitude is often impossible. The Supreme Court has recently noted " 'the uncertainty of diagnosis in this field and the tentativeness of professional judgment.' *Greenwood* v. *United States,* 350 U.S. 366, 375, 76 S.Ct. 410, 100 L.Ed. 412 (1956)." *Drope* v. *Missouri,* 420 U.S. 162, 95 S.Ct. 896, 43 L.Ed.2d 103 (February 19, 1975). Error and uncertainty considered alone must often be accepted without labeling them negligence. Yet we cannot accept the position of the United States which would confine the legal responsibility of the Hospital in this case to a narrow reading of section 24-301(b) of our Code. Pointing to Mr. Morgan's commitment to the Hospital August 12, 1966, "until he is mentally competent to stand trial" (Tr. II, 33), the United States relies upon section 301 as confining the Hospital's legal responsibility. The section provides:

> Ahenever an accused person confined to a hospital for the mentally ill is restored to mental competency in the opinion of the superintendent of said hospital, the superintendent shall certify such fact to the clerk of the court in which the indictment, information, or charge against the accused is pending and such certification shall be sufficient to authorize the court to enter an order thereon adjudicating him to be competent to stand trial, . . . unless the accused or the Government objects, in which event, the court, after hearing without a jury, shall make a judicial determination of the competency of the accused to stand trial. . . .

24 D.C.Code § 301(b).

This court has held that the duty of the Hospital under section 301 calls for a report in substantial detail going beyond a bare conclusion as to competency to be tried.[7] We shall enlarge upon this subject shortly but now refer to a particular aspect of the report to the court in this case. The report about Mr. Morgan went beyond a certification of his competency to be tried. It advised the court, unqualifiedly, that he was "recovered." Thus, the issue of negligence confronted the District Court, apart from whether or not the legal responsibility of the Hospital under section 301 was to report only as to Mr. Morgan's competency to be tried.

We are cited to no case claiming damages due to injury resulting from a hospital's negligence in connection with its obligation to a court regarding the mental condition of

[7]In *Washington* v. *United States,* 390 F.2d 444, 453, n.25 (D.C.Cir. 1967), we pointed out:

> The Judicial Conference of the District of Columbia has condemned the use of conclusory labels in hospital competency reports. In October 1965, the Conference recommended that "The report of a courtordered pretrial mental examination should be made in substantial detail, recounting what was done to get at the facts concerning the accused's mental condition and what those facts are, not merely the conclusions the psychiatrists have drawn from these facts."

The Superintendent of St. Elizabeths at the time of the trial of this case said he was aware that this was necessary.

one who has been committed to the hospital for determination of his competency to be tried on a pending charge. There are cases, including our own, which have enunciated standards for determining a hospital's negligence in other circumstances. See, for example, *Lucy Webb Hayes National Training School* v. *Perotti,* 136 U.S.App. D.C. 122, 419 F.2d 704 (1969); *Washington Hospital Center* v. *Butler,* 127 U.S.App.D.C. 379, 384 F.2d 331 (D.C.Cir. 1967); *Underwood* v. *United States,* 356 F.2d 92 (5th Cir. 1966). And numerous cases cited to us have involved problems of actionable negligence of physicians alleged to have led to injury to patients.

A very recent case is *Tarasoff* v. *Regents of the University of California,* 13 Cal.3d 177, 118 Cal.Rptr. 129, 529 P.2d 553 (1974), rehearing granted March 12, 1975.[8] There is also the recent case of Homere v. State, 361 N.Y.S.2d 820 (1974). The Court of Claims of New York there approved the rule that a hospital is not liable under the state tort claims act for "an honest error of professional judgment", *Id.* at 823; but the court held the state was liable for injuries inflicted on two persons by a psychiatric patient whose release from a state hospital was due to the negligent failure of the hospital to reconvene, in the special circumstances of the case, including a history of violence, a three-psychiatrist "commission" to reevaluate the patient's condition before his release. *Id.* at 824.

The basic standard to govern our decision on the issue of negligence is well-settled, and may be stated as requiring "that degree of care which a reasonably prudent person would have exercised under the same or similar circumstances." *Washington Hospital Center* v. *Butler, supra,* 384 F.2d at 335.[9] And see, *Tarasoff* v. *Regents of the University of California, supra.*

Fair v. *United States,* 234 F.2d 288 (5th Cir. 1956), involved liability under the Tort Claims Act for alleged negligence in the release of an Air Force officer from a base hospital which resulted in three homicides. The court, in reversing the dismissal of the complaint, referred to the applicable standard as stated by the Supreme Court in *Schulz* v. *Pennsylvania Railroad Co.,* 350 U.S. 523, 525, 76 S.Ct. 608, 100 L.Ed. 668 (1956):

> In considering the scope of the issues entrusted to juries in cases like this, it must be borne in mind that negligence cannot be established by direct, precise evidence such as can be used to show that a piece of ground is or is not an acre. Surveyors can measure an acre. But measuring negligence is different. The definitions of negligence are not definitions at all, strictly speaking. Usually one discussing the subject will say that negligence consists of doing that which a person of reasonable prudence would not have done, or of failing to do that which a person of reasonable prudence would have done under like circumstances. Issues of negligence, therefore, call for the exercise of common sense and sound judgment under the circumstances of particular cases.

[8] When a "hospital has notice or knowledge of facts from which it might reasonably be concluded that a patient would be likely to harm himself *or others* unless preclusive measures were taken, then the hospital must use reasonable care in the circumstances to prevent such harm." (*Vistica* v. *Presbyterian Hospital* (1967), 67 Cal.2d 465, 469, 62 Cal.Rptr. 577, 580, 432 P.2d 193, 196.) (Emphasis added.) A mental hospital may be liable if it negligently permits the escape or release of a dangerous patient (*Underwood* v. *United States* (5th Cir. 1966), 356 F.2d 92; *Fair* v. *United States* (5th Cir. 1956), 234 F.2d 288).
118 Cal.Rptr. at 134, 529 P.2d at 558, n.8.

[9] Our present case was not tried on the theory that negligence is to be determined on the basis of expert opinion as to reasonable prudence, *see,* Lucy Webb Hayes National Training School v. Perotti, *supra,* 419 F.2d at 710–711; *Washington Hospital Center* v. *Butler, supra,* 384 F.2d at 336.

234 F.2d at 295.

The standard to be applied, however, must take into consideration the uncertainty which accompanies psychiatric analysis. In that area, as we have suggested, negligence may not ordinarily be found short of serious error or mistake, and not necessarily when the error or mistake is serious. The concept of "due care" in appraising psychiatric problems, assuming proper procedures are followed, must take account of the difficulty often inevitable in definitive diagnosis. Nevertheless, applying the standard we have indicated as applicable, we approve the District Court's finding of negligence, as we shall more fully explain. To hold otherwise in light of the certainty of the Hospital's advice to the court that Morgan had recovered, would run counter to that degree of uncertainty, to which we have referred, in psychiatric evaluation and analysis.

2. On the basis of the record reviewed as above to the extent deemed requisite for passing upon the issue, Judge Curran found negligence in the Hospital's "failure to transmit adequate information to the court concerning the patient's mental condition." 357 F.Supp. at 439.[10]

The evidence at trial demonstrated that the Hospital knew that Morgan had been found by the District of Columbia General Hospital to suffer from a "moderately severe organic brain syndrome," "actual brain damage." There was also testimony of a doctor at the Hospital, pointed to by Judge Curran, that the Hospital's own findings did not really differ from the advice given to the court by the District of Columbia General Hospital.

The Hospital's Clinical Record entries of October 21, 1966, had stated: "[P]atient's family can definitely not be used as a community resource as they are afraid of him." The psychological tests of Morgan reported in the October 25, 1966, "Psychological Summary," as we have noted, contained a conclusion, under the label "General Impression," that outstanding in the results of the test "is organic brain damage . . ." The Psychiatric Case Study of October 26, 1966, records, "patient's wife called the police . . . [Morgan] had threatened to kill her . . . the eighth time . . . arrested for similar reasons." The October 27, 1966, report referred to the psychological tests as follows:

> Psychological testing revealed marked evidence of organicity. . . .
>
> . . . Those who know him best feel that he is ready soon to return to Court for trial.
>
> Acute Brain Syndrome Associated with Alcoholic Intoxication. (Recovered).
> . . . Mentally competent to stand trial.
>
> Condition on Discharge: Recovered.

Soon thereafter, on December 19, 1966, the Hospital reported to the Court of General Sessions the opinion of the physicians,

> that Mr. Morgan has recovered from his mental disorder, Acute Brain Syndrome Associated With Alcohol Intoxication. . . . [t]here is indication that he was suffering

[10] Additional rulings of the judge respecting negligence are set forth, *supra,* 167 U.S.App.D.C. p. 175, 511 F.2d p. 413.

> from a mental disorder on or around July 9, 1966, [the date of the assault was July 7] from which he has now recovered. . . .

For the full text of this report see, 167 U.S.App.D.C. p. 174, 511 F.2d p. 412, *supra*.

Upon Morgan's release January 30, 1967, followed by the homicide on March 26, 1967, in turn followed by the indictment and commitment to St. Elizabeths, this time by the District Court, ample evidence accumulated to give support to the District Court's finding on the whole evidence that the Hospital's report to the court had been so inadequate as to justify characterizing it as negligent. Any doubt that the standard of care appropriate to the circumstances was not met is removed by testimony growing out of the recommitment of Morgan to the Hospital after he had killed his wife, as he had threatened to do. The United States urges, however, that this later change in the position of the doctors was due to a change in Morgan's condition rather than that the chronic condition had existed when the letter that he had recovered was sent to the court under date of December 19, 1966. But the trial court on all the evidence reasonably concluded otherwise. The evidence supports the court's conclusion that the chronic condition the doctors later agreed upon, as represented by their testimony after the homicide, reflected Morgan's actual condition at the earlier period. Moreover, the testimony at trial that the psychological tests, referred to in the October 25 report, which showed organic brain damage due to the effects of a long history of alcohol consumption, could refer to either an acute or a chronic condition, the former being the way it was described by the Hospital to the Court of General Sessions, does not persuade us that the report was informative enough to avoid considering it to be the consequence of negligence. It gave no indication whatever of uncertainty as to his condition, justified by the Hospital record, or the danger to his wife should he be released.

The trial court was not required in finding negligence to go so far as to find, as it did, that the Hospital knew of the underlying chronic condition. It is sufficient that in the exercise of due care in the circumstances it should at least have indicated uncertainty. The inadequacy of the report appears also from its complete omission to inform the court with greater detail of his mental condition as a basis for guidance to the court, including some reference to the special orientation of his condition toward danger to his wife should he be released.[11] The evidence in sum called for something more than a definite characterization of his condition as having been only acute, and recovered. At trial the doctor who in the interim had become Superintendent of the Hospital testified that when the report to the court in December, 1966, that he had recovered was made, if Morgan had continued to suffer from a brain injury and the Hospital knew he posed a danger to his wife, it surely should have been in the report. He felt, however, that the

[11]The allegations made by Mrs. Morgan in her affidavit are referred to several times in the Hospital record. Her statement reads:

> Husband came home after drinking and assaulted me by kicking me in the back choked me and beating me in head with fists. I managed to escape him from the house and he stated "get you black ass out of here" and if I came back he would "murder" me and if he finds me anywhere he'll kill me on the spot. He has been acting this way for the past five or six months and has got to the point where he drinks constantly and has not worked for the past week. I have nine children the oldest is 19 and youngest four and he uses foul language in front of them constantly. I have been in fear to return home ever since Thursday and have been living with friends. I was here in the U. S. Attorney's office last week and have been here in past months. I have had him arrested before for drunkeness and fighting before.

We have outlined heretofore in this opinion the continuity of his attitude toward and threats to his wife while at St. Elizabeths.

report was adequate on competency since it advised the court of the basis for that finding, quite a different matter.

There can be no serious question, in our analysis of the situation, that the Hospital was advising the court, for its use and the use of those officials responsible for participating in the proceedings, that his stay at the Hospital was no longer desirable from any standpoint—he was discharged by the Hospital as recovered. There was no indication that, being competent to stand trial, there was any other matter to be considered with respect to his mental condition. The report thus went beyond a report on competency to stand trial.

The earlier report to the court by the District of Columbia General Hospital, which became part of the records of St. Elizabeths reflected the connection between his abusive treatment of Mrs. Morgan and his mental condition. And we have referred to the testimony regarding a family visit to Mr. Morgan at St. Elizabeths, which disclosed his continued threats to his wife and her fear for herself should he be released. The numerous Hospital records accumulated during his months there make clear the relationship between his long, excessive use of alcohol and his mental condition associated with his threats and physical abuse of his wife. There was thus imposed upon the institution a duty to carry out its public responsibility so as to reflect these circumstances.[12]

We have referred several times to the statement in the report of the Hospital to the Court of General Sessions that Mr. Morgan was recovered, and we have related that statement to the issue of negligence. We desire to emphasize, however, that our position on that issue does not depend upon the communication of that particular conclusion to the court. The shortcomings of the Hospital resided also in its failure to inform the court fully enough to enable it to pass intelligently upon whatever conclusion the Hospital might have reached. Even had the Hospital advised the court only that Mr. Morgan was competent to be tried, acceptance by the court of that conclusion would have led to the same consequences, hereinafter described in Part IV, as followed from the report submitted. The information in possession of the Hospital about Mr. Morgan's condition imposed upon it an obligation, in reporting to the court on his competency, to communicate a review of that information, including reference to his dangerousness to others, particularly his wife. The obligation so to do arose from the important function of the Hospital to aid the court and the prosecutorial officers in arriving at a course of action on their part protective of society.

A jury would have been justified in finding negligence. Though such a finding by a judge as trier of the facts, as here, may not be equated altogether with that of a jury, it

[12] The statement that there is or is not a duty begs the essential question—whether the plaintiff's interests are entitled to legal protection against the defendant's conduct. It is therefore not surprising to find that the problem of duty is as broad as the whole law of negligence, and that no universal test for it ever has been formulated. It is a shorthand statement of a conclusion, rather than an aid to analysis in itself. It is embedded far too firmly in our law to be discarded, and no satisfactory substitute for it, by which the defendant's responsibility may be limited, has been devised. But it should be recognized that "duty" is not sacrosanct in itself, but only an expression of the sum total of those considerations of policy which lead the law to say that the particular plaintiff is entitled to protection.

There is little analysis of the problem of duty in the courts. Frequently it is dealt with in terms of what is called "proximate cause," usually with resulting confusion. In such cases, the question of what is "proximate" and that of duty are fundamentally the same: whether the interests of the plaintiff are to be protected against the particular invasion by the defendant's conduct. (Footnotes omitted).

Prosser, Law of Torts, ch. 9, pp. 325-26 (4th ed. 1971).

is entitled to weight at our hands. Our consideration of the record leads us to no different conclusion.

The trial judge also found negligence in the failure of the Hospital to follow its own standards of care concerning the diagnosis of the patient. In light of what we have held, it is not necessary to consider this aspect of the case.

IV
The Question of Proximate Cause

Liability for compensation for injury alleged to have been caused by negligence follows only if it is proven that the negligence was a proximate cause of the injury. An intervening cause which is independent of the negligence absolves the defending negligent actor of liability. The standard to guide the fact-finder is no stricter now than when stated by the Supreme Court in *Milwaukee and St. Paul Railway Co.* v. *Kellogg,* 94 U.S. 469, 474–75, 24 L.Ed. 256 (1896):

> The true rule is, that what is the proximate cause of an injury is ordinarily a question for the jury. It is not a question of science or of legal knowledge. It is to be determined as a fact, in view of the circumstances of fact attending it. The primary cause may be the proximate cause of a disaster, though it may operate through successive instruments, as an article at the end of a chain may be moved by a force applied to the other end, that force being the proximate cause of the movement, or as in the oft-cited case of the squib thrown in the marketplace. 2 Bl. Rep. 892. The question always is, Was there an unbroken connection between the wrongful act and the injury, a continuous operation? Did the facts constitute a continuous succession of events, so linked together as to make a natural whole, or was there some new and independent cause intervening between the wrong and the injury? It is admitted that the rule is difficult of application. But it is generally held, that, in order to warrant a finding that negligence, or an act not amounting to wanton wrong, is the proximate cause of an injury, it must appear that the injury was the natural and probable consequence of the negligence or wrongful act, and that it ought to have been foreseen in the light of the attending circumstances.

Of special relevance to an aspect of our case is the Restatement of Torts, § 448 (1965), p. 480:

> The act of a third person in committing an intentional tort or crime is a superseding cause of harm to another resulting therefrom although the actor's negligent conduct created a situation which afforded an opportunity to the third person to commit such a tort or crime, unless the actor at the time of his negligent conduct realized or should have realized the likelihood that such a situation might be created, and that a third person might avail himself of the opportunity to commit such a tort or crime.

See *Underwood* v. *United States,* 356 F.2d 92, 99 (5th Cir. 1966) as an application of this position.

Moreover,

> . . . where it is evident that the influence of the actor's negligence is still a substantial factor, mere lapse of time, no matter how long, is not sufficient to prevent it from being the legal cause of the other's harm.

Restatement of Torts, § 433, comment on Clause (c) at p. 434 (1965).

Nor is liability avoided because a causative negligence may concur with another of like character.

> The rule is settled by innumerable authorities that if injury be caused by the concurring negligence of the defendant and a third person, the defendant is liable to the same extent as though it had been caused by his negligence alone.

Miller v. *Union Pacific R. Co.,* 290 U.S. 227, 236, 54 S.Ct. 172, 174, 78 L.Ed. 285 (1933).

> Injury consequent upon the concurring negligence of two or more persons subjects each to liability . . . "It is no defense for a wrongdoer that a third party shared the guilt of the same wrongful act, nor can he escape liability for the damages he has caused on the ground that the wrongful act of a third party contributed to the injury." *Miller* v. *Union Pac. R.R.,* 290 U.S. 227, 236, 54 S.Ct. 172, 174, 78 L.Ed. 285 (1933). . . .

Washington Hospital Center v. *Butler, supra,* 384 F.2d at 339 n. 29. And see, *Hanna* v. *Fletcher,* 97 U.S.App.D.C. 310, 231 F.2d 469 (1956), cert. denied, sub nom. *Guchner Iron Works, Inc.* v. *Hanna,* 351 U.S. 989, 76 S.Ct. 1051, 100 L.Ed. 1501 (1956), with its special discussion also as to the responsibility of the jury in determining proximate cause.

What we have said in Part III goes a way to indicate our answer to the question of proximate cause. Mr. Morgan's release upon entry of the nolle prosequi was a natural consequence of the position of the Hospital conveyed to the court. That position contained no information which might have led the court to follow a course other than release. None of the factors in his history known to the Hospital, indicative of a possibly chronic or other unstable mental condition was suggested to the court. No mention was made of the close connection between his brain syndrome, his excessive use of alcohol, and his threats to kill his wife.

The unqualified report that Morgan was recovered is shown by the evidence as a whole to have been seriously mistaken, and to have resulted from a lack of the care required of the Hospital. A careful appraisal communicated to the court, though it included the opinion that Morgan was competent to be tried, would not have stated unqualifiedly that he had recovered; it would have embodied a significantly fuller account of his condition, with some reference to the connection between his condition and the danger to his wife if he were at liberty. The absence of a report of this or comparable character must be considered to have been a substantial factor leading to his release. The effect was to close the door as it were to steps by either, or both, court and prosecution looking to his return to the Hospital as incompetent to stand trial, or for further observation and treatment, or leading either, or both, court and prosecution to initiate steps toward civil commitment. Had an adequate report been formulated based on his history known to the Hospital the institution itself no doubt would not have discharged him as recovered, even though competent to stand trial. It would have awaited consideration of the situation by the court. Certainty that any one or more of the courses we have mentioned would have been followed is not required to be established in order to find against the Hospital on negligence as a cause of the release of Mr. Morgan. As this court held in *Christie* v. *Callahan,* 75 U.S.App.D.C. 133, 124 F.2d 825 (1941), on an issue of proximate cause related to injury allegedly due to negligence in radiation treatment by a hospital,

> there is no requirement that the circumstances, to justify the inferences sought, negative every other positive or possible conclusion. The law is not so exacting that it requires proof of negligence or causation by testimony so clear that it excludes every other speculative theory. (Footnotes omitted.)

Id. at 840.

We accordingly accept as adequately supported by the evidence the conclusion of the District Court that the negligence of the Hospital was a substantial factor which contributed to the release of Mr. Morgan, as part of the continuing course of events which link the negligence of the Hospital to the death of Mrs. Morgan as a proximate cause of it.

The consequences of the release, as they developed, were foreseeable. Morgan promptly resumed his drinking. This triggered the pattern of the past, ending now fatally for his wife.[13] The homicide of course was a wrongful act intervening between his release and the death, but the fact that he would again attack his wife was foreseeable, even that he might do so with fatal consequences. The homicide was closely related to the very reason he had been committed originally to the Hospital—one of many drunken assaults upon his wife. The brain syndrome from which he suffered, due to his heavy drinking for many years, had been accompanied by recurring physical assaults upon her, not free of threats to her life. These were known manifestations of the mental condition which brought him to the Hospital. His release led to drink which activated the brain damage from which he suffered. The homicide was the consequence, or so in reason could it be found. The tragic culmination did not occur for 56 days after his release, during 20 days of which, however, he was in confinement or under public care because of his alcoholic affliction, which was a part of the foreseeable pattern. The lapse of time is of no controlling legal significance. It introduced no foreign or unforeseeable factor as an unrelated and independent cause of the tragedy, for the Hospital "at the time of [its] negligent conduct realized or should have realized the likelihood that such a situation might be created . . . ," with the result which followed. Restatement of Torts, § 448, *supra*. That the result was fatal to his wife did not break the chain of causation.

Affirmed.

TAMM, Circuit Judge, concurring with whom MCGOWAN, Circuit Judge, joins:

I concur in Judge Fahy's well reasoned opinion. Specifically, I agree that since proximate causation is a question of fact, the scope of our review is limited to determining whether the trial judge's finding of proximate causation was clearly erroneous. I believe that Judge Fahy amply demonstrates that Judge Curran's finding was not clearly erroneous. I also agree that under the statutory scheme St. Elizabeth's Hospital owes a duty to the courts to disclose information in its possession that would undermine or cast doubt on its diagnosis, as well as to divulge facts consonant with that diagnosis. However, in considering Judge Fahy's opinion, I became concerned with the relationship between the hospital's obligation of disclosure and its duty of reasonable care in making its diagnosis. I therefore take this opportunity to set forth what I believe to be the relationship between the two, and how their interaction affects the hospital's liability.

[13]At the uncontested trial for murder a physician on the staff of the Hospital testified that the connection between Mr. Morgan's condition and the murder was pretty clear cut: "It was not merely the fact that he had been drinking, but alcohol, in the case of a brain damaged individual, impairs his judgment and his restraint and his capacity to restrain himself. And all of this had—I think it was pretty clearly related to this condition which I referred to as chronic brain syndrome."

It is obvious that the courts cannot make informed judgments concerning the necessity or desirability of civil commitment proceedings without the expert guidance of the staff of institutions such as St. Elizabeth's. Nevertheless, the commitment decision is a legal, rather than a medical one; the court must convert medical findings and opinions into legal conclusions having the profoundest effect on an individual's liberty. The court cannot intelligently fulfill its responsibility unless it knows of facts that are dissonant to the hospital's diagnosis as well as those facts that are consonant to it.

While this duty is owed to the courts, appellees are logical persons to enforce it. Unless persons injured by the hospital's failure to properly perform its functions can recover for their injury, society's ability to insure that the hospital conscientiously performs its duties is rendered haphazard at best.

However, private enforcement of the duty of disclosure is not a panacea, for, as I perceive our holding, the potential range of recovery for breach of the hospital's duty of disclosure is narrowly confined. Initially, recovery in the case *sub judice* must be predicated upon the fact that the hospital's diagnosis was incorrect even if it were not negligent. As Judge Curran pointed out: "There is no explanation how Morgan could have become incompetent from his drinking during three weeks of freedom and the subsequent diagnosis of chronic brain syndrome associated with alcohol associated with behavioral reaction." *Hicks* v. *United States,* 357 F.Supp. 434, 439 (D.D. C.1973). If the original diagnosis, "acute brain syndrome associated with alcohol—recovered," had been correct, I fail to see how there would be a causal connection between the hosiital's conduct and the homicide. Unfortunately, acts of violence are constantly commited for reasons that are not associated with mental dysfunction as we know it, and this case would then fall into this category.

Moreover, the hospital can discharge its obligation, even if its diagnosis is incorrect, by disclosing information in its possession that could reasonably aid the court in carrying out its sunctions. I do not suggest, nor do I believe that my brethren suggest, that the hospital alter its normal diagnostic procedures out of fear that it will be charged with the failure to disclose information that would have been discovered had the hospital performed further tests. Such problems remain in the realm of the reasonableness of the diagnostic procedures, where the judgments of the institution and its staff6 must be given great deference. *See Drope* v. *Missouri,* 420 U.S. 162, 95 S.Ct. 896, 43 L.Ed.2d 103 (1975). I am certain that the courts in this jurisdiction will be diligent in insuring that issues involving negligence in diagnosis or treatment are not confused with negligent disclosure.

Finally, I agree with Judge Fahy that the trial judge's finding of negligence cannot be set aside. The negligence issue is one that is submitted to the trier of fact and we do not approach the issue *de novo.* On this record, it was reasonable for the trial judge to find that the hospital breached its duty in failing to disclose information of recognized importance.

Locality rule. In a bygone era the question courts would ask in attempting to establish the applicable standard was, "How would the ordinary practitioner with the same or similar training, *in the same or similar community,* have acted under the same or similar circumstances?" The italicized portion of his hypothetical question has effectively been deleted in most jurisdictions. Referred to as the "locality rule," the notion here was that rural practitioners did not have the same opportunities for postgraduate education and training as urban practitioners and tended to see different types of problems; it was therefore unreasonable to hold the rural practitioner to the same standard of care as the urban practitioner. For years the courts invoked this "locality rule," especially with respect to physicians who were general practitioners. Physicians who held themselves out as specialists tended to be held to the same standard as other specialists throughout the country. With the advent of faster transportation, the proliferation of professional journals, and opportunities for exposure to myriad sources of postgraduate education, rural practitioners cannot make the same claims that they once did. Further, the widespread availability of medicines and "miracle drugs" has had the effect of "equalizing" the kinds of treatment (and diseases) found from locality to locality. The result has been that the locality rule has become less and less a factor in determinations as to the applicable standard of care. Still, it is an issue that is in some quarters hotly debated. A sharply divided Arkansas Supreme Court wrote in 1975 that modern avenues of communication had obviated the need for a locality rule in that state. Just one year later the court reversed itself, opining in part as follows:

> We are not convinced that we have reached the time when the same postgraduate medical education, research, and experience is equally available to all physicians, regardless of the community in which they practice. The opportunities for doctors in small towns, of which we have many, to leave a demanding practice to attend seminars and regional medical meetings cannot be the same as those for doctors practicing in clinics in larger centers. It goes without saying that the physicians in these small towns do not and cannot have the clinical and hospital facilities available in the larger cities where there are large, modern hospitals, and medical centers or the same advantage of observing others who have been trained, or have developed expertise, in the use of new skills, facilities and procedures, of consulting and exchanging views with specialists, other practitioners and drug experts, of utilizing closed circuit television, special radio networks or of studying in extensive medical libraries found in larger centers.

The case of *Hirshberg* v. *State,* 91 Misc.2d 590, 398 N.Y.S.2d 470 (Ct.Cl. 1977), which appears below, is illustrative of the courts' dissatisfaction with, and in this case rejection of, the locality rule.

Hirshberg v. *State,* 91 Misc.2d 590, 398 N.Y.S.2d 470 (Ct.Cl. 1977)

ROBERT J. MANGUM, J. This claim seeks damages for the wrongful death, pain and suffering of claimant's intestate (hereinafter "decedent"). A reading of the papers before the court indicates proper compliance with this court's rules respecting the filing of claims.

On November 15, 1973 at 10 o'clock in the morning decedent is alleged to have swallowed 100 aspirin. Thereafter, at about 2:00 P.M. he attempted suicide by jumping in front of a school bus. The driver of the vehicle took decedent to the Monticello police. After contacting decedent's psychiatrist, who was an employee of the State, they were advised to take decedent to the Monticello Community Hospital. While there, decedent received no medical treatment because the two doctors on call were unavailable and a third physician could not be reached. The nurse did report to the psychiatrist that decedent's vital signs appeared within normal limits. No query was made regarding what kind of examination had been conducted at that time.

Decedent was then brought to his psychiatrist's office located in a county mental health clinic. He arrived about 3:40 in the afternoon. While there, a superficial examination revealed some symptomatology of aspirin toxicity, or salicylate poisoning. A rapid pulse rate and complaints of nausea and ringing in the ears were noted. This doctor, however, did not believe decedent ingested the quantity of aspirin claimed. No other tests were taken to remove any ambiguity observed by the symptoms, i.e., blood pressure, respiration. Recognizing his clinic did not possess the necessary facilities to care for decedent, the doctor decided to transport him to Middletown State Hospital. While en route decedent vomited. They arrived at the hospital between the hours of 4:30 and 5:00 that afternoon.

The admission application attached to decedent's Middletown State Hospital record describes his having taken aspirin. It is conspicuous, however, in the absence of any recommended course of treatment, omitting to describe what care decedent had received for the consumption of the aspirin, and the failure to list any physical symptoms and complaints. In a report prepared on January 8, 1974, following decedent's death, this same physician, decedent's psychiatrist, claimed he had reviewed decedent's history and symptomatology with the nursing supervisor upon admission. He stated he advised the nurse that decedent should receive only clear fluids.

This physician recognized that his clinic was designed only for treatment of mental disorders and that other community medical facilities had to be relied upon for medical assistance and somatic therapy.

The decedent was admitted to Middletown Hospital at about 5:30 in the afternoon. The admitting physician did not conduct a physical examination because the patient had come into the hospital after the normal time for such procedure. His examination before trial reveals the following colloquy.

Q. Did the doctor tell you what was done to clear the patient at the hospital (Monticello)?
A. No, he didn't tell me. I didn't ask. I took it for granted, when he told me everything is okay.
Q. Did he tell you any steps had been taken with respect to the removal of any aspirin or the contents of his stomach?
A. No.
Q. Did you ask him?
A. I didn't.
Q. Did the doctor use the words he was cleared by Monticello hospital?
A. He told me he was in Monticello hospital.
Q. Is it that he told you the patient was merely at the hospital or did he tell you that the hospital had cleared him?
A. I don't remember now. I know that he said that he was in the hospital and I didn't ask any questions.
Q. Do you recall any other discussion with (the doctor)?
A. No, nothing.

Later in the same examination this admitting physician claimed he did not see any signs of intoxication. Though no tests were performed, he was relying on the fact that the patient was in the general hospital and had been seen by his colleague.

The admitting doctor was only licensed to practice medicine in the Republic of Yugoslavia. He was not licensed to practice medicine within the State of New York. While at Middletown State Hospital he was participating in a psychiatric residency program.

Bearing in mind all of the foregoing, this unlicensed physician placed decedent on suicide alert and prescribed 100 milligrams of thorazine. He did not advise the medical staff on duty to notify him of any irregular reaction to the medication or to observe for other signs of toxicity. Consequently, he was not informed decedent vomited 10 minutes after receiving the medicine at 7 o'clock.

Decedent expired at about 11 P.M. on the evening of his admission. An autopsy conducted the next day at the hospital determined the cause of death as salicylate poisoning and, among other findings, aspiration of stomach contents into lungs. "An analysis of the blood serum drawn at the time of autopsy revealed a salicylate level of 202 mgs%."

A physician is required to possess that reasonable degree of learning and skill that is possessed by the average member of the medical profession. He has a duty to exercise ordinary and reasonable care in the application of such professional knowledge and skill. In addition, the physician must use his best judgment in the application of that knowledge and skill. The foregoing propositions represent the "three component duties" that form the basic theory of medical malpractice.

The rule does not hold a physician "liable for a mere error of judgment, provided he does what he thinks is best after careful examination." (*Pike* v. *Honsinger,* 155 NY 201, 210.) In the usual case, proof of the absence of these duties is dependent upon the testimony of experts. The underlying reason is that the subject matter to be inquired about may be presumed to be outside the common knowledge and experience of ordinary jurors and the inferences and facts are of such a nature as to require special knowledge or skill. An expert witness is not necessary in every case. This is particularly evident where the conditions are "of such a character as to warrant the inference of want of care from the testimony of laymen or in the light of the knowledge and experience of the jurors themselves." (*Benson* v. *Dean,* 232 NY 52, 56; *Meiselman* v. *Crown Hgts. Hosp.,* 285 NY 389; *Cassano* v. *Hagstrom,* 5 NY2d 643, 649, dissenting opn.)

Where expert opinion is not necessary recovery may be permitted on a theory of simple negligence. In those circumstances the trier of fact measures liability upon the reasonable man doctrine.

The facts of this case are punctuated with evidence of malpractice, negligence and a want of the exercise of any reasonable judgment.

The attending or admitting physician was not licensed to practice medicine within the State of New York. At the time of administering to decedent he apparently was seeking to qualify as a psychiatrist pursuant to the authority vested in the Commissioner of Mental Hygiene. (Mental Hygiene Law, § 13.25.) This law permits the commissioner to certify a New York State licensed physician as a qualified psychiatrist provided he holds either acceptable professional recognition or meets certain requirements referred to as "Standards of equivalency." (14 NYCRR 2.1, 2.2.) Since this doctor was without such certification or other licensed qualification in this State, he did not possess the skill or professional judgment to " 'essentially unsupervised, provide ordinary and reasonable psychiatric medical treatment and care to this decedent.' " (*Cohen* v. *State of New York,* 51 AD2d 494, 495–496.)

Moreover, no informed judgment was ever made after careful examination. As previously discussed, the attending physician did not conduct more than a cursory examination because of the lateness of the hour of admission. He prescribed medication of a dangerous nature about which the potential side effects of shock and irregularity of heart beat (*Brown* v. *State of New York,* 56 AD2d 672, affd 42 NY2d 959) must be presumed to have been known. Instead of guarding against reasonably foreseeable risks and hazards (*Excelsior Ins. Co. of N. Y.* v. *State of New York,* 296 NY 40) the attending physician ignored the warning of others and the available signs of toxicity. Even when decedent vomited after receiving the thorazine, no one was instructed or exercised the good judgment of notifying the physician who ordered the medication.

The failure to have examined decedent more thoroughly upon admission, the absence of any attention to the available history (*O'Neil* v. *State of New York,* 66 Misc 2d 936), prescribing drugs when only fluids were ordered by a qualified physician (*Taylor* v. *State of New York,* Claim No. 59390, filed July 26, 1977), omitting to report decedent's reaction to the medication, failure to call a specialist on internal medicine (*Meiselman* v. *Crown Hgts. Hosp.,* 285 NY 389, *supra*), the lack of concern for any precautions and the baseless assumption that others had effectively tended to the salicylate poisoning, warrant a finding of mindless professional care and treatment, tantamount to gross negligence.

Since the wrong is hardly "'an honest error of professional judgment made by qualified and competent persons' (*St. George* v. *State of New York,* 283 App. Div. 245, 248, affd. 308 N.Y. 681), the State cannot seek refuge behind the veil that generally protects a doctor's medical judgment." (*O'Neil* v. *State of New York, supra,* p 940.)

Here the psychiatrists, involved in this case, recognized their own lack of sophistication concerning internal medicine and the need for a specialist. Notwithstanding, none were consulted. If a practitioner has reason to doubt, and under circumstances should doubt his competence and experience to handle a particular case, good judgment dictates the consulting of those more knowledgeable (*Benson* v. *Dean,* 232 NY 52, 59, *supra*) or as indicated here, conducting appropriate blood tests to determine the level of aspirin poisoning.

In *Pike* v. *Honsinger* (155 NY 201, *supra*) decided in 1898, the Court of Appeals established that the medical care, skill and diligence required of a physician was determined by the standards of the community in which he practiced. The "locality rule" represented the favored malpractice doctrine in jurisdictions throughout the country at the time.* The rule had its genesis in the generally accepted theory that doctors in small communities lacked the same opportunities and resources to keep abreast as other members of their profession situated in large urban medical centers. Parenthetically, the professional competency of members of the legal profession has never been measured by a similar consideration.

Since, over the past 80 years, the medical profession has enjoyed numerous technological advances, more universal training experience expanded means of obtaining knowledge without regard to geographic considerations, re-evaluation of the rule is not without merit.

The locality rule has always had two practical difficulties: (1) scarcity of professional people in a community who were either qualified or willing to testify about local

*Curiously, England has apparently never adopted the locality rule. (*Pederson* v. *Dumouchel,* 72 Wn 2d 73, 79; cf. Nathan, Medical Negligence [Butterworth & Co., Ltd., 1957], p. 21.)

standards; (2) giving effect to a local standard of care below that which is generally found acceptable. "Negligence cannot be excused on the ground that others in the same locality practice the same kind of negligence." (*Pederson* v. *Dumouchel, supra,* p 78.) The impreciseness of the rule may also be gleaned from the following observation: "[i]f a physician fails to employ his expertise or best judgment, and that omission causes injury, he should not automatically be freed from liability because in fact he adhered to acceptable practice. There is no policy reason why a physician, who knows or believes there are unnecessary dangers in the community practice, should not be required to take whatever precautionary measures he deems appropriate." (*Toth* v. *Community Hosp. at Glen Cove,* 22 NY2d 255, 263.)

An expanding number of jurisdictions are permitting "medical witnesses from localities other than that in which the defendant practices to testify, in a malpractice case, to the standard of care that the defendant should have observed." (Ann. 37 ALR3d 424, Malpractice-Care-Nonlocal Testimony, § 2 [a].) In some States the archaic locality rule has been broadened to include "similar communities." This test, however, while less confining does not eradicate all the disadvantages inherent in the local community standard. The potentially careless and improper standard adopted by physicians of a particular community is still an issue.

Today, "there is no lack of opportunity for a physician or surgeon to keep abreast of the advances made in his profession and to be familiar with the latest methods and practices adopted." (*Pederson* v. *Dumouchel, supra,* p 78.) The "distinctions based on geography are no longer valid in view of modern developments in transportation, communication and medical education, all of which tend to promote a certain degree of standardization within the profession." (*Brune* v. *Belinkoff,* 354 Mass 102, 105.) Rural areas are not primitive societies too distant in time and place to take advantage of advanced learning. Neither do medical schools provide different degrees of instruction dependent upon where one intends to practice his specialty.

In this State there are appellate cases in which an emphasis has been on a general standard, free of any locality considerations. Citing from *Pike* v. *Honsinger* (155 NY 201, *supra*) the Appellate Division, First Department, omitted any reference to locality when it stated a physician "promises by implication to use the skill and learning of the average physician" (*Stone* v. *Goodman,* 241 App Div 290, 295). Again, in a decision recently affirmed by the Court of Appeals the Appellate Division, Third Department, enumerated the "three component duties" of a physician without any reference to a locality requirement. (*Hale* v. *State of New York,* 53 AD2d 1025, *supra.*)

A change in the locality rule would not require doctors to employ the best method considered by others so long as "a method which is accepted by respectable medical authority is adopted." (*Gielskie* v. *State of New York,* 10 AD2d 471, 474, affd 9 NY2d 834; *Schreiber* v. *Cestari,* 40 AD2d 1025, 1026.)

The more progressive principle adopted in sister States places the emphasis upon professional proficiency rather than geographical proximity. Unsuited as the locality rule is to present day conditions, this court respectfully urges, and will in this case adopt, acceptance of a rule promulgated by other jurisdictions. A qualified medical practitioner should be subject to liability, in a malpractice action, if he fails to exercise that degree of care and skill expected of the average practitioner in the class to which he belongs, having regard for the circumstances under which he must act, the advances of his profession and the medical resources reasonably available. (*Carbone* v. *Warburton,* 11 NJ 418; *Pederson* v. *Dumouchel,* 72 Wn 2d 73, 79; *Brune* v. *Belinkoff,* 354 Mass 102, 109.) Of course the financial resources and territorial expanse of an area as well as its population density and patient's particular requirements will always have a bearing in determining the skill and care required.

The rigid locality rule of the 19th century, however, should give way to a principle consonant with the realities of contemporary medical knowledge and practice. No greater justification exists for the abandonment of the local community test than in cases involving the State of New York. The State administers dozens of hospitals throughout our territorial limits. It does not practice medicine according to the different standards established in each of the communities in which it has a facility. In this context the community standard is addressed to a policy of State-wide import developed by the State's own regulations and statutory requirements.

Claimant's expert was qualified to testify in this case for the purpose of informing the court of the acceptable standard of medical care that, under the circumstances, should have been utilized. Gastric lavage, administering of fluids and blood test are some nondrastic procedures that could have been employed. A thorough physical examination to check and monitor heart beat, blood pressure and respiratory functions was necessary to determine whether the aspirin poisoning had subsided or increased. The immediate reporting of any violent reaction from the thorazine to the physician in charge was another standard of acceptable care omitted. Further, prescribing thorazine in the first instance, a central nervous system depressant, was contraindicated.

The autopsy report verified death resulting from aspirin poisoning. Considering the time period involved, the procedures available for treatment, and the apparent symptoms that should have given rise to alarm in the professionally tutored, the State's failure to evaluate more thoroughly, treat or render any medical care, together with the administering of thorazine, effectively precluded decedent from recovering from the poisoning. Judged by a fair preponderance of the credible evidence, it is reasonably certain that even the most conservative measures taken at an early hour would have saved decedent's life.

"Even where symptoms are capable of several interpretations, normal and prudent medical procedure would dictate the use of available tests and an extensive examination, which not only could have clarified the ambiguities, but detected that which was ascertainable and frustrated the otherwise natural consequences of the negligence." (*O'Neil* v. *State of New York,* 66 Misc 2d 936, 944, *supra.*)

In evaluating damages there was no evidence, other than mild discomfort, of any pain. Decedent's potential for employment appeared to be limited to nonstress situations with little social interaction. The evidence revealed decedent had previous emotional conflicts requiring the assistance of professional attention. At the time of his death decedent was an unemployed, unmarried 27-year-old male, with a life expectancy of 43.8 years. Offers of employment from previous applications were received following his death. There was some evidence he worked part time for Western Union. Funeral expenses, together with all burial costs, aggregated $2,328. Bearing in mind all of the foregoing, together with decedent's emotional problems, educational and vocational experiences, the court awards claimant $35,000, plus interest to be computed from the date of decedent's death, November 15, 1973, to the date of entry of judgment.

Motions made by counsel for defendant at the close of claimant's case and at the end of the entire trial to dismiss the claim, upon which the court reserved decision, are denied.

Best judgment rule. Practitioners are legally required to possess the education and expertise that could reasonably be expected from the ordinary member of the profession. They are further required to use reasonable and ordinary care in the application of professional expertise. There is also the requirement that they use their best judgment in the application of professional expertise. The courts have consistently held that practitioners are not insurers of good results and that an error in judgment does not constitute malpractice, if the proper standard of care was followed. This principle and its application is illustrated below in *Belk* v. *Schweizer,* 268 N.C. 50, 149 S.E.2d 565 (1966) and in *Spadaccini* v. *Dolan,* 63 App.Div.2d 110, 407 N.Y.S.2d 840 (1978). The *Belk* case also speaks to the issue of the higher standard of care that is required of those professionals who hold themselves out to the public as specialists. Specialists will be held to the higher standard of the ordinary practitioner in the field.

Belk v. *Schweizer,* 268 N.C. 50, 149 S.E.2d 565 (1966)

PARKER, C.J. This is a summary of the allegations of fact in the complaint: Defendant, Dr. Donald C. Schweizer, is a practicing physician in the city of Greensboro, and holds himself out to be a specialist in the field of obstetrics and gynecology. Plaintiff, Joan E. Belk, a young married woman, visited defendant in his office on 19 May 1959 for medical services. At that time defendant, performing routine services for plaintiff, discovered she had a small ulcer at the mouth of her womb, and he treated her for this condition. On 9 November 1959 she went to defendant's office and explained to him that her last menstrual date was 4 August 1959. On 18 November 1959 she started a vaginal bleeding and called the defendant. Defendant was out of town on this occasion, and she was treated by his assistant. On 23 November 1959 plaintiff saw defendant in his office, and explained to him that she had been bleeding for approximately twelve days, had suffered great pain, was swollen, and had a temperature. On 27 November 1959 she was examined by defendant, at which time she was still bleeding. On 1 December 1959 she returned to defendant's office, and explained to him that she had had chills and fever the night before, was bleeding heavily and passing clots, was having severe cramps and pain, and was swollen. On 1 December 1959 defendant hospitalized her for an operation known as a D and C. (It was stipulated that a D and C is a dilatation and curettage.) She inquired of defendant as to the possibility of her having a tubular pregnancy. Defendant ran certain laboratory tests and told her that it could not be a tubular pregnancy. She remained in the hospital from 1 December 1959 to 3 December 1959. On 5 December 1959 she contacted defendant by telephone, stating to him that she had a temperature, was experiencing great pain in her back and side, was bleeding extensively, was swollen, and her complexion was discolored. The defendant did not come to see her nor did he request her to come to his office nor go to the hospital. From the symptoms given to him on the telephone, without seeing her, he diagnosed her illness as a kidney infection and proceeded to prescribe medicine for a kidney infection. Plaintiff's husband on several occasions asked defendant what should be done for plaintiff, and defendant said he would hospitalize her if her husband thought it necessary. During this period defendant prescribed a large amount of the narcotic Demerol to relieve her pain. On 7 December 1959 she contacted another physician in Greensboro, Dr. Francis Berry, who came to see her, advised her she was in a very serious condition, and told her to return the next day to defendant. Plaintiff returned the following day to see the defendant, who attempted manually to examine her for a pelvic mass, but due to the pain this caused her, he was unable to make a successful examination. Defendant told her on this occasion that he did not know what was wrong with her, and to feel free to call another physician. Her condition became progressively worse, and she had a high temperature and was still bleeding. She contacted Dr. Francis Berry. She was placed in a hospital and was operated on by Dr. Berry for a ruptured tubular pregnancy. She remained in the hospital for twelve days.

Since that time she has been treated continuously by physicians and surgeons as a result of the negligence of defendant in failing to diagnose her illness as being caused by a tubular pregnancy. She avers and believes that if the tubular pregnancy had been diagnosed in apt time that these operations and expenses would not have been necessary.

The complaint alleges in substance that defendant was negligent in the following respects: (1) At all times complained of defendant did not possess the degree of professional learning, skill and ability which other physicians similarly situated ordinarily possessed, and he failed to exercise reasonable care and diligence in his application of his knowledge and skill to plaintiff's case; (2) he failed and neglected to use proper methods in his treatment of plaintiff from 9 November 1959 to 9 December 1959; (3) in examining plaintiff he did not use the care and methods used by physicians engaged in medical practice in Greensboro, and he negligently failed to correctly diagnose her condition; (4) he diagnosed plaintiff's illness as a kidney infection without seeing her, from a telephone examination; (5) he failed and refused to visit with plaintiff or to hospitalize her at a time when he knew or in the exercise of reasonable diligence should have known that her condition was serious and required immediate attention; (6) he was negligent in failing to notify plaintiff that the treatment which he was giving her had failed and to initiate other treatments and to attempt other diagnosis; (7) in the exercise of reasonable diligence he should have discovered that plaintiff had a tubular pregnaniy and should have treated her for the same; (8) he was negligent in that he failed to hospitalize plaintiff and perform an exploratory operation in order to properly diagnose her condition, particularly in view of the fact that he was unable to examine her manually due to the fact that she was in a swollen condition and suffering extreme pain; (9) defendant knew or should have known that tubular pregnancy was very serious, would undoubtedly rupture and cause severe consequences to plaintiff, but nevertheless he treated plaintiff conservatively while not ruling out the possibility that plaintiff had a tubular pregnancy; and (10) other allegations of negligence of a similar nature.

Defendant in his answer admits that he saw plaintiff on the occasions alleged in her complaint, but he denies that he was guilty of negligence in any respect.

The parties offered evidence in support of the allegations of fact in their pleadings.

The deposition of Dr. Lonis L. Schurter, consisting of 36 pages in the record, was read to the jury by plaintiff. Plaintiff has no other medical evidence, except that it read to the jury an adverse examination of defendant. Defendant offered in his behalf the testimony of six doctors, which appears in the record on pages 134 through 345.

Plaintiff assigns as error the part of the charge of the court to the jury appearing in parentheses:

> In response to a hypothetical question regarding the failure of Dr. Schweizer to do a culdoscopy or a cul-de-sac puncture on Mrs. Belk at the time of the D & C and while she was under anesthetic, Dr. Schurter stated that he had an opinion satisfactory to himself as to whether the treatment and examination was in accordance

with approved medical practices in the community of Greensboro. (His answer is difficult of comprehension generally, because he does not say that he thinks at this stage a culdoscopic examination—no, his answer is difficult of comprehension generally, but he does say that he thinks at this stage a culdoscopic examination would be diagnostic, and that is the virtue, is the diagnostic examination.)

Plaintiff further assigns as error the following part of the judge's charge:

The defendant further contends that the evidence of Dr. Schurter, introduced by the plaintiff, is the evidence of a doctor who has never practiced in the specialty of obstetrics and gynecology exclusively; that Dr. Schurter's opinions are vague and indefinite; . . .

Even if we concede that the second part of the charge challenged by plaintiff was a statement of a contention of the defendant rather than the expression of the statement of an opinion by the judge as to the credibility of Dr. Schurter's testimony, still it would seem that the statement of the court that Dr. Schurter's testimony was difficult of comprehension could be construed by the jury as a statement of an opinion by the court that Dr. Schurter's testimony in this respect was so confused and vague that it had little probative value, and that such expression of opinion by the court of Dr. Schurter's testimony was highly prejudicial, if not utterly disastrous, to plaintiff's case, particularly when Dr. Schurter was plaintiff's only medical witness other than the adverse examination of defendant, and was in many respects plaintiff's principal witness.

G.S. 1-180 reads: "No judge, in giving a charge to the petit jury, either in a civil or criminal action, shall give an opinion whether a fact is fully or sufficiently proven, that being the true office and province of the jury, but he shall declare and explain the law arising on the evidence given in the case. . . ." Moore, J., speaking for the Court, said in *Upchurch* v. *Funeral Home,* 263 N.C. 560, 140 S.E. 2d 17: "The slightest intimation from the judge as to the weight, importance or effect of the evidence has great weight with the jury, and, therefore, we must be careful to see that neither party is unduly prejudiced by any expression from the bench which is likely to prevent a fair and impartial trial."

The court in its charge may not intimate or express an opinion as to the facts, the weight of the evidence, or the credibility of the witnesses, either directly or indirectly, in any manner, and if the judge does intimate or express such an opinion, it is prejudicial. 4 Strong's N. C. Index, Trial § 35.

"The law imposes on the trial judge the duty of absolute impartiality. The expression of an opinion by the trial court on an issue of fact to be submitted to a jury, being prohibited by statute, is a legal error." *Nowell* v. *Neal,* 249 N.C. 516, 107 S.E. 2d 107.

In *S.* v. *Benton,* 226 N.C. 745, 40 S.E. 2d 617, the court instructed the jury, "The evidence as testified to by the witnesses has been rather clear." The Court held that under the circumstances of the case the expression, "The evidence as testified to by the witnesses has been rather clear," must have been understood by the jury to have referred to the State's witnesses, and not defendant's, and was held for error as an expression of an opinion by the court upon the weight of the evidence. In *S.* v. *Horne,* 171 N.C. 787, 88 S.E. 433, the Court in its charge to the jury stated: "The State calls your attention to the fact that Dr. Stovall gave an admirably lucid account of what he conceived to be and his opinion of the mental condition of the defendant." The Court held that this expression was well calculated to weigh heavily against defendant, and awarded a new trial. In *S.* v. *Bryant,* 189 N.C. 112, 126 S.E. 107, the court made the following statement: "This witness has the weakest voice or the shortest memory of any witness I ever saw." The Court held that this expression of opinion entitled defendant to a new trial. As to other cases involving prejudicial comments on witnesses by the trial judge, see: *Sneed* v. *Greath,* 8 N.C. 309; *Noland* v. *McCracken,* 18 N.C. 594; *McRae* v. *Lawrence,* 75 N.C. 289; *S.* v. *Rogers,* 173 N.C. 755, 91 S.E. 854.

Defendant makes these contentions: The burden of proof is on the appellant not only to show error but to show that he was prejudiced to the extent that the verdict of the jury was thereby probably influenced against him. *Freeman* v. *Preddy,* 237 N.C. 734, 76 S.E. 2d 159. The Court said in *Freeman* v. *Preddy, supra:*

> In applying this rule, we have consistently held that when, upon a consideration of the whole record, it clearly appears that the appellant, under no aspect of the testimony, is entitled to recover and that the evidence considered in the light most favorable to him is such that the trial judge would have been fully justified in giving a peremptory instruction, or directing a verdict, against him on the determinative issue or issues, any error committed during the trial will be deemed harmless. [Citing authority.]

Higgins, J., in a clear and accurate statement of the law as to the duties a physician owes his patient, said for the Court in *Hunt* v. *Bradshaw,* 242 N.C. 517, 88 S.E. 2d 762:

> A physician or surgeon who undertakes to render professional services must meet these requirements: (1) He must possess the degree of professional learning, skill and ability which others similarly situated ordinarily possess; (2) he must exercise reasonable care and diligence in the application of his knowledge and skill to the patient's case; and (3) he must use his best judgment in the treatment and care of his patient. [Citing authority.] If the physician or surgeon lives up to the foregoing requirements he is not civilly liable for the consequences. If he fails in any one particular, and such failure is the proximate cause of injury and damage, he is liable.

A physician, who holds himself out as having special knowledge and skill in the treatment of a particular organ or disease, is required to bring to the discharge of his duty to a patient employing him as such specialist, not merely the average degree of skill possessed by general practitioners, but that special degree of skill and knowledge which physicians similarly situated who devote special study and attention to the treatment of such organ or disease ordinarily possess regard being had to the state of scientific knowledge at the time. 70 C.J.S., Physicians and Surgeons, p. 949.

A qualified physician or surgeon does not guarantee or insure the correctness of his diagnosis, and ordinarily he is not responsible for a mistake in diagnosis if he uses the requisite degree of skill and care. Generally stated, a qualified physician or surgeon is not liable for an honest error or mistake in judgment if he applies ordinary and reasonable skill and care, keeps within recognized and approved methods, and forms his judgment after a careful and proper examination or investigation. He is not charged with the duty of omniscience, and ordinarily is not an insurer. In order to afford a basis for an action for malpractice, the want of skill or care must be a proximate cause of the injury or death of the patient. 70 C.J.S., Physicians and Surgeons, § 48, a, c, d, e.

This case presents for review very difficult questions of medicine and of law. A very large part of the evidence in the case consists of the nature and characteristics of tubular pregnancy, the medical problem presented thereby, the treatment rendered to plaintiff by defendant, and as to whether the methods used are or are not generally approved and recognized in the profession in the Greensboro area or in similar localities.

Plaintiff alleged in her complaint "that at all times herein complained of, the defendant did not possess the degree of professional learning, skill and ability which other physicians similarly situated, ordinarily possessed." Plaintiff introduced no evidence in support of this allegation in her complaint.

In applying the rule quoted from *Freeman* v. *Preddy, supra,* it cannot be said, in our opinion, after a careful examination of all the evidence in the light most favorable to plaintiff, and particularly plaintiff's evidence tending to show the care, treatment, and lack of attention given her by defendant who held himself out as an expert in the field of obstetrics and gynecology, that plaintiff under no aspect of the evidence is entitled to recover.

For error in the charge, plaintiff is entitled to a

New trial.

Spadaccini v. *Dolan*, 63 App.Div.2d 110, 407 N.Y.S.2d 840 (1978)

FEIN, J.

Defendants Westchester Square Hospital and Doctors Sherman, Di Salvo and Nisi appeal from a judgment entered after trial on a jury verdict in favor of plaintiff in this action to recover damages for the wrongful death of Santo Spadaccini and for the conscious pain and suffering allegedly endured by him during the period he lingered in the hospital prior to his death on April 19, 1970. The jury returned a verdict in favor of plaintiff on the cause of action for wrongful death in the sum of $350,000, apportioned 80% against the doctors and 20% against the hospital and, on the cause of action for conscious pain and suffering, in the sum of $25,000 against the doctors and $25,000 against the hospital.

On this appeal, defendant doctors assign as error the failure of the Trial Justice to instruct the jury that mere error of judgment is not malpractice particularly after having advised counsel, at the conference held prior to closing statements pursuant to CPLR 4110-b, that the court would charge the jury in substance that defendant doctors were required to exercise reasonable care in the care and treatment of decedent, but could not be held liable for mere error of judgment. It is undisputed that no instruction was given to the effect that the doctors could not be held liable for mere error of judgment. The doctors contend they were entitled to such a charge on the facts of this case. They assert that in any event reversal is required because the court deviated in this respect from the commitment made to counsel prior to closing statements.

Defendant hospital contends that (1) the proof against it was insufficient for submission to the jury; and (2) plaintiff failed to make out a prima facie case. All defendants further claim that (1) the verdict in both the death action and the survival action for conscious pain and suffering was excessive; (2) the jury's apportionment was improper; and (3) the judgment entered in the sum of $50,000 on the cause of action for conscious pain and suffering, 50% against the doctors and 50% against the hospital was improper in view of the jury's 80%-20% apportionment on the wrongful death cause. Defendants also claim that the verdict for pain and suffering was in the total sum of $25,000 and that even in that amount, it was excessive.

Essentially this is a case where the decedent received successful surgical treatment, but allegedly died as a result of improper attention and treatment following surgery.

For several days decedent complained of a swelling of the tongue and pain in the mouth. He was referred to Westchester Square Hospital by Dr. Procario, a general practitioner, who called in Dr. Sherman, a head, neck and plastic surgery specialist. Dr. Sherman diagnosed the condition as Ludwig's Angina and advised that immediate surgery was required. In diagnosing the condition as Ludwig's Angina, Dr. Sherman noted a severe infection, evidenced by marked swelling under the chin and marked edema of the floor of the mouth. The condition is usually caused by a dental infection which can spread from the bottom front of the mouth in toward the back of the tongue and, if not treated, can cause swelling on the outside of the neck. Primary treatment is administration of antibiotics and/or surgery.

Subsequent to decedent's admission, Dr. Sherman performed the operation on March 27, 1970, consisting of an incision and drainage through the neck to the floor of the mouth. Following the operation, decedent was placed in a private room to insure necessary isolation precautions because of the severe infection. Dr. Sherman had ordered that a tracheotomy set be placed in the room in the event of any upper respiratory difficulty. Decedent was not placed in an intensive care unit, nor does it appear that there was an intensive care unit in the hospital, other than a coronary care unit for treatment of coronary patients. Although certain precautions were taken, the private room in which decedent was confined was admittedly not made the equivalent of an intensive care unit (ICU). It did not have the equipment normally found in such a unit. Nor did it have an ICU nurse or doctor constantly present in the event of an emergency. Although decedent did have a private room with a private duty nurse, this was not the equivalent of ICU confinement.

Subsequent to the operation, decedent developed pneumonia in the left lung, at which point Dr. Procario called in Dr. Nisi and his partner, Dr. Di Salvo, internists. They rendered medical treatment to decedent during the postoperative period. None of the doctors ordered a tracheotomy either during the operation or during the postoperative period, a procedure which even defendants' expert, Dr. Cohen, testified "should always be considered in a case of Ludwig's Angina in order to prevent respiratory distress." Plaintiff's expert, Dr. Greene, also testified to the necessity of a tracheotomy to assure the protection of the patient's airway where there is a threat of respiratory obstruction. Indeed the presence of a tracheotomy set in decedent's room indicated some awareness by all of the treating physicians as to the possible or potential need to administer a tracheotomy.

Plaintiff's primary claim of negligence against the doctors was their failure to order an elective prophylactic tracheotomy or a tracheotomy during the postoperative period and their failure to insure that decedent was placed in an intensive care unit or the equivalent. The sufficiency and the adequacy of the medical treatment accorded decedent was clearly a question for resolution by the jury.

As to defendant hospital, plaintiff's allegation of negligence concerned the manner in which the hospital reacted when decedent went into respiratory arrest and a code 54 was announced throughout the hospital. Code 54 is an emergency code indicating that a patient is in immediate danger of death. It indicates that the patient is in distress and needs immediate resuscitation and emergency treatment. The evidence was sufficient for a finding that there was a delay of some 15 minutes between the time the code 54 was issued and the time a doctor responded thereto.

The evidence was adequate to present a jury question as to whether defendant hospital and its staff timely responded to the emergency code. According to the proof, decedent began choking and turning blue at 7:55 P.M. The code 54 was not called until

8:00 P.M. and a tracheotomy was not begun until at least 8:15 P.M. We find the evidence sufficient to present a question for the jury whether the delay in responding after the code 54 call was turned in conformed to proper and accepted medical practice and was a proximate cause of the death. The hospital entries leave much to be desired. Even assuming the accuracy of the hospital record, there appears to have been at least a 15-minute delay during which Mr. Spadaccini went into cardiac arrest and sustained the irreversible brain damage which led to his death some 21 days later on April 19, 1970. The proof was sufficient for a jury to find that the hospital did not timely respond to the code 54. On the basis of the evidence, it cannot be ruled as a matter of law, as the hospital apparently contends on this appeal, that by the time the code 54 was sounded or within a minute thereafter irreversible brain damage already existed, which the hospital was powerless to prevent. These were questions for the jury, which by its verdict resolved them against the hospital.

The primary legal issue raised by the doctors is the sufficiency of the trial court's charge to the jury and its refusal to charge "error of judgment," in the face of the court's advice to counsel prior to summation that it would in substance instruct the jury as to the applicable malpractice principles announced by the Court of Appeals in *Pike* v. *Honsinger* (155 NY 201), embodied in PJI 2:150, including the "error of judgment" charge. Defendants contend that the refusal of the court to charge as indicated violated the statute (CPLR 4110-b), since it prejudiced counsel who tailored his closing statement to the substance of what he anticipated would be contained in the charge to the jury. Defendants further claim that it was error not to instruct the jury as to "error of judgment," which defendants claim is a standard instruction in any malpractice case and required in this case.

We disagree. The court's refusal to use the "error of judgment" language was proper. Such a charge under the facts here presented would have been unwarranted. We further conclude that no prejudice resulted to defendant doctors. They have failed to demonstrate that they were misled to their prejudice at the conference held with the court at which the court advised the respective parties of "proposed action" which would be taken with respect to requests to charge which had been submitted (CPLR 4110-b).

The law applicable in medical malpractice cases was succinctly set forth in *Pike* v. *Honsinger* (*supra,* pp 209–210): "The law relating to malpractice is simple and well settled, although not always easy of application. A physician and surgeon, by taking charge of a case, impliedly represents that he possesses, and the law placed upon him the duty of possessing, that reasonable degree of learning-and skill that is ordinarily possessed by physicians and surgeons in the locality where he practices, and which is ordinarily regarded by those conversant with the employment as necessary to qualify him to engage in the business of practicing medicine and surgery. Upon consenting to treat a patient, it becomes his duty to use reasonable care and diligence in the exercise of his skill and the application of his learning to accomplish the purpose for which he was employed. He is under the further obligation to use his best judgment in exercising his skill and applying his knowledge. The law holds him liable for an injury to his patient resulting from want of the requisite knowledge and skill, or the omission to exercise reasonable care, or the failure to use his best judgment. The rule in relation to learning and skill does not require the surgeon to possess that extraordinary learning and skill which belong only to a few men of rare endowments, but such as is possessed by the average member of the medical profession in good standing. Still, he is bound to keep abreast of the times, and a departure from approved methods in general use, if it injures the patient, will render him liable, however good his intentions may have been. The rule of reasonable care and diligence does not require the exercise of the highest possible degree of care, and to render a physician and surgeon liable, it is not enough that there has been a less degree of care than some other medical man might have shown, or less than even he himself might have bestowed, but there must be a want of ordinary and reasonable care, leading to a bad result. . . . The rule requiring him to use his best judgment does not hold him liable for mere error of judgment, provided he does what he thinks is best after careful examination. His implied engagement with his patient does not guarantee a good result, but he promises by implication to use the skill and learning of the average physician, to exercise reasonable care and to exert his best judgment in the effort to bring about a good result. [Citing cases.]''

Toth v. *Community Hosp. at Glen Cove* (22 NY2d 255) recognized that a specialist should be held to the degree of care and treatment expected of specialists in the community where he practices. That case served to differentiate between the degree of care to which a specialist is held as opposed to that to which a general practitioner is held, by giving cognizance to the superior knowledge, skill and intelligence of the specialist in treatment rendered to patients in the area of his specialty. The substantive law set forth in these two cases was adopted in the formulation of the standard instruction set forth in the New York Pattern Jury Instructions (PJI 2:150). However, as observed by the trial court in this case, the Pattern Jury instructions are only intended as a guide to the Trial Justice. There may be situations where, as here, portions of what is recommended in Pattern Jury Instructions need not or should not be charged. As the instructions themselves advise it is the Trial Justice's primary responsibility to instruct the jury on the applicable law in the case. It is also the responsibility of attorneys in representing their clients at the trial, to submit requests to charge which are warranted by the actual evidence and the relevant law so that a meaningful discussion may be had between counsel and the court as to the applicable law in relation to the proof adduced.

Here, in a conference held at the close of the evidence in accordance with CPLR 4110-b, defendant doctors requested that the court charge as follows: ''18. If you find that there was an error of judgment made by any of the defendants—the court is not suggesting that there was or was not—you are not to infer or to attribute negligence from such mere error of judgment since the standard of care required of a physician allows for errors of judgment reasonably to be expected in the context of the circumstances in which doctor or doctors operated and treated.'' No basis was shown for such a charge. However, in conjunction with this request, the Trial Justice restated the *Pike* v. *Honsinger* (155 NY 201, *supra*) standard as follows: ''What you're talking about is the rule in performing a medical service the doctor's [*sic*] obligated to use his best judgment, to use reasonable care in exercise of his knowledge and ability. The rule requiring him to use his best judgment does not make him liable for a mere error of judgment provided he does what he thinks is best after careful consideration. The rule of reasonable care does not require every possible degree of care; it requires only that he exercise that degree of care that a reasonable prudent doctor—or we can name the specialist—would exercise under the similar circumstances.'' The court further stated: ''If that's your request, in substance, that's what I will charge.'' Plaintiff's attorney had no objection and defendants' attorney responded that such a charge would be satisfactory.

When the Trial Justice delivered his instructions to the jury, he did not use the ''mere error of judgment'' language. However he did properly charge the rule of reasonable care.

He instructed the jury as follows: "By undertaking to perform a medical service he does not, nor does the law require him to guarantee a good result. He is liable only for negligence or, as I said, as it's sometimes called, malpractice, the terms are used interchangeably in connection with the doctor. A doctor who renders a medical service is obligated to have that reasonable degree of knowledge and ability that is expected of specialists who do that particular operation or treatment in the community where he practices, and that's the City of New York. The law recognizes that there are differences in the ability of doctors, just as there are in the ability of people engaged in other activities. To practice his profession, a doctor is not required to be possessed of the extraordinary knowledge and ability that belongs to a few men in rare endowments, but he is required to keep abreast of the times and to practice in accordance with the approved methods and means of treatment in general use or, as has been stated in the course of this trial, in accordance with medically accepted standards and practices in the community. The standard to which he is held is measured by the degree of knowledge and ability of the average surgeon or internist in good standing in the community where he practices. If a patient should die while undergoing medical care and that death results from the doctor's lack of knowledge or ability, or his failure to exercise reasonable care, which means the failure to comply with or conform with the medically accepted standards and practices in his community, then he is responsible for the deaths [*sic*] that is a result of his acts and in this respect, you are to decide the issues as I set them forth as to the malpractice or the negligence of the doctors."

The court also charged "proximate cause." The court, however, did not use the following language from *Pike* v. *Honsinger* (*supra,* p 210), which is also set forth in PJI 2:150: "The rule requiring him to use his best judgment does not hold him liable for a mere error of judgment, provided he does what he thinks is best after careful examination." Defendants claim that such a charge is standard and must be given in every malpractice case. The contention however, lacks merit. Each case must stand or fall on its own facts. With few exceptions, it cannot be said that any particular legal standard must be charged in every conceivable case. If the facts do not require a particular instruction a Trial Justice should not give it. Merely because a particular instruction is generally given in a particular type of case and is included in the standard PJI instruction and comes from a leading case does not require it in every case of that genre. The court's instruction on the law, is, rather, to be molded by the applicable facts.

Pike v. *Honsinger* (155 NY 201, *supra*) sets forth two applicable standards of care to be applied in malpractice cases. The first, which was correctly charged here, holds the doctor to the standard of care measured by the knowledge and ability of the average physician or specialist in good standing in the community where he practices. This is the standard of reasonable care. Liability is premised upon the failure to exercise reasonable care, so measured. A doctor is also subject to a separate duty which requires him to use his best judgment, but which does not make him liable for a mere error of judgment, provided he does what he thinks is best after careful examination. This latter instruction was not given in this case. Nor, on the facts presented, would it have been appropriate for the court to so charge the jury. An error of judgment charge is appropriate in a case where a doctor is confronted with several alternatives and, in determining appropriate treatment to be rendered, exercises his judgment by following one course of action in lieu of another. That is not the situation here.

Here, the evidence was sufficient for a jury to find that one of three preventative measures should have been taken in the treatment rendered to Mr. Spadaccini in order to avoid or guard against the consequences of respiratory arrest: (1) placement of the patient in an intensive care unit (ICU) or his confinement in the equivalent of an ICU setup, including a nurse trained in ICU procedures and full equipment necessary to be employed where a patient is under intensive care supervision; or (2) a prophylactic, preventative elective tracheotomy; or (3) a tracheotomy in the postoperative period to assure proper respiration. Except for the jury issue as to whether the unit used was sufficient, the doctors took none of these measures. This is undisputed. Hence there was no issue to submit to the jury as to whether defendant doctors exercised their best judgment in electing to proceed with one course of treatment in lieu of another. Rather, the facts raised in issue and the court properly submitted for disposition by the jury whether the conduct of defendants in failing to follow any of these procedures conformed to accepted standards of medical care, the standard of reasonable care charged by the court. The "error of judgment" charge implies the exercise of some judgment in choosing from among two or more available alternatives. Where a physician is confronted with alternate means of treatment and elects to follow none of the alternatives, it is unnecessary to charge error of judgment, since the issue is preserved by the required charge as to whether the doctor exercised the degree of care a reasonably prudent doctor or specialist would have exercised under the same circumstances.

This is clearly demonstrated by the procedure utilized by the Trial Justice. He submitted a verdict sheet to the jury on which the jury reported its verdict in pertinent part, as follows: "2. In accordance with my charge was Dr. Sherman negligent in treating the decedent, in any or all of the following respects:

"a. without a prophylactic, preventative or elective tracheotomy Yes X No ______

"b. without placing decedent in an Intensive Care unit or its equivalent? Yes X No ______

"c. without a tracheotomy in the post-operative period (3/27–2/29) Yes X No ______". The jury's answers are significant. They were not misled.

In the course of his charge describing the verdict sheet the Trial Justice carefully, clearly and properly charged the jury that they were to determine with respect to each of these questions whether the doctors were negligent in failing to perform the tracheotomy or to put the decedent in an intensive care unit or its equivalent. He instructed the jury they were to determine their answers based upon the evidence and the standard of reasonable care he had charged. The jury was charged that it was to determine as to each alternative whether the failure to utilize it was negligence. This is all defendants were entitled to by way of jury instructions. To the extent that error of judgment is appropriate to this case it was implicit in the charge as given and the verdict sheet. The jury was plainly and clearly and properly advised of the standard by which to determine whether the failure of the doctors to adopt any of these alternatives was or was not negligence. This is all that the "error of judgment" words could properly cover. The failure to use them was not error.

Nor is it conceivable that counsel was misled. We do not have the benefit of the summations, which were not transcribed, but it is obvious competent counsel would and undoubtedly did discuss these alternatives and ground his argument on the contention that the decision not to adopt any of them was not negligence because it did not deviate from the reasonable care standard measured by the skill, learning, care and judgment of physicians and surgeons practicing in the community.

. . . .

It is fairly clear that the jury's verdict on the conscious pain and suffering claim was in the amount of $25,000 against the hospital and $25,000 against the doctors. The total verdict on that cause, accordingly, was $50,000, apportioned 50% against the hospital and 50% against the doctors. The fact that the jury had apportioned damages for wrongful death at 80% against the doctors and 20% against the hospital is not dispositive and does not preclude a different apportionment on recoverable damages for conscious pain and suffering. Decedent lingered for a 21-day period prior to his death. However, we find the award of damages for pain and suffering in the amount of $50,000 to be excessive and would reduce the award on that cause of action to the sum of $25,000, which, under the circumstances of this case, should be apportioned in the same manner as the jury apportionment with respect to damages for wrongful death, i.e., 80% against defendant doctors and 20% against defendant hospital. Although defendants claim that decedent was in a coma during the 21-day period after the respiratory and cardiac arrest episode on March 29, 1970, there is sufficient evidence for a jury to have found that he was conscious during part of that period of time. Mrs. Spadaccini testified that she had visited her husband every day and on two occasions he opened his eyes and appeared to be crying. She also observed that he was trying to form words but was unable to do so. Under the circumstances, the record is sufficient to sustain the jury's finding of conscious pain and suffering, reduced to the extent directed.

. . . .

Accordingly the judgment, Supreme Court, Bronx County (David Levy, J.), entered April 13, 1977, should be reversed, on the law and on the facts, and the matter remanded for a new trial with costs to abide the event unless plaintiff stipulates to reduce the verdict to $200,000 as damages for wrongful death and $25,000 as damages for conscious pain and suffering, both damage awards to be apportioned on the basis of 80% against defendant doctors and 20% against defendant hospital, in which event the judgment, as so modified, should be affirmed, without costs.

. . . .

Lane and Sullivan, JJ., concur with Fein, J.; Sandler, J., concurs in result only; Silverman, J. P., dissents in part in an opinion.

Judgment, Supreme Court, Bronx County, entered on April 13, 1977, reversed, on the law and on the facts, and the matter remanded for a new trial, with $60 costs and discursements of this appeal to abide the event, unless plaintiff, within 20 days after service by appellants upon plaintiff a copy of the order of this court, with notice of entry thereof, stipulates to reduce the verdict to $200,000 as damages for wrongful death and $25,000 as damages for conscious pain and suffering, both damage awards to be apportioned on the basis of 80% against defendant doctors and 20% against defendant hospital, in which event the judgment, as so modified, is affirmed, without costs and without disbursements.

Judicial review of profession's standard of care. Customarily it is the profession and not the judiciary that sets the applicable standard of care. However, in the case of *Helling* v. *Carey,* 83 Wash.2d 514, 519 P.2d 981 (1974), which appears below, the court, in essence, set a new and higher standard for the profession. As detailed below, the court heard undisputed expert testimony attest to the fact that it was not customary and usual for ophthalmologists to routinely give a pressure test for glaucoma to patients under forty years of age. Yet if the patient, Barbara Helling (thirty-two years old at the time she had consulted opthalmologist Thomas Carey), had been given such a test and her condition had been properly diagnosed and treated, she would not have suffered the severe loss of vision that she did. The Supreme Court of Washington found the defendant ophthalmologist to be negligent as a matter of law for not performing the pressure test. In his majority opinion, Justice Hunter quoted from a decision handed down in *The Matter of T. J. Hooper,* 60 F2d 737 (1932):

> [A] whole calling may have unduly lagged in the adoption of new and available devices. . . . Courts must in the end say what is required; there are precautions so imperative that even their universal disregard will not excuse their omission.

This case presents an important reminder to professionals that if the standard set by their respective profession and professional organizations is deficient or not up to date enough or in other ways fails to meet their responsibility to and the needs of the citizenry, the courts are prepared to assign liability when called upon to do so.

Note that Justice Utter alluded in his opinion to the pressure test for glaucoma being harmless, reliable, and inexpensive. This assertion has not gone uncontested. Bradford (1974) has argued that the pressure test poses a risk of damage to the eye, that it does not always reliably indicate the existence of glaucoma, and it is inexpensive only if it were to be given alone. We might add that if it were given alone in the State of Washington the practitioner might well be liable for not performing other tests in combination. The point here is that the court treads on shaky ground once it begins to take it upon itself to set standards for the profession.

Generally, *Helling* has spurred no rash of similar standard-setting decisions. In one subsequent Washington case the court reiterated that the decision in *Helling* was a consequence of the unique fact situation presented (see *Meeks* v. *Max,* 550 P.2d 1158). In *Barton* v. *Owen,* 139 Cal.Rptr. 494, a California court voiced agreement with the principle in *Helling* that custom is not an absolute standard to be applied in determinations of negligence. Still, in the vast majority of the malpractice actions that come before the courts, the standards of the profession comprise the yardstick against which a professional's actions are judged. The case of *Hirshberg* v. *State* (p. 125) provides a clear example of a deviation from the applicable standard by a physician who had a license to practice medicine only in the Republic of Yugoslavia. Note that in *Hirshberg* the "acceptable practice" standard is applied, while in the case of *Baker* v. *United States* (p. 100) the locality rule is applied.

Helling v. *Carey,* 83 Wash.2d 514, 519 P.2d 981 (1974)

HUNTER, J.—This case arises from a malpractice action instituted by the plaintiff (petitioner), Barbara Helling.

The plaintiff suffers from primary open angle glaucoma. Primary open angle glaucoma is essentially a condition of the eye in which there is an interference in the ease with which the nourishing fluids can flow out of the eye. Such a condition results in pressure gradually rising above the normal level to such an extent that damage is produced to the optic nerve and its fibers with resultant loss in vision. The first loss usually occurs in the periphery of the field of vision. The disease usually has few symptoms and, in the absence of a pressure test, is often undetected until the damage has become extensive and irreversible.

The defendants (respondents), Dr. Thomas F. Carey and Dr. Robert C. Laughlin, are partners who practice the medical specialty of ophthalmology. Ophthalmology involves the diagnosis and treatment of defects and diseases of the eye.

The plaintiff first consulted the defendants for myopia, nearsightedness, in 1959. At that time she was fitted with contact lenses. She next consulted the defendants in September 1963, concerning irritation caused by the contact lenses. Additional consultations occurred in October 1963; February 1967; September 1967; October 1967; May 1968; July 1968; August 1968; September 1968; and October 1968. Until the October 1968 consultation, the defendants considered the plaintiff's visual problems to be related solely to complications associated with her contact lenses. On that occasion, the defendant, Dr. Carey, tested the plaintiff's eye pressure and field of vision for the first time. This test indicated that the plaintiff had glaucoma. The plaintiff, who was then 32 years of age, had essentially lost her peripheral vision and her central vision was reduced to approximately 5 degrees vertical by 10 degrees horizontal.

Thereafter, in August of 1969, after consulting other physicians, the plaintiff filed a complaint against the defendants alleging, among other things, that she sustained severe and permanent damage to her eyes as a proximate result of the defendants' negligence. During trial, the testimony of the medical experts for both the plaintiff and the defendants established that the standards of the profession for that specialty in the same or similar circumstances do not require routine pressure tests for glaucoma upon patients under 40 years of age. The reason the pressure test for glaucoma is not given as a regular practice to patients under the age of 40 is that the disease rarely occurs in this age group. Testimony indicated, however, that the standards of the profession do require pressure tests if the patient's complaints and symptoms reveal to the physician that glaucoma should be suspected.

The trial court entered judgment for the defendants following a defense verdict. The plaintiff thereupon appealed to the Court of Appeals, which affirmed the judgment of the trial court. *Helling* v. *Carey,* 8 Wn. App. 1005 (1973). The plaintiff then petitioned this court for review, which we granted.

In her petition for review, the plaintiff's primary contention is that under the facts of this case the trial judge erred in giving certain instructions to the jury and refusing her proposed instructions defining the standard of care which the law imposes upon an ophthalmologist. As a result, the plaintiff contends, in effect, that she was unable to argue her theory of the case to the jury that the standard of care for the specialty of ophthalmology was inadequate to protect the plaintiff from the incidence of glaucoma, and that the defendants, by reason of their special ability, knowledge and information, were negligent in failing to give the pressure test to the plaintiff at an earlier point in time which, if given, would have detected her condition and enabled the defendants to have averted the resulting substantial loss in her vision.

We find this to be a unique case. The testimony of the medical experts is undisputed concerning the standards of the profession for the specialty of ophthalmology. It is not a question in this case of the defendants having any greater special ability, knowledge and information than other ophthalmologists which would require the defendants to comply with a higher duty of care than "that degree of care and skill which is expected of the average practitioner in the class to which he belongs, acting in the same or similar circumstances.'' *Pederson* v. *Dumouchel,* 72 Wn.2d 73, 79, 431 P.2d 973 (1967). The issue is whether the defendants' compliance with the standard of the profession of ophthalmology, which does not require the giving of a routine pressure test to persons under 40 years of age, should insulate them from liability under the facts in this case where the plaintiff has lost a substantial amount of her vision due to the failure of the defendants to timely give the pressure test to the plaintiff.

The defendants argue that the standard of the profession, which does not require the giving of a routine pressure test to persons under the age of 40, is adequate to insulate the defendants from liability for negligence because the risk of glaucoma is so rare in this age group. The testimony of the defendant, Dr. Carey, however, is revealing as follows:

> Q. Now, when was it, actually, the first time any complaint was made to you by her of any field or visual field problem? A. Really, the first time that she really complained of a visual field problem was the August 30th date. [1968] Q. And how soon before the diagnosis was that? A. That was 30 days. We made it on October 1st. Q. And in your opinion, how long, as you now have the whole history and analysis and the diagnosis, how long had she had this glaucoma? A. I would think she probably had it ten years or longer. Q. Now, Doctor, there's been some reference to the matter of taking pressure checks of persons over 40. What is the incidence of glaucoma, the statistics, with persons under 40? A. In the instance of glaucoma under the age of 40, is less than 100 to one per cent. The younger you get, the less the incidence. It is thought to be in the neighborhood of one in 25,000 people or less. Q. How about the incidence of glaucoma in people over 40? A. Incidence of glaucoma over 40 gets into the two to three per cent category, and hence, that's where there is this great big difference and that's why the standards around the world has been to check pressures from 40 on.

The incidence of glaucoma in one out of 25,000 persons under the age of 40 may appear quite minimal. However, that one person, the plaintiff in this instance, is entitled to the same protection, as afforded persons over 40, essential for timely detection of the evidence of glaucoma where it can be arrested to avoid the grave and devastating result of this disease. The test is a simple pressure test, relatively inexpensive. There is no judgment factor involved, and there is no doubt that by giving the test the evidence of glaucoma can be detected. The giving of the test is harmless if the physical condition of the eye permits. The testimony indicates that although the condition of the plaintiff's eyes might have at times prevented the defendants from administering the pressure test, there is an absence of evidence in the record that the test could not have been timely given.

Justice Holmes stated in *Texas & P. Ry.* v. *Behymer,* 189 U.S. 468, 470, 47 L. Ed. 905, 23 S. Ct. 622 (1903):

> What usually is done may be evidence of what ought to be done, but what ought to be done is fixed by a standard of reasonable prudence, whether it usually is complied with or not.

In *The T.J. Hooper,* 60 F.2d 737 (2d Cir. 1932), Justice Hand stated on page 740:

> [I]n most cases reasonable prudence is in fact common prudence; but strictly it is never its measure; a whole calling may have unduly lagged in the adoption of new

> and available devices. It never may set its own tests, however persuasive be its usages. *Courts must in the end say what is required; there are precautions so imperative that even their universal disregard will not excuse their omission.*

(Italics ours.)

Under the facts of this case reasonable prudence required the timely giving of the pressure test to this plaintiff. The precaution of giving this test to detect the incidence of glaucoma to patients under 40 years of age is so imperative that irrespective of its disregard by the standards of the opthalmology profession, it is the duty of the courts to say what is required to protect patients under 40 from the damaging results of glaucoma.

We therefore hold, as a matter of law, that the reasonable standard that should have been followed under the undisputed facts of this case was the timely giving of this simple, harmless pressure test to this plaintiff and that, in failing to do so, the defendants were negligent, which proximately resulted in the blindness sustained by the plaintiff for which the defendants are liable.

There are no disputed facts to submit to the jury on the issue of the defendants' liability. Hence, a discussion of the plaintiff's proposed instructions would be inconsequential in view of our disposition of the case.

The judgment of the trial court and the decision of the Court of Appeals is reversed, and the case is remanded for a new trial on the issue of damages only.

HALE, C.J., and ROSELLINI, STAFFORD, WRIGHT, and BRACHTENBACH, JJ., concur.

UTTER, J. (concurring)—I concur in the result reached by the majority. I believe a greater duty of care could be imposed on the defendants than was established by their profession. The duty could be imposed when a disease, such as glaucoma, can be detected by a simple, well-known harmless test whose results are definitive and the disease can be successfully arrested by early detection, but where the effects of the disease are irreversible if undetected over a substantial period of time.

The difficulty with this approach is that we as judges, by using a negligence analysis, seem to be imposing a stigma of moral blame upon the doctors who, in this case, used all the precautions commonly prescribed by their profession in diagnosis and treatment. Lacking their training in this highly sophisticated profession, it seems illogical for this court to say they failed to exercise a reasonable standard of care. It seems to me we are, in reality, imposing liability, because, in choosing between an innocent plaintiff and a doctor, who acted reasonably according to his specialty but who could have prevented the full effects of this disease by administering a simple, harmless test and treatment, the plaintiff should not have to bear the risk of loss. As such, imposition of liability approaches that of strict liability.

Strict liability or liability without fault is not new to the law. Historically, it predates our concepts of fault or moral responsibility as a basis of the remedy. Wigmore, *Responsibility for Tortious Acts: Its History,* 7 Harv. L. Rev. 315, 383, 441 (1894). As noted in W. Prosser, *The Law of Torts* § 74 (3d ed. 1964) at pages 507, 508:

> There are many situations in which a careful person is held liable for an entirely reasonable mistake. . . . in some cases the defendant may be held liable, although he is not only charged with no moral wrongdoing, but has not even departed in any way from a reasonable standard of intent or care. . . . There is "a strong and

> growing tendency, where there is blame on neither side, to ask, in view of the exigencies of social justice, who can best bear the loss and hence to shift the loss by creating liability where there has been no fault.''

(Footnote omitted.) Tort law has continually been in a state of flux. It is ''not always neat and orderly. But this is not to say it is illogical. Its central logic is the logic that moves from premises—its objectives—that are only partly consistent, to conclusions—its rules—that serve each objective as well as may be while serving others too. It is the logic of maximizing service and minimizing disservice to multiple objectives.'' Keeton, *Is There a Place for Negligence in Modern Tort Law?,* 53 Va. L. Rev. 886, 897 (1967).

When types of problems rather than numbers of cases are examined, strict liability is applied more often than negligence as a principle which determines liability. Peck, *Negligence and Liability Without Fault in Tort Law,* 46 Wash. L. Rev. 225, 239 (1971). There are many similarities in this case to other cases of strict liability. Problems of proof have been a common feature in situations where strict liability is applied. Where events are not matters of common experience, a juror's ability to comprehend whether reasonable care has been followed diminishes. There are few areas as difficult for jurors to intelligently comprehend as the intricate questions of proof and standards in medical malpractice cases.

In applying strict liability there are many situations where it is imposed for conduct which can be defined with sufficient precision to insure that application of a strict liability principle will not produce miscarriages of justice in a substantial number of cases. If the activity involved is one which can be defined with sufficient precision, that definition can serve as an accounting unit to which the costs of the activity may be allocated with some certainty and precision. With this possible, strict liability serves a compensatory function in situations where the defendant is, through the use of insurance, the financially more responsible person. Peck, *Negligence and Liability Without Fault in Tort Law, supra* at 240-41.

If the standard of a reasonably prudent specialist is, in fact, inadequate to offer reasonable protection to the plaintiff, then liability can be imposed without fault. To do so under the narrow facts of this case does not offend my sense of justice. The pressure test to measure intraocular pressure with the Schiotz tonometer and the Goldman applanometer takes a short time, involves no damage to the patient, and consists of placing the instrument against the eyeball. An abnormally high pressure requires other tests which would either confirm or deny the existence of glaucoma. It is generally believed that from 5 to 10 years of detectable increased pressure must exist before there is permanent damage to the optic nerves.

Although the incidence of glaucoma in the age range of the plaintiff is approximately one in 25,000, this alone should not be enough to deny her a claim. Where its presence can be detected by a simple, well-known harmless test, where the results of the test are definitive, where the disease can be successfully arrested by early detection and where its effects are irreversible if undetected over a substantial period of time, liability should be imposed upon defendants even though they did not violate the standard existing within the profession of ophthalmology.

The failure of plaintiff to raise this theory at the trial and to propose instructions consistent with it should not deprive her of the right to resolve the case on this theory on appeal. Where this court has authoritatively stated the law, the parties are bound by those principles until they have been overruled. Acceptance of those principles at trial does not constitute a waiver or estop appellants from adapting their cause on appeal to such a rule as might be declared if the earlier precedent is overruled. *Samuelson* v. *Freeman,* 75 Wn.2d 894, 900, 454 P.2d 406 (1969).

FINLEY and HAMILTON, JJ., concur with UTTER, J.

Petition for rehearing denied July 31, 1974.

Expert testimony and the standard of care. Usually expert testimony is required to determine if the applicable standard of care was met. As stated in *Lawless* v. *Calaway,* 147 P.2d 604, "Ordinarily, a doctor's failure to possess or exercise the requisite learning or skill can be established only by the testimony of experts." Exceptions to this case include situations in which the court invokes the doctrine of *res ipsa loquitur* (see page 99 above) and the even rarer situation where the court takes it upon itself to define the standard (see the discussion of *Helling* v. *Carey* above). A third situation in which the need for expert testimony is obviated is that in which the court invokes the doctrine of common knowledge. The application of this doctrine is illustrated in *Steinke* v. *Bell,* 107 A.2d 825, wherein the defendant dentist had been sued for malpractice after extracting the wrong tooth. The court rejected the argument of the defense that the plaintiff could not recover unless expert testimony was introduced. The court opined that a jury was competent to determine the applicable standard:

> We think laymen, looking at this case in the light of their common knowledge and experience, can say that a dentist engaged to remove a lower left second molar is not acting with the care and skill normal to the average member of the profession if, in so doing, he extracts or causes to come out an upper right lateral incisor. Expert testimony was therefore not necessary under the circumstances of this case.

The distinction between the doctrine of common knowledge and the *res ipsa loquitur* doctrine is that in cases involving the application of the latter, the plaintiff is required to prove only injury and not a standard of care or a specific act or omission. In contrast, the doctrine of common knowledge is applied after damages have already been proved and after the fact of the commission or omission of the professional has been established. The invocation of the doctrine of common knowledge in essence transforms the case from one of professional malpractice to one of ordinary negligence.

Expert witnesses must usually be licensed members of the profession whose standards they profess to know (*Hull* v. *Plume,* 37 A.2d 53; *Rawleigh* v. *Donoho,* 283 Ky. 480, 38 S.W.2d 227). Yet when considering mental health professionals, this judicial tradition, like many others, cannot be applied in a straightforward, clear-cut manner. As the court in *Matter of Wellington,* 340 N.E.2d 131, observed, "the question whether a nonmedical psychologist is qualified to give expert testimony of the issue of mental condition or competency has not received uniform treatment in the courts of this country." Other related questions have not received uniform treatment or have yet to be tested in the courts. For example, can both psychologists and psychiatrists of the same therapeutic school qualify as experts in malpractice litigation involving either a psychologist or a psychiatrist, or will the court rule that a psychoanalytically oriented psychiatrist is not qualified to give testimony as to the standard of care offered by a psychoanalytically oriented psychologist? Who will qualify as an expert in litigation involving psychotherapists who are not licensed psychologists, psychiatrists, or social workers but merely self-proclaimed "therapists"? Will expert testimony be required—even admissable—in such cases? These and many related questions remain to be addressed by the courts.

PROXIMATE CAUSE

As we have noted, a basic element needed to show malpractice or negligence is proximate cause. Proximate cause has been defined as "that cause which as a natural and continuous sequence, unbroken by any intervening cause, produces the injury without which it would not have occurred" (*Reder* v. *Hanson,* 338 F.2d 244). Foreseeability is a factor that figures prominently in determinations of proximate cause. In malpractice litigation the issue of foreseeability frequently relates to questions as to whether the practitioner knew or should have known that his actions would result in a specific outcome. Rothblatt and Leroy (1973, p. 264) have addressed themselves to the difficulties attendant on foreseeing the consequences of mental health care as well as the difficulty in proving proximate causation:

> Besides proving that the psychiatrist has breached the requisite standard of care in some specific detail, the plaintiff must also demonstrate causation and damage. Because the natural pathological development and prognosis of mental disease is not well known, it is frequently difficult to state to a reasonable degree of medical certainty whether the application or omission of a particular procedure at a specified time caused mental injury to the patient. Thus it is often difficult for the plaintiff to prove the element of causation. The task is simplified, however, if the alleged negligence in some manner caused or encouraged the patient to sustain or inflict tangible physical injuries upon himself or others. Indeed, this characteristic is typical of almost every successful suit. In this situation, proof of the injuries in addition to proof that ordinary and prudent therapeutic techniques would have prevented the damage may sustain the burden of proof.
>
> The plaintiff who complains of exclusively mental injuries may also have a difficult time proving the element of damages. Not only are his allegations intangible and difficult to demonstrate to the judge and jury, but they also tend to be somewhat speculative because of the state of knowledge about mental illness. Even where improper procedures have been used to institutionalize a person in need of mental care, the courts may absolve physicians from liability by finding that the patient was not injured by receiving the treatment he needed.

In *Hicks* v. *United States* (1975) (p. 109 above), the section of the opinion dealing with the problem of determining proximate cause is set forth.

REFERENCES FOR CHAPTER II

Bradford, R. T. A unique decision. *Journal of Legal Medicine,* 1974, *2,* 52–55.

Harris, M. Tort liability of the psychotherapist. *University of San Francisco Law Review,* 1973, *8,* 405–436.

Rothblatt, H. B. & Leroy, D. H. Avoiding psychiatric malpractice. *California Western Law Review,* 1973, *9,* 260–272.

CHAPTER III

Nature and Causes of Action

A "CAUSE OF ACTION" is the basis for a lawsuit. Malpractice litigation involving mental health professionals usually contains allegations of negligent diagnosis and/or negligent care and treatment. The preceding chapter traced the development of a standard against which the care to which a patient is entitled can be measured. The present chapter deals with specific applications of this standard to sundry aspects of professional practice.

DIAGNOSIS-RELATED LIABILITY

The rendering of an improper diagnosis or the failure to render a diagnosis may subject a health professional to liability for malpractice. In the medical malpractice literature, such as in *Naccarato* v. *Grob,* 384 Mich. 248, 180 N.W.2d 788 (1970), there are cases in which practitioners have been held liable for the failure to use a diagnostic test when it is customary and usual to do so (see also *Smith* v. *Yohe,* 194 A.2d 167; *Estate of Davies,* 248 N.W.2d 344); the failure to interpret test data correctly: *Green* v. *State,* 309 S.2d 706; the failure to respond appropriately to an adverse reaction to a test: *Dill* v. *Miles,* 310 P.2d 896; and the failure to detect inaccurate laboratory findings that should have been recognized as inaccurate: *Johnson* v. *St. Paul Mercury Insurance Company,* 219 S.2d 524, and *Price* v. *Neyland,* 320 F.2d 624. In this context Feegel (1974, p. 48) has advised physicians that to assume laboratory infallibility is to leave oneself "wide open to a liability suit when, following an adverse result, the patient's attorney points out that a reasonable and prudent physician should have known that the reported lab results were inconsistent with the clinical picture." Liability may be avoided if a misdiagnosis does not affect treatment (*see Black* v. *Caruso,* 9 Cal.Rptr. 634; *Romberg* v.

Morgan, 218 N.W.2d 492), or if correct treatment follows the misdiagnosis (*McManus* v. *Donlin,* 127 N.W.2d 22; *Hall* v. *Bacon,* 453 P. 816).

In considering the subject of diagnosis in the mental health field, special questions, issues and problems over and above those that attend the subject of diagnosis in the medical field emerge. One such issue or problem is the lack of "hard" data on which many mental diagnoses are based. With the exception of cases involving suspected brain tumors or other neurological impairments, the diagnoses mental health professionals are called upon to make are more apt to be based on analysis of interview data, historical data, and/or psychological test data than on analysis of blood, urinc, x-rays or rclatcd "physical" findings. Subjectivity and the allowance for a wide range of opinion tends to increase with the lack of tangible evidence. Opinions as to the etiology of the diagnosed condition are likely to vary widely as a function of the school of psychotherapy to which the practitioner subscribes. Thus two practitioners may agree on the diagnosis but may radically disagree as to the suspected mental and environmental events and conditions that predisposed the patient to, or brought about, the diagnosed condition. Although such uncertainty exists in many other areas of health practice, nowhere is there more room for speculation and contrasting opinion than the mental health field. Related to this point about the potentiality for varying opinions as to the etiology of the diagnosed condition, the point must be made that diagnosis has little relation to the treatment modality in the mental health field. In this context Slovenko (1978) has noted that, "Given the same diagnosis, a person may be involved in individual or group psychotherapy, or in primal scream or behavior therapy, hypnotherapy, drug therapy, or electroshock, or being hospitalized."

Actions against mental health professionals alleging misdiagnosis have frequently involved charges that the practitioner negligently failed to recognize a patient or client's suicidal or homicidal tendencies. Another frequent allegation is that the practitioner negligently diagnosed mental illness instead of sanity and this diagnosis resulted in improper commitment. The following cases are illustrative of the way the courts have applied legal principles in arbitrating disputes involving claims of misdiagnosis. Note that in cases involving death by suicide or homicide that the suicide or homicide is viewed by the courts as an end result that does not in and of itself presuppose or create any underlying liability for the professional. The terms "suicide" and "homicide" are merely descriptive of an injury; the factual circumstances of liability will be considered in the same manner as in any other malpractice action, and the usual legal principles will be applied to determine whether or not the practitioner failed to exercise due care in rendering a diagnosis.

Some representative cases involving misdiagnosis are reprinted below. In *Dinnerstein* v. *United States,* 486 F.2d 34 (2d Cir., 1973), the court takes up the issue of whether it was proper to allow unrestricted movement to a hospitalized mental patient who subsequently committed suicide. At issue in *Meier* v. *Ross General Hospital,* 71 Cal.Rptr. 903, 445 P.2d 519, is the question of whether a hospital with an "open door" policy of treatment should have placed a suicidal patient in a room with an openable window. In *Merchants National Bank & Trust Co. of Fargo* v. *United States,* 272 F.Supp. 409 (D.N.D. 1967), the court deals with the question of the liability of a hospital and its staff following the release of a mental patient who subsequently committed homicide.

Dinnerstein v. *United States,* 486 F.2d 34 (2d Cir. 1973)

Before KAUFMAN, Chief Judge, and SMITH and MULLIGAN, Circuit Judges.

J. JOSEPH SMITH, Circuit Judge:

This action arose out of the suicide of plaintiff's husband while a patient at the Veterans Administration Hospital in West Haven, Connecticut.[1] The only question on appeal is the validity of the district court's finding that the hospital officials and staff were negligent in permitting Mr. Dinnerstein's death. Both parties agree that under the Tort Claims Act, Connecticut law applies, and that under that law the proper standard of care is that standard which other hospitals in the area have and afford similar patients. The parties disagree, however, as to whether the evidence presented at trial—most notably the expert psychiatric testimony—sufficiently supports the court's finding of negligence. Since we find the evidence to be sufficient, we affirm.

I

For as long as six years before his death on January 4, 1969, Howard Dinnerstein had suffered recurrent periods of depression serious enough to require voluntary psychiatric care. On January 31, 1968, he ran his car into a highway bridge abutment. Though little damage was done to the car and none to himself, Dinnerstein told his wife that the "accident" had actually been a suicide attempt. The same day he was admitted—again voluntarily—to the V.A. Hospital in West Haven; he remained there under observation until February 12. The hospital records indicate that at the time its staff doctors considered Dinnerstein a "suicide risk." Though the records also indicate that Dinnerstein was gradually accorded greater freedom of movement—from complete restriction on January 31 to full privileges on February 2—his release on February 12 was nevertheless "against medical advice."

In the fall of 1968, business pressures apparently drove Dinnerstein back into his depression. Dr. Gottlieb, Dinnerstein's new private psychiatrist, convinced him to admit himself to St. Raphael's Hospital in New Haven on November 5, 1968. Dr. Gottlieb testified that his reasons for hospitalizing Dinnerstein in November included protecting him from possible suicide. On November 9, Dinnerstein's condition took a turn for the worse: He would not leave his bed nor do anything for himself. However, by November 14 he had improved enough to be granted walking privileges; and on November 28, he was again discharged.

But in December the cycle again turned downward, and Dinnerstein was treated by Dr. Gottlieb no less than seven times. As he was going steadily downhill, Dr. Gottlieb again recommended hospitalization. At the V.A. Hospital, the physician on duty, Dr. Talan, informed Dinnerstein that the individual therapy he was seeking was not available. Depressed further by this, Dinnerstein refused to admit himself. However, on the

[1]The government has never disputed that Dinnerstein's fall was a suicide.

following day, January 3, 1969, he decided to accept the V.A. offer of group therapy. During the admission session, Dr. Clark of the V.A. staff diagnosed Dinnerstein's condition as a "Depressive Reaction." However, he later testified that he did not consider Dinnerstein to be suicidal.

Though Dr. Clark was aware of Dinnerstein's prior history from both the V.A. records of his February hospitalization and from a telephone conversation between Dr. Talan and Dr. Gottlieb on January 2, he did not order any restrictions or special supervision for Dinnerstein in assigning him to a seventh-floor ward. Dr. Clark also discontinued a regime of anti-depressant drugs Dinnerstein had followed up to that time in order to obtain a more accurate reading of his psychological state.

The V.A. records indicate that on the evening of January 3, Dinnerstein complained to Dr. Clark that he had become even more depressed since arriving at the hospital because of the inadequacy of the group therapy program. However, despite these complaints, Dr. Clark issued no additional orders either to supervise Dinnerstein more closely or to give him anti-depressant medication. At approximately 3:00 P.M. on the following day, January 4, Dinnerstein walked to the lavatory on the seventh floor and leaped to his death from an unsecured window.

II

The government's first contention is that as a matter of Connecticut law, the district court's finding of negligence cannot stand because no psychiatric expert testified that the appropriate standard of medical care was not satisfied. This argument misstates the law. Rather it is clear that expert medical testimony is necessary only to provide the trier of fact with the proper standard of medical care against which to measure the defendant's actions. It is the trier of fact, and not the expert witness, who must then evaluate the evidence to determine whether or not that standard was actually met. *Slimak* v. *Foster,* 106 Conn. 366, 370–71, 138 A. 153, 155 (1927). Indeed, the trier of fact may even base a finding of negligence on the expert testimony of the defendant-doctor. *Snyder* v. *Pantaleo,* 143 Conn. 290, 294, 122 A.2d 21, 24 (1956); *Allen* v. *Giuliano,* 144 Conn. 573, 575 135 A.2d 904, 906 (1957); *Console* v. *Nickou,* 156 Conn. 268, 274, 240 A.2a 895, 898 (1968); *Levett* v. *Etkind,* 158 Conn. 567, 575, 265 A.2d 70, 73 (1969).

Here there was clear testimony from three psychiatric experts—Dr. Gottlieb, Dr. Talan, and Dr. Rubenstein, a government witness—that the hospital should have restricted Dinnerstein *if* there was reason to believe he was suicidal. Indeed, this standard of care is so obvious that expert testimony seems hardly necessary.

Nevertheless, when one remembers the fact that unlike blood pressures or pulse rates, emotional states cannot be calibrated with precision, medical expertise again becomes relevant. That is, the question for expert guidance—but still for ultimate determination by the trier of fact—was whether it was reasonably foreseeable on the basis of Dinnerstein's prior history that he would commit suicide. The government correctly notes that all of the expert witnesses, including Dr. Gottlieb, testified that they did not consider Dinnerstein to be suicidal on his admission to the hospital. However, despite this testimony on the narrow question of whether Dinnerstein exhibited suicidal tendencies on the day he was admitted, the trial court—relying primarily on the hospital's own records and the conversations between Dr. Gottlieb and Dr. Talan—nevertheless found:

> [T]hat the Hospital knew or should have known of the real possibility of a suicide attempt, that it failed to take appropriate measures to guard Dinnerstein against that danger, that it was its duty to do so, and that, having failed to act with due care in the discharge of that duty, the United States is liable to the plaintiff for the losses caused thereby. . . .
>
> At the least, for the first few days of Dinnerstein's admission his movements should have been restricted so that he could be closely watched. As he was assigned to a ward on the seventh floor, measures should have been taken to see that he could not jump from a window. His own denial upon admission of suicidal ideation and even Dr. Gottlieb's belief that he was not imminently suicidal, cannot excuse the complete absence of precautions to insure the safety of a patient with a suicidal gesture in his past, a long history of psychiatric treatment for recurrent and severe depression, previous hospitalization to protect against possible suicide. . . .

In our review of this finding, the government urges that we reconsider the evidence unrestrained by the "clearly erroneous" test of Rule 52(a).[2] However, while we agree that a finding of negligence is reviewable as a matter of law, we cannot accept the government's invitation to conduct a broad, almost *de novo,* inquiry into the basic facts of this case. As we have previously stated:

> The standard of review to be applied to a district court's finding of negligence is not the "clearly erroneous" standard . . . for a finding of negligence is reviewable as a matter of law. Nevertheless, the lower court finding "[will] ordinarily stand unless the [lower] court manifests an incorrect conception of the applicable law." *Cleary* v. *United States Lines Co.,* 411 F.2d 1009 (2 Cir. June 2, 1969), citing *Radovich* v. *Cunard Steamship Co.,* 364 F.2d 149, 152 (2 Cir. 1966) and *Esso Standard Oil S.A.* v. *S.S. Gasbras Sul.,* 387 F.2d 573 (2 Cir.), cert. denied, 391 U.S. 914, 88 S.Ct. 1808, 20 L.Ed.2d 653 (1968).

[2]The government cites *Mamiye Bros.* v. *Barber Steamship Lines, Inc.,* 360 F.2d 774 (2d Cir. 1966), cert. denied, 385 U.S. 835, 87 S.Ct. 80, 17 L.Ed.2d 70 (1966), for the proposition that our review of this finding of negligence must also be free of the clearly erroneous rule in order to insure a uniformity of result among the several courts in this circuit. However, *Mamiye Bros.* applied only where contrary decisions rest "on exactly the same facts. . . ." *Id.* at 777.

Baker v. *United States,* 226 F.Supp. 129 (S.D.Iowa 1964), aff'd 343 F.2d 222 (8th Cir. 1965), cited by the government, while strikingly similar to the case at bar does not satisfy this test. In *Baker* the patient, who had been referred to a V.A. hospital by a private physician who had noted suicidal tendencies, was also assigned to an open ward after a V.A. doctor concluded he was not a suicide risk. Three days later, Baker left his ward and jumped into a open well on the hospital grounds. The trial judge, noting that modern psychiatric theory requires some "calculated risks," found no negligence, and the Eighth Circuit affirmed.

Assuming, *arguendo,* that we must reconcile our result here with *Baker,* a case from another circuit which may or may not be correct, there is one important point of distinction between the two sets of facts. In *Baker,* there is no suggestion that hospital officials had any reason to believe the patient's psychological condition was further deteriorating after his initial admission examination. Here, by contrast, it is undisputed that Dinnerstein told Dr. Clark that he was becoming even more depressed—apparently due to the lack of either individual therapy or anti-depressant medication, or both.

Two other federal decisions finding no negligence in the suicides of government patients are similarly distinguishable by the fact that in both there was no evidence of recent suicide tendencies or attempts. See, *White* v. *United States,* 244 F.Supp. 127, 129–131 (E.D.Va.1965), aff'd, 359 F.2d 989 (4th Cir. 1966) (last suicidal "gesture" occurred fourteen years before actual suicide; the Fourth Circuit held that the finding of non-negligence, while "highly debatable," was not reversible); *Frederic* v. *United States,* 246 F.Supp. 368, 371 (E.D.La.1965) (patient, hospitalized for non-psychiatric reasons, had never previously attempted nor threatened suicide).

Hendry v. *United States,* 418 F.2d 774, 784 (2d Cir. 1969).

Here there is no doubt that the trial court applied the proper legal standard: If Dinnerstein's suicide was reasonably foreseeable, the hospital staff was clearly negligent in assigning him to an unsupervised and unrestricted room on the seventh floor.

We further hold that even without the benefit of the clearly erroneous rule, the finding that Dinnerstein's suicide was sufficiently foreseeable to demand greater supervision is amply supported by the record. The hospital officials should certainly have been aware of Dinnerstein's prior hospitalization history contained in their own records. Similarly, Dr. Gottlieb, who testified that he considered Dinnerstein's condition in late December to be the same or worse than it was in November when he was hospitalized partially to prevent a suicide attempt, informed Dr. Talan that Dinnerstein had exhibited "negativism and unpredictability" as recently as November 9th. This diagnosis certainly should have been made available to Dr. Clark, the admitting physician.

Moreover, Dr. Clark himself admitted that soon after his admission, Dinnerstein expressed dissatisfaction and further depression with the treatment he was receiving. Yet despite these complaints, Dr. Clark continued to deprive Dinnerstein of antidepressant drugs he had been receiving, so as to evaluate his psychological condition.

From these facts, when combined with a six-year history of deepening depression, it was not at all unreasonable for the trial court to conclude that Dinnerstein should have been supervised more closely. This is not to suggest that every potential suicide must be locked in a padded cell. The law and modern psychiatry have now both come to the belated conclusion that an overly restrictive environment can be as destructive as an overly permissive one.[3] But while we must accept some calculated risks in order to insure the patient's legal rights and provide him with the most effective therapy,[4] we must also admit that errors in judgment do occur and that when they do, medical authorities must assume their rightful share of the responsibility.[5] Here, in short, we cannot say the trial court erred in concluding that the hospital staff was negligent in allowing Dinnerstein—an emotional unknown quantity—unrestricted movement on the seventh floor.

The judgment is affirmed.

[3]See, e.g., Perr, Suicide Responsibility of Hospital and Psychiatrist, 9 Clev.-Mar. L.R. 427, 439-40 (1960).

[4]See, generally, B. Ennis, Prisoners of Psychiatry (1972); T. Szasz, Law, Liberty and Psychiatry (1963); Note, Civil Commitment of the Mentally Ill: Theories and Procedures, 79 Harv.L.R. 1288 (1966). Cf. *Jackson* v. *Indiana,* 406 U.S. 715, 92 S.Ct. 1845, 32 L.Ed.2d 435 (1972) (due process standards applied to competency statutes).

[5]See, *Lucy Webb Hayes National Training School for Deaconesses and Missionaries* v. *Perotti,* 136 U.S.App.D.C. 122, 419 F.2d 704, 707-708 (1969) (Bazelon, C. J.):

> The mental hospital functions in this new model as a repair shop rather than as a human junkyard. Confinement and physical restraint are no longer the defining qualities of hospitalization. Since the emphasis is upon treatment, the atmosphere of the hospital should encourage recovery by allowing the patient to assume progressively greater and greater responsibility.
>
> Since confinement and restraint may deny the patient the sense of responsibility and self-control essential to his recovery, the argument runs, limitations upon his freedom of movement are appropriate only when necessary for the safety of the patient or others. And since the restraint required for absolute safety may be inconsistent with effective therapy, calculated risks must sometimes be taken.
>
> . . . Real challenges and real responsibility for the patient imply the risk of real failures, however. Some patients will prove unready for responsibility, and may injure themselves or others. In a real sense these failures are the inevitable cost of any treatment program oriented toward returning patients to the community. But the law nevertheless must allocate at least the economic losses occasioned thereby.

Meier v. *Ross General Hospital,* 71 Cal.Rptr. 903, 445 P.2d 519

TOBRINER, Justice.

Plaintiffs, the widow and minor children of decedent Kurt Meier, brought this action against defendants Ross General Hospital and James M. Stubblebine, to recover damages for the alleged wrongful death of the decedent. While a patient in the psychiatric wing of the hospital and under the care and supervision of Dr. Stubblebine, decedent committed suicide by jumping headfirst through an open window of his second floor room. Following a trial before a jury, the verdict favored both defendants. Plaintiffs appeal from the judgment.

The assignment of errors includes the following question: Did the trial court commit prejudicial error in rejecting a requested instruction which explained that plaintiffs were not to be deprived of the benefit of a res ipsa loquitur presumption because of decedent's "voluntary action or contribution" (cf. *Ybarra* v. *Spangard* (1944) 25 Cal.2d 486, 489, 154 P.2d 687, 162 A.L.R. 1258) if such action or contribution were not the "responsible cause" of death? (See *Vistica* v. *Presbyterian Hospital* (1967) 67 Cal.2d 465, 470-471, 62 Cal.Rptr. 577, 432 P.2d 193.) We hold that such a refusal constituted error,[1] because *Vistica* requires such an explanation whenever the facts of a case support a theory of liability based on a duty to protect plaintiff (decedent) from his own actions, voluntary or involuntary. (*Vistica* v. *Presbyterian Hospital, supra,* 67 Cal.2d 465, 470-471, 62 Cal.Rptr. 577, 432 P.2d 193.)

Furthermore, we hold that the conditional res ipsa instruction, properly qualified, should be given in this case. If those charged with the care and treatment of a mentally disturbed patient know of facts from which they could reasonably conclude that the patient would be likely to harm himself in the absence of preclusive measures, then they must use reasonable care under the circumstances to prevent such harm. (*Wood* v. *Samaritan Institution* (1945) 26 Cal.2d 847, 853, 161 P.2d 556.) Given this duty and the fact that defendants placed decedent, following an attempted suicide, in a second floor room with a fully openable window, the jury could find from the fact of decedent's suicidal plunge through this window that defendants more probably than not breached the duty of care owed to decedent. Even in the absence of expert testimony which describes the probability that the death or injury resulted from negligence, the jury may competently decide that defendant more probably than not breached his duty of care when the evidence supports a conclusion that the cause of the accident (here, the openable window) was not inextricably connected with a course of treatment involving the exercise of medical judgment beyond the common knowledge of laymen.

Finally, we conclude that we must reverse the judgment and remand for a new trial because the jury's verdict may have been based on the erroneous instruction; prejudice appears from the probability of a determinative application of an erroneous instruction,

[1]The Court of Appeal declined to consider this determinative issue on appeal because the plaintiffs, having failed to raise the point in their opening brief, could not do so later without "good reason." (3 Witkin, Cal. Procedure, Appeal, § 155, pp. 2341-2342.) During the course of this litigation the case of *Vistica* v. *Presbyterian Hospital, supra,* 67 Cal.2d 465, 62 Cal.Rptr. 577, 432 P.2d 193, proceeded through the courts. On October 10, 1967, three and one-half months after the plaintiffs had filed their closing brief, the Supreme Court decided *Vistica;* that decision decisively affected the proper disposition of the present case. Thereafter plaintiffs sought and obtained permission to file a supplemental brief and defendants responded by letter.

The circumstances outlined above provide a satisfactory basis for the unusual practice of considering a point raised for the first time after the opening briefs have been filed.

and this court should not speculate upon the actual basis of the verdict. (*Robinson* v. *Cable* (1961) 55 Cal.2d 425, 428, 11 Cal.Rptr. 377, 359 P.2d 929.)

On July 5, 1962, decedent Kurt Meier attempted to commit suicide by slashing his wrists. After treatment for his physical injury, the decedent's family brought him to the Ross General Hospital. Defendant Stubblebine, director of the hospital's psychiatric wing, attended decedent upon his admission and during his hospitalization became his personal physician.

The hospital had adopted the "open door" policy for its psychiatric patients. This method of treatment de-emphasizes physical restraint by providing a "homelike" atmosphere in the hospital. The patients are free to move about and even to leave the hospital if they are so inclined. No mechanical security devices are regularly used; the doors are not locked; the windows are not barred.

The policy rests upon the premise that freedom of movement and personal responsibility of patients, even potential suicides, improve the process of their rehabilitation and reduce possible emotional stress. The proponents of the "open door" policy concede, however, that the lessening of physical security exposes a potentially suicidal patient to greater risk. They assert that no amount of security or physical restraint short of rendering the patient unconscious can effectively prevent suicide. Nevertheless, recognizing the risk of suicide in certain patients, the proponents of "open door" therapy normally employ larger staffs to facilitate surveillance and administer chemotherapy to those patients whose symptomatic restlessness and agitation indicate severe depression which may lead to suicide.

The window through which the decedent jumped was not barred in any way; it had no security screen; it was fully openable by means of a crank. The crank could have been removed, and the window secured at a fixed width, by removing a screw. Evidence introduced by plaintiffs at trial indicated that other hospitals employ security windows of a type which would have prevented the accident in this case. Plaintiffs also offered evidence which tended to show that secured windows would not have been incompatible with the "open door" policy. Defendant physician and other defense experts testified that the operation of the psychiatric facilities at Ross Hospital, including the openable windows, comported with accepted hospital and medical standards. Plaintiffs produced no expert witness.

To alleviate decedent's depression, defendant Stubblebine had prescribed a program of chemotherapy. The record indicates, however, that decedent refused to take the medication as prescribed. Although various members of the hospital staff saw and observed decedent on several occasions, the record does not reveal whether the hospital supplied any formal observation or guard. On July 13, 1962, while decedent was alone in his room, he plunged through the window to his death.

At trial, plaintiffs characterized the openable window in decedent's room as an invitation to commit suicide, a patent violation of defendant's duty of care to the decedent, and a fact of negligence wholly unrelated to the "open door" policy. Plaintiffs also attacked the adequacy of the chemotherapy prescribed and administered to the decedent. In answer, defendants described the treatment and supervision given decedent while in the hospital as exceeding the standard of due care and comporting with good medical practice. Defendants' expert witnesses testified that the "open door" policy as administered at Ross Hospital complied with accepted professional standards. Defendants suggested that the openable window constituted as much a part of "open door" therapy as the unlocked doors. Finally, defendants offered evidence of the difficulty, bordering on impossibility, of preventing an attempted suicide by any sort of physical restraint.[2]

The trial judge gave three distinct negligence instructions: ordinary negligence, medical malpractice, and the questionable res ipsa loquitur instruction. The jury's verdict (10 to 2) favored both defendants.

The trial judge instructed the jury on the doctrine of res ipsa loquitur: "With respect to the doctrine of res ipsa loquitur mentioned by counsel we have this question for you to decide in this case. The question is stated in this way: Whether the accident involved occurred under the following three conditions. First, that it is the kind of accident which ordinarily does not occur in the absence of someone's negligence; second, that it was caused by an agency or instrumentality in the exclusive control of the defendants; and third, that the accident was not due to any voluntary action or contribution on the part of the decedent. And only in the event that you should find all these conditions to exist, you are instructed that an inference arises that a proximate cause of the occurrence was some negligent conduct on the part of the defendants."

Although this instruction meets the requirements set forth by this court in *Ybarra* v. *Spangard, supra,* 25 Cal.2d 486, 489, 154 P.2d 687, 162 A.L.R. 1258, we held in *Vistica* v. *Presbyterian Hospital, supra,* 67 Cal.2d 465, 468–469, 62 Cal.Rptr. 577, 432 P.2d 193, that an instruction must be measured by the circumstances of the case in which it was given. (Cf. *Adams* v. *American President Lines* (1944) 23 Cal.2d 681, 688, 146 P.2d 1; *Schroeder* v. *Baumgarteker* (1927) 202 Cal. 626, 629, 262 P. 740.) In the present case, the plaintiffs offered an instruction which would have explained to the jury that "A plaintiff may properly rely on res ipsa loquitur although he [the decedent] participated in events leading to the accident if the evidence excludes his conduct as the responsible cause." The trial judge refused to give this qualification. We held in *Vistica* v. *Presbyterian Hospital, supra,* 67 Cal.2d at pages 470–471, 62 Cal.Rptr. 577, 432 P.2d 193, that just such a qualification must be given whenever the facts of a case support a theory of liability based on a duty to protect plaintiff (decedent) from his own actions, voluntary or involuntary.

The rationale for our holding in *Vistica* rested on the probability that the jury would misunderstand the trial condition to the res ipsa instruction to mean that the doctrine could never apply when the decedent's voluntary actions contributed to the accident. The purpose of this condition is to eliminate the possibility that the decedent was responsible for the accident. As Prosser states: ". . . [T]he requirement [absence of any action on the part of the decedent contributing to the accident] may easily be misunderstood. The plaintiff [decedent] is seldom entirely static, and it is not necessary that he be completely inactive, but merely that there be evidence removing the inference of his own responsibility." (Prosser on Torts (2d ed. 1955) § 42, p. 208.) In the present case, decedent had attempted suicide and had been placed in the hospital because of his depressed state and physical injuries. Under such circumstances, we have held that those charged with the care and treatment of a patient, who know of facts from which it might reasonably be concluded that a patient would be likely to harm himself in the absence of preclusive measures, must use reasonable care to prevent such harm. (Wood v. Samaritan Inst., supra, 26 Cal.2d 847, 853, 161 P.2d 556; Vistica v. Presbyterian Hospital, supra, 67 Cal.2d 465, 468–470, 62 Cal.Rptr. 577, 432 P.2d 193.) The same considerations which led us in *Vistica* to qualify the standard conditional res ipsa

[2]Defendant Stubblebine testified that patients have committed suicide in a padded cell, while secured and immobilized, by biting their tongues and bleeding to death.

loquitur instruction require us to hold in the present case that the trial judge erred in not giving plaintiffs' requested instruction.

Defendants argue that any error in the form in which the trial judge instructed the jury on res ipsa loquitur must be adjudged harmless. They contend that, when the question of negligence involves a determination of what constitutes proper medical treatment the jury cannot competently assess the "probabilities of negligence" without the assistance of expert witnesses and that, therefore, the trial judge should not have given any res ipsa instruction in the first instance. They point out that the res ipsa loquitur instruction may properly be given in medical malpractice cases only when laymen (the jury) can infer as a matter of common knowledge that the accident would not have occurred unless the defendant were negligent, or when expert testimony supports the same inference, namely, that the accident was more probably than not caused by defendant's negligence. (Siverson v. Weber (1962) 57 Cal.2d 834, 836, 22 Cal.Rptr. 337, 372 P.2d 97; cf. Prosser, Res Ipsa Loquitur in California (1949) 37 Cal.L.Rev. 183, 193, 210–212.) Since plaintiffs here could offer no expert testimony on the "probabilities of negligence," defendants contend that the trial court should not have given the res ipsa instruction because the propriety of treatment for mentally ill patients raises questions of professional judgment and accepted medical practice which fall outside the realm of lay or common knowledge.

Defendants' contention raises the issue whether, as a matter of law, the jury could find, without the aid of expert testimony, the conditions precedent to an application of the doctrine of res ipsa loquitur. Stated differently, could the jury find from the mere occurrence of the accident under the circumstances that it probably was the result of negligence by someone and that defendant is probably the person who is responsible? (Clark v. Gibbons (1967) 66 Cal.2d 399, 408, 58 Cal.Rptr. 125, 426 P.2d 525.) The former probability must concern us here: defendants assert that the jury requires the aid of experts because the questions raised lie exclusively within the province of medical science.

The facts of this case preclude our acceptance of defendants' contention. Ordinarily, if a plaintiff seeks to hold a hospital or a physician liable for a breach of a duty as to the medical care and treatment of a patient, the courts refuse to give a res ipsa loquitur instruction unless the plaintiff has produced some expert testimony[3] which supports an inference of negligence from the fact of the accident itself. (Siverson v. Weber, supra, 57 Cal.2d 834, 22 Cal.Rptr. 337, 372 P.2d 97; cf. Quintal v. Laurel Grove Hosp. (1964) 62 Cal.2d 154, 41 Cal.Rptr. 577, 397 P.2d 161; Clark v. Gibbons, supra, 66 Cal.2d 399, 58 Cal.Rptr. 125, 426 P.2d 525.)[4] The reason for this requirement appears from the following statement: "The law demands only that a physician or surgeon have the degree of learning and skill ordinarily possessed by practitioners of the medical

[3]Under our law, the plaintiff may call the defendant physician and make him the plaintiff's "expert witness" for the purposes of this requirement. (Code Civ. Proc., § 2055; Lawless v. Calaway (1944) 24 Cal.2d 81, 89–91, 147 P.2d 604.)

[4]*Quintal* and *Clark* permit the application of res ipsa loquitur to cases in which the only basis for the jury's competence to determine the "probabilities of negligence" are the rarity of the accident and some expert testimony supporting *a* negligent cause. That this development constitutes a more liberal interpretation of the scope of res ipsa loquitur has been noted (see *Clark* v. *Gibbons, supra,* 66 Cal.2d 399, 421–424, 58 Cal.Rptr. 125, 426 P.2d 525, Traynor, C. J., concurring; cf. Prosser, Res Ipsa Loquitur in California, supra, 37 Cal.L.Rev. 183, 189–196.) We mention these recent precedents in this context only to point out that the present case is not governed by them. For the reasons presented *infra,* we hold that the question of res ipsa must go to the jury even without any expert testimony when the facts support a finding of probable negligence without regard to the propriety of any distinctly "medical" course of treatment.

profession in the same locality and that he exercise ordinary care in applying such learning and skill to the treatment of his patient. . . . Ordinarily, a doctor's failure to possess or exercise the requisite learning or skill can be established only by the testimony of experts.'' (*Lawless* v. *Calaway, supra,* 24 Cal.2d 81, 86, 147 P.2d 604, 606.)

The courts, however, have established an exception to this requirement for the testimony of experts if the subject matter of the litigation is such that laymen could infer *as a matter of common knowledge* that the injury would not have occurred unless the defendant were negligent. (Note, The Application of Res Ipsa Loquitur in Medical Malpractice Cases [1966] 60 Nw.L.Rev. 852, 857-864.) The requirement for expert testimony disappears if ''during the performance of surgical or other skilled operations an ulterior act or omission occurs, the judgment of which does not require scientific opinion to throw light upon the subject.'' (*Ales* v. *Ryan* [1936] 8 Cal.2d 82, 98, 64 P.2d 409, 417; see, e.g., *Leonard* v. *Watsonville Community Hosp.* [1956] 47 Cal.2d 509, 305 P.2d 36, leaving a clamp in the incision following abdominal surgery; *Davis* v. *Memorial Hosp.* [1962] 58 Cal.2d 815, 26 Cal.Rptr. 633, 376 P.2d 561, rectal abscess following routine pre-surgical enema; *Friedman* v. *Dresel* [1956] 139 Cal.App.2d 333, 293 P.2d 488, failure to examine or X-ray hip despite complaints of pain in that area.)

In order to sustain the application of res ipsa loquitur in the particular circumstances of this case, however, we need not rely upon the above ''common knowledge'' exception to the requirement of expert testimony in medical malpractice cases. An obvious instance in which we do not call for expert testimony arises when the facts of a case support a finding of negligence of the ordinary type unrelated to questions involving *materia medica*.[5] (Cf. *Ales* v. *Ryan, supra,* 8 Cal.2d 82, 100, 64 P.2d 409.)

In this case Dr. Stubblebine, testifying as plaintiffs' witness under Code of Civil Procedure section 2055, acknowledged that a secured type of window was compatible with the ''open door'' policy.

> Q. Did you consider the fact that he [decedent] might go out the window?
> A. Not very much, because there were so many other means available, closer at hand, more certain.
> Q. You didn't know what means he might take?
> A. No.
> Q. The window was one of them?
> A. Yes.
> Q. You gave the window no concern at all? * * *
> [Objection.] * * *
> Q. Your answer was 'not very much.' Did you consider it—to what extent did you consider it?

[5]When the evidence is conflicting, or subject to different inferences, as to whether the alleged negligence is to be measured by reference to the ordinary standard of due care or by reference to the standard of good medical practice set by physicians of good standing in the community, a question of fact arises which must be left to the jury under proper instructions. (Cf. *Davis* v. *Memorial Hospital, supra,* 58 Cal.2d 815, 817, 26 Cal.Rptr. 633, 376 P.2d 561.) Such a question emerges in a case like the one before us in which the facts show a possibly negligent act or omission (i.e., leaving decedent alone in a room with an openable window) which defendant seeks to justify as part of a course of ''medical'' treatment involving the exercise of professional judgment (''open door'' therapy). The jury must determine whether the defendants instituted a course of conduct, or act or omission, for a good faith ''medical'' reason. The appropriate standard of care to be applied depends on the results of such a determination. (See fn. 6, *infra*.)

A. I don't know how much weight I gave it. I was more concerned about the many other ways.
Q. You told me that the cranks of the windows—they would crank open?
A. Yes.
Q. And the crank may be removed?
A. Yes.
Q. You could open it a certain distance and remove the crank, and the only way you could close or open it further would be with the crank?
A. Yes.
Q. Did you give any thought to providing proper ventilation, to remove the crank and—.
A. No.

. . . .

Q. You could have a secured type of window and still leave the doors open, and it would still be the open door policy?
A. Yes.

. . . .

Q. The kind of window a facility might have doesn't change the fact it might otherwise be an open type hospital?
A. That is correct.

No testimony introduced by defendants, either specifically or substantially or as a matter of law, rebutted the inference from Dr. Stubblebine's statement that the openable window did not constitute an essential, or even relevant, element of the "open door" policy.

The jury could therefore find negligence in the present case without regard to the propriety or impropriety of an asserted medical justification. We hold that the trial court must submit a conditional res ipsa instruction, even absent expert testimony on the "probabilities of negligence," when the evidence supports a conclusion that the cause of the accident (the openable window) was not inextricably bound up in a course of treatment involving the exercise of medical judgment beyond the common knowledge of laymen.[6] In brief, the "open door" policy does not necessarily call for an openable window; the objectives of the policy can be achieved without leaving an openable window available to the patient.

Having established that the trial judge committed error by failing to give the res ipsa instruction as qualified by *Vistica,* we turn to the question whether plaintiffs suffered prejudice by the error. In *Vistica,* we held erroneous, for reasons similar to those expressed in this opinion, a conditional res ipsa instruction that lacked the qualification as to the *responsible* contribution by decedent to the accident. We said there: "Where it seems probable that the jury's verdict may have been based on the erroneous instruction, prejudice appears, and this court should not speculate upon the basis of the verdict. (*Robinson* v. *Cable,* 55 Cal.2d 425, 428, 11 Cal.Rptr. 377, 359 P.2d 929.)" (*Vistica* v. *Presbyterian Hospital, supra,* 67 Cal.2d 465, 470–471, 62 Cal.Rptr. 577, 581, 432 P.2d 193, 197.)

[6]The judge should instruct the jury, however, that if it finds that defendants allowed the decedent to remain in the room with an openable window for a good faith medical reason that is inextricably bound up in a course of treatment involving the exercise of medical judgment beyond the knowledge of common laymen, they must assess this medical reason in the light of the standard of medical learning and skill prevalent in the community. The need for expert testimony in such a case will depend upon whether in such a case matter in issue falls within the "common knowledge" exception discussed *supra* at page 910.

In this case, in the context of perhaps necessarily complex and confusing instructions, we could not lightly find an absence of prejudice. We have concluded, as in *Vistica,* that if the res ipsa loquitur instruction had been rendered, it is reasonably probable that plaintiffs would have prevailed. Since we have found that the erroneous instruction could have deprived plaintiffs of a proper application of this doctrine to the present case and that it is reasonably probable that a result more favorable to the appealing party would have been reached in the absence of the error (*People* v. *Watson* [1956] 46 Cal.2d 818, 836, 299 P.2d 243), we must reverse the judgment.

The plaintiffs assign as errors rulings rendered and instructions given other than those we have discussed. For the benefit of a proper disposition of this case on remand, we shall briefly pass on these points.

First, plaintiffs contend that the trial judge erred in refusing to admit a brochure from the manufacturer of a drug (Mallaril) administered to decedent, which showed the drug to be contraindicated for severely depressed patients. This assignment of error would not, standing alone, require a reversal because plaintiffs' counsel obtained an admission of the contraindication from defendant Stubblebine on cross-examination. Furthermore, the plaintiffs do not present an adequate record for challenging this ruling since they laid no foundation for admission of the brochure and presented no properly informative offer of proof. (*Douillard* v. *Woodd* [1942] 20 Cal.2d 665, 670, 128 P.2d 6; *Carey* v. *Lima, Salmon & Tully Mortuary* [1959] 168 Cal.App.2d 42, 46, 335 P.2d 181; *Blackburn* v. *Union Oil Co.* [1949] 90 Cal.App.2d 775, 778, 204 P.2d 69.) For the purposes of retrial, however, we believe that the court should permit the introduction into evidence of such a brochure, not to establish the standard of care, but to show that the physician administering the drug had *notice* of the contraindication. *Sanzari* v. *Rosenfeld* [1961] 34 N.J. 128, 139, 140, 167 A.2d 625, 631.)

Second, plaintiffs contend that in view of the facts of this case, the trial judge committed prejudicial error in rendering the following instruction: "In determining whether defendant's [Stubblebine's] learning, skill and medical conduct fulfill the duties imposed upon him by law, as they have been stated to you, you are not permitted to set up arbitrarily, a standard of your own. The standard was set by the learning, skill and care ordinarily possessed and practiced by others of the same profession in good standing, in the same or a similar locality and under similar circumstances at the same time. It follows, therefore, that the only way you may properly learn the standard is through evidence presented in this trial by physicians and surgeons called as expert witnesses."

Although the questioned instruction complies with the decisional rules prescribing the standard of care for medical malpractice cases (*Simone* v. *Sabo* [1951] 37 Cal.2d 253, 257, 231 P.2d 19; *Lawless* v. *Calaway, supra,* 24 Cal.2d 81, 86, 147 P.2d 604), plaintiffs argue that since they did not challenge the validity of any *medical* diagnosis or treatment, the instruction as framed worked error. The record of the case belies this contention. Plaintiffs challenged the adequacy of the program of chemotherapy to accomplish its purpose, namely, to alleviate the decedent's depression and reduce the risk of suicide. Plaintiffs suggested that defendant Stubblebine did not correctly assess the risk of suicide on the part of the decedent, a diagnostic problem. Finally, defendants' asserted justification for the openable window necessarily presented a medical issue, namely, the "open door" policy.

Although issues of medical malpractice did arise in the case, the facts also supported a finding of ordinary negligence without regard to the propriety of any controverted medical diagnosis or treatment. Recognizing this, the trial judge instructed the jury on ordinary negligence, announcing as the standard of care that conduct which, under the circumstances, a reasonably prudent person should follow. The judge attempted to distinguish the two sets of instructions by preceding the word "conduct" in the medical malpractice instruction with the word "medical." Plaintiffs correctly assert that these two sets of instructions caused confusion. On remand, the trial judge should make clear to the jury that the medical malpractice and ordinary negligence instructions are perfectly consistent, that it is for the jury to decide which instruction will guide them in determining the standard of care, and that this decision will depend on how it characterizes the conduct which led to the injury: whether the conduct was based on good faith medical reasons or whether the conduct was without any peculiarly "medical" justification.

In this respect plaintiffs argue that the trial judge should have instructed the jury on the "common knowledge" exception to the rule requiring expert testimony as to the standard of care in medical malpractice cases. As we have explained, the res ipsa loquitur instruction could properly rest upon a finding, here, of negligence of the ordinary type unrelated to questions involving *materia medica.* We have previously discussed for purposes of retrial the matter of an instruction on the "common knowledge" exception (*supra,* p. 910).

Third, plaintiffs challenge the trial court's instruction BAJI 214-A (Revised) to the effect that when a physician chooses one of alternative accepted methods of treatment, with which other physicians disagree, and which is in fact unsuccessful, the jury may not automatically deem him negligent. Although this instruction correctly states the rule (*Huffman* v. *Lindquist* [1951] 37 Cal.2d 465, 473–475, 234 P.2d 34, 29 A.L.R.2d 485), plaintiffs again argue that its rendition here constituted error because no issue of alternative medical treatment arose. Plaintiffs, however, urged at trial that defendants should have used greater physical restraint to protect decedent from taking his life; the line of questioning on the issue of chemotherapy suggested that defendant Stubblebine should have administered more or different drugs to decedent. The evidence thus supported the application of this instruction.

Fourth, plaintiffs object to the following rendered instruction: "A physician is not responsible for routine matters performed by him in his absence by a nurse not selected by him but employed by the hospital in which his patient is being treated." This instruction is normally proper. (*Sherman* v. *Hartman* [1955] 137 Cal.App.2d 589, 596, 290 P.2d 894.) In the present case, however, plaintiffs urged two theories of recovery against defendant Stubblebine: One asserted his liability as decedent's personal physician; the other, the doctor's liability in his capacity as director of the hospital's psychiatric wing. Plaintiffs argue that defendant Stubblebine, in his capacity as director of the wing, selected the nurses, or at least may be fairly assumed to have concurred in their selection, and that the nurses worked for him as their superior. Since the record contained no evidence, however, that defendant Stubblebine did participate in the selection of the nurses, the trial court properly gave this instruction.

Fifth, plaintiffs claim that the trial judge committed error in giving an instruction which quoted from section 423 of title 17 of the California Administrative Code. This section deals with the requirements for providing hospital rooms with windows "which shall be openable." We concede that this section bears some relation to the issues raised by this case; we believe, however, that the net effect of such an instruction would be to confuse, rather than to assist, the jury. The official requirement that the windows be openable in design bears little relationship to the question whether defendants should have locked, secured, or screened them. Although the instruction could lead the jury to believe defendants' behavior had received the benefit of some sort of official sanction, we doubt that the instruction caused prejudicial error. To avoid any such confusion on remand, however, the trial judge should eliminate such an instruction, preserving defendants' right to introduce the code section into evidence and argue its relevance to the jury.

Sixth, plaintiffs contest the propriety of an instruction limiting the liability of the hospital to action taken by defendant physician only in the exercise of his capacity as the director of the psychiatric wing and not in his performance as decedent's personal physician. Although we recognize the ambiguity inherent in the presentation of the dual theories of liability against defendant Stubblebine, we cannot, merely to eliminate possible confusion, adopt a rule which would extend the liability of the hospital beyond its legal limitations. Plaintiffs argue that this potential dual liability unfairly enables the hospital to divorce itself from amenability for defendant physician's negligent application of his knowledge or from his careless conduct. The trial judge, however, did give a sufficient and clear instruction that the hospital would be liable for any acts or omissions of the doctor in his capacity as director of the psychiatric wing.

Finally, plaintiffs object to an instruction which told the jury that it could not find negligence merely because another treatment acceptable to, or even preferred by, other physicians could have avoided the death. Plaintiffs claim the instruction superfluous because they did not raise any issue of an alternative form of treatment. As we pointed out *supra,* the record renders plaintiffs' contention untenable. The instruction constitutes a proper statement of the rule that, in determining whether defendants breached a standard of care owed decedent, the jury may not engage in "but-for" reasoning.

The judgment is reversed and the case remanded to the trial court for a new trial in accordance with this opinion.

TRAYNOR, C.J., and MCCOMB, PETERS, MOSK, BURKE and SULLIVAN, JJ., concur.

Merchants National Bank & Trust Co. of Fargo v. *United States*, 272 F.Supp. 409 (D.N.D. 1967)

Memorandum of Decision

RONALD N. DAVIES, District Judge.

This is an action brought by the Merchants National Bank and Trust Company of Fargo, a corporation, as Administrator and Personal Representative of the Estate of Eloise A. Newgard, deceased, against the United States of America, to recover damages by reason of the alleged negligent conduct of the defendant's agents and employees which resulted in the killing of Eloise A. Newgard by her husband, William Bry Newgard,[1] in Detroit Lakes, Minnesota, July 31, 1965. Jurisdiction is predicated upon Title 28, U.S.C.A. § 1346 et seq., commonly described as the Federal Tort Claims Act. The suit is brought on behalf of the three minor children of the decedent: Elizabeth, born September 16, 1955, Ann Marie, born April 13, 1958, and Robert William, born December 28, 1960.

Basically, the questions here presented are factual in nature, necessitating a somewhat detailed statement of the evidence developed upon trial.

[1]He will be referred to hereafter as Newgard, as not to confuse his name with that of his father, William S. Newgard.

Early in the morning of January 17, 1965, Dr. Mack V. Traynor, a Fargo physician, was called to the Newgard apartment in Fargo, North Dakota, by Newgard's wife, Eloise. She was frantic-voiced and said she needed help. The doctor, promptly responding to the call, found Newgard glassy-eyed and making senseless talk about horses, cattle "and God most of the time." Dr. Traynor felt Newgard was completely psychotic. Earlier that same morning Eloise had telephoned her pastor, Reverend Richard C. Faust, who knew both Newgard and his wife. He, too, came to the apartment. A daughter, Elizabeth, admitted him. Eloise asked for his help. From elsewhere in the apartment Newgard was shouting "get him out." Reverend Faust says that Newgard finally appeared, yelling that he was "the reincarnation of Jesus Christ." He was clad in boxer shorts and T-shirt. Newgard pulled his shorts down, exposed himself and said he was "going to repopulate the world." Newgard accused his wife of unfaithfulness and threatened to kill her. Reverend Faust also understood Newgard to say that the "God of Fire" would repopulate the world.

Both the Newgards had taught Sunday school in his church, but Reverend Faust had so many complaints about Newgard, he was forced to relieve him of his teaching assignment. Reverend Faust later in the morning of January 17, 1965, was able to get Newgard to St. Luke's Hospital in Fargo by literally marching him there through the streets.

Dr. Albert C. Kohlmeyer, a well qualified psychiatrist, saw Newgard the same day in the Neuropsychiatric Institute section of the hospital. He found him very agitated, "carrying on" about religious ideas and testified that Newgard thought "he was Christ or some representative of Christ." Because of his delusional ideas, the psychiatrist thought Newgard was psychotic and although he saw Newgard only a couple of days, it was his belief that Newgard's illness had been coming on for a long time. Dr. Kohlmeyer felt Newgard was a schizophrenic, chronic, with acute exacerbation, paranoid type.

On January 19, 1965, the Cass County, North Dakota, Mental Health Board after a hearing, ordered Newgard committed to the State Hospital at Jamestown, North Dakota. Later because he was a veteran, an amended order was issued by the board, making the commitment a dual one so that Newgard could eventually be transferred to the Veterans Administration Hospital at Fort Meade,[2] South Dakota. Effective March 23, 1965, Newgard was transferred to Meade where he was admitted to a ward and placed under the direct supervision of Dr. Leonard S. Linnell, a medical doctor and psychiatrist. This was Dr. Linnell's first position as a psychiatrist since completion of his residency in psychiatry at the University of Minnesota and the Veterans Administration Hospital in Minneapolis.

Dr. Linnell had access to the records of Newgard from the North Dakota State Hospital at Jamestown, which he says he studied, he had access to the mental health records and the commitment papers which he studied and, of course, at all times while Newgard was at Meade he had access to any of Newgard's files and records of whatever kind or nature.

For a number of weeks Newgard was treated with tranquilizers and saw a clinical psychologist, Dr. Jesse H. Craft, weekly, for psychotherapy and examinations. During the course of Newgard's treatment and care he was interviewed by Dr. Linnell about once a week. The psychiatrist also sent Newgard to Dr. Truman M. Cheney, a voca-

[2]All future references to the Veterans Administration Hospital at Fort Meade, South Dakota, are simply to "Meade."

tional psychologist, for testing and reporting his job aptitudes. Newgard was given various jobs around the hospital, a procedure followed by Meade in the treatment of hospital patients and which is followed in hospitals of a similar nature. On or about May 25, 1965, Newgard received a letter from his father according to Dr. Linnell, advising Newgard an uncle had died. Newgard got permission from Dr. Linnell to attend the funeral and for that purpose was given a pass for one week's leave of absence "to his parents' home in North Dakota." Dr. Linnell told Newgard to go to the funeral and to his parents' home and to return to the hospital and not to make any other visits. It is quite evident that Dr. Linnell did not know where or when the funeral was to be held or even the city in North Dakota in which Newgard's parents lived. Nor did he consult any other member of the staff at Meade prior to releasing Newgard to attend a funeral conducted at Leeds, North Dakota, which was already over long before Newgard reached Fargo by bus on the day thereof. Dr. Linnell did, however, have Mrs. Lois Powers, a social worker at Meade, telephone Eloise Newgard as the patient's guardian, that Newgard was to be released to attend his uncle's funeral.

Mrs. Newgard, frightened for her life, sought help from people in Fargo who eventually got in touch with County Judge Paul M. Paulsen, Chairman of the Cass County Mental Health Board, who had Newgard taken into custody at the bus station in Fargo. Here it is noteworthy that Dr. Linnell called Judge Paulsen by long distance telephone on the day Newgard was released, ostensibly to attend the funeral and visit his parents' home. Dr. Linnell told Judge Paulsen, referring to Newgard, "Nobody need to be afraid because this man is cured and he wouldn't hurt anybody." Judge Paulsen thereupon told Dr. Linnell that everyone who knew about Newgard, his condition and his commitment, felt Newgard was far from well mentally and that he was a dangerous man and should not have been released. Dr. Linnell told Judge Paulsen also that "there is nothing to worry about; this man I have told not to stop in Fargo" and "not to try to see his wife." The Cass County Mental Health Board met next day and directed the sheriff of Cass County to return Newgard to Meade. On May 27, 1965, Cass County deputies Dewey Eagle and Archie Vraa did so.

After Newgard's return to Meade the authorities there began thinking about getting Newgard work in the Meade area. Sometime early in July, 1965, Eloise Newgard learned that Dr. Linnell and the Meade authorities were about to discharge Newgard, and very much concerned for her safety, called Meade and talked to Dr. Curt L. Rosenbaum, Meade's Chief of Staff. Dr. Rosenbaum says she was upset and hung up on him. Dr. Rosenbaum himself never diagnosed Newgard, although he conceded there was no way it could be said Newgard's condition was in complete remission when he arrived at Meade. Dr. Harland T. Hermann, Chief of Psychiatry at Meade, evaluated Newgard's case thereafter. Unfortunately his written report was in some manner lost since it could not be found in the Meade records and files, but Dr. Hermann remembers making it and Dr. Linnell remembers seeing it. Dr. Hermann advised Dr. Linnell not to discharge Newgard.[3]

Sometime before July 18, 1965, Dr. Truman M. Cheney, Counseling Psychologist at Meade, had made arrangements to put Newgard on leave at the ranch owned by Mr. and Mrs. Clarence A. Davis located some ten miles north of Belle Fourche, South Dakota. Dr. Cheney told Mr. Davis that Newgard had had "a mental disturbance, a nervous breakdown" and that Newgard wanted hard work to forget some of his

[3]Dr. Linnell on June 30, 1965, had signed an outright discharge for Newgard, "MHB" (Maximum Hospital Benefit).

troubles and for rehabilitation purposes. Mr. Davis had never before had a Meade patient working on his ranch.

On July 18, 1965, Newgard was released by Dr. Linnell on work leave to rancher Davis. When asked what instructions he had received from Dr. Cheney with respect to Newgard, Mr. Davis replied:

> None whatsoever that I can recall. I don't believe there was anything said about any way that he would conduct himself, that he thought that he was completely arrested from his troubles and just needed a chance to work and get better rehabilitated again. But there was no reservations made of what I should do with him or for him; or there was no given pattern where I should pay the money or who I should give the money to or whether he was free to come and go. I assumed from the way they talked that I was to pay him and he was to come and go as he pleased.

Dr. Cheney on the other hand testified he had told Mr. Davis that Newgard had an emotional problem, that he might be nervous, that Newgard was upset because his wife was suing him for divorce, and that he had instructed Mr. Davis to call Meade if Newgard gave indication of unusual behavior.

Dr. Cheney conceded, on cross-examination, that he had not told Mr. Davis what constituted "unusual behavior." It is Dr. Cheney's testimony that Dr. Linnell told him that Newgard could work in the immediate Fort Meade area, but that he would have to be kept in South Dakota and "more or less" under hospital surveillance. Dr. Cheney did not tell Mr. Davis that Newgard was under any hospital surveillance, that he could not leave South Dakota, or even that he was a mental patient.

Dr. Linnell testified that he received reports from Dr. Cheney that Newgard was doing well in his work and adjusting on the Davis ranch. This testimony is flatly contradicted by Dr. Cheney himself who testified that his only contact with Mr. Davis after Newgard was first placed on the Davis ranch, was after Newgard had gone to Detroit Lakes and killed his wife.

The second weekend when Newgard left the Davis ranch for the last time, Mr. Davis believed he was "going back to Sturgis" and took Newgard, with another employee, into Sturgis and let them off at the hotel in Belle Fourche. At no time during Newgard's stay at the Davis ranch was Mr. Davis ever contacted by any representative of Meade. So far as Mr. Davis was concerned he had simply hired another farmhand, quite free to come and go as he chose. Newgard told Mr. Davis he was "bitter about the way he had been used" but Mr. Davis did not understand what Newgard meant, nor did the latter amplify his statement. Newgard did tell Mrs. Davis that he was bitter toward his wife "because she had served those divorce papers on him" and Mrs. Davis remembers telling a newsman after Eloise Newgard's death that Newgard had told her "he resented the fact that his wife had him committed." Newgard also told Mrs. Davis he had bought a car like his wife's, some carpeting and other things, none of which find any evidentiary support in this record.

Dr. Russell O. Saxvik, a psychiatrist, former North Dakota State Health Officer and former Superintendent of the North Dakota State Hospital at Jamestown, testified he was acquainted with the standards of practice in mental hospitals in this area. He thought Jamestown State Hospital and Meade standards were comparable. He testified further that the Davises should have been given specific instructions with respect to Newgard, which the Court finds were not given. He further testified that a mental hospital would want to know the whereabouts of a patient on leave and that Mr. and Mrs. Davis should have been told to notify Meade immediately, if Newgard left the ranch, and that Meade in turn should have alerted the committing health board, which in the instant case was Cass County, North Dakota. Not one of these things was done in Newgard's case, although clearly the standards of practice in the area required that they be done. Moreover, Dr. Rosenbaum, one of the Government's own expert witnesses, testified that when a man has gone from an area in which he was given leave of absence "the matter should have been pursued, no question about that at all."

It develops that on July 24, 1965, Newgard left the ranch for the weekend. He was to have returned Monday, July 26th, but Newgard went to his parents' home at Mayville, North Dakota. His wife Eloise had no idea he was in Mayville and was there herself only for a brief visit. Newgard wanted his wife to return with him to Fargo but she declined. Newgard then called Mr. Davis, advising him he would return to work on the ranch on Tuesday, which he did. On the night of Friday, July 31, 1965, Mr. Davis again took Newgard into Belle Fourche, having paid him his wages. Newgard got possession of a car and ultimately drove to his mother-in-law's home in Detroit Lakes, Minnesota, where on July 31, 1965, he first attempted to run Eloise Newgard down with the car and failing that, got out of the vehicle, shot and killed her.

The Government sought to make much of Eloise Newgard's meeting her husband in Mayville, Sunday, July 25, 1965, which was entirely circumstantial so far as she was concerned as the record reflects, and to make much of Eloise's alleged failure to telephone Meade as to his whereabouts. It ought not to be forgotten that Eloise A. Newgard was a well trained and responsible registered nurse; that she had worked in a hospital for mental patients; that she knew Newgard was mentally ill and under the supervision of Meade; that she knew he was going back to the ranch and supposedly, at any rate, that Newgard was under the care and supervision of Meade personnel. Her conduct was that of any normally prudent person with any common sense. She wanted him away from her because of his mental illness and her deathly fear of him. She encouraged his going back to South Dakota; and he went back.

Similarly the Government made much of Eloise Newgard visiting her husband at Meade in mid June, 1965, when she journeyed down to South Dakota with her mother, Mrs. Danielson, and the three Newgard children. On that occasion Eloise Newgard talked to Mrs. Lois Powers, the social worker, and to Dr. Linnell. There was a good deal of testimony concerning Eloise's attitude and conduct at Meade, but one inference is clearly drawn from the credible evidence in this action, and that is that Dr. Linnell believed almost everything Newgard told him without investigating or causing to be investigated any of Newgard's statements. Dr. Linnell quite evidently preferred "exaggeration" to "delusional" in describing Newgard's statements and appeared convinced that Eloise Newgard needed psychiatric help herself.

The evidence supports the inference that had Dr. Linnell devoted more of his time and talents to Newgard and less of them attempting to diagnose Newgard's wife, conceivably she would never have met so tragic and untimely a death. This Court thinks it abundantly clear, from the record in this case, that Dr. Linnell knew that Eloise Newgard was afraid of her husband, and it is utterly incredible that she would not have mentioned it to Dr. Linnell or that he would not have questioned her about it at their conference in Meade in June, 1965. Yet that is Dr. Linnell's testimony.

Because of the completely groundless statements by Newgard concerning his wife's fidelity and the nature of his statements to Reverend Faust, Deputy Sheriffs Eagle and Vraa on the same subject, and in the light of Dr. Linnell's seeming preoccupation with having Eloise Newgard seek psychiatric help herself, it seems singularly appropriate to point out some of the testimony received in this case concerning Eloise A. Newgard. Dr. William E. G. Lancaster, an able and experienced physician, a retired member of the Fargo Clinic, and for some 35 years a member of the Cass County Mental Health Board, who knew her well, said she was "as stable a nurse as we ever had." C. Warner Litten, Manager of the Fargo Clinic, who hired and supervised Mrs. Newgard, said "She was the finest nurse I ever employed." The evidence shows Eloise A. Newgard to have been a fine Christian woman, a splendid mother, and a faithful wife.

Dr. Linnell ignored and rejected every warning signal that Newgard was delusional at Meade and every warning signal that Eloise A. Newgard had every reason to be in mortal fear of her husband because of his prior conduct and the nature of some of the letters he wrote her while a patient at Meade. Dr. Linnell felt the recommittal order of the Cass County Mental Health Board of May 27, 1965, was "incorrect." Along with its recommittal order the Cass board sent to Meade Newgard's letter to his wife dated May 22, 1965. Dr. Linnell still referred to Newgard's cattle deals as "not a case of delusional thinking, it was exaggeration." Donald E. Frees, a social worker at the Veterans Administration Hospital in Fargo, made a thorough, comprehensive and very revealing report on the family history of the Newgards at the request of Meade. Dr. Linnell saw this instrument and conceded that he had no information that would provide him any basis for disregarding the information in Mr. Frees' report. Yet it is clear from the evidence that Dr. Linnell ignored the report. Had he even heeded the warning implicit in the summary of the social worker, Mr. Frees, which suggested that Newgard had become quite astute at manipulating people, it might have given the doctor pause, but it did not. It is worth noting that Dr. Rosenbaum testified that psychiatrists could not rely upon what a patient tells them in a mental hospital and that is why they have social service reports. Dr. Rosenbaum was shown Mr. Frees' report and testified that it was better than average.

One of the Government witnesses testifying was Dr. Jesse H. Craft, a clinical psychologist on the Meade staff, who evaluated Newgard. Dr. Craft gave Newgard certain tests and submitted a written evaluation to Dr. Linnell as a diagnostic aid to the psychiatrist. His testing showed, among other things, clues of organic brain damage. Dr. George B. Kish, the Chief Clinical Psychologist at Meade, testified that he did not agree with Dr. Craft that there was evidence of brain damage, even though Dr. Kish had not read all the reports on Newgard. Dr. Craft had been questioned under oath by Mr. Olin M. Stansbury, Jr., a Field Examiner for the Veterans Administration and one of the Government's attorneys in this trial. These questions and answers had been reduced to writing and sworn to before Mr. Stansbury on December 10, 1965. Paradoxically, when plaintiff's counsel demanded to see Dr. Craft's statement, which on its face was styled "deposition," the Government vigorously objected that it was the "work product" of Government lawyers. Dr. Linnell had been similarly questioned under oath twice, on December 9th and December 12th, 1965. But when plaintiff's attorney asked for copies of Dr. Linnell's sworn statements Government counsel promptly produced them without objection or without any reference to "work product."

We now examine the record to see whether it may be determined why the Government's position was so flexible with respect to Dr. Linnell's prior interrogation and so inflexible with respect to the questioning of Dr. Craft. Among the questions asked of Dr. Craft by Mr. Stansbury on December 10, 1965, under oath, were these:

Q. Have you been informed of the facts on the commitment to the effect that he had choked his wife and had a loaded pistol in the home the day that his wife had asked for his commitment?
A. No, he didn't tell me anything about that.

Q. Did you ever have access to the VA Hospital Correspondence File in which a copy of that transcript is available?
A. No, I didn't.
Q. Had anyone ever told you about that?
A. Not that I recall.
Q. Now, in view of that fact, if in fact it were true, would you have taken his show of jealously [*sic*] after July 1st more seriously in your recommendations to the Team before they placed him out on leave of absence?
A. *I certainly would if there had been any indication that he had any serious intent toward the wife. I certainly would have recommended against his going.*
Q. Maybe I'm not making myself clear, Doctor, but what I have in mind is if you had all the information that you have had before July 18th with the exception of the fact that you would have been furnished the information from the commitment to the effect that he had tried to choke his wife on or about January 17th, 1965, would that one more piece of information made you hesitant in agreeing with the Team that he should be released on a leave of absence? Just the one fact that one time previously he had tried to choke his wife or had threatened to and apparently had a loaded gun available in the home to do damage.
A. *I certainly wouldn't have recommended his release had I known that he had any such ideas or had behaved in that way.*
Q. Why?
A. *Because it would have shown more evidence of his homicidal—rather it would have shown evidence of homicidal thinking which I was completely unaware of* [Emphasis mine.]

There follows a series of questions by Mr. Stansbury and answers by Dr. Craft which clearly show that Mr. Stansbury sought to rehabilitate Dr. Craft's testimony, which was patently damaging to the Government's position. In the posture of this lawsuit that course of conduct with Dr. Craft, the Government's own witness, falls just short of being reprehensible.

The plaintiff alleges that the Government, acting through its duly authorized agents employed by the Veterans Administration, undertook the custody, care and treatment of Newgard, knowing him to be an insane and incompetent person with homicidal tendencies, and that the Government's inexcusable negligence was the proximate cause of Eloise A. Newgard's death on July 31, 1965, at the hands of her husband.

The plaintiff's burden in this type of case is not an easy one, but it has successfully borne it, in proving, by a preponderance of the relevant, material and credible evidence, that the negligence of the defendant acting by and through its duly authorized agents and employees was indeed the sole and proximate cause of the death of Eloise A. Newgard, and the damages sustained by the plaintiff as a result of her slaying.

The Government argued that modern psychiatry was on trial in this lawsuit. I reject that argument. It is not overstatement to suggest, however, that the *modi operandi* of some of its practitioners are. And that of some psychologists as well.

The Government contends by way of affirmative defense that the United States is exempt from liability under § 2680(a) of Title 28 U.S.C.A. which provides that § 1346(b) shall not apply to:

> (a) Any claim based upon an act or omission of an employee of the Government, exercising due care, in the execution of a statute or regulation, whether or not such statute or regulation be valid, or based upon the exercise or performance or the

failure to exercise or perform a discretionary function or duty on the part of a federal agency or an employee of the Government, whether or not the discretion involved be abused.

It is the Government's position that the granting of the leave of absence to Newgard to work on the Davis ranch near Belle Fourche was the exercise of due care in the execution of a Veterans Administration regulation, and that this falls within the exception set out in § 2680.

Considering the circumstances under which Newgard was placed on leave of absence at the Davis ranch, as disclosed by the credible evidence, the Government's agents and employees not only did not exercise due care; in the view of this Court they exercised no care at all.

The test of liability under the Federal Tort Claims Act is set out in § 2674, the first paragraph of which reads:

> The United States shall be liable, respecting the provisions of this title relating to tort claims, in the same manner and to the same extent as a private individual under like circumstances, but shall not be liable for interest prior to judgment or for punitive damages.

The Fourth Circuit Court of Appeals pointed out in *Somerset Seafood Co.* v. *United States,* 193 F.2d 631, 634, that:

> . . . The Act must be given a liberal construction to ward off the obvious evil which the Act was passed to prevent—the cumbersome and unwieldy practice of seeking relief in Congress by private bills. The jurisdiction granted to the federal District Courts by § 1346(b) of the Act is couched in quite broad and very expansive language. See, *United States* v. *Aetna Casualty & Surety Co.*, 338 U.S. 366, 383, 70 S.Ct. 207, 94 L.Ed. 171; *American Stevedores* v. *Porello,* 330 U.S. 446, 453, 67 S.Ct. 847, 91 L.Ed. 1011; *United States* v. *Travis,* 4 Cir., 165 F.2d 546, 547.

Again, the Fourth Circuit in *White* v. *United States,* 317 F.2d 13, 17 (1963), speaking through Judge J. Spencer Bell, said:

> . . . While the policy embodied in the Veterans Administration Regulations that patients should be allowed the maximum of freedom warranted by their condition is a discretionary decision, the application of that policy to an individual case is not within the category of policy decisions exempted by the statute. The application of that policy to the individual case is an administrative decision at the operational level which if negligently done will make the Government liable—whether it involves substandard professional conduct (malpractice) or simple negligence in custodial care. . . .

This Court is of the opinion that in the case of Newgard the defendant's agents were tortiously negligent both in the matter of substandard professional conduct on the part of Dr. Linnell, and because of gross negligence on the part of Dr. Linnell and Dr. Cheney in the careless custodial care of Newgard. Moreover, Dr. Craft was negligent in not bringing to the attention of the appropriate Meade personnel a letter from Newgard while the latter was on the Davis ranch, in which Newgard made reference to returning to North Dakota and selling some cattle. Newgard's cattle dealings[4] were just

[4]Sometime during late 1964 or early 1965 Newgard told his pastor, Reverend Faust, he was giving $50,000.00 to the church "through some cattle deal."

as delusional as his horse dealings. The Government did produce one John J. Froehlich, a farmer, who on January 9, 1965, made "a deal" with Newgard for twelve head of quarter horses for $2400.00. Newgard got the horses and Mr. Froehlich got a bad check. Through the efforts of Eloise A. Newgard Mr. Froehlich got eleven of the twelve horses back. Somewhat crestfallen Mr. Froehlich concluded, after Newgard's check was returned, that Newgard really was not a horse dealer after all. Because of Newgard's well known delusional thinking, Dr. Craft was negligent in not seeing that the letter was at least placed in Newgard's file where presumably some Meade personnel, in due course, would have read it. Dr. Craft does not even know what happened to the letter.

Nor may it be said that Dr. Curt L. Rosenbaum, Meade's Chief of Staff, was not negligent. It was he who received the telephone call from Eloise A. Newgard. Routinely he put a note of the conversation in Newgard's file, but at no time did he direct anyone at Meade to pursue the matter of Eloise Newgard's phone call further to determine what caused her to be upset and allegedly to have hung up the phone on him. Dr. Rosenbaum, as the supervisor of all professional services at Meade, did discuss the matter with Dr. Harland T. Hermann, Meade's Chief of Psychiatry, and suggested Newgard should not be released because of his wife's feelings, but he did not, as he should have, follow through on the matter.

Dr. Hermann, a man with impressive credentials as a psychiatrist, conceded that Newgard's leave of absence was not a full discharge and that Newgard was to return to Meade for reevaluation. There is, of course, no question about whether Newgard was a patient under the control of Meade at the time of Eloise A. Newgard's murder. He was.

It is a fair and reasonable inference from the testimony and evidence in this case that the psychiatrists and psychologists at Meade believed Newgard's unsubstantiated and uninvestigated stories about his business ventures and his statements about his wife and that no one placed any credence in the statements of Eloise A. Newgard, Dr. Lancaster, Judge Paulsen, Mr. Rutland, Dr. Kohlmeyer, or Dr. Hubert A. Carbonne.[5] Dr. Carbonne, the record shows, is a psychiatrist certified by the American Board of Psychiatry and Neurology in 1950 and is also a man with impressive qualifications.

It is also a fair and reasonable inference to be drawn from the evidence that Dr. Linnell felt there was something wrong with Eloise A. Newgard; that she was not interested in anything but keeping Newgard away from her; that she did not visit him often enough at Meade; and that her physical fear of Newgard was groundless. Dr. Linnell not only failed to use the facilities available to him to attempt to verify the things Newgard was telling him, and which Dr. Linnell mistakenly described as "exaggeration", but obviously completely ignored the contents of the social service report from Fargo which certainly should have alerted him to the fact that there was something seriously wrong with Newgard.

It is important to note that Dr. Carbonne testified that the purpose of a social worker's report is "to contribute as much information as can possibly be gathered to be presented for the purpose of understanding the patient's problems and *arriving at a diagnosis*." (Emphasis mine.)

Judgment for plaintiff.

[5]Dr. Carbonne, the Superintendent of the Jamestown Hospital, on February 2, 1965, signed the Diagnosis Impression of Newgard, reciting: "Schizophrenic reaction, catatonic type. Recommendation: Continued hospitalization. Patient should be evaluated for electro-convulsive therapy. Impairment: Severe."

LACK OF INFORMED CONSENT

Definition of informed consent. "Informed consent" is a court-made doctrine with a definition and rationale that are succinctly stated in the following excerpt from the opinion in *Sard* v. *Hardy,* 281 Md. 432, 379 A.2d 1014 (1977):

> The doctrine of informed consent, which we shall apply here, follows logically from the universally recognized rule that a physician, treating a mentally competent adult under non-emergency circumstances, cannot properly undertake to perform surgery or administer other therapy without the prior consent of his patient. . . . In order for the patient's consent to be effective, it must have been an "informed" consent, one that is given after the patient has received a fair and reasonable explanation of the contemplated treatment or procedure. . . .
>
> The fountainhead of the doctrine of informed consent is the patient's right to exercise control over his own body, at least when undergoing elective surgery, by deciding for himself whether or not to submit to the particular therapy. . . . Other courts have bottomed the physician's duty to disclose on the fiducial quality of the physician-patient relationship. . . . Whatever its source, the doctrine of informed consent takes full account of the probability that unlike the physician, the patient is untrained in medical science, and therefore depends completely on the trust and skill of his physician for the information on which he makes his decision. . . .
>
> Simply stated, the doctrine of informed consent imposes on a physician, before he subjects his patient to medical treatment, the duty to explain the procedure to the patient and to warn him of any material risks or dangers inherent in or collateral to the therapy, so as to enable the patient to make an intelligent and informed choice about whether or not to undergo such treatment. . . .
>
> This duty to disclose is said to require a physician to reveal to his patient the nature of the ailment, the nature of the proposed treatment, the probability of success of the contemplated therapy and its alternatives, and the risk of unfortunate consequences associated with such treatment. . . . The law does not allow a physician to substitute his judgment for that of the patient in the matter of consent to treatment.

The opinion in *Sard* discusses the three elements and attributes of the cause of action arising from a practitioner's failure to obtain informed consent prior to treatment: (1) the scope of the practitioner's duty to warn, and whether the duty is to be measured by a professional standard of care or a general reasonableness standard; (2) whether expert medical testimony is required to prove the standard of care; and (3) the appropriate test for proving causal connection between the failure to disclose and any injury or damage that might result.

The notion that physicians—and we might add other health service providers—have a legal duty to make a full and frank disclosure of all facts pertinent to the illness and the treatment was clearly enunciated in the case of *Natanson* v. *Kline,* 350 P.2d 1093 and 354 P.2d 670 (1960).

Natanson v. *Kline*, 186 Kan. 393, 350 P.2d 1093 (1960)

SCHROEDER, Justice.

This is an action for malpractice against a hospital and the physician in charge of its radiology department to recover for injuries sustained as the result of radiation therapy with radioactive cobalt, alleged to have been given in an excessive amount.

The plaintiff (appellant), Irma Natanson, suffering from a cancer of the breast, had a radical left mastectomy performed on May 29, 1955. At the direction of Dr. Crumpacker, the surgeon who performed that operation, the plaintiff engaged Dr. John R. Kline, a radiologist, for radiation therapy to the site of the mastectomy and the surrounding areas.

Dr. Kline, a licensed physician and specialist in radiation therapy, was head of the radiology department at St. Francis Hospital at Wichita, Kansas. The plaintiff seeks damages for injuries claimed to have been sustained as a result of alleged acts of negligence in the administration of the cobalt radiation treatment. Dr. Kline and the hospital were named as a defendants (appellees).

The case was tried to a jury which returned a verdict in favor of both defendants. The plaintiff's motion for a new trial having been denied, this appeal followed specifying various trial errors.

The questions controlling the decision herein relate to the giving of instructions by the trial court.

It will be unnecessary to relate in detail all the facts presented by the evidence as abstracted, consisting of more than three hundred pages, to dispose of the issues on appeal.

The jury was submitted two special questions. In the first it found that the defendants were not guilty of any act or acts of negligence which were the proximate cause of plaintiff's injury. The jury having found in the negative on the first, the second question required no answer.

It must be conceded, insofar as the evidence is concerned, that all presumptions are, and must be, in favor of the verdict. All issues of fact have been resolved in favor of the defendants. *Lord* v. *Hercules Powder Co.*, 161 Kan. 268, 167 P.2d 209; and *Beye* v. *Andres*, 179 Kan. 502, 296 P.2d 1049.

The appellant contends, however, the uncontradicted evidence shows the defendants negligent as a matter of law.

Dr. Kline was called by the plaintiff to testify in the trial court and in great detail counsel examined Dr. Kline to educate the court and jury concerning cobalt radiation therapy in the treatment of cancer. A short summary in rough will serve as a basis for further discussion.

The purpose of any irradiation therapy is to destroy tissue. The theory of destruction of cancer by irradiation therapy is that when treatment is given in a series of doses (fractionation in medical terms), the greater ability of normal tissue to recover from irradiation effects enables it to survive while the cancerous tissue is destroyed.

Dosages of irradiation are expressed in roentgen. All forms of irradiation have some point of maximum, or one hundred per cent, dosage and diminish as they penetrate deeper into the body. In the case of X-rays the point of maximum dosage is in the skin. In the case of cobalt irradiation the maximum dosage is received at a point about five millimeters beneath the outer surface of the skin. The primary advantages of cobalt irradiation over X-ray irradiation are deeper penetration and less skin injury. The amount of X-ray which can be administered is governed in a large measure by the amount which the skin can tolerate. The amount of cobalt irradiation which can be administered is governed by the tolerance of the tissues lying five millimeters below the outer surface of the skin.

By ''equilibrium'' dose in relation to radioactive cobalt is meant the maximum dose, which occurs about five millimeters below the outer surface of the skin. ''Tumor'' dose means the quantity received at the known or assumed depth of the tumor.

Dr. Kline ordered the administration of cobalt irradiation for the appellant in ''routine fashion.'' To him and to his assistant, Dr. Somers, this meant a tumor dose of 4,400 roentgen delivered to the supraclavicular area in a period of sixteen days. For this purpose the tumor was assumed to extend from outer surface in front to outer surface behind. ''Routine fashion'' also meant a dosage of 4,800 roentgen delivered over the outer two centimeters of the remainder of the left chest from a point at the rear portion of the left side of the patient's body around past the breast bone in a period of twenty-three days. It also meant an approximately equal dosage to the outer two centimeters over the breast bone including the chain of lymph nodes running longitudinally along each side of the breast bone.

Material to further discussion is the fact that the prescription or outline of treatment called for 4,800 roentgen to be delivered to the outer two centimeters of the chest wall. It also directed that this treatment be delivered by means of rotating beam. According to the testimony of the appellant's husband the rotational equipment had not been installed and ready for use at the time of the appellant's first treatment. It was installed and ready for use soon thereafter.

A radiologist, who administers cobalt irradiation treatment with rotational equipment, must have the assistance of a specialist in physics. Dr. Kline's assistant was a hospital employee by the name of Darter who determined by necessary computations how to administer the desired quantity of radiation, ordered by Dr. Kline, by means of a moving beam. Darter had graduated from Wichita University with a B.S. degree the preceding spring and had a six months' special course on irradiation therapy at Massachusetts Institute of Technology. His actual experience with radioactive cobalt therapy began with the installation of the unit at the St. Francis Hospital on January 29, 1955, some four months before the appellant's treatment began.

Highly summarized, the evidence upon which the appellant relies is that the radioactive cobalt beam was delivered at an angle to the chest wall in an effort to avoid injury to the lungs. In making the calculations to achieve the tumor doses (one and one-half to two centimeters deep), the equilibrium doses (five millimeters deep) were not calculated by Darter.

Dr. Paul A. Roys, an assistant professor of physics at Wichita University, who was a specialist in the field of nuclear physics of which radiation physics is a part, was called to testify concerning his calculations of the roentgen delivered to various parts of the appellant's chest wall in accordance with the time chart and dosages administered to the appellant as a result of Darter's calculations. From Dr. Roys' calculations the equilibrium doses administered at several segments of the chest wall were from 5,670 roentgen to 6,260 roentgen at a depth of five millimeters. It was in these segments where the appellant's injuries were sustained.

Dr. Kline had previously testified that the soft tissues of the chest wall could tolerate about 5,000 roentgen in twenty-four or twenty-five days; that the cartilage could tolerate about 5,500 roentgen over a period of twenty-eight days, and ordinarily bone would stand a larger amount. The appellant argues the effect upon her of the administration of amounts ranging from 5,670 roentgen to 6,280 roentgen certainly corroborates Dr. Kline's testimony. The entire chest, skin, cartilage and bone were completely destroyed in those areas.

There was other evidence which contradicted the appellant's theory, however. When Dr. Kline was called as a witness on his own behalf, he stated the prescribed dosage of 4,400 roentgen was intended as a minimum dosage, and was the smallest dosage which would be effective and had to be given, even though he knew that portions of the chest would receive a much higher dosage. He testified that a doctor has to take a chance in the treatment of cancer, that he knew there was danger of injury from such treatment, but that he took a calculated risk. This risk is determined to a large extent by the tolerance of the individual concerned. Some patients have a much higher tolerance than others. He further testified that he had treated approximately seventy-five breast and cancer cases since the treatment of the appellant, all of which were treated in the same manner with the same number of roentgens directed to be given.

Dr. Hare, a radiologist from Los Angeles, was called to testify for the appellees. He said that for five years he had been using 6,000 roentgen up to 9,000 roentgen on the treatment of cancer cases.

At the time treatment started the appellant had an ulcer about the size of a quarter under her left arm which remained from the mastectomy. It had not stopped draining. After treatment started the drainage increased and, according to the appellant, she understood the treatment was to shrink the area but instead it seemed to be growing larger.

There is no issue presented by the record as to the relationship between Dr. Kline and the St. Francis Hospital. The petition pleaded that the defendants were engaged in a joint adventure or in the alternative that the defendant physician was acting within the scope of his employment as agent, servant and employee of the defendant hospital. The answer of the defendant hospital admitted that the defendant physician "was in charge of its radiology department." Moreover, the pleadings raised no issues between the defendants.

Upon the foregoing evidence on the state of the record presented herein, it cannot be said the appellees were guilty of negligence as a matter of law. At best it may be said, upon all the facts and circumstances presented by the record, there was evidence from which a jury could find that the proximate cause of the appellant's injury was the negligence of the defendants. On the other hand a jury, *properly instructed,* would be justified in finding for the appellees.

We shall next consider whether the jury was properly instructed.

The code of civil procedure requires the court to give general instructions to the jury, with or without request having been made for the same. (G.S.1949, 60-2909, *Fifth.*) This provision has frequently been interpreted to require the court to define the issues and state at least generally the law applicable thereto. *Bushey* v. *Coffman,* 109 Kan. 652, 201 P. 1103; *Knox* v. *Barnard,* 181 Kan. 943, 317 P.2d 452; and *Schmid* v. *Eslick,* 181 Kan. 997, 317 P.2d 459. The trial court in summarizing the pleadings for the jury in its instructions was quite brief. Aside from general factual recitations the material portions of this summarization given in instruction No. 1 are as follows:

> In this case the plaintiff Irma Natanson . . . alleges . . . *that Dr. Kline and personnel of St. Francis Hospital administered to the plaintiff a series of cobalt radiation treatments in such a negligent manner* that the skin, flesh and muscles beneath her

> left arm sloughed away and ribs of her left chest were so burned that they became necrotic, or dead; . . .
>
> The defendants then filed their answers in the case in which they allege that the treatments were properly administered and that they were not guilty of any negligence toward the plaintiff. [Emphasis added]

Then followed the usual instruction (No. 2) that the foregoing statement taken from the pleadings set forth the various claims and contentions of the parties against each other, and that such claims and contentions are to be considered only as they may have been proved by evidence presented during the trial of the case.

Instruction No. 3 reads in part:

> This is a lawsuit based upon negligence. In the conduct of human affairs, the law imposes upon us the obligation to use due and proper care to avoid hurt or injury to others. Thus, negligence may be defined as a violation of the duty to use due and proper care. The term, 'due and proper care' means, in this case, such care as medical specialists in radiology in this community would ordinarily and reasonably use under the same or similar circumstances.

The court then instructed that negligence is never presumed—it must be proved by a preponderance or greater weight of the evidence; it defined preponderance or greater weight of the evidence and instructed that negligence may be established by circumstantial evidence.

Instruction No. 4 given by the court reads:

> The law does not require that treatments given by a physician to a patient shall attain nearly perfect results. He is not responsible in damages for lack of success or honest mistakes or errors of judgment unless it be shown that he did not possess that degree of learning and skill ordinarily possessed by radiologists of good standing in his community, or that he was not exercising reasonable and ordinary care in applying such skill and learning to the treatment of the patient. And if among radiologists more than one method of treatment is recognized, it would not be negligence for the physician to have adopted any of such methods if the method he did adopt was a recognized and approved method in the profession at the time and place of treatment.

On this appeal the court is not concerned with the general instructions on negligence or instruction No. 4, which correctly states the law. The cases upon which the appellees rely to substantiate these instructions are sound law. *Tefft* v. *Wilcox,* 6 Kan. 46; *Sly* v. *Powell,* 87 Kan. 142, 123 P. 881; *Paulich* v. *Nipple,* 104 Kan. 801, 180 P. 771; *James* v. *Grigsby,* 114 Kan. 627, 220 P. 267; *Riggs* v. *Gouldner,* 150 Kan. 727, 96 P.2d 694; *Cummins* v. *Donley,* 173 Kan. 463, 249 P.2d 695; and *Goheen* v. *Graber,* 181 Kan. 107, 309 P.2d 636.

The amended petition pleaded negligence in eight specific particulars, one or more of which presented issues which the jury was required to determine on the basis of the evidence presented. It was proper for the trial court to exclude those specific allegations of negligence enumerated in the amended petition concerning which there was no evidence, but it should have set forth those specific allegations of negligence concerning which there was evidence. The general summarization, consisting of the italicized portion of instruction No. 1 heretofore quoted, was insufficient to meet this obligation of the trial court.

The answers filed by both of the defendants in the lower court denied the specific allegations of negligence alleged in the amended petition and pleaded "the plaintiff assumed the risk and hazard of said treatment."

One of the alleged grounds of negligence, concerning which there was evidence before the jury, was that Dr. Kline failed to warn the appellant the course of treatment which he undertook to administer involved great risk of bodily injury or death.

The appellant requested and the trial court refused to give the following instruction:

> You are instructed that the relationship between physician and patient is a fiduciary one. The relationship requires the physician to make a full disclosure to the patient of all matters within his knowledge affecting the interests of the patient. Included within the matters which the physician must advise the patient are the nature of the proposed treatment and any hazards of the proposed treatment which are known to the physician. Every adult person has the right to determine for himself or herself whether or not he will subject his body to hazards of any particular medical treatment.
>
> You are instructed that if you find from the evidence that defendant Kline knew that the treatment he proposed to administer to plaintiff involved hazard or danger he was under a duty to advise plaintiff of that fact and if you further find that defendant Kline did not advise plaintiff of such hazads then defendant Kline was guilty of negligence.

There was evidence from which the jury could have found that the appellant fully appreciated the danger and the risk of the radiation treatment. The appellant's husband testified:

> Q. Yes, how did it happen you went there for the conference with Dr. Kline?
> A. We, of course, made a periodic visit to Dr. Crumpacker after the operation, and he told us that as a precautionary measure Mrs. Natanson should go to the St. Francis Hospital and take the cobalt treatment. He explained to us that the cobalt was a new therapy; that it was much more powerful than the x-ray they had used previously. He suggested we see Dr. Kline.

On cross examination he testified:

> Q. Just a question or two. Mr. Natanson, when you and your wife went to see Dr. Crumpacker, did you have a discussion with him about the purpose of the irradiation?
> A. Yes.
> Q. And, was the general objection of irradiation explained to you?
> A. Yes.
> Q. And, that was when Mrs. Natanson was with you?
> A. Yes.
> Q. Now, did you consult any radiologist other than Dr. Kline in determining anything about this irradiation?
> A. No, sir.
>
> . . . .
>
> Q. Now, I take it that it was Dr. Crumpacker's thought or suggestion at least to you that Dr. Kline be consulted?
> A. Yes.

Q. And, up to the time you engaged Dr. Kline, Dr. Crumpacker had been the doctor on the case?
A. Yes.

There was also testimony from the appellant and her husband that Dr. Kline did not inform the appellant the treatment involved any danger whatever. The testimony of Dr. Kline, a radiologist with special training in cobalt irradiation, was that he knew he was "taking a chance" with the treatment he proposed to administer and that such treatment involved a "calculated risk". He testified there was always a danger of injury in the treatment of cancer. Insofar as the record discloses Dr. Kline did not testify that he informed the appellant the treatment involved any danger. His only testimony relevant thereto was the following:

Q. Now, tell us what transpired when you first met with the Natansons?
A. I could not completely recall that meeting. It was such a long time ago.
Q. Just tell us what you can recall of it?
A. I remember Mr. and Mrs. Natanson coming in to see me. I can't remember if I met them in my office or whether we were downstairs. I remember in a very vague way. I remember in a vague way that we discussed the treatment, about how long it took, the number of areas we would irradiate. I have a recollection of that. I remember we took her into the treatment room. She was marked out, measured. I believe the marking out and measurement was done by Mr. Darter. Her first treatment occurred the first day she came. I am not sure of that but I think so.
Q. Have you told us everything you recall?
A. Yes.

No other evidence appears in the record concerning the subject.

The appellees argue that we are here concerned with a case where the patient consented to the treatment, but afterwards alleges that the nature and consequences of the risks of the treatment were not properly explained to her. They point out this is not an action for assault and battery, where a patient has given no consent to the treatment.

What appears to distinguish the case of the unauthorized surgery or treatment from traditional assault and battery cases is the fact that in almost all of the cases the physician is acting in relatively good faith for the benefit of the patient. While it is true that in some cases the results are not in fact beneficial to a patient, the courts have repeatedly stated that doctors are not insurers. The traditional assault and battery involves a defendant who is acting for the most part out of malice or in a manner generally considered as "anti-social." One who commits an assault and battery is not seeking to confer any benefit upon the one assaulted.

The fundamental distinction between assault and battery on the one hand, and negligence such as would constitute malpractice, on the other, is that the former is intentional and the latter unintentional. *Hershey* v. *Peake,* 115 Kan. 562, 223 P. 1113; and *Maddox* v. *Neptune,* 175 Kan. 465, 264 P.2d 1073.

We are here concerned with a case where the patient consented to the treatment, but alleges in a malpractice action that the nature and consequences of the risks of the treatment were not properly explained to her. This relates directly to the question whether the physician has obtained the informed consent of the patient to render the treatment administered.

The treatment of a cancer patient with radioactive cobalt is relatively new. Until the use of atomic energy appeared in this country, X ray was the type of radiation treatment used for such patients. Radioactive cobalt is manufactured by the Atomic Energy Commission in a neutron pill by bombarding the stable element of cobalt in its pure state. This makes the cobalt unstable and by reason thereof it is radioactive. The radioactive cobalt emits two homogeneous beams of pure energy called gamma rays, very close in character, which are far more powerful than the ordinary X rays. It produces no other rays to be filtered out. This makes it desirable for use in the treatment of cancer patients. The cobalt machine may be compared to a three million volt X ray machine.

Radioactive cobalt is so powerful that the Atomic Energy Commission specifies the construction of the room in which the cobalt unit is to be placed. The walls of the room are made of concrete forty inches thick and the ceiling, also concrete, is twenty-four inches thick. The room is sunken down in a courtyard outside the hospital. A passageway off the control room about ten feet long leads to the treatment room. All controls are placed in the outer control room and, when the radiation treatment is administered to a patient, the operator in the outer room looks through a specially designed thick lead quartz glass which gives a telescopic view. A periodic report of radiation outside the room must be made to the Atomic Energy Commission in accordance with regulations. These facts were given by Dr. Kline in his testimony.

These facts are not commonly known and a patient cannot be expected to know the hazards or the danger of radiation from radioactive cobalt unless the patient is informed by a radiologist who knows the dangers of injury from cobalt irradiation. While Dr. Kline did not testify that the radiation he gave the appellant caused her injury, he did state cobalt irradiation could cause the injury which the appellant did sustain.

What is the extent of a physician's duty to confide in his patient where the physician suggests or recommends a particular method of treatment? What duty is there upon him to explain the nature and probable consequences of that treatment to the patient? To what extent should he disclose the existence and nature of the risks inherent in the treatment?

We have been cited to no Kansas cases, nor has our research disclosed any, dealing directly with the foregoing questions. A recent article by William A. Kelly published in the Kansas Law Review entitled "The Physician, The Patient, And The Consent" (8 Kan.L.Rev. 405), reviews many malpractice cases dealing with the consent of the patient, but the article fails to deal with the problem of disclosure involving on one hand the right of the patient to decide for himself and on the other a possible therapeutic ground for withholding information which may create tension by depressing or exciting the patient. This subject has been touched upon in an article by Charles C. Lund, M.D.; "The Doctor, The Patient, And The Truth" (19 Tenn.L.Rev. 344 [1946]), and in an article by Hubert Winston Smith, LL.B.; M.D.; "Therapeutic Privilege To Withhold Specific Diagnosis From Patient Sick With Serious Or Fatal Illness" (19 Tenn.L.Rev. 349 [1946]). Allan H. McCoid, Associate Professor of Law, University of Minnesota, has written two recent articles, one "A Reappraisal Of Liability For Unauthorized Medical Treatment" (41 Minn.L.Rev. 381), published in March, 1957, and the other "The Care Required Of Medical Practitioners" (12 Vanderbilt L.Rev. 549, 586), published in June, 1959.

The courts frequently state that the relation between the physician and his patient is a fiduciary one, and therefore the physician has an obligation to make a full and frank disclosure to the patient of all pertinent facts related to his illness. We are here concerned with a case where the physician is charged with treating the patient without consent on the ground the patient was not fully informed of the nature of the treatment or its consequences, and, therefore, any "consent" obtained was ineffective. An effort will be made to review the cases from foreign jurisdictions most nearly in point with the question presently at hand, although none may be said to be directly in point.

In 1958 the Supreme Court of Minnesota in *Bang* v. *Charles T. Miller Hospital,* 251 Minn. 427, 88 N.W.2d 186, had an assault case before it, and thought not alleged as a malpractice action for negligence, a new trial was granted on the ground that a fact issue was presented for the jury to determine whether the patient consented to the performance of the operation. There the patient went to a urologist because of urinary trouble and apparently consented to a cystoscopic examination and a prostate operation. He was not informed that part of the procedure of a transurethral prostatic resection would be the tying off of his sperm ducts. In the opinion the court said:

> While we have no desire to hamper the medical profession in the outstanding progress it has made and continues to make in connection with the study and solution of health and disease problems, it is our opinion that a reasonable rule is that, where a physician or surgeon can ascertain in advance of an operation alternative situations and no immediate emergency exists, a patient should be informed of the alternative possibilities and given a chance to decide before the doctor proceeds with the operation. By that we mean that, in a situation such as the case before us where no immediate emergency exists, a patient should be informed before the operation that if his spermatic cords were severed it would result in his sterilization, but on the other hand if this were not done there would be a possibility of an infection which could result in serious consequences. Under such conditions the patient would at least have the opportunity of deciding whether he wanted to take the chance of a possible infection if the operation was performed in one manner or to become sterile if performed in another. [251 Minn. at pages 434, 435, 88 N.W.2d at page 190.]

A malpractice action was before the Fifth Circuit Court in *Lester* v. *Aetna Casualty & Surety Company,* 240 F.2d 676. The patient was given electro-shock treatments prescribed by a psychiatrist and suffered a bad result. In affirming the jury's finding the court held the patient's wife gave sufficient legal consent, and said:

> The basic, the fundamental, difficulty which confronts plaintiff on this appeal is that he presents his case as though it were one of a person being deprived by another of due process of law, instead of grounding it upon the well settled principles that a physician must, except in real and serious emergencies, acquaint the patient or, when the circumstances require it, some one properly acting for him, of the diagnosis and the treatment proposed, and obtain consent, thereto express or implied, and, consent obtained must proceed in accordance with proper reasonable medical standards *and in the exercise of due care....* [240 F.2d at page 679. Emphasis added.]

The appellees rely upon the Canadian case of *Kenny* v. *Lockwood* [1932], 1 D.L.R. 507, where a patient alleged the defendants falsely and recklessly, without caring whether it was true or false, and without reasonable ground for believing it to be true, represented the operation to be "simple," and that her hand "would be all right in three weeks.'' No evidence was presented to suggest fraud or recklessness and the plaintiff's argument proceeded mainly upon the duty which it was said the defendants owed to the plaintiff, due to the peculiar relation set up between a surgeon and his patient. The Ontario trial judge concluded that it was the duty of the defendant doctors to ''enlighten the patient's mind in a plain and reasonable way as to what her ailment was, as to what were the risks of operating promptly, what were the risks of delaying the operation, and what the risks of not operating at all. Having discharged that duty, it was their further duty to secure from the patient a decision or consent as to what course is to be followed, and if that decision or consent is not had and the surgeons operate and the operation turns out badly the surgeons are liable. Such a relationship is established between a person of special skill and knowledge and a person of no skill or knowledge upon the facts required for the making of a decision that, unless the person with the special skill and knowledge discharges the duty which he owes of placing the patient in a position to make a decision, that person, when he is employed and paid because of his special skill and knowledge, has failed to perform his duty, and that breach of duty makes him liable in damages for untoward results.'' (*Kenny* v. *Lockwood Clinic Ltd.* [1931], 4 D.L.R. 906, 907.)

The trial court found for the plaintiff but on appeal the judgment was reversed, the appellate court saying there was some testimony that the doctors had explained all details to the plaintiff, although the extracts contained in the opinion indicate that the doctor admitted to having said that the operation was not a very serious one and that he had not clearly presented the alternatives to the plaintiff. In the court's opinion it was said:

> . . . the duty cast upon the surgeon was to deal honestly with the patient as to the necessity, character and importance of the operation and its probable consequences and whether success might reasonably be expected to ameliorate or remove the trouble, but that such duty does not extend to warning the patient of the dangers incident to, or possible in, any operation, nor to details calculated to frighten or distress the patient.'' [p. 525.]

The court concluded upon the evidence presented:

> That the defendant Stoddart reasonably fulfilled the duty laid upon him arising out of the relationship of surgeon and patient, not being guilty of 'negligence in word' or 'economy of truth' nor of misleading the plaintiff, and so is not liable for breach of the duty. . . . [p. 526.]

In the opinion it was said the duty of a surgeon is to be honest in fact and to express his honest belief, and if he does so he ought not to be judged as if he had warranted a perfect cure nor to be found derelict in his duty on any meticulous criticism of his language.

The conclusion to be drawn from the foregoing cases is that where the physician or surgeon has affirmatively misrepresented the nature of the operation or has failed to point out the probable consequences of the course of treatment, he may be subjected to a claim of unauthorized treatment. But this does not mean that a doctor is under an obligation to describe in detail all of the possible consequences of treatment. It might be argued, as indicated by the authors of the various law review articles heretofore cited, that to make a complete disclosure of all facts, diagnoses and alternatives or possibilities which may occur to the doctor could so alarm the patient that it would, in fact, constitute bad medical practice. There is probably a privilege, on therapeutic grounds, to withhold the specific diagnosis where the disclosure of cancer or some other dread disease would seriously jeopardize the recovery of an unstable, temperamental or severely depressed patient. But in the ordinary case there would appear to be no such warrant for suppressing facts and the physician should make a substantial disclosure to the patient prior to the treatment or risk liability in tort.

Anglo-American law starts with the premise of thorough-going self determination. It follows that each man is considered to be master of his own body, and he may, if he be of sound mind, expressly prohibit the performance of life-saving surgery, or other medical treatment. A doctor might well believe that an operation or form of treatment is desirable or necessary but the law does not permit him to substitute his own judgment for that of the patient by any form of artifice or deception.

The mean between the two extremes of absolute silence on the part of the physician relative to the treatment of a patient and exhaustive discussion by the physician explaining in detail all possible risks and dangers was well stated by the California District Court of Appeal in *Salgo* v. *Leland Stanford, Etc. Bd. Trustees,* 1957, 154 Cal.App.2d 560, 317 P.2d 170. There the court had before it a malpractice action wherein the defendants were charged with *negligence*. The patient, his wife and son testified that the patient was not informed anything in the nature of an aortography was to be performed. Two of the doctors contradicted this, although admitting that the details of the procedure involving injection of a radio-opaque substance into the aorta and the possible dangers therefrom were not explained. As a result of the aortography the patient was paralyzed from the waist down. The trial court gave a rather broad instruction on the duty of the physician to disclose to the patient "all the facts which mutually affect his rights and interests and of the surgical risk, hazard and danger, if any." 154 Cal.App.2d at page 578, 317 P.2d at page 181. On appeal, the instruction was held to be overly broad, the court stating:

> . . . A physician violates his duty to his patient and subjects himself to liability if he witholds any facts which are necessary to form the basis of an intelligent constant by the patient to the proposed treatment. Likewise the physician may not minimize the known dangers of a procedure or operation in order to induce his patient's consent. At the same time, the physician must place the welfare of his patient above all else and this very fact places him in a position in which he sometimes must choose between two alternative courses of action. One is to explain to the patient every risk attendant upon any surgical procedure or operation, no matter how remote; this may well result in alarming a patient who is already unduly apprehensive and who may as a result refuse to undertake surgery in which there is in fact minimal risk; it may also result in actually increasing the risks by reason of the physiological results of the apprehension itself. The other is to recognize that each patient presents a separate problem, that the patient's mental and emotional condition is important and in certain cases may be crucial, and that in discussing the element of risk a certain amount of discretion must be employed consistent with the full disclosure of facts necessary to an informed consent. . . .
>
> The instruction given should be modified to inform the jury that the physician has such discretion consistent, of course, with the full disclosure of facts necesary to an informed consent. [154 Cal.App.2d at page 578, 317 P.2d at page 181]

The appellees rely upon *Hunt* v. *Bradshaw,* 1955, 242 N.C. 517, 88 S.E.2d 762, a North Carolina case. This was a malpractice action against a physician wherein the patient sought damages alleged to have resulted from the negligent failure of the defendant (1) to use reasonable care and diligence in the application of his knowledge and skill as a physician and surgeon, and (2) to exercise his best judgment in attempting to remove a small piece of steel from plaintiff's body. On these allegations of negligence the plaintiff contended, among other things, that the defendant advised the plaintiff the operation was simple, whereas it was serious and involved undisclosed risks. The plaintiff's evidence was sufficient to justify a finding the operation was of a very serious nature. The court after reviewing the evidence said:

> . . . Upon Dr. Bradshaw's advice the operation was decided upon. It is understandable the surgeon wanted to reassure the patient so that he would not go to the operating room unduly apprehensive. Failure to explain the risks involved, therefore, may be considered a mistake on the part of the surgeon, *but under the facts* cannot be deemed such want of ordinary care to import liability.
>
> Proof of what is in accord with approved surgical procedure and what constitutes the standard of care required of the surgeon in performing an operation, like the advisability of the operation itself, are matters not within the knowledge of lay witnesses but must be established by the testimony of qualified experts. . . .
>
> Plaintiff's expert testimony is sufficient to justify the finding the injury and damage to plaintiff's hand and arm resulted from the operation. But, as in cases of ordinary negligence, the fact that injury results is not proof the act which caused it was a negligent act. The doctrine *res ipsa loquitur* does not apply in cases of this character. . . .
>
> Of course, it seems hard to the patient in apparent good health that he should be advised to undergo an operation, and upon regaining consciousness finds that he has lost the use of an arm for the remainder of his life. Infallibility in human beings is not attainable. The law recognizes, and we think properly so, that the surgeon's hand, with its skill and training, is, after all, a human hand, guided by a human brain in a procedure in which the margin between safety and danger sometimes measures little more than the thickness of a sheet of paper.
>
> The plaintiff's case fails because of lack of expert testimony that the defendant failed, either to exercise due care in the operation, or to use his best judgment in advising it. . . . [242 N.C. at pages 523, 524, 88 S.E.2d at page 766. Emphasis added.]

Under *the facts* presented by the case it does not appear the allegations of negligence were sufficient to encompass the failure of the physician to inform the patient of the risks.

An X-ray case upon which the appellees rely is *Costa* v. *Regents of Univ. of California,* 116 Cal.App.2d 445, 254 P.2d 85. This was a malpractice action against a hospital and certain doctors for alleged negligence in the X-ray treatment of cancer to the area of the lower jaw which resulted in necrosis of tissue. It was alleged the X-ray treatment was too drastic and extensive. While the circumstances were in many respects similar to the case at bar, it did not involve any failure of the physicians to disclose the risks. It was claimed a less drastic and extensive treatment should have been undertaken by the doctors. The court said:

> . . . The expert evidence showed clearly that the exact extent of the cancer under the surface and the absence of hidden involvements cannot in a case like appellant's be decided with such certainty that it can be safely relied on for the purpose of restricting the treatment within narrow limits. There was no expert evidence what-

> ever that on the data available to defendants they ought in good practice to have restricted X-ray treatment to a less drastic procedure or that the diagnostic methods now indicated by appellant if used would have yielded certainty and should have led to restriction to less dangerous treatment. Several experts testified that said methods (X-ray pictures and biopsy) could not be relied on for the purpose. In fighting so dangerous a condition as here involved, physicians may take serious risks and in doing so must rely on their judgment in deciding how far to go. See *Callahan* v. *Hahnemann Hospital,* 1 Cal.2d 447, 35 P.2d 536. To hold them responsible in the cases where the bad chance unfortunately materializes would be evidently unjust and most dangerous if physicians were deterred from going to the extent which gives their patient the best chance of survival. [116 Cal.App.2d at page 457, 254 P.2d at page 92.]

The Costa case has nothing to do with the duty to inform the patient of the hazardous character of proposed treatment. The more recent case of the same court in *Salgo* v. *Leland Stanford, Etc. Bd. Trustees, supra,* covers the subject specifically.

In our opinion the proper rule of law to determine whether a patient has given an intelligent consent to a proposed form of treatment by a physician was stated and applied in *Salgo* v. *Leland Stanford, Etc. Bd. Trustees, supra.* This rule in effect compels disclosure by the physician in order to assure that an informed consent of the patient is obtained. The duty of the physician to disclose, however, is limited to those disclosures which a reasonable medical practitioner would make under the same or similar circumstances. How the physician may best discharge his obligation to the patient in this difficult situation involves primarily a question of medical judgment. So long as the disclosure is sufficient to assure an informed consent, the physician's choice of plausible courses should not be called into question if it appears, all circumstances considered, that the physician was motivated only by the patient's best therapeutic interests and he proceeded as competent medical men would have done in a similar situation.

Turning now to the facts in the instant case, the appellant knew she had a cancerous tumor in her left breast which was removed by a radical mastectomy. Pathological examination of the tissue removed did not disclose any spread of the cancer cells into the lymphatics beyond the cancerous tumor itself. As a precautionary measure the appellant's ovaries and fallopian tubes were removed, which likewise upon pathological examination indicated no spread of the cancer to these organs. At the time the appellant went to Dr. Kline as a patient there was no immediate emergency concerning the administration of cobalt irradiation treatment such as would excuse the physician from making a reasonable disclosure to the patient. We think upon all the facts and circumstances here presented Dr. Kline was obligated to make a reasonable disclosure to the appellant of the nature and probable consequences of the suggested or recommended cobalt irradiation treatment, and he was also obligated to make a reasonable disclosure of the dangers within his knowledge which were incident to, or possible in, the treatment he proposed to administer.

Upon the record here presented Dr. Kline made no disclosures to the appellant whatever. He was silent. This is not to say that the facts compel a verdict for the appellant. Under the rule heretofore stated, where the patient fully appreciates the danger involved, the failure of a physician in his duty to make a reasonable disclosure to the patient would have no causal relation to the injury. In such event the consent of the patient to the proposed treatment is an informed consent. The burden of proof rests throughout the trial of the case upon the patient who seeks to recover in a malpractice action for her injury.

In considering the obligation of a physician to disclose and explain to the patient in language as simple as necessary the nature of the ailment, the nature of the proposed treatment, the probability of success or of alternatives, and perhaps the risks of unfortunate results and unforeseen conditions within the body, we do not think the administration of such an obligation, by imposing liability for malpractice if the treatment were administered without such explanation where explanation could reasonably be made, presents any insurmountable obstacles.

The appellant's requested instruction on the duty of a physician to make a disclosure to his patient was too broad. But this did not relieve the trial court of its obligation to instruct on such issue under the circumstances here presented, since the issue was raised by the pleadings. On retrial the instruction should be modified to inform the jury that a physician has such discretion, as heretofore indicated, consistent with the full disclosure of facts necessary to assure an informed consent by the patient.

On retrial of this case the first issue for the jury to determine should be whether the administration of cobalt irradiation treatment was given with the informed consent of the patient, and if it was not, the physician who failed in his legal obligation is guilty of malpractice no matter how skillfully the treatment may have been administered, and the jury should determine the damages arising from the cobalt irradiation treatment. If the jury should find an informed consent was given by the patient for such treatment, the jury should next determine whether proper skill was used in administering the treatment.

The primary basis of liability in a malpractice action is the deviation from the standard of conduct of a reasonable and prudent medical doctor of the same school of practice as the defendant under similar circumstances. Under such standard the patient is properly protected by the medical profession's own recognition of its obligations to maintain its standards.

The appellant requested and the trial court refused to give the following instruction:

> You are instructed that under the terms of the contract between defendant Kline and defendant Hospital it was the duty of defendant Kline to supervise the work of all of the personnel in the radiology department. If you find that plaintiff's injury was the result of the negligence of personnel in the department your verdict shall be in favor of plaintiff and against both defendants.

Nowhere in the written instructions was there anything to indicate that either defendant could be chargeable with the negligence of anyone other than the negligence of Dr. Kline personally, unless it is to be construed from the generalization of the pleadings contained in the court's instruction No. 1. This generalization at best would be confusing to a jury on this point.

> A physician is responsible for an injury done to a patient through the want of proper skill and care in his assistant, and through the want of proper skill and care in his apprentice, agent, or employee. The fact that a physician's assistant is a member of the same or a similar profession does not make the rule of respondent superior inapplicable, and a physician is liable not only for negligence of laymen employed by him, but also for the negligence of nurses or other physicians in his employ.
>
> . . . .
>
> Corporations, or persons other than physicians, who treat patients for hire with the expectation of profit are liable for negligence or malpractice on the part of the

> physicians or nurses employed by them. [70 C.J.S. Physicians and Surgeons § 54e, pp. 978, 979, and see cases cited therein]

Although the court did not think it necessary to go into the doctrine of *respondeat superior,* see the facts in *Rule* v. *Cheeseman,* 181 Kan. 957, 317 P.2d 472.

In *Gray* v. *McLaughlin,* 207 Ark. 191, 179 S.W.2d 686, an X-ray specialist or roentgenologist was held liable for injuries caused by the X-ray technician employed by him.

In an action for damages founded on malpractice it is the duty of the trial court to instruct the jury with respect to the law governing the case, explaining the precise questions at issue. This includes, under the evidence presented by the record in the instant case, the responsibility of the physician for the acts or omissions of others under his supervision. (See, 70 C.J.S. Physicians and Surgeons § 64, p. 1016, and cases cited.)

A party is entitled to have the trial court give an instruction to the jury which is essential to his theory of the case when there is sufficient evidence to support such theory. *Kreh* v. *Trinkle,* 185 Kan. 329, 343 P.2d 213.

In our opinion the refusal of the trial court to give the requested instruction was prejudicial and constituted reversible error. It was Dr. Somers, not Dr. Kline, who prescribed use of rotational therapy. Dr. Somers was an assistant to Dr. Kline. It was the hospital's employee, Darter, referred to by Dr. Kline as his physicist, who made the computations which resulted in administration of a dosage in excess of tolerance limits, if the jury were to give credence to the appellant's theory of the evidence, and Dr. Kline was chargeable with knowledge of the quantity and effect of the irradiation he caused to be administered to the appellant. *Agnew* v. *Larson,* 82 Cal.App.2d 176, 185 P.2d 851.

While counsel for the appellees made no objection to the testimony of Dr. Roys, they set forth in detail his testimony in a counter abstract to show he was not a physician but was testifying by virtue of an academic degree. Inferentially this may suggest Dr. Roys, not being a physician of the same school of practice as Dr. Kline, was incompetent to establish negligence concerning medical practice and treatment. *Goheen* v. *Graber,* 181 Kan. 107, 309 P.2d 636.

It is the customary practice, however, for a radiologist to have a physicist make his calculations where cobalt irradiation therapy treatments are given by a rotational beam to patients. This was confirmed not only by Dr. Kline but also by Dr. Hare. In fact, Dr. Kline testified that he did not know how to make the calculations necessary to make the irradiation administered meet the requirements for the radiation prescribed. He said he could not even understand the calculations when they had been made by others. It must be observed this is not unusual because the radiologist is not trained in nuclear physics, a specialty in itself. Dr. Roys was a technician of the same type as Darter, and, in fact, was the professor at Wichita University under whom Darter studied. Thus, there could be no legitimate objection to the competency of Dr. Roys to testify relative to the calculations made.

The appellees contend that no issue was raised in the pleadings or in the evidence at the trial, so far as the jury was concerned, which would exempt the hospital from liability for the acts of Dr. Kline under the doctrine of *respondeat superior* and that by reason thereof no instruction was required. The simple answer is that the appellees are privileged to make this admission, but the jury is entitled by an appropriate instruction to know about it. The appellees argue the appellant does not claim that Darter made any error in computation. While this is true, Darter did not, under the appellant's theory, make enough calculations to know that an excessive equilibrium dosage was administered five millimeters beneath the skin. Under these circumstances, the appellees' argument has no merit.

The appellant contends the trial court erred in failing to instruct that the jury might consider the fact of injury as evidence of negligence, citing *George* v. *Shannon,* 92 Kan. 801, 142 P. 967. On the facts presently before the court this point is not well taken. The appellant alleges injury as a result of burns from cobalt irradiation therapy. This is not a *res ipsa loquitur* case and no presumption of negligence of a physician is to be indulged from the fact of injury or adverse result of his treatment of the patient. *Cummins* v. *Donley,* 173 Kan. 463, 249 P.2d 695, and cases cited therein.

In *Costa* v. *Regents of Univ. of California, supra,* it was contended, among other things, that necrosis did not ordinarily follow treatment from cancer X-ray and that this circumstance amounted to proof of negligence. In rejecting the contention the California court said:

> . . . The result of the same treatment is not always the same in all cases and on all patients. When the result of a treatment is less favorble or more prejudicial than in the great majority of cases such need not indicate that the treatment was negligently performed, but may as well be the result of individual differences in reaction or the less favorable circumstances of the case. . . . [116 Cal.App.2d at pge 461, 254 P.2d at page 95]

The expert testimony in the instant case confirms the correctness of the above statement. But see, *King* v. *Ditto,* 142 Or. 207, 19 P.2d 1100.

Upon the record presented it is apparent the appellees were united in interest; therefore, pursuant to G.S.1949, 60-2907, the appellees were obligated in the exercise of their peremptory challenges in empaneling the jury to challenge jointly.

In conclusion we hold the trial court committed reversible error in the matter of instructing the jury. It has been held when the instructions to the jury define the issues and state the pertinent law with accuracy, the failure of the court to emphasize some particular point of law deemed important by a party litigant does not constitute error, especially when such party does not object to the instructions as given nor ask for a further instruction to supplement them. *Kiser* v. *Skelly Oil Co.,* 136 Kan. 812, 18 P.2d 181. In the instant case the instructions given to the jury did not define the issues and state the pertinent law with accuracy, and further instructions were requested. By reason of the errors heretofore noted the appellant should be granted a new trial.

The judgment of the lower court is reversed with directions to grant a new trial.

PARKER, C. J., and PRICE, J., dissent.

Natanson v. *Kline*, 187 Kan. 186, 354 P.2d 670 (1960)

SCHROEDER, Justice.

Within the time allotted after the decision of the court herein was announced the appellees filed motions for rehearing. Thereafter, pursuant to request, leave was granted the Kansas Medical Society on May 12, 1960, to file its brief amicus curiae in support of the appellees' motions for rehearing. Finding nothing, upon consideration of the motions for rehearing and the brief of amicus curiae in support thereof, which warrants a reconsideration of the case, the motions for rehearing are denied.

Recognizing, however, that this is a case of first impression in Kansas and one establishing judicial precedent of the highest importance to the medical profession, an attempt will be made to clarify Syllabus ¶ 4 and the corresponding portion of the opinion concerning which counsel are apprehensive.

Perhaps in preoccupation over the *legal* obligation of a physician to his patient, the court has not adequately emphasized procedural aspects of the case, or reiterated fundamental doctrine in the law of negligence sufficiently to completely avoid efforts to misconstrue the opinion.

It is charged that the court has confused a malpractice suit, where negligence is an essential element, with an assault and battery case, where negligence is not an essential element, thereby giving rise to a hybrid action which is neither one of negligence nor one of assault and battery, but may be a combination of the two.

It is argued the only way the court's opinion can be justified is to say that the duty of a physician to disclose to his patient the risks and hazards of a proposed form of treatment is an absolute one, and the matter is not to be judged by such disclosures as a reasonable medical practitioner would make under the same or similar circumstances.

In support of the argument, that the court has imposed an absolute duty upon the physician, the following paragraph is isolated from context:

> On retrial of this case the first issue for the jury to determine should be whether the administration of cobalt irradiation treatment was given with the informed consent of the patient, and if it was not, the physician who failed in his legal obligation is guilty of malpractice no matter how skillfully the treatment may have been administered, and the jury should determine the damages arising from the cobalt irradiation treatment. If the jury should find an informed consent was given by the patient for such treatment, the jury should next determine whether proper skill was used in administering the treatment. [*Natanson* v. *Kline,* 186 Kan. 393, 411, 350 P.2d 1093, 1107]

A casual reading of this paragraph in context would indicate that reference is there being made to the *order* in which the jury is to consider the issues presented on retrial of the case, and not to an enumeration of the various elements which must be established by the evidence to prove each of the issues stated.

The gravamen of the plaintiff's complaint was malpractice or the failure of the defendants to properly perform the duties which devolved upon them—a failure which resulted in the alleged injuries to the plaintiff. Thus it was incumbent upon the plaintiff to prove and establish (1) that the defendants failed to perform their duty; and (2) that the plaintiff's injuries were the direct and proximate result of such failure.

The petition alleged that the injuries were "a direct and proximate result of the defendants' negligence and carelessness" and then set forth eight specific grounds of negligence, including:

> (*g*) He [Dr. Kline] failed to warn plaintiff that the course of treatment which he undertook to administer involved great risk of bodily injury or death.

The answers of both defendants denied generally the allegations of asserted negligence, and in addition thereto, affirmatively pleaded that the plaintiff "assumed the risk and hazard of the treatment." Thus, at the trial the defendants were fully aware that *the informed consent of the patient to the hazards of the treatment was an issue of fact in the case.* This is true because as a defense assumption of risk is applicable only where the plaintiff is equally competent with the defendant to judge concerning the risks and hazards. See, *Taylor* v. *Hostetler,* 186 Kan. 788, 352 P.2d 1042, and cases cited therein. These affirmative allegations of the defendants presupposed an informed consent by the patient with full knowledge of the risks and hazards of the treatment.

The court held after reviewing the record presented on this appeal that a physician violates his duty to his patient and *subjects himself to liability for malpractice,* where no immediate emergency exists *and upon facts and circumstances particularly set forth in the opinion,* if he makes *no disclosure* of significant facts within his knowledge which are necessary to form the basis of an intelligent consent by the patient to the proposed form of treatment (Syllabus ¶ 4).

In other words, on the fact and circumstances presented by the record the appellant was entitled to some explanation concerning the risks and hazards inherent in the administration of cobalt irradiation treatment which Dr. Kline proposed to administer to her. For this treatment she was Dr. Kline's patient and not the patient of Dr. Crumpacker, by whom she was referred to Dr. Kline.

The appellant was entitled to a reasonable disclosure by Dr. Kline so that she could intelligently decide whether to take the cobalt irradiation treatment and assume the risks inherent therein, or in the alternative to decline this form of precautionary treatment and take a chance that the cancerous condition in her left breast had not spread beyond the lesion itself which had been removed by surgery. There was no emergency calling for immediate attention. The appellant had recovered from the surgery. In addition to the evidence related in the opinion her husband testified:

Q. Now directing your attention to approximately the 5th or 6th day of June, 1955, I would like to have you describe for us the general apparent condition of the health of Mrs. Natanson?

A. Mrs. Natanson at that particular time was very, very well. She had gone through the two operations and had made a very, very fine recovery. She was able to use her arm because of the therapy; she had almost the complete use of the left arm again. The breast had healed fully. There were actually no scars—just the one large scar but there was a thickness there. We were living a very normal life after the big scare we had.

Q. Now, directing your attention to the first week of June, 1955, I will ask you whether or not Mrs. Natanson ever recovered to the point where she was able to do her own housework?

A. Yes, she had.

But contrary to the legal obligation imposed upon a physician to make a reasonable disclosure to his patient of the inherent risks and hazards of a proposed form of treatment, Dr. Kline gave the appellant no explanation whatever. He made no disclosures. He was silent. On this state of the record Dr. Kline failed in his legal duty to make a reasonable disclosure to the appellant who was his patient *as a matter of law.*

Conceivably, in a given case as indicated in the opinion, no disclosures to a patient may be justified where such practice, under given facts and circumstances, is established by expert testimony to be in accordance with that of a reasonable medical practitioner under the same or similar circumstances. But on the state of the record here presented the appellant was not required to produce expert medical testimony to show that the failure of Dr. Kline to give any explanation or make any disclosures was contrary to accepted medical practice. To hold otherwise would be a failure of the court to perform its solemn duty.

Whether or not a physician has advised his patient of the inherent risks and hazards in a proposed form of treatment is a *question of fact* concerning which lay witnesses are competent to testify, and the establishment of such fact is not dependent upon expert medical testimony. It is only when the facts concerning the actual disclosures made to the patient are ascertained or ascertainable by the trier of the facts, that the expert testimony of medical witnesses is required to establish whether such disclosures are in accordance with those which a reasonable medical practitioner would make under the same or similar circumstances.

The question then remains whether such failure on the part of Dr. Kline to make a reasonable disclosure to the appellant was a proximate cause of her injury. As indicated in the opinion the mere fact that Dr. Kline was silent does not compel a verdict for the appellant. It was said:

> . . . Under the rule heretofore stated where the patient fully appreciates the danger involved, the failure of a physician in his duty to make a reasonable disclosure to the patient would have no causal relation to the injury. In such event the consent of the patient to the proposed treatment is an informed consent. The burden of proof rests throughout the trial of the case upon the patient who seeks to recover in a malpractice action for her injury. [*Natanson* v. *Kline, supra,* 186 Kan. at page 410, 350 P.2d at page 1106]

Negligence is an essential element of malpractice, and the foregoing statement recognizes that a causal relation must be established by the patient, between the negligent act of the physician and the injury of the patient, to sustain the burden of proof where damages are sought in a malpractice action for injury. Prior to a discussion of the manner in which the court instructed the jury it was said in the opinion:

> . . . At best it may be said, upon all the facts and circumstances presented by the record, there was evidence from which a jury could find that the proximate cause of the appellant's injury was the negligence of the defendants. On the other hand a jury, *properly instructed,* would be justified in finding for the appellees. [*Natanson* v. *Kline, supra,* 186 Kan. at page 398, 350 P.2d at page 1098]

After making the foregoing statement in the opinion, discussion was directed to the instructions of the court without further specific attention to the issue of proximate cause. If, of course, the appellant would have taken the cobalt irradiation treatments even though Dr. Kline had warned her that the treatments he undertook to administer involved great risk of bodily injury or death, it could not be said that the failure of Dr. Kline to so inform the appellant was the proximate cause of her injury. While the appellant did not directly testify that she would have refused to take the proposed cobalt irradiation treatments had she been properly informed, we think the evidence presented by the record *taken as a whole* is sufficient and would authorize a jury to infer that had she been properly informed, the appellant would not have taken the cobalt irradiation treatments.

Two days after the decision of this court was announced, the Supreme Court of Missouri handed down its opinion in *Mitchell* v. *Robinson,* 334 S.W.2d 11, 12, on April 11, 1960, wherein the Missouri court reached the same conclusion as this court on the duty of a physician to inform his patient of the hazards of treatment. There the patient had a rather severe emotional illness but was not mentally incompetent. The treatment prescribed was "combined electro-shock and insulin subcoma therapy." A sharp conflict developed in the testimony as to whether the patient was informed of the risks of the treatment. Serious hazards incident to shock treatment were admitted, to-wit: fractured bones, serious paralysis of limbs, irreversible coma and even death, and further that there were no completely reliable or successful precautions. The patient as a result of treatment went into convulsions which caused the fracture of several vertebrae and sued the physicians in a malpractice action on the ground that he was not informed of the risks inherent in the treatment. The "essentially meritorious problem" before the court was whether upon the record there was any evidence to support the jury's finding of negligence. In the opinion the court said:

> In the particular circumstances of this record, considering the nature of Mitchell's illness and this rather new and radical procedure with its rather high incidence of serious and permanent injuries not connected with the illness, the doctors owed their patient in possession of his faculties the duty to inform him generally of the possible serious collateral hazards; and in the detailed circumstances there was a submissible fact issue of whether the doctors were negligent in failing to inform him of the dangers of shock therapy. [At page 19]

As always, an effort is made by the court to present an opinion in logical sequence, so that consideration of subsequent issues is dependent upon the disposition of issues previously determined, and if opinions are analyzed in this manner misinterpretations will be minimized.

PARKER, C.J., and PRICE, J., are of the opinion the judgment of the trial court should be affirmed, and therefore dissent.

Competency or ability to give informed consent. The patient may express consent to treatment verbally or in writing. Alternatively, the consent may be implied by behavior or by law. Consent may be nullified at any time by the consenting patient or it may in effect be nullified by law if (1) the consenting person was legally incapable of giving fully informed consent to treatment or (2) the consent was obtained under conditions of duress or fraud. In *Kaimowitz* v. *Michigan Department of Mental Health,* 42 U.S.L.W. 2063 (Mich.Cir.Ct. 1973), which appears below, the court ruled an involuntarily confined mental patient was not competent to give informed and adequate consent to experimental psychosurgery.

Kaimowitz v. *Michigan Department of Mental Health,* 42 U.S.L.W. 2063 (Mich.Cir.Ct. 1973)

The record in this case demonstrates that animal experimentation and non-intrusive human experimentation have not been exhausted in determining and studying brain function. Any experimentation on the human brain, especially when it involves an intrusive, irreversible procedure in a non-life-threatening situation, should be undertaken with extreme caution, and then only when answers cannot be obtained from animal experimentation and from non-intrusive human experimentation.

Psychosurgery should never be undertaken upon involuntarily committed populations, when there is a high-risk low-benefit ratio as demonstrated in this case. This is because of the impossibility of obtaining truly informed consent from such populations. The reasons such informed consent cannot be obtained are set forth in detail subsequently in this opinion.

The physician cannot experiment without restraint or restriction. He must consider first of all the welfare of his patient. This concept is universally accepted by the medical profession, the legal profession, and responsible persons who have thought and written on the matter.

Furthermore, he must weigh the risk to the patient against the benefit to be obtained by trying something new. The risk-benefit ratio is an important ratio in considering any experimental surgery upon a human being. The risk must always be relatively low, in the non-life threatening situation to justify human experimentation.

Informed consent is a requirement of variable demands. Being certain that a patient has consented adequately to an operation, for example, is much more important when doctors are going to undertake an experimental, dangerous, and intrusive procedure than, for example, when they are going to remove an appendix. When a procedure is experimental, dangerous, and intrusive, special safeguards are necessary. The risk-benefit ratio must be carefully considered, and the question of consent thoroughly explored.

To be legally adequate, a subject's informed consent must be competent, knowing and voluntary.

To be competent to give his consent, the patient must rationally understand the nature of the procedure, its risks, and other relevant information. Even if an involuntarily detained patient can intellectually comprehend his circumstances, the very nature of his incarceration diminishes his capacity to consent to psychosurgery. He is particularly vulnerable as a result of his mental condition, his involuntarily confinement, and the effects of "institutionalization." In an institution, most decisions are made for the patients. Institutionalization strips the individual of the support that permits him to maintain his sense of self-worth and the value of his own physical and mental integrity. His capacity to consent to irreversible experimental psychosurgery is clearly diminished.

The second element of an informed consent, knowledge of the risk involved and the procedures, is also absent. The evidence in this case indicates that the facts surrounding experimental brain surgery are profoundly uncertain; knowledgeable consent to psychosurgery is literally impossible in view of lack of knowledge in the field.

The third element of an informed consent is voluntariness. The most important thing to an involuntarily detained mental patient is freedom. When freedom is dependent upon a patient's cooperation with the authorities, it is impossible for the patient to be free of ulterior forms of restraint or coercion when giving his consent to experimental surgery. The institutional environment is inherently coercive. Patients who are involuntarily confined cannot reason as equals with the doctors and administrators. This inherent inequality in their position makes them incapable of voluntarily giving an informed consent to undergo psychosurgery.

The law has always been meticulous in scrutinizing inequality in bargaining power and the possibility of undue influence in commercial fields and in the law of wills. It also has been most careful in excluding from criminal cases confessions where there was no clear showing of their completely voluntary nature after full understanding of the consequences. No lesser standard can apply to involuntarily detained mental patients.

The keystone to any intrusion upon the body of a person must be full, adequate and informed consent. The integrity of the individual must be protected from invasion into his body and personality not voluntarily agreed to. Consent is not an idle or symbolic act; it is a fundamental requirement for the protection of the individual's integrity.

We therefore conclude that involuntarily detained mental patients cannot give informed and adequate consent to experimental psychosurgical procedures on the brain.

The three basic elements of informed consent—competency, knowledge, and voluntariness—cannot be ascertained with a degree of reliability warranting resort to use of such an invasive procedure. . . .

Freedom of speech and expression, and the right of all men to disseminate ideas, popular or unpopular, are fundamental to ordered liberty. Government has no power or right to control men's minds, thoughts, and expressions. This is the command of the First Amendment. And we adhere to it in holding an involuntarily detained mental patient may not consent to experimental psychosurgery.

For, if the First Amendment protects the freedom to express ideas, it necessarily follows that it must protect the freedom to generate ideas. Without the latter protection, the former is meaningless.

Experimental psychosurgery, which is irreversible and intrusive, often leads to the blunting of emotions, the deadening of memory, the reduction of affect, and limits the ability to generate new ideas. Its potential for injury to the creativity of the individual is great, and can impinge upon the right of the individual to be free from interference with his mental processes.

The State's interest in performing psychosurgery and the legal ability of the involuntarily detained mental patient to give consent must bow to the First Amendment, which protects the generation and free flow of ideas from unwarranted interference with one's mental processes.

To allow an involuntarily detained mental patient to consent to the type of psychosurgery proposed in this case, and to permit the State to perform it, would be to condone State action in violation of basic First Amendment rights of such patients, because impairing the power to generate ideas inhibits the full dissemnation of ideas. . . .

There is no privacy more deserving of constitutional protection than that of one's mind. . . .

Intrusion into one's intellect, when one is involuntarily detained and subject to the control of institutional authorities, is an intrusion into ones constitutionally protected right of privacy. If one is not protected in his thoughts, behavior, personality and identity, then the right of privacy becomes meaningless.

Before a State can violate one's constitutionally protected right of privacy and obtain a valid consent for experimental psychosurgery on involuntarily detained mental patients, a compelling State interest must be shown. None has been shown here.

The practitioner is relieved of his or her duty to disclose and obtain an informed consent in emergency-type situations where time may be of the essence and/or the patient may be in no condition to provide fully informed consent. Another exceptional situation is one in which a practitioner invokes his or her "therapeutic privilege" and proceeds to supply the patient with only limited information about the nature of the treatment and its possible risks, benefits, consequences, and alternatives. "Therapeutic privilege" is a judicially created concept that was meant to be applied primarily in situations in which the practitioner's full disclosure, while attempting to obtain consent, might itself cause the patient to suffer "harmful effects." This issue is discussed in *Canterbury* v. *Spence,* 464 F.2d 772 (D.C.Cir. 1972). In practice, "therapeutic privilege" is frequently invoked in the courtroom as a defense against liability for malpractice in negligence or battery actions involving allegations of failure to conform to informed consent requirements, as it was in *Woods* v. *Brumlop,* 71 N.M. 221, 377 P.2d 520 (1962), which appears below.

Woods v. *Brumlop,* 71 N.M. 221, 377 P.2d 520 (1962)

NOBLE, Justice.

A jury awarded Beulah Anne Woods $5,889.58 damages against Doctor Brumlop for malpractice, and the decisive question is whether testimony of the plaintiff was admissible as to the cause of a claimed loss of hearing and whether in the absence of medical testimony that the treatment prescribed caused a loss of hearing it should have been submitted to the jury as an element of damages.

The action originally was against Doctor Brumlop and Doctor Gonzales for malpractice. A verdict was directed in favor of Doctor Gonzales, and the case was submitted to the jury against Doctor Brumlop alone.

Plaintiff was referred to Doctor Brumlop for psychiatric treatment by her physician. After consultation and some routine psychiatric treatments, Doctor Brumlop advised that plaintiff should submit to electroshock treatments. Doctor Brumlop refused to give the treatments herself and suggested that plaintiff enter the New Mexico Mental Hospital for the treatments. After further consultations with her original physician, who likewise recommended the treatments, plaintiff entered the State Hospital where the electroshock treatments were administered by Doctor Gonzales. Doctor Gonzales, without consultation or recommendation by Doctor Brumlop, but upon his own diagnosis, determined to administer the electroshock treatments. Plaintiff claims to have received injuries consisting of a compression fracture to her spine and loss of hearing as a result of the treatments.

Several grounds are urged for reversal. We consider submission of the question of a claimed loss of hearing and the cost of a hearing aid as elements of damage caused by the electroshock treatments to be decisive and, therefore, consider it first.

Perhaps we should point out at the outset that plaintiff's claim for damages against defendant Brumlop, who did not administer the treatments which caused her injury, is based upon two theories. First, the doctor failed to inform and advise plaintiff of the dangers inherent in the electroshock treatments. Secondly, the doctor, upon direct inquiry by plaintiff, told her that no harmful results could occur, knowing that statement to be untrue; that the plaintiff had no knowledge of such and that this resulted in plaintiff having no basis upon which to predicate her consent to the treatments. We shall discuss the denial of a motion for directed verdict later.

As we have pointed out, plaintiff claimed as one of the injuries sustained by her as a result of the treatments, a loss of hearing and $175.00 as the expense of a hearing aid. The particular complaint is that the causal relation between the claimed loss of hearing and the treatment prescribed was not established by competent evidence. There was no medical testimony establishing the causal relationship, and it is contended that the lay testimony of plaintiff as to the cause of a physical condition is inadmissible. The evidence was objected to at the time it was offered and was the subject of a motion to strike the testimony and to not permit the jury to consider loss of hearing and the cost of the hearing aid as an element of damage, made at the conclusion of all the evidence. Denial of the motion is urged as error requiring reversal. We agree that its denial requires a remand for new trial.

The defendant is liable only for injuries inflicted on the plaintiff by reason of the electroshock treatment and is in no way responsible for plaintiff's loss of hearing occasioned by any other means. The burden of proving with reasonable certainty the causal connection between the treatment and plaintiff's loss of hearing rested upon the plaintiff. *Hebenstreit* v. *Atchison, Topeka & Santa Fe Ry.*, 65 N.M. 301, 336 P.2d 1057, and cases there cited.

The annotator at 66 A.L.R.2d 1127 states the rule as to the admissibility of lay testimony as to the cause of a physical condition as follows:

> . . . where the subject matter is wholly scientific or so far removed from the usual and ordinary experience of the average man that expert knowledge is essential to the formation of an intelligent opinion, only an expert can competently give opinion evidence as to the cause of death, disease, or a physical condition.

The testimony objected to here was that of plaintiff:

> Q. Now Mrs. Woods, in addition to the pain and discomfort that you had in your back after this first shock treatment was given, did you experience any other physical effects?
> A. The treatment destroyed most of my hearing.

There was also the admission of the cost of a hearing aid. A medical expert in hearing and ear troubles testified that he had treated plaintiff prior to the shock treatments for inner-ear trouble and had tested her hearing and found her to be hard of hearing. The medical expert, however, testified that in his opinion the cause when he examined her was audiosclorosis. He said that he was unable to form an opinion as to whether shock treatment could result in loss of hearing. The only testimony that such loss of hearing was caused by the shock treatments, therefore, was the lay testimony of plaintiff.

In *Pacific Employers Ins. Co.* v. *Industrial Accident Commission,* 47 Cal.App.2d 494, 118 P.2d 334, it was said that the pathological cause of an ailment is a scientific question upon which it is necessary to obtain scientific knowledge and only the opinions of experts are of any value.

In an action for punitive damages for willful and malicious trespass to land, the court in *Ruland* v. *Zenith Const. Co.,* Okl., 283 P.2d 540, held a husband is incompetent, not being an expert, to testify that his wife became ill, nervous and sick because of the alleged wrongful conduct of the defendant. In a malpractice action against a physician for causing the administration of medicine containing arsenic, it was held in *Hawkins* v. *McCain,* 239 N.C. 160, 79 S.E.2d 493, that the evidence of lay witnesses that they told the plaintiff not to continue to take medicine because it was apparently killing her was properly excluded because it constituted "nothing more than mere conjecture or surmise . . . as to cause and effect in a field of knowledge in which only an expert could give a competent opinion," that is, whether the health of plaintiff had been injuriously affected by taking the medicine.

The following exchange between the court and counsel for plaintiff at the time objection was made to submitting the issue of loss of hearing as an element of damage indicates that counsel for plaintiff admitted that a causal connection had not been medically established. It was contended that the issue should remain because otherwise it would affect the credibility of the testimony of plaintiff.

> THE COURT: Mr. Hall, it is the Court's understanding from your statements that you have given up your claim of loss of hearing due to the electroshock treatments.
>
> MR. HALL: I didn't make that as an official part of the record; however I think I indicated to the Court during the recess period that we had been unable medically to connect it up as being any loss. I would like to be in a position to argue the matter [to] the jury, however, and retain it in the case, in order to explain, because it is going to be raised on the credibility of the witness. There are degrees of loss of hearing and she may have contributed more of a loss than actually occurred after it, or it may have been or may not have been due to the electroshock treatment and all that. I would like to keep it in the case, although I am inclined to believe that the Jury would be justified in throwing it out because we haven't medically connected it up.

In *Hebenstreit* v. *Atchison, Topeka & Santa Fe Ry., supra,* the medical expert testified that it would be a matter of pure speculation to state the extent of aggravation caused by the trauma. This court there said:

> Uncertainty as to the amount of damages one may be entitled to receive will not prevent a recovery, but it is well settled that a judgment based on conjecture, surmise or speculation can not be sustained, and that is what we have here.
>
> If Dr. Tanney with his superior knowledge of the condition of Mrs. Hebenstreit through the years could not give an approximation of the extent of the aggravation or acceleration, we are at a loss to understand how the members of the jury could do so.

We think these decisions demonstrate that the cause and effect of a physical condition lies in a field of knowledge in which only a medical expert can give a competent opinion. Not having shown a peculiar knowledge, the plaintiff's testimony as to the cause of her loss of hearing was inadmissible. There being no medical testimony to support her contention that loss of hearing was caused by the treatments, and in view of the testimony of the medical expert in this case, we feel that the jury could have had no basis other than conjecture, surmise or speculation upon which to consider whether plaintiff's claimed loss of hearing was caused by the shock treatments.

Plaintiff now argues that it does not appear that loss of hearing was an issue submitted to the jury. We cannot agree. The court instructed the jury as a part of instruction No. 5:

> . . . Second, did the electric shock treatments cause the disabilities or injuries that the complaint has alleged she suffered as a result of these treatments? . . .

Loss of hearing was not only alleged but testified to by plaintiff.

By instruction No. 13, the court charged the jury they might "consider the plaintiff's physical condition prior to the injury and consider the physical condition of the plaintiff at this time and what it would have been but for the injury."

These, together with the court's refusal to strike the allegation of loss of hearing upon motion at the close of all the testimony, make it clear to us that loss of hearing was submitted to the jury as an element of damages.

We think the error complained of is substantial and requires a reversal of the judgment appealed from and that the cause must be remanded for a new trial.

Since there must be a new trial, we think it proper to comment on the issue as to whether there was substantial evidence upon which to submit the issue of defendant's liability to the jury. This question was raised by defendant's motion for a directed verdict.

In considering a motion for directed verdict, the evidence must be viewed in its aspect most favorable to the plaintiff, including all reasonable inferences to be drawn from it, and all unfavorable testimony and inferences must be disregarded. It is only where there is no fact for the jury to determine or where the court, in the exercise of its sound discretion, would be required to set aside a verdict if favorable to one side, rather than to the other, that the court should direct a verdict. *Landers* v. *Atchison, T. & S. F. Ry.*, 68 N.M. 130, 359 P.2d 522; *Ferris* v. *Thomas Drilling Co.*, 62 N.M. 283, 309 P.2d 225.

While the claimed failure of defendant to advise plaintiff of the dangers inherent in the recommended treatment was alleged as a breach of defendant's duty to her patient, plaintiff, at the trial and now, relies entirely upon her contention and allegation that the breach of duty was the failure of defendant to tell plaintiff the truth in answer to a direct inquiry as to the dangers that might result from such treatment, and upon plaintiff's reliance upon defendant's alleged statement that no harm could result to her from such treatment. The testimony is directly conflicting upon this question. Defendant insists that she did fully discuss the inherent dangers with plaintiff, plaintiff maintaining the contrary that the doctor told her that no harm could result from the treatments.

The question is immediately presented—what is the extent of a physician's duty to explain to his patient the nature and probable consequences of a treatment recommended or prescribed? To what extent must the doctor disclose the existence and nature of the risks inherent in the treatment? An answer to these questions is pertinent in determining that duty as well, in an answer to a direct inquiry by the patient.

Courts have frequently said that the relation between a physician and his patient is one of trust and confidence and that the physician has the duty to make a full and frank disclosure to the patient of all pertinent facts relative to his illness and the treatment prescribed or recommended therefor. *Los Alamos Medical Center* v. *Coe,* 58 N.M. 686, 275 P.2d 175, 50 A.L.R. 2d 1033; *Natanson* v. *Kline,* 186 Kan. 393, 350 P.2d 1093; *Batty* v. *Arizona State Dental Board,* 57 Ariz. 239, 112 P.2d 870; *Pashley* v. *Pacific Elec. Co.*, 25 Cal.2d 226, 153 P.2d 325; *Macaulay* v. *Booth,* 53 Cal.App.2d 757, 128 P.2d 386.

Plaintiff testified that she would not have consented to the treatments if she had been aware of the probable dangers resulting therefrom. The real basis for the rule requiring disclosure is to give the patient a basis upon which to exercise judgment as to whether he will consent to the treatment. Without the disclosure by the doctor it is said that the patient is not informed and that, therefore, any consent obtained is ineffectual. An adult person, if he be of sound mind, is considered to have the right to determine for himself whether a recommended treatment or surgery shall be performed upon him, and to have the right even to expressly prohibit life-saving surgery or other medical treatment. *Natanson* v. *Kline, supra.*

In regard to the duty of a doctor to advise his patient as to the probable consequences of a treatment and the dangers connected with it, the author of an article in 41 Minn.L.Rev. 381, 427, has this to say:

> . . . The proper solution of this problem, in the opinion of the author, is to recognize that the doctor owes a duty to his patient to make reasonable disclosure of all

> significant facts, i.e., the nature of the infirmity (so far as reasonably possible), the nature of the operation and some of the more probable consequences and difficulties inherent in the proposed operation. It may be said that a doctor who fails to perform this duty is guilty of malpractice. . . .

The views of the author were approved in *Mitchell* v. *Robinson,* (Mo.1960), 334 S.W.2d 11, 79 A.L.R.2d 1017. In *Salgo* v. *Leland Stanford, etc. Board of Trustees,* 154 Cal.App.2d 560, 317 P.2d 170, it was said that:

> A physician violates his duty to his patient and subjects himself to liability if he withholds any facts which are necessary to form the basis of an intelligent consent by the patient to the proposed treatment. Likewise the physician may not minimize the known dangers of a procedure or operation in order to induce his patient's consent. . . .

See, also, *Bang* v. *Charles T. Miller Hospital,* 251 Minn. 427, 88 N.W.2d 186; *Lester* v. *Aetna Cas. & Sur. Co.,* (C.C.A. 5), 240 F.2d 676. Compare *Natanson* v. *Kline, supra,* and *Di Filippo* v. *Preston,* Del., 173 A.2d 333, where it is held that the duty to warn the patient of inherent dangers in the treatment must be established by medical testimony.

An exception to the rule requiring a disclosure of the dangers of a treatment procedure, of course, is an actual emergency where the patient is in no condition to determine for himself. Some courts have said that another exception is where an explanation of every risk attendant upon a treatment procedure may well result in alarming a patient who is already apprehensive and who may, as a result, refuse to undertake surgery or a treatment in which there is a minimal risk or where such disclosure may result in actually increasing the risk by reason of the psychological results of the apprehension itself. Actually some courts recognize a further exception that each patient is to be treated as a separate problem on the theory that the patient's mental and emotional condition is important, and that a certain amount of discussion consistent with full disclosure of facts necessary to an informed consent should be employed. Defendant argues for an application for one of these exceptions on the ground that the patient here was emotionally upset and the treatment was recognized as an aid in recovery from such emotional unbalance, and that a disclosure of the dangers would only tend to increase the emotional, mental condition of the patient. She relies on *Hunt* v. *Bradshaw,* 242 N.C. 517, 88 S.E.2d 762; *Amerine* v. *Hunter,* (Tex.Civ.App.), 335 S.W.2d 643; *Bernath* v. *Le Fever,* 325 Pa. 43, 189 A. 342. Cf. *Simone* v. *Sabo,* 37 Cal.2d 253, 231 P.2d 19; *Schloendorff* v. *Society of New York Hospital,* 211 N.Y. 125, 105 N.E. 92, 52 L.R.A.,N.S., 505. This contention of defendant, however, is not available on appeal. Defendant neither offered any testimony nor requested an instruction on the question as to whether a disclosure of the risks involved in the treatment would alarm an emotionally upset and apprehensive patient to the extent that it would not be proper medical practice to disclose such risks to the plaintiff. Defendant's defense was that she did advise plaintiff of the risks and dangers of the electroshock treatment. This was denied by plaintiff and she further claimed that the doctor expressly told her in answer to an inquiry that no danger could result from the treatment. Plaintiff testified that had she known of the dangers attendant upon the treatment, she would not have permitted it to have been performed.

A physician who misleads a patient by not only failing to give a warning of reasonable and recognized risks inherent in a treatment after which the patient would have refused the treatment, but by affirmatively assuring her that there are no risks, knowing such statement to be untrue, is liable for the harmful consequences of the treatment. Such a failure to disclose, or the giving of an untrue answer as to the probable consequences of a treatment constitutes malpractice; and a doctor who fails to so advise his client, or gives an untrue answer as to such consequences, is liable for malpractice unless his failure to do so comes within one of the exceptions to the rule requiring candor and disclosure. Under the circumstances of this case, a fact issue was presented for determination by the jury upon which there was no necessity for expert medical testimony.

A careful review of the evidence convinces us there was no error in the denial of defendant's motion for a directed verdict.

Other questions presented and argued have either been disposed of by what we have said, or have been found to be without merit.

The judgment appealed from will be reversed and remanded with instructions to grant a new trial.

It is so ordered.

COMPTON, C.J., and CHAVEZ, J., concur.

CARMODY and MOISE, JJ., not participating.

The continuing controversy about informed consent. Controversy surrounding judicial interpretations of the doctrine of informed consent is reflected in strong, sometimes impassioned arguments. For example, in her *Emory Law Journal* article "Informed Consent: The Illusion of Patient Choice," Rice (1974) presented a strident criticism of the judiciary for interpretations of therapeutic privilege that in essence allowed for *de facto* substitution of the physician's judgment for that of the patient. Focusing on the doctrine from a perspective sympathetic to the medical practitioner in a *Resident and Staff Physician* article called "Informed Consent: Descent to Absurdity," Ravitch (1974) presented a parody of the lengths to which practitioners are being compelled to go to ensure that their patients' consents are informed. How much information needs to be conveyed by whom in what types of cases? Is it sufficient for a physician to recite a "laundry list" of pros and cons of a particular procedure or must there be a veritable meeting of the minds? In the future will medical assistants, paraprofessionals, and hospital attorneys be encouraged to play a greater role in informing patients and obtaining consents? What are the limits, if any, of therapeutic privilege? The current situation is that there still exists a wide variety of opinion when it comes to questions concerning the nature and adequacy of a physician's disclosure and the standard by which the disclosure should be measured.

Because of uncertainties with respect to patients' capacity to provide fully informed consent to treatment, fact situations involving informed consent (or the lack of it) are more likely to fall into "gray" legal areas when cases in the mental health field as opposed to the health field in general are considered. Consider for the purposes of illustration the following account of the first electroshock treatment by the Italian psychiatrist Ugo Cerletti. Impastato (1960) writes that when it came to using electricity on humans, most of the medical experimenters in the 1930s were "timid and feared causing death, irreversible brain changes and epileptic states'' but ''Cerletti was the least fearful'' and he ''experimented on many pigs which were placed at his disposal at the slaughter house in Rome'' (p. 1113). Impastato went on:

> Now came the search for Rome's first patient. For obvious reasons this was not a simple matter. Then, luckily, a patient from North Italy was admitted to the clinic who was a catatonic schizophrenic and who spoke an incomprehensible gibberish. He was unable to give his name or to state anything about himself. No one could identify him. Dr. Cerletti decided he should be the historic patient. Following adequate preparations the first treatment was given in 1938. Present were Cerletti, Bini, Longhi, Accornero, Kalinowsky and Fleischer. The patient was brought in, the machine was set at 1/10 of a second and 70 volts and the shock given. Naturally, the low dosage resulted in a petit mal reaction. After the electric spasm, which lasted a fraction of a second, the patient burst out into song. The Professor suggested that another treatment with a higher voltage be given. The staff objected. They stated that if another treatment were given the patient would probably die and wanted further treatment postponed until the morrow. The Professor knew what that meant. He decided to go ahead right then and there, but before he could say so the patient suddenly sat up and pontifically proclaimed, no longer in a jargon, but in clear Italian: ''Non una seconda! Mortifera!'' (Not again, it will kill me). This made the Professor think and swallow, but his courage was not lost. He gave the order to proceed at a higher voltage and a longer time: and the first electroconvulsion in man ensued. Thus was born EST out of one man and over the objection of his assistants. (pp. 1113-1114)

From Impastato's account we can surmise that Rome's first electroshock patient was in no condition to provide fully informed consent to the treatment. But even if he—or his next of kin if such persons could be located—were able to offer informed consent to the treatment, what would Cerletti have disclosed? That the treatment might cause death, irreversible brain changes, and epileptic states? That the treatment had never before been attempted on humans, only on pigs? Applying contemporary legal and ethical standards to this historical event, perhaps the more interesting question concerns Cerletti's decision to proceed with a second shock treatment in spite of the patient's protest in clear Italian, ''Not again, it will kill me!'' Clearly, Cerletti did not have the consent of the patient to proceed with the treatment. Cerletti did not even have the approval of his assistants to proceed at a higher voltage and a longer time. One wonders whether Cerletti would have been able to convince a court that he knew better than the patient what was in the patient's best interests. Impastato's account does not tell us whether or not the patient survived Cerletti's treatment.

In psychotherapy, as opposed to other physical forms of therapy, the course of treatment is not usually predictable, and the consequences of the treatment may be quite variable. In a case study reported by Cohen and Smith (1976) entitled ''Socially Reinforced Obsessing: Etiology of a Disorder in a Christian Scientist,'' the authors presented the case of ''Mary,'' a twenty-eight-year-old mother and housewife who had been referred to a clinic for treatment of her obsession with disease as well as other complaints. The authors hypothesized that this woman's exposure to Christian Science and that religion's emphasis on "thought cures" to diseases (e.g., "demonstrating" over disease with thoughts such as, "My child doesn't have a cold, there's no such thing as colds"); combined with the ambivalence and guilt she suffered as a result of not seeking traditional medical counsel, contributed to the etiology of this woman's obsessive disorder. The publication of this case study precipitated a spate of articles that focused on various issues touched on in it. Representative of those articles that discussed the issue of informed consent was a comment by Halleck (1976) which raised the question, "Did the treatment of a highly religious person succeed at the expense of her abandoning her religious beliefs?" Halleck went on to caution that "it would seem that the ethical issues could be minimized . . . if the consumer could be adequately forewarned of possible consequences of treatment."

A reply to the points made by Halleck (1976) as well as the other commentators on Cohen and Smith (1976) appears in Cohen (1977) and Cohen (1979, pp. 76-83). A reply was also made in portions of a symposium on religion and psychotherapy presented at the annual convention of the American Psychological Association (Cohen, 1978). The relevant portions of that symposium are reprinted below.

Recently, a forum for the discussion of the issue of informed consent to treatment evolved in the *Journal of Consulting and Clinical Psychology* after the publication of Cohen and Smith's, "Socially Reinforced Obsessing: Etiology of a Disorder in a Christian Scientist." As reported in that case study, a sometime Christian Scientist named Mary presented with obsessive symptomatology which appeared to be related to and exacerbated by her religious involvements. In his comment on the case study, Seymour Halleck asked, "Did the treatment of a highly religious person succeed at the expense of her abandoning her religious beliefs?" Halleck went on to caution that "it would seem that the ethical issues could be minimized . . . if the consumer could be adequately forewarned of possible consequences of treatment."

In an article that restated Halleck's position, James C. Coyne argued that, like surgeons preparing to operate and lawyers preparing to litigate, psychotherapists preparing to do therapy must forewarn their clients of possible consequences and obtain their fully informed consent. In using the Cohen and Smith article as a point of departure from which to talk about preparation for surgery and litigation, Coyne overlooked the fact that Mary had been seen in treatment for fifteen weeks before she revealed her Christian Science background. It is, of course, impossible to forewarn a patient of the possibility of the modification of her religious beliefs fifteen weeks before the patient elects to reveal those beliefs. Still, Coyne's article raises some questions. Should therapists be obliged [i.e., other than in the usual course of obtaining demographic data] to delve into their clients' religious beliefs before beginning a course of treatment? If so, should physicians be required to delve into the religious beliefs of their patients before prescribing birth control pills? Should pharmacists be obligated to carefully question a suspected Catholic customer before selling him contraceptives?

I would agree that patients' informed consent to psychotherapeutic treatment should be ethically, if not legally, mandated. However, I have grave doubts about how theory can be put into practice in this context. There will be exceedingly difficult questions to be answered. Who should be informed of what under what conditions? How much information is necessary to make a consent fully informed? Which patients, by virtue of their mental states, are incompetent to give consent? Perhaps the most basic question concerns the incapability of psychotherapists to predict changes in their patients' lives that were not targeted for change when therapy was begun. Some academicians may pontificate on the notion that clinicians have been "naively anti-ecological" in that they haven't anticipated the effects of therapeutic intervention in areas of their patients' lives that were not targeted for change. But most clinician/scholars will candidly admit that they cannot begin to predict all of the life changes that will take place in their patients as a result of psychotherapy. We don't need one-shot surveys or laboratory analogue studies to tell us that there is often a ripple effect during a course of treatment. Read the work of Albert Ellis or Carl Rogers or any other clinician/scholar to begin to appreciate the myriad changes that take place in clients after a course of psychotherapy. Not all of the changes that take place were targeted for change when therapy was begun. The point here is that when it comes to the remarkably complex field of human relations, how precise or accurate can a therapist be in forecasting to his clients possible outcomes? In this context, the analogy of the singularly complex enterprise of psychotherapy to surgery and litigation seems particularly ill-chosen and inappropriate.

The case study of Mary was indeed a rather unique set of circumstances in the psychological literature. Christian Scientists typically do not go to medical doctors or psychologists with their problems—they go to Christian Science practitioners. Mary was a patient who *voluntarily* sought a form of treatment which, by its very nature, tended to compromise her religious beliefs. It can be seen now that the answer to Halleck's question, "Did the treatment of a highly religious person succeed at the expense of her abandoning her religious beliefs?" is "No, she had abandoned them beforehand as evidenced by her voluntary desire to receive treatment." As I have pointed out elsewhere, this patient appeared to be seeking out values she could live with. "But can a Christian Scientist be effectively treated in psychotherapy by a non-Christian Scientist?" asks one of the commentators. Two questions in reply: "Can a Jew be effectively treated by a non-Jew? Can a Democrat be treated by a Republican?" My answer to all three questions: Yes, Yes, and Yes . . .

Judicious use of the principles of informed consent may just be the answer to the difficult questions attendant to the issue of control in psychotherapy. However, whether truly informed consent to treatment is more a reality or an ideal remains to be seen. Once we, as psychotherapists, are alerted to our handicap in being able to provide the warning for a fully informed consent to take place, we are more apt to be sensitive to the issue of control. With sensitivity to that issue we can take on the treatment of clients of varied religious persuasions and, where appropriate, help those clients to make their religion work for and not against them.

It can be seen from the material above that the issues attendant to the legal concept of informed consent as regards psychotherapy are multifaceted and complex. Readers interested in pursuing other material written on Cohen and Smith (1976) are urged to consult Coyne (1976), Halleck (1976), London (1976), McLemore and Court (1977), and Stokes (1977), as well as Cohen (1977) and Cohen (1979, pp. 76–83). More information on the concept of informed consent in general can be found in Burt (1979); Glass (1970); Goin, Burgoyne, and Goin (1976); Harper and James (1956, pp. 211–237); Katz (1972); and Waitzkin and Stoeckle (1976).

ABUSE OF PSYCHOTHERAPEUTIC PROCESS

As of the printing of this book, no cases have been reported in which liability has been imputed solely on the ground of misapplication of the psychotherapeutic process. Rather, liability arises out of abuse of the process, misuse of the transference, and/or a breach of the trust that has been placed in the professional. The following case of *Roy* v. *Hartogs,* 81 Misc.2d 350, 366 N.Y.S.2d 297 (Civ.Ct. 1975), *aff'd,* 85 Misc.2d 891, 381 N.Y.S.2d 587 (Sup.Ct. 1976), is illustrative of this abuse of the psychotherapeutic process.

Roy v. *Hartogs,* 85 Misc.2d 891, 381 N.Y.S.2d 587 (Sup.Ct. 1976)

Per Curiam. A complaint should not be dismissed on the opening statement of counsel unless, accepting as true all facts stated in the opening and resolving in plaintiff's favor all material facts in issue, plaintiff nevertheless is precluded from recovery as a matter of law (*Rivera* v. *Board of Educ. of City of N.Y.,* 11 AD2d 7, 8, 9). Counsel asserted in the opening statement that the defendant, a psychiatrist, had treated the plaintiff, as his patient, during the period March, 1969 through September, 1970. It was further averred that, during the last 13 months of her treatment, plaintiff was induced to have sexual intercourse with the defendant as part of her prescribed therapy. As a result of this improper treatment, counsel alleged that the plaintiff was so emotionally and mentally injured that she was required to seek hospitalization on two occasions during 1971.

The right of action to recover a sum of money for seduction has been abolished by article 8 of the Civil Rights Law and the predecessor legislation found in article 2-A of the Civil Practice Act. These statutes were passed, as a matter of public policy, so that marriages should not be entered into because of the threat or danger of an action to recover money damages and the embarrassment and humiliation growing out of such action (*Fearon* v. *Treanor,* 272 NY 268, 274). However, this legislation did not abolish all causes of action wherein the act of sexual intercourse was either an ''incident of'' or ''contributed to'' the ultimate harm or wrong (*Tuck* v. *Tuck,* 14 NY2d 341). In this proceeding, the injury to the plaintiff was not merely caused by the consummation of acts of sexual intercourse with the defendant. Harm was also caused by the defendant's failure to treat the plaintiff with professionally acceptable procedures (cf. *Zipkin* v. *Freeman,* 436 SW2d 753, 761, 762 [Mo, 1969]; cf. *Anclote Manor Foundation* v. *Wilkinson,* 263 So.2d 256, 257 [Fla. 1972]). By alleging that his client's mental and emotional status was adversely affected by this deceptive and damaging treatment, plaintiff's counsel asserted a viable cause of action for malpractice in his opening statement (*Tuck* v. *Tuck, supra,* p. 345).

Generally, evidence of other acts or transactions, even of a similar nature, are not admissible where such acts can only be deemed relevant through the inference that the party would follow the same course in the transaction in issue (21 NY Jur, Evidence, § 181). However, the physical condition of the defendant in this appeal became relevant when he stated that he did not have sexual intercourse after 1965 because of a hydrocele (21 NY Jur, Evidence, § 187; 29 Am Jur 2d, Evidence, § 439). At that juncture, the testimony of witness Stern was correctly received in rebuttal on defendant's physical condition in 1969 and 1970 when he was treating the plaintiff. Because witnesses Cuttler and Sherwood were unaware of defendant's physical capability during the period in issue, their testimony was properly stricken by the court below. In the context of this protracted trial, the jurors were not so unduly influenced by this stricken testimony as to warrant a reversal on this ground (*Mercadante* v. *Barry Transp. Co.*, 23 AD2d 653, affd 17 NY2d 462).

Since the brief and unsolicited meeting between juror Smith and witness Sherwood occurred after the rendition of the verdict on liability, the defendant cannot meritoriously contend that the resolution of the liability issue was tainted by juror misconduct. The propriety of the transfer from Supreme Court to Civil Court (CPLR 325, subd [d]) was not raised below and will not be considered, for the first time, upon appeal.

The award of $50,000 in compensatory damages for defendant's aggravation of plaintiff's pre-existing mental disorders, is, however, in our opinion excessive. Plaintiff's condition was of long standing, and began years before she became defendant's patient. There is no evidence to support a permanent worsening of the condition by defendant's acts; nor is there proof demonstrating a permanent impairment of her ability to work in a position comparable to that she had before or during the period she was defendant's patient. Given the fact that she may recover only for the aggravation of her condition by defendant (*Schneider* v. *New York Tel. Co.*, 249 App. Div. 400), we conclude that an award of more than $25,000 would be excessive.

The jury's finding, implicit in its award of punitive damages, that the defendant was actuated by evil or malicious intentions when the parties had sexual intercourse was against the predominating weight of the credible evidence. Viewing all the facts and circumstances incident to the occurrences most favorably to the plaintiff as disclosed in this record (*Sanders* v. *Rolnick*, 188 Misc 627, affd 272 App Div 803), the weight of the evidence did not justify the jury's finding that defendant's conduct, while inexcusable, was so wanton or reckless as to permit an award for punitive damages (*Hedrick* v. *Jebiley*, 198 NYS2d 346; 14 NY Jur, Damages, §§ 177, 179; *Walker* v. *Sheldon*, 10 NY2d 401; cf. *Conners* v. *Walsh*, 131 NY 590; *Da Costa* v. *Technico Constr. Corp.*, 74 Misc 2d 583, affd 78 Misc 2d 1100, lv to app den NYLJ, Dec. 31, 1974, p 2, col 1). The other points of error raised in defendant's brief are clearly without merit and need not be explored in this decision.

Judgment, entered July 29, 1975, reversed and new trial ordered limited to the issue of compensatory damages, with $30 costs to appellant to abide the event that plaintiff recovers less than $25,000 in compensatory damages, unless respondent within 10 days after service of a copy of the order entered hereon with notice of entry, stipulates to reduce the recovery to $25,000, in which event judgment modified accordingly and as modified, affirmed without costs.

MARKOWITZ, P.J. (concurring). I concur in the *Per Curiam* but would like to add the following observations.

The subject matter of this case was highly sensational forcing the participants to operate in a charged atmosphere rather than the calm almost cloistered climate of the routine civil courtroom. However, since this State has not closed the door on all actions merely because sexual relations are part of the core facts, and does permit civil prosecutions where the wrong alleged is grounded on conventional tort (*Tuck* v. *Tuck*, 14 NY2d 341) there is no question that the facts adduced in this record were properly presented to the jury as a possible basis for malpractice which had a causal connection to plaintiff's subsequent psychotic episodes.

While cultists expound theories of the beneficial effects of sexual psychotherapy, the fact remains that all eminent experts in the psychiatric field including the American Psychiatric Association abjure sexual contact between patient and therapist as harmful to the patient and deviant from accepted standards of treatment of the mentally disturbed.

Dr. Ernest Jones, in his encyclopedic treatment of "The Life and Work of Sigmund Freud" (New York, Basic Books, Inc. 1953) sets forth (vol 3, p 163) a letter written by Freud to a colleague which is relevant to the discussion here.

It reads in pertinent part as follows:

"13. XII. 1931

"Lieber Freund: . . .

". . . You have not made a secret of the fact that you kiss your patients and let them kiss you . . .

"Now I am assuredly not one of those who from prudishness or from consideration of bourgeois convention would condemn little erotic gratifications of this kind. . . . But that does not alter the facts . . . that with us a kiss signifies a certain erotic intimacy. We have hitherto in our technique held to the conclusion that patients are to be refused erotic gratifications. You know too that where more extensive gratifications are not to be had milder caresses very easily take over their role, in love affairs, on the stage, etc.

"Now picture what will be the result of publishing your technique. There is no revolutionary who is not driven out of the field by a still more radical one. A number of independent thinkers in matters of technique will say to themselves: why stop at a kiss? Certainly one gets further when one adopts 'pawing' as well, which after all doesn't make a baby. And then bolder ones will come along who will go further to peeping and showing—and soon we shall have accepted in the technique of analysis the whole repertoire of demiviergerie and petting parties, resulting in an enormous increase of interest in psychoanalysis among both analysts and patients. The new adherent, however, will easily claim too much of this interest for himself, the younger of our colleagues will find it hard to stop at the point they originally intended, and God the Father Ferenczi gazing at the lively scene he has created will perhaps say to himself: may be after all I should have halted in my technique of motherly affection *before* the kiss.

"Sentences like 'about the dangers of neocatharsis' don't get very far. One should obviously not let oneself get into the danger. I have purposely not mentioned the increase of calumnious resistances against analysis the kissing technique would bring, although it seems to me a wanton act to provoke them. . . .

With cordial greetings
Your
Freud"

Thus from the font of psychiatric knowledge to the modern practioner we have common agreement of the harmful effects of sensual intimacies between patient and therapist.

Of interesting note is an annotation entitled Civil Liability of Doctor or Psychologist for Having Sexual Relationship With Patient (Ann 33 ALR 3d 1393), in which the notewriters state: "Apart from Nicholson v Han [12 Mich App 35, a case whose facts are not applicable here] research has failed to disclose any case in which the courts have discussed or passed upon the civil liability of a doctor or a psychologist, as such, who, while the doctor-patient relationship subsisted, had established a sexual relationship with a patient." However, where the sexual contacts are themselves the prescribed course of treatment and where such treatment is outside of accepted professional standards, what remains is a simple malpractice action as to which research would be merely cumulative.

On the question of punitive damages, such recovery is allowed in cases where the wrong complained of is morally culpable, or is actuated by evil and reprehensible motives, not only to punish the defendant but to deter him as well as others, from indulging in similar conduct in the future. (*Walker* v. *Sheldon,* 10 NY2d 401, 404.)

In the instant case all that has been established is professional incompetence. It was established that plaintiff was influenced to participate on a theory that it would solve her problems.

Sex under cloak of treatment is an acceptable and established ground for disciplinary measures taken against physicians either by licensing authorities or professional organizations (see Ann 15 ALR 3d 1179). Whether defendant acted in such manner as to seriously affect his performance as a practitioner in the psychiatric field should be left to these more competent fora, rather than by seeking deterrence by way of punitive damages. The only thing that the record herein supports is that his prescribed treatment was in negligent disregard of the consequences. For that, and that alone, he must be held liable.

Riccobono, J. (dissenting). The plaintiff pursued her action for malpractice by alleging that over a period of some 13 months the defendant made sexual advances towards her with a lewd and lascivious motive and that he did in fact engage in sexual intercourse and other acts of carnal knowledge with her, in a purported furtherance of psychiatric treatment. Plaintiff further asserts that instead of assisting and curing her, the defendant's therapeutic methods caused her permanent mental and emotional harm. This harm, it is alleged, was caused by the defendant's failure to treat the plaintiff by acceptable medical procedures.

The right of action to recover a sum of money for seduction was abolished by virtue of former article 2-A of the Civil Practice Act, now section 80-a of the Civil Rights Law. Article 8 of the Civil Rights Law must be liberally construed to effectuate this purpose (Civil Rights Law, § 84). This legislation was passed as a matter of public policy because of the threat or danger of an action to recover money damages and the embarrassment and humiliation emanating from such scandalous causes of action.

In the case at bar, although the plaintiff was suffering from a number of emotional problems her competency was never placed in issue. Is it not fair to infer, therefore, that she was capable of giving a knowing and meaningful consent? For almost one and a-half years while this "meaningful" relationship continued, the plaintiff was not heard to complain. Upon the defendant terminating the relation, this lawsuit evolves.

The defendant obviously did not help his cause by denying what the jury found to be the fact, viz, that the defendant did have sexual relations with the plaintiff. Nevertheless, however ill-advised or ill-conceived was the choice of his defense, in my view this did not constitute malpractice. The plaintiff was still obliged to prove her case by the preponderance of the credible evidence, regardless of the defendant's defense.

I neither condone the defendant's reprehensible conduct, nor maintain that it was not violative of his professional ethics and Hippocratic oath. If, however, the defendant has committed a crime, let him be brought before the criminal halls of justice. For violation of his Hippocratic oath, if there be any, let him suffer the sanctions of the Medical Ethics Board or other appropriate medical authority. But let him not be convicted of his acts of misfeasance and malfeasance by virtue of an action in malpractice. I might parenthetically add, that if the plaintiff is to succeed I am in total agreement with my colleagues that the plaintiff is not entitled to punitive damages and am likewise in full accord that her recovery should not exceed $25,000.

The relief sought by this plaintiff constitutes the closest approach to a conventional action for seduction, and hence must be treated as such. This is barred by section 80-a of the Civil Rights Law (*Fernandez* v. *Lazar,* NYLJ, Sept. 15, 1971, p 19, col 6 [NY Sup Ct, LEFF, J.]; *Nicholson* v. *Han,* 12 Mich App 35). As so inextricably intertwined, I would reverse and dismiss the complaint.

MARKOWITZ, P.J., and TIERNEY, J., concur, MARKOWITZ, P.J., in concurring memorandum; RICCOBONO, J., dissents in separate memorandum.

TREATMENT WITH MEDICATION

The courts have demonstrated a reluctance to find physical or mental harm as a result of the use of words alone. This state of affairs can at least in part be attributed to the difficulty in establishing that the verbal therapy was the proximate cause of the injury. When psychotherapeutic treatment is coupled with the use of medication, however, the possible exposure to liability increases severalfold. This is true because the courts will now readily be able to analyze more "concrete" issues such as foreseeability, informed consent to treatment, physical and behavioral effects of the drug, and aspects of the situation relating to the prescription of the drug. The following cases of *Rennie* v. *Klein,* 462 F.Supp. 1131 (D.N.J. 1978), and *Blanton* v. *United States,* 428 F.Supp. 360 (D.D.C. 1977), illustrate how the courts have tended to deal with allegations of improper treatment with medication. Note that where there has been an involuntary administration of a drug or the lack of informed consent, it is the patient's constitutional right of privacy that is said to have been violated.

Rennie v. *Klein,* 462 F.Supp. 1131 (D.N.J. 1978)

Opinion

BROTMAN, District Judge.

This matter is before the court on the motion of plaintiff, John E. Rennie, for a preliminary injunction pursuant to Fed.R.Civ.P. 65. Plaintiff is an involuntary patient of Ancora Psychiatric Hospital, a state institution. He seeks to enjoin the defendant psychiatrists and officials at Ancora from forcibly administering drugs to him in the absence of an emergency situation. The complaint is grounded on 42 U.S.C. § 1983, with jurisdiction pursuant to 28 U.S.C. § 1343. The following are the court's findings of fact and conclusions of law, Fed.R.Civ.P. 52.

Findings of Fact

I. Procedural History

The complaint in this action was filed on December 22, 1977. While the complaint is stated in six counts, plaintiff essentially charged defendants with violations of four rights: (1) the right to refuse medication in non-emergent circumstances, (2) the right to treatment, (3) the right of access to counsel, and (4) the right to be free from physical abuse while in custody.

On the same date, counsel for Mr. Rennie, Sheldon Gelman of the New Jersey Public Advocate's Office, and counsel for the state officials, Steven D. Wallach, Deputy Attorney General, appeared in chambers on an application for a temporary restraining order. The parties agreed that only the issue of the right to refuse medication would be considered on the motion for a preliminary injunction. In an order prepared that day and filed December 30th, it was ordered that plaintiff not be medicated against his will beyond a maintenance dosage except in emergencies. Counsel agreed, after consultation with the state psychiatrists, that a maintenance dosage would be 15 mg. of prolixin hydrochloride per day. Dr. Marvin Greenberg, plaintiff's expert, was named temporary consultant to the court.

On January 13, 1978, hearings on the motion for preliminary injunction began. The court conducted fourteen days of hearings; the final day was April 28, 1978. Testimony was taken from hospital officials and employees; three Ancora psychiatrists, Dr. Rotov, Direitor of the state Division of Mental Health and Hospitals, three psychiatrists from outside the state system produced by plaintiff, and two outside psychiatrists produced by defendant.[1] Counsel were then allowed to prepare proposed findings and briefs.

During the lengthy course of these hearings, plaintiff attempted suicide by swallowing an overdose of pills on April 10, 1978. Transcript, Volume X, page 5, April 12, 1978 (hereafter cited in the form Tr. X, 5, 4/12/78). Defendants moved to remove the temporary restraining order on April 12. Instead, the court reserved decision and requested that all doctors involved in Mr. Rennie's case convene on April 14, to attempt to reach a consensus on the future course of plaintiff's treatment. The psychiatrists agreed that plaintiff should be treated immediately with an antidepressant medication, followed by the use of lithium carbonate when his depression lifted. There was disagreement over when an antipsychotic drug should be used. On the representation that the lithium-antidepressant regime would be commenced and that plaintiff consented thereto, the temporary restraining order was dissolved by order dated April 18, 1978.

It should be noted that on April 12, Dr. Max Pepernik, Medical Director of Ancora, had stated that if any antipsychotic medication (these drugs are also called "psychotropies") were resumed as treatment, it would not be prolixin because of plaintiff's aversion to that drug. Tr. X, 14. Based on the hearings, the court certainly agrees that this is appropriate. However, much of the court hearing was devoted to examining studies of this particular drug. Defendants argue that, to the extent plaintiff seeks to enjoin the use of prolixin, this case is moot since defendants are not now using that drug and have indicated no plans to do so. Defendants' Proposed Findings of Fact, No. 23, June 23, 1978.

On May 19, 1978, plaintiff brought the parties before this court seeking to restrain the hospital's use of thorazine, another psychotropic drug. Since the April 28 hearing, it was reported that the hospital gave Mr. Rennie every possible chance on lithium but that he was dangerous to himself, other patients, and the staff. After placing Mr. Rennie in restraints for three days, the decision was made to medicate him with

[1]Drs. Greenberg, Pepper, and Limoges were called by plaintiff. Drs. Stinnett and Heller were the state's two outside consultants.

thorazine. Relief was denied plaintiff pending briefing by the parties and the issuance of this opinion, unless plaintiff was prepared to put forward further medical testimony. Thus, while the issue as to prolixin may be moot, defendants have used other drugs of the same type since April. Since the testimony indicates that the benefits and detrimental side effects of all psychotropic drugs are similar, the case as a whole is not moot.

II. The Plaintiff's Personal History

John Rennie is a highly intelligent[2] 38 year old white divorced male. Before his psychiatric difficulties began, he worked as a pilot and a flight instructor. His first symptoms of mental illness appeared in December 1971. Def. Exh. 2, Case History. Serious problems commenced early in 1973, in the wake of his twin brother's death in an airplane accident.

His medical history is lengthy and can only be highlighted here. His first admission to Ancora Psychiatric Hospital was on April 1, 1973. He was depressed and suicidal, and diagnosed as a paranoid schizophrenic. Mellaril, an antipsychotic drug, was given, and plaintiff was released on April 5 to the Fairmont Farms Hospital, a private facility. Def. Exh. 2; Testimony of Dr. Ortanez, Tr. II, 100, 1/19/78.

There followed a revolving door series of readmissions and releases. His second admission was from May 2, 1973 to June 1, 1973, with plaintiff exhibiting similar suicidal ideas and religious delusions. By his third admission, from February 18 to February 26, 1974, he began to exhibit some aggressive and abusive symptoms. Thorazine, another antipsychotic drug, was used. Delusions that he was Christ continued in the fourth admission in March 1974. Tr. II, 102–04.

Subsequent admissions showed further trials of different medicines. During the sixth admission, from April 9 to May 7, 1974 on a voluntary commitment, there is the first indication of a refusal to take medication. He was discharged against medical advice. His eighth admission, on a voluntary commitment from August 26 to September 10, 1974, was initiated when the Secret Service brought him to state authorities after he threatened to kill President Ford. His behavior again was abusive and assaultive. This type of assaultive behavior continued during his ninth admission from September 18 to October 12, 1974, so that the hospital placed him on homicidal precautions. Def. Exh. 2; Testimony of Dr. Ortanez, Tr. II, 100–04. He was also on homicidal precautions during his tenth admission in January 1975. His eleventh admission was involuntary and lengthy, from November 16, 1975 to June 9, 1976. His behavior was erratic, alternating between being depressed and suicidal to manic and homicidal. There was a suicide attempt on December 14 by an overdose of mellaril. Ortanez, Tr. II, pp. 37–38. Both psychotropic drugs, such as haldol, mellaril and prolixin decanoate, as well as lithium, were utilized. During this hospitalization, his diagnosis for a time was changed to manic depressive illness. Def. Exh. 2.

Throughout this period, plaintiff was inconsistent in his attitude toward the various medications, refusing at times and cooperating at others. Ortanez, Tr. III, 101. One of many causes of his repeated discharges and readmissions is his failure to continue taking medications after he has left the hospital's custody.

[2]Testimony of Dr. Marvin Heller, Tr. XIII, 23, 4/25/78. No dulling of the intellect or reduction in IQ has appeared throughout the course of his psychiatric difficulties. Testimony of Dr. Marvin Greenberg, Tr. 1, 77, 1/13/78.

Plaintiff's twelfth and present admission to Ancora began on August 10, 1976, pursuant to an involuntary commitment. N.J.S.A. 30:4-27. Although committed, he has never been declared incompetent. *See* N.J.S.A. 30:4-24.2(c). The admitting diagnosis was manic depressive illness, circular type. He was placed on lithium and on suicidal and homicidal precautions. Later psychotropic drugs were added. Again, at various times, medication was refused. In December 1976, the Public Advocate's Office became involved in Mr. Rennie's case. After conversation with Mr. Gelman, the hospital agreed that medication would not be forced against the patient's will. Following an injection or prolixin decanoate on January 5, 1977, plaintiff became extremely psychotic and threatened suicide. During 1977, plaintiff was shifted between a number of medications, including thorazine, prolixin, etrafon, haldol, elavil, and lithium. Frequent incidents of fights with other patients and attendants were reported. Suicidal and delusional periods were also reported.

One particular incident prior to the commencement of this lawsuit should be noted. On November 17, 1977, plaintiff reported that evening shift attendants beat him with sticks while he was tied to a bed. The next day he pointed out the sticks, which were hidden at the nurses' station. Tr. IX, 7, 4/12/78. The investigation that followed resulted in the suspension of one employee for three days. Plaintiff and the attendant remained together in the same ward. Tr. IX, 45; Tr. II, 81.

In brief fashion, this summarizes plaintiff's history to December 1977, when this suit was commenced. The events of that month will be discussed further, *infra*.

III. Ancora Psychiatric Hospital

Ancora Psychiatric Hospital is a state facility for the mentally ill in Hammonton, New Jersey. It has been accredited by the Joint Commission on Accreditation of Hospitals. Dr. Ortanez and Dr. Bugaoan were the patient's treating psychiatrists during the time relevant to this litigation.

During most of his current admission, plaintiff has been housed in a barren, bleak ward; it has been described as more like a prison than a hospital. Greenberg, Tr. I, 46-7. Plaintiff sometimes has difficulty obtaining a pillow for his bed. His days contain long blocks of unproductive and unstructured time. Testimony of John Rennie, Tr. XIV, 165-67, 4/28/78. In general, doctors at Ancora do not have sufficient time for each patient. Testimony of Dr. Josefina Bugaoan, Tr. V, 61-63, 1/17/78. However, as a result of this lawsuit, the doctors are spending more time with Mr. Rennie. Tr. V, 64-65.

IV. The Medication

A. Benefits of Psychotropic Drugs

Prolixin or Fluphenazine belongs to a group of chemicals variously described as antipsychotic or psychotropic drugs. It comes in long-acting (prolixin decanoate) and short-acting (prolixin hydrochloride) form. Prolixin Decanoate is the only psychotropic drug to come in a form that will last approximately two weeks. Bugaoan, Tr. IV, 124, 1/16/78; Zander, *Prolixin Decanoate: A Review of the Research,* in 2 Mental Disability L.Rep. 37 (1977).

Many other major tranquilizers exist which are very similar to prolixin hydrochloride, both in therapeutic action and side effect. Plotkin, *Limiting the Therapeutic*

Orgy: Mental Patients' Right to Refuse Treatment, 72 Nw.U.L.Rev. 461, 475 (1977). These include thorazine, mellaril, haldol and trilafon. There is no evidence supporting the superiority of any one of these drugs. Bozzuto, *Use of antipsychotic agents for schizophrenia,* 1977 Drug Therapy 40.

In the past twenty years, psychotropic drugs have played an increasingly important role in the treatment of mental illness, and are now widely used. Psychotropic drugs tend to shorten hospital stays and allow patients to function in the community. Many consider use of these drugs necessary in any treatment program, especially for schizophrenics. Winick, *Psychotropic Medication and Competence to Stand Trial,* 1977 Am.B.Found.Res.J. 769, 773-74; Zander, *supra.* Dr. Stinnett went so far as to testify that the failure to treat an acutely psychotic patient with drugs would be malpractice, Tr. XI, 85; *see also,* Tr. II, 145 (quoting a 1976 National Institute of Mental Health report); *cf. Whitree* v. *State,* 56 Misc.2d 693, 290 N.Y.S.2d 486, 501 (1968); *Nason* v. *Superintendent of the Bridgewater State Hospital,* 353 Mass. 604, 233 N.E.2d 908, 910 (1968).

More studies exist demonstrating the efficacy of the psychotropic drugs in the treatment of schizophrenia than for any other mode of treatment. DuBose, *Of the Parens Patriae Commitment Power and Drug Treatment of Schizophrenia: Do the Benefits to the Patient Justify Involuntary Treatment?,* 60 Minn.L.Rev. 1149, 1167 (1976). Defendants offered a number of studies establishing the efficacy of prolixin in the treatment of schizophrenics. May, et al., *Schizophrenia—A Follow-up Study of Results of Treatment,* 33 Arch. Gen'l Psychiatry, 474, 474-78, 481-86 (1976); *Bozzuto, supra* at 44; E. Spohn, et al., *Phenothiazine Effects on Psychological and Psychophysiological Dysfunction in Chronic Schizophrenics,* 34 Arch. Gen'l Psychiatry 633 (1977). *See also* Zander, *supra.*

Of course, the research is not conclusive. Double blind testing is difficult because a placebo group will not experience the usual side effects. Thus the patient and the testers may know that he is unmedicated. Also no studies can conclusively compare the pain of schizophrenic mental states and physical side effects of medication simply because both are subjective experiences. Zander, *supra* at 41; Stinnett, Tr. XI, 81. Furthermore, new studies raise questions about recidivism and the efficacy of using psychotropic medication in every case. Gunderson, *Drugs and Psychosocial Treatment of Schizophrenia Revisited,* Dec. 1977 Psychiatry Digest 25; Simpson, et al., *Psychotic Exacerbation Produced by Neuroleptics,* 37 Diseases of the Nervous System 367 (1976). Patients do react idosyncratically to any particular psychotropic drug. Plotkin, *supra* at 475.

However, the court can appropriately make certain generalizations even at this stage of scientific knowledge. Psychotropic drugs are effective in reducing thought disorder in a majority of schizophrenics. With first admission patients, success rates of as high as 95% have been obtained. *See* May, *supra;* DuBose, *supra* at 1176. Success rates are less impressive with chronic patients. DuBose, *supra* at 1173. However, no other treatment modality has achieved equal success in the treatment of schizophrenics. *Cf.* Bugaoan, Tr. IX, 153-54 (quoting from Hollister, *Choice of Antipsychotic Drugs,* 127 Amer.J. Psychiatry 104, 104 (1970)).

Furthermore, psychotropic drugs are required in order for some patients to effectively participate in and benefit from other types of therapy, such as individual or group psychotherapy and occupational therapy. Comment, *Forced Drug Medication of Involuntarily Committed Mental Patients,* 20 St.Louis U.L.J. 100, 112 (1975); Winick, *supra* at 781; Ortanez, Tr. III, 92; Testimony of Dr. Max Pepernik, Tr. VII, 29, 2/24/78.

In sum, psychotropic drugs are widely accepted in present psychiatric practice. A. Brooks, *Law, Psychiatry and the Mental Health System* 878 (1974). They are the treatment of choice for schizophrenics today. *Cf.* Testimony of Dr. Bertram Pepper, Tr. VIII, 32, 3/27/78; Pepernik, Tr. VII, 16.

B. Side Effects of Psychotropic Drugs

Unfortunately, all of the psychotropic drugs cause dysfunctions of the central nervous system called extrapyramidal symptoms, as well as other side effects. All these vary among individuals. Zander, *supra* at 39. On the average, among all patients, no one drug is much worse than the others at any given therapeutic dosage.[3]

A number of short term autonomic side effects have commonly been reported. These include blurred vision, dry mouth and throat, constipation or diarrhea, palpitations, skin rashes, low blood pressure, faintness and fatigue. Winick, *supra* at 782 n. 66; Plotkin, *supra* at 476; DuBose, *supra* at 1203; Bugaoan, Tr. V, 84. These side effects tend to diminish after a few weeks. Ortanez, Tr. II, 139; Pepernik, Tr. VII, 23. Sudden death may also be a side effect in rare cases. Stinnett, Tr. XI, 50; Pepper, VIII, 24.

Among the extrapyramidal side effects, the two most common are akinesia and akathesia. Akinesia refers to a state of diminished spontaneity, and feeling of weakness and muscle fatigue. Zander, supra; Rifkin, et al., *Fluphenazine Decanoate, Oral Fluphenazine, and Placebo in Treatment of Remitted Schizophrenics,* 34 Arch. Gen'l Psychiatry 1215, 1216 (1977). Patients with severe cases of akinesia had to be dropped from the Rifkin study of prolixin. Akathesia is a subjective state and refers to an inability to be still; a motor restlessness which may produce a shaking of the hands or arms or feet or an irresistable desire to keep walking or tapping the feet. Pepper, Tr. VIII, 22; Zander, *supra;* Winick, *supra;* Bugaoan, Tr. IV, 36. Both of these side effects are temporary and terminate either during or after the drug regime; the effects can also be treated with antocholinergic or antiparkinsonian drugs such as cogentin. Stinnett, Tr. XI, 95; DuBose, *supra* at 1203. However cogentin has side effects of its own, including blurred vision and salivation. Pepper, VIII, 28.

A potential permanent side effect of prolixin and other antipsychotic medication is tardive dyskinesia. Tardive dyskinesia is characterized by rhythmical, repetitive, involuntary movements of the tongue, face, mouth, or jaw, sometimes accompanied by other bizarre muscular activity. Winick, *supra;* Zander, *supra;* DuBose, *supra;* Greenberg, Tr. I, 28. The risk of this disorder is greatest in elderly patients, especially women, and is associated with prolonged use. Zander, *supra* at 40.

Finally, it should be mentioned that British researchers have suggested a link between prolixin and suicidal depression. Zander, *supra*. It is too early for scientists, much less the court, to draw any firm conclusions from this research. Stinnett, Tr. XI, 37.

C. Lithium Carbonate

As lithium is another drug previously used and presently recommended by some doctors in Mr. Rennie's case, a short discussion is appropriate. Lithium carbonate is

[3]Long-acting prolixin may be worse than the short-acting medications. Zander, *supra* at 39. However, as prolixin has been eliminated as the drug of choice, the court will not focus on this distinction.

now established as the most effective treatment available for mania, an affective disorder marked by extreme elation, hyperactivity, grandiosity, and accelerated thinking and speaking. It also prevents the recurrence of both the manic and depressive episodes which alternately afflict patients with bipolar manic-depression. Winick, *supra* at 787; Pepper, Tr. VIII, 40; Testimony of Dr. Richard F. Limoges, Tr. XII, 27-29, 4/20/78. However, in a bipolar case, an antidepressant such as tofranil, amitripyene or imipramine must be added to prevent depression. Tr. VIII, 40; Tr. XII, 29.

V. The Appropriate Treatment for Mr. Rennie

A. Plaintiff's Condition as of December 1977

It is at this juncture appropriate to resume the history of Mr. Rennie and the events which raised the forced medication issue. In early December 1977, the staff of Ancora felt that plaintiff was highly homicidal, and that his general condition was deteriorating. Bugaoan, Tr. III, 137-39. On December 5, a meeting was convened attended by Dr. Bugaoan, Dr. Pepernik, Dr. Ortanez, and the members of plaintiff's treatment team to discuss the situation. Ex. D-2; Bugaoan, Tr. IV, 94. The next day, Dr. Pepernik sought and received permission from the Attorney General's office to administer medication without consent. At a hospital treatment team meeting on December 7, a multi-modal treatment plan for plaintiff was formulated, including the administration of prolixin hydrochloride. The decision to compel medication was made to prevent plaintiff from harming other patients, staff, and himself and to ameliorate his delusional thinking pattern. Prolixin was chosen because, in the decanoate form, it is the only injectable long-acting drug. Tr. IV, 121. It was thought that in the post-hospitalization period, it would be easiest to maintain Mr. Rennie on prolixin decanoate, with one injection every two weeks, since he had a history of failing to continue his medication once released. In the month following the initiation of the prolixin regime, Mr. Rennie's condition improved markedly. Ex. D-2; Tr. II, 129-30. After his dosage was lowered to 15 mg/day by the court order of December 30, it was reported that his behavior was controllable. However the staff psychiatrists felt the dosage to be insufficient to treat his thought disorder. Tr. III, 86.

B. Plaintiff's Diagnosis

Obviously, before drugs can be prescribed, plaintiff's condition must be known. Perhaps the question most contested during the hearings was plaintiff's proper diagnosis. While psychotropic drugs are generally regarded as the treatment of choice for schizophrenia, lithium, with an antidepressant, is the treatment of choice for manic depression. As plaintiff is presently willing to take lithium,[4] this case would be moot if manic depression were the consensus diagnosis.

As noted earlier, at various times during plaintiff's prior hospitalizations, diagnoses of both schizophrenia and manic depression were offered. There is a thin line between these two illnesses. Pepper, Tr. XIV, 78, 4/28/78. No expert indicated any medical agreement as to whether the two disorders arise from different environmental causes,

[4]In the past, Mr. Rennie has refused lithium, stating it made him too depressed. Greenberg, Tr. I, 35. His assessment of the drug was correct. At the time, the hospital apparently would not give him an antidepressant in addition to the lithium. Perhaps as a result of these hearings, all now agree that lithium is best at curbing the manic side of manic depression, and that in a bipolar case such as plaintiff's, an antidepressant such as tofrinil is also necessary. *See* Order Dissolving Temporary Restraining Order 4/18/78; Tr. XI, 139; Pepper, VIII, 40; Heller, XIII, 41, 4/25/78; Limoges, XII, 29.

or represent different physiological states within the brain. Instead, the testimony concentrated on symptomatology. Furthermore, there was little testimony on how the psychopharmacological substances work in the brain. This emphasis on symptoms and lack of certainty about causation and physiopathology demonstrates the tentativeness of much psychiatric diagnosis as compared to the usual physical diagnosis. The experts who testified concerning Mr. Rennie's disorder are in great disagreement. Drs. Heller and Bugaoan believe plaintiff is schizophrenic. Tr. XII, 40. Drs. Ortanez and Pepernik give a diagnosis of schizophrenia, affective type. Tr. III, 71, Tr. X, 109, but Ortanez agrees that plaintiff has also shown a manic depression symptoms at times. Tr. III, 75. Dr. Stinnett diagnoses plaintiff as manic depressive, but offers schizo-affective disorder as a possible alternative diagnosis. Tr. XI, 15. Finally, Drs. Limoges and Pepper feel that plaintiff suffers only from manic depression. Tr. XII, 32; VIII, 31.

There is much overlap between the two diagnoses and disagreement among experts. Manic depression is basically a mood disorder, while schizophrenia is primarily a thought disorder, characterized by delusions, hallucinations, and faulty logic. However, manic depressives can also show thought disorders at the manic end of the mood swing. But, true schizophrenia is characterized by sustained rather than episodic periods of thought disorder. Further, a manic depressive's periods of thought disorder will be tied to his mood swings, unlike a schizophrenic's cognitive dysfunctions. In addition, schizophrenics can show mood disorder as a secondary symptom. This is called schizophrenia, affective type, or schizo-affective disorder. Stinnett, Tr. XI, 20; Ortanez, Tr. III, 71.

The problem facing the doctors diagnosing Mr. Rennie is obviously complex. Simplified for the lawyer's mind, one of the key inquiries is whether Rennie's assertions that he is the "alpha omega," Tr. VII, 25, or Christ, are firm and fixed schizophrenic delusions or mere grandiosity characteristic of his manic euphoria. Dr. Limoges believes the latter and thus would only prescribe lithium and an antidepressant to combat plaintiff's manic depression. Tr. XII, 26, 118-19.

Dr. Stinnett however testified that while his diagnosis was manic depression, the distinction is largely academic. He found the symptoms to warrant both antipsychotic medication and lithium. An antipsychotic was deemed necessary both to curb the patient's perceived delusions and to control the destructive aspects of his behavior. Tr. XI, 22-23. While Dr. Ortanez lacks Dr. Stinnett's experience and expertise,[5] as the treating physician Dr. Ortanez also believed that both antipsychotics and lithium would be appropriate based on his perception of combined symptoms.

A little knowledge can be dangerous, and this court is hesitant to diagnose mental illness and prescribe medication. But it is possible to draw these conclusions. Plaintiff is acutely psychotic at times. Stinnett, Tr. XI, 135. Aside from his adverse reaction to psychotropics, the best course of treatment for Mr. Rennie would combine psychotropic medication with lithium and an antidepressant. However, the position that he has no fixed delusions, thus making use of a psychotropic unnecessary, is, at the least, a reasonable proposition.

C. Use of Pharmaco-therapy as the Sole Therapy

Defendants have produced at least one study, May, *supra,* demonstrating that drugs alone are an effective means of curing schizophrenia. Testimony has also indicated that

[5] In this case, opportunity to observe Mr. Rennie's everchanging symptoms may be the best way to arrive at an appropriate diagnosis. None of the outside experts besides Dr. Greenberg had this luxury.

drugs must be used initially to bring Mr. Rennie into contact with reality before any other therapy may be usefully employed. Bugaoan, Tr. III, 143; Stinnett, Tr. XI, 16; Heller, Tr. XIII, 33.

However, the court rejects any solution to the problems of this case which would allow Mr. Rennie to be treated with an antipsychotropic drug alone. Dr. Stinnett expressed in the strongest possible terms that both pharmacotherapy and psychotherapy would have to be used to improve Mr. Rennie's conditions and not one without the other. The court fully accepts Dr. Stinnett's recommendation. Dr. Pepper concurred in stating that medicine cannot be successful outside of a good total treatment plan. Tr. VIII, 34. Only in the context of a trusting relationship achieved through psychotherapy can medicine be employed in a rational way. Tr. XI, 16.

D. Plaintiff's Reaction to Psychotropics

John Rennie suffers from many of the side effects described above. He experiences blurred vision and a dry mouth. Rennie, Tr. XIV, 144, 4/28/78. On thorazine, his blood pressure has dropped. Tr. I, 35. He also suffers from akathesia on prolixin, getting uncontrollable tremors. Tr. XIV, 144. This, and the fact that he feels his senses are dulled, are his two principal reasons for refusal of prolixin. Tr. I, 35. Despite the hospital's assertion that Mr. Rennie has faked akathesia, Bugaoan, Tr. IV, 125 this court is convinced that the akathesia is real and extremely unpleasant. Pepper, Tr. VIII, 22; Heller, Tr. XIII, 22. The hospital doctors are to be faulted for ignoring plaintiff's subjective reports of akathesia while on prolixin. Stinnett, Tr. XI, 55.

Mr. Rennie also has shown wormlike movements of the tongue. This is a preliminary symptom which is possibly indicative that tardive dyskinesia may develop if medication is continued. Pepper, Tr. XIV, 34. Thus, there is a risk of permanent damage from psychotropic medication in Mr. Rennie's case, and Mr. Rennie requires extremely close monitoring if these drugs are to be continued.

E. The Efficacy of Forced Medication

As noted above, a trusting relationship or therapeutic alliance between psychiatrist and patient is essential for a drug regimen to succeed. Stinnett, Tr. XI, 16; Limoges, XII, 73. Plaintiff has demonstrated that psychotropic drugs are less efficacious in a hostile or negative environment. Stinnett, XI, 35, 108; Pepper, VIII, 57. As a corollary to this even if the best drug is prescribed, if the patient is unwilling to accept it, the positive effects are greatly lessened, especially in terms of long range benefits. Pepper, Tr. VIII, 76; Limoges, Tr. 72; *O'Connor* v. *Donaldson,* 422 U.S. 563, 579, 95 S.Ct.2486, 45 L.Ed.2d 396 (1975) (Burger, C. J., concurring).

F. Plaintiff's Competency to Make Medication Decisions

John Rennie's psychiatric problems are of a cyclical nature, so that on some days he is psychotic. Dr. Pepper testified that plaintiff's refusal of prolixin is not a product of his mental disorder. Tr. XIV, 123. However, Dr. Stinnett found that during his examination on February 25, 1978, Mr. Rennie was not capable of making a decision on treatment in his best interests. Tr. XI, 112. The court feels that Dr. Pepernik's assessment is most accurate, and that Mr. Rennie's wishes should be taken into account on any treatment decision. But the court finds that his capacity to participate in the refusal of medicine or the choice of medicine is somewhat limited, depending on the day. Tr. VII, 24; *cf.* Shwed, *Protecting the Rights of the Mentally Ill,* 64 A.B.A.J.

564, 566 (1978); Comment, *Forced Drug Medication, supra* at 113. The court does believe that Mr. Rennie's reports of his subjective reactions to particular drugs are generally accurate.

Conclusions of Law

I. Introduction—New Jersey Law

A New Jersey state court has recently been faced with a factual situation very similar to this case. *In re Hospitalization of B,* 156 N.J.Super. 231, 383 A.2d 760 (Law Div. 1977) involved an involuntarily committed patient who was refusing prolixin. B had not responded to all conventional therapies, and the treating physician sought the court's permission to administer a psychotropic drug. B had not been declared incompetent. N.J.Ct.R. 4:83.

Looking to the New Jersey statutes, the court quoted N.J.S.A. 30:4-24.2(d)(1), which states that:

> No medication shall be administered unless at the written order of a physician. Notation of each patient's medication shall be kept in his treatment records. At least weekly, the attending physician shall review the drug regimen of each patient under his care. All physician's orders or prescriptions shall be written with a termination date, which shall not exceed 30 days. Medication shall not be used as punishment, for the convenience of staff, as a substitute for a treatment program, or in quantities that interfere with the patient's treatment program. Voluntarily committed patients shall have the right to refuse medication.

Based on this statute the court held that involuntarily committed patients do not have the right to refuse medication. Involuntary patients "are protected by nothing more than the court's review, the occasional consultation of an independent expert and the promised administrative procedure." 156 N.J.Super. at 238, 383 A.2d at 764. Thus, plaintiff is proceeding under § 1983 to determine if the state scheme is constitutionally defective.

New Jersey does recognize the emerging right to treatment of mental patients. N.J.S.A. 30:4-24.1; *State* v. *Carter,* 64 N.J. 382, 393-04, 316 A.2d 449 (1974); *see also Wyatt* v. *Aderholt,* 503 F.2d 1305 (5th Cir. 1974).

II. Standards on a Preliminary Injunction

Generally, four factors are to be considered on an application for a preliminary injunction: (1) whether the moving party has shown that it is likely to prevail on the merits, (2) whether the movant has demonstrated that he would be irreparably harmed if the preliminary injunction is denied, (3) whether the grant of the injunction would harm other interested parties to a greater extent than it would benefit movant, and (4) whether the public interest would be served. *A. O. Smith Corp.* v. *F. T. C.,* 530 F.2d 515, 525 (3rd Cir. 1976). Defendants argue that there can be no showing of probability of success on the merits where novel legal issues are raised.

Certainly the issue of a federal right to refuse medication is novel and complex. However, the case has not followed the usual course of a preliminary injunction hearing. Hearings have been held on fourteen dates over a period of four months. The court has heard testimony from nine psychiatrists. Counsel have aided the court with excellent briefs. Thus, while more information is always desirable, the court feels that it should not avoid a consideration of the merits in this instance merely because the issues are novel.

III. Abstention

Defendants argue that this court should abstain in this case so as to allow a state appellate court to consider the issue. Abstention is only appropriate in narrowly limited special circumstances. *Zwickler* v. *Koota,* 389 U.S. 241, 248, 88 S.Ct. 391, 19 L.Ed.2d 444 (1967). It is proper when a federal constitutional claim is premised on an unsettled question of state law and where a state court decision on the state law issue might avoid the constitutional problem. *Frederick L.* v. *Thomas,* 557 F.2d 373, 381 (3rd Cir. 1977).

In this case, the state statute is clear. N.J.S.A. 30:4–24.2(d)(1) provides that voluntary patients may refuse medication, and thus by implication, involuntary patients may not. A recent state case, *In re Hospitalization of B, supra,* has settled the point. The fact that an appellate court has not decided the issue is not dispositive.

Furthermore, abstention is discretionary. *Frederick L., supra* at 382. It would be inequitable to send plaintiff back to state court at this stage of the proceedings. Therefore, the court will not abstain.

IV. The Federal Constitutional Issues

The plaintiff alleges numerous constitutional grounds in support of his position. These claims generally track the course charted in *Scott* v. *Plante,* 532 F.2d 939 (3rd Cir. 1976). *See also Souder* v. *McGuire,* 423 F.Supp. 830 (M.D.Pa.1976). Scott, a patient of Trenton State Hospital, had five pro se complaints dismissed by the district court. One claim challenged the involuntary administration of medications, including thorazine, mellaril, and trilafon. The Third Circuit, in reversing the motion to dismiss, outlined in dictum how such a claim could establish a constitutional deprivation.

> . . . [E]xisting case law points to at least three[9] conceivable deprivations that may accompany the involuntary administration of such substances by state officers acting under color of state law to inmates confined in a state institution. . . . [T]he involuntary administration of drugs which affect mental processes . . . could amount, under an appropriate set of facts, to an interference with Scott's rights under the first amendment. *See Mackey* v. *Procunier,* 477 F.2d 877 (9th Cir. 1973); *Kaimowitz* v. *Dep't of Mental Health,* Civ. No. 73-19434-AW (Mich. Cir. Ct., Wayne County, July 10, 1973). Moreover, on this record we must assume that Scott, though perhaps properly committable, has never been adjudicated an incompetent who is incapable of giving an informed consent to medical treatment. Under these circumstances due process would require, in the absence of an emergency, that some form of notice and opportunity to be heard be given to Scott or to someone standing *in loco parentis* to him before he could be subjected to such treatment. Finally, under certain conditions, Scott's claim may raise an eighth amendment

[9]A possible fourth constitutional deprivation might include invasion of the inmate's right to bodily privacy . . . *See, e. g., Roe* v. *Wade,* 410 U.S. 113, 93 S.Ct. 705, 35 L.Ed.2d 147 . . . (1973).

issue respecting cruel and unusual punishment. *See Knecht* v. *Gillman,* 488 F.2d 1136 (8th Cir. 1973); *Mackey* v. *Procunier, supra* at 878.

A. *Cruel and Unusual Punishment*

As Dr. Rotov testified, Tr. VI, 141, 2/23/78, there is great potential for the abuse of psychotropic medication, and careful scrutiny is required when they are involuntarily administered. Comment, *Advances in Mental Health: A Case for the Right to Refuse Treatment,* 48 Temp.L.Q. 354, 364 (1975). The court will assume that the eighth amendment prohibition on cruel and unusual punishment does apply to protect persons confined in mental institutions. *See Ingraham* v. *Wright,* 430 U.S. 651, 669 n. 37, 97 S.Ct. 1401, 51 L.Ed.2d 711 (1977).

The question is whether use of antipsychotic drugs in plaintiff's case is justified as treatment or whether it can be classified as punishment by the court. *Knecht* v. *Gillman,* 488 F.2d 1136, 1138 (8th Cir. 1973). A number of cases have found eighth amendment violations despite claims of therapeutic value. *Knecht, supra; Mackey* v. *Procunier,* 477 F.2d 877 (9th Cir. 1973); *Pena* v. *New York State Division for Youth,* 419 F.Supp. 203, 207 (S.D.N.Y.1976); *Nelson* v. *Heyne,* 355 F.Supp. 451, 455 (N.D.Ill.1972). However, each case is clearly distinguishable from the one at bar. In *Knecht,* the drug apomorphine was found to have no proven therapeutic value and its use was not recognized as acceptable medical practice. 488 F.2d at 1138, 1140; *see* Plotkin, *supra* at 494. Furthermore, while the behavior modification program was believed to have long-term benefits, the adverse effects seemed *unnecessarily* harsh. Comment, *The Right Against Treatment: Behavior Modification and the Involuntarily Committed,* 23 Cath.U.L.Rev. 774, 782 (1974). In *Nelson, Pena,* and *Mackey,* the courts found that the drugs were used improperly and for punishment rather than as part of an ongoing psychotherapeutic program. *Cf. Welsh* v. *Likins,* 373 F.Supp. 487, 503 (D.Minn.1974).

In contrast, psychotropic drugs have been proven effective. Furthermore, the Ancora staff has established that they were trying to use prolixin as an integral component of an overall treatment program. While the side effects of prolixin are serious, they are not *unnecessarily* harsh in light of the potential benefits. Accordingly, the court finds no eighth amendment violation. Prolixin was justifiably administered as treatment, not punishment.

B. *First Amendment*

Another constitutional argument advanced in support of a right to refuse treatment is a first amendment right to freedom of expression, including both the right to communicate and the right to think. Plotkin, *supra* at 494. Plaintiff argues in this case that drugs may be used to punish or suppress truthful expression critical of the institution. Certainly plaintiff has a history of justifiably criticizing hospital procedure. However, there is no evidence that the hospital administered the medications in this case in an attempt to suppress those statements.

Plaintiff also argues that the use of drugs interferes with his mental processes and thus deprives him of his right to mentation. *Kaimowitz* v. *Dept. of Mental Health,* Civ.No. 73-19434 (Cir. Ct. Wayne County, Michigan July 10, 1973), *reprinted in* A. Brooks, *Law, Psychiatry and the Mental Health System, supra* at 902; *Scott, supra* at 946; Comment, *Advances in Mental Health, supra* at 366. In *Kaimowitz,* the court held that an adult may not give legally adequate consent to experimental psychosurgery, in part because of first amendment protection of the freedom to generate ideas. Any court must be deeply concerned with potential state control of individual thought and carefully scrutinize instances of forced psychiatric treatment.

In the case at bar, the court does not believe that first amendment analysis requires the use of drugs to be enjoined. First, Dr. Greenberg indicated that plaintiff's ability to perform on intelligence tests has not been impaired. Most importantly, plaintiff has indicated a desire to be cured of his mental illness. In his action, he is asserting a right to be treated, and has testified that he *wants* to be cured, not warehoused. Tr. XIV, 170. Thus, the hospital's efforts to alter his thinking disorder cannot be seen as a first amendment violation. The court need not reach the question of whether insane or disordered thought is within the scope of first amendment protection. Comment, *Advances in Mental Health, supra* at 366-67.

However, plaintiff also claims that a side effect of prolixin is that it dulls his senses and makes it difficult for him to speak. These side effects are temporary and expected to last only a few days or a couple of weeks, Pepernik, Tr. VII, 23, perhaps two months at the outside, Stinnett, Tr. XI, 132. This effect on mentation differs sharply from the problem faced in *Kaimowitz*. The patient in that case was to be subjected to experimental psychosurgery. The effects would be irreversible and unpredictable, the dangers to the patient substantial, and the benefits uncertain, with no scientifically established therapeutic effect. More specifically as to effects on the mental processes, psychosurgery flattens emotional responses and leads to lack of abstract reasoning ability, loss of capacity for new learning, and impairment of memory. *Kaimowitz, supra* at 909. In sum, if forced medication is otherwise proper, the temporary dulling of the senses accompanying it does not rise to the level of the first amendment violations found in *Kaimowitz*.

C. *The Right to Privacy*

(1) INDIVIDUAL INTERESTS

The court believes that any right to refuse medication in the absence of an emergency is best founded on the emerging right of privacy. The right of privacy is broad enough to include the right to protect one's mental processes from governmental interference. *Kaimowitz, supra* at 919; *Mackey* v. *Procunier,* 477 F.2d 877, 878 (9th Cir. 1973); *Stanley* v. *Georgia,* 397 U.S. 557, 565, 89 S.Ct. 1243, 22 L.Ed.2d 542 (1969); Comment, *Advances in Mental Health, supra* at 367; Comment, *The Right Against Treatment, supra* at 785. Additionally, privacy has been used to establish an individual's autonomy over his own body. *Roe* v. *Wade,* 410 U.S. 113, 93 S.Ct. 705, 35 L.Ed.2d 147 (1973); *Runnels* v. *Rosendale,* 499 F.2d 733, 735 (9th Cir. 1974); Comment, *Forced Drug Medication, supra* at 104. In other contexts, courts have established a constitutional right of privacy "broad enough to encompass a patient's decision to decline medical treatment under certain circumstances." *In re Quinlan,* 70 N.J. 10, 40, 355 A.2d 647, 663 (1976). This court holds that the right to refuse treatment extends to mental patients in non-emergent circumstances. *Bell* v. *Wayne County General Hospital at Eloise,* 384 F.Supp. 1085, 1100 (E.D.Mich.1974) (three-judge court); DuBose, *supra* at 1160; Zander, *supra* at 50. This accords with the usual common law rule against involuntary medical treatment. *Winters* v. *Miller,* 446 F.2d 65, 68 (2nd Cir. 1971); *Scott* v. *Plante, supra.* Only where the government shows some strong countervailing interest can the right to refuse be qualified. *See* 1 Report and Recommendation of the President's Commission on Mental Health 44 (1978);

DuBose, *supra;* SZASZ, *Involuntary Psychiatry,* 45 U. of Cin.L.Rev. 347, 356–57 (1976); Zander, *supra.*

The court feels that the recognition of a right to refuse treatment in a non-emergency situation is practical. The testimony has indicated that involuntary treatment is much less effective than the same treatment voluntarily received. The psychiatric experts stated that it is more likely that a patient will consent to desirable treatment when consulted before action is taken, and when he feels that he has some real control over his fate, than when he feels totally at the mercy of the hospital doctors.

Furthermore, only the patient can really know the discomfort associated with side effects of particular drugs. Again, the experts agree that they must rely on their patients for evidence of subjective feelings of pain associated with drug usage. Individual autonomy demands that the person subjected to the harsh side effects of psychotropic drugs have control over their administration.

It is also difficult for any person, even a doctor, to balance for another the possibility of a cure of his schizophrenia with the risks of permanent disability in the form of tardive dyskinesia. Whether the potential benefits are worth the risks is a uniquely personal decision which, in the absence of a strong state interest, should be free from state coercion.

Finally, the testimony in this case underscores the fact that psychiatric diagnosis and therapy is uncertain, with great divergence of opinion in any given case. *O'Connor* v. *Donaldson,* 422 U.S. 563, 579, 95 S.Ct. 2486, 45 L.Ed.2d 396 (Burger, C. J., concurring). This also weighs toward leaving the final decision with the patient rather than deferring to doctors. Thus, the court concludes that it is appropriate to recognize a right to refuse treatment.

(2) STATE INTEREST

The constitutional right to refuse treatment cannot be absolute. *Jacobson* v. *Massachusetts,* 197 U.S. 11, 25 S.Ct. 358, 49 L.Ed. 643 (1905). The President's Commission charges all concerned with mental health laws to pay "careful attention to the circumstances and procedures under which the right may be qualified." Commission on Mental Health, *supra* at 44. Based on the evidence in this case, the court has identified three factors to be considered in overriding the patient's right to refuse.

First, the state's police power is often cited as one justification for the initial confinement of the mentally ill. The police power permits the state to confine a mentally ill person who presents a danger to himself or other members of society. *O'Connor* v. *Donaldson,* 422 U.S. 563, 575–77, 95 S.Ct. 2486, 45 L.Ed.2d 396 (1975); Note, *Wyatt* v. *Stickney—A Constitutional Right to Treatment for the Mentally Ill,* 34 U.Pitt.L.Rev. 79, 82–83 (1972). The fact that the patient is dangerous in free society may give the state power to confine, but standing alone it does not give the power to treat involuntarily. *Winters* v. *Miller, supra* at 70. Once confined, the patient cannot hurt those outside.

However, the other patients in the hospital also have a constitutional right to protection from harm. Commission on Mental Health, *supra* at 44; *Runnels* v. *Rosendale, supra* at 735; *Goodman* v. *Parwatikar,* 570 F.2d 801, 804 (8th Cir. 1978); *Welsch* v. *Likins,* 373 F.Supp. 487, 503 (D.Minn.1974). If a patient cannot be confined without endangering other patients and staff, and yet he refuses medication that would curb his dangerous tendencies, this would be one factor to weigh in overriding his decision to refuse. Comment, Forced Drug Medication, *supra* at 107.

The court found in this case that Mr. Rennie had shown frequent assaultive behavior while at Ancora. At times, this behavior led the Ancora staff to put him in restraints. Mr. Rennie has also complained bitterly about the use of restraints. However, in light of the hospital's duty to safeguard other patients and staff, plaintiff cannot both refuse his medication and be left free to inflict harm on others.

A second justification for involuntary confinement and treatment is the doctrine of parens patriae, under which the state cares for those unable to care for themselves. Note, *Wyatt* v. *Stickney—Constitutional Right to Treatment, supra* at 82–83. It is clear that mental illness is not the equivalent of incompetency, which renders one incapable of giving informed consent to medical treatment. *Scott* v. *Plante, supra;* Plotkin, *supra* at 490, 496; Comment, *Advances in Mental Health, supra* at 371; N.J.S.A. 30:4-24.2(c). Therefore, before the state can use parens patriae as a basis for medication, some hearing on the issue of competency must be held. *Scott* v. *Plante, supra.*

The factfinder of such a hearing must determine the extent to which the refusal of treatment is based on the underlying mental illnesses. Often, a characteristic of the illness is the inability to recognize and understand the severity of the problem. The greater the lack of insight, the stronger the impetus to override the right to individual autonomy. As stated by Judge Bazelon, "how real is the promise of individual autonomy for a confused person set adrift in a hostile world?" Bazelon, *Institutionalization, Deinstitutionalization and the Adversary Process,* 75 Colum.L.Rev. 897, 907 (1975).

If a factfinder is swayed to allow involuntary medication in part because of the patient's diminished capacity to care for himself, he should also consider the ability of the hospital to provide a reasonable full treatment plan. Since *Rouse* v. *Cameron,* 125 U.S.App.D.C. 366, 373 F.2d 451 (1966), courts have increasingly been recognizing a right to treatment. If a hospital cannot provide reasonable treatment services beyond the forcing of medication, one would doubt the appropriateness of allowing that institution to act in parens patriae. *Cf. Naughton* v. *Bevilacqua,* 458 F.Supp. 610 (D.R.I.1978), which held that prolixin could not be used solely to control a patient's behavior, without a habilitative purpose.

In the instant case, the court has found Mr. Rennie's decision-making powers to be somewhat impaired. However, the prior refusal of lithium without an antidepressant was well-founded, and the refusal of prolixin also had a rational basis. As previously noted, prolixin has been discontinued. If the state again seeks to medicate Mr. Rennie without his consent, the court will have to evaluate the basis for using that particular drug when the occasion arises. As part of that inquiry, it will be relevant to determine if Mr. Rennie understands that the alternative to accepting treatment may be permanent custody at Ancora.

As a final consideration, many courts and commentators have employed the concept of least restrictive alternatives in regard to the choice of a custodial setting. *Welsch* v. *Likins, supra* at 501; *Gary W.* v. *State of La.,* 437 F.Supp. 1209, 1217 (E.D.La.1976); *Eubanks* v. *Clarke,* 434 F.Supp. 1022, 1028 (E.D.Pa.1977); *Bazelon, supra* at 901; *Barnett, Treatment Rights of Mentally Ill Nursing Home Residents,* 126 U.Pa.L.Rev. 578, 590 (1978); Flaschner, *Legal Rights of the Mentally Handicapped: A Judge's Viewpoint,* 60 A.B.A.J. 1371 (1974). The court feels that this concept should be extended to the choice of medications. Comment, *Advances in Mental Health, supra* at 376; Winick, *supra* at 813; Commission on Mental Health, *supra* at 44. Under this theory, a patient "may challenge the forced administration of drugs on the basis that alternative treatment methods should be tried before a more intrusive technique like psychotropic medication is used.'' Winick, *supra*.

In Mr. Rennie's case, psychotherapy had not proved effective. However, plaintiff's experts stated that lithium plus an antidepressant would be a reasonable therapy to which plaintiff would consent. Dr. Heller agreed that lithium and tofrinil was worth a trial: Tr. XIII, 41. Under these circumstances, the hospital is required to give Mr. Rennie a fair trial on the agreed upon lithium and tofrinil regime before seeking to medicate involuntarily the plaintiff. The notion of least restrictive alternatives can also be applied to the threat of tardive dyskinesia. If plaintiff is likely to contract tardive dyskinesia through renewed administration of psychotropic drugs, the cure would be worse than the illness, and involuntary medication would not be permitted.

Although another hearing may be required, the court does not intend to necessitate multiple hearings. The court wishes to avoid a cyclical situation where prohibition of treatment causes a patient's incompetency, upon which his doctors can then overturn his refusal and treat him with drugs, which then help him to regain competency and his refusal right. Instead, the court will, as much as possible, look to the proper treatment over the long term. Consideration of the least restrictive alternative is part of this long-term analysis.

To summarize, if the trial of lithium and tofrinil has failed and the state seeks to administer another drug which is refused by the plaintiff, the drug can only be administered in an emergency. For a long range program, the state must come back to court for further hearings. On the evidence to date, the court does not believe that tardive dyskinesia is likely at this time; only a preliminary symptom *possibly* indicative of the disease has been shown. The court would find that all less restrictive alternatives have been exhausted if the lithium and tofrinil regime was given a fair trial. The court does find Mr. Rennie dangerous to others on the ward at times. Both his dangerousness and the rationality behind any new refusal would have to be evaluated at a new hearing. Furthermore, perhaps because he is a litigant, Mr. Rennie seems to be receiving an adequate treatment regime.

D. *Due Process*

In light of the extended nature of these hearings, Mr. Rennie certainly has received all the process to which he is due. However, in view of this court's practical experiences during this hearing, it is perhaps appropriate to comment on what the court feels are the shortcomings of the state's new Bulletin 78-3 regarding psychotropic medication, which appears as an appendix to this opinion.

First, the court finds that there is a sufficient liberty interest so that due process attaches. To go from a state of confinement to confinement plus forced medication involves a major change in the conditions of confinement, so that *Meachum* v. *Fano,* 427 U.S. 215, 96 S.Ct. 2532, 49 L.Ed.2d 451 (1975) is inapposite. A drug regimen subjects a patient to harsh side effects and possible permanent disability, effects different in kind than the differences between places of confinement. Furthermore, a hearing is required to insure that the use of drugs in a particular case does not violate the first or eighth amendments or the right of privacy. Thus, in the absence of emergency, some due process hearing is required prior to the forced administration of drugs. *Scott* v. *Plante, supra. See also Clonce* v. *Richardson,* 379 F.Supp. 338, 349 (W.D.Mo. 1974); Plotkin, *supra* at 491; Winick, *supra* at 816; *Winters* v. *Miller, supra* at 71. *Cf.* Bazelon, *supra* at 909.

A due process hearing is also required because there is great risk of hospital error. As we have seen, hospital records are difficult even for the staff to use. Entries are sometimes missed, and the complete drug history is not always clear. This underscores the need for systematic review of the decision to medicate involuntarily.

Initially, patients must be informed of and participate in the decision-making aspects of their treatment. *In re W. S., Jr.*, 152 N.J.Super. 298, 377 A.2d 969 (Juv. and Dom.Rel.Ct.1977).

Patients are entitled to a lawyer to assist them. Counsel is necessary to cope with the problems of law, to make skilled inquiry into the facts, and to insure proper procedures. *Bell, supra* at 1092 (quoting *In re Gault,* 387 U.S. 1, 36, 87 S.Ct. 1428, 18 L.Ed.2d 527 (1967)); *cf.* Bazelon, *supra* at 910. It is clear in this case that without the tireless efforts of Mr. Gelman and his staff at the Public Advocate's Office, Mr. Rennie could not effectively have made an argument before a factfinder and brought his case before this court. *See, Scott, supra* at 950.

Independent psychiatrists are also essential to a fair hearing. Unless the state elects to set up some form of independent administrative board to review treatment decisions, the patient is entitled to an outside psychiatrist of his choice to evaluate the need for medication. *See* Senator Menza's Bill, Senate No. 1032 (October 23, 1975), vetoed March 4, 1976.

A hospital-retained psychiatrist is not sufficient. As Dr. Pepper testified, psychiatrists are as objective as lawyers when representing a client. When Dr. Pepernik and Dr. Stinnett reviewed plaintiff's files, they began with the assumption that the choice of prolixin was correct. Dr. Heller was also influenced by having the hospital doctors refer him to specific sections of the charts. Patients refusing treatment must be entitled to an outside consultant of their choice so that all of the facts can be aired.

The court also notes that once the outside consultants and hospital psychiatrists began talking, it was possible to reach areas of agreement and a fuller understanding of Mr. Rennie's problem. Thus, it believes that the presence of independent doctors will aid rather than inhibit treatment.

Finally, the patient's lawyer and psychiatrist must have access to hospital records to determine comprehensively the position of their client. Where the patient cannot reasonably afford an attorney or a psychiatrist, the state must supply them.

V. Conclusion

As the involuntary medication of prolixin was terminated, no injunction need issue on that point. Due to the time required for briefing and preparation of this opinion, over four months have passed since the parties were last in court. Accordingly, the court is not fully aware of the present status of Mr. Rennie and what effect an injunction would have.[6] Therefore, no injunction will issue at the moment. If Mr. Rennie now refuses any drug which the Ancora doctors seek to administer in a nonemergency situation, the court will upon notice restrain the administration of the drug and immediately schedule hearings to examine (1) plaintiff's physical threat to patients and staff at the institution, (2) plaintiff's capacity to decide on his particular treatment, (3) whether any less restrictive treatments exist, and (4) the risk of permanent side effects from the proposed treatment.

[6]It is the court's understanding that as of the date of this opinion Mr. Rennie is not receiving psychotropic drugs, and may soon be released from Ancora.

Appendix: Division of Mental Health and Hospitals Administrative Bulletin 78-3

March 1, 1978

SUBJECT: The Administration of Psychotropic Medication to Voluntary and Involuntary Patients

I. *Introduction*

A. *Issue*

Division guidelines governing the administration of psychotropic medication to voluntary and involuntary psychiatric hospital patients.

B. *Objectives*

1. To fulfill our ethical, professional and statutory responsibilities in improving the condition of psychiatric hospital patients;
2. To provide patients with the opportunity to participate in the development of their own individual treatment plans;
3. To provide for *medical review* of the treating physician's medication determination;
4. To utilize the patient's treatment team in formulating clinical care.

C. *Legislative Parameters*

1. Every individual who is mentally ill is entitled to medical care and other professional services in accordance with accepted standards. N.J.S.A. 30:4-24.1. New Jersey courts have also recognized that a psychiatric hospital patient has an affirmative right to receive treatment and that a hospital has a correlative responsibility to attempt to improve the condition of its patients.
2. Each patient has the right to participate in planning for his own treatment to the extent that his condition permits. N.J.S.A. 30:4-24.1.
3. (a) Voluntary patients have the right to refuse medication. N.J.S.A. 30:4-24.2. d (1).
   (b) The chief executive officer of a state or county psychiatric hospital is authorized to give consent for psychiatric treatment to patients declared legally incompetent by a court or patients under the age of 21 under certain conditions. See N.J.S.A. 30:4-7.1 - 7.6.
   (c) Patients have the right to be free from unnecessary or excessive medication. N.J.S.A. 30:4-24.1 d (1) [30:4-24.2 d (1)].
   (d) Medication may not be used as punishment, for the convenience of staff, or as a substitute for a treatment program. N.J.S.A. 30:4-24.1 d (1) [30:4-24.2 d (1)].
   (e) Notation of each patient's medication shall be kept in his treatment records. At least weekly, the attending physician shall review the drug regimen of each patient under his care. All physicians' prescriptions shall be written with a termination date, which shall not exceed 30 days. N.J.S.A. 30:4-24.2 d (1).

D. *Judicial Parameters*

Although existing case law is not clear with respect to the administration of medication to involuntary patients, in December 1977 a New Jersey County District Court Judge held, in the case of, *in Re Mark B.*, that under certain conditions, "Involuntarily committed patients do not have the right to refuse medication."

II. *The Involuntary Administration of Medication*

Definitions

1. A patient is considered incompetent only if he has been adjudicated incompetent by a court.
2. Medication is considered a necessary part of a patient's treatment plan when either:
   (a) The patient is incapable, without medication, of participating in any treatment plan available at the hospital that will give him a realistic opportunity of improving his condition; or
   (b) Although it is possible to devise a treatment plan that is available at the hospital and will give the patient a realistic opportunity of improving his condition; either:
      (1) a treatment plan which includes medication would probably improve the patient's condition within a significantly shorter time period; or
      (2) there is a significant possibility that the patient will harm himself or others before improvement of his condition is realized, if medication is not administered.

A. *Emergency Administration of Medication*

The procedures described in this Bulletin are not intended to preclude the administration of psychotropic medication to a patient in an emergency. Therefore, if a physician certifies that it is essential to administer psychotropic medication in order to prevent the death of or serious consequences to a patient, the Chief Executive Officer is authorized to consent to the administration of the medication recommended by the physician's certification. If it is impossible to comply with this procedure without jeopardizing the life of the patient, the medication may be administered on a physician's order.

B. If a patient refuses to take the psychotropic medication that has been prescribed for him, the attending physician shall speak to the patient and *attempt to explain:* his assessment of the patient's condition; his reasons for prescribing the medication; the benefits and risks of taking the medication; and the advantages and disadvantages of alternative courses of action.

If the patient still refuses to take the medication and the physician still believes that medication is a necessary part of the patient's treatment plan:

(a) The physician should tell the patient that the matter will be discussed at a meeting of the patient's treatment team;
(b) If the patient's clinical condition permits, the physician should invite the patient to attend the meeting of the treatment team.
(c) The physician should suggest that the patient discuss the matter with a person of his own choosing, such as a relative or friend.

C. The treatment team shall meet to discuss the physician's recommendation and the patient's response.

(1) If the patient is present, the team shall attempt to formulate a treatment plan that is acceptable to the patient and the team. The patient may agree to take medication unconditionally or under certain conditions that are acceptable to the physician.
(2) If the patient is not present, the team and the physician shall discuss the physician's recommendation and the patient's response, and shall document their respective conclusions.

D. If, after the team meeting, the physician still believes that medication is a necessary part of the patient's treatment plan and the patient still refuses to take the prescribed medication,
Then:

Case 1: *Patients Adjudicated Incompetent by a Court*

(1) If there is a consensus in regard to the necessity of the medication, the physician shall attempt to secure the consent of the patient's guardian. If the patient's guardian, after reasonable notice of the proposed action and a request for consent, refuses or neglects to execute and submit a writing expressing either the grant or denial of consent,
Then, The Chief Executive Officer may consent to the administration of medication.

(2) If there is disagreement between the team and the physician in regard to medication, then the medical director (or his designee) shall conduct a personal examination of the patient and a review of the record. If the medical director (or his designee) agrees with the physician, the physician shall attempt to secure the consent of the guardian.
If the patient's guardian, after reasonable notice of the proposed action and a request for consent, refuses or neglects to execute and submit a writing expressing either the grant or denial of consent,
Then, The Chief Executive Officer may consent to the administration of the medication.

Case 2: *Patients Who Have Not Been Adjudicated Incompetent by a Court*

Part I—Voluntary Patients

Medication may not be administered to a voluntary patient who refuses to accept it.

Part II—Involuntary Patients

The medical director (or his designee) must conduct a personal examination of the patient and a review of the record. If the medical director (or his designee) agrees with the necessity for medication, the medication may be administered as a part of the patient's documented individualized treatment plan.

E. *Miscellaneous*

1. *Independent Evaluations*

Whenever the medical director (or his designee) is asked to review a medication decision, the medical director shall be authorized to retain an independent psychiatric consultant to evaluate the patient's need for medication. This would be indicated particularly in cases where there is disagreement between the treating physician and the team.

If the patient is evaluated by an independent psychiatric consultant invited by the hospital and the consultant recommends a treatment plan that does not include the administration of medication, then the medical director in the report filed in the treatment record, shall address the conclusions and recommendations of the consultant.

2. *Review*

In addition to the reviews mandated by N.J.S.A. 30:24.2 d (1), the medical director (or his designee) shall review each week the treatment program of each involuntary patient, who is refusing to accept medication voluntarily, to determine:

(a) Whether the patient is still refusing his prescribed medication;
(b) Whether medication is still a necessary part of the patient's treatment plan; and
(c) Whether the other components of the patient's treatment plan are being implemented.

3. *Documentation*
Each step of the procedures outlined above shall be documented in the patient's chart.

s/ Michail Rotov
Michail Rotov, M.D., Director
Division of Mental Health and Hospitals

On Renewed Motion for Preliminary Injunction

This is a renewed motion for a preliminary injunction pursuant to Fed.R.Civ.P. 65 by plaintiff John E. Rennie, an involuntary patient of Ancora Psychiatric Hospital. He seeks to enjoin the defendant psychiatrists and officials at Ancora from forcibly administering drugs to him in the absence of an emergency situation. The complaint is grounded on 42 U.S.C. § 1983, with jurisdiction pursuant to 28 U.S.C. § 1343.

This court held fourteen days of hearings on the original motion between January 13 and April 28, 1978, and issued its opinion November 9, 1978. 462 F.Supp. 1131. Although the opinion discussed the facts of the case and legal issues at length, the court did not issue an injunction since the record did not reflect the plaintiff's then current status. Furthermore, the court had been informally advised by counsel that plaintiff's condition had improved substantially, and release from the hospital was contemplated. The opinion left the courthouse door open for plaintiff to reapply for immediate injunctive relief if his condition worsened and the hospital again attempted to medicate plaintiff against his will in a non-emergent situation.

Unfortunately, the plaintiff's condition has greatly deteriorated in recent weeks, and as a result the hospital on December 2, 1978 began to administer the antipsychotic drug thorazine without plaintiff's consent. Plaintiff renewed his motion for an injunction on December 6, and a hearing was held the following day. After hearing the testimony of plaintiff's witnesses and the arguments of counsel, the court denied the motion. The following are the court's findings of fact and conclusions of law, Fed.R.Civ.P. 52, which supplement the findings and conclusions set forth in the November 9 opinion.

Findings of Fact

I. Plaintiff's Condition

Mr. Rennie's mental health began to deteriorate within a few days after the November 9 issuance of the earlier opinion. He became increasingly manic, exhibiting grandiose behaviors. Transcript of December 7 hearing, pages 43-60, hereinafter cited as Tr. 43-60. By November 14, he was transferred to a closed ward and placed on homicidal precautions. His behavior has become increasingly abusive and assaultive, and he has suffered from inability to sleep and hallucinations. Tr. 31-37. He has been in restraints much of the time since November 14, and is currently in a state described by his treating psychiatrist, Dr. Engrazio Balita, as floridly psychotic. Tr. 28. His physical condition has also deteriorated, and he has suffered dehydration, abnormal fluctuations in temperature, and probable infection. Tr. 28–31. Dr. Balita testified that these complications have imperilled his life. Tr. 28.

Mr. Rennie has been on a maintenance dosage of lithium carbonate. However, while on a furlough from Ancora the first week of November, he stopped taking this medication, Tr. 45, and refused it upon returning to the hospital.[1] Tr. 48. However, after appeals from his counsel, Mr. Gelman, he began taking lithium November 14 and attained a maintenance level of the drug in his blood on November 24. Tr. 50–58.

As the lithium failed to stabilize plaintiff's condition, Dr. Balita began emergency injections of thorazine on December 2, and at a treatment team meeting December 5 recommended that thorazine be forcefully administered in accordance with Administrative Bulletin 78–3. This recommendation was approved at the meeting, and reviewed and approved the following day by Dr. Max Pepernik, the Ancora Medical Director. Tr. 9, 27.

II. The Four Factors

In the November 9 opinion, the court stated four factors which must be considered in determining if an injunction should issue. These are (1) plaintiff's physical threat to patients and staff at the institution, (2) plaintiff's capacity to decide on his particular treatment, (3) whether any less restrictive treatments exist, and (4) the risk of permanent side effects from the proposed treatment. These factors will now be applied to the current situation.

Plaintiff has repeatedly threatened patients and staff during the past few weeks, and has been put on homicidal precautions by the hospital. Tr. 49, 53. It has often been necessary to place him in restraints to protect the plaintiff himself as well as others in the institution. Tr. 68.

The court accepts Mr. Gelman's representation that in his current psychotic thrall Mr. Rennie has still knowingly refused to consent to injection of thorazine. Tr. 4. But as the court indicated in its November 9 opinion, his capacity to participate in the choice of medication is limited. Plaintiff's failure to take lithium the last several weeks is additional evidence of his limited capacity to make treatment decisions, as the expert testimony is almost unanimous that lithium is a helpful drug with only minor side effects to Mr. Rennie. It should be noted that he has not only refused lithium while in his current manic state, but also early in November when his condition had markedly improved.

Analyzing plaintiff's behavior, the court concludes that while his refusal of thorazine is partly motivated by a rational desire to avoid harmful and unpleasant side effects, it is also prompted by an irrational desire to rebel against the hospital and its doctors. Therefore the court finds that plaintiff's capacity is severely limited, particularly at the present time, but also over the course of his illness. However, if plaintiff continues his present cooperation with the doctors in taking lithium for a few months, the court might reconsider this finding of lack of capacity. On the other hand, Mr.

[1]Dr. Balita testified that plaintiff's persistence in refusing lithium was buoyed by the court's November 9 opinion (though that opinion approved use of that drug). Tr. 30. The doctor also stated that Mr. Rennie's discussion of the opinion in a hospital ward for the criminally insane encouraged other patients in that ward to refuse medication. Tr. 49.

Rennie need not consent to psychotropic medication to demonstrate capacity, as his refusal of these drugs at this time has, at the least, a rational basis. The court may reconsider this finding at a later time, however.

As was stated in the court's earlier opinion, the lithium regime must be given a fair trial as a less restrictive treatment. Plaintiff's expert, Dr. William T. Carpenter, testified that lithium has not yet had a complete chance, Tr. 211, but this is partly because plaintiff has failed to take the medication. Tr. 46.

Even plaintiff's expert indicated that a psychotropic was essential to stabilize Mr. Rennie. He recommended that thorazine be administered for at least one week or until Mr. Rennie's condition had stabilized to the point where he could be released from restraints and lithium and psychotherapy could be effectively employed. Tr. 114.

The court therefore finds there is currently no less restrictive alternative to thorazine, other than constant restraints, which will safeguard plaintiff and others in the hospital, and no alternative treatment which offers a reasonable chance of alleviating plaintiff's current acute psychosis. The court further finds that this situation will continue until the plaintiff's condition has stabilized and improved, and until plaintiff demonstrates a convincing willingness to participate in a lithoum and psychotherapy regime.

Finally, the court must consider the risk of permanent side effects. The court is concerned about tardive dyskinesia which, as stated in the earlier opinion, is a cure worse than the mental disorder itself. While Dr. Carpenter testified that he had observed mild abnormal movements of the jaw and extremities at an August 24 examination of Mr. Rennie, Tr. 91-92, plaintiff's counsel conceded that plaintiff has no symptomatic movements at this time. Tr. 79. Dr. Carpenter concluded that Mr. Rennie may have had a very mild, reversible case of tardive dyskinesia, and at least has a predisposition to the disease. Tr. 92-93. However, he also indicated that short-term use of thorazine does not pose a significant threat, though he cautioned against use of thorazine for more than four weeks, particularly if the drug does not greatly affect Mr. Rennie's psychosis. He also stated Mr. Rennie should be watched closely for manifestations of tardive dyskinesia symptoms. Tr. 115-25.

The court agrees that close scrutiny is vitally necessary, but does not believe that the threat of the disease is salient enough to preclude use of thorazine at this time.

Conclusions of Law

As plaintiff's capacity is severely limited, and as thorazine injections provide the least restrictive means to stabilize plaintiff's condition in order that lithium and psychotherapy may be used (with or without thorazine), and in order that the hospital may safely remove plaintiff from restraints, no injunction will be issued.[2]

The court has indicated its desire to avoid multiple hearings by examining the situation over the long term at this injunction hearing. However, the need to administer thorazine for a week or two became readily apparent, and the court did not require defendants to call their witnesses and provide their long-term treatment plan.[3] Neither

[2]The Attorney General has indicated that he may wish to appeal this decision despite the favorable outcome because of the court's statements on the law. The court will consider an application for certification to appeal under 28 U.S.C. § 1292(b) when such a petition is made. Subsection (b) certification may be used for the purpose of avoiding serious harm to a litigant *pendente lite* from an erroneous interlocutory order. *Katz* v. *Carte Blanche Corp.*, 496 F.2d 747, 754 (3rd Cir.), *cert. denied*, 419 U.S. 885, 95 S.Ct. 152, 42 L.Ed.2d 125 (1974).

[3]A plan will be required by the pre-trial order in this case, so that long-term use of psychotropics may be fully considered when the consent to treatment issue is tried.

did the treatment team evaluation of December 5 indicate how long thorazine will be used. Furthermore, as plaintiff's counsel, Mr. Gelman, conceded at the hearing, it was not the best time in plaintiff's view to decide his long-term care. Tr. 72.

But consistent use of lithium for several weeks is required to demonstrate plaintiff's renewed capacity to choose his treatment, as well as to enable the hospital and this court to confidently assume that lithium and psychotherapy alone may be given a realistic trial through proper use. Therefore, this decision should be conclusive for at least two months, barring any significant evidence of tardive dyskinesia or drastic change in any other relevant factor in the court's decision. The court is still very concerned about the possibility of tardive dyskinesia and urges the hospital to monitor Mr. Rennie closely for signs of this disease. Furthermore, the court stresses that the hospital should carefully consider the need for continued administration of thorazine in light of objective medical evidence and plaintiff's refusal of the drug. The court hopes that reasoned action by both parties will preclude the need for further applications for preliminary injunctive relief.

Both parties have also asked the court to clarify the procedure for seeking an injunction established in the November 9 opinion and the definition of the term emergency used in the opinion. These procedures will apply to any later appeal by plaintiff for injunctive relief on this issue. Emergency signifies a sudden, significant change in the plaintiff's condition which creates danger to the patient himself or to others in the hospital. While restraints can always eliminate this danger, Tr. 68, this is a realistic alternative only if a few hours' confinement are adequate to calm the plaintiff. Otherwise the hospital is not required to place the plaintiff in permanent restraints rather than forcefully medicate.

The emergency is deemed to last until the administrative procedures under Bulletin 78-3 may be followed, but no longer than 72 hours regardless. At that time, plaintiff may, if he wishes, seek a temporary restraining order by notifying the court and the state, and presenting evidence that psychotropics are being forcefully administered. Then the court will issue the restraining order and immediately schedule a preliminary injunction hearing, to be held within 72 hours if possible, to consider the right to refuse treatment under the four stated factors.

Order

Application by plaintiff on his renewed motion for preliminary injunction being heard by the court on the 7th day of December, 1978; and

The court having considered the testimony of Dr. William T. Carpenter (plaintiff's medical expert psychiatrist) and Dr. Engrazio Balita (employee of defendant and plaintiff's treating psychiatrist at Ancora), exhibits, briefs and argument of counsel; and

For the reasons stated in the court's opinion of December 12, 1978,

It is on this 12th day of December, 1978, ORDERED that the renewed motion for a preliminary injunction is denied.

Blanton v. *United States,* 428 F.Supp. 360 (D.D.C. 1977)

Memorandum Opinion and Order

GESELL, District Judge.

This complaint, brought under the Federal Tort Claims Act, 28 U.S.C. § 1346, *et seq.*, alleges negligence based on medical malpractice occurring in a Navy Regional

Medical Center at Oakland, California, where Mary Elizabeth Blanton, wife of a Coast Guard officer, was admitted for childbirth on March 6, 1973.

I. Facts

Mrs. Blanton's blood is Rh negative and her husband's blood is Rh positive. The child born on March 7 had Rh positive blood. The Blantons desired to have more than this one child. The Blantons and the attending physicians knew, however, that if Mrs. Blanton again became pregnant with an Rh positive fetus a reaction of great danger to the fetus and the mother might occur, perhaps causing a stillbirth or the birth of a defective child. This reaction can be completely avoided in 99 percent of the cases by administering a passive anti-D antibody of proper strength almost immediately after birth. There were at the time at least two proprietary names for such a drug, Rho-Gam and Hyp-Rho-D. Mrs. Blanton having given birth successfully to a child by her prior marriage had received Rho-Gam, knew it was effective in her case, and took special precautions to advise the doctors and staff of her special situation and her desire to receive Rho-Gam. When the time came she was asked whether she would be willing to take Hyp-Rho-D instead as part of an experiment then being conducted at the hospital in conjunction with Cutter Laboratories, Inc., the manufacturer, to determine whether Hyp-Rho-D had effectiveness beyond its FDA-approved shelf life. Mrs. Blanton refused to participate in the experiment, insisted on Rho-Gam, spoke to an attending physician, and her chart was marked for Rho-Gam. When she received her shot the nurse said "here is your Rho-Gam." In fact, Mrs. Blanton received a shot of outdated Hyp-Rho-D without her consent or knowledge as part of the experiment. While the medical staff learned of the mistake by March 10, 1973, Mrs. Blanton was not advised until August, 1973.

Mrs. Blanton was immediately shocked and upset when she learned of the mistake and feared she could not have any more children. She broke into tears. Anxiety, depression and anger developed. The episode had a strong emotional impact causing physical symptoms such as nervousness, muscle pains, nausea, indigestion, loss of sleep and menstrual irregularities. She consulted private physicians, took various blood tests and she and her husband became amateur experts in fetal obstetrics related to the Rh factor. They read the scientific literature, consulted medical friends and sought some positive assurance that they could successfully produce another child without the hazards that would arise should the fetus be Rh positive.

A blood test taken at the hospital six months after the birth found a negative anti-D titer and thus showed no danger that the feared reaction would occur with a subsequent pregnancy. Medically this test at six months is considered the most predictive test of future pregnancies. While the results of the Hyp-Rho-D experiment are not fully known, all preliminary indications are favorable to using the drug for a longer shelf life period and the preponderance of the evidence established that Hyp-Rho-D was just as effective as Rho-Gam. The possibility of the feared reaction should a second fetus be Rh positive has for all practical purposes, within medical knowledge, been successfully treated.

II. Liability

Given these facts the United States strenuously argues that no cause of action exists under the Federal Tort Claims Act. This Act provides at 23 U.S.C. § 2680(h) that there is no waiver of sovereign immunity for "any claim arising out of assault, battery . . . misrepresentation, deceit or interference with contract rights." It is urged that the instant claim is either in misrepresentation or in battery and hence exempted from the Act's grant of jurisdiction to this Court.

In this case, Medical Center personnel had at least two duties to the patient: (1) the exercise of due care in the administration of the drug, and (2) the accurate description of the drug that was administered. The clear violation here of the duty of accurate description may be a misrepresentation or battery and thus not actionable under the Federal Tort Claims Act. *Ramirez* v. *United States,* Civil No. 74-532-E (S.D.Cal., Oct. 30, 1975); *Sawyer* v. *United States,* Civil No. 75-246-N (S.D.Cal., Oct. 30, 1975); *Rowell* v. *United States,* Civil No. 75-245-GT (S.D.Cal., Oct. 30, 1975). However, this need not be reached for the issue of whether due care was violated in the administration of Hyp-Rho-D rather than Rho-Gam would still remain. *Hungerford* v. *United States,* 307 F.2d 99 (9th Cir. 1962).

Mrs. Blanton was not simply given one drug that was inaccurately represented as another. The shelf life of the Hyp-Rho-D had been exceeded and the drug was of unknown effectiveness. It was, in effect, a "new drug" without FDA approval and must be presumed dangerous. *See* 21 U.S.C. § 355. It was administered despite the availability of a drug of known effectiveness and proven reliability. The hospital violated accepted medical standards and its duty of due care. Only had plaintiff consented to the experiment would the United States be immune from liability in tort.

Judgment for wife; judgment for United States on husband's claim.

TREATMENT USING ELECTROSHOCK THERAPY

Distinct from strictly verbal therapy and psychotherapy with medication, electroshock therapy is a treatment modality unto itself. This method of treatment involves the passing of an electrical current through the brain that is sufficient to induce a convulsion and a loss of consciousness. The pioneers of this method of treatment (e.g., Meduna, 1936) had observed that psychosis seemed to be incompatible with epilepsy. It was noted that after an epileptic seizure, psychotic symptoms would remit. Proceeding on the assumption that coma states and psychotic states were somehow antagonistic to one another, some psychiatrists began inducing comas as a means of treating psychosis. The assumption that psychotic symptoms would remit as a function of the induction of a coma state has since been proved false (Hoch, 1943; Kalinowsky & Hippius, 1969). Meduna himself in his later years "recognized with admirable candor that the coma therapies were crudely empirical and compared them to kicking a Swiss watch" (Redlich & Freedman, 1966, p. 336). Still, electroshock therapy remains a widely practiced treatment today (Asnis, Fink & Saferstein, 1978), one thought to have particular applicability in cases involving severe depression, involutional melancholia, and suicidal ideation (Freedman & Kaplan, 1967). The precise mechanism by which this treatment method works is unknown, though one investigator has delineated fifty theories as to the mechanism (Gordon, 1948).

From a legal perspective, cases involving situations in which electroshock was used have for the most part involved claims of failure to obtain proper consent to treatment and failure to meet the prescribed standard of care in administering the treatment and/or tending to posttreatment complications. Illustrative of these situations are the cases of *Price* v. *Sheppard,* 307 Minn. 250, 239 N.W.2d 905 (1976), and *McDonald* v. *Moore,* 323 So.2d 635 (Fla. Dist. Ct. App. 1975), which follow.

Price v. *Shepard,* 307 Minn. 250, 239 N.W.2d 905 (1976)

Considered and decided by the court en banc.

YETKA, Justice.

This appeal from a summary judgment entered in the Ramsey County District Court involves an action against the medical director of the Minnesota Security Hospital at St. Peter, Dr. Charles G. Sheppard, for (1) assault and battery, and (2) violation of plaintiff Dwight Price's civil rights under 42 U.S.C.A. § 1983.[1] The claims arise out of the administration of a series of 20 electroshock treatments, given against the express wishes of plaintiff Willa Mae Price, Dwight's mother and natural guardian, while Dwight, a minor, was under involuntary commitment in the Minnesota Security Hospital at St. Peter.

Defendant's motion for summary judgment on Count I, alleging assault and battery, was granted March 22, 1974, based on the court's ruling that the defendant, acting in his official capacity, was immune from suit. Summary judgment was also granted on Count IV, alleging violation of Dwight's civil rights, on November 29, 1974. The court ruled that the electroshock treatments were neither cruel and unusual punishment under the Eighth Amendment of the United States Constitution, nor a violation of Dwight's right to privacy. We affirm.

Dwight Price was committed to the Hastings State Hospital September 8, 1971, by order of the Ramsey County Probate Court, which found Dwight to be "mentally ill-inebriate." The commitment petition was brought by Dwight's mother, Willa Mae Price, apparently in order to secure treatment for Dwight for a developing drug and alcohol problem. Several attempts at voluntary treatment, prior to the commitment proceedings, had proved unsuccessful.

Shortly after being admitted to Hastings, Dwight allegedly attempted to strangle one of the hospital staff. Because Hastings was not equipped to handle dangerous patients, Dwight was transferred to the Security Hospital at St. Peter on September 11, 1971.[2]

Dwight's condition, upon his admission at St. Peter was diagnosed as simple

[1]42 U.S.C.A. § 1983, provides as follows: "Every person who, under color of any statute, ordinance, regulation, custom, or usage, of any State or Territory, subjects, or causes to be subjected, any citizen of the United States or other person within the jurisdiction thereof to the deprivation of any rights, privileges, or immunities secured by the Constitution and laws, shall be liable to the party injured in an action at law, suit in equity, or other proper proceeding for redress."

Plaintiffs' complaint included two other claims, one for negligence in administering the electroshock treatments and one for the intentional infliction of mental distress to Mrs. Price; however, that part of the lower court's order relating to those claims is not challenged on appeal.

[2]While the removal of the minor plaintiff from Hastings to St. Peter was later determined to be invalid by a review board at Hastings, that fact seems to be without any particular significance to the issues on appeal, and none is demonstrated by plaintiffs.

schizophrenia. He was treated with tranquilizing and antidepressant medications, but apparently failed to respond and continued to be aggressive and assaultive to the staff and other patients. For this reason, Dr. Sheppard prescribed electroshock therapy.

He sought Mrs. Price's consent to administer the electroshock treatments. Through her attorney Mrs. Price arranged for an independent medical examination by Dr. William Chalgren,[3] a Mankato psychiatrist, for the purpose of determining the advisability of the proposed treatment. Dr. Chalgren examined Dwight November 27, 1971, and recommended that drug treatment continue but that if Dwight did not respond favorably, electroshock treatment be given.

Dr. Chalgren's recommendations were followed by the staff at St. Peter, but Dwight's condition did not improve. Accordingly, on December 22, 1971, without the consent of Mrs. Price, electroshock therapy began and was continued to February 11, 1972. Dwight was released from St. Peter June 19, 1972.

The issues raised on this appeal are:

(1) Does the administration of electroshock therapy to an involuntarily committed minor patient of a state mental hospital, without the consent of the minor's guardian, violate his rights (a) to be free from cruel and unusual punishment, and (b) of privacy?

(2) Is a state official entitled to immunity from an action for damages for acts performed by him in good faith and which he could not reasonably have known would violate the constitutional rights of another?

1. We do not agree with the claim that the electroshock therapy was cruel and unusual punishment for the reason that the record does not suggest, nor have plaintiffs demonstrated, how those treatments, under the circumstances of this case, can be regarded as "punishment." While plaintiffs are certainly correct in the statement that the characterization of electroshock therapy by defendant as "treatment" does not insulate it from Eighth Amendment scrutiny,[4] that alone does not establish that the treatments were "punishment."

The Supreme Court's decision in *Trop* v. *Dulles,* 356 U.S. 86, 78 S.Ct. 590, 2 L.Ed.2d 630 (1958), involving the question of whether a law which provided for loss of United States citizenship upon conviction of desertion from the military violated the Eighth Amendment, is instructive.

> ... In deciding whether or not a law is penal, this Court has generally based its determination upon the purpose of the statute. If the statute imposes a disability for the purposes of punishment—that is, to reprimand the wrongdoer, to deter others, etc.—it has been considered penal. But a statute has been considered nonpenal if it imposes a disability, not to punish, but to accomplish some other legitimate governmental purpose. The Court has recognized that any statute decreeing some adversity as a consequence of certain conduct may have both a penal and a nonpenal effect. The controlling nature of such statutes normally depends on the

[3]Plaintiffs imply that Dr. Chalgren was less than candid with Mrs. Price in failing to disclose that he was, on occasion, a consultant to the St. Peter Security Hospital. Plaintiffs imply in their brief that her consultation with Dr. Chalgren was tainted, a conclusion we are not willing to draw. Beyond the bare fact that Dr. Chalgren was an occasional consultant to the Security Hospital, there is nothing to suggest collusiveness with hospital staff. On the contrary, the opposite is suggested from the fact that Dr. Chalgren recommended treatment which differed from that prescribed by the hospital, specifically that electroshock therapy be postponed, and that it be resorted to if other less serious forms of treatment failed.

[4]*Trop* v. *Dulles,* 356 U.S. 86, 78 S.Ct. 590, 2 L.Ed.2d 630 (1958); *Knecht* v. *Gillman,* 488 F.2d 1136 (8 Cir. 1973); *Vann* v. *Scott,* 467 F.2d 1235 (7 Cir. 1972); *Inmates of Boys' Training School* v. *Afflect,* 346 F.Supp. 1354 (D.R.I. 1972).

> evident purpose of the legislature. The point may be illustrated by the situation of an ordinary felon. A person who commits a bank robbery, for instance, loses his right to liberty and often his right to vote. If, in the exercise of the power to protect banks, both sanctions were imposed for the purpose of punishing bank robbers, the statutes authorizing both disabilities would be penal. But because the purpose of the latter statute is to designate a reasonable ground of eligibility for voting, this law is sustained as a nonpenal exercise of the power to regulate the franchise. [356 U.S. 96, 78 S.Ct. 595, 2 L.Ed.2d 639]

Applying the *Trop* rationale, if the electroshock treatments given the minor plaintiff served legitimate purpose rather than deterrence or reprimand, the Eighth Amendment claim must fail. Cf. *Knecht* v. *Gillman,* 488 F.2d 1136, 1138 (8 Cir. 1973).

It is difficult to perceive, on the record before the court, how the electroshock therapy administered to the plaintiff could be regarded as anything but treatment. The purpose of Dwight's presence in the state's mental hospital system was not to reprimand him or deter him from certain behavior but rather for the treatment of his mental problems and developing chemical dependency. Moreover, the decision to administer electroshock therapy was not triggered by any single incident nor did it involve an isolated treatment, both of which would be more characteristic of punishment. Rather, the decision to administer a series of 20 treatments over a substantial period of time was made after other forms of treatment failed to show any curative effect on Dwight's condition, diagnosed as schizophrenia.

The circumstances of this case are simply unlike those presented in *Knecht* v. *Gillman, supra.* Inmates of the Iowa Security Medical Facility, confined there for examination, diagnosis, and treatment of mental disorders, for minor violations of hospital protocol, were given injections of a drug which caused the inmate to vomit for 15 minutes to an hour. Although characterized as aversive therapy, the apparent purpose of administering the drug in response to a violation of protocol was to reprimand the inmate.

In *Inmates of Boys' Training School* v. *Afflect,* 346 F.Supp. 1354 (D.R.I.1972), also cited by plaintiffs in support of their claim, the retributive nature of the challenged conduct is even more clear. For committing infractions of the institution's rules, inmates of a juvenile corrections institution were isolated in cold, dark cells containing only a toilet and mattress. Finally, in *Vann* v. *Scott,* 467 F.2d 1235 (7 Cir. 1972), cited by plaintiffs, the court did not decide whether the incarceration of runaway juveniles was punishment but on the contrary indicated that under some circumstances, where it served the purpose of safeguarding the lives and welfare of juveniles, it would not be. Cf. *Robinson* v. *California,* 370 U.S. 660, 82 S.Ct. 1417, 8 L.Ed.2d 758 (1962).

Under the circumstances of this case, where electroshock therapy involving multiple treatments over a substantial period of time was prescribed for an involuntarily committed patient of a state mental hospital who had failed to respond to other forms of treatment, we hold that the administration of such electroshock treatments, absent the effective consent of the patient or his guardian, is not cruel or unusual punishment.

2. Plaintiffs second claimed violation of the minor's civil rights—the right of privacy—is more troublesome, primarily because that emerging right is currently so ill-defined. While its origins are said to date back to the late nineteenth century, its birth as an independent constitutional right, clearly denominated as such, is generally regarded as coming in *Griswold* v. *Connecticut,* 381 U.S. 479, 85 S.Ct. 1678, 14

L.Ed.2d 510 (1965), where the court overturned a statute prohibiting the use of contraceptives by married couples.

The right has since served as the basis of decisions striking down a Georgia statute prohibiting possession of obscene materials in one's home, *Stanley* v. *Georgia,* 394 U.S. 557, 89 S.Ct. 1243, 22 L.Ed.2d 542 (1969); extending the *Griswold* ruling to include unmarried individuals, *Eisenstadt* v. *Baird,* 405 U.S. 438, 92 S.Ct. 1029, 31 L.Ed.2d 349 (1972); and overturning a Texas statute prohibiting abortions, *Roe* v. *Wade,* 410 U.S. 113, 93 S.Ct. 705, 35 L.Ed.2d 147 (1973). The right remains, however, an extremely amorphous one.

We recognize that it is far too early in the evolution of the right of privacy to offer any single definition or rule of what the right entails. Only its broadest contours have been sketched. We do feel, however, because of the importance of that emerging right, it is appropriate for us, at this time, to set forth more than our bare conclusion that the right of privacy is or is not involved.

At the core of the privacy decisions, in our judgment, is the concept of personal autonomy—the notion that the Constitution reserves to the individual, free of governmental intrusion, certain fundamental decisions about how he or she will conduct his or her life.[5] Like other constitutional rights, however, this right is not an absolute one and must give way to certain interests of the state, the balance turning on the impact of the decision on the life of the individual. As the impact increases, so must the importance of the state's interest. Some decisions, we assume, will be of little consequence to the individual and a showing of a legitimate state interest will justify its intrusion; other decisions, on the other hand, will be of such major consequence that only the most compelling state interest will justify the intrusion.

But once justified, the extent of the state's intrusion is not unlimited. It must also appear that the means utilized to serve the state's interest are necessary and reasonable, or, in other words, in light of alternative means, the least intrusive.[6]

To summarize, our understanding of at least one aspect of the privacy decisions to

[5]See, Henkin, *Privacy and Autonomy,* 74 Col.L.Rev. 1410; Note, On Privacy: Constitutional Protection for Personal Liberty, 48 N.Y.U.L.Rev. 670; Tribe, *The Supreme Court 1972 Term,* 87 Harv.L.Rev. 1.

[6]*Roe* v. *Wade,* 410 U.S. 113, 93 S.Ct. 705, 35 L.Ed.2d 147 (1973), aptly illustrates the balancing process. The decision involved was whether to terminate a pregnancy, a decision the state had completely assumed by prohibiting abortion. Step one for the court was assessing the impact of the decision on the life of the individual.

"... The detriment that the State would impose upon the pregnant woman by denying this choice altogether is apparent. Specific and direct harm medically diagnosable even in early pregnancy may be involved. Maternity, or additional offspring, may force upon the woman a distressful life and future. Psychological harm may be imminent. Mental and physical health may be taxed by child care. There is also the distress, for all concerned, associated with the unwanted child, and there is the problem of bringing a child into a family already unable, psychologically and otherwise, to care for it. In other cases, as in this one, the additional difficulties and continuing stigma of unwed motherhood may be involved." *Roe* v. *Wade,* 410 U.S. 153, 93 S.Ct. 727, 35 L.Ed.2d 177. The court concluded that the decision was of such fundamental importance and impact that only a compelling state interest could justify the state's intrusion.

The state advanced two interests: (1) the preservation and protection of the health of the pregnant woman, and (2) the protection of prenatal life. Recognizing both as legitimate state interests, the court nevertheless concluded that in the early stages of pregnancy neither one was "compelling." However, as the pregnancy progressed those interests became compelling, the first at the stage when the mortality rate in abortion surpassed that in childbirth, and the second when the fetus became viable.

In determining the necessity and reasonableness of the alternative means of serving the state's interest in the health of the mother—regulation of the abortion procedure or prohibition of abortion—the court settled on the former being the least intrusive means that adequately served the state's interest. Obviously there were no alternatives to protect prenatal life.

date is that where the state proposes to intrude into a fundamental decision affecting the conduct of an individual's life, in order to justify that intrusion, it must first demonstrate a legitimate and important state interest. The sufficiency of the interest will be directly dependent on the impact of the decision on the individual's life. And secondly, the means it intends to utilize in serving that interest must, in light of the alternatives, be the least intrusive.

The question in the case before us is whether the state, consistent with Dwight Price's right of privacy, can assume the decision of whether Dwight, an involuntarily committed mental patient, will undergo psychiatric treatment. We observe that the more fundamental decision, whether he was to undergo hospitalization, was assumed by the state at the commitment proceeding, the validity of which is not contested.

The impact of the decision on the individual is unquestionably great, for the result is the alteration of the patient's personality. The state's interest in assuming the decision is in acting as *parens patriae,* fulfilling its duty to protect the well-being of its citizens who are incapable of so acting for themselves. Under the circumstances of this case, that interest can be articulated as the need for the state to assume the decision-making role regarding the psychiatric treatment for one who, presumptively, based on the fact of commitment on the ground of mental illness,[7] is unable to *rationally* do so for himself. If that interest of the state is sufficiently important to deprive an individual of his physical liberty, it would seem to follow that it would be sufficiently important for the state to assume the treatment decision. We hold that it is.

> Under the *parens patriae* rationale, an individual may be committed when he lacks capacity to make a rational decision concerning hospitalization, and the treatment or custodial care available would be beneficial enough to outweigh the deprivations which commitment would impose on him. Inherent in an adjudication that an individual should be committed under the state's *parens patriae* power is the decision that he can be forced to accept the treatments found to be in his best interest; it would be incongruous if an individual who lacks capacity to make a treatment decision could frustrate the very justification for the state's action by refusing such treatments. [Note, *Developments in the Law—Civil Commitment of the Mentally Ill,* 87 Harv.L.Rev. 1190, 1344 (1974)]

The more important question, we believe, involved in the state's assumption of the treatment decision is the necessity and reasonableness of the means utilized by the state in treating an involuntarily committed patient. The techniques generally available to treat psychological disorders range in degree of severity and coerciveness from the least intrusive forms such as milieu therapy (behavior changes produced by manipulation of the patient's environment) and psychoanalysis, to drug, aversion, or electroconvulsive therapy, and ultimately to psychosurgery. Some of these techniques require in the voluntary participation of the patient in order to be effective, while others can be effective when involuntarily imposed. As the techniques increase in severity, so do the risks of serious and long-lasting psychological or neurological damage.[8]

[7]While Minn.St. 253A.18, subd. 1, provides that "[c]ommitment . . . is not a judicial determination of legal incompetency," a finding that a person is mentally ill, one of the grounds for commitment, requires evidence that "clearly shows that his customary self-control, judgment, and discretion in the conduct of his affairs [including medical care] is lessened to such an extent that hospitalization is necessary for his own welfare or the protection of society. . . ." Minn.St. 253A.07, subd. 17(a).

[8]Note, 45 So.Cal.L.Rev. 616, 621 to 633.

Whether the administration of electroshock treatments, one of the most intrusive forms of treatment, was necessary and reasonable in the treatment of Dwight Price is a question we cannot reach. We believe, and so hold, that whatever the answer to that question may be, on the record before us the defendant is immune from liability under 42 U.S.C.A. § 1983.[9]

The Supreme Court has recently considered the qualified immunity possessed by state officials acting in their official capacity, *O'Connor* v. *Donaldson,* 422 U.S. 563, 95 S.Ct. 2486, 45 L.Ed.2d 396 (1975); *Wood* v. *Strickland,* 420 U.S. 308, 95 S.Ct. 992, 43 L.Ed.2d 214 (1975); *Scheuer* v. *Rhodes,* 416 U.S. 232, 94 S.Ct. 1683, 40 L.Ed.2d 90 (1974). In *O'Connor,* the court summarized the nature of that immunity:

> . . . [T]he relevant question for the jury is whether [the state official] "knew or reasonably should have known that the action he took within his sphere of official responsibility would violate the constitutional rights of [the plaintiff], or if he took the action with the malicious intention to cause a deprivation of constitutional rights or other injury to [the plaintiff]." . . . [*Wood* v. *Strickland,* 420 U.S. 322, 95 S.Ct. 1001, 43 L.Ed.2d 225.] For purposes of this question, an official has, of course, no duty to anticipate unforeseeable constitutional developments. [Citations omitted.]

It seems abundantly clear, given the vagueness of the constitutional right of privacy, that the defendant could not reasonably have known that the administration of electroshock treatments to Dwight Price violated a "clearly established" constitutional right. *Wood* v. *Strickland,* 420 U.S. 322, 95 S.Ct. 1001, 43 L.Ed.2d 225.

Moreover, it is evident from the record that the defendant acted without malice and in good faith. Less intrusive means of treatment were employed by the defendant for a period of 3 months without success. Dwight continued to be assaultive and for that reason required confinement to his room most of the time, a circumstance which the defendant believed was a substantial obstacle to recovery and which could be corrected by electroshock. He followed the recommendation of the plaintiff's own doctor and continued the less intrusive forms of treatment for a further period before commencing the electroshock treatments. Proper medical procedures were followed in administering the treatments, and their administration did not contravene any state statute or regulation. In short, measured by accepted conduct at that time, the defendant's actions were proper.

Because the potential impact of the more intrusive forms of treatment is so great, we are reluctant in those cases where the patient or guardian refuse their consent, to leave the imposition of the more intrusive forms of treatment solely within the discretion of

[9]We also believe that defendant is protected from liability for assault and battery because, while the electroshock therapy here was performed without the consent of the minor patient's guardian, defendant was privileged to institute such therapy as part of his duty to provide care to an involuntarily committed, mentally ill patient. See, Minn.St. 253A.02, subd. 9. In *Campbell* v. *Glenwood Hills Hospitals, Inc.,* 273 Minn. 525, 536, 142 N.W.2d 255, 262 (1966), we alluded to the duty of care owed involuntarily committed patients by the state and refused there to find the defendant doctors liable for a battery arising out of a course of treatment "determined and effected by competent institutional doctors who would have been at fault if they had not attempted to help plaintiff." Similarly, the institutional doctor's privilege to pursue reasonable lines of therapy in good faith in conformance with existing procedures authorizing treatment after a commitment order protects the defendant doctor from tort liability in the instant case. In the future, of course, institutional doctors must comply with the new procedures set forth in this opinion for authorizing more severe forms of therapy, e.g., electroshock therapy, in order to remain protected by this privilege from tort liability.

medical personnel at our state hospitals. For that reason, we adopt the following procedure for future cases:

(1) If the patient is incompetent to give consent or refuse consent or his guardian other than persons responsible for his commitment also refuses his consent, before more intrusive forms of treatment may be utilized, the medical director of the state hospital must petition the probate division of the county court in the county in which the hospital is located for an order authorizing the prescribed treatment;[10]

(2) the court shall appoint a guardian ad litem to represent the interests of the patient;[11]

(3) in an adversary proceeding, pursuant to the petition, the court shall determine the necessity and reasonableness of the prescribed treatment.

In making that determination the court should balance the patient's need for treatment against the intrusiveness of the prescribed treatment. Factors which should be considered are (1) the extent and duration of changes in behavior patterns and mental activity effected by the treatment, (2) the risks of adverse side effects, (3) the experimental nature of the treatment, (4) its acceptance by the medical community of this state, (5) the extent of intrusion into the patient's body and the pain connected with the treatment, and (6) the patient's ability to competently determine for himself whether the treatment is desirable.[12]

We cannot draw a clear line between the more intrusive forms of treatment requiring this procedural hearing and those which do not. Certainly this procedure is not intended to apply to the use of mild tranquilizers or those therapies requiring the cooperation of the patient. On the other hand, given current medical practice, this procedure must be followed where psychosurgery or electroshock therapy is proposed.

Affirmed.

McDonald v. *Moore,* 323 So.2d 635 (Fla. Dist. Ct. App. 1975)

Before PEARSON, HAVERFIELD and NATHAN, JJ.

Per Curiam

This is an appeal by Gary P. McDonald, plaintiff in the trial court, from a judgment on a jury verdict for compensatory damages in the amount of $5,000 in the plaintiff's favor, in an action for malpractice against Dr. Thomas Earl Moore. McDonald contends that the amount of the verdict is inadequate due to the trial court's striking his claim for punitive damages.

The plaintiff, a narcotics addict, underwent treatment by Dr. Moore, a psychiatrist. The treatment included daily prescriptions for methadone. McDonald agreed to permit

[10]It is recommended, for purposes of economy, that the necessity and reasonableness of more intrusive forms of treatment be considered at the commitment hearing. This would, of course, depend on a sufficiently extensive diagnosis and history of the patient's disorder, and should not become merely a matter of form. Also, for economy, if the committing court is reasonably convenient to the state hospital, it would be desirable to return to it since it would be already familiar with the case, having previously appointed a guardian ad litem for the patient.

[11]Those considered for appointment as guardian ad litem should not include those responsible for the patient's commitment.

[12]Note, 45 So.Cal.L.Rev. 616, 658; Note, Developments in the Law—Civil Commitment of the Mentally Ill, 87 Harv.L.Rev. 1190, 1347; *Kaimowitz* v. *Michigan Dept. of Mental Health* (summarized in 42 U.S.L.W. 2063, July 31, 1973).

Dr. Moore to perform a series of six electric shock treatments in order to cure his addiction to methadone without the pain of withdrawal. During the fifth treatment, McDonald complained of extreme pain in his left shoulder. The doctor minimized the importance of his complaint and convinced McDonald to proceed with the sixth treatment on the next day. After the sixth treatment, McDonald discovered that his shoulder had been dislocated and fractured by the shock treatments. The evidence showed that Dr. Moore failed to warn McDonald of the danger of a shoulder fracture and that he did not administer a muscle relaxant before the electric shock. One of the plaintiff's medical experts testified that it was not the usual practice to give shock treatments without utilizing the muscle relaxant; the other testified that such omission fell below the standard of care. They both testified that failure to advise the patient of the risk of fractures encountered with shock treatments was conduct below the standard of care.

During the trial, after the plaintiff had presented all of his evidence relating to the issue of punitive damages, the trial court struck his claim for punitive damages.

In the recent case of *Buie* v. *Barnett First National Bank of Jacksonville,* Fla. 1972, 266 So.2d 657, 659, the Florida Supreme Court stated:

> Punitive or exemplary damages are allowable, however, solely as punishment or "smart money" to be inflicted for the malicious or wanton state of mind with which the defendant violated plaintiff's legal right, and can only be imposed in cases where either by direct or circumstantial evidence some reasonable basis for an inference of wantonness, actual malice, deliberation, gross negligence, or utter disregard of law on defendant's part may be legitimately drawn by the jury trying the case. [Quoting *Winn* v. *Lovett Grocery Co.* v. *Archer*, 126 Fla. 308, 171 So. 214, 222, 223.]

In *Richards Company* v. *Harrison,* Fla.App. 1972, 262 So.2d 258, 262, the First District Court of Appeal also stated that punitive damages are allowable in circumstances where the defendant:

> ... acts willfully or with such gross negligence as to indicate a wanton disregard of the rights of others. Punitive damages need not flow from an intentional course of conduct or intent to inflict damages but may also be allowed in such cases where there is that entire want of care which would raise the presumption of a conscious indifference to the consequences of one's action or inaction.

The record presented in the instant case fails to demonstrate wanton disregard for the plaintiff's rights or an entire want of care raising a presumption of conscious indifference to the consequences. Thus, we cannot say that the trial judge committed reversible error in striking the claim for, and refusing to charge the jury on, punitive damages.

McDonald's other two points, as well as the points raised on appeal by Dr. Moore, are not well taken and will not be discussed.

Affirmed.

ASSAULT AND BATTERY

Legally, an assault is said to have occurred when one individual, without his consent, is placed in apprehension of a harmful or offensive touching by another person. A battery is said to have occurred when the nonconsensual harmful or offensive touching has taken place. A "harmful" touching is usually defined as one that causes pain, injury, and the like. An "offensive" touching is usually defined as one that would be offensive to a reasonable person's sense of dignity. In the olden days when psychotherapy was referred to as "the talking cure," a casebook on the subject of malpractice and the mental health profession might not have even had a section on assault and battery. Today, however, with the advent of psychiatric medication, electroshock treatment, other physical forms of treatment, and individual and group therapy methods that call for therapist-patient and patient-patient touching, the potential for liability on the grounds of assault and/or battery has risen dramatically.

Hammer v. *Rosen,* 7 N.Y.2d 376, 198 N.Y.S.2d 65 (1960), which appears below, exemplifies the view that any physical contact construed as assaultive between therapist and patient is unacceptable. But what if the "assaultive" contact could be shown to have been necessary to calm the patient? What are the implications of such a holding for the development of new or novel modes of therapy? Should a practitioner be released from liability when the therapist-patient or patient-patient touching is consensual? These are some of the many questions yet to be dealt with by the courts in this area.

Hammer v. *Rosen,* 7 N.Y.2d 376, 198 N.Y.S.2d 65 (1960)

Opinion per FULD, J.

Div. 383; *People* v. *Malkin,* 250 N.Y. 185; *People* v. *Dorthy,* 156 N.Y. 237; *Paretta* v. *Yuhas*, 273 App. Div. 977, 298 N.Y. 756; *People* v. *Weinberger*, 239 N.Y. 307.

FULD, J. Alice Hammer, suffering from schizophrenia, was treated for some seven years by Dr. Rosen, a psychiatrist. In 1955 she and her father instituted this action, the patient seeking damages for malpractice, the father, for breach of contract and for fraud.[1] Their efforts have been signally unsuccessful. The trial court dismissed the malpractice and fraud causes of action at the close of the plaintiffs' case, while the jury, following submission to it of the contract cause, returned a verdict in favor of the defendant, and the Appellate Division, by a divided court, affirmed the resulting judgment. Although we agree with the disposition made of the other counts, we believe, as did the dissenting justice in the Appellate Division, that the count charging malpractice should have been submitted to the jury.

With respect to the evidence, it is necessary merely to point out that the testimony given by three of the plaintiff's witnesses, indicating that the defendant had beaten Alice on a number of occasions, made out a prima facie case of malpractice which, if uncontradicted and unexplained and credited by the jury, would require a verdict for the plaintiff.

With respect to the defendant's contentions seeking to justify the dismissal—that the action was barred by the Statute of Limitations, that there was no expert testimony

[1]Alice was represented by a guardian ad litem; her father, Max Hammer, having died before trial, was replaced by the executors of his estate.

that the acts of assault with which he was charged constituted improper treatment or malpractice and that there was no proof of injury—we may be almost as brief.

Since Alice was insane at the time the cause of action arose, section 60 of the Civil Practice Act effected an extension of the time within which to commence this action. And, since she was still insane when the suit was begun, the defense based on the Statute of Limitations must fail, and it matters not that she had not actually been adjudged incompetent. (See *Thlocco* v. *Magnolia Petroleum Co.*, 141 F.2d 934, cert. denied 323 U.S. 785; *Browne* v. *Smith*, 119 Col. 469; but see, contra, *Chilford* v. *Central City Cold Stor. Co.*, 166 Misc. 780.) Indeed, even if section 60 had not extended the time to commence the action, the defense would still be unavailing in view of the plaintiff's evidence that the beatings complained of were part and parcel of a continuing course of psychiatric treatment which did not terminate until 1955, the very year in which the action was begun. (See *Nervick* v. *Fine*, 195 Misc. 464, 465; *Sly* v. *Van Lengen*, 120 Misc. 420; *Huysman* v. *Kirsch*, 6 Cal. 2d 302, 307-308; *De Haan* v. *Winter*, 258 Mich. 293, 296-297; *Schanil* v. *Branton*, 181 Minn. 381, 382; *Williams* v. *Elias*, 140 Neb. 656, 660; *Peteler* v. *Robinson*, 81 Utah 535, 546.)

As to the second of the defendant's arguments—that there was no expert testimony to support the plaintiff's charge of malpractice—the simple answer is that the very nature of the acts complained of bespeaks improper treatment and malpractice and that, if the defendant chooses to justify those acts as proper treatment, he is under the necessity of offering evidence to that effect. In point of fact, the defendant can hardly urge that the plaintiff must call an expert to demonstrate the impropriety of the assaultive acts charged against him in view of the acknowledgment, contained in his brief in this court, that any mode of treatment which involves assaults upon the patient is "fantastic."

And, finally, as to the defendant's claim that there was insufficient proof of injury, we simply call attention to our recent statement that "The damages recoverable in malpractice are for personal injuries, including the pain and suffering which naturally flow from the tortious act." (*Robins* v. *Finestone*, 308 N.Y. 543, 546.) On the evidence presented, a jury would have been warranted in finding that defendant's acts had caused the plaintiff pain and suffering.

The judgment appealed from should be modified by reversing so much thereof as dismissed the malpractice cause of action, a new trial granted as to such cause, with costs to abide the event, and, as so modified, judgment affirmed.

Chief Judge Desmond and Judges Dye, Froessel, Van Voorhis, Burke and Foster concur.

Judgment accordingly.

Administration of drugs as assault and battery. Given that *Hammer* rules that practitioners generally have no right to "assault" patients, the question arises as to whether the administration of a drug for the benefit of the patient and in the course of developing a new method of treatment, but without the patient's consent, amounts to an actionable assault. *Stowers* v. *Wolodzko*, 386 Mich. 119, 191 N.W.2d 355 (1971), which appears below, is reflective of current judicial opinion on this issue. In *Stowers* we see the view that the patient at all times retains the right to control the treatment. Thus the administration of a drug without consent—regardless of the beneficial or suspected beneficial results—is deemed an assault and trespass upon the body of the patient. Note that the issue of assault and battery is taken up also in *Roy* (p. 204) and *Price* (p. 234).

Stowers v. *Wolodzko*, 386 Mich. 119, 191 N.W.2d 355 (1971)

Before the Entire Bench.

SWAINSON, Justice.

This case presents complicated issues concerning the liability of a doctor for actions taken subsequent to a person's confinement in a private mental hospital pursuant to a valid court order. The facts are seriously in dispute, both parties being in disagreement as to precisely what did occur. A full statement of the allegations of both parties is necessary in order that a proper framework be developed in an effort to resolve the legal issues involved.

Plaintiff, a housewife, resided in Livonia, Michigan, with her husband and children. She and her husband had been experiencing a great deal of marital difficulties and she testified that she had informed her husband two months previous to the events giving rise to this cause of action that she intended to file for a divorce.

On December 6, 1963, defendant appeared at plaintiff's home and introduced himself as "Dr. Wolodzko." Dr. Wolodzko had never met either plaintiff or her husband before he came to the house. He stated that he had been called by the husband, who had asked him to examine plaintiff. Plaintiff testified that defendant told her that he was there to ask about her husband's back. She testified that she told him to ask her husband, and that she had no further conversation with him or her husband. She testified that he never told her that he was a psychiatrist.

Dr. Wolodzko stated in this deposition (taken December 1, 1966) that he told plaintiff he was there to examine her. However, upon being questioned upon this point, he stated that he could "not specifically" recollect having told plaintiff that he was there to examine her. He stated in his deposition that he was sure that the fact he was a psychiatrist would have come out, but that he couldn't remember if he had told plaintiff that he was a psychiatrist.

Plaintiff subsequently spoke to Dr. Wolodzko at the suggestion of a Livonia policewoman, following a domestic quarrel with her husband. He did inform her at that time that he was a psychiatrist.

On December 30, 1963, defendant Wolodzko and Dr. Anthony Smyk, apparently at the request of plaintiff's husband and without the authorization, knowledge, or consent of plaintiff, signed a sworn statement certifying that they had examined plaintiff and found her to be mentally ill. Such certificate was filed with the Wayne county probate court on January 3, 1964, and on the same date an order was entered by the probate court for the temporary hospitalization of plaintiff until a sanity hearing could be held. The judge ordered plaintiff committed to Ardmore Acres, a privately operated institution, pursuant to the provisions of M.C.L.A. 330.21, M.S.A. 14.811.

Plaintiff was transported to Ardmore Acres on January 4, 1964. Precisely what transpired on this date is greatly in dispute by the parties.

Plaintiff testified that on the evening of January 4, 1964, she was in her bedroom, partially undressed; that her children and her husband were upstairs; that the doorbell rang and she went to the door; that there were two men in white jackets at the door and Dr. Wolodzko was behind some shrubs outside the door; that the two men pushed past her into the house, the doctor following. Plaintiff further testified that the two men grabbed her, and defendant told her he was there to take her to an institution because she was mentally ill. He showed her a court order, but refused to allow her to read it. She asked to use the telephone, received no response, then asked to be allowed to get dressed, and went down a hallway, picked up the telephone and dialed the operator. Plaintiff testified that defendant called out, "Grab her, don't let her use the telephone." The ambulance attendants took the telephone away from her and pushed her into the bedroom, where she got dressed. She told defendant she did not want to go and pleaded with him to let her use the telephone to contact relatives or an attorney. His alleged response was to tell the ambulance driver to get a strait jacket. Plaintiff then told them that a strait jacket would not be necessary, and agreed to accompany them.

Defendant stated in his deposition that he went to plaintiff's home on January 4, 1964, and that when he arrived only the plaintiff and her family were present. He said that the ambulance and the two attendants arrived a quarter to one-half hour later. He said he couldn't recall that he told plaintiff he had a court order, or that he told the ambulance attendants to seize her and take her from the house, but that it was possible he had done so. In response to a question, he stated he could not recall that she had tried to use the telephone, or that it was taken from her. He stated that he was called to plaintiff's home by her husband to re-examine her, and did not know that she was to be sent to a hospital. He could not recall telling her that she had to go with him or that she would be tied to a stretcher if she refused.

However at the trial, defendant, on cross-examination, testified that on January 4, 1964, he made arrangements to meet Mr. Stowers and the ambulance people outside the Stowers' house. He stated that he met them on a corner some distance from the house and told the husband that the ambulance should stay out of sight. He went to see Mrs. Stowers and then her husband called the ambulance people, and when they came in he went upstairs with Mr. Stowers and the two children. He further testified that he issued no instructions to the ambulance attendants and did not see Mrs. Stowers attempt to use the telephone.

Robert Brooks, one of the ambulance attendants who took Mrs. Stowers to the hospital, testified that he met the defendant and Mr. Stowers on a corner near the Stowers' home. Upon being signaled, he went to the home and Mrs. Stowers opened the door. Mrs. Stowers was behind the door and he told her why he was there. He stated that the children were hysterical, that the plaintiff became violent, that they grabbed her, that she got loose and ran into the bedroom, that they followed her and during the resulting melee the bed was broken. In response to a question from plaintiff's counsel, the ambulance attendant stated that he had been in the business for 13 years and had taken five to six people a week to mental institutions. He testified that he did not recall plaintiff trying to use the telephone and that he was not told to use a strait jacket to restrain her.

The parties are in substantial agreement as to what occurred at Ardmore Acres. Defendant requested permission to treat the plaintiff on several different occasions, and she refused. For six days, she was placed in the "security room," which was a bare room except for the bed. The windows of the room were covered with wire mesh. During five of the six days, plaintiff refused to eat, and at all times refused medication. Defendant telephoned orders to the hospital and prescribed certain medication. He visited her often during her stay.

When plaintiff arrived at the hospital she was refused permission to receive or place telephone calls, or to receive or write letters. Dr. Wolodzko conceded at the trial that plaintiff wished to contact her brother in Texas by telephone and that he forbade her to do so. After nine days, she was allowed to call her family, but no one else. Plaintiff testified on direct examination that once during her hospitalization she asked one of her children to call her relatives in Texas and that defendant took her to her room and told her, "Mrs. Stowers, don't try that again. If you do, you will never see your children again." It is undisputed that plaintiff repeatedly requested permission to call an attorney and that Dr. Wolodzko refused such permission.

At one point when plaintiff refused medication, on the written orders of defendant, she was held by three nurses and an attendant and was forcibly injected with the medication. Hospital personnel testified at the trial that the orders concerning medication and deprivation of communication were pursuant to defendant's instructions.

Plaintiff, by chance, found an unlocked telephone near the end of her hospitalization and made a call to her relatives in Texas. She was released by court order on January 27, 1964.

Plaintiff filed suit alleging false imprisonment, assault and battery, and malpractice, against defendant Wolodzko, Anthony Smyk and Ardmore Acres. Defendants Ardmore Acres and Smyk were dismissed prior to trial. At the close of plaintiff's proofs, defendant moved for a directed verdict. The court granted the motion as to the count of malpractice only, but allowed the counts of assault and battery and false imprisonment to go to the jury. At the conclusion of the trial, the jury returned a verdict for plaintiff in the sum of $40,000. The court denied defendant's motion for judgment notwithstanding verdict, but granted a conditional order for a new trial unless a remittitur was filed for the excess above $30,000. The Court of Appeals[1] reversed the order for remittitur and reinstated the jury verdict of $40,000. We granted leave to appeal. 383 Mich. 794.

I.

Defendant has raised five issues on appeal. The first issue is whether a jury could find defendant Wolodzko liable for assault and battery for treating plaintiff, who was temporarily hospitalized pursuant to M.C.L.A. 330.21, M.S.A. 14.811, after the plaintiff had refused such treatment?

Defendant contends that his treatment of plaintiff was required regardless of her consent because of the contract he had made with her husband to provide medical care for her. He implies that a husband has an almost absolute right to force his wife, if he believes her to be incompetent, to receive any medical treatment that he desires for her. He cites several cases which he contends stand for this proposition. None of them are on point.

One of the cases most frequently cited by defendant is *Maben* v. *Rankin* (1961), 55 Cal.2d 139, 10 Cal.Rptr. 353, 358 P.2d 681. The Court of Appeals stated concerning the *Maben Case* (fn. 12, pp. 125–126, 172 N.W.2d p. 502):

> Defendant often cites this case in support of a number of his assertions, but recognizes that the California statutes differ, as do the facts, from our problem here. California statutes provided for what could amount to 90 days hospitalization without a court order upon the certificate of one doctor. No certificate was necessary for the treatment which may ensue, subject to the statutory liability of the doctor for any negligence in that treatment. The patient was also permitted by

[1] *Stowers* v. *Wolodzke* (1969), 19 Mich.App. 115, 172 N.W.2d 497.

statute to contact others and inform them of his detention. The detention had to cease after 90 days unless the patient wished to remain, or unless the court then issued an order continuing the detention or unless a relative or friend obtained two doctors' certificates in support of continued detention. Any California statute in any way similar to our temporary detention statute was not before the *Maben* court. See West's Annotated California Codes, Welfare and Institutions, §§ 5750, 5750.1-5750.3 [repealed 1965, see §§ 6030-6033], 5751 [renumbered § 6250], 5752 [renumbered § 6251].

This Court stated in *In re LaFreniere's Estate* (1949), 323 Mich. 562, 36 N.W.2d 147, that:

> The general rule is that a husband is primarily liable for the payment of his wife's reasonable medical, hospital and funeral expenses.

City of Detroit v. *Eisele* (1961), 362 Mich. 684, 108 N.W.2d 763, stands for the same proposition. However, this does not mean that a husband can force medical care upon his wife. Rather, this means that once medical care has been consented to by a wife, the husband must pay for it. These cases are, therefore, not on point.

Likewise, *Johnson* v. *Borland* (1947), 317 Mich. 225, 26 N.W.2d 757, and *Wood* v. *Vroman* (1921), 215 Mich. 449, 184 N.W. 520, are not on point. In *Johnson* v. *Borland* (a malpractice action), the Court held that a physician who rendered services gratuitously had the duty of exercising reasonable and ordinary care, skill and diligence.

Wood v. *Vroman, supra,* stands for the same proposition. However, there is no question of defendant's malpractice in this case and, thus, both *Johnson* and *Wood* are not relevant to our determination in this situation.[2]

Defendant contends that under the probate court order he had not only the right, but the duty, to give plaintiff medical care and treatment. He contends that since there was no evidence of malpractice, he could not be liable for assault and battery because of the care and treatment he gave plaintiff at the hospital. He relies on *Dabkowski* v. *Davis* (1961), 364 Mich. 429, 111 N.W.2d 68, and *Olepa* v. *Mapletoff* (1966), 2 Mich.App. 734, 141 N.W.2d 350. In *Dabkowski,* plaintiff sued two physicians for false imprisonment and assault and battery. Plaintiff's husband had applied to the probate court to have her committed to a State hospital as a mentally ill person. The two defendants certified that plaintiff should be committed to the Kent County Receiving Hospital, and the probate court so ordered. Plaintiff was taken to the Kent County Receiving Hospital where she remained for 11 hours and was then released upon rescission of the emergency order. The trial court dismissed plaintiff's action, and this Court affirmed. The doctors had acted pursuant to M.C.L.A. 330.21, M.S.A. 14.811, the same statute involved in this case. The Court stated (364 Mich. pp. 433-434, 111 N.W.2d p. 70):

> It is clear that the statements of opinion by the doctors in the certificates before us are absolutely privileged. They were submitted while a sanity proceeding of plaintiff was pending, related to the emergency commitment of the plaintiff, and were submitted to the court having jurisdiction in the premises.

[2]*Fortner* v. *Koch* (1935), 272 Mich. 273, 261 N.W. 762, and *Buchanan* v. *Kull* (1949), 323 Mich. 381, 35 N.W.2d 351, both deal with the necessity of a surgeon using reasonable and ordinary care until the physician-patient relationship is terminated. The question we are dealing with here, however, is whether the physician-patient relationship was created in the first instance.

Thus, our Court has held that a physician is not liable for statements he makes in connection with the temporary commitment of a patient. However, that is not the issue before us. The issue here is: Whether once a patient is admitted to the hospital pursuant to M.C.L.A. 330.21 M.S.A. 14.811, may the doctor then give treatment without the patient's consent?

The trial court ruled as a matter of law that the defendant could not be found guilty for any actions taken up to the time plaintiff was hospitalized. Thus, insofar as *Dabkowski* and *Mapletoff* were applicable (i.e., up to the time of commitment), the trial court correctly applied and followed them in this case. These cases, however, do not state a defense to the actions of the doctor subsequent to plaintiff's admission to Ardmore Acres.

The Court of Appeals held that defendant was liable under M.C.L.A. 330.21, M.S.A. 14.811. That statute provides:

> The . . . *husband* . . . of a person *alleged* to be mentally ill, mentally handicapped or epileptic, . . . *may petition* the probate court of said county for an order directing the admission of said person to a hospital, home or institution for the care of the mentally ill, . . . such petition to contain a statement giving the facts and not the conclusions upon which the allegation of such mental disease is based and because of which the application for the order is made. Upon receiving such petition the court shall fix a day for hearing thereof and shall appoint 2 reputable physicians to make the required examination of such alleged mentally diseased person; such physicians shall file their report duly certified to with the court on or before such hearing. . . . The court shall also take proofs as to the alleged mental condition or epilespy of such person, and fully investigate the facts, and, if no jury is requested, the probate court shall determine the question of such alleged mental disease of such person. . . . *Pending such proceedings for admission* into the proper home, hospital or institution, *if it shall appear, upon the certificate of 2 legally qualified physicians, to be necessary and essential so to do, the court may order such alleged mentally diseased person* to be placed in the custody of some suitable person, or to be removed to *any hospital,* home or retreat to be detained until such petition can be heard and determined or to be removed to *any state hospital for the mentally diseased for custody and treatment. The period of such temporary detention shall not exceed 60 days* . . . [Emphasis added]

The Court of Appeals stated (19 Mich.App. p. 122, 172 N.W.2d p. 500):

> Reference to the statute quoted above shows that treatment of a patient temporarily detained in a *state* hospital is authorized by law, but that no mention of treatment of a patient in a *private* hospital, such as Ardmore Acres, is made. Therefore, no mandatory nor implied duty of the defendant to treat plaintiff attached by reason of the court order. The result is that the treatment of plaintiff as a patient becomes subject to the same examination by the jury as if there was no court action involved at all.

Defendant points out that this is the first such interpretation made of M.C.L.A. 330.21, M.S.A. 14.811. This is a case of first impression on this point. The Court of Appeals' decision is the first interpretation as to whether there is a distinction between treatment in a State hospital and a private institution.

In 2 OAG, 1955–56, No. 2847, p. 693 (Nov. 26, 1956), a similar problem was dealt with involving treatment under the Michigan statutes for patients removed to a regional diagnostic center for diagnostic care. The Attorney General stated:

> On the one hand, the statute clearly provides that the patient is referred for diagnosis, care and treatment. On the other, the sole purpose of the referral is to obtain diagnosis. *At the time of the diagnostic referral, no judicial determination of mental illness has taken place. . . .*
>
> Prior to final adjudication by the court, any treatment given without consent of the patient, *other than that necessary to keep him on the premises and to prevent his injuring himself or others, is given at the peril of the superintendent, and may give rise to liability for assault or for trespass. . . .*
>
> It should be emphasized, however, *that the patient referred for diagnosis has not been determined to be insane,* and for this reason superintendents should be advised that they *may be incurring a personal risk by administering any care and treatment not clearly and demonstrably essential to the making of the diagnosis, or to the safeguarding of the patient.* [Emphasis added]

We have an analogous situation with temporary commitment under M.C.L.A. 330.21, M.S.A. 14.811. While the patient has been certified to be mentally ill by two doctors under the statute, there has not been a determination of insanity. The statements of the Attorney General as to liability for assault when a patient is removed for diagnostic care does apply in this situation.

We, therefore, hold that the Court of Appeals was correct in its construction of M.C.L.A. 330.21, M.S.A. 14.811. The statute does not authorize defendant to administer any care to the plaintiff which is not necessary to keep a person on the premises or to prevent harm to the patient or to others. (2 OAG, 1955-56, *supra*)

Defendant concedes that he did treat the plaintiff in this case and that if his treatment was not privileged, he would be liable for assault and battery. We hold that the treatment was not privileged because of M.C.L.A. 330.21, M.S.A. 14.811, and that a jury, under the evidence, could find defendant liable for assault and battery. Thus, we do not find merit in defendant's first issue on appeal.

II.

The second issue involves whether or not there was evidence from which a jury could find false imprisonment.

"False imprisonment is the unlawful restraint of an individual's personal liberty or freedom of locomotion." 35 C.J.S. False Imprisonment § 1, p. 621. It is clear that plaintiff was restrained against her will. Defendant, however, contends that because the detention was pursuant to court order (and hence not unlawful), there can be no liability for false imprisonment. However, defendant was not found liable for admitting or keeping plaintiff in Ardmore Acres. His liability stems from the fact that after plaintiff was taken to Ardmore Acres, defendant held her incommunicado and prevented her from attempting to obtain her release, pursuant to law. Holding a person incommunicado is clearly a restraint of one's freedom, sufficient to allow a jury to find false imprisonment.

Defendant contends that it was proper for him to restrict plaintiff's communication with the outside world. Defendant's witness, Dr. Sidney Bolter, testified that orders restricting communications and visitors are customary in cases of this type. Hence, defendant contends these orders were lawful and could not constitute the basis for an action of false imprisonment. However, the testimony of Dr. Bolter is not conclusive on this point.

Psychiatry is a relatively new professional discipline and, as with all disciplines, there is a great deal of controversy within the profession as to precisely what methods of treatment should be used. Psychiatrists have a great deal of power over their patients. In the case of a person confined to an institution, this power is virtually unlimited. All professions (including the legal profession) contain unscrupulous individuals who use their position to injure others. The law must provide protection against the torts committed by these individuals. In the case of mental patients, in order to have this protection, they must be able to communicate with the outside world. In our country, even a person who has committed the most abominable crime has the right to consult with an attorney. *Miranda* v. *Arizona* (1966), 384 U.S. 436, 86 S.Ct. 1602, 16 L.Ed.2d 694, 10 A.L.R.3d 974.

Our Court and the courts of our sister States have recognized that interference with attempts of persons incarcerated to obtain their freedom may constitute false imprisonment.[3] Further we have jealously protected the individual's rights by providing that a circuit judge "who wilfully or corruptly refuses or neglects to consider an application, action, or motion for habeas corpus, is guilty of malfeasance in office." M.C.L.A. 600.4313, M.S.A. 27A.4313.

Hoff v. *New York* (1939), 279 N.Y. 490, 492, 493, 18 N.E.2d 671, 672, involved an action against the superintendent of a state hospital for diverting a letter containing a writ of habeas corpus from the plaintiff to his attorney. The lower courts dismissed the complaint, and the New York Court of Appeals reversed, holding that the complaint stated a cause of action. The plaintiff's wife had requested that the superintendent forward all mail to her and he had done so in accordance with her instructions. The court stated:

> The right of persons, deprived of liberty, to challenge in the courts the legality of their detention is safeguarded by the Constitution of the United States and by the Constitution of the State. . . . Doubtless the superintendent acted in the honest belief that the claimant was insane. Nevertheless, his act delayed for a time a test of the claimant's sanity which, when made, resulted in his discharge.
>
> We can find no basis for any claim that the superintendent's action was justifiable. . . .
>
> The right of the superintendent in the exercise of a reasonable discretion to censor the ordinary mail written by a patient who has been adjudged insane is not challenged. The question is whether the superintendent of a State hospital for the insane may in the exercise of his discretion obstruct or delay a challenge of the legality of detention by a patient held under a court order. To that question one answer is clearly dictated. The State cannot under the Constitution withhold the privilege of the writ of habeas corpus. . . . An officer of the State who detains a man under command of the State may not by indirection accomplish what the Constitution forbids to the State. He may not lawfully withhold from a person so detained the opportunity to apply for a writ of habeas corpus.

[3]For somewhat different fact situations where our Court has held that actions which delay a person's release may constitute false imprisonment, see *Linnen* v. *Banfield* (1897), 114 Mich. 93, 72 N.W. 1, and *Oxford* v. *Berry* (1918), 204 Mich. 197, 170 N.W. 83.

The reasoning of the New York Court of Appeals is applicable to our case. Although plaintiff was not attempting to use a writ of habeas corpus, she was attempting to communicate with a lawyer or relative in order to obtain her release. Defendant prevented her from doing so. We agree with the reasoning of the New York court and hold that the actions on the part of defendant constitute false imprisonment.

A person temporarily committed to an institution pursuant to statute certainly must have the right to make telephone calls to an attorney or relatives. We realize that it may be necessary to restrict visits to a patient confined to a mental institution. However, the same does not apply to the right of a patient to call an attorney or relative for aid in obtaining his release. This does not mean that an individual has an unlimited right to make numerous telephone calls, once he is confined pursuant to statute. Rather, it does mean that such an individual does have a right to communicate with an attorney and/or a relative in an attempt to obtain his release.

Dr. Bolter was unable to give any valid reason why a person should not be allowed to consult with an attorney. We do not believe there is such a reason. While problems may be caused in a few cases because of this requirement, the facts in the instant case provide cogent reasons as to why such a rule is necessary. Mrs. Stowers was able to obtain her release after she made the telephone call to her relatives and they, in turn, obtained an attorney for her. Prior to this, because of the order of no communications, she was virtually held a prisoner with no chance of redress. We, therefore, agree with the Court of Appeals that there was sufficient evidence from which a jury could find that Dr. Wolodzko had committed false imprisonment.[4]

III.

The third issue involves whether there was evidence from which a jury could find that defendant had committed the tort of assault and battery. Defendant contends that because he was acting pursuant to a court order, there could be no liability for assault and battery. However, as we pointed out in Part I, hereof, M.C.L.A. 330.21, M.S.A. 14.811, only authorizes treatment in a State institution. As we stated, *supra:*

> Prior to final adjudication by the court, any treatment given without consent of the patient, other than that necessary to keep him on the premises and to prevent his injuring himself or others, is given at the peril of the superintendent, and may give rise to liability for assault or for trespass.

The Court of Appeals pointed out (19 Mich.App. p. 126, 172 N.W.2d p. 503):

> The sanctity of one's body is such that a possible absence of pain and suffering in its unwarranted and nonconsensual touching does not eliminate the need for protec-

[4]Defendant, at oral argument and in his Reply Brief, cites *Maniaci* v. *Marquette University* (1971), 50 Wis.2d 287, 184 N.W.2d 168, as holding that there can be no false imprisonment in cases analogous to our facts. In *Maniaci,* the plaintiff was a 16-year old girl who was prevented by school officials from leaving the University and was committed to Milwaukee County General Hospital under a temporary commitment order pursuant to statute. The Supreme Court reversed a jury verdict for damages for false imprisonment and held that there could be a trial on the issue of abuse of process. However, the facts are clearly distinguishable from our case. The plaintiff in *Maniaci* was a minor and the University officials were acting in *loco parentis.* Moreover, she was *not* prevented from communicating with other individuals to obtain her release. A social worker at the hospital contacted a Leonard McGravey and informed him that Miss Maniaci was being held in the hospital. He, in turn, came to the hospital and was allowed to visit her at 11:00 P.M. that same evening. Also, she was released at 9:00 A.M. the next morning. Mrs. Stowers was held for 23 days. Thus, the ability to communicate with others to try to obtain her release was not denied to Miss Maniaci as it was to Mrs. Stowers.

> tion from, or compensation for, such touching in the absence of a court order or an emergency. Any submission by plaintiff, no matter how benign, was not voluntary. It was not necessary that she violently resist at every juncture as a prerequisite to recovery for assault and battery if her lack of consent was clearly manifested.

We agree with the Court of Appeals on this point. Because there was no authority given by the court order pursuant to M.C.L.A. 330.21, M.S.A. 14.811, there clearly was a nonconsensual touching of the plaintiff. Given the evidence of this case (and, indeed, defendant does not contend that he did not order certain medication and shots to be given plaintiff), there was sufficient evidence that the jury could find that defendant committed assaultand battery on the plaintiff.

The Court of Appeals is affirmed. Costs to plaintiff.

T. M. KAVANAGH, C.J., and BLACK, ADAMS, BRENNAN, T. G. KAVANAGH, and WILLIAMS, JJ., concur.

SEXUAL OR MARITAL HARM

For understandable reasons, the actual frequency with which sexual encounters between patients and their therapists occurs is not known. Studies addressing this and related questions have yielded varying estimates (Butler, 1975; Butler & Zelen, 1977; Holroyd & Brodsky, 1977; Kardener, Fuller & Mensh, 1973; Perrs, 1976). Some mental health professionals have attempted to rationalize sexual contact with patients on grounds such as (a) such contact was needed to reassure the patient of his/her sexual desirability; (b) such contact was needed to treat the patient's sexual problem; (c) such contact was needed to enhance the patient's self-concept; and (d) the use of sexual energy, up to and including sexual intercourse, can have a healing effect for the patient. McCartney (1966) theorized that some patients needed to work out transference-related problems by doing more than talking about them. McCartney advised therapists to engage in therapeutic nudity, touching and intercourse with the caveat that therapists should "remain objective and yet react sexually appropriately in order to lead the immature person into full maturity."

Despite advice such as that offered by McCartney, most mental health professionals believe that it is difficult, if not impossible, for a therapist to remain objective with her/his pants down. As Masters and Johnson (1966) observed, "It's damn hard to be in bed and be objective at the same time." Holroyd and Brodsky (1977) have also cited the loss of objectivity as a danger attendant to patient-therapist sexual activity. In more cases than not, such activity would appear to cater to the needs of the therapist and not the patient. Discussing his observations concerning male therapists who had had sex with their patients, Dahlberg (1970) wrote that "these aging men, some in a depressive and needy period, somehow let themselves be convinced by their patients' fantasies that they might recapture their youth." Marmor (1976) has pointed out that the activity may be a product of the therapist's unconscious hostility toward the opposite sex combined with a sadistic need to exploit, humiliate, and ultimately reject. He went on to observe that "most erotic breaches of the therapist–patient relationship occur with women who are physically attractive, almost never with the aged, the infirm, or the ugly, thus giving the lie to the oft-heard rationalization on the part of such therapists that they were acting in the interest of the patient!''

A study by Taylor and Wagner (1976) analyzed data relating to the outcomes of patient–therapist sex. In that study it was found that in 47 percent of the cases the outcome was negative, in 32 percent of the cases the effects were mixed, and in 21 percent of the cases there were positive effects reported for either the patient or the therapist. In another study the potentially positive effects of the sexual activity *for the therapist* was more apparent. Butler and Zelen (1977) reported as follows:

> The data revealed that the therapists' own personal needs and motivations overwhelmingly contributed to the sexual contact, and that the therapists acknowledged their needs as a factor in this sexual behavior (although not necessarily at that time). Ninety percent reported having been ''vulnerable,'' ''needy,'' and/or ''lonely'' when the sexual contact occurred. These high-need states were related to unsatisfying marriages, recent separations and/or divorces. One might assume the therapists shifted their source of gratification to their patients during these vulnerable or needy periods of time. (p. 142)

The problem of patient–therapist sex is not new. Rather, it dates back to the time when psychotherapy was first developing as a legitimate medical enterprise. One of the psychoanalysts in Freud's coterie, Sandor Ferenczi, attempted to rationalize his kissing and hugging of patients by arguing that he was providing emotional restitution for the love and support that the patient was denied as a child. According to Marmor (1976), Ferenczi was strongly reprimanded by Freud for taking such liberties and Freud warned that a similar rationalization might lead other therapists to take even greater liberties. In agreement with the majority of mental health professionals, Marmor (1976) does not condone sexual interaction between patients and psychotherapists on the grounds that such interaction ''fosters a serious confusion between reality and fantasy in the patient, with inevitably antitherapeutic results.'' The American Psychiatric Association (1973) has straightforwardly deemed therapist–patient sex to be unethical. The American Psychological Association made a similar statement in its 1977 revision of the Code of Ethics, Principle Six.

Despite the fact that professional organizations have universally decried therapist–patient sexual interaction under any circumstances, knotty legal questions remain. Keeping in mind that the judiciary is concerned with protecting the conditions by which new or novel treatments can be developed, and keeping in mind that the legislative and judicial climate is one that is fiercely protective of the patient's right to treatment, what if sexual interaction was mutually consented to and contracted for in the context of a therapeutic relationship? As Serban has pointed out, ''On the one hand, the right-to-treatment law in New York assumes that any patient, even the psychotic patient, is aware and knowledgeable enough to accept or refuse any form of treatment; on the other hand, the implication of *Roy* v. *Hartogs* is that the patient was not aware of the nature of the 'treatment'—a 'treatment' which was pursued on a regular basis for thirteen months'' (cited in Cohen, 1979, p. 96; see also Serban & Gidynski, 1974, for a discussion of how current mental hygiene laws may be unrealistic with respect to the suppositions they make concerning the competencies of psychotic patients).

Another difficult legal question arises when a professional claims that he or she is not acting within the context of a professional relationship at the time that the sexual interaction takes place. This was the claim made by Martin Shepard, a psychiatrist who had his license to practice medicine revoked by the New York State Board of Regents on the grounds of sexual misconduct with patients. Appearing on the NBC network ''Tomorrow'' program (aired February 22, 1979), Shepard explained that at one time he was working at ''a center in New York that was modeled after Esalen in California'' that offered workshops and was not for the treatment of sick people. Shepard was intimate with some of the people in the groups that he led, and he wrote about those intimacies in a book, Shepard went on:

> I wasn't counseling them, I—they never said they considered me their doctor, I never considered them patients of mine but I was there as a group facilitator or a group leader or whatever. So the State, in its ultimate wisdom, decided that since I was a group leader and I had credentials after my name, all these people must have thought of me as a doctor. And, uh, therefore if I were writing about intimacies with them, I was taking advantage of a doctor-patient relationship.[1]

Legal questions surrounding the burgeoning number of sex therapy clinics in this country are bound to emerge with greater frequency in the near future. Does therapy that requires sexual relations give rise to the tort of interference with the marital relationship of the patient? What of the use of sexual surrogates? Currently, the way prostitution, pimping, pandering, and related statutes (e.g., the Mann Act) are written, certain sex therapy clinics might be construed as being in violation of laws proscribing sex on a free-for-service basis—regardless of the alleged ''therapeutic'' benefit to be derived.

The following cases of *Anclote Manor Foundation* v. *Wilkinson,* 263 So.2d 256 (Fla.Dist.Ct.App. 1972), and *Nicholson* v. *Han,* 12 Mich.App. 35, 162 N.W.2d 313 (1968), are representative of actions brought against mental health professionals that address the issue of sexual or marital harm. These cases, like *Roy* v. *Hartogs* (p. 204) have been brought for malpractice and/or breach of contract. See also *Morra* v. *State Bd. of Examiners of Psychologists,* 212 Kan. 103, 510 P.2d 614 (1973), and *Cooper* v. *Bd. of Medical Examiners,* 49 Cal.App.3d 931, 123 Cal.Rptr. 563 (1975).

Anclote Manor Foundation v. *Wilkinson*, 263 So.2d 256 (Fla.Dist.Ct.App., 1972)

HOBSON, Judge.

Appellant appeals a final judgment entered in favor of appellee on an action for breach of contract arising out of appellant's agreement with the appellee to render

[1]See Cohen (1979, pp. 97-98) for further excerpts of the ''Tomorrow'' transcript.

psychiatric and medical services to appellee's wife. Appellee's wife was a patient at appellant's hospital for approximately two years for which appellee paid the appellant $28,627.50.

A psychiatrist who was a full-time employee of the appellant was assigned to treat appellee's wife. Appellee's wife was under the direct supervision of such psychiatrist during the entire period that she was a patient. While appellee's wife was still a patient the psychiatrist told her that he was going to divorce his wife and he wanted to marry her.

Each and every one of the expert witnesses testified that the "acting out" of the psychiatrist's feelings toward appellee's wife (known as countertransference) was conduct below acceptable psychiatric and medical standards. On March 1, 1966, approximately ten days subsequent to the psychiatrist "acting out" his feelings toward appellee's wife, she was discharged from appellant's hospital. Prior to her discharge, on February 22, 1966, appellee filed for a divorce. Subsequently, on April 12, 1966, a final decree of divorce was entered divorcing appellee and his wife. The following year appellee's wife committed suicide. Between the date of her discharge and her death by suicide the appellee's wife's only brother was killed in Viet Nam and her grandmother passed away.

The issues were submitted to a jury and a verdict was returned in the amount of $28,600.

Appellant contends that there is no competent evidence in the record from which the jury could determine what, if any, damages appellee suffered as the result of the conduct of the psychiatrist who was appellant's full-time employee. Appellee contends that he is entitled to full reimbursement for monies paid under the contract on the theory that where there is a breach of contract on the part of a physician which destroys the possibility of any benefit which could have been anticipated under skillful treatment in the first instance, he is entitled to recover all expenses incurred by him in the entire course of treatment of his wife. We agree that this is the correct measure of damages if supported by the evidence. Appellee argues that there is sufficient evidence in the record to pose a jury question as to whether or not the breach of contract destroyed the possibility of any benefit which could have been anticipated under skillful treatment in the first instance.

There is sufficient evidence in the record, when considered in the light of the correct instructions given to the jury, to sustain the jury's finding that there was a breach of contract and that the appellee is entitled to recover the total sum paid by him under the contract.

Appellant also challenges the admissibility into evidence of testimony concerning the divorce and suicide of appellee's wife both of which occurred subsequent to her discharge. When this evidence is viewed in light of the expert testimony that the psychiatrist's conduct might have adverse effects upon her, it then becomes a question of the weight to be given such evidence by the jury and not of its admissibility. It is also noted that the *appellant* introduced testimony to the effect that subsequent to the patient's discharge and prior to her suicide, her brother was killed in Viet Nam and a grandmother passed away. This evidence was also weighed by the jury as to its effect on the patient.

Next, appellant challenges the correctness of the judge determining as a matter of law that the psychiatrist was guilty of malpractice. Suffice it to say that each and every expert testified that the psychiatrist's conduct was below acceptable psychiatric standards.

The other two points raised by appellant have been considered and found to be without merit. Therefore, the judgment appealed is affirmed.

Affirmed.

LILES, A.C.J., and MCNULTY, J., concur.

Nicholson v. *Han*, 12 Mich.App. 35, 162 N.W.2d 313 (1968)

LESINSKI, C.J. The circuit court granted defendant's motion for accelerated judgment[1] and entered an order for summary judgment of dismissal[2] from which the plaintiff appeals. The court believed the substance of the plaintiff's claim to be in the nature of an action for "alienation of affections, charging criminal conversation and seduction of a person over the age of 18 or more years" and therefore barred by statute.[3]

Defendant's motion for summary judgment was "governed by GCR 1963, 117, which permits such motion to be based, as it was here, on the ground that plaintiff's complaint failed to state a claim upon which relief can be granted. For the purpose of that motion, both at the trial and appellate levels, every well-pleaded allegation [of fact] in the complaint is assumed to be true." *Bielski* v. *Wolverine Insurance Company* (1967), 379 Mich 280, 283. Accordingly, the following facts and allegations of fact which frame the legal issues are taken from the amended complaint and other papers filed in this cause.

Mr. Nicholson, the plaintiff herein, and his wife Marilyn, were experiencing marital difficulties. In December, 1960, plaintiff had occasion to consult the defendant, Dr. Maolin Han, a licensed physician, concerning an injury to plaintiff's left foot. During the course of treatment, plaintiff told the doctor about his marital problems and received an offer of help. The plaintiff avers that defendant offered to reconcile plaintiff's marital problems through the use of psychiatry and other means and warranted that his marital relations would improve. Defendant told plaintiff that he had been successful with other patients. The plaintiff and his wife consulted defendant in his role as a psychiatrist and marriage counselor in December, 1960, and in 1961 and 1962; however, the plaintiff's marital situation deteriorated to such a point that Marilyn Nicholson obtained a divorce in February, 1962. The plaintiff had occasion to visit Northville State Hospital in the fall of 1964 and saw there a hospital record relating to his wife. The record revealed that Marilyn Nicholson told her physicians that she had been intimate with defendant. Later Marilyn Nicholson told plaintiff that her personal relationship with the doctor began in 1961 and continued into 1964. The plaintiff claims no knowledge of the relationship between defendant and his wife until he saw the hospital record in the fall of 1964.

The plaintiff brought this action against defendant charging him with utilizing the doctor-patient relationship to seduce plaintiff's wife. The amended complaint contains five counts alleging: (1) breach of contract, (2) malpractice, (3) assault and battery, (4) trespass on the case (negligence) and (5) fraud. Each count contains an allegation to the effect that defendant used the pretext of rendering psychiatric and marriage counseling services to deprive plaintiff of the services, companionship, and marital relationship of

[1] GCR 1963, 116.

[2] GCR 1963, 117.

[3] CLS 1961, § 600.2901 (Stat Ann 1962 Rev § 27A.2901); CL 1948, §§ 551.301, 551.302 (Stat Ann 1957 Rev §§ 25.191, 25.192).

his wife by inducing her to engage in a sexual relationship and to divorce plaintiff. The plaintiff stated in opposition to the motions for accelerated and summary judgment that "there can be no doubt that plaintiff's amended complaint includes elements which used to be recoverable through actions for criminal conversation or alienation of affections. However, that fact does not immunize defendant from suit."

The lower court found plaintiff's entire claim to be based upon torts abolished by statute and dismissed the action. The plaintiff appeals the court's ruling as respects counts 1 and 5 of the amended complaint for breach of contract and fraud.

The question before us is whether counts 1 and 5 of the amended complaint plead causes of actions unaffected by the statutory bar. CL 1948, § 551.301 (Stat Ann 1957 Rev § 25.191), reads as follows:

> All civil causes of action for alienation of affections, criminal conversation, and seduction of any person of the age of 18 years or more, and all causes of action for breach of contract to marry are hereby abolished.

The provisions of CL 1948, § 551.301, *supra,* were substantially re-enacted as CLS 1961, § 600.2901 (Stat Ann 1962 Rev § 27A.2901), in the following language:

> The following causes of action are abolished:
>
> (1) alienation of the affections of any person, animal, or thing capable of feeling affection, whatsoever;
>
> (2) criminal conversation;
>
> (3) seduction of any person of the age of 18 years or more;
>
> (4) breach of contract to marry.

In *Miller* v. *Kretschmer* (1965), 374 Mich 459, 461, the Supreme Court concluded that "the reenactment of the above section [CL 1948, § 551.301], as modified by the legislature, has unquestionably spelled out a legislative decision to abolish all actions for alienation of affections." *Miller* v. *Kretschmer, supra,* teaches that the ambit of the re-enacted statute extends beyond the orthodox action for alienation of a spouse for loss of consortium, conjugal society, and assistance of the other spouse.

We have momentarily digressed from our main inquiry concerning the nature of the appealed counts to make plain the fact that Michigan courts have taken the statute to mean exactly what it says. Further, it has been held that a bare reading of the statute is sufficient and no interpretation is necessary when the language employed by the legislature is plain, certain, and unambiguous. *Van Antwerp* v. *State* (1952), 334 Mich 593. And "a plain and unambiguous statute is to be applied, and not interpreted, since such a statute speaks for itself, and any attempt to make it clearer is a vain labor and tends only to obscurity." *City of Lansing* v. *Township of Lansing* (1959), 356 Mich 641, 649.

A reading of the statute here in question reveals no ambiguity or delphic meaning in the clear language employed by the legislature.

Count 1 alleges that defendant failed to perform a special agreement to reconcile and improve plaintiff's marital problems through the use of psychiatry and other means, "in that he failed to constructively counsel plaintiff and his wife and in that defendant failed to use psychiatry and in that he in fact induced plaintiff's wife to become friendly and intimate and to have sexual intercourse with defendant and induced plaintiff's wife to obtain a divorce from plaintiff."[4]

[4]Count 5 of the amended complaint claiming fraud contains identical language.

The plaintiff cites *Stewart* v. *Rudner* (1957), 349 Mich 459, and *Johnson* v. *Caldwell* (1963), 371 Mich 368, in support of his proposition that defendant doctor made a special agreement enforceable under Michigan law. In the *Stewart Case,* the Court found that the language of the parties gave rise to an express promise on the part of the defendant physician to perform a caesarean section and that he breached the special agreement by failing to perform the operation at the mother's full term. In the *Johnson Case,* the language of the parties again indicated that the physician had made a special agreement to treat the plaintiff during and after pregnancy. The failure to provide proper *post partum* treatment was held a breach of contract.

The Court said in *Stewart* v. *Rudner, supra,* pp. 467, 468:

We have now to consider the contract made. A doctor and his patient, of course, have the same general liberty to contract with respect to their relationship as other parties entering into consensual relationship with one another, and a breach thereof will give rise to a cause of action. It is proper to note, with respect to the contracts of physicians, that certain qualitative differences should be observed, since the doctor's therapeutic reassurance that his patient will be all right, not to worry, must not be converted into a binding promise by the disappointed or quarrelsome. These qualifications we have in mind as we proceed.

This Court considers the above language especially salutary in this case where the plaintiff alleges a special agreement to effect a psychiatric cure related to the marital relationship. The warranties and representations alleged by plaintiff to show a special agreement to reconcile a marriage are, in another sense, *qualitatively different* from the special agreements found in the *Stewart* and *Johnson Cases*. This is not to say that a patient and his doctor cannot make an express contract for psychiatric services containing a warranty of "cure," but such must very clearly appear from what was said by the parties at the time of making. The Court held in *McInerney* v. *Detroit Trust Co.* (1937), 279 Mich 42, 46, that "an express contract may be defined as one in which the terms were openly uttered and avowed at the time of making." See, also, *Woods* v. *Ayres* (1878), 39 Mich 345.

We are persuaded moreover that the substantial cause of action pleaded in count 1 is for alienation of affections and criminal conversation, not for breach of contract.

It is stated in 1 Am Jur 2d, Actions, § 8, p. 549:

> The determination of whether an action is on contract or in tort requires knowledge of the source or origin of the duty, the nature of the grievance, and what is said concerning them in the pleading in the cause. The form cannot always be determined from the character of the damages claimed, although the relief demanded has in some cases been considered controlling. When the facts are plainly and distinctly stated, the action will be regarded either as one in tort or as one in contract, depending, first, upon the character of the remedy such facts indicate, and, second, upon what is the most complete and ample redress that the law affords upon the facts stated.[5]

[5]The negligent breach of a contract involving misfeasance gives rise to an action for tort. See *Clark* v. *Dalman* (1967), 379 Mich 251; *Hart* v. *Ludwig* (1956), 347 Mich 559; and *Chase* v. *Clinton County* (1928), 241 Mich 478. And cases involving the statute of limitations have required that a determination be made whether the pleaded action was essentially a contract or tort. See *Baatz* v. *Smith* (1960), 361 Mich 68; and *Coates* v. *Milner Hotels, Inc.* (1945), 311 Mich 233.

Justice TALBOT SMITH put the matter admirably in a strong dissent in *Baatz* v. *Smith* (1960), 361 Mich 68, 76:

"The pleader insists he is relying on the contractual cause of action, and so, in truth, the declaration reads, but it is hopeless to rely upon verbiage alone, unless the wheel has come full circle and lawsuits will once more, as in medieval times, stand or fall upon the words employed in the writ.

> We should be determining the cause of action pleaded, examine the essential allegations of the complaint as a whole, stressing neither particular words nor particular allegations taken out of context. [Footnote omitted.] If the substantial cause of action pleaded is a tort action, the tort limitation would follow. If contract, the longer period.

Count 1 does not allege two substantial causes of action. It is founded on allegations of breach of contract; but the gravamen of the action sounds in tort, that is, the substance of the allegations denominate a tort. *Clark* v. *Dalman* (1967), 379 Mich 251. "The authorities are uniform in holding that the nature of the action with respect to whether it is based on a breach of contract or sounds in tort must be determined by the gravamen, or essential facts or grievance as alleged, to be ascertained from a consideration of the pleading as a whole. 1 CJS, Actions, § 46, p 1100." *Williamson* v. *Pacific Greyhound Lines* (1944), 67 Cal App 2d 250 (153 P2d 990, 992).

The gist of the action for alienation of affections was "plaintiff's loss of his wife's society, services, and comfort by means of the tortious conduct of the defendant." *Perry* v. *Lovejoy* (1883), 49 Mich 529, 531. The gist of the action for criminal conversation was proof of an actual marriage plus adulterous intercourse. *Perry* v. *Lovejoy, supra*. The action for alienation of affections necessarily involves intent to induce the spouse to separate and malice is conclusively presumed in the case of adultery. See 27 Am Jur, Husband and Wife, § 523, p 125. It is clear that the facts alleged in count 1 of the amended complaint place it squarely within the abolished actions, *i.e.*, the fact of plaintiff's marriage, the adulterous intercourse, the inducement to obtain a divorce and resulting loss of society, loss of services, pain and suffering rising from the marital relationship.

We are likewise persuaded that the claim of fraud in count 5 of the amended complaint falls squarely within the abolished actions. For here too, what is alleged constitutes an action for alienation of affections and criminal conversation in the same language found in count 1, and no action can be based thereon.

Affirmed, with costs to appellee.

MCGREGOR and CANHAM, JJ., concurred.

BREACH OF CONFIDENTIALITY

The confidentiality issue in general. Individuals have a right of privacy. As noted by Shah (1969, p. 57), "the concept of privacy recognized the freedom of the individual to pick and choose for himself the time, circumstances, and particularly the extent to which he wishes to share with or withhold from others his attitudes, beliefs, behavior, and opinions." The Fifth Amendment of the Constitution ensures the right of privacy with respect to information that may be self-incriminating, i.e., you cannot be compelled to testify against your own self-interest. States, as a matter of public policy (not constitutional right), have enacted statutes that have extended the right of the individual to refuse to disclose certain information. The privilege has been extended to those persons with whom the individual shares a special relationship, e.g., attorney, physician, psychologist, priest, husband/wife, and so on. Below we have reprinted the governing New York law of evidence as an example of statutes that establish the privileged nature of communications made in the course of professional relationships.

In addition to the statute law and rules of privilege, there is a practice or custom derived not only from statute but also from professional standards of practice and codes of ethics of a duty not to disclose information (i.e., the rule of confidentiality) obtained in the course of treatment.

Patients of mental health professionals have a right to expect that the confidentiality of the patient–therapist relationship and the communications therein will be assured. In general, mental health professionals have been granted by law the same right to privileged communication as that enjoyed by physicians and lawyers. It is important to note here the distinction between rules of confidentiality and the concept of privileged communication, a distinction of which few mental health professionals are aware (Swoboda, Elwork, Sales & Levine, 1978; Jagim, Wittman & Noll, 1978). As stated succinctly by Jagim et al. (1978, p. 459), "Whereas confidentiality concerns matters of communication outside the courtroom, privilege protects clients from disclosure in judicial proceedings."

Breach of confidentiality serves as the basis of a malpractice action. The practitioner who fails to exercise reasonable care in maintaining the confidentiality of patient communications may be subject to disciplinary action by his or her professional association and/or disciplinary action by the administrative body charged with the regulation and control of the profession. Also noteworthy is the fact that some patients have brought suit against physicians under a theory of breach of contract. The claim here is that the practitioner breached an implied contract to maintain confidentiality.

Below in *Horne* v. *Patton,* 291 Ala. 701, 287 So.2d 824 (1973), we find a general consideration of the multiple theories upon which confidentiality is based. As shown in the excerpts from the case of *Doe* v. *Roe,* 93 Misc.2d 201, 400 N.Y.S.2d 668 (Sup.Ct. 1977), there is a duty on the part of the psychiatrist—as well as other mental health professionals—not to disclose information obtained in the course of the therapist–patient relationship. This duty not to disclose is an affirmative duty imposed upon the practitioner, and its breach constitutes an invasion of the patient's right to privacy. Also existing in every jurisdiction are laws stating that certain communications made by patients to practitioners cannot be required to be disclosed by a court of law. Below in *In re Lifschutz,* 2 Cal.3d 415, 85 Cal.Rptr. 829, 467 P.2d 557 (1970), it is pointed out that the waiver of privilege is the right of the patient, not the practitioner, and this right is enforceable by the patient. After setting forth *Doe,* we will proceed to point out that the therapist–patient privilege, like the physician–patient and attorney–client privilege, is not absolute.

New York Evidence Law § 4504(a) (McKinney 1962)

§ 4504. Physician, Dentist and Nurse

(a) Confidential information privileged. Unless the patient waives the privilege, a person authorized to practice medicine or dentistry, or a registered professional or licensed practical nurse, shall not be allowed to disclose any information which he acquired in attending a patient in a professional capacity, and which was necessary to enable him to act in that capacity.

New York Civil Practice Law and Rules § 4507 (McKinney 1963)

The confidential relations and communications between a psychologist, registered under provisions of article one hundred fifty-three of the education law, and his client are placed on the same basis as those provided by law between attorney and client, and nothing in this article shall be construed to require any such privileged communication to be disclosed.

Horne v. *Patton,* 291 Ala. 701, 287 So.2d 824 (1973)

BLOODWORTH, Justice.

Plaintiff Larry Horne comes here on a voluntary nonsuit assigning as error the trial court's ruling in sustaining defendant's demurrer to his complaint.

This case is alleged to have arisen out of the disclosure by Dr. Patton, defendant herein, to plaintiff's employer of certain information acquired in the course of a doctor-patient relationship between plaintiff Horne and defendant doctor, contrary to the expressed instructions of patient Horne. Plaintiff Horne's original complaint asserted that the alleged conduct constituted a breach of fiduciary duty and an invasion of the plaintiff's right of privacy. Demurrer to this complaint was sustained. Subsequently, three amended counts were filed and demurrer to these counts was also sustained. Plaintiff thereupon took a voluntary nonsuit and filed this appeal.

There are sixty-eight assignments of error on this appeal. Appellant has expressly waived all but twenty-two, relating to the trial court's sustaining of defendant's demurrer to the complaint as last amended.

Count I of the amended complaint alleges in substance that defendant is a medical doctor, that plaintiff was a patient of defendant doctor for valuable consideration, that plaintiff instructed defendant doctor not to release any medical information regarding plaintiff to plaintiff's employer, and that defendant doctor proceeded to release full medical information to plaintiff's employer without plaintiff's authorization. Count I further alleges that the doctor–patient relationship between plaintiff and defendant was a confidential relationship which created a fiduciary duty from the defendant–doctor to the plaintiff–patient, that the unauthorized release of said information breached said fiduciary duty, moreover that said disclosure violated the Hippocratic Oath which defendant had taken and therefore constitutes unprofessional conduct. Plaintiff avers that as a direct and proximate result of the release of said information, plaintiff was dismissed from his employment.

Count II alleges the same basic facts but avers that the release of said information was an unlawful and wrongful invasion of the plaintiff's privacy.

Count III alleges, in substance, that plaintiff entered into a physician–patient contractual relationship for a consideration with the defendant, whereby through common custom and practice, impliedly, if not expressly, defendant agreed to keep confidential personal information given to him by his patient, that plaintiff believed the defendant would adhere to such an implied contract, with the usual responsibility of the medical profession and the traditional confidentiality of patient communications expressed in the Hippocratic Oath taken by the defendant. Count III goes on to allege that defendant breached said contract by releasing full medical information regarding the plaintiff to plaintiff's employer.

It is defendant's initial contention that this court cannot review appellant's assignments of error because they are deficient, relying primarily upon Alldredge v. Alldredge, 288 Ala. 625, 264 So.2d 182. Appellant's assignments of error are in the following form:

47. The court erred in sustaining ground No. 1 of Defendant's demurrer to the complaint as last amended and filed June 20, 1972.

The other assignments of error are in the same form assigning as error the trial court's sustaining the remaining twenty-one grounds of defendant's demurrer.

Furthermore, decisions from states with testimonial privilege statutes are not necessarily inopposite. Where the tort duty is based upon breach of the statute or the public policy expressed by the statute, this may be true. However, whether or not testimony may be barred at trial does not necessarily control the issue of liability for unauthorized extra-judicial disclosures by a doctor.

This was recognized by the Supreme Court of Nebraska in the case of *Simonsen* v. *Swenson,* 104 Neb. 224, 177 N.W. 831 (1920). There the court, after noting that Nebraska had a testimonial privilege statute, stated that such statute did not apply to non-testimonial disclosures and therefore had no bearing upon the case at hand involving extra-judicial disclosures. In seeking a source of a duty of secrecy on the part of the defendant doctor, the court pointed to a licensing provision that included "betrayal of a professional secret to the detriment of a patient" as unprofessional conduct. From this expression of policy the court derived a legal duty of secrecy on the part of the defendant doctor, viz:

> By this statute, it appears to us, a positive duty is imposed upon the physician, both for the benefit and advantage of the patient as well as in the interest of general public policy. The relation of physician and patient is necessarily a highly confidential one. It is often necessary for the patient to give information about himself which would be most embarrassing or harmful to him if given general circulation. This information the physician is bound, not only upon his own professional honor and the ethics of his high profession, to keep secret, but by reason of the affirmative mandate of the statute itself. A wrongful breach of such confidence, and a betrayal of such trust, would give rise to a civil action for the damages naturally flowing from such wrong. . . .

See also the discussions of policy in the *Hammonds* v. *Aetna Casualty & Surety Co., Berry* v. *Moench* and *Smith* v. *Driscoll, supra.*

It should be noted that Alabama has a very similar statute which gives the state licensing board for the healing arts the power and imposes on it the duty of suspending or revoking a doctor's license who wilfully betrays a professional secret. Title 46, § 257(21), Code of Alabama 1940, as last amended, reads as follows:

> The state licensing board for the healing arts shall have the power and it is its duty to suspend for a specified time, to be determined in the discretion of the board, or revoke any license to practice the healing arts or any branch thereof in the state of Alabama whenever the licensee shall be found guilty of any of the following acts or offenses; . . .
>
> (14) Wilful betrayal of a professional secret;

Moreover, the established ethical code of the medical profession itself unequivocally recognizes the confidential nature of the doctor–patient relationship. Each physician upon entering the profession takes the Hippocratic Oath. One portion of that required pledge reads as follows:

> Whatever in connection with my professional practice, or not in connection with it, I see or hear, in the life of men, which ought not be spoken of abroad, I will not divulge, as reckoning that all such should be kept secret.

This pledge has been reaffirmed in the Principles of Medical Ethics promulgated by the American Medical Association in Principle 9, viz:

> A physician may not reveal the confidences entrusted to him in the course of medical attendance, or the deficiencies he may observe in the character of patients, unless he is required to do so by law or unless it becomes necessary in order to protect the welfare of the individual or of the community. [American Medical Association, Principles of Medical Ethics, 1957, § 9 (Published by AMA)]

When the wording of Alabama's state licensing statute is considered alongside the accepted precepts of the medical profession itself, it would seem to establish clearly that public policy in Alabama requires that information obtained by a physician in the course of a doctor–patient relationship be maintained in confidence, unless public interest or the private interest of the patient demands otherwise. Is it not important that patients seeking medical attention be able to freely divulge information about themselves to their attending physician without fear that the information so revealed will be frivolously disclosed? As the New Jersey Supreme Court so aptly pointed out, what policy would be served by according the physician the right to gossip about a patient's health.

Only two courts have refused to recognize any duty on the part of the physician not to disclose. They are *Collins* v. *Howard,* 156 F.Supp. 322 (S.D.Ga., 1957) and *Quarles* v. *Sutherland,* 215 Tenn. 651, 389 S.W.2d 249 (1965). Neither the reasoning nor the result of either of these two cases is impressive. Both opinions fail to adequately separate the issue of testimonial privilege and the duty of confidentiality in extra-judicial communications. This problem is further complicated in that both cases involve disclosures in the context of pending litigation, such that the plaintiffs suffered no injury by virtue of the allegedly wrongful disclosures. Moreover, both courts found that no doctor–patient relationship existed on the facts there involved.

It is thus that it must be concluded that a medical doctor is under a general duty not to make extra-judicial disclosures of information acquired in the course of the doctor–patient relationship and that a breach of that duty will give rise to a cause of action. It is, of course, recognized that this duty is subject to exceptions prompted by the supervening interests of society, as well as the private interests of the patient himself. Whether or not the alleged disclosure by the defendant doctor in the instant case falls within such an exception, is not now an issue before this court.

The trial court erred in sustaining the demurrer to Count I.

Count II

The gravamen of Count II is that defendant's release to plaintiff's employer of information concerning plaintiff's health constituted an invasion of plaintiff's privacy.

This court has recognized the right of a person to be free from unwarranted publicity or unwarranted appropriation or exploitation of one's personality, publicization of one's private affairs with which the public has no legitimate concern, or the wrongful intrusion of one's private activities in such manner as to outrage or cause mental suffering, shame or humiliation to a person of ordinary sensibilities. *Norris* v. *Moskin Stores, Inc.*, 272 Ala. 174, 132 So.2d 321 (1961); *Abernathy* v. *Thornton,* 263 Ala. 496, 83 So.2d 235 (1955); *Smith* v. *Doss,* 251 Ala. 250, 37 So.2d 118 (1947).

Whether or not unauthorized disclosure of a person's medical record constitutes an invasion of this right of privacy is likewise a question of first impression in Alabama. Looking to other jurisdictions which have considered this question, those courts have almost uniformly recognized such disclosure as a violation of the patient's right of privacy. See cases collected at 20 A.L.R.3d 1109, 1114–15.

As a federal district court so aptly stated in *Hammonds* v. *Aetna Casualty & Surety Co.,* 243 F.Supp. 793 (N.D.Ohio, 1965), involving disclosure of medical information concerning the patient to the patient's insurer:

> When a patient seeks out a doctor and retains him, he must admit him to the most private part of the material domain of man. Nothing material is more important or more intimate to man than the health of his mind and body. Since the layman is unfamiliar with the road to recovery, he cannot sift the circumstances of his life and habits to determine what is information pertinent to his health. As a consequence, he must disclose all information in his consultations with his doctor—even that which is embarrassing, disgraceful or incriminating. To promote full disclosure, the medical profession extends the promise of secrecy referred to above. The candor which this promise elicits is necessary to the effective pursuit of health; there can be no reticence, no reservation, no reluctance when patients discuss their problems with their doctors. But the disclosure is certainly intended to be private. If a doctor should reveal any of these confidences, he surely effects an invasion of the privacy of his patient. We are of the opinion that the preservation of the patient's privacy is no mere ethical duty upon the part of the doctor; there is a legal duty as well. The unauthorized revelation of medical secrets, or *any* confidential communication given in the course of treatment, is tortious conduct which may be the basis for an action in damages.

Unauthorized disclosure of intimate details of a patient's health may amount to unwarranted publicization of one's private affairs with which the public has no legitimate concern such as to cause outrage, mental suffering, shame or humiliation to a person of ordinary sensibilities. Nor can it be said that an employer is necessarily a person who has a legitimate interest in knowing each and every detail of an employee's health. Certainly, there are many ailments about which a patient might consult his private physician which have no bearing or effect on one's employment. If the defendant doctor in the instant case had a legitimate reason for making this disclosure under the particular facts of this case, then this is a matter of defense.

The trial court erred in sustaining the demurrer to Count II.

Count III

The gravamen of Count III is that the alleged disclosure breached an implied contract to keep confidential all personal information given to defendant doctor by his patient. This count alleges that defendant doctor entered into a physician-patient contractual relationship wherein the plaintiff agreed to disclose to defendant all facts which would help him in his diagnosis and treatment of the plaintiff, that defendant agreed to treat the plaintiff to the best of his medical ability, and to keep confidential all personal information given to him by the plaintiff. It is alleged that this agreement is implied from the facts through common custom and practice.

This court has often stated that an implied contract arises where there are circumstances which, according to the ordinary course of dealing and the common understanding of men, show a mutual intent to contract. See, e.g., *Broyles* v. *Brown Engineering Company,* 275 Ala. 35, 151 So.2d 767 (1963). Defendant admits in his brief that the facts and circumstances alleged are such as to show a mutual intent to contract according to the ordinary course of dealing between a physician and his patient. The point of difference between the parties appears to be whether or not there is an implied term in the ordinary course of dealing between a doctor and patient that information disclosed to the doctor will be held in confidence.

Again, this question is one of first impression in this state. Few courts have considered this question. One of the fullest discussions on this point appears in *Hammonds* v. *Aetna Casualty & Surety Co., supra,* viz:

> Any time a doctor undertakes the treatment of a patient, and the consensual relationship of physician and patient is established, two jural obligations (of significance here) are simultaneously assumed by the doctor. Doctor and patient enter into a simple contract, the patient hoping that he will be cured and the doctor optimistically assuming that he will be compensated. As an implied condition of that contract, this Court is of the opinion that the doctor warrants that any confidential information gained through the relationship will not be released without the patient's permission. Almost every member of the public is aware of the promise of discretion contained in the Hippocratic Oath, and every patient has a right to rely upon this warranty of silence. The promise of secrecy is as much an express warranty as the advertisement of a commercial entrepreneur. Consequently, when a doctor breaches his duty of secrecy, he is in violation of part of his obligations under the contract.

A Pennsylvania court in *Clayman* v. *Bernstein,* 38 Pa.D & C 543 (1940), appears also to have recognized an implied term of confidentiality in the doctor-patient contract as it permitted the husband of a patient to maintain suit against a doctor for threatened disclosure of medical information concerning his wife:

> It would seem, moreover, that the act of defendant directly violated the rights of the husband. He is the person who is liable for his wife's medical treatment and it is with him that the contract of employment of defendant as a physician is made. Such

> a contract contains many implied provisions upon the breach of which the husband has a right of action. The most common of these perhaps are actions for negligence or malpractice, although they might sound in tort independent of contract. It may very well be, however, that a breach of trust or confidence, so necessarily associated with a contract of this type, may occur. Is not the unauthorized act of taking this photograph such a breach? . . .

Although the Tennessee Supreme Court denied there was a cause of action in tort for unauthorized disclosure of medical information concerning a patient, it admitted that there might be a breach of an implied contract. *Quarles* v. *Sutherland,* 215 Tenn. 651, 389 S.W.2d 249, 252 (1965).

We have not been cited to, nor have we found in our research, any case in which a cause of action for the breach of an implied contract of confidentiality on the part of the doctor has been rejected. Moreover, public knowledge of the ethical standards of the medical profession or widespread acquaintance with the Hippocratic Oath's secrecy provision or the AMA's Principles of Ethics or Alabama's medical licensing requirements of secrecy (which is a common provision in many states) singly or together may well be sufficient justification for reasonable expectation on a patient's part that the physician has promised to keep confidential all information given by the patient.

Again, of course, any confidentiality between patient and physician is subject to the exceptions already noted where the supervening interests of society or the private interests of the patient intervene. These are matters of defense.

The trial court erred in sustaining demurrer to Count III.

The judgment of the trial court is therefore due to be reversed and remanded.

Reversed and remanded.

HEFLIN, C.J., and HARWOOD and JONES, JJ., concur.

MERRILL, MADDOX, and FAULKNER, JJ., concur in the result.

MCCALL, J., dissents.

MCCALL, Justice (dissenting).

In Count III, the plaintiff relies on the breach of an alleged implied contract that the defendant would not divulge his medical findings about the plaintiff to the latter's employer. If there is no legal duty not to make such a disclosure, then there can be no implied contract not to disclose the information. In my opinion there is no legal duty not to make the disclosure in this case.

Alabama is a common law state. Tit. 1, § 3, Code of Alabama, 1940; *Hollis* v. *Crittendern,* 251 Ala. 320, 37 So.2d 193. At common law no privilege between physician and patient existed as to communications between physician and patient. This is the rule in the absence of a contrary statute. 58 Am.Jur. Witnesses, § 401, notes 20 and 1 on page 232. While statutes have been enacted in most states making communications between physician and patient privileged from compulsory disclosure in courts of justice, Alabama has not enacted such a law. The common law therefore remains in effect. In 61 Am.Jur.2d Physicians, Surgeons, Etc., § 101, it is said that at common law neither the patient nor the physician has the privilege to refuse to disclose in court a communication of one to the other, nor does either have a privilege that the communication not be disclosed to a third person. *Quarles* v. *Sutherland,* 215 Tenn. 651, 389 S.W.2d 249, 20 A.L.R.2d 1103, citing 1 Morgan, Basic Problems of Evidence, Ch. 5 (1954); 8 Wigmore, Evidence § 2380 (3rd Ed. 1961). In *Quarles, supra,* a store physician, who treated the plaintiff, immediately after her fall in the store, sent a copy of his report of findings to her lawyer and to the store's lawyer also, although he was requested not to send any medical report to anyone until notified by the plaintiff's lawyer.

The Tennessee Supreme Court said:

> We have made a thorough search of the statutes of this State, and have found no statute which would alter the common law rule in this regard. While the arguments for and against making doctor–patient communications privileged are many, our Legislature has not seen fit to act on the matter and, therefore, we must apply the common law rule as set forth above. For a thorough treatment of the subject see Chafee, "Privileged Communication: Is Justice Served or Obstructed by Closing the Doctor's Mouth on the Witness Stand?" 52 Yale L.Jour. 607 (1943).
>
> Petitioner cites T.C.A. sec. 63-618 concerning grounds for revocation of license, and T.C.A. sec 63-619 defining unprofessional conduct for our consideration. We have carefully studied these provisions and have concluded they are merely administrative provisions concerning the licensing of physicians. The standards set out therein are merely ethical in nature, and the nonadherence to these standards might constitute grounds for the revocation of the physician's license. Our view is that the statutes cited concern only the power of the State of Tennessee to revoke or continue a physician's license, and would have no application to the case sub judice. *Henderson* v. *Knoxville,* 157 Tenn. 477, 9 S.W.2d 697, 60 A.L.R. 652 (1928).
>
> We are aware that physicians and surgeons are required by the ethics of their profession to preserve the secrets of their patients which have been communicated to them or learned from symptoms or examination of other bodily conditions. However, under the common law, applicable in this case, this ethical requirement is not enforceable by law and, therefore, a demurrer to a cause of action wholly dependent upon an alleged 'patient–physician privilege' must be sustained.

It is important to observe that the information allegedly revealed by the physician in the present complaint did not constitute gossiping about his patient's health or a frivolous disclosure of information, as the court alluded to in *Hague* v. *Williams,* 37 N.J. 328, 181 A.2d 345.

In *Hague* v. *Williams, supra,* the court said:

> This is not to say that the patient enjoys an absolute right, but rather that he possesses a limited right against such disclosure, subject to exceptions prompted by the superventing interest of society. . . .

The court held that where the public interest or the private interest of a patient so demands, disclosure may be made to a person with a legitimate interest in the patient's health, and, where in the course of examining an infant patient the physician became aware of a pathological heart condition, the physician was not barred from disclosing such condition to an insurer to whom the parents had applied for life insurance on the infant, the court holding that when the parents made a claim for insurance, they lost any rights to nondisclosure that they may have had. *Hague, supra*, p. 349. In my opinion the overriding competing interest and responsibility of an employer for the welfare of all of his employees, to the public who come to his establishment and who buy his merchandise, and to the furtherance of his own business venture, should entitle him to be free from the shackles of secrecy that would prevent a physician from disclosing to the employer critical information concerning the physical or mental condition of his employees.

Doe v. *Roe*, 93 Misc.2d 201, 400 N.Y.S.2d 668 (Sup.Ct. 1977)

Opinion of the Court

MARTIN B. STECHER, J.

This action for an injunction and for damages for breach of privacy is a matter of first impression in this State, and so far as I am able to ascertain, a matter of first impression in the United States. It arises out of the publication, verbatim, by a psychiatrist of a patient's disclosures during the course of a lengthy psychoanalysis. I have made and filed detailed findings of fact which are briefly summarized here.[1]

Dr. Joan Roe is a physician who has practiced psychiatry for more than 50 years. Her husband, Peter Roe, has been a psychologist for some 25 years. The plaintiff had her late, former husband were each patients of Dr. Roe for many years. The defendants, eight years after the termination of treatment, published a book which reported verbatim and extensively the patients' thoughts, feelings, and emotions, their sexual and other fantasies and biographies, their most intimate personal relationships and the disintegration of their marriage. Interspersed among the footnotes are Roe's diagnosis of what purport to be the illnesses suffered by the patients and one of their children.

The defendants allege that the plaintiff consented to this publication. This defense is without substance. Consent was sought while the plaintiff was in therapy. It was never obtained in writing. In Dr. Roe's own words consent "was there one day and not there another day. That was the nature of the illness I was treating, unreliable." I need not deal with the value of an oral waiver of confidentiality given by a patient to a psychiatrist during the course of treatment. It is sufficient to conclude that not only did the defendants fail to obtain the plaintiff's consent to publication, they were well aware that they had none.

The plaintiff seeks to prevail on any or all of four theories: that violation of CPLR 4504 (subd [a]) gives rise to a cause of action;[2] that the provisions of section 6509 of the Education Law and the regulations of the Commissioner of Education (8 NYCRR 60.1 [d] [3])[3] establish a public policy whose breach gives rise to a cause of action in tort; that the physician-patient relationship is contractual and in it there is implied the physician's promise to obey the Hippocratic oath[4] whose violation gives rise to a cause of action for breach of contract; and, finally, "in light of the expanding recognition of invasion of privacy actions" (*Doe* v. *Roe,* 42 AD2d 559, 560, affd 32 NY2d 902, cert granted 417 US 907, cert dsmd 420 US 307) a separate cause of action exists for

[1]By prior order this file has been sealed from indiscriminate viewing and pseudonyms have been used in the title of the action and in the other documents. I see every reason to continue that arrangement (cf. *Munzer* v. *Blaisdell,* 268 App Div 9).

[2]CPLR 4504 (subd [a]) provides in part: "Unless the patient waives the privilege, a person authorized to practice medicine . . . shall not be allowed to disclose any information which he acquired in attending a patient in a professional capacity, and which was necessary to enable him to act in that capacity."

[3]Subdivision (9) of section 6509 of the Education Law provides: "Each of the following is professional misconduct: . . . (9) Committing unprofessional conduct, as defined by the board of regents in its rules or by the commissioner in regulations approved by the board of regents."

8 NYCRR 60.1 (d) (3) provides in part, "Unprofessional conduct in the practise of medicine shall include . . . the revealing of facts, data or information obtained in a professional capacity relating to a patient or his records without first obtaining the consent of the patient."

[4]Every physician is presumed to have taken the oath of Hippocrates [460?–377? B. C.] which states in part, "I will abstain [in treating patients] . . . from whatever is deleterious and mischievous. . . . Whatever, in connection with my professional practise, or not in connection with it, I may see or hear in the lives of men which ought not to be spoken abroad I will not divulge, as reckoning that all such should be kept secret."

unreasonably publicizing elements of plaintiff's life which ought to have been left in confidence.

The defendants contend not only that there was no unlawful disclosure, the patient's identity having been fully concealed, but that no right of action exists even if the plaintiff is recognizable in this volume. The defendants assert that neither the "evidentiary privilege" contained in CPLR 4504 (subd [a]) nor the regulations of the Commissioner of Education, by their history, are intended to give rise to a cause of action for their violation; that the only cause of action for invasion of privacy recognized in the State of New York is the statutory cause of action set forth in sections 50 and 51 of the Civil Rights Law; that the invasion of privacy concept as developed in the Federal courts and elsewhere is a constitutional guarantee of a right to privacy against intrusion by governments and has no reference to non-State action; that the volume in question is of such scientific merit that the professional need which it fills transcends the patient's right of nondisclosure; that the plaintiff is guilty of laches in bringing this action; and, finally, that the defendants' right to publication is protected by the First Amendment to the United States Constitution.

The few New York cases dealing with a physician's unauthorized disclosure of a patient's confidences usually turn on other issues, restrict themselves for the most part to a discussion of the effect of the current evidentiary statute (CPLR 4504, subd [a]) or its predecessor (Civ Prac Act, § 352) and in their dicta reach contradictory conclusions. In *Munzer* v. *Blaisdell* (183 Misc 773, affd 269 App Div 970) a patient in a State psychiatric institution sued its director for unauthorizedly releasing his case record in violation of the Mental Hygiene Law. The cause of action founded on section 352 of the Civil Practice Act was dismissed because there was no physician-patient relationship between the parties. The court did, however, offer the opinion (p 775) that "where the statutory duty is violated, the patient is entitled to redress; for it is well settled that, where a positive duty is imposed by statute, a breach of that duty will give rise to a cause of action for damages on the part of the person for whose benefit the duty was imposed; and, in such cases, if the statute itself does not provide a remedy, the common law will furnish it. *Willy* v. *Mulledy* 78 N.Y. 310, 314; *Racine* v. *Morris,* 201 N.Y. 240, 244; *Amberg* v. *Kinley,* 214 N.Y. 531, 535; 3 Cooley on Torts [4th ed.], § 477, p 361.) This principle was recognized by the decision of the Appellate Division in the case at bar (see *Munzer* v. *Blaisdell,* 268 App. Div. 9)."

In *Clark* v. *Geraci* (29 Misc 2d 791), the court found that the patient had waived the privilege and stated in a dictum that CPLR 4504 (subd [a]), section 6509 of the Education Law and the regulations issued thereunder (8 NYCRR 60.1 [d] [3]) provided no cause of action for breach of confidentiality. *Felis* v. *Greenberg* (51 Misc 2d 441) on the other hand expresses the view that such disclosure gives rise to a cause of action but turns on the sufficiency of a pleading alleging the publication of false information. *Curry* v. *Corn* (52 Misc 2d 1035) suggests that violation of CPLR 4504 (subd [a]) was not intended by the Legislature to create an independent cause of action; but there the physician's disclosure was to the plaintiff's husband and the court held that a husband is entitled, as a matter of right, to be informed of his wife's medical condition. In *Hammer* v. *Polsky* (36 Misc 2d 482) the court, in a dictum, said that neither section 352 of the Civil Practice Act nor the regulations issued under the Education Law will support a cause of action; but as in *Munzer* v. *Blaisdell* (183 Misc 777) recovery was denied on the ground that no physician-patient relationship was alleged to have existed.

The most frequently cited cases arising in other jurisdictions suffer from the same limitations. Although in *Smith* v. *Driscoll* (94 Wash 441, 442) the court said that "for so palpable a wrong, the law provides a remedy," the case turned on a question of pleading. A dictum in *Simonsen* v. *Swenson* (104 Neb 224) suggests the availability of a remedy for violation of the duty of secrecy, but the issue involved what the court held to be a limited right of disclosure of the existence of a communicable disease. The court in *Berry* v. *Moench* (8 Utah 2d 191) expressed the opinion that violation of evidentiary statutes gives rise to a cause of action, but like *Felis* v. *Greenberg* (*supra*) the action was for libel, the issue turning on whether or not the physician's disclosures were truthful. *Alexander* v. *Knight* (197 Pa Super Ct 79) similarly contains such dicta, but the action was for personal injuries sustained in an automobile accident.

In *Hague* v. *Williams* (37 NJ 328, 336) the court states that despite the absence of a common-law physician-patient privilege (cf. *Matter of City Council of City of N.Y.* v *Goldwater,* 284 NY 296; *Buffalo Loan, Trust & Safe Deposit Co.* v. *Knights Templar & Masonic Mut. Aid Assn.,* 126 NY 450, 455; *Quarles* v. *Sutherland,* 215 Tenn 651; Ann., 20 ALR3d 1109; *Clark* v. *Geraci,* 29 Misc 2d 791, *supra;* 8 Wigmore, Evidence [3d ed], § 2380) "[a] patient should be entitled to freely disclose his symptoms and condition to his doctor in order to receive proper treatment without fear that those facts may become public property" and that a physician "was under a general duty not to disclose frivolously the information received from [the patient], or from an examination of the patient." The court, however, concluded that a physician was perfectly justified in disclosing to an insurer the heart condition of a child whose parents had applied for a policy of life insurance on that child's life.

None of the post Civil Practice Act cases had considered the effect of the repeal of section 354 of the Civil Practice Act. Section 352 of the Civil Practice Act which prohibited disclosure, was carried forward verbatim into the new statute (CPLR 4504, subd [a]). Section 354 of the Civil Practice Act limited the application of section 352 providing in part that it applied "to any examination of a person as a witness," but this language was excluded from the new statute leaving only the broad prohibition without limitation that "a person duly authorized to practice medicine . . . shall not be allowed to disclose any information which he acquired in attending a patient in a professional capacity, and which was necessary to enable him to act in that capacity."

Were this case to turn exclusively on the application of CPLR 4504 (subd [a]) it might be argued that had the Legislature intended, on adoption of the Civil Practice Law and Rules, to create a new cause of action where none existed before (cf. *Matter of City Council of City of N. Y.* v. *Goldwater, supra*), it would have said so explicitly. Obviously, this case does not depend on so limited an approach; but I am of the opinion that the Legislature, in excluding from the new statute the opening words of section 354 of the Civil Practice Act (quoted *supra*), intended to reinforce the public policy of this State expressed in numerous statutes and regulations (cf. CPLR 4504, subd [a]; 4507, 4508; Education Law, §§ 6509-6511; Mental Hygiene Law, § 15.13, subds [c], [d]; § 35.11; Public Health Law, § 2803-c, subd 3, par f; § 2805-e, subd 3; § 3371; 8 NYCRR 60.1 [d] [3]) prohibiting physicians, persons in allied fields and medical institutions from disclosing without authorization of the patient, information discovered in attending the patient. I believe it clear, from the statutory and regulatory schemes set forth above that the Legislature did not intend to confine the prohibition to trials and other formal hearings whose proceedings are governed by a practice act (cf. *Matter of City Council of City of N. Y.* v. *Goldwater, supra*) but intended that " 'the statute [CPLR 4504, subd (a)] have a broad and liberal construction to carry out its policy' " (*Matter of City Council of City of N. Y.* v. *Goldwater, supra,* p 301, citing

Buffalo Loan, Trust & Safe Deposit Co. v. *Knights Templar & Masonic Mut. Aid Assn., supra*).

As hereafter indicated there are theories on which liability may be predicated other than violation of the CPLR (4504, subd [a]) the licensing and disciplinary statutes (Education Law, § 6509 *et seq.*) and what I perceive as this State's public policy. In two of the very few cases which have come to grips with the issue of wrongful disclosure by physicians of patients' secrets (*Hammonds* v. *Aetna Cas. & Sur. Co.*, 243 F Supp 793; *Horne* v. *Patton,* 291 Ala 701) the courts predicated their holdings on the numerous sources of obligation which arise out of the physician-patient relationship. In *Hammonds* (*supra*) an insurance carrier, defending an action brought by a patient of the physician, tricked the physician into revealing confidential data by telling him that the patient intended a medical malpractice action. Both physician and insurance carrier were held liable in damages for the wrongful disclosure on theories of public policy;[5] the privileged communication statute; the State licensing statute; the implied covenant not to disclose whose breach is a contractual violation;[6] invasion of privacy and breach of a fiduciary duty to which a trust doctrine should be applied. The court was "of the opinion that the preservation of the patient's privacy is no mere ethical duty upon the part of the doctor; there is a legal duty as well. The unauthorized revelation of medical secrets, or *any* confidential communication given in the course of treatment, is tortious conduct which may be the basis for an action in damages" (pp 801-802).

Horne v. *Patton* (*supra*) was a case of first impression in Alabama, a State without a testimonial privilege statute, but which had a licensing statute (Ala Code, tit 46, § 257 [21]; now Ala Code, § 34-24-35, subd 14) which, like our own statute (Education Law, § 6509 *et seq.*) and regulations (8 NYCRR 60.1 [d] [3]) permitted revocation of the physician's license for "[w]ilful betrayal of a professional secret." The court (p 830) sustained the complaint seeking an injunction and damages and recognized the "right of a person to be free from unwarranted publicity or unwarranted appropriation or exploitation of one's personality, publicization of one's private affairs with which the public has no legitimate concern, or the wrongful intrusion of one's private activities in such a manner as to outrage or cause mental suffering, shame or humiliation to a person of ordinary sensibilities." Its conclusions were also based on obligations arising from the Hippocratic oath and the principles of medical ethics of the American Medical Association;[7] the State licensing and disciplinary statute; the fiduciary nature of the relationship; and the implied covenant of secrecy in the contract between the parties. It held (p 829) that "public policy in Alabama requires that information obtained by a physician in the course of a doctor-patient relationship be maintained in confidence." The court (pp 829-830) "concluded that a medical doctor is under a general duty not to make extra-judicial disclosures of information acquired in the course of the doctor-patient relationship and that a breach of that duty will give rise to a cause of action."

[5] "[w]hen a course of conduct is cruel or shocking to the average man's conception of justice, such course of conduct must be held to be obviously contrary to public policy, though such policy has never been so written in the bond, whether it be Constitution, statute, or decree of court" (p 796).

[6] "[a]lmost every member of the public is aware of the promise of discretion contained in the Hippocratic Oath, and every patient has a right to rely upon this warranty of silence. The promise of secrecy is as much an express warranty as the advertisement of a commercial entrepreneur" (p 801).

[7] "A physician may not reveal the confidences entrusted to him in the course of medical attendance, or the deficiencies he may observe in the character of patients, unless he is required to do so by law or unless it becomes necessary in order to protect the welfare of the individual or of the community." (American Med Assn., Principles of Medical Ethics, 1957, § 9.)

I too find that a physician, who enters into an agreement with a patient to provide medical attention, impliedly covenants to keep in confidence all disclosures made by the patient concerning the patient's physical or mental condition as well as all matters discovered by the physician in the course of examination or treatment. This is particularly and necessarily true of the psychiatric relationship, for in the dynamics of psychotherapy "[t]he patient is called upon to discuss in a candid and frank manner personal material of the most intimate and disturbing nature . . . He is expected to bring up all manner of socially unacceptable instincts and urges, immature wishes, perverse sexual thoughts—in short, the unspeakable, the unthinkable, the repressed. To speak of such things to another human requires an atmosphere of unusual trust, confidence and tolerance. . . . Patients will be helped only if they can form a trusting relationship with the psychiatrist." (Heller, Some Comments to Lawyers on the Practice of Psychiatry, 30 Temple L Rev 401, 405-406.)

There can be little doubt that under the law of the State of New York and in a proper case, the contract of private parties to retain in confidence matter which should be kept in confidence will be enforced by injunction and compensated in damages (*Karpinski* v. *Ingrasci,* 28 NY2d 45; *Bates Chevrolet Corp.* v. *Haven Chevrolet,* 13 AD2d 27, 16 AD2d 917, affd without opn 13 NY2d 644; *Millet* v. *Slocum,* 4 AD2d 528, affd without opn 5 NY2d 734; *Lynch* v. Bailey, 300 NY 615; *Clark Paper & Mfg. Co.* v. *Stenacher,* 236 NY 312).

The contract between the plaintiff and Dr. Roe is such a contract. The contention that such enforcement of a private agreement not to disclose information received in confidence somehow offends the United States Constitution would seem to be disputed by implication in *Kewanee Oil Co.* v. *Bicron Corp.* (416 US 470). The cases cited by the defendants in support of their theory that First Amendment rights are somehow involved do not support their contention. *Time, Inc.* v. *Hill* (385 US 374) involves a right to publish a matter of general public interest. *New York Times Co.* v. *Sullivan* (376 US 254) involved the right to publish matters critical of, or even offensive to, public officials. Reliance on the defamation cases (*New York Times Co.* v. *Sullivan, supra; Garrison* v. *Louisiana,* 379 US 64; *Curtis Pub. Co.* v. *Butts,* 388 US 130; *St. Amant* v. *Thompson,* 390 US 727; *Gertz* v. *Robert Welch, Inc.,* 418 US 323; *Cox Broadcasting Corp.* v. *Cohn,* 420 US 469; *Time Inc.* v. *Firestone,* 424 US 448; *Chapadeau* v. *Utica Observer-Dispatch,* 38 NY2d 196) would appear to be misplaced. In none of them is a contractual duty to maintain a confidence involved. On the other hand, in *United States* v. *Marchetti* (466 F2d 1309, cert den 409 US 1063) an agreement by an agent of the Central Intelligence Agency not to disclose information acquired during his service with the agency was sufficient to enjoin the publication in a book by Marchetti of matter reasonably deemed by the CIA to be in violation of that contract.

The complaint alleges a cause of action for breach of privacy under sections 50 and 51 of the Civil Rights Law. These statutes have not been violated for the defendants did not use the plaintiff's "name, portrait or picture" in their book. We are not, of course, limited to the theory set forth in the complaint, but may consider any cause of action revealed by the pleadings and proof (*Diemer* v. *Diemer,* 8 NY2d 206) and can even amend the pleadings on the court's own motion after trial (*Princiotto* v. *Materdomini,* 45 AD2d 883). A motion to amend this cause of action has been granted and a cause of action for breach of privacy has been established—if such a cause of action is recognized in this State apart from the Civil Rights Law.

The expression "right of privacy" is not without confusion and has been applied to varying rights and causes of action. Among the cases cited by the plaintiff in support of its contention are *Roe* v. *Wade* (410 US 113), *Griswold* v. *Connecticut* (381 US 479) and *Drake* v. *Covington County Bd. of Educ.* (371 F Supp 974). In each of these cases there is a judicial recognition that the individual has rights of privacy which may not be infringed upon by a government. Such right of privacy, of course, is not involved in this litigation.

In *Nader* v. *General Motors Corp.* (25 NY2d 560, 572) a case decided under the law of the District of Columbia, Judge (now Chief Judge) BREITEL, in a concurring opinion, said that "scholars in trying to define the elusive concept of the right of privacy, have, as of the present, subdivided the common law right into separate classifications, most significantly distinguishing between unreasonable intrusion and unreasonable publicity (Restatement, 2d, Torts, Tent. Draft No. 13 [April 27, 1967], §§ 652A, 652B, 652D; Prosser, Torts [3d ed.], pp 832–837). This does not mean, however, that the classifications are either frozen or exhausted, or that several of the classifications may not overlap." The *Nader* case is a classic case of "unreasonable intrusion." At bar is a claim of "unreasonable publicity" (cf. *Time, Inc.* v. *Hill,* 385 US 374, *supra*).

Ever since *Roberson* v. *Rochester Folding Box. Co.* (171 NY 538), the courts of this State have held uniformly (cf. *Waters* v. *Moore,* 70 Misc 2d 372) that no cause of action for invasion of privacy will be recognized apart from that authorized by sections 50 and 51 of the Civil Rights Law. Only this year the Appellate Division, First Department, reaffirmed this view (*Wojtowicz* v. *Delacorte Press,* 58 AD2d 45).[8] Stated differently, to date there has not been recognized in this State a common-law right of privacy. The right of privacy urged here, however, is not a common-law right. The right of privacy with which we deal arises from two other sources: the public policy (discussed *supra*) of the State of New York proclaimed by statute (CPLR 4504, subd [a]; 4507, 4508; Education Law, §§ 6509-6511; Mental Hygiene Law, § 15.13, subds [c], [d]; § 35.11; Public Health Law, § 2803-c, subd 3, par f; § 2805-e, subd 3; § 3371; 8 NYCRR 60.1 [d] [3]) which bars a physician from disclosing a patient's confidences; and the implied promise of confidentiality which every physician makes to his patient. It is in this context that the Appellate Division, First Department, upheld and expanded the preliminary injunction previously granted in this case saying "[i]n light of the expanding recognition of invasion of privacy actions [citing cases] and in view of the confidentiality accorded the physician-patient relationship, we believe that plaintiff has alleged a cognizable claim for relief" (*Doe* v. *Roe,* 42 AD2d 559, 560).

Every patient, and particularly every patient undergoing psychoanalysis, has such a right of privacy. Under what circumstances can a person be expected to reveal sexual fantasies, infantile memories, passions of hate and love, one's most intimate relationship with one's spouse and others except upon the inferential agreement that such confessions will be forever entombed in the psychiatrist's memory, never to be revealed during the psychiatrist's lifetime or thereafter? The very needs of the profession itself require that confidentiality exist *and be enforced.* As pointed out in *Matter of Lifschutz* (2 Cal 3d 415, 421) "a large segment of the psychiatric profession concurs in Dr. Lifschutz's strongly held belief that an absolute privilege of confidentiality is essential to the effective practice of psychotherapy" (cf. Ann., 20 ALR3d 1109–

[8]It has been predicted (*Galella* v. *Onassis,* 487 F2d 986, 995) that the New York Court of Appeals, when again faced with the issue, will abandon *Roberson* v. *Rochester Folding Box Co.* (*supra*), but this case need not turn on such prediction.

1112). Despite the fact that in no New York case has such a wrong been remedied due, most likely, to the fact that so few physicians violate this fundamental obligation, it is time that the obligation not only be recognized but that the right of redress be recognized as well.

What label we affix to this wrong is unimportant (although the category of wrong could, under certain circumstances—such as determining the applicable Statute of Limitations—be significant). "'It is generally accepted that "There is no necessity whatever that a tort must have a name. New and nameless torts are being recognized constantly," (Prosser, Torts [2d ed.], p. 3.) What is important is that there must be the infliction of intentional harm, resulting in damage, without legal excuses or justification. (See *Aikens* v. *Wisconsin,* 195 U.S. 194, 204; *Rager* v. *McCloskey,* 305 N. Y. 75, 81; *Ruza* v. *Ruza,* 286 App. Div. 767, 769; *Knapp Engraving* v. *Keystone Photo,* [1 AD2d 170].)'" (*Morrison* v. *National Broadcasting Co.,* 24 AD2d 284, 291, quoting *Penn-Ohio Steel Corp.* v. *Allis-Chalmers Mfg. Co.,* 7 AD2d 441, 443-444.)

The defendants contend that the physician's obligation of confidentiality is not absolute and must give way to the general public interest. The interest, as they see it in this case, is the scientific value of the publication.

It is not disputed that under our public policy the right of confidentiality is less than absolute. The evidentiary statute itself (CPLR 4504, subd [a]) contains its own exceptions. Despite the duty of confidentiality courts have recognized the duty of a psychiatrist to give warning where a patient clearly presents a danger to others (*Tarasoff* v. *Regents of Univ. of Cal.,* 529 P2d 553, 555 [Sup Ct Cal], to disclose the existence of a contagious disease [P.H.L. 2101]; *Hoffmann* v. *Blackmon,* 241 So 2d 752 [Fla]; *Wojcik* v. *Aluminum Co. of Amer.,* 18 Misc 2d 740), to report the use of "controlled substances" in certain situations (Public Health Law, §§ 3355, 3373), and to report gunshot and other wounds (Penal Law, § 265.25). In no case, however, has the curiosity or education of the medical profession superseded the duty of confidentiality. I do not reach the question of a psychiatrist's right to publish case histories where the identities are fully concealed[9] for that is not our problem here, nor do I find it necessary to reach the issue of whether or not an important scientific discovery would take precedence over a patient's privilege of nondisclosure. I do not consider myself qualified to determine the contribution which this book may have made to the science or art of psychiatry. I do conclude, however, that if such contribution was the defendants' defense they have utterly failed in their proof that this volume represented a major contribution to scientific knowledge. The evidence is to the contrary and this defense must necessarily fail.

Nor is the argument available that by enjoining the further distribution of this book the court will be engaging in a "prior restraint" on publication. The Supreme Court long ago recognized that "liberty of speech, and of the press, is . . . not an absolute right, and the State may punish its abuse" (*Near* v. *Minnesota,* 283 US 697, 708). That the action contemplated here is not a "prior restraint" is clear. In *Kingsley Books*

[9]It is interesting to observe that a leading professional organization, The Group for the Advancement of Psychiatry, in its Report No. 45 [New York, NY, 1960] concurs in the conclusion that conflicts between ethical obligations and scientific advance must be resolved in favor of the ethical consideration. It said,

"When the psychiatrist describes the details of the life history of his patient, his job problems, et cetera, the possibility of recognition is very high.

"For this reason clinical data may have to be disguised with consequent impairment of the objective scientific value. Sometimes material may be so impossible to camouflage that it should not be published at all, in spite of its scientific value.

"Such ethical requirements take priority over research objectives."

v. *Brown* (354 US 436) Justice FRANKFURTER distinguished prior restraint from the situation at bar. Contrasting the unconstitutional statute in *Near* v. *Minnesota* (*supra*) with the New York statute (Code Crim Pro, § 22-a, now CPLR 6330), Justice FRANKFURTER said (p 445), "The two cases are no less glaringly different when judged by the appropriate criteria of constitutional law. Minnesota empowered its courts to enjoin the dissemination of future issues of a publication because its past issues had been found offensive. In the language of Mr. Chief Justice HUGHES, 'This is of the essence of censorship.' 283 U. S., at 713. As such, it was found unconstitutional. This was enough to condemn the statute wholly apart from the fact that the proceeding in *Near* involved not obscenity but matters deemed to be derogatory to a public officer. Unlike *Near*, § 22-a is concerned solely with obscenity and, as authoritatively construed, it studiously withholds restraint upon matters not already published and not yet found to be offensive."

There is no prior restraint in the case at bar. The book has been published and it does offend against the plaintiff's right of privacy, contractual and otherwise, not to have her innermost thoughts offered to all for the price of this book. There is no prior restraint and, therefore, no censorship within constitutional meaning.

As I have indicated in the separately filed findings of facts, the defense of laches is groundless. Publication occurred 10 years after Dr. Roe last discussed the book with the plaintiff, eight years after treatment stopped. As soon as the plaintiff heard of the impending publication, she protested, orally through a mutual friend and in writing through her attorney. Dr. Roe's evasive and misleading answer to the attorney should serve to still any claim of laches.

The liability of Dr. Roe to respond in damages is clear; and Mr. Poe's liability is equally clear. True, he and the plaintiff were not involved in a physician-patient relationship and he certainly had no contractual relationship to her. But, the conclusion is unassailable that Poe, like anyone else with access to the book, knew that its source was the patient's production in psychoanalysis. He knew as well as, and perhaps better than Roe, of the absence of consent, of the failure to disguise. If anyone was the actor in seeing to it that the work was written, that it was manufactured, advertised and circulated, it was Poe. He is a coauthor of the book and a willing, indeed avid, coviolator of the patient's rights and is therefore equally liable (*Hammonds* v. *Aetna Cas. & Sur. Co.*, 243 F Supp 793, *supra*).

The plaintiff seeks punitive damages and suggests that a proper measure of those damages, in addition to compensatory damage, is approximately $50,000, the sum plaintiff has thus far expended on and incurred for attorneys' fees. (Given the history of this action with appeals to the United States Supreme Court, it is reasonable to assume that she shall continue to incur expenses.) Under the English rule, an allowance of costs to the prevailing party includes attorneys' fees assessed by the court. Early in the judicial history of the United States, this country and nearly all if not all, jurisdictions within it, determined that except for extraordinary circumstances, attorneys' fees were not a proper element of costs unless provided for by statute. It has been held that in the Federal courts where jurisdiction is attained other than by diversity of citizenship, attorneys' fees may be awarded under general Federal equity jurisdiction where a losing litigant has acted "in bad faith, vexatiously, wantonly, or for oppressive reasons" (*Hall* v. *Cole*, 412 US 1, 5; to the same effect see *International Assn. of Machinists* v. *Texas Steel Co.*, 538 F2d 1116; *Vaughan* v. *Atkinson*, 369 US 527, 530; *Universal Oil Co.* v. *Root Refining Co.*, 328 US 575, 580; *Rich Co.* v. *Industrial Lbr. Co.*, 417 US 116, 129–130; see, contra, *Alyeska Pipeline Co.* v. *Wilderness Soc.*, 421

US 240, revg *Wilderness Soc.* v. *Morton,* 495 F2d 1026). It would appear that as punitive damages or otherwise, attorneys' fees are not available in this case there being no statutory authority providing for them. (*City of Buffalo* v. *Clement Co.,* 28 NY2d 241, 262-263.)

In order to warrant an award of punitive damages, it must have been affirmatively demonstrated that the wrong committed was willful and malicious, that the act complained of was "morally culpable or . . . actuated by evil and reprehensible motives not only to punish the defendant but to deter him as well as others" (*Walker* v. *Sheldon,* 10 NY2d 401, 404). Where the act complained of is willful, malicious and wanton, punitive damages are sometimes available to "express indignation at the defendants' wrong rather than a value set on plaintiff's loss" (*Gostowski* v. *Roman Catholic Church,* 262 NY 320, 324-325). Certainly, the acts of the defendants here are such as to warrant an expression of indignation and punishment for the purpose of deterring similar acts by these defendants or others. The difficulty, however, is that the defendants' acts were not willful, malicious or wanton—they were merely stupid. I have no doubt that the defendants were of the opinion that they had sufficiently concealed the identity of the plaintiff and her family. I have no doubt that in addition to the commercial success they hoped to have, they believed that they were rendering a public service in publishing what they considered an in depth description of the plaintiff's family. But there was no motive to harm. Under these circumstances, punitive damages are not available.

On turning to compensatory damages, we are confronted by the defendants' contention that the information concerning the book acquired by the plaintiff's university students and colleagues be excluded from consideration. They argue that these people acquired their information as a consequence of newspapers reporting the filing of this suit. They say, inferentially, that had plaintiff not brought this action she would have been spared that particular embarrassment, and therefore, having brought the action, she must bear its consequences.

This argument must be rejected for the same reason we reject the demand for attorneys' fees. An underlying principle of American law is that a person having a cognizable claim is entitled or even encouraged to pursue that claim in the courts and that which discourages a person from seeking redress, such as the imposition of substantial costs as a penalty for losing his suit, is rejected. (Cf. *Alyeska Pipeline Co.* v. *Wilderness Soc.,* 421 US, at p 251). So it is here. The plaintiff clearly had a meritorious cause of action and we encourage her to assert her rights. If a consequence of that assertion of rights was further damaging publicity, the loss must fall, not on the plaintiff, but on the defendants, whose conduct made this lawsuit necessary. The wrongful publication and not the commencement of suit was the proximate cause of the damage.

The plaintiff has suffered damage as a consequence of this publication. She suffered acute embarrassment on learning the extent to which friends, colleagues, employer, students and others, had read or read of the book. Her livelihood, as indicated in the findings, was threatened; but fortunately, the actual cash loss was only some $1,500. Medical attention, principally treatment with Dr. Lowenfeld, cost an additional $1,400. But beyond these sums the plaintiff suffered in health. She had insomnia and nightmares. She became reclusive as a consequence of the shame and humiliation induced by the book's publication and her well-being and emotional health were significantly impaired for three years. In my opinion the fair and reasonable value of the injury she sustained—to the extent it can be compensated in damages—is $20,000.

Damages, of course, do not provide an adequate remedy; for should the book circulate further, beyond the 220 copies already sold, the damage must accrue anew. The plaintiff is entitled to a judgment permanently enjoining the defendants, their heirs, successors and assigns from further violating the plaintiff's right to privacy whether by circulating this book or by otherwise disclosing any of the matters revealed by the plaintiff to Dr. Roe in the course of psychotherapy. On settlement of the judgment suggestions will be entertained concerning the disposition of any remaining volumes or parts thereof.

In re Lifschutz, 85 Cal.Rptr. 829, 2 Cal.3d 415, 467 P.2d 557 (1970)

TOBRINER, Justice.

Dr. Joseph E. Lifschutz, a psychiatrist practicing in California, seeks a writ of habeas corpus to secure his release from the custody of the Sheriff of the County of San Mateo. Dr. Lifschutz was imprisoned after he was adjudged in contempt of court for refusing to obey an order of the San Mateo County Superior Court instructing him to answer questions and produce records relating to communications with a former patient. Dr. Lifschutz contends that this underlying court order was invalid as unconstitutionally infringing his personal constitutional right of privacy, his right effectively to practice his profession, and the constitutional privacy rights of his patients. He also attacks the order, or more specifically, the statutory provisions which authorize the compulsion of his testimony in these circumstances, as unconstitutionally denying him the equal protection of the laws since, under California law, clergymen could not be compelled to reveal certain confidential communications under these circumstances.

The instant proceeding arose out of a suit instituted by Joseph F. Housek against John Arabian on June 3, 1968, for damages resulting from an alleged assault. Housek's complaint alleged that the assault caused him "physical injuries, pain, suffering and severe mental and emotional distress." Defendant Abrabian deposed the plaintiff and during the course of that deposition Housek stated that he had received psychiatric treatment from Dr. Lifschutz over a six-month period approximately 10 years earlier. Nothing in the record indicates that the plaintiff revealed the nature or contents of any conversation with or treatment by Dr. Lifschutz.

Arabian then subpenaed for deposition Dr. Lifschutz and all of his medical records relating to the treatment of Housek. (Code Civ.Proc. §§ 2016, 2019, subd. [a].) Although Dr. Lifschutz appeared for the deposition, he refused to produce any of his medical records and refused to answer any questions relating to his treatment of patients; the psychiatrist declined even to disclose whether or not Housek had consulted him or had been his patient. Although notified, neither plaintiff Housek nor his attorney were present at this deposition and neither has appeared in any of the subsequent hearings related to this proceeding. Housek has neither expressly claimed a psychotherapist-patient privilege, statutory or constitutional, nor expressly waived such a privilege.

In response to the psychiatrist's refusal to cooperate, defendant Arabian moved for an order of the superior court compelling the production of the subpenaed records and the answers to questions on deposition (Code Civ.Proc. § 2034, subd. [a]). Relying on the patient-litigant exception of section 1016 of the Evidence Code, the superior court determined that because the plaintiff, in instituting the pending litigation, had tendered as an issue his mental and emotional condition, the statutory psychotherapist-patient (Evid. Code, § 1014) privilege did not apply. On December 20, 1968, the court therefore ordered Dr. Lifschutz to comply with the subpena and to answer questions posed during deposition.[1] On January 15, 1969, defendant attempted to continue with the deposition of Dr. Lifschutz as ordered by the superior court, but petitioner remained resolute in his refusal to respond or produce records. Thereafter, petitioner sought a writ of prohibition to restrain the superior court from enforcing its order; the writ was denied by the Court of Appeal, a petition for hearing was denied by this court, and finally a petition for certiorari to the United States Supreme Court was similarly denied.

The superior court held another hearing on December 5, 1969; when Dr. Lifschutz again refused to comply with the order, the court adjudged him in contempt (Code Civ.Proc. § 1209, subd. 5)[2] and ordered him to be confined in the custody of the Sheriff of San Mateo County (Code Civ.Proc. § 1219). After the Court of Appeal on December 8, 1969, denied without opinion a petition for habeas corpus, this court agreed to hear the case and ordered the petitioner released on his own recognizance pending our determination of the cause.

Dr. Lifschutz presents a novel challenge, attempting to raise far-reaching questions of constitutional law. From the affidavits and correspondence included in the record we note that a large segment of the psychiatric profession concurs in Dr. Lifschutz's strongly held belief that an absolute privilege of confidentiality is essential to the effective practice of psychotherapy.

We recognize the growing importance of the psychiatric profession in our modern, ultracomplex society. The swiftness of change—economic, cultural, and moral—produces accelerated tensions in our society, and the potential for relief of such emotional disturbances offered by psychotherapy undoubtedly establishes it as a profession essential to the preservation of societal health and well-being. Furthermore, a growing consensus throughout the country, reflected in a trend of legislative enactments,[3]

[1]The order read in full: "The witness, Joseph E. Lifschutz, is hereby ordered to answer the questions involved in the taking of his deposition and to comply with the production requirements of the subpoena duces tecum issued in this proceeding (the declaration therefor being filed herein on October 11, 1968).

"The matter will be continued for 30 days during which time said JOSEPH E. LIFSCHUTZ will comply with this order at a time during said period agreed upon by the parties, or on proper notice in the absence of agreement.

"Motion for sanctions and attorney's fees denied."

[2]Section 1209, subdivision 5, provides: "The following acts or omissions in respect to a court of justice, or proceedings therein, are contempts of the authority of the court: . . . 5. Disobedience of any lawful judgment order, or process of the court: . . . ."

[3]Until 20 years ago, no statutes dealt specifically with the question of the privilege for psychotherapeutic communications; protection was available only under the terms of existing physician-patient privileges. Such privilege only applied to medical practitioners who fell within the terms of various state statutes; often psychiatrists were covered, but clinical psychologists, though using many of the same techniques of psychotherapy, were not. In the nineteen-fifties and sixties several states, responding to the demands of organized spokesmen of psychology, enacted new privilege statutes, often granting psychologist-patient communications much broader protection than was provided by existing physician-patient privileges. (See Ferster, "Statutory Summary of Physician-Patient Privileged Communication Laws" in Allen, Ferster & Ruben, Readings in Law & Psychiatry [1968] pp. 161-165.) In 1960 California enacted such a statute, providing: "[T]he confidential relations and communications between psychologist and client shall be placed upon the same basis as those provided by law between attorney and client. . . ." (Bus. & Prof.Code, § 2904 [since repealed].)

Although commentators who analyzed the need for a privilege in this specific area unanimously supported the position that greater protection be extended to communications of psychotherapeutic treatment (see, e.g., Louisell, The Psychologist in Today's Legal World: Part II [1957] 41 Minn.L.Rev. 731; Slovenko, Psychiatry and a Second Look at the Medical Privilege [1960] 6 Wayne L.Rev. 175), they pointed out the anomaly of affording more protection to patients of psychologists than to patients of psychiatrists, as most of the existing statutory schemes did. To eliminate this irrational distinction, California enacted the current psychotherapist-patient privilege (Evid.Code, § 1014) in 1965.

acknowledges that an environment of confidentiality of treatment is vitally important to the successful operation of psychotherapy. California has embraced this view through the enactment of a broad, protective psychotherapist-patient privilege.

The nature of the actual interests involved in this case can only be properly evaluated against the California statutory background. Although petitioner, in pressing for judicial acceptance of a genuine and deeply held principle, seeks to cast the issue involved in this case in the broadest terms, we must properly address, in reality, a question of more modest dimensions. We do not face the alternatives of enshrouding the patient's communication to the psychotherapist in the black veil of absolute privilege or of exposing it to the white glare of absolute publicity. Our choice lies, rather, in the grey area.

Properly viewed, the broadest issue before our court is whether the Legislature, in attempting to accommodate the conceded need of confidentiality in the psychotherapeutic process with general societal needs of access to information for the ascertainment of truth in litigation, has unconstitutionally weighted its resolution in favor of disclosure by providing that a psychotherapist may be compelled to reveal relevant confidences of treatment when the patient tenders his mental or emotional condition in issue in litigation. For the reasons discussed below, we conclude that, under a properly limited interpretation, the litigant-patient exception to the psychotherapist-patient privilege, at issue in this case, does not unconstitutionally infringe the constitutional rights of privacy of either psychotherapists or psychotherapeutic patients. As we point out, however, because of the potential of invasion of patients' constitutional interests, trial courts should properly and carefully control compelled disclosures in this area in the light of accepted principles.

I. *The order requiring Dr. Lifschutz to answer appropriate questions concerning communications with a patient does not infringe the psychotherapist's constitutional rights.*

The primary contention of Dr. Lifschutz's attack on the judgment of contempt consists of the assertion of a constitutional right of a psychotherapist to absolute confidentiality in his communications with, and treatment of, patients. Although, as we understand it, the alleged right draws its substance primarily from the psychological needs and expectations of patients. Dr. Lifschutz claims that the Constitution grants him an absolute right to refuse to disclose such confidential communications, regardless of the wishes of a patient in a particular case.[4] In separating the interest of the

[4]Although at numerous points in his legal argument, petitioner asserts that his challenge is raised on behalf of his patient's rights as well as his own, the facts of this case demonstrate that the psychotherapist's interests and the patient's wishes do not always coincide on this issue. (See also *Commonwealth ex rel. Romanowicz* v. *Romanowicz* [1968], 213 Pa.Super. 382, 248 A.2d 238, 240 [psychiatrist compelled to testify if patient so desires].) Although under circumstances in which a patient cannot easily or effectively affirm his own rights, a physician may be granted standing to assert the constitutional rights of his patients (see, e.g., *Griswold* v. *Connecticut* [1965] 381 U.S. 479, 481, 85 S.Ct. 1678, 14 L.Ed.2d 510), in the instant case the patient, whose rights Dr. Lifschutz presumably seeks to protect, is a party to the action, and had full opportunity to challenge the disclosures which have so far been sought but declined to do so. Under these facts it would be inappropriate to find that Dr. Lifschutz could assert his patient's constitutional rights.

Moreover, petitioner has himself asserted that although the constitutional interests of his patient are inextricably involved, the constitutional right that he claims is a right of psychotherapists. At the contempt proceeding petitioner's attorney stated: "[F]rankly, I am very pleased that the particular patient, the plaintiff Housek, has taken no part in these proceedings because it presents the issue with perfect clarity. We are not on anyone's side here. We're just on the side of the doctor and medicine itself, because he is saying that no matter what the patient wants to do—. . . . Now what I'm saying is that a doctor has an independent duty to all of his patients not to let any patient make him violate his oath that he has given to all patients at once. So it is his own privilege. . . ."

psychotherapist from that of the patient for the purposes of analyzing this contention, we conclude that the compelled disclosure of relevant information obtained in a confidential communication does not violate any constitutional privacy rights of the psychotherapist.

Petitioner founds his far-reaching constitutional claim on the United States Supreme Court decision of *Griswold* v. *Connecticut, supra,* 381 U.S. 479, 85 S.Ct. 1678. In *Griswold* the court struck down a state criminal statute prohibiting the use of contraceptives as an unconstitutional infringement of a marital right of privacy. Although, as we explain in section III, infra, the *Griswold* decision is relevant to an evaluation of the general scope of permissible intrusions into confidential relations between a patient and a psychotherapist, the decision does not support Dr. Lifschutz's claim for a constitutional right independent of the rights of individual patients.

Dr. Lifschutz apparently seeks support for his position in the fact that the defendants in *Griswold* were a licensed physician and the head of a birth control clinic who had counselled married couples on the use of contraceptives, rather than the married individuals themselves. The *Griswold* court quite explicitly explained, however, that the constitutional privacy interests and rights underlying its decision were those of the "patients" of the birth control clinic, rather than of physicians. "We think that appellants have standing to raise *the constitutional rights of the married people* with whom they had a professional relationship. . . . *The rights of husband and wife,* pressed here, are likely to be diluted or adversely affected unless those rights are considered in a suit involving those who have this kind of confidential relation to them." (Italics added.) (381 U.S. at p. 481, 85 S.Ct. at p. 1679.)[5] It is the depth and intimacy of the *patients'* revelations that give rise to the concern over compelled disclosure; the psychotherapist, though undoubtedly deeply involved in the communicative treatment, does not exert a significant privacy interest separate from his patient.[6] We cannot accept petitioner's reliance on the *Griswold* decision as establishing broad constitutional privacy rights of psychotherapists.

In addition to his claim as to a "right of privacy," petitioner urges that the provisions of the Evidence Code requiring a psychotherapist to reveal confidential matters under some circumstances unconstitutionally impair the practice of his profession. This position rests on two distinct legal contentions: first, that the impairment is so severe as to constitute an unconstitutional "taking" of a valuable property right, the doctor's right to practice psychotherapy; and second, that compelled disclosure of any psychotherapeutic communication renders the continued practice of psychotherapy impossible and thus unconstitutionally constricts the realm of available medical treatment. Although psychotherapists should, of course, be entitled to the constitutional protections requisite to the right to practice their profession (see *Yakov* v. *Board of Medical Examiners* [1968] 68 Cal.2d 67, 75, 64 Cal.Rptr. 785, 435 P.2d 553), we doubt that the disclosure involved here goes so far as to constitute the claimed unconstitutional deprivation of that right.

[5]Since the *Griswold* defendants' "criminal" activities included the general dissemination of information concerning contraceptives and birth control, it has been persuasively argued that the convictions may have contravened the First Amendment rights of the individual physician-defendants. (See, e.g., Dixon, The Griswold Penumbra: Constitutional Charter For an Expanded Law of Privacy [1965] 64 Mich.L.Rev. 197, 213.) The Supreme Court, however, chose not to address that problem.

[6]Indeed, in many instances a patient may desire to have a psychotherapist testify as to confidential communications. (See, e.g., *Hampton* v. *Hampton* [1965] 241 Or. 277, 405 P.2d 549.) The granting of petitioner's broad contention could foreclose access to psychotherapeutic sessions even when the patient has no desire to preserve his "privacy."

Insofar as petitioner's argument rests on the economic loss that psychotherapists may suffer as a result of the disclosure requirement, his position runs contra to the current trend of constitutional adjudication involving the regulation of economic interests. Legal requirements prescribing mandatory disclosure of confidential business records are of course regular occurrences (see, e.g., *Shapiro* v. *United States* [1948] 335 U.S. 1, 32-33, 68 S.Ct. 1375, 92 L.Ed. 1787; *Hickman* v. *Taylor* [1947] 329 U.S. 495, 511-513, 67 S.Ct. 385, 91 L.Ed. 451; *In re Sidebotham* [1938] 12 Cal.2d 434, 436, 85 P.2d 453), and although all compelled disclosures may interfere to some extent with an individual's performance of his work, such requirements have been universally upheld so long as the compelled disclosure is reasonable in light of a related and important governmental purpose. (E.g., *Greyhound Corp.* v. *Superior Court* [1961] 56 Cal.2d 355, 394, 15 Cal.Rptr. 90, 364 P.2d 266.) In order to facilitate the ascertainment of truth and the just resolution of legal claims, the state clearly exerts a justifiable interest in requiring a businessman to disclose communications, confidential or otherwise, relevant to pending litigation. (Cf., e.g., *Wilson* v. *United States* [1911] 221 U.S. 361, 372-376, 31 S.Ct. 538, 55 L.Ed. 771; *Blair* v. *United States* [1919] 250 U.S. 273, 279-282, 39 S.Ct. 468, 63 L.Ed. 979.) Although we appreciate, as petitioner suggests, that because of the peculiar nature of psychotherapy, the debilitating effect of disclosure is particularly acute, the incidental infringement of the psychotherapist's economic interest in such practice does not succumb to constitutional challenge so long as the circumstances of disclosure are properly confined to serve a legitimate governmental interest. (Cf. *Day-Brite Lighting, Inc.* v. *Missouri* [1952] 342 U.S. 421, 423-424, 72 S.Ct. 405, 96 L.Ed. 469; *Nebbia* v. *New York* [1934] 291 U.S. 502, 537, 54 S.Ct. 505, 78 L.Ed. 940.) Moreover, because, as we explain below, the patient-litigant exception at issue involves only that special instance in which a patient has chosen to forego the confidentiality of the privilege, we question whether the deterrence of patients and the impairment to the practice of psychotherapy will be as great as petitioner anticipates.

The second basis of petitioner's contention raises a more serious problem. Petitioner claims that if the state is authorized to compel disclosure of some psychotherapeutic communications, psychotherapy can no longer be practiced successfully.[7] He asserts that the unique nature of psychotherapeutic treatment, involving a probing of the patient's subconscious thoughts and emotions, requires an environment of total confidentiality and absolute trust. Petitioner claims that unless a psychotherapist can truthfully assure his patient that all revelations will be held in strictest confidence and never disclosed, patients will be inhibited from participating fully in the psychotherapeutic process and proper treatment will be impossible. Petitioner concludes that the patient-litigant exception involved here conflicts with the preservation of an environment of absolute confidentiality and unconstitutionally constricts the field of medical practice.

Petitioner's argument, resting as it does on assertions of medical necessity, exemplifies the type of question to which the judiciary brings little expertise. Although

[7]Petitioner's contention that the recognition of a privilege is necessary to the preservation of a given occupation or profession is by no means unique to psychotherapy. In the past, organized occupational groups of journalists, accountants, and social workers, among others, have sought the establishment of a legal privilege and have proclaimed, on principle, that required revelation of information received in confidence would mean the destruction of their calling. (See generally, 8 Wigmore, Evidence [McNaughton rev. 1961] § 2286, pp. 532-537.) In many instances such organized groups have been able to convince state legislatures of the wisdom of their position and as a result statutory privileges have been created; the broad psychotherapist-patient privilege enacted in California is such an example.

petitioner has submitted affidavits of psychotherapists who concur in his assertion that total confidentiality is essential to the practice of their profession, we cannot blind ourselves to the fact that the practice of psychotherapy has grown, indeed flourished, in an environment of a non-absolute privilege. No state in the country recognizes as broad a privilege as petitioner claims is constitutionally compelled.[8] Whether psychotherapy's development has progressed only because patients are ignorant of the existing legal environment can only be a matter for speculation; psychotherapists certainly have been aware of the limitations of their recognized privilege for some time. (See, e.g., Hollender, Privileged Communication and Confidentiality [1965] 26 Diseases of the Nervous System 169 [paper and round table discussion]; Sidel, Confidential Information and the Physician [1961] 264 New England J. of Med. 1133, 1136.)

Petitioner's broad assertion, moreover, overlooks the limited nature of the intrusion into psychotherapeutic privacy actually at issue in this case. As we explain more fully in part III infra, the patient-litigant exception of section 1016 of the Evidence Code compels disclosure of only those matters which the patient himself has chosen to reveal by tendering them in litigation. We do not know, of course, to what extent patients are deterred from seeking psychotherapeutic treatment by the knowledge that if, at some future date, they choose to place some aspect of their mental condition in issue in litigation, communications relevant to that issue may be revealed. We can only surmise that an understanding of the limits of section 1016, and the realization that the patient retains control over subsequent disclosure, may provide a measure of reassurance to the prospective patient.

The statutory provisions challenged here do not attempt to narrow the scope of psychotherapeutic treatment, by proscribing, for example, the discussion of certain subjects (cf. *Poe* v. *Ullman* [1961] 367 U.S. 497, 513-515, 81 S.Ct. 1752, 6 L.Ed.2d 989 [Douglas, J., dissenting] [state statute barring advice on the use of contraceptives]). Instead, the provisions are intended to serve the important state interest of facilitating the ascertainment of truth in legal proceedings. Although petitioner argues that, as a matter of social as well as medical policy, the benefits to be derived from a broadening of the existing privilege would outweigh the detriments resulting from a narrowing of evidence available in litigation, the balancing of those alternatives remains with the Legislature.

II. *The presence of a legislatively created absolute clergyman-penitent privilege does not render the absence of such an absolute psychotherapist-patient privilege a denial of equal protection.*

Section 1034 of the Evidence Code provides that: "a clergyman . . . has a privilege to refuse to disclose a penitential communication if he claims the privilege"; the code provides no exceptions to the clergyman-penitent privilege comparable to the numerous exceptions to the psychotherapist-patient privilege. (See Evid.Code, §§ 1016-1026.) Petitioner contends that the Legislature, in so distinguishing between clergymen and psychotherapists, has denied psychotherapists the equal protection of the laws in violation of the Fourteenth Amendment.

The potential range of confidential communications spans a large area: a conducive

[8]Indeed, only six states have any laws specifically granting to the psychiatric relationship any special protection, over and above that given to medical communications generally. (See Slawson, Patient-Litigant Exception: Hazard to Psychotherapy [1969] 21 Arch.Gen.Psychiat. 347, 348.)

environment for such communications may be produced by numerous social (marriage), business (attorney-client), medical (physician-patient), or spiritual (clergyman-penitent) settings. Although the preservation of each of these varied relationships compels some measure of confidentiality, the differing degrees of nondisclosure essential to the relationship and the value of preserving the particular confidential aspect involved, has led states to adopt a variety of different kinds of privileges. The distinction drawn in the California Evidence Code between clergymen and participants in other privileged communications parallels the distinction recognized in the 44 states that have established a distinct clergyman-penitent or ''priest-penitent'' privilege. (See generally, 8 Wigmore, Evidence, supra, § 2395, at pp. 873-877, and Supp. at pp. 53-54.)

Petitioner maintains, however, that, given the purpose of the clergyman-penitent privilege, the distinction between clergymen and psychotherapists cannot stand. Dr. Lifschutz characterizes the ''modern'' purpose of the clergyman-penitent privilege as fostering a ''sanctuary for the disclosure of emotional distress'': as so characterized, relevant distinctions between clergymen and psychotherapists do diminish. Petitioner's portrayal of the clergyman-penitent privilege, however, while perhaps identifying one of the supporting threads of the statutory provision, does not reflect a complete analysis of the foundation of the privilege.

Realistically, the statutory privilege must be recognized as basically an explicit accommodation by the secular state to strongly held religious tenets of a large segment of its citizenry. As the Law Revision Commission Comment accompanying the adoption of California's current privilege explains: ''At least one underlying reason seems to be that the law will not compel a clergyman to violate—nor punish him for refusing to violate—the tenets of his church which require him to maintain a secrecy as to confidential statements made to him in the course of his religious duties.'' Wigmore, in his treatise, similarly relates the purpose of the privilege in a question and answer format: ''Does the penitential relation deserve recognition and countenance? In a state where toleration of religion exists by law, and where a substantial part of the community professes a religion practising a confessional system, this question must be answered in the affirmative.'' (8 Wigmore, Evidence, *supra,* § 2396 at p. 878; see also Stoyles, The Dilemma of the Constitutionality of the Priest-Penitent Privilege—The Application of the Religion Clauses [1967] 29 U.Pitt.L.Rev. 27, 51.)

Recognizing that the toleration of religious beliefs and practices forms the basis for this privilege, we cannot say that the Legislature acted irrationally in granting the privilege to clergymen and not to psychotherapists. Although in some circumstances clergymen and psychotherapists perform similar functions and serve similar needs, fundamental and significant differences remain. While many psychotherapists are no doubt strongly committed to the ''tenets'' of their profession,[9] as indeed Dr. Lifschutz has exhibited by his determined action in the instant proceeding, the source of this

[9]We note that this court has not been apprised of any present, established ''tenet'' of the medical profession that would be violated by petitioner's compliance with the order of the trial court. Section 9 of the ''Principles of Medical Ethics'' adopted by the American Medical Association, which petitioner submitted to the trial court, proclaims: ''A physician may not reveal the confidences entrusted to him in the course of medical attendance, or the deficiencies he may observe in the character of patients, *unless he is required to do so by law* or unless it becomes necessary in order to protect the welfare of the individual or of the community.'' (Italics added.) Although there has been some criticism of this present principle (see, e.g., Sidel, Confidential Information and the Physician, supra, 264 New England J. of Med. 1133), we are not aware of any modification of the ''official'' principle of confidentiality.

commitment can be reasonably distinguished from the distinctive religious conviction out of which the penitential privilege flows.

We have no occasion in the instant case to address the contention, which petitioner obliquely proffers, that because of its "accommodation of religion" purpose, the clergyman-penitent privilege itself frames an unconstitutional establishment of religion. Petitioner does not seek to compel disclosure of a penitential communication, nor will he achieve any benefit from a decision invalidating the statutory privilege. Under these circumstances this court cannot properly comment on this potentially difficult constitutional question.[10]

III. *Under the facts of this case petitioner could assert no statutory authority to refuse to comply with requested disclosures.*

Although, as we have discussed above, Dr. Lifschutz on his own behalf can claim no constitutional privilege to avoid disclosure, he may in some circumstances assert the statutory privilege of his patient.[11] Evidence Code, section 1012 recognizes communications between patient and psychotherapist, diagnosis by the psychotherapist, and advice given during the therapy relationship as privileged communications. Section 1015 provides that: "[t]he psychotherapist who received or made a communication subject to the privilege whenever he is present when the communication is sought to be disclosed and is authorized to claim the privilege under subdivision (c) of Section 1014." Section 1014, subdivision (c), indicates that the psychotherapist cannot claim the privilege of the patient "if there is no holder of the privilege in existence or if he is otherwise instructed by a person authorized to permit disclosure." The record in the present case shows no express instructions from plaintiff Housek directing Dr. Lifschutz to decline the privilege against disclosure. Thus, under Evidence Code, section 1015 Dr. Lifschutz could generally assert the privilege of his patient to prevent disclosure of privileged communications.

The psychotherapist, however, cannot assert his patient's privilege if that privilege has been waived or if the communication in question falls within the statutory exceptions to the privilege. Evidence Code, section 912, subdivision (a), provides that: "... the right of any person to claim a privilege provided by Section ... 1014 (psychotherapist-patient privilege) ... is waived with respect to a communication protected by such privilege if any holder of the privilege, without coercion, has disclosed a significant part of the communication or has consented to such disclosure made by anyone. Consent to disclosure is manifested by any statement or other conduct of the holder of the privilege indicating his consent to the disclosure, including his failure to claim the privilege in any proceeding in which he has the legal standing and opportunity to claim the privilege."

Since Housek, the holder of the privilege (see Evid.Code, § 1013), disclosed at a prior deposition that he had consulted Dr. Lifschutz for psychiatric treatment, he has waived whatever privilege he might have had to keep such information confidential. (Cf. *In re Kaplan* [1960] 8 N.Y.2d 214, 203 N.Y.S.2d 836, 168 N.E.2d 660.)

[10]See generally, Stoyles, The Dilemma of the Constitutionality of the Priest-Penitent Privilege—The Application of the Religion Clauses, supra, 29 U.Pitt.L.Rev. 27.

[11]The statutory privilege established in section 1014 of the Evidence Code is a privilege of the patient, not of the psychotherapist. (Evid.Code, § 1013; cf. *City and County of San Francisco* v. *Superior Court* [1951] 37 Cal.2d 227, 233, 231 P.2d 26.)

The questions posed to Dr. Lifschutz, however, have inquired only into whether he treated Mr. Housek, and whether he possessed records regarding this patient. Defendant has not yet asked Dr. Lifschutz about the nature of his treatment of the plaintiff, his diagnosis, or the content of any communication. Certainly, in admitting the existence of a psychotherapist-patient relationship, plaintiff has not disclosed "a significant part of the communication" (Evid.Code, § 912) between himself and Dr. Lifschutz so as to waive his right subsequently to claim the privilege as to other elements of the communication.

Defendant contended in the superior court, however, that *any* communication between the plaintiff and Dr. Lifschutz has lost its privileged status because the plaintiff has filed a personal injury action in which he claims recovery for "mental and emotional distress." Defendant relies on section 1016 of the Evidence Code, the patient-litigant exception to the psychotherapist-patient privilege, which provides that: "[t]here is no privilege under this article as to a communication relevant to an issue concerning the mental or emotional condition of the patient if such issue has been tendered by: (a) the patient. . . ." To avoid the necessity for further contempt proceedings or delaying appellate review in the instant case, we have considered whether defendant has accurately identified the proper reach of the patient-litigant exception.

As we explain more fully below, the patient-litigant exception allows only a limited inquiry into the confidences of the psychotherapist-patient relationship, compelling disclosure of only those matters directly relevant to the nature of the specific "emotional or mental" condition which the patient has voluntarily disclosed and tendered in his pleadings or in answer to discovery inquiries. Furthermore, even when confidential information falls within this exception, trial courts, because of the intimate and potentially embarrassing nature of such communications, may utilize the protective measures at their disposal to avoid unwarranted intrusions into the confidences of the relationship.

In interpreting this exception we are necessarily mindful of the justifiable expectations of confidentiality that most individuals seeking psychotherapeutic treatment harbor. As has been aptly pointed out by Judge Edgerton in *Taylor* v. *United States* (1955) 95 U.S.App.D.C. 373, 222 F.2d 398, 401 (quoting from Guttmacher, M., et al., Psychiatry and the Law [1952] p. 272), "The psychiatric patient confides more utterly than anyone else in the world. He exposes to the therapist not only what his words directly express; he lays bare his entire self, his dreams, his fantasies, his sins, and his shame. Most patients who undergo psychotherapy know that this is what will be expected of them, and that they cannot get help except on that condition. . . . It would be too much to expect them to do so if they knew that all they say—and all that the psychiatrist learns from what they say—may be revealed to the whole world from a witness stand."

We believe that a patient's interest in keeping such confidential revelations from public purview, in retaining this substantial privacy, has deeper roots than the California statute and draws sustenance from our constitutional heritage. In *Griswold* v. *Connecticut, supra,* 381 U.S. 479, 484, 85 S.Ct. 1678, 1681, 14 L.Ed.2d 510, the United States Supreme Court declared that "Various guarantees [of the Bill of Rights] create zones of privacy," and we believe that the confidentiality of the psychotherapeutic session falls within one such zone. (Cf. *People* v. *Belous* (1969) 71 A.C. 996, 1005-1006, 80 Cal.Rptr. 354, 458 P.2d 194.) Although *Griswold* itself involved only the marital relationship, the open-ended quality of that decision's rationale evidences its far-reaching dimension. (See generally, Dixon, The Griswold Penumbra: Constitutional Charter for An Expanded Law of Privacy, *supra,* 64 Mich.L.Rev. 197.)[12] Indeed, the decision's concern for valued aspects of individual privacy may ultimately aid in protecting man from the dehumanization of an ever-encroaching technological environment. The retention of a degree of intimacy in interpersonal relations and communications lies at the heart of the broad rationale of *Griswold;* the opinion itself significantly followed the teachings of *NAACP* v. *Alabama ex rel. Patterson* (1958) 357 U.S. 449, 78 S.Ct. 1163, 2 L.Ed.2d 1488 which struck down a state statute requiring an association to disclose its membership list as an unconstitutional impingement upon the members' rights of privacy and anonymity. (Cf. *Talley* v. *California* [1960] 362 U.S. 60, 80 S.Ct. 536, 4 L.Ed.2d 559.)

Even though a patient's interest in the confidentiality of the psychotherapist-patient relationship rests, in part, on constitutional underpinnings, all state "interference" with such confidentiality is not prohibited. In section 1016 we do not deal with a provision which seeks to proscribe the association of psychotherapist and patient entirely,[13] but instead we encounter a provision carefully tailored to serve the historically important state interest of facilitating the ascertainment of truth in connection with legal proceedings. (See, e.g., *Blair* v. *United States* [1919] 250 U.S. 273, 279-281, 39 S.Ct. 468, 63 L.Ed. 979; *Wilson* v. *United States* [1911] 221 U.S. 361, 372-373, 31 S.Ct. 538, 55 L.Ed. 771; *Blackmer* v. *United States* [1932] 284 U.S. 421, 52 S.Ct. 252, 76 L.Ed. 375.)[14] In the past this state interest has been viewed as substantial enough to compel the disclosure of a great variety of confidential material. (See, e.g., *Chronicle Pub. Co.* v. *Superior Court* [1960] 54 Cal.2d 548, 574, 7 Cal.Rptr. 109, 354 P.2d 637; *Green* v. *Superior Court* [1963] 220 Cal.App.2d 121, 33 Cal.Rptr. 604; *Tatkin* v. *Superior Court* [1958] 160 Cal.App.2d 745, 753-754, 326 P.2d 201; *Garland* v. *Torre* [2d Cir. 1958] 259 F.2d 545, 548-549, cert. den. 358 U.S. 910, 79 S.Ct. 237, 3 L.Ed.2d 231.) Moreover, since the exception compels disclosure only in cases in which the patient's own action initiates the exposure, "intrusion" into a patient's privacy remains essentially under the patient's control. As such, we find no constitutional infirmity in it.

Although no previous cases have arisen under the patient-litigant exception to the psychotherapist-patient privilege, decisions applying an analogous exception to the physician-patient privilege[15] have identified two distinct grounds for the exception.

[12]The breadth of the principles of privacy and individual freedom recognized in *Griswold* is illustrated by the variety of the cases which have subsequently embraced that decision's conclusions. (See, e.g., *Stanley* v. *Georgia* [1969] 394 U.S. 557, 564, 89 S.Ct. 1243, 22 L.Ed.2d 542 [right to view all books and films in the privacy of one's home]; *Roberts* v. *Clement* [E.D.Tenn.1966] 252 F.Supp. 835, 848 [Darr, J., concurring] [right to practice nudism in private]; *Finot* v. *Pasadena City Board of Education* [1967] 250 Cal.App.2d 189, 197-198, 58 Cal.Rptr. 520 [right of adult teacher to wear beard]; cf. *Jessin* v. *County of Shasta* [1969] 274 A.C.A. 810, 821, 79 Cal.Rptr. 359 [right to obtain voluntary sterilization].)

[13]Cf. *Roberts* v. *Clement, supra,* 252 F.Supp. 835, 849 (Darr, J., concurring) (state statute prohibiting the practice of nudism unconstitutional under *Griswold*).

[14]The justification for compelling disclosure of relevant psychotherapeutic communications when the patient himself has raised an issue of his mental condition has been recognized even by commentators who are strongly in favor of broadening the current psychotherapist-patient privilege. Two "model" psychotherapist-patient privilege acts, drafted by such proponents, have included a provision recognizing a patient-litigant exception. (See Model Psychotherapist-Patient Privilege [1968] 4 Harv.J.Legis. 307, 322; Fisher, The Psychotherapeutic Profession and the Law of Privileged Communication [1964] 10 Wayne L.Rev. 609, 644.)

[15]The present patient-litigant exception to the physician-patient privilege (Evid. Code, § 996) which parallels the exception to the psychotherapist-patient privilege precisely, superseded section 1881, subdivision 4, of

First, the courts have noted that the patient, in raising the issue of a specific ailment or condition in litigation, in effect dispenses with the confidentiality of that ailment and may no longer justifiably seek protection from the humiliation of its exposure.[16] Second, the exception represents a judgment that, in all fairness, a patient should not be permitted to establish a claim while simultaneously foreclosing inquiry into relevant matters.[17] As we explained in *City and County of San Francisco* v. *Superior Court, supra,* 37 Cal.2d 227, 232, 231 P.2d 26, 28 (the *Catton* case), "The whole purpose of the [physician-patient] privilege is to preclude the humiliation of the patient that might follow disclosure of his ailments. When the patient himself discloses those ailments by bringing an action in which they are in issue, there is no longer any reason for the privilege. The patient-litigant exception precludes one who has placed in issue his physical condition from invoking the privilege on the ground that disclosure of his condition would cause him humiliation. He cannot have his cake and eat it too."

Although defendant reads the above quoted language of the *Catton* case as implying that the patient-litigant exception contemplates an automatic, complete waiver of privilege whenever a patient institutes a claim for any physical or mental injury, we find nothing in either the rationale of the exception as explained in the *Catton* case, or in the cases applying the exception,[18] to justify the breadth of this description. In previous physician-patient privilege cases the exception has been generally applied only to compel disclosure of medical treatment and communication concerning the very injury or impairment that was the subject matter of the litigation.[19] There is certainly nothing to suggest that in the context of the more liberal psychotherapist-patient privilege this exception should be given a broader reading.[20]

---

the Code of Civil Procedure, the initial patient-litigant exception enacted in 1917 and the section under which most of the relevant case law arose. Section 1881, subdivision 4, limited the physician-patient privilege by providing: "[W]here any person brings an action to recover damages for personal injuries, such action shall be deemed to constitute a consent by the person bringing said action that any physician who has prescribed for or treated said person and *whose testimony is material in said action* shall testify." (Italics added.)

[16]See *Moreno* v. *New Guadalupe Mining Co.* (1917) 35 Cal.App. 744, 755, 170 P. 1088, 1092 ("clearly a patient should not be permitted to describe—'at length to the jury in a crowded courtroom the details of his supposed ailment and then neatly suppress the available proof of his falsities by wielding a weapon, nominally termed a privilege.' [4 Wigmore, § 2389, p. 3360.]").

[17]Cf. *Koump* v. *Smith* (1969) 25 N.Y.2d 287, 294, 303 N.Y.S.2d 858, 864, 250 N.E. 2d 857 ("A party should not be permitted to assert a mental or physical condition in seeking damages or in seeking to absolve himself from liability and at the same time assert the privilege in order to prevent the other party from ascertaining the truth of the claim and the nature and extent of the injury or condition."); *Schlagenhauf* v. *Holder* (1964) 379 U.S. 104, 126, 85 S.Ct. 234, 13 L.Ed. 2d 152 (Douglas, J., dissenting); 4 Harv. J.Legis. 307, 323, *supra.*

[18]See, e.g., *Phillips* v. *Powell* (1930) 210 Cal. 39, 42, 290 P. 441, 443 ("Pursuant to the provisions of section 1881, subdivision 4, of the Code of Civil Procedure, the bringing of the action to recover damages for personal injuries constitutes a waiver of the privilege, provided the testimony is material to the issues"); *San Francisco Unified Sch. Dist.* v. *Superior Court* (1961) 55 Cal.2d 451, 454, 11 Cal.Rptr. 373, 375, 359 P.2d 925, 927 ("when the patient himself discloses *those ailments* by bringing an action in which they are in issue, there is no longer any reason for the privilege." [Italics added.]).

[19]For example, in *Ballard* v. *Pacific Greyhound Lines* (1946) 28 Cal.2d 357, 360, 170 P.2d 465, the plaintiff, injured in a bus accident, had consulted a physician concerning the injuries she sustained therein. When the patient later sued the bus company for damages, the court permitted the defendant to examine the physician concerning the injuries of which plaintiff complained, finding the patient-litigant exception directly applicable. (Accord, *San Francisco Unified Sch. Dist.* v. *Superior Court, supra,* 55 Cal.2d 451, 454, 11 Cal.Rptr. 373, 374, 359 P.2d 925, 926 [exception applicable to doctor who had been consulted "to diagnose and treat [the plaintiff] for the injuries for which recovery is now sought"].)

[20]Our reliance on precedents rendered in the context of the physician-patient privilege is not intended to suggest that authorities involving the physician-patient privilege will always be helpful in resolving issues concerning the psychotherapist-patient privilege. In the past the physician-patient privilege has been the

If the provision had as broad an effect as is suggested by petitioner, it might effectively deter many psychotherapeutic patients from instituting any general claim for mental suffering and damage out of fear of opening up all past communications to discovery. This result would clearly be an intolerable and overbroad intrusion into the patient's privacy, not sufficiently limited to the legitimate state interest embodied in the provision and would create opportunities for harassment and blackmail.

In light of these considerations, the "automatic" waiver of privilege contemplated by section 1016 must be construed not as a complete waiver of the privilege but only as a limited waiver concomitant with the purposes of the exception. Under section 1016 disclosure can be compelled only with respect to *those mental conditions* the patient-litigant has "disclose[d] . . . by bringing an action in which *they* are in issue" (*City and County of San Francisco* v. *Superior Court, supra,* 37 Cal.2d 227, 232, 231 P.2d 26); communications which are not directly relevant to those specific conditions do not fall within the terms of section 1016's exception and therefore remain privileged. Disclosure cannot be compelled with respect to other aspects of the patient-litigant's personality even though they may, in some sense, be "relevant" to the substantive issues of litigation.[21] The patient thus is not obligated to sacrifice all privacy to seek redress for a specific mental or emotional injury; the scope of the inquiry permitted depends upon the nature of the injuries which the patient-litigant himself has brought before the court.

In some situations, the patient's pleadings may clearly demonstrate that his entire mental condition is being placed in issue and that records of past psychotherapy will clearly be relevant. Thus in *In re Cathey* (1961) 55 Cal.2d 679, 12 Cal.Rptr. 762, 361 P.2d 426, for example, a mental patient confined in a prison hospital sought release contending, inter alia, that he was not a "dangerous" or "violent" individual as the state mental health officials asserted; when the officials offered Cathey's medical records to substantiate their position, he claimed such records were privileged. This court, analogizing the facts before it to those of the patient-litigant exception to the physician-patient privilege,[22] found that "petitioner himself caused his mental condi-

---

subject of rather severe criticism (see, e.g., Chafee, Privileged Communications: Is Justice Served or Obstructed by Closing the Doctor's Mouth on the Witness Stand? [1943] 52 Yale L.J. 607; 8 Wigmore, Evidence, *supra,* § 2380a, at pp. 828-832), and in response the application of the privilege has been limited in a variety of circumstances (see, e.g., Evid. Code, §§ 998, 999, 1007). The psychotherapist-patient privilege, on the other hand, won legislative recognition in the face of legal antipathy toward privileges generally (see Louisell, The Psychologist in Today's Legal World: Part II, *supra,* 41 Minn.L.Rev. 731, 731-732); the Legislature acknowledged that the unique nature of psychotherapeutic treatment required and justified a greater degree of confidentiality than was legally afforded other medical treatment (see Legislative Committee Com. to Evid.Code, § 1014). Even commentators who concurred in the criticism of the general physician-patient privilege noted that the psychotherapeutic privilege rested on a much sounder basis and supported its adoption. (See, e.g., Louisell, *supra,* at pp. 740-746.) The differences that exist between these two medically oriented privileges caution against blind application of the precedents of the physician-patient privilege in future psychotherapist-patient privilege cases.

[21]Thus in the instant case, for example, defendant would not be authorized to undertake an examination of psychotherapeutic communications to determine if the plaintiff has ever exhibited aggressive tendencies or had other personal attributes that might be related to the assault. The plaintiff has not disclosed such elements of his mental condition merely by instituting an action for damages resulting from an assault and thus the exception of section 1016 is not applicable. (Cf. *Carlton* v. *Superior Court* [1968] 261 Cal.App.2d 282, 289-290, 67 Cal.Rptr. 568, 68 Cal.Rptr. 469; *Koump* v. *Smith, supra,* 25 N.Y.2d 287, 294, 299, 303 N.Y.S.2d 858, 864, 868-869, 250 N.E.2d 857.)

[22]The present psychotherapist-patient privilege was not yet enacted at the time *Cathey* was decided. Because the then existing statutory "patient-litigant" exception was, by its terms, limited to personal injury actions, the court reached its decision by analogy rather than by direct application of a statutory provision.

tion to be put in issue by his applications for habeas corpus and the averments of his briefs. . . .'' (55 Cal.2d at p. 691, 12 Cal.Rptr. at p. 768, 361 P.2d at p. 432.) In such a case, section 1016 will of course be applicable.

In other cases, however, the determination of the specific ''mental condition'' in issue may present more complex problems. The difficulties involved in analyzing the applicability of the exception in the instant case may be illustrative. The plaintiff's complaint, containing the typical allegations of ''mental and emotional distress'' arising out of a physical assault, does not specifically identify the nature of the ''mental or emotional condition'' at issue. In incorporating this allegation in his complaint, plaintiff obviously neither disclosed his entire medical history if treatment for mental or emotional conditions nor realistically waived his interest in maintaining the confidentiality of that treatment. The generality of the claim, however, does create the possibility that some feature of plaintiff's psychological history will be directly relevant to the determination of whether his emotional or mental distress can be properly attributed to the alleged assault. Although we doubt that the 10-year-old therapeutic treatment sought to be discovered from Dr. Lifschutz would be sufficiently relevant to a typical claim of ''mental distress'' to bring it within the exception of section 1016, we cannot determine from the present state of the record whether plaintiff's ''mental and emotional'' distress is merely the ''normal'' distress experienced as a result of physical assault or whether it includes unusual or particularly serious elements upon which prior history may be directly relevant.

Because only the patient, and not the party seeking disclosure, knows both the nature of the ailments for which recovery is sought and the general content of the psychotherapeutic communications, the burden rests upon the patient initially to submit some showing that a given confidential communication is not directly related to the issue he has tendered to the court. (Cf.Evid.Code, § 404 [person claiming privilege against incrimination bears burden of showing proffered evidence might tend to incriminate him].) A patient may have to delimit his claimed ''mental or emotional distress'' or explain, in general terms, the object of the psychotherapy[23] in order to illustrate that it is not reasonably probable that the psychotherapeutic communications sought are directly relevant to the mental condition that he has placed in issue. In determining whether communications sufficiently relate to the mental condition at issue to require disclosure, the court should heed the basic privacy interests involved in the privilege (cf. *Wiesenberger* v. *W. E. Hutton & Co.* [S.D.N.Y.1964] 35 F.R.D. 556, 557–558); in general, the statutory psychotherapist-patient privilege ''[is to] be liberally construed in favor of the patient.'' (Cf. *Carlton* v. *Superior Court, supra,* 261 Cal.App.2d 282, 288, 67 Cal.Rptr. 568, 572, 68 Cal.Rptr. 469; *Newell* v. *Newell* [1956] 146 Cal.App.2d 166, 177, 303 P.2d 839.)

Even when the confidential communication is directly relevant to a mental condition tendered by the patient, and is therefore not privileged, the codes provide a variety of protections that remain available to aid in safeguarding the privacy of the patient.

[23]Although ordinarily a patient cannot be required to disclose privileged information in order to claim the privilege (Evid. Code, § 915, subd. [a]), because the privileged status of psychotherapeutic communications under the patient-litigant exception depends upon the *content* of the communication, a patient may have to reveal some information about a communication to enable the trial judge to pass on his claim of irrelevancy. Upon such revelation, the trial judge should take necessary precautions to protect the confidentiality of these communications; for example, he might routinely permit such disclosure to be made *ex parte* in his chambers. (Compare the procedure suggested in Evid.Code, § 915, subd. [b].) (See also Developments in the Law—Discovery [1964] 74 Harv.L.Rev. 940, 1017–1018.)

When inquiry into the confidential relationship takes place before trial during discovery, as in the instant case, the patient or psychotherapist may apply to the trial court for a protective order to limit the scope of the inquiry or to regulate the procedure of the inquiry so as to best preserve the rights of the patient. Section 2019, subdivision (b), subsection (1), of the Code of Civil Procedure grants the court broad discretion to issue "any . . . order which justice requires to protect the party or witness from annoyance, embarrassment or oppression." Section 2019, subdivision (b), subsection (1), specifically enumerates a number of protective orders that might be particularly helpful to a patient-litigant. For example, the section provides that, upon good cause shown, the court may direct that at the oral deposition[24] "[1] certain matters shall not be inquired into or [2] that the scope of the examination shall be limited to certain matters, books, [or] documents, . . . or [3] that the examination shall be held with no one present except the parties to the action and their . . . counsel, or [4] that after being sealed the deposition shall be opened only by order of the court. . . ." (Bracketed numbers added.) (See *Chronicle Pub. Co.* v. *Superior Court, supra,* 54 Cal.2d 548, 575, 7 Cal.Rptr. 109, 354 P.2d 637; cf. *Reynolds Metals Co.* v. *Yturbide* [9th Cir. 1958] 258 F.2d 321, 333, cert. den. 358 U.S. 840, 79 S.Ct. 66, 3 L.Ed.2d 76.) Such a protective order may be sought at any time during the deposition, and, in appropriate cases, the trial court may issue such an order on its own motion. (Code Civ.Proc. § 2019, subd. [d].)

When the questioning of the psychotherapist or patient as to confidential communications occurs at the trial itself, the danger of publicity and embarrassment is increased. Of course, unless the information sought is directly relevant to the issue as revealed by the evidence at trial, the communication is privileged and no disclosure can be compelled. Moreover, as with any evidence, the court retains discretion to "exclude evidence if its probative value is substantially outweighted by the probability that its admission will . . . (b) create substantial danger of undue prejudice, ..." (Evid.Code, § 352.)[25] In this area, the careful exercise of this discretion is necessary to provide substantial protection for the patient's legitimate interests;[26] without this element of court supervision intensive examinations of psychotherapists and patients may often ultimately result in substantially more harm than benefit.

In sum, we conclude that no constitutional right enables the psychotherapist to assert an absolute privilege concerning all psychotherapeutic communications. We do not believe the patient-psychotherapist privilege should be frozen into the rigidity of absolutism. So extreme a conclusion neither harmonizes with the expressed legislative intent nor finds a clear source in constitutional law. Such an application would lock the patient into a vice which would prevent him from waiving the privilege without the

[24]Although section 2019, subdivision (b), only applies to oral deposition, other discovery sections specifically provide that similar protective orders can be obtained to limit inquiries sought under their discovery devices. (See § 2020, subd. [d]; § 2030, subd. [b]; § 2033, subd. [a].)

[25]Necessary information will often be accessible without delving deeply into specific intimate factual circumstances and such searching probes ought to be avoided whenever possible. The psychotherapist's general conclusions about specific emotional symptoms will often suffice to convey the needed information while preserving the patient's dignity and interest in privacy.

[26]The draftsmen of two separate versions of "model" legislation in this field each suggested that only a "conditional" patient-litigant exception be adopted; under this suggestion, disclosure would be compelled only upon a finding of the court that it would be in "the best interests of justice." (See Fisher, The Psychotherapeutic Profession and the Law of Privileged Communications, *supra,* 10 Wayne L.Rev. 609, 644; Model Psychotherapist-Patient Privilege, *supra,* 4 Harv. J.Legis. 307, 322.) Similar protection can be afforded under the California statutory scheme through a sensitive exercise of the trial court's discretionary authority.

psychotherapist's consent. The question whether such a ruling would have the medical merit claimed by petitioner must be addressed to the Legislature; we can find no basis for such a ruling in legal precedent or principle.

Furthermore, the existence of a broad statutory privilege in clergymen does not deny psychotherapists the equal protection of the laws. Finally, although we recognize the legitimacy and importance of the concern over governmentally sanctioned intrusions into a patient's psychotherapeutic history, the patient-litigant exception, as properly limited, does not necessarily entail an overbroad intrusion into the patient's privacy.

Inasmuch as plaintiff had already disclosed that he had consulted Dr. Lifschutz for psychotherapeutic treatment, petitioner could not properly have refused to answer at least that question concerning the communications; since neither plaintiff nor the psychotherapist has as yet made any claim that the subpenaed records are not directly relevant to the specific "mental and emotional" injuries for which plaintiff is claiming relief, Dr. Lifschutz had no right to refuse to produce the records. Thus the trial court's order requiring the production of records and the answering of questions was valid; the trial court properly adjudged Dr. Lifschutz in contempt of court for intentionally violating that valid court order.[27]

The order to show cause is discharged and the petition for writ of habeas corpus is denied.

MOSK, Acting C.J., MCCOMB, PETERS, BURKE, and SULLIVAN, J.J., and *MOLINARI, J. pro tem., concur.

Limitations on the applicability of the rule of confidentiality. Professionals' ethical codes have generally taken cognizance of a duty to breach confidentiality under extraordinary conditions. For example, in the Hippocratic Oath the sentence that intimates that disclosure of doctor-patient communications is appropriate under some circumstance goes "whatsoever I see or hear in my attendance on the sick, *which ought not to be noised abroad,* I will keep silence thereon" (emphasis ours). The Oath contains no clarification about what "ought not to be noised abroad." Equally ambiguous is the line in the code of ethics of the American Medical Association that goes, "Confidence . . . should never be revealed unless the law requires it or if necessary to

[27]At oral argument petitioner raised the additional argument that the civil contempt provisions of section 1219 of the Code of Civil Procedure, providing that an individual who is in contempt because of his "omission to perform an act which is yet in [his] power . . . to perform" may be confined until he performs the act, constitutes "cruel and unusual" punishment as applied to him. Petitioner contends that the application of the section will result in life imprisonment if the doctor refuses to betray his professional convictions. The short answer to petitioner's complaint is that civil contempt, as contrasted with criminal contempt, has traditionally been viewed as non-punitive, for its purpose is only to compel compliance with a lawful order of the court; petitioner, key to his jail cell in pocket (see *Uphaus* v. *Wyman* [1960] 364 U.S. 388, 404, 81 S.Ct. 153, 5 L.Ed.2d 148 [Douglas, J., dissenting]), can secure his own release at any time by following the court order. Confinement until compliance, under civil contempt, has universally been upheld as consistent with constitutional strictures. (See, e.g., *Shillitani* v. *United States* [1966] 384 U.S. 364, 370, 86 S.Ct. 1531, 16 L.Ed.2d 622; *Uphaus* v. *Wyman* [1959] 360 U.S. 72, 81 82, 79 S.Ct. 1040, 3 L.Ed.2d 1090.) Furthermore, petitioner misjudges the possible duration of his confinement; he can only be confined so long as the underlying litigation remains alive. (Cf. *Shillitani* v. *United States, supra,* 384 U.S. 364, 371-372, 86 S.Ct. 1531.) When the trial is concluded or the litigation is otherwise terminated, imprisonment for civil contempt must cease. (See *Ex parte Rowe* [1857] 7 Cal. 175, 177; cf. *Morelli* v. *Superior Court* [1969] 1 Cal.3d 328, 332, 82 Cal.Rptr. 375, 461 P.2d 655.)

*Assigned by the Chairman of the Judicial Council.

protect the welfare of individuals or the community.'' The code of ethics of the American Psychological Association specifies that safeguarding confidential information is a ''primary obligation'' of psychologists but one that may be breached ''after most careful deliberation and when there is clear and imminent danger to an individual or to society.'' It can therefore be surmised that professionals by and large do not disagree with the spirit of decisions such as *Tarasoff;* they disagree with the idea of being legally—as opposed to ethically—mandated to reveal confidential communications under certain circumstances. Such a feeling seems at least to run through the tone of one psychiatrist's comments on the opinion in *Tarasoff:*

> It is with a sense of despair that one reads the opinion and recognizes that the increasing manifest violence in our world today has persuaded one of our nation's most distinguished courts to create standards of practice and procedures that ally the psychotherapist more with the goal of protecting society that with that of healing patients. It is not that psychiatrists reject the need to counterbalance these functions; in fact, most psychiatrists attempt to fulfill both responsibilities. However, we have done so with procedures that have not mandated us to routinely perform a duty that is counter to our powers of prescience. (Gurevitz, 1977)

Short of the duty to warn endangered third parties of their peril, there are a variety of situations in which courts have upheld practitioners' decisions to breach confidentiality when such a breach occurred in good faith, on a proper occasion, and with a legitimate interest to be furthered by the divulgence of the information. Illustrative of such a situation is *Clark* v. *Geraci,* 29 Misc.2d 791, 208 N.Y.S.2d 560 (Sup.Ct. 1960), which appears below, a case in which the defendant psychiatrist divulged, in response to an official request for information as to the plaintiff's condition, that the plaintiff suffered from a drinking problem. Soon thereafter the plaintiff was fired from his civilian position as an accountant for the United States Air Force. The court rejected the plaintiff's argument that the mere divulgence of the confidential matter had caused his dismissal. The court also held the practitioner's duty to the United States government to be above that of the duty to the patient.

Further discussion of exceptions to the usual rules of confidentiality and privilege appear herein in the following chapter in the section on defamation (page 394). Note that complaints alleging breach of confidentiality as a cause of action frequently concurrently allege related causes of action such as defamation and invasion of privacy.

Clark v. *Geraci,* 29 Misc.2d 791, 208 N.Y.S.2d 564 (Sup.Ct. 1960)

BENJAMIN BRENNER, J. Plaintiff, an accountant, long in the civilian employ of the United States Air Force, was discharged therefrom following receipt of a letter addressed to it by his doctor, the defendant, which established that plaintiff's absences were due to alcoholism. The doctor had alerted plaintiff that the letter was requested by the Air Force because the underlying cause of plaintiff's illness had not been set out in prior medical certificates issued by him in behalf of the plaintiff to explain such absences. The formal notice of discharge listed plaintiff's repeated absences, recited the doctor's letter and rejected plaintiff's attempt to attribute the absences to a series of misfortunes. It is plaintiff's contention that he requested the doctor not to send the letter, that his discharge was due directly to it and that he could not find permanent employment thereafter.

On trial plaintiff urged three theories of action: (1) that in mailing the letter the doctor committed an unlawful act which constituted malpractice for the reason that it divulged a confidential communication; (2) that even if the mailing of the letter were lawful it is actionable for prima facie tort in that it was deliberately sent against plaintiff's specific plea that it be withheld, and (3) that the contents of the letter were untrue and thus gave rise to an action in negligence.

A doctor is indeed a confidante of medical information and knowledge that come to him while treating his patient. Dr. Geraci learned that plaintiff had taken to drink as a means of meeting his social problems. He repeatedly treated him for asthmatic bronchitis and respiratory infections which were the ill effects thereof. His disclosure of that information is defined as unprofessional conduct by section 30 of article 2 of the Regulations of the Commissioner of Education, made pursuant to the Education Law:

"4. 'Unprofessional conduct [in the practice of medicine' shall include but not be] limited to the following: . . .

"(c). The revealing of facts, data, or information obtained in a professional capacity relating to a patient or his records without first obtaining consent of the patient or his duly authorized representative, except if duly required by a court of competent jurisdiction." (N. Y. Off. Comp. of Codes, Rules & Regulations [13th Suppl.], p. 407.)

He is, by another statute, specifically enjoined from giving evidence of such information when called upon to testify as a witness (Civ. Prac. Act, § 352). So, while no principle of common law is violated (Wigmore, Evidence [3d ed.], § 2380), disclosure is plainly reprehensible as indicated by the statutory law in this State, accepted usage and the Hippocratic oath, for information possessed by the doctor of the illness of his patient has long been thought of as a protected professional confidence upon which every patient may rely.

Yet I have been unable to discover, nor have the parties brought to my attention, any New York case dealing with the subject, apart from the giving of testimony in an action at law. Other jurisdictions have recognized that a disclosure may be actionable. (*Berry* v. *Moench,* 8 Utah2d 191; *Simonsen* v. *Swenson,* 104 Neb. 224; *Smith* v. *Driscoll,* 94 Wash. 441.) I believe that the cause should also be recognized in this State because the duty of secrecy is implied by our statutory law and widely conceived in the doctor-patient relationship.

It is, however, the doctor's claim that he had an overriding duty to make a disclosure of the underlying cause of plaintiff's illnesses and absences when required by a military unit of the United States Government so to do, especially since he had previously supplied incomplete information. The delicate balance of conflicting duties must thus be weighed (*Berry* v. *Moench, supra; Simonsen* v. *Swenson, supra*) to determine the doctor's paramount duty. Was the duty to divulge the employee's weakness, which conceivably could be used to rid the Government of a worthless servant and thereby save public funds, greater than the duty to maintain a confidential professional communication?

Had the disclosure risen to the level of a need to safeguard the security of the Government or the safety of the public, as in a case of a disclosure of a communicable disease (*Simonsen* v. *Swenson, supra*), it would, of course, be quite simple to find that the doctor's duty to disclose overrode his duty to remain silent. In view of the prior incomplete medical certificates requested by the plaintiff and supplied by the doctor to explain the former's absences, it may similarly be said that his right, if not duty to his Government, to make a full disclosure of the facts superseded his duty to the patient to remain silent.

This leads directly to the issue of waiver. The prior requested medical certificates not only set forth the *fact* of illness but described plaintiff's trouble to have consisted of ailments without disclosure that many of them, such as the bronchial and respiratory difficulties, were due to alcoholism. These requested certificates constituted plaintiff's waiver of the privilege at least as to those illnesses which were described. The question is, assuming it to be true that plaintiff had specifically requested the doctor not to dispatch the letter, whether, having previously asked for and permitted incomplete disclosures as to the *nature* of his illness, such waiver of privilege could be limited or terminated. If section 352 of the Civil Practice Act were directly applicable and the privilege even partially waived as to testimony upon trial, we know that such waiver would be complete and not thereafter subject to termination, restriction or qualification. (*Apter* v. *Home Life Ins. Co.*, 266 N. Y. 333.) The plaintiff knew that the nature of his illness had been set out in the certificates requested by him but he insists that the underlying cause thereof, namely alcoholism, could not legally be disclosed. He not only waived the disclosure of the secret to the extent that they told of the effects of his habitual inebriation, but was aware that the certificates were true only as far as they went. Having placed the doctor in the position of telling but part of the truth, he is estopped from preventing his divulging the remainder. In the circumstances there could be no qualification, limitation or termination of the waiver.

The second theory of action is that regardless of the lawful character of the disclosure, the same constituted a prima facie tort because it was deliberately and willfully made with knowledge that it would bring about plaintiff's discharge.

Prima facie tort arose out of the dictum enunciated in *Mogul S.S. Co.* v. *McGregor* (23 Q.B.D. 598, 613, affd. [1892] A.C. 25) that "intentionally to do that which is calculated in the ordinary course of events to damage, and which does, in fact, damage another in that other person's property or trade, is actionable if done without just cause or excuse." The doctrine was espoused by Mr. Justice HOLMES who said "*prima facie*, the intentional infliction of temporal damage is a cause of action, which . . . requires a justification if the defendant is to escape." (*Aikens* v. *Wisconsin,* 195 U.S. 194.) The theory of prima facie tort was accepted in New York (*Beardsley* v. *Kilmer,* 236 N.Y. 80) if the sole motivation for the acts complained of were the intent to harm the plaintiff. And in *Al Raschid* v. *News Syndicate Co.* (265 N.Y. 1, 4) the court said: "Even a lawful act done solely out of malice and illwill to injure another may be actionable." Intent to harm and not merely intent to do the act (*Ruza* v. *Ruza,* 286 App.Div. 767) seems to be one of the necessary ingredients of prima facie tort. And if there be justification the action does not lie. In *Beardsley* v. *Kilmer* (*supra*) the malicious character of the act was required to be unmixed and exclusive to render a lawful act unlawful. So in *Reinforce, Inc.*, v. *Birney* (308 N.Y. 164) it was said that even if the motivation be mixed there may be sufficient justification though there is some intent to do harm.

The court must weigh the conflicting interests of the public and the private parties (*Brandt* v. *Winchell,* 3 N.Y.2d 628) to determine if an otherwise lawful act has become unlawful or if there be justification, even if the motives are malevolent.

The evidence produced upon trial is overwhelmingly in favor of the defendant that even if the letter caused the discharge the doctor intended no harm. Certainly the doctor's act was justified by reason of his concept of duty to his Government. No malice could be attributed to him but even if some intent to do harm was part of his motivation, it was so mixed with thoughts of right and duty as to exonerate him. In any event, there is nothing in the evidence to contradict the doctor's testimony that he felt compelled to make a full breast of the matter and that the letter was sent under the justifiable belief that it was a communication needed by the Government. Thus reasonable self-interest is alone justification sufficient to bar the suit based upon prima facie tort (*Spivak* v. *Delma Studios,* 15 Misc.2d 760).

The third basis for the claim is that the doctor was negligent because the letter set forth more than was required and that it was in fact untruthful. A statement of part of the truth may be evidence of lack of care; not so, as here, a narration of the whole truth, for only less than all the facts tend to mislead. Moreover, one cannot be charged with telling more than is required when he is specificially asked to do so to clear up doubtful information previously supplied. Nor are the statements of the fact of alcoholism and periods of depression untrue and actionable because they differ from prior statements of respiratory and bronchial illness when the causes and effects are thereby explained.

In addition to the legal bars to plaintiff's suit is the overwhelming proof that plaintiff's discharge was due essentially to his absences and not to the disclosure. While the formal notice of discharge did make reference to the doctor's letter and pointed out that it contradicted plaintiff's attempted explanation for his absences, it is clear on plaintiff's own testimony, that the Air Force gave him further opportunity to improve his attendance record even after the letter had been received—an opportunity which plaintiff apparently failed to satisfy, as shown by his continued absences thereafter. It is for the reasons stated that judgment for the defendant was directed.

Affirmative duty to warn. The privileged status of information deriving from physician-patient, attorney-client, and related communications within the context of a special relationship is not absolute. As Justice Tobriner put it with reference to the status of psychotherapist-patient communications in *In re Lifschutz,* "We do not face the alternatives of enshrouding the patient's communications to the psychotherapist in the black veil of absolute privilege or of exposing it to the white glare of publicity. Our choice lies, rather, in the grey area." The Supreme Court of California ventured into that "grey area," so to speak, four years later in its holding in *Tarasoff* v. *Regents of University of California,* 17 Cal.3d 425, 131 Cal.Rptr. 14, 551 P.wd 334 (1976), which appears below. In that case the issues concerning the psychotherapist's duty to the patient versus the duty to society at large were discussed at length. The court concluded that the psychotherapist is obliged to keep communications confidential "unless . . . disclosure is necessary to avert danger to others." In the words of Justice Tobriner, "[P]rotective privilege ends where the public peril begins."

Subsequent to *Tarasoff,* a California court dealing with a case that involved a suicide, did not apply the duty-to-warn rule. In *Bellah* v. *Greenson,* 181 Cal.App.3d 614, 146 Cal.Rptr. 535 (1978), which appears below, the court noted that suicide was not equivalent to impending danger of violent assault on the public. The court held confidentiality to be of the utmost importance in effecting treatment of suicidal persons in ruling that no duty to warn the decedent's parents existed. The court stated: "We conclude that *Tarasoff* v. *Regents* requires only that a therapist disclose the contents of a confidential communication where the risk to be prevented thereby is the danger of violent assault and not where the risk of harm is self-inflicted harm" (citations omitted).

Tarasoff v. *Regents of University of California*, 13 Cal.3d 425, 131 Cal.Rptr. 14, 551 P.2d 334 (1976)

TOBRINER, Justice.

On October 27, 1969, Prosenjit Poddar killed Tatiana Tarasoff.[1] Plaintiffs, Tatiana's parents, allege that two months earlier Poddar confided his intention to kill Tatiana to Dr. Lawrence Moore, a psychologist employed by the Cowell Memorial Hospital at the University of California at Berkeley. They allege that on Moore's request, the campus police briefly detained Poddar, but released him when he appeared rational. They further claim that Dr. Harvey Powelson, Moore's superior, then directed that no further action be taken to detain Poddar. No one warned plaintiffs of Tatiana's peril.

Concluding that these facts set forth causes of action against neither therapists and policemen involved, nor against the Regents of the University of California as their employer, the superior court sustained defendants' demurrers to plaintiffs' second amended complaints without leave to amend.[2] This appeal ensued.

Plaintiffs' complaints predicate liability on two grounds: defendants' failure to warn plaintiffs of the impending danger and their failure to bring about Poddar's confinement pursuant to the Lanterman-Petris-Short Act (Welf. & Inst.Code, § 5000ff.) Defendants, in turn, assert that they owed no duty of reasonable care to Tatiana and that they are immune from suit under the California Tort Claims Act of 1963 (Gov.Code, § 810ff.).

We shall explain that defendant therapists cannot escape liability merely because Tatiana herself was not their patient. When a therapist determines, or pursuant to the standards of his profession should determine, that his patient presents a serious danger of violence to another, he incurs an obligation to use reasonable care to protect the intended victim against such danger. The discharge of this duty may require the therapist to take one or more of various steps, depending upon the nature of the case. Thus it may call for him to warn the intended victim or others likely to apprise the victim of the danger, to notify the police, or to take whatever other steps are reasonably necessary under the circumstances.

In the case at bar, plaintiffs admit that defendant therapists notified the police, but argue on appeal that the therapists failed to exercise reasonable care to protect Tatiana in that they did not confine Poddar and did not warn Tatiana or others likely to apprise

[1]The criminal prosecution stemming from this crime is reported in *People* v. *Poddar* (1974) 10 Cal.3d 750, 111 Cal.Rptr. 910, 518 P.2d 342.

[2]The therapist defendants include Dr. Moore, the psychologist who examined Poddar and decided that Poddar should be committed; Dr. Gold and Dr. Yandell, psychiatrists at Cowell Memorial Hospital who concurred in Moore's decision; and Dr. Powelson, chief of the department of psychiatry, who countermanded Moore's decision and directed that the staff take no action to confine Poddar. The police defendants include Officers Atkinson, Brownrigg and Halleran, who detained Poddar briefly but released him; Chief Beall, who received Moore's letter recommending that Poddar be confined; and Officer Teel, who, along with Offiier Atkinson, received Moore's oral communication requesting detention of Poddar.

her of the danger. Defendant therapists, however, are public employees. Consequently, to the extent that plaintiffs seek to predicate liability upon the therapists' failure to bring about Poddar's confinement, the therapists can claim immunity under Government Code section 856. No specific statutory provision, however, shields them from liability based upon failure to warn Tatiana or others likely to apprise her of the danger, and Government Code section 820.2 does not protect such failure as an exercise of discretion.

Plaintiffs therefore can amend their complaints to allege that, regardless of the therapists' unsuccessful attempt to confine Poddar, since they knew that Poddar was at large and dangerous, their failure to warn Tatiana or others likely to apprise her of the danger constituted a breach of the therapists' duty to exercise reasonable care to protect Tatiana.

Plaintiffs, however, plead no relationship between Poddar and the police defendants which would impose upon them any duty to Tatiana, and plaintiffs suggest no other basis for such a duty. Plaintiffs have, therefore, failed to show that the trial court erred in sustaining the demurrer of the police defendants without leave to amend.

2. *Plaintiffs can state a cause of action against defendant therapists for negligent failure to protect Tatiana.*

The second cause of action can be amended to allege that Tatiana's death proximately resulted from defendants' negligent failure to warn Tatiana or others likely to apprise her of her danger. Plaintiffs contend that as amended, such allegations of negligence and proximate causation, with resulting damages, establish a cause of action. Defendants, however, contend that in the circumstances of the present case they owed no duty of care to Tatiana or her parents and that, in the absence of such duty, they were free to act in careless disregard of Tatiana's life and safety.

In analyzing this issue, we bear in mind that legal duties are not discoverable facts of nature, but merely conclusory expressions that, in cases of a particular type, liability should be imposed for damage done. As stated in *Dillon* v. *Legg* (1968) 68 Cal.2d 728, 734, 69 Cal.Rptr. 72, 76, 441 P.2d 912, 916: "The assertion that liability must . . . be denied because defendant bears no 'duty' to plaintiff 'begs the essential question—whether the plaintiff's interests are entitled to legal protection against the defendant's conduct. . . . [Duty] is not sacrosanct in itself, but only an expression of the sum total of those considerations of policy which lead the law to say that the particular plaintiff is entitled to protection.' (Prosser, Law of Torts [3d ed. 1964] at pp. 332-333.)"

In the landmark case of *Rowland* v. *Christian* (1968) 69 Cal.2d 108, 70 Cal.Rptr. 97, 443 P.2d 561, Justice Peters recognized that liability should be imposed "for an injury occasioned to another by his want of ordinary care or skill" as expressed in section 1714 of the Civil Code. Thus, Justice Peters, quoting from *Heaven* v. *Pender* (1883) 11 Q.B.D. 503, 509 stated: "whenever one person is by circumstances placed in such a position with regard to another . . . that if he did not use ordinary care and skill in his own conduct . . . he would cause danger of injury to the person or property of the other, a duty arises to use ordinary care and skill to avoid such danger."

We depart from "this fundamental principle" only upon the "balancing of a number of considerations"; major ones "are the foreseeability of harm to the plaintiff, the degree of certainty that the plaintiff suffered injury, the closeness of the connection between the defendant's conduct and the injury suffered, the moral blame attached to the defendant's conduct, the policy of preventing future harm, the extent of the burden to the defendant and consequences to the community of imposing a duty to exercise care with resulting liability for breach, and the availability, cost and prevalence of insurance for the risk involved.''[4]

The most important of these considerations in establishing duty is foreseeability. As a general principle, a ''defendant owes a duty of care to all persons who are foreseeably endangered by his conduct, with respect to all risks which make the conduct unreasonably dangerous.'' (*Rodriguez* v. *Bethlehem Steel Corp.* [1974] 12 Cal.3d 382, 399, 115 Cal.Rptr. 765, 776, 525 P.2d 669, 680; *Dillon* v. *Legg, supra,* 68 Cal.2d 728, 739, 69 Cal.Rptr. 72, 441 P.2d 912; *Weirum* v. *R.K.O. General, Inc.* [1975] 15 Cal.3d 40, 123 Cal.Rptr. 468, 539 P.2d 36; see Civ.Code, § 1714.) As we shall explain, however, when the avoidance of foreseeable harm requires a defendant to control the conduct of another person, or to warn of such conduct, the common law has traditionally imposed liability only if the defendant bears some special relationship to the dangerous person or to the potential victim. Since the relationship between a therapist and his patient satisfies this requirement, we need not here decide whether foreseeability alone is sufficient to create a duty to exercise reasonably care to protect a potential victim of another's conduct.

Although, as we have stated above, under the common law, as a general rule, one person owed no duty to control the conduct of another[5] (*Richards* v. *Stanley* [1954] 43 Cal.2d 60, 65, 271 P.2d 23; *Wright* v. *Arcade School Dist.* [1964] 230 Cal.App.2d 272, 277, 40 Cal.Rptr. 812; Rest.2d Torts [1965] § 315), nor to warn those endangered by such conduct (Rest.2d Torts, *supra,* § 314, com. c.; Prosser, Law of Torts [4th ed. 1971] § 56, p. 341), the courts have carved out an exception to this rule in cases in which the defendant stands in some special relationship to either the person whose conduct needs to be controlled or in a relationship to the foreseeable victim of that conduct (see Rest.2d Torts, *supra,* §§ 315–320). Applying this exception to the present case, we note that a relationship of defendant therapists to either Tatiana or Poddar will suffice to establish a duty of care; as explained in section 315 of the Restatement Second of Torts, a duty of care may arise from either ''(a) a special relation . . . between the actor and the third person which imposes a duty upon the actor to control the third person's conduct, or (b) a special relation . . . between the actor and the other which gives to the other a right of protection.''

Although plaintiffs' pleadings assert no special relation between Tatiana and defendant therapists, they establish as between Poddar and defendant therapists the special relation that arises between a patient and his doctor or psychotherapist.[6] Such a rela-

[3]Omitted (this and some subsequent footnotes have been omitted for the sake of brevity).

[4]See *Merrill* v. *Buck* (1962) 58 Cal.2d 552, 562, 25 Cal.Rptr. 456, 375 P.2d 304; *Biakanja* v. *Irving* (1958) 49 Cal.2d 647, 650, 320 P.2d 16; *Walnut Creek Aggregates Co.* v. *Testing Engineers Inc.* (1967) 248 Cal.App.2d 690, 695, 56 Cal.Rptr. 700.

[5]This rule derives from the common law's distinction between misfeasance and nonfeasance, and its reluctance to impose liability for the latter. (See Harper and Kime, *The Duty to Control the Conduct of Another* [1934] 43 Yale L.J. 886, 887.) Morally questionable, the rule owes its survival to ''the difficulties of setting any standards of unselfish service to fellow men, and of making any workable rule to cover possible situations where fifty people might fail to rescue. . . .'' (Prosser, Torts [4th ed. 1971] § 56, p. 341.) Because of these practical difficulties, the courts have increased the number of instances in which affirmative duties are imposed not by direct rejection of the common law rule, but by expanding the list of special relationships which will justify departure from that rule. (See Prosser, *supra,* § 56, at pp. 348–350.)

[6]The pleadings establish the requisite relationship between Poddar and both Dr. Moore, the therapist who treated Poddar, and Dr. Powelson, who supervised that treatment. Plaintiffs also allege that Dr. Gold personally examined Poddar, and that Dr. Yandell, as Powelson's assistant, approved the decision to arrange Poddar's commitment. These allegations are sufficient to raise the issue whether a doctor–patient or

tionship may support affirmative duties for the benefit of third persons. Thus, for example, a hospital must exercise reasonable care to control the behavior of a patient which may endanger other persons.[7] A doctor must also warn a patient if the patient's condition or medication renders certain conduct, such as driving a car, dangerous to others.[8]

Although the California decisions that recognize this duty have involved cases in which the defendant stood in a special relationship *both* to the victim and to the person whose conduct created the danger,[9] we do not think that the duty should logically be constricted to such situations. Decisions of other jurisdictions hold that the single relationship of a doctor to his patient is sufficient to support the duty to exercise reasonable care to protect others against dangers emanating from the patient's illness. The courts hold that a doctor is liable to persons infected by his patient if he negligently fails to diagnose a contagious disease (*Hofmann* v. *Blackmon* [Fla.App.1970] 241 So.2d 752), or, having diagnosed the illness, fails to warn members of the patient's family (*Wojcik* v. *Aluminum Co. of America* [1959] 18 Misc.2d 740, 183 N.Y.S.2d 351, 357-358; *Davis* v. *Rodman* [1921] 147 Ark. 385, 227 S.W. 612; *Skillings* v. *Allen* [1919] 143 Minn. 323, 173 N.W. 663; see also *Jones* v. *Stanko* [1928] 118 Ohio St. 147, 160 N.E. 456).

Since it involved a dangerous mental patient, the decision in *Merchants Nat. Bank & Trust Co. of Fargo* v. *United States* (D.N.D.1967) 272 F.Supp. 409 comes closer to the issue. The Veterans Administration arranged for the patient to work on a local farm, but did not inform the farmer of the man's background. The farmer consequently permitted the patient to come and go freely during nonworking hours; the patient borrowed a car, drove to his wife's residence and killed her. Notwithstanding the lack of any "special relationship" between the Veterans Administration and the wife, the court found the Veterans Administration liable for the wrongful death of the wife.

In their summary of the relevant rulings Fleming and Maximov conclude that the "case law should dispel any notion that to impose on the therapists a duty to take precautions for the safety of persons threatened by a patient, where due care so requires, is in any way opposed to contemporary ground rules on the duty relationship. On the contrary, there now seems to be sufficient authority to support the conclusion that by entering into a doctor-patient relationship the therapist becomes sufficiently

---

therapist-patient relationship, giving rise to a possible duty by the doctor or therapist to exercise reasonable care to protect a threatened person of danger arising from the patient's mental illness, existed between Gold or Yandell and Poddar. (See Harney, Medical Malpractice [1973] p. 7.)

[7]When a "hospital has notice or knowledge of facts from which it might reasonably be concluded that a patient would be likely to harm himself *or others* unless preclusive measures were taken, then the hospital must use reasonable care in the circumstances to prevent such harm." (*Vistica* v. *Presbyterian Hospital* [1967] 67 Cal.2d 465, 469, 62 Cal.Rptr. 577, 580, 432 P.2d 193, 196.) (Emphasis added.) A mental hospital may be liable if it negligently permits the escape or release of a dangerous patient (*Semler* v. *Psychiatric Institute of Washington, D. C.* [4th Cir. 1976] 44 U.S.L.Week 2439; *Underwood* v. *United States* [5th Cir. 1966] 356 F.2d 92; *Fair* v. *United States* [5th Cir. 1956] 234 F. 2d 288). *Greenberg* v. *Barbour* (E.D.Pa. 1971) 322 F.Supp. 745, upheld a cause of action against a hospital staff doctor whose negligent failure to admit a mental patient resulted in that patient assaulting the plaintiff.

[8]*Kaiser* v. *Suburban Transp. System* (1965) 65 Wash.2d 461, 398 P.2d 14; see *Freese* v. *Lemmon* (Iowa 1973) 210 N.W.2d 576 (concurring opn. of Uhlenhopp, J.).

[9]*Ellis* v. *D'Angelo* (1953) 116 Cal.App.2d 310, 253 P.2d 675, upheld a cause of action against parents who failed to warn a babysitter of the violent proclivities of their child: *Johnson* v. *State of California* (1968) 69 Cal.2d 782, 73 Cal.Rptr. 240, 447 P.2d 352, upheld a suit against the state for failure to warn foster parents of the dangerous tendencies of their ward: *Morgan* v. *City of Yuba* (1964) 230 Cal.App.2d 938, 41 Cal.Rptr. 508, sustained a cause of action against a sheriff who had promised to warn decedent before releasing a dangerous prisoner, but failed to do so.

involved to assume some responsibility for the safety, not only of the patient himself, but also of any third person whom the doctor knows to be threatened by the patient." (Fleming & Maximov, *The Patient or His Victim: The Therapist's Dilemma* [1974] 62 Cal.L.Rev. 1025, 1030.)

Defendants contend, however, that imposition of a duty to exercise reasonable care to protect third persons is unworkable because therapists cannot accurately predict whether or not a patient will resort to violence. In support of this argument amicus representing the American Psychiatric Association and other professional societies cites numerous articles which indicate that therapists, in the present state of the art, are unable reliably to predict violent acts; their forecasts, amicus claims, tend consistently to overpredict violence, and indeed are more often wrong than right.[10] Since predictions of violence are often erroneous, amicus concludes, the courts should not render rulings that predicate the liability of therapists upon the validity of such predictions.

The role of the psychiatrist, who is indeed a practitioner of medicine, and that of the psychologist who performs an allied function, are like that of the physician who must conform to the standards of the profession and who must often make diagnoses and predictions based upon such evaluations. Thus the judgment of the therapist in diagnosing emotional disorders and in predicting whether a patient presents a serious danger of violence is comparable to the judgment which doctors and professionals must regularly render under accepted rules of responsibility.

We recognize the difficulty that a therapist encounters in attempting to forecast whether a patient presents a serious danger of violence. Obviously we do not require that the therapist, in making that determination, render a perfect performance; the therapist need only exercise "that reasonable degree of skill, knowledge, and care ordinarily possessed and exercised by members of [that professional specialty] under similar circumstances." (*Bardessono* v. *Michels* [1970] 3 Cal.3d 780, 788, 91 Cal.Rptr. 760, 764, 478 P.2d 480, 484; *Quintal* v. *Laurel Grove Hospital* [1964] 62 Cal.2d 154, 159–160, 41 Cal.Rptr. 577, 397 P.2d 161; see 4 Witkin, Summary of Cal.Law [8th ed. 1974] Torts, § 514 and cases cited.) Within the broad range of reasonable practice and treatment in which professional opinion and judgment may differ, the therapist is free to exercise his or her own best judgment without liability; proof, aided by hindsight, that he or she judged wrongly is insufficient to establish negligence.

In the instant case, however, the pleadings do not raise any question as to failure of defendant therapists to predict that Poddar presented a serious danger of violence. On the contrary, the present complaints allege that defendant therapists did in fact predict that Poddar would kill, but were negligent in failing to warn.

Amicus contends, however, that even when a therapist does in fact predict that a patient poses a serious danger of violence to others, the therapist should be absolved of any responsibility for failing to act to protect the potential victim. In our view, however, once a therapist does in fact determine, or under applicable professional standards reasonably should have determined, that a patient poses a serious danger of violence to others, he bears a duty to exercise reasonable care to protect the foreseeable victim of

[10]See, e.g., *People* v. *Burnick* (1975) 14 Cal.3d 306, 325–328, 121 Cal.Rptr. 488, 535 P.2d 352; Monahan, *The Prevention of Violence*, in Community Mental Health in the Criminal Justice System (Monahan ed. 1975); Diamond, *The Psychiatric Prediction of Dangerousness* (1975) 123 U.Pa.L.Rev. 439; Ennis and Litwack, *Psychiatry and the Presumption of Expertise: Flipping Coins in the Courtroom* (1974) 62 Cal.L.Rev. 693.

that danger. While the discharge of this duty of due care will necessarily vary with the facts of each case,[11] in each instance the adequacy of the therapist's conduct must be measured against the traditional negligence standard of the rendition of reasonable care under the circumstances. (Accord *Cobbs* v. *Grant* [1972] 8 Cal.3d 229, 243, 104 Cal.Rptr. 505, 502 P.2d 1.) As explained in Fleming and Maximov, *The Patient or His Victim: The Therapist's Dilemma* (1974) 62 Cal.L.Rev. 1025, 1067: "... the ultimate question of resolving the tension between the conflicting interests of patient and potential victim is one of social policy, not professional expertise. . . . In sum, the therapist owes a legal duty not only to his patient, but also to his patient's would-be victim and is subject in both respects to scrutiny by judge and jury."

Contrary to the assertion of amicus, this conclusion is not inconsistent with our recent decision in *People* v. *Burnick, supra,* 14 Cal.3d 306, 121 Cal.Rptr. 488, 535 P.2d 352. Taking note of the uncertain character of therapeutic prediction, we held in *Burnick* that a person cannot be committed as a mentally disordered sex offender unless found to be such by proof beyond a reasonable doubt. (14 Cal.3d at p. 328, 121 Cal.Rptr. 488, 535 P.2d 352.) The issue in the present context, however, is not whether the patient should be incarcerated, but whether the therapist should take any steps at all to protect the threatened victim; some of the alternatives open to the therapist, such as warning the victim, will not result in the drastic consequences of depriving the patient of his liberty. Weighing the uncertain and conjectural character of the alleged damage done the patient by such a warning against the peril to the victim's life, we conclude that professional inaccuracy in predicting violence cannot negate the therapist's duty to protect the threatened victim.

The risk that unnecessary warnings may be given is a reasonable price to pay for the lives of possible victims that may be saved. We would hesitate to hold that the therapist who is aware that his patient expects to attempt to assassinate the President of the United States would not be obligated to warn the authorities because the therapist cannot predict with accuracy that his patient will commit the crime.

Defendants further argue that free and open communication is essential to psychotherapy (see *In re Lifschutz* [1970] 2 Cal.3d 415, 431–434, 85 Cal.Rptr. 829, 467 P.2d 557); that "Unless a patient . . . is assured that . . . information [revealed by him] can and will be held in utmost confidence, he will be reluctant to make the full disclosure upon which diagnosis and treatment . . . depends." (Sen.Comp. on the Judiciary, comment on Evid.Code, § 1014.) The giving of a warning, defendants contend, constitutes a breach of trust which entails the revelation of confidential communications.[12]

[11]Defendant therapists and amicus also argue that warnings must be given only in those cases in which the therapist knows the identity of the victim. We recognize that in some cases it would be unreasonable to require the therapist to interrogate his patient to discover the victim's identity, or to conduct an independent investigation. But there may also be cases in which a moment's reflection will reveal the victim's identity. The matter thus is one which depends upon the circumstances of each case, and should not be governed by any hard and fast rule.

[12]Counsel for defendant Regents and amicus American Psychiatric Association predict that a decision of this court holding that a therapist may bear a duty to warn a potential victim will deter violence-prone persons from seeking therapy, and hamper the treatment of other patients. This contention was examined in Fleming and Maximov, The Patient or His Victim: The Therapist's Dilemma (1974) 62 Cal.L.Rev. 1025, 1038–1044; they conclude that such predictions are entirely speculative. In *In re Lifschutz, supra,* 2 Cal. 3d 415, 85 Cal.Rptr. 829, 467 P.2d 557, counsel for the psychiatrist argued that if the state could compel disclosure of some psychotherapeutic communications, psychotherapy could no longer be practiced successfully. (2 Cal.3d at p. 426, 85 Cal.Rptr. 829, 467 P.2d 557.) We rejected that argument, and it does not appear that our

We recognize the public interest in supporting effective treatment of mental illness and in protecting the rights of patients to privacy (see *In re Lifschutz, supra,* 2 Cal.3d at p. 432, 85 Cal.Rptr. 829, 467 P.2d 557), and the consequent public importance of safeguarding the confidential character of psychotherapeutic communication. Against this interest, however, we must weigh the public interest in safety from violent assault. The Legislature has undertaken the difficult task of balancing the countervailing concerns. In Evidence Code section 1014, it established a broad rule of privilege to protect confidential communications between patient and psychotherapist. In Evidence Code section 1024, the Legislature created a specific and limited exception to the psychotherapist-patient privilege: "There is no privilege . . . if the psychotherapist has reasonable cause to believe that the patient is in such mental or emotional condition as to be dangerous to himself or to the person or property of another and that disclosure of the communication is necessary to prevent the threatened danger."[13]

We realize that the open and confidential character of psychotherapeutic dialogue encourages patients to express threats of violence, few of which are ever executed. Certainly a therapist should not be encouraged routinely to reveal such threats; such disclosures could seriously disrupt the patient's relationship with his therapist and with the persons threatened. To the contrary, the therapist's obligations to his patient require that he not disclose a confidence unless such disclosure is necessary to avert danger to others, and even then that he do so discreetly, and in a fashion that would preserve the privacy of his patient to the fullest extent compatible with the prevention of the threatened danger. (See Fleming and Maximov, *The Patient or His Victim: The Therapist's Dilemma* [1974] 62 Cal.L.Rev. 1025, 1065-1066.)[14]

The revelation of a communication under the above circumstances is not a breach of trust or a violation of professional ethics; as stated in the Principles of Medical Ethics of the American Medical Association (1957), section 9: "A physician may not reveal the confidence entursted to him in the course of medical attendance . . . *unless he is required to do so by law or unless it becomes necessary in order to protect the welfare*

---

decision in fact adversely affected the practice of psychotherapy in California. Counsel's forecast of harm in the present case strikes us as equally dubious.

We note, moreover, that Evidence Code section 1024, enacted in 1965, established that psychotherapeutic communication is not privileged when disclosure is necessary to prevent threatened danger. We cannot accept without question counsels' implicit assumption that effective therapy for potentially violent patients depends upon either the patient's lack of awareness that a therapist can disclose confidential communications to avert impending danger, or upon the therapist's advance promise never to reveal nonprivileged threats of violence.

[13]Fleming and Maximov note that "While [section 1024] supports the therapist's less controversial *right* to make a disclosure, it admittedly does not impose on him a *duty* to do so. But the argument does not have to be pressed that far. For if it is once conceded . . . that a duty in favor of the patient's foreseeable victims would accord with general principles of tort liability we need no longer look to the statute for a source of duty. It is sufficient if the statute can be relied upon . . . for the purposes of countering the claim that the needs of confidentiality are paramount and must therefore defeat any such hypothetical duty. In this more modest perspective, the Evidence Code's 'dangerous patient' exception may be invoked with some confidence as a clear expression of legislative policy concerning the balance between the confidentiality values of the patient and the safety values of his foreseeable victims." (Emphasis in original.) Fleming and Maximov, *The Patient or His Victim: The Therapist's Dilemma* (1974) 62 Cal.L.Rev. 1025, 1063.

[14]Amicus suggests that a therapist who concludes that his patient is dangerous should not warn the potential victim, but institute proceedings for involuntary detention of the patient. The giving of a warning, however, would in many cases represent a far lesser inroad upon the patient's privacy than would involuntary commitment.

of the individual or of the community."[15] (Emphasis added.) We conclude that the public policy favoring protection of the confidential character of patient-psychotherapist communications must yield to the extent to which disclosure is essential to avert danger to others. The protective privilege ends where the public peril begins.

Our current crowded and computerized society compels the interdependence of its members. In this risk-infested society we can hardly tolerate the further exposure to danger that would result from a concealed knowledge of the therapist that his patient was lethal. If the exercise of reasonable care to protect the threatened victim requires the therapist to warn the endangered party or those who can reasonably be expected to notify him, we see no sufficient societal interest that would protect and justify concealment. The containment of such risks lies in the public interest. For the foregoing reasons, we find that plaintiffs' complaints can be amended to state a cause of action against defendants Moore, Powelson, Gold, and Yandell and against the Regents as their employer, for breach of a duty to exercise reasonable care to protect Tatiana.[16]

Finally, we reject the contention of the dissent that the provisions of the Lanterman-Petris-Short Act which govern the release of confidential information (Welf. & Inst.Code, §§ 5328–5328.9) prevented defendant therapists from warning Tatiana. The dissent's contention rests on the assertion that Dr. Moore's letter to the campus police constituted an "application in writing" within the meaning of Welfare and Institutions Code section 5150, and thus initiates proceedings under the Lanterman-Petris-Short Act. A closer look at the terms of section 5150, however, will demonstrate that it is inapplicable to the present case.

Section 5150 refers to a written application only by a professional person who is "[a] member of the attending staff . . . of an evaluation facility designated by the county," or who is himself "designated by the county" as one authorized to take a person into custody and place him in a facility designated by the county and approved by the State Department of Mental Hygiene. The complaint fails specifically to allege that Dr. Moore was so empowered. Dr. Moore and the Regents cannot rely upon any inference to the contrary that might be drawn from plaintiff's allegation that Dr. Moore intended to "assign" a "detention" on Poddar; both Dr. Moore and the Regents have expressly conceded that neither Cowell Memorial Hospital nor any member of its staff has evern been designated by the County of Alameda to institute involuntary commitment proceedings pursuant to section 5150.

Furthermore, the provisions of the Lanterman-Petris-Short Act defining a therapist's duty to withhold confidential information are expressly limited to "information and records *obtained in the course of providing services* under Division 5 (commencing with Section 5000), Division 6 (commencing with Section 6000), or Division

[15]See also Summary Report of the Task Force on Confidentiality of the Council on Professions and Associations of the American Psychiatric Association (1975).

[16]Moore argues that after Powelson countermanded the decision to seek commitment for Poddar, Moore was obliged to obey the decision of his superior and that therefore he should not be held liable for any dereliction arising from his obedience to superior orders. Plaintiffs in response contend that Moore's duty to members of the public endangered by Poddar should take precedence over his duty to obey Powelson. Since plaintiffs' complaints do not set out the date of Powelson's order, the specific terms of that order, or Powelson's authority to overrule Moore's decisions respecting patients under Moore's care, we need not adjudicate this conflict; we pass only upon the pleadings at this stage and decide if the complaints can be amended to state a cause of action.

7 (commencing with Section 7000)'' of the Welfare and Institutions Code (Welf. & Inst. Code, § 5328). (Emphasis added.) Divisions 5, 6 and 7 describe a variety of programs for treatment of the mentally ill or retarded.[17] The pleadings at issue on this appeal, however, state no facts showing that the psychotherapy provided to Poddar by the Cowell Memorial Hospital falls under any of these programs. We therefore conclude that the Lanterman-Petris-Short Act does not govern the release of information acquired by Moore during the course of rendition of those services.

Neither can we adopt the dissent's suggestion that we import wholesale the detailed provisions of the Lanterman-Petris-Short Act regulating the disclosure of confidential information and apply them to disclosure of information *not governed by the act*. Since the Legislature did not extend the act to control all disclosures of confidential matter by a therapist, we must infer that the Legislature did not relieve the courts of their obligation to define by reference to the principles of the common law the obligation of the therapist in those situations not governed by the act.

Relying on *Johnson,* we conclude that defendant therapists in the present case are not immune from liability for their failure to warn of Tatiana's peril. *Johnson* held that a parole officer's determination whether to warn an adult couple that their prospective foster child had a background of violence ''present[ed] no . . . reasons for immunity'' (*Johnson* v. *State of California, supra,* at p. 795, 73 Cal.Rptr. 240, 447 P.2d 352), was ''at the lowest, ministerial rung of official action'' (*id.,* at p. 796, 73 Cal.Rptr., at p. 250, 447 P.2d, at p. 362), and indeed constituted ''a classic case for the imposition of tort liability.'' (*Id.,* p. 797, 73 Cal.Rptr., p. 251, 447 P.2d, p. 363; cf. *Morgan* v. *County of Yuba, supra,* 230 Cal.App.2d 938, 942-943, 41 Cal.Rptr. 508.) Although defendants in *Johnson* argued that the decision whether to inform the foster parents of the child's background required the exercise of considerable judgmental skills, we concluded that the state was not immune from liability for the parole officer's failure to warn because such a decision did not rise to the level of a ''basic policy decision.''

We also noted in *Johnson* that federal courts have consistently categorized failures to warn of latent dangers as falling outside the scope of discretionary omissions immunized by the Federal Tort Claims Act.[22] (See *United Air Lines, Inc.* v. *Wiener* [9th Cir. 1964] 335 F.2d 379, 397-398, cert. den. *sub nom. United Air Lines, Inc.* v. *United States,* 379 U.S. 951, 85 S.Ct. 452, 13 L.Ed.2d 549 [decision to conduct

[17]Division 5 includes the Lanterman-Petris-Short Act and the Short-Doyle Act (community mental health services). Division 6 relates to programs for treatment of persons judicially committed as mentally disordered sex offenders or mentally retarded. Division 7 encompasses treatment at state and county mental hospitals, the Langley Porter Neuropsychiatric Institute and the Neuropsychiatric Institute of the U.C.L.A. Medical Center.

[18]Omitted.

[19]Omitted.

[20]Omitted.

[21]Omitted.

[22]By analogy, section 830.8 of the Government Code furnishes additional support for our conclusion that a failure to warn does not fall within the zone of immunity created by section 820.2. Section 830.8 provides: ''Neither a public entity nor a public employee is liable . . . for an injury caused by the failure to provide traffic or warning signals, signs, markings or devices described in the Vehicle Code. Nothing in this section exonerates a public entity or public employee from liability for injury proximately caused by such failure if a signal, sign, marking or device . . . was necessary to warn of a dangerous condition which endangered the safe movement of traffic and which would not be reasonably apparent to, and would not have been anticipated by, a person exercising due care.'' The Legislature thus concluded at least in another context that the failure to warn of a latent danger is not an immunized discretionary omission. (See *Hilts* v. *County of Solano* [1968] 265 Cal.App.2d 161, 174, 71 Cal.Rptr. 275.)

military training flights was discretionary but failure to warn commercial airline was not]; *United States* v. *Washington* [9th Cir. 1965] 351 F.2d 913, 916 [decision where to place transmission lines spanning canyon was assumed to be discretionary but failure to warn pilot was not]; *United States* v. *White* [9th Cir. 1954] 211 F.2d 79, 82 [decision not to "dedud" army firing range assumed to be discretionary but failure to warn person about to go onto range of unsafe condition was not]; *Bulloch* v. *United States* (D.Utah 1955) 133 F.Supp. 885, 888 [decision how and when to conduct nuclear test deemed discretionary but failure to afford proper notice was not]; *Hernandez* v. *United States* [D.Hawaii 1953] 112 F.Supp. 369, 371 [decision to erect road block characterized as discretionary but failure to warn of resultant hazard was not].)

We conclude, therefore, that the therapist defendants' failure to warn Tatiana or those who reasonably could have been expected to notify her of her peril does not fall within the absolute protection afforded by section 820.2 of the Government Code. We emphasize that our conclusion does not raise the specter of therapists employed by the government indiscriminately being held liable for damage despite their exercise of sound professional judgment. We require of publicly employed therapists only that quantum of care which the common law requires of private therapists. The imposition of liability in those rare cases in which a public employee falls short of this standard does not contravene the language or purpose of Government Code section 820.2.

7. Conclusion

For the reasons stated, we conclude that plaintiffs can amend their complaints to state a cause of action against defendant therapists by asserting that the therapists in fact determined that Poddar presented a serious danger of violence to Tatiana, or pursuant to the standards of their profession should have so determined, but nevertheless failed to exercise reasonable care to protect her from that danger. To the extent, however, that plaintiffs base their claim that defendant therapists breached that duty because they failed to procure Poddar's confinement, the therapists find immunity in Government Code section 856. Further, as to the police defendants we conclude that plaintiffs have failed to show that the trial court erred in sustaining their demurrer without leave to amend.

The judgment of the superior court in favor of defendants Atkinson, Beall, Brownrigg, Hallernan, and Teel is affirmed. The judgment of the superior court in favor of defendants Gold, Moore, Powelson, Yandell, and the Regents of the University of California is reversed, and the cause remanded for further proceedings consistent with the views expressed herein.

WRIGHT, C.J., and SULLIVAN and RICHARDSON, JJ., concur.

MOSK, Justice (concurring and dissenting).

I concur in the result in this instance only because the complaints allege that defendant therapists did in fact predict that Poddar would kill and were therefore negligent in failing to warn of that danger. Thus the issue here is very narrow; we are not concerned with whether the therapists, pursuant to the standards of their profession, "should have" predicted potential violence; they allegedly did so in actuality. Under these limited circumstances I agree that a cause of action can be stated.

Whether plaintiffs can ultimately prevail is problematical at best. As the complaints admit, the therapists *did* notify the police that Poddar was plannint to kill a girl identifiable as Tatiana. While I doubt that more should be required, this issue may be raised in defense and its determination is a question of fact.

I cannot concur, however, in the majority's rule that a therapist may be held liable for failing to predict his patient's tendency to violence if other practitioners, pursuant to the "standards of the profession," would have done so. The question is, what standards? Defendants and a responsible amicus curiae, supported by an impressive body of literature discussed at length in our recent opinion in *People* v. *Burnick* (1975) 14 Cal.3d 306, 121 Cal.Rptr. 488, 535 P.2d 352, demonstrate that psychiatric predictions of violence are inherently unreliable.

In *Burnick,* at pages 325-326, 121 Cal.Rptr. at page 501, 535 P.2d at page 365, we observed: "In the light of recent studies it is no longer heresy to question the reliability of psychiatric predictions. Psychiatrists themselves would be the first to admit that however desirable an infallible crystal ball might be, it is not among the tools of their profession. It must be conceded that psychiatrists still experience considerable difficulty in confidently and accurately *diagnosing* mental illness. Yet those difficulties are multiplied manyfold when psychiatrists venture from diagnosis to prognosis and undertake to predict the consequences of such illness: " 'A diagnosis of mental illness tells us nothing about whether the person so diagnosed is or is not dangerous. Some mental patients are dangerous, some are not. Perhaps the psychiatrist is an expert at deciding whether a person is mentally ill, but is he an expert at predicting which of the persons so diagnosed are dangerous? Sane people, too, are dangerous, and it may legitimately be inquired whether there is anything in the education, training or experience of psychiatrists which renders them particularly adept at predicting dangerous behavior. Predictions of dangerous behavior, no matter who makes them, are incredibly inaccurate, and there is a growing consensus that psychiatrists are not uniquely qualified to predict dangerous behavior and are, in fact, less accurate in their predictions than other professionals.' " (*Murel* v. *Baltimore City Criminal Court* [1972] . . . 407 U.S. 355, 364-365, fn. 2, 92 S.Ct. 2091, 32 L.Ed.2d 791, 796-797 [Douglas, J., dissenting from dismissal of certiorari].)" (Fns. omitted.) (See also authorities cited at p. 327 & fn. 18 of 14 Cal.3d, 121 Cal.Rptr. 488, 535 P.2d 352.)

The majority confidently claim their opinion is not offensive to *Burnick,* on the stated ground that *Burnick* involved proceedings to commit an alleged mentally disordered sex offender and this case does not. I am not so sanguine about the distinction. Obviously the two cases are not factually identical, but the similarity in issues is striking: in *Burnick* we were likewise called upon to appraise the ability of psychiatrists to predict dangerousness, and while we declined to bar all such testimony (*id.* at pp. 327-328, 121 Cal.Rptr. 488, 535 P.2d 352) we found it so inherently untrustworthy that we would permit confinement even in a so-called civil proceeding only upon proof beyond a reasonable doubt.

I would restructure the rule designed by the majority to eliminate all reference to conformity to standards of the profession in predicting violence. If a psychiatrist does in fact predict violence, then a duty to warn arises. The majority's expansion of that rule will take us from the world of reality into the wonderland of clairvoyance.

CLARK, Justice (dissenting).

Until today's majority opinion, both legal and medical authorities have agreed that confidentiality is essential to effectively treat the mentally ill, and that imposing a duty on doctors to disclose patient threats to potential victims would greatly impair treatment. Further, recognizing that effective treatment and society's safety are necessarily intertwined, the Legislature has already decided effective and confidential treatment is preferred over imposition of a duty to warn.

The issue whether effective treatment for the mentally ill should be sacrificed to a system of warnings is, in my opinion, properly one for the Legislature, and we are bound by its judgment. Moreover, even in the absence of clear legislative direction, we must reach the same conclusion because imposing the majority's new duty is certain to result in a net increase in violence.

The majority rejects the balance achieved by the Legislature's Lanterman-Petris-Short Act. (Welf. & Inst. Code, § 5000 et seq., hereafter the act.)[1] In addition, the majority fails to recognize that, even absent the act, overwhelming policy considerations mandate against sacrificing fundamental patient interests without gaining a corresponding increase in public benefit.

Statutory Provisions

Although the parties have touched only briefly on the nondisclosure provisions of the act, amici have pointed out their importance. The instant case arising after ruling on demurrer, the parties must confront the act's provisions in the trial court. In these circumstances the parties' failure to fully meet the provisions of the act would not justify this court's refusal to discuss and apply the law.

Having a grave impact on future treatment of the mentally ill in our state, the majority opinion clearly transcends the interests of the immediate parties and must discuss all applicable law. It abdicates judicial responsibility to refuse to recognize the clear legislative policy reflected in the act.

Effective 1 July 1969, the Legislature created a comprehensive statutory resolution of the rights and duties of both the mentally infirm and those charged with their care and treatment. The act's purposes include ending inappropriate commitment, providing prompt care, protecting public safety, and safeguarding personal rights. (§ 5001.) The act applies to both voluntary and involuntary commitment, and to both public and private institutions; it details legal procedure for commitment; it enumerates the legal and civil rights of persons committed; and it spells out the duties, liabilities and rights of the psychotherapist. Thus the act clearly evinces the Legislature's weighing of the countervailing concerns presently before us—when a patient has threatened a third person during psychiatric treatment.

Reflecting legislative recognition that disclosing confidences impairs effective treatment of the mentally ill, and thus is contrary to the best interests of society, the act establishes the therapist's duty to *not* disclose. Section 5328 provides in part that "[a]ll information and records obtained in the course of providing services . . . to either voluntary or involuntary recipients of services *shall* be confidential." (Italics added.) Further, a patient may enjoin disclosure in violation of statute and may recover the greater of $500 or three times the amount of actual damage for unlawful disclosure. (§ 5330.)

However, recognizing that some private and public interests must override the patient's, the Legislature established several limited exceptions to confidentiality.[2] The

[1]All statutory references, unless otherwise stated, are to the Welfare and Institutions Code.

[2]Section 5328 provides: "All information and records obtained in the course of providing services under Division 5 (commencing with Section 5000), Division 6 (commencing with Section 6000), or Division 7 (commencing with Section 7000), to either voluntary or involuntary recipients of services shall be confidential. Information and records may be disclosed only: [¶] (a) In communications between qualified professional persons in the provision of services or appropriate referrals, or in the course of conservatorship proceedings. The consent of the patient, or his guardian or conservator must be obtained before information or records may be disclosed by a professional person employed by a facility to a professional person not

limited nature of these exceptions and the legislative concern that disclosure might impair treatment, thereby harming both patient and society, are shown by section 5328.1. The section provides that a therapist may disclose "to a member of the family of a patient the information that the patient is presently a patient in the facility or that the patient is seriously physically ill . . . if the professional person in charge of the facility determines that the release of such information is in the best interest of the patient." Thus, disclosing even the fact of treatment is severely limited.

As originally enacted the act contained no provision allowing the therapist to warn anyone of a patient's threat. In 1970, however, the act was amended to permit disclosure in two limited circumstances. Section 5328 was amended, in subdivision (g), to allow disclosure "[*t*]*o governmental law enforcement agencies* as needed for the protection of federal and state elective constitutional officers and their families." (Italics added.) In addition, section 5328.3 was added to provide that when "necessary for the protection of the patient or *others* due to the patient's disappearance from, without prior notice to, a designated facility and his whereabouts is unknown, notice of such disappearance *may* be made to *relatives and governmental law enforcement*

---

employed by the facility who does not have the medical responsibility for the patient's care. [¶] (b) When the patient, with the approval of the physician in charge of the patient, designates persons to whom information or records may be released, except that nothing in this article shall be construed to compel a physician, psychologist, social worker, nurse, attorney, or other professional person to reveal information which has been given to him in confidence by members of a patient's family; [¶] (c) To the extent necessary for a recipient to make a claim, or for a claim to be made on behalf of a recipient for aid, insurance, or medical assistance to which he may be entitled; [¶] (d) If the recipient of services is a minor, ward, or conservatee, and his parent, guardian, or conservator designates, in writing, persons to whom records or information may be disclosed, except that nothing in this article shall be construed to compel a physician, psychologist, social worker, nurse, attorney, or other professional person to reveal information which has been given to him in confidence by members of a patient's family; [¶] (e) For research, provided that the Director of Health designates by regulation, rules for the conduct of research. Such rules shall include, but need not be limited to, the requirement that all researchers must sign an oath of confidentiality as follows:

____
Date

As a condition of doing research concerning persons who have received services from ________________ (fill in the facility, agency or person), I, ____________, agree not to divulge any information obtained in the course of such research to unauthorized persons, and not to publish or otherwise make public any information regarding persons who have received services such that the person who received services is identifiable. I recognize that unauthorized release of confidential information may make me subject to a civil action under provisions of the Welfare and Institutions Code.

____
Signed

[¶] (f) To the courts, as necessary to the administration of justice. [¶] (g) To governmental law enforcement agencies as needed for the protection of federal and state elective constitutional officers and their families. [¶] (h) To the Senate Rules Committee or the Assembly Rules Committee for the purposes of legislative investigation authorized by such committee. [¶] (i) If the recipient of services who applies for life or disability insurance designates in writing the insurer to which records or information may be disclosed. [¶] (j) To the attorney for the patient in any and all proceedings upon presentation of a release of information signed by the patient, except that when the patient is unable to sign such release, the staff of the facility, upon satisfying itself of the identity of said attorney, and of the fact that the attorney does represent the interests of the patient, may release all information and records relating to the patient except that nothing in this article shall be construed to compel a physician, psychologist, social worker, nurse, attorney, or other professional person to reveal information which has been given to him in confidence by members of a patient's family. [¶] The amendment of subdivision (d) of this section enacted at the 1970 Regular Session of the Legislature does not constitute a change in, but is declaratory of, the preexisting law."

Subdivisions (g), (h), and (i) were added by amendment in 1972. Subdivision (j) was added by amendment in 1974.

Section 5328, specifically enumerating exceptions to the confidentiality requirement, does not admit of an interpretation importing implied exceptions. (*County of Riverside* v. *Superior Court,* 42 Cal.App.3d 478, 481, 116 Cal.Rptr. 886.)

agencies designated by the physician in charge of the patient or the professional person in charge of the facility or his designee." (Italics added.)

Obviously neither exception to the confidentiality requirement is applicable to the instant case.

Not only has the Legislature specifically dealt with disclosure and warning, but it also has dealt with therapist and police officer liability for acts of the patient. The Legislature has provided that the therapist and the officer shall not be liable for prematurely releasing the patient. (§§ 5151, 5154, 5173, 5278, 5305, 5306.)

Ignoring the act's detailed provisions, the majority has chosen to focus on the "dangerous patient exception" to the psychotherapist-patient privilege in Evidence Code sections 1014, 1024 as indicating that "the Legislature has undertaken the difficult task of balancing the countervailing concerns." (*Ante,* p. 440, p. 26 of 131 Cal.Rptr., p. 346 of 551 P.2d.) However, this conclusion is erroneous. The majority fails to appreciate that when disclosure is permitted in an evidentiary hearing, a fourth interest comes into play—the court's concern in judicial supervision. Because they are necessary to the administration of justice, disclosures to the courts are excepted from the nondisclosure requirement by section 5328, subdivision (f). However, this case does not involve a court disclosure. Subdivision (f) and the Evidence Code sections relied on by the majority are clearly inapposite.

The provisions of the act are applicable here. Section 5328 (see fn. 2, *supra*) provides, "*All information and records obtained in the course of providing services under Division 5 . . . shall be confidential.*" (Italics added.) Dr. Moore's letter describing Poddar's mental condition for purposes of obtaining 72-hour commitment was undisputedly a transmittal of information designed to invoke application of division 5. As such it constituted information obtained in providing services under division 5. This is true regardless of whether Dr. Moore has been designated a professional person by the County of Alameda. Although section 5150 provides that commitment for 72 hours' evaluation shall be based on a statement by a peace officer or person designated by the county, section 5328 prohibits disclosure of *all information,* not just disclosure of the committing statement or disclosure by persons designated by the county. In addition, section 5330 gives the patient a cause of action for disclosure of confidential information by "an individual" rather than the persons enumerated in section 5150.

Moreover, it appears from the allegations of the complaint that Dr. Moore is in fact a person designated by the county under section 5150. The complaint alleges that "On or about August 20, 1969, defendant Dr. Moore notified Officers Atkinson and Teel, he would give the campus police a letter of diagnosis on Prosenjit Poddar, so the campus police could pick up Poddar and take him to Herrick Hospital in Berkeley where Dr. Moore would assign a 72-hour Emergency Psychiatric Detention on Prosenjit Poddar." Since there is no allegation that Dr. Moore was not authorized to sign the document, it must be concluded that under the allegations of the complaint he was authorized and thus a professional person designated by the county.

Whether we rely on the facts as stated in the complaint that Dr. Moore is a designated person under section 5150 or on the strict prohibitions of section 5328 prohibiting disclosure of "*all information,*" the imposition of a duty to warn by the majority flies directly in the face of the Lanterman-Petris-Short Act.

Under the act, there can be no liability for Poddar's premature release. It is likewise clear there exists no duty to warn. Under section 5328, the therapists were under a duty *to not disclose,* and no exception to thatduty is applicable here. Establishing a duty to warn on the basis of general tort principles imposes a Draconian dilemma on therapists—either violate the act thereby incurring the attendant statutory penalties, or ignore the majority's duty to warn thereby incurring potential civil liability. I am unable to assent to such.

If the majority feels that it must impose such a dilemma, then it has an obligation to specifically enumerate the circumstances under which the Lanterman-Petris-Short Act applies as opposed to the circumstances when "general tort principles" will govern. The majority's failure to perform this obligation—leaving to the therapist the subtle questions as to when each opposing rule applies—is manifestly unfair.

Duty to Disclose in the Absence of Controlling Statutory Provision

Even assuming the act's provisions are applicable only to conduct occurring after commitment, and not to prior conduct, the act remains applicable to the most dangerous patients—those committed. The Legislature having determined that the balance of several interests requires nondisclosure in the graver public danger commitment, it would be anomalous for this court to reweigh the interests, requiring disclosure for those less dangerous. Rather, we should follow the legislative direction by refusing to require disclosure of confidential information received by the therapist either before or in the absence of commitment. The Legislature obviously is more capable than is this court to investigate, debate and weigh potential patient harm through disclosure against the risk of public harm by nondisclosure. We should defer to its judgment.

Common Law Analysis

Entirely apart from the statutory provisions, the same result must be reached upon considering both general tort principles and the public policies favoring effective treatment, reduction of violence, and justified commitment.

Generally, a person owes no duty to control the conduct of another. (*Richards* v. *Stanley* [1954] 43 Cal.2d 60, 65, 271 P.2d 23; *Wright* v. *Arcade School Dist.* [1964] 230 Cal.App.2d 272, 277, 40 Cal.Rptr. 812; Rest.2d Torts [1965] § 315.) Exceptions are recognized only in limited situations where (1) a special relationship exists between the defendant and injured party, or (2) a special relationship exists between defendant and the active wrongdoer, imposing a duty on defendant to control the wrongdoer's conduct. The majority does not contend the first exception is appropriate to this case.

Policy generally determines duty. (*Dillon* v. *Legg* [1968] 68 Cal.2d 728, 734, 69 Cal.Rptr. 72, 441 P.2d 912.) Principal policy considerations include forseeability of harm, certainty of the plaintiff's injury, proximity of the defendant's conduct to the plaintiff's injury, moral blame attributable to defendant's conduct, prevention of future harm, burden on the defendant, and consequences to the community. (*Rowland* v. *Christian* [1968] 69 Cal.2d 108, 113, 70 Cal.Rptr. 97, 443 P.2d 561.)

Overwhelming policy considerations weigh against imposing a duty on psychotherapists to warn a potential victim against harm. While offering virtually no benefit to society, such a duty will frustrate psychiatric treatment, invade fundamental patient rights and increase violence.

The importance of psychiatric treatment and its need for confidentiality have been recognized by this court. (*In re Lifschutz* [1970] 2 Cal.3d 415, 421-422, 85 Cal.Rptr. 829, 467 P.2d 557.) "It is clearly recognized that the very practice of psychiatry vitally depends upon the reputation in the community that the psychiatrist will not tell."

(Slovenko, *Psychiatry and a Second Look at the Medical Privilege* [1960] 6 Wayne L.Rev. 175, 188.)

Assurance of confidentiality is important for three reasons.

Deterrence from Treatment

First, without substantial assurance of confidentiality, those requiring treatment will be deterred from seeking assistance. (See Sen. Judiciary Com. comment accompanying § 1014 of Evid.Code; Slovenko, *supra,* 6 Wayne L.Rev. 175, 187–188; Goldstein and Katz, *Psychiatrist-Patient Privilege: The GAP Proposal and the Connecticut Statute* [1962] 36 Conn.Bar J. 175, 178.) It remains an unfortunate fact in our society that people seeking psychiatric guidance tend to become stigmatized. Apprehension of such stigma—apparently increased by the propensity of people considering treatment to see themselves in the worst possible light—creates a well-recognized reluctance to seek aid. (Fisher, *The Psychotherapeutic Professions and the Law of Privileged Communications* [1964] 10 Wayne L.Rev. 609, 617; Slovenko, *supra,* 6 Wayne L.Rev. 175, 188; see also Rappeport, *Psychiatrist-Patient Privilege* [1963] 23 Md.L.J. 39, 46–47.) This reluctance is alleviated by the psychiatrist's assurance of confidentiality.

Full Disclosure

Second, the guarantee of confidentiality is essential in eliciting the full disclosure necessary for effective treatment. (*In re Lifschutz, supra,* 2 Cal.3d 415, 431, 85 Cal.Rptr. 829, 467 P.2d 557; *Taylor* v. *United States* [1955], 95 U.S.App.D.C. 373, 222 F.2d 398, 401; Goldstein and Katz, *supra,* 36 Conn.Bar J. 175, 178; Heller, *Some Comments to Lawyers on the Practice of Psychiatry* [1957] 30 Temp.L.Q. 401; Guttmacher and Weihofen, *Privileged Communications Between Psychiatrist and Patient* [1952] 28 Ind.L.J. 32, 34.)[3] The psychiatric patient approaches treatment with conscious and unconscious inhibitions against revealing his innermost thoughts. "Every person, however well-motivated, has to overcome resistances to therapeutic exploration. These resistances seek support from every possible source and the possibility of disclosure would easily be employed in the service of resistance." (Goldstein and Katz, *supra,* 36 Conn.Bar J. 175, 179; see also, 118 Am.J.Psych. 734, 735.) Until a patient can trust his psychiatrist not to violate their confidential relationship, "the unconscious psychological control mechanism of repression will prevent the recall of past experiences." (Butler, *Psychotherapy and Griswold: Is Confidentiality a Privilege or a Right?* [1971] 3 Conn.L.Rev. 599, 604.)

Successful Treatment

Third, even if the patient fully discloses his thoughts, assurance that the confidential relationship will not be breached is necessary to maintain his trust in his psychiatrist—the very means by which treatment is effected. "[T]he essence of much psychotherapy

[3]One survey indicated that five of every seven people interviewed said they would be less likely to make full disclosure to a psychiatrist in the absence of assurance of confidentiality. (See, Comment, *Functional Overlap Between the Lawyer and Other Professionals: Its Implications for the Doctrine of Privileged Communications* [1962] 71 Yale L.J. 1226, 1255.)

is the contribution of trust in the external world and ultimately in the self, modelled upon the trusting relationship established during therapy.'' (Dawidoff, *The Malpractice of Psychiatrists,* [1966] Duke L.J. 696, 704.) Patients will be helped only if they can form a trusting relationship with the psychiatrist. (*Id.* at p. 704, fn. 34; Burham, *Separation Anxiety* [1965] 13 Arch.Gen. Psychiatry 346, 356; Heller, *supra,* 30 Temp.L.Q. 401, 406.) All authorities appear to agree that if the trust relationship cannot be developed because of collusive communication between the psychiatrist and others, treatment will be frustrated. (See, e.g., Slovenko [1973] Psychiatry and Law, p. 61; Cross, *Privileged Communications Between Participants in Group Psychotherapy* [1970] Law and the Social Order, 191, 199; Hollender, *The Psychiatrist and the Release of Patient Information* [1960] 116 Am.J. Psychiatry 828, 829.)

Given the importance of confidentiality to the practice of psychiatry, it becomes clear the duty to warn imposed by the majority will cripple the use and effectiveness of psychiatry. Many people, potentially violent—yet susceptible to treatment—will be deterred from seeking it; those seeking it will be inhibited from making revelations necessary to effective treatment; and, forcing the psychiatrist to violate the patient's trust will destroy the interpersonal relationship by which treatment is effected.

Violence and Civil Commitment

By imposing a duty to warn, the majority contributes to the danger to society of violence by the mentally ill and greatly increases the risk of civil commitment—the total deprivation of liberty—of those who should not be confined.[4] The impairment of treatment and risk of improper commitment resulting from the new duty to warn will not be limited to a few patients but will extend to a large number of the mentally ill. Although under existing psychiatric procedures only a relatively few receiving treatment will ever present a risk of violence, the number making threats is huge, and it is the latter group—not just the former—whose treatment will be impaired and whose risk of commitment will be increased.

Both the legal and psychiatric communities recognize that the process of determining potential violence in a patient is far from exact, being fraught with complexity and uncertainty. (E.g., *People* v. *Burnick* [1975] 14 Cal.3d 306, 326, 121 Cal.Rptr. 488, 535 P.2d 352, quoting from *Murel* v. *Baltimore City Criminal Court* [1972] 407 U.S. 355, 364-365, fn. 2, 92 S.Ct. 2091, 32 L.Ed.2d 791 [Douglas, J., dissenting from dismissal of certiorari]; Ennis and Litwack, *Psychiatry and the Presumption of Expertise: Flipping Coins in the Courtroom,* 62 Cal.L.Rev. 693, 711-716; Rector, *Who Are the Dangerous?* [July 1973] Bull. of Amer.Acad. of Psych. & L. 186; Kozol, Boucher and Garofalo, *The Diagnosis and Treatment of Dangerousness* [1972] 18 Crime & Delinquency 371; Justice and Birkman, *An Effort to Distinguish the Violent From the Nonviolent* [1972] 65 So.Med.J. 703.)[5] In fact precision has not even been attained in

[4]The burden placed by the majority on psychiatrists may also result in the improper deprivation of two other constitutionally protected rights. First, the patient's constitutional right of privacy (*In re Lifschutz, supra,* 2 Cal.3d 415, 85 Cal.Rptr. 829, 467 P.2d 557) is obviously encroached upon by requiring the psychotherapist to disclose confidential communications. Secondly, because confidentiality is essential to effective treatment, the majority's decision also threatens the constitutionally recognized right to receive treatment. (*People* v. *Feagley* [1975] 14 Cal.3d 338, 359, 121 Cal.Rptr. 509, 535 P.2d 373; *Wyatt* v. *Stickney* [M.D.Ala.1971] 325 F. Supp. 781, 784, affd. sub nom. *Wyatt* v. *Aderholt* [5th Cir. 1974] 503 F.2d 1305; *Nason* v. *Superintendent of Bridgewater State Hosp.* [1968] 353 Mass. 604, 233 N.E.2d 908.)

[5]A shocking illustration of psychotherapists' inability to predict dangerousness, cited by this court in *People*

predicting who of those having already committed violent acts will again become violent, a task recognized to be of much simpler proportions. (Kozol, Boucher and Garofalo, *supra,* 18 Crime & Delinquency 371, 384.)

This predictive uncertainty means that the number of disclosures will necessarily be large. As noted above, psychiatric patients are encouraged to discuss all thoughts of violence, and they often express such thoughts. However, unlike this court, the psychiatrist does not enjoy the benefit of overwhelming hindsight in seeing which few, if any, of his patients will ultimately become violent. Now, confronted by the majority's new duty, the psychiatrist must instantaneously calculate potential violence from each patient on each visit. The difficulties researchers have encountered in accurately predicting violence will be heightened for the practicing psychiatrist dealing for brief periods in his office with heretofore nonviolent patients. And, given the decision not to warn or commit must always be made at the psychiatrist's civil peril, one can expect most doubts will be resolved in favor of the psychiatrist protecting himself.

Neither alternative open to the psychiatrist seeking to protect himself is in the public interest. The warning itself is an impairment of the psychiatrist's ability to treat, depriving many patients of adequate treatment. It is to be expected that after disclosing their threats, a significant number of patients, who would not become violent if treated according to existing practices, will engage in violent conduct as a result of unsuccessful treatment. In short, the majority's duty to warn will not only impair treatment of many who would never become violent but worse, will result in a net increase in violence.[6]

---

v. *Burnick, supra,* 14 Cal.3d 306, 326-327, fn. 17, 121 Cal.Rptr. 488, 535 P.2d 352, is cited and discussed in Ennis, Prisoners of Psychiatry: Mental Patients, Psychiatrists, and the Law (1972): "In a well-known study, psychiatrists predicted that 989 persons were so dangerous that they could not be kept even in civil mental hospitals, but would have to be kept in maximum security hospitals run by the Department of Corrections. Then, because of a United States Supreme Court decision, those persons were transferred to civil hospitals. After a year, the Department of Mental Hygiene reported that one-fifth of them had been discharged to the community, and over half had agreed to remain as voluntary patients. During the year, only 7 of the 989 committed or threatened any act that was sufficiently dangerous to require retransfer to the maximum security hospital. Seven correct predictions out of almost a thousand is not a very impressive record. [¶] Other studies, and there are many, have reached the same conclusion: psychiatrists simply cannot predict dangerous behavior." (*Id.* at p. 227.) Equally illustrative studies are collected in Rosenhan, *On Being Sane in Insane Places* (1973) 13 Santa Clara Law. 379, 384; Ennis and Litwack, *Psychiatry and the Presumption of Expertise: Flipping Coins in the Courtroom, supra,* 62 Cal.L.Rev. 693, 750-751.

[6]The majority concedes that psychotherapeutic dialogue often results in the patient expressing threats of violence that are rarely executed. (*Ante,* p. 441, p. 27 of 131 Cal.Rptr., p. 347 of 551 P.2d.) The practical problem, of course, lies in ascertaining which threats from which patients will be carried out. As to this problem, the majority is silent. They do, however, caution that a therapist certainly "should not be encouraged routinely to reveal such threats; such disclosures could seriously disrupt the patient's relationships with his therapist and with the persons threatened." (*Id.*)

Thus, in effect, the majority informs the therapists that they must accurately predict dangerousness—a task recognized as extremely difficult—or face crushing civil liability. The majority's reliance on the traditional standard of care for professionals that "therapist need only exercise 'that reasonable degree of skill, knowledge, and care ordinarily possessed and exercised by members of [that professional specialty] under similar circumstances' " (*ante,* p. 438, p. 25 of 131 Cal.Rptr., p. 345 of 551 P.2d) is seriously misplaced. This standard of care assumes that, to a large extent, the subject matter of the specialty is ascertainable. One clearly ascertainable element in the psychiatric field is that the therapist cannot accurately predict dangerousness, which, in turn, means that the standard is inappropriate for lack of a relevant criterion by which to judge the therapist's decision. The inappropriateness of the standard the majority would have us use is made patent when consideration is given to studies, by several eminent authorities, indicating that "[t]he chances of a second psychiatrist agreeing with the diagnosis of a first psychiatrist 'are barely better than 50-50; or stated differently, there is about as much chance that a different expert would come to some different conclusion as there is that the other would agree.' " (Ennis and Litwack, *Psychiatry and the Presumption of Expertise: Flipping Coins in the Courtroom, supra,* 62 Cal.L.Rev. 693, 701, quoting. Ziskin, Coping With Psychiatric and Psychological Testimony, 126.) The majority's attempt to apply a

The second alternative open to the psychiatrist is to commit his patient rather than to warn. Even in the absence of threat of civil liability, the doubts of psychiatrists as to the seriousness of patient threats have led psychiatrists to overcommit to mental institutions. This overcommitment has been authoritatively documented in both legal and psychiatric studies. (Ennis and Litwack, *Psychiatry and the Presumption of Expertise: Flipping Coins in the Courtroom, supra,* 62 Cal.L.Rev. 693, 711 et seq.; Fleming and Maximov, *The Patient or His Victim: The Therapist's Dilemma,* 62 Cal.L.Rev. 1025, 1044–1046; Am. Psychiatric Assn. Task Force Rep. 8 [July 1974] Clinical Aspects of the Violent Individual, pp. 23–24; see Livermore, Malmquist & Meehl, *On the Justifications for Civil Commitment,* 117 U.Pa.L.Rev. 75, 84.) This practice is so prevalent that it has been estimated that "as many as twenty harmless persons are incarcerated for every one who will commit a violent act." (Steadman and Cocozza, *Stimulus/Response: We Can't Predict Who is Dangerous* [Jan. 1975] 8 Psych. Today 32, 35.)

Given the incentive to commit created by the majority's duty, this already serious situation will be worsened, contrary to Chief Justice Wright's admonition "that liberty is no less precious because forfeited in a civil proceeding than when taken as a consequence of a criminal conviction." (*In re W.* [1971] 5 Cal.3d 296, 307, 96 Cal.Rptr. 1, 9, 486 P.2d 1201, 1209.)

Conclusion

In adopting the act, the Legislature fully recognized the concerns that must govern our decision today—adequate treatment for the mentally ill, safety of our society, and our devotion to individual liberty, making overcommitment of the mentally ill abhorrent. (§ 5001.) Again, the Legislature balanced these concerns in favor of nondisclosure (§ 5328), thereby promoting effective treatment, reducing temptation for overcommitment, and ensuring greater safety for our society. Psychiatric and legal expertise on the subject requires the same judgment.

The tragedy of Tatiana Tarasoff has led the majority to disregard the clear legislative mandate of the Lanterman-Petris-Short Act. Worse, the majority impedes medical treatment, resulting in increased violence from—and deprivation of liberty to—the mentally ill.

We should accept legislative and medical judgment, relying upon effective treatment rather than on indiscriminate warning.

The judgment should be affirmed.

McComb, J., concurs.

LIABILITY FOR NEGLIGENCE OF ASSOCIATES AND ASSISTANTS

Recalling his involvement as a defendant in four malpractice suits, one psychiatrist advised his colleagues as follows:

---

normative scheme to a profession which must be concerned with problems that balk at standardization is clearly erroneous.

In any event, an ascertainable standard would not serve to limit psychiatrist disclosure of threats with the resulting impairment of treatment. However compassionate, the psychiatrist hearing the threat remains faced with potential crushing civil liability for a mistaken evaluation of his patient and will be forced to resolve even the slightest doubt in favor of disclosure or commitment.

> I never saw three of these plaintiffs, nor did I talk to the families. In the other case I saw the plaintiff patient only for ½ hour. My associates and partners were not negligent in these cases, but the plaintiff thought so.
>
> The point is that as a senior partner I was considered responsible for the actions of my associates, even though I had never seen the patients. This is an important point to be remembered by every senior physician. The senior officer in every organization is legally responsible for every act of his juniors, both omission and commission. (Robinson, 1962, p. 780)

Indeed, practitioners can and have been held liable for the tortious conduct of their partners, employees, and agents. Beyond ordinary partnership liability, a discussion of the doctrine of *respondeat superior* is pertinent here. Frequently referred to as vicarious liability, the doctrine of *respondeat superior* holds that a "master" is responsible for the acts of his, her, or its (the "master" may be a corporate entity) "servants." Sagall and Reed (1975) reviewed how the doctrine has been applied to hospital attending physicians and chiefs of service in medical malpractice cases. In *Baxter* v. *Morningside,* 10 Wash.App. 893, 521 P.2d 946 (1974), which appears below, the court invokes the doctrine despite the fact that the agent is a volunteer. In *Graddy* v. *New York Medical College,* 19 App.Div.2d 426, 243 N.Y.S.2d 940 (1963), which also appears below, we see the court deal with the question of imputed negligence to a professional who is neither agent, employer, nor partner.

Psychologists, psychiatrists, and other mental health professionals who supervise the work of training psychotherapists must be responsive to the needs of the supervisee and of the patient if they are to avoid liability under the doctrine of *respondeat superior*. In too many training institutions today, psychotherapy supervision is set up on a *pro forma* once-a-week or once-a-month basis. It would seem to the present authors that this standard, upon which the profession has expressed approval by its silence, is too low. If some harm or injury befalls the patient of the student psychotherapist because the supervisor improperly failed to take into account the specific and unique needs of the patient and the supervisee, then it would seem that the doctrine of *respondeat superior* would be applicable.

A related issue of interest when discussing the potential for liability of associates and assistants is that of the psychiatric team. First conceived of by Healy (1915) and later popularized by Kanner (1957), the team is a group of professionals from varied disciplines who bring to bear a number of viewpoints on a specific problem. In the mental health field the team concept usually brings together a psychiatrist, a psychologist and a social worker at the least. In recent years other professionals have joined the team (e.g., reading specialists, psychiatric nurses, speech therapists, and so forth). Although there is as yet no case law to illustrate this point, it would seem that as the team concept gains in popularity and as membership in the team is extended to more professionals (and nonprofessionals), the potential liability of the individual team member would increase.

Another one of the "gray areas" of the law, namely that of unlicensed assistants, in this area was discussed by Cohen (1979, pp. 236-237):

> One of the many gray areas of the law affecting mental health professionals is the law concerning the use of assistants and paraprofessionals in the private practice of psychotherapy. The rise of community psychology, behavioral treatment, and other factors has prompted an unparalleled rise in the frequency with which unlicensed persons have been utilized by licensed practitioners to aid in the treatment of psychological problems. Although mental health professionals are permitted to employ assistants, the extent of responsibility they can legally delegate to an assistant in the treatment of patients remains to be defined by law. We can say that the law does not permit mental health professionals—or any other licensed professionals—to delegate their responsibilities in toto to an unlicensed competent to perform the services he is performing. This caution is based on an interpretation of Section 29.1 (9,10) of the Rules of the New York State Board of Regents Relating to Definitions of Unprofessional Conduct (effective October 1, 1977), which reads as follows:
>
> 9. Practicing or offering to practice beyond the scope permitted by law, or accepting and performing professional responsibilities which the licensee knows or has reason to know that he or she is not competent to perform, or performing without adequate supervision professional services which the licensee is authorized to perform only under the supervision of a licensed professional, except in an emergency situation where a person's life or health is in danger.
> 10. Delegating professional responsibilities to a person when the licensee delegating such responsibilities knows or has reason to know that such person is not qualified by training, by experience, or by licensure to perform them.
>
> In New York as well as other states the relationship of an assistant to a licensed professional is, legally, akin to an "extension" of the professional himself. However, a nonprofessional cannot legally function in a way so as to get the "cloak" of being a licensed professional by reason of his association with the licensed professional. If an employee of a professional is functioning in such a capacity that a reasonable person could confuse the employee with being a licensed professional, the professional is said to be "lending out" his license, and he may be subject to disciplinary action such as revocation of his license.

Baxter v. *Morningside, Inc.*, 10 Wn. App. 893, 521 P.2d 946

ARMSTRONG, J.—On November 10, 1970, an automobile collision occurred when defendant Carl Hoffer attempted to make a left turn at the Randall Road interchange on the Aberdeen freeway in Thurston County. The driver of the vehicle involved in the collision and her passengers commenced actions against defendant Hoffer and, on the theory of respondeat superior, against defendant Morningside, Inc., a charitable corporation. Plaintiffs contend that defendant Hoffer was acting for the benefit of Morningside as its agent, and that at the time of the incident in question he was acting within the scope of the agency.

A summary judgment on the issue of liability was entered against defendant Hoffer on December 18, 1970. Subsequent to the entry of that judgment, plaintiffs as well as defendant Morningside filed motions for summary judgment. The trial court granted a summary judgment dismissing defendant Morningside on April 30, 1973, finding no vicarious liability as a matter of law. The sole issue on appeal is whether the trial court properly ruled as a matter of law that Morningside was not vicariously responsible for the tort of Hoffer under the doctrine of respondeat superior. We hold that the trial court erred.

The record discloses that Mr. Hoffer is a retired state employee who, since his retirement, had been employed by Morningside, Inc., on a salaried part-time basis. Mr. Hoffer was assigned to a woodshop where he assisted in the instruction and training of youngsters in the use of hand tools and equipment. Morningside frequently received donations of lumber and material, and as part of Hoffer's duties he would go out and pick up the materials for use in various projects. During this period of employment Mr. Hoffer sometimes used his own vehicle for such trips, and after Morningside acquired a truck, he often used that vehicle.

Mr. Hoffer terminated his status as a salaried employee in October of 1970, but expressed a willingness to run errands and perform other tasks as a volunteer, contingent upon need and his availability. The record reflects that Hoffer's offer was welcomed and accepted by Morningside, and that on several occasions following Hoffer's termination of paid employment, Morningside did in fact solicit and accept his gratuitous services.

On the date of the incident in question, Irene Jones, Mr. Hoffer's former supervisor at Morningside, called Mr. Hoffer and requested his help. He was told that a timber company in Shelton had donated items that could not be left out in the weather to deteriorate, and which needed to be transported to Morningside's warehouse in Olympia. At the time Morningside's truck was disabled, and the parties agreed that Hoffer would obtain a trailer to pull behind his own vehicle. On Hoffer's second return trip from Shelton, as a result of his negligence, a collision occurred involving Hoffer's vehicle and the vehicle in which plaintiffs were riding. There is no question but that Hoffer was acting as a volunteer when the accident happened. However, we note the executive director of Morningside, Inc., averred that the only difference between Hoffer's activities on the day in question and prior work he had done as a salaried employee was volunteer rather than staff status.

Plaintiffs seek to predicate vicarious tort liability against Morningside, Inc., on these facts under the doctrine of respondeat superior. Plaintiffs may impose vicarious liability against Morningside only if it is established that Morningside engaged defendant Hoffer to perform services in Morningside's affairs and that Morningside controlled, or had the right to control, Hoffer's physical conduct in the performance of the service. *Jackson* v. *Standard Oil Co.,* 8 Wn. App. 83, 91, 505 P.2d 139 (1972); *McLean* v. *St. Regis Paper Co.,* 6 Wn. App. 727, 496 P.2d 571 (1972); *see Hollingbery* v. *Dunn,* 68 Wn.2d 75, 79, 411 P.2d 431 (1966).

In this regard, it may be emphasized that it is not de facto control nor actual exercise of a right to interfere with or direct the work which constitutes the test, but rather, the *right to control* the negligent actor's physical conduct in the performance of the service. *Cassidy* v. *Peters,* 50 Wn.2d 115, 120, 309 P.2d 767 (1957); W. Seavey, *Agency* § 84, at 142 (1964). For example, the *Cassidy* case involved young salesmen employed by a partnership to sell ice cream from motor scooters equipped with refrigerator boxes. There the court found that a master-servant relationship existed, although the court noted at page 121:

> [T]hat the partners exercised no direct control or supervision over the drivers while they were covering their routes; but as a practical matter, direct supervision was uncalled for and virtually impossible. It is not a necessary element of control.

Similarily, in *Swam* v. *Aetna Life Ins. Co.*, 155 Wash. 402, 284 P. 792 (1930), cited with approval in *Cassidy* v. *Peters, supra,* the court held that a man engaged to repair a windmill was a servant even though he was under no obligation to repair, could have quit the job at any time he saw fit, or could have been discharged at any time, and there appeared to be no particular supervision involved.

It should also be emphasized that although the appellate courts of this state have not heretofore addressed the question of the effect of volunteer status upon the existence of the master-servant relationship, Mr. Hoffer's status as a volunteer worker for Morningside, Inc., does not necessarily preclude a finding that a master-servant relationship existed. Other jurisdictions considering this issue have uniformly held that consideration or monetary compensation is not necessary to create the relation. *State* v. *Tug Go-Getter,* 299 F.Supp. 269, 276 (D. Ore. 1969); *Bollman* v. *Kark Rendering Plant,* 418 S.W.2d 39 (Mo. 1967); *Chavez* v. *Sprague,* 209 Cal.App.2d 101, 25 Cal.Rptr. 603 (1962). We believe the rule to be that where one volunteers or agrees to assist another, to do something for the other's benefit, or to submit himself to the control of the other, even without an agreement for or expectation of reward, if the one for whom the service is rendered consents to its being performed under his direction and control, then the service may be rendered within the scope of a master-servant relationship. Restatement (Second) of Agency §§ 225, 221 (1958); *Scottsdale Jaycees* v. *Superior Court,* 17 Ariz. App. 571, 499 P.2d 185 (1972).

For example, in *Duffy* v. *Harden,* 179 N.W.2d 496 (Iowa 1970), the Supreme Court of Iowa held there was sufficient evidence to establish a master-servant relationship where a driver, with the owner's knowledge and consent, had been gratuitously repairing the owner's automobile and after a test drive negligently pushed the disabled vehicle onto the traveled portion of a highway at night. The court in *Duffy* relied heavily on the opinion of the Supreme Court of Minnesota in *Frankie* v. *Twedt*, 234 Minn. 42, 47 N.W.2d 482 (1951). The court in that case found sufficient evidence to establish a master-servant relationship where a driver was given permission to use the owner's automobile for the driver's pleasure, but with the understanding that he would call for the owner at his place of employment at 1:30 A.M. to take him home. The accident in that case occurred as the driver was on his way to pick up the owner. The court noted that the existence of a mutual agreement controlling the time, destination and purpose of the trip was a significant factor bearing on the requisite right of control. *Frankie* v. *Twedt, supra* at 49.

Upon applying the foregoing principles to the instant facts, we are of the opinion it was established that when Morningside engaged Hoffer to transport the donated items to their warehouse, Morningside controlled and had the right to control Hoffer's physical conduct in the performance of the service. A master-servant relationship therefore existed.

Mr. Hoffer had performed very similar services for Morningside in the past as part of his duties as a salaried employee. It is true that the salaried relationship had been terminated. However, an ongoing volunteer relationship between Hoffer and Morningside continued. On the date in question it was Hoffer's former employment supervisor who called Hoffer by telephone and solicited his services, which services, it was conceded, differed in nature from previous services as a paid employee only in that the service was rendered by one with volunteer rather than staff status. We deem it particularly significant that the result of this telephone call and solicitation was a mutual agreement between Hoffer and Morningside controlling the time, destination, purpose and especially the means of Hoffer's undertaking. The time of performance was implicitly agreed to be as soon as reasonably possible because it was imperative that the materials not be left out in the weather to deteriorate. The parties explicitly agreed upon the destination and purpose of the trip; namely, to transport the donated items from Shelton to Morningside's warehouse in Olympia. The parties also explicitly agreed that it would be necessary for Hoffer to use his own vehicle and to obtain a trailer as the means to accomplish the desired result. Because of the nature of the service to be performed, any further control, such as direct supervision of the loading or operation of the motor vehicle, would have been uncalled for, impractical, and was not necessary to establish the requisite right of control which vicarious liability contemplates. *Cassidy* v. *Peters, supra* at 121; *Frankle* v. *Twedt, supra.*

Usually the question of control or right of control is one of fact for the jury. *Jackson* v. *Standard Oil Co., supra* at 91. However, this is true only where the facts as to the agreement between the parties are in dispute, or are susceptible of more than one interpretation. If the facts are undisputed, as in this case, and, without weighing the credibility of witnesses, there can be but one reasonable conclusion drawn from the facts, the nature of the relationship between the parties becomes a question of law. *Hollingbery* v. *Dunn, supra* at 80; Restatement (Second) of Agency § 220, comment *c* (1958); 57 C.J.S. *Master & Servant* § 530 (1948).

In this case the material facts were undisputed, the negligence of defendant Hoffer had previously been established, and both sides filed motions for summary judgment to determine the existence or nonexistence of the master-servant relationship. At that stage of the proceedings, the pleadings, affidavits, and depositions on file clearly indicated that no genuine issue of material fact existed as to the vicarious liability of defendant Morningside for the negligence of defendant Hoffer. The record clearly indicated that as a matter of law Hoffer was acting within the scope of a master-servant relationship. It was therefore error to deny the plaintiffs' motion for summary judgment.

The judgment in favor of defendant Morningside, Inc., is reversed, and the cause remanded for entry of judgment against defendant Morningside, Inc., on the issue of liability, and for a determination of the amount of damages sustained.

PEARSON, C.J., and PETRIE, J., concur.

Graddy v. *New York Medical College*, 19 App.Div.2d 426, 243 N.Y.S.2d 940 (1963)

BERGAN, J. Upon an adequate record it has been found that plaintiff suffered injury resulting from negligence in the course of surgical treatment by defendant Edward G. Bell, who does not appeal. A vicarious liability has also been imposed on defendant-appellant Alvin M. Street, who took no part in the medical or surgical management of plaintiff's treatment, but who had office and financial arrangements with Dr. Bell in the practice of medicine.

The liability thus imposed on Dr. Street cuts deeper than any case thus far reported in New York, and, as far as we have observed, in other jurisdictions. The problem presented is of significance in the practice of medicine and in affecting liability resting on the arrangements made by physicians for the care and treatment of each other's patients.

The record demonstrates that both Dr. Street and Dr. Bell were specialists in otolaryngology. They shared one medical office which they used at different periods of the day and shared the services of a secretary and the use of professional equipment and office supplies. There was no partnership between them in the practice of medicine; each had separate patients and billed these patients as individual practitioners. But a patient of one physician would, in his absence, be treated by the other if the patient consented. In such case the physician would bill his own patient for the service and pay half of it to the other who had performed the service.

Plaintiff had consulted Dr. Street in April, 1959 and had been treated on two occasions for complaints referable to his nose and throat. Dr. Street had advised against surgical treatment. Dr. Street himself became ill and did not thereafter see plaintiff, who on May 11 came back to the office where he was told that Dr. Street was ill and that Dr. Bell, who was then in the office, was caring for his patients. Plaintiff related the same symptoms he had previously given Dr. Street and Dr. Bell advised surgery, which he himself undertook to perform on May 13 at the Flower and Fifth Avenue Hospitals, one of the defendants in the case.

A verdict having been returned by the jury against Dr. Bell, the court, which had by consent not submitted the issue of Dr. Street's liability but had held it subject to his view of the law after the verdict came in, ruled that Dr. Street was liable for Dr. Bell's negligence and directed judgment accordingly. The nexus of relationship, as the court saw it, was the financial interest which Dr. Street would have in the fee for the services performed by Dr. Bell. In the opinion of the court the fact that Dr. Street left it to Dr. Bell to exercise his own professional judgment "upon his—Dr. Street's—patients, to the latter's economic advantage" was decisive. Respondent on this appeal argues that if a label must be put on the relationship "it is that of joint venturers."

In the absence of some recognized traditional legal relationship such as partnership, master and servant, or agency, between physicians in the treatment of patients, the imposition of liability on one for the negligence of the other has been largely limited to situations of joint action in diagnosis or treatment or some control of the course of treatment of one by the other. In *Bing* v. *Thunig* (2 N.Y.2d 656), for example, liability was imposed on a hospital for the negligence of nurses employed by the hospital; in *Mrachek* v. *Sunshine Biscuit* (308 N.Y. 116), liability was similarly imposed on a business corporation, under very limited circumstances, for the negligence of a physician in its employ. (See, *e.g., Matter of Bernstein* v. *Beth Israel Hosp.,* 236 N.Y. 268.)

Where physicians actually participate together in diagnosis and treatment, they may each incur a liability for the negligence of the other even though a more active part in the treatment may have been taken by one of them. (*Rodgers* v. *Canfield,* 272 Mich. 562, 564), but the Supreme Court of Michigan noted that any act of negligence "by one, in the absence of the other, unless concerted, could not be attributed to the nonparticipant."

A family physician who participated in the diagnosis of a fracture for which a cast was negligently applied by a specialist and continued in active charge of the case after the cast was applied was held jointly negligent (*Morrill* v. *Komasinski,* 256 Wis. 417). This is the general rule: "Physicians employed together by the patient, and diagnosing or treating the case together, without withdrawal by, or discharge of, either, owe the same duty and are jointly liable for any negligence." (70 C.J.S., Physicians and Surgeons, § 54, subd. c, p. 977.) For a discussion of the rule applicable to medical partnership and agency in rendering medical care, see *Simons* v. *Northern Pacific Ry. Co.* (94 Mont. 355). As to liability where one physician is the employee of another, see *Moulton* v. *Huckleberry* (150 Ore. 538).

But a referral of a patient by one physician to another competent physician, absent partnership, employment, or agency, upon abundant authority, does not impose a liability on the referring physician. (*Nelson* v. *Sandell,* 202 Iowa 109; *Nash* v. *Royster,* 189 N. C. 408; *Moore* v. *Lee,* 109 Tex. 391; *Mayer* v. *Hipke,* 183 Wis. 382.) An exhaustive discussion of the problem appears in *Smith* v. *Beard* (56 Wyo. 375) which, although not quite in point, has some parallel to the case now before us.

The general rule, synthesized from the authorities in many States on this subject, is that "a physician who is unable or unwilling to assume or continue the treatment of a case, and recommends or sends another physician who is not his employee, agent, or partner, is not liable for injuries resulting from the latter's want of skill or care unless he did not exercise due care in making the recommendation or substitution." (70 C.J.S., Physicians and Surgeons, § 54, subd. d, p. 978.)

Although the movement of the law has been in the direction of broadening the base of derived liability to others from the professional acts of physicians, this has been largely achieved by looking differently than we formerly did at the highly individualized independence of judgment of a physician in the area of professional diagnosis and treatment. Even in situations when he would normally be regarded as under control of another, a physician had been treated as an "independent contractor" and liability for his negligence was not passed on (*Schloendorff* v. *Society of N.Y. Hosp.,* 211 N.Y. 125, 129).

But this limitation of liability has been broken through in situations of control to which the physician has submitted himself. Although the rule of liability is broadening out in this area, we think it ought not be extended to rest on a situation where there is neither a legal nor an actual control of the treating physician by the other physician and the relationship between them upon which responsibility is sought to be imputed turns upon a shared office and an agreement to service each other's patients for a shared fee.

This is something less, and quite different from, a relationship of master and servant or agency upon which vicarious liability has thus far rested. The implications of such an enlarged liability would tend to discourage a physician from arranging to have another care for his patients on his illness or absence and thus curtail the availability of medical service.

On the whole this extension of liability should not be made on the record now before us. If splitting of fees in the absence of active participation in the service or of a written partnership agreement was professionally irregular (Education Law, § 6514) that should be dealt with rather by appropriate disciplinary action than by an extension of vicarious liability. Thus, in our view, the judgment against appellant Street should not stand.

The judgment against the Flower and Fifth Avenue Hospitals and against the New York Medical College, concerning which no distinction from the hospital is suggested on appeal, rests on a different base. By formal concession in the record, Dr. Cesar Vijil, a resident in anesthesiology, was an employee of the hospital. Dr. Vijil was a graduate in medicine of a Central American medical school but had not been admitted to practice in New York.

It could be found he was assigned by someone in the hospital's department of anesthesiology to plaintiff's case, although the exact process of assignment is open to some dispute. The medical proof in the record is adequate to find that in the steps taken to administer anesthesia to the plaintiff, and particularly in the failure to recognize early the development of symptoms in the patient indicating grave physical peril, the anesthetist failed to follow standard procedures and could be found negligent. In these circumstances the hospital becomes liable. (*Bing* v. *Thunig*, 2 N.Y.2d 656, *supra*.) Indeed, the hospital on appeal does not stress an absence of liability but rests its case largely on purported errors on the trial which we regard as insufficient to disturb the verdict.

The liability imposed on defendants Fierro and Berger, doing business as Flower Anesthetists Associates, is based on a purported control of Dr. Vijil by these two defendants in the administration of anesthesia in the hospital and also upon their purported peripheral participation in the anesthesia given to plaintiff. There is also a suggestion in the record that Dr. Vijil was to some extent an employee of the associates.

Dr. Frank Fierro and Dr. Howard C. Berger were partners in the practice of medicine and in the specialty of anesthesiology in the hospital. Dr. Fierro was chairman of the department of anesthesiology at the hospital. He had a general responsibility for the administration of anesthesia. Dr. Vijil worked as a resident under the supervision of this department. There is proof that plaintiff in a prior operation, some 15 years earlier, had experienced difficulty in taking anesthesia and this became known to the house staff physician at Flower, who took the history on plaintiff's admission and noted this in the chart. Dr. Bell also knew of this and testified he told Dr. Berger about it before the operation.

There was some proof to the effect that Dr. Berger accompanied Dr. Vijil to the operating room and was there before or at the time the procedure started, but during the operation Dr. Vijil was alone with the operating surgeon and attending nurses. All this spells out a sufficient control of the anesthetist and a responsibility for the procedures followed, together with the specific signal of unusual reaction to anesthesia in the patient that the jury could find, to bring home a liability to the defendants Fierro and Berger.

The verdict of $150,000 is, however, heavily excessive. The apparent cessation of vital functions from cardiac arrest due to the effects of anesthesia until resuscitation procedures were successful, caused a cerebral anoxia. Plaintiff was unconscious for several days. Plaintiff's neurologist conceded that any permanent injury sustained by reason of cerebral anoxia would have become manifest a short time after the operation. But on June 18, 1959, a month after the operation, the neurologist found plaintiff to be neurologically normal except for some unsteadiness of gait. He had fairly good retention in a memory test and his speech was normal. Three months after the operation it was observed at the Eastview Hospital that the "only mental symptoms noted is a slight memory defect which causes him to make frequent repetitious statements." In our view the later psychological symptoms observed in plaintiff are not sufficiently attributed to this single incident to justify a verdict in this magnitude and the record suggests there are other causes which contributed to his physical and mental condition.

The judgment should be modified on the law and the facts by dismissing the complaint as to defendant Street and directing entry of judgment for such defendant; and by reversing, on the law, on the facts and in the exercise of discretion, the judgment as to defendants New York Medical College, Flower and Fifth Avenue Hospitals, Frank Fierro and Howard C. Berger, doing business as Flower Anesthetists Associates, and directing a new trial as to such defendants, unless plaintiff stipulates to accept $75,000 in lieu of the award by verdict, in which event the judgment should be modified to that extent and affirmed as thus modified, without costs.

BOTEIN, P.J., RABIN, EAGER and STEUER JJ., concur.

Judgment unanimously modified on the law and the facts by dismissing the complaint as to defendant Street and directing entry of judgment for such defendant; and by reversing, on the law, on the facts and in the exercise of discretion, the judgment as to defendants New York Medical College, Flower and Fifth Avenue Hospitals, Frank Fierro and Howard C. Berger, doing business as Flower Anesthetists Associates, and directing a new trial as to such defendants, unless plaintiff stipulates to accept $75,000 in lieu of the award by verdict, in which event the judgment is modified to that extent and affirmed as thus modified, without costs. Settle order on notice.

LIABILITY ARISING FROM REFERRAL TO ANOTHER PRACTITIONER

Private practitioners are not legally obligated to accept into treatment anyone and everyone who wishes to engage them. The practitioner may not have available the number of hours needed to serve the patient properly; the patient may not be able to afford the practitioner's fee for the service; the practitioner may feel that he or she does not have the proper expertise to deal with the presenting problem—there are any number of reasons why a practitioner may refer a patient to another practitioner. The referral is in and of itself an act of judgment, and it is possible for this act to result in liability for malpractice. Liability will be imputed to the referring practitioner if it can be shown that he or she knew or should have known that the practitioner to whom the patient was referred to was incompetent to treat the problem, which is illustrated below in the case of *Cestone* v. *Harkavy,* 243 App.Div. 732, 277 N.Y.S.2d 438 (1935). Conversely, the practitioner who refers a patient to a competent practitioner is not held liable for the actions of the practitioner to which the patient was referred. This point is discussed below in the case of *Brandt* v. *Grubin,* 131 N.J.Super., 182, 329 A.2d 82 (1974). Note, however, that the practitioner who is negligent in treating a patient before referring the patient may be held liable for subsequent acts by other practitioners not breaking the causality chain—such acts being viewed by the court as complicating or aggravating the effects of the original negligence.

Cestone v. *Harkavy,* 243 App. Div. 732, 277 N.Y.S.2d 438 (1935)

PER CURIAM.

In an action for damages for wrongfully causing death, order denying defendant's motion to dismiss the complaint affirmed, with $10 costs and disbursements; with leave to defendant to answer within ten days from the entry of the order herein. The complaint sufficiently alleges that the operating surgeon was incompetent and unskillful to the knowledge of defendant at the time he selected such surgeon and recommended him to the decedent, and the defendant was therefore negligent in so selecting and recommending him. *Stage* v. *Michigan Central Railroad Co.,* 199 App. Div. 675, 191 N Y.S. 824, and cases cited.

Affirmed, with leave to defendant to answer.

Brandt v. *Grubin*, 13 N.J.Super. 182, 329 A.2d 82 (1974)

DREIER, J.D.C., Temporarily Assigned. In this medical malpractice action defendant Dr. Charles J. Grubin has moved for summary judgment. This case raises an issue of first impression in New Jersey concerning the alleged abandonment by a physician who had referred a patient for specialized services.

Both *R.* 4:46-2 and the cases interpreting this rule and its predecessor *R.* 4:58-3 dictate that this court must find that there is an absence of dispute as to material facts, and must give to plaintiff all favorable inferences reasonably to be drawn from the expert's report, depositions and interrogatories. *Judson* v. *Peoples Bank & Trust Co. of Westfield,* 17 *N.J.* 67, 74-76 (1954). This court, therefore, has searched the depositions and other documents supporting plaintiff's position to see if there is a palpably genuine issue as to any material fact. From that point of departure, the following facts appear.

Defendant Dr. Grubin is a licensed and practicing physician of the State of New Jersey engaged in the general practice of medicine. He is alleged to have been the physician of plaintiff, the decedent's mother, but her depositions show his earlier services had been limited to signing one or two death certificates for the family. On October 25, 1971, and for some time prior thereto, decedent, George F. Brandt, Jr., then 21 years of age, was alleged to have experienced periods of anxiety, loneliness and insomnia, as described by Dr. Grubin. On this date (and perhaps one other occasion) decedent consulted Dr. Grubin for examination, care and treatment of these conditions.

In answers to interrogatories Dr. Grubin stated:

> The patient was seen on 10/25/71. He came to defendant's office at 123 Hillside Avenue, Hillside, New Jersey. He showed symptoms of anxiety, loneliness and insomnia. He presented a history of having LSK [*sic*] but no other drugs. He gave an impression of schizophrenia and was referred to Elizabeth Mental Hygiene Clinic or the Mount Carmel Guild Mental Hygiene Clinic in Cranford. He was given a prescription of thorazine 10 mmgs. #15 one or two three times daily no refills. . . .

At his deposition Dr. Grubin characterized the decedent's mental condition on October 25, 1971 as "an anxiety syndrome." He admitted that he was not a psychiatrist, but nevertheless prescribed thorazine to be taken by decedent "to take the edge off his anxiety." He admitted that the principal contraindication for the use or prescription of thorazine is depression, and the second most important contraindication is liver disease. With respect to depression as a contraindication, he noted that "the literature says in the presence of depression thorazine should be used very cautiously and that's all I have to see and I don't touch it.

After this one visit, and perhaps an additional contact a few days later (see Mrs. Freda's deposition quoted *infra*), decedent did not return to Dr. Grubin. A month later, on November 21, 1971, decedent was treated at the Elizabeth General Hospital Emergency Room and was again advised to go to the Union County Psychiatric Clinic for further treatment. Two days later (on November 23, 1971) he was again admitted into the hospital's medical ward, and then placed in the psychiatric ward just prior to his suicide on November 26, 1971.

On the subject of Dr. Grubin's later alleged unavailability, decedent's sister, Mrs.

Frances Freda, stated in her depositions that the family attempted repeatedly to contact Dr. Grubin the week prior to decedent's confinement at Elizabeth General Hospital on November 23, 1971. She testified that "for the whole weekend we tried to reach Dr. Grubin and we just got a series of runarounds," and further:

> My mother's neighbor was there also. She even attempted to get in touch with Dr. Grubin. We called the priest to come. He said he needs a doctor. There was nothing he could do. I mean, it just seemed that Dr. Grubin was evasive.
>
> At one point my mother called him and spoke with the nurse again. We explained to him all these times it was an emergency, that we had to speak to him immediately. We told him who we were, who we were calling for, and this last time when my mother called she asked him has Dr. Grubin returned yet and the nurse said, "Returned? He's always been here. He hasn't gone anyplace." It was as if, you know, we are lying, that we are calling him and we never really talked to any of the answering services. We waited and Dr. Grubin wasn't there from what we gathered from the answering service, that's as far as I can remember.

Plaintiff has submitted an expert report from Dr. Lewis J. Vorhaus II, of New York City. This report is over seven single-spaced typewritten pages in length, less than a page of which concerns the actions of Dr. Grubin. Although the basis for Dr. Grubin's alleged liability is set forth in one paragraph, in reality three separate claims are made. Set apart, these are:

> With respect to Dr. Grubin I think that he was also guilty of departing from accepted standards of practice in not adequately assessing the seriousness of the situation when he saw the patient in his office. It was not enough that he merely suggest to the patient that he get psychiatric help. He obviously was not competent to make judgments for himself or to follow directions given by a physician. Responsibility for this should have been placed in the hands of the family and they should have been notified about the seriousness of his problem.
>
> The treatment that was given was totally inadequate. If there was any question in Dr. Grubin's mind about the severity of the psychiatric problem he should have seen to it that the patient got psychiatric consultation and evaluation before making any recommendations whatsoever. Simply to give the patient a small dose of thorazine and tell the patient to get psychiatric help was clearly inadequate for the needs of the situation.
>
> With respect to his further conduct there apparently is a difference of opinion between the mother of the decedent and the doctor. She claims she tried to reach him and he did not respond to her calls. He claims he got no calls. This would be a matter obviously for the jury to decide. I can only say that if it can be demonstrated that he did not respond to calls for help from the patient's mother and failed to call her back when she sought his help subsequent to his first examination of the boy then this too would be a departure from accepted standards of practice in that he failed to meet his obligations toward the patient or failed to be adequately responsive to the needs in this case.

In short, the three claims of malpractice are Dr. Grubin's (1) inadequate assessment of the "seriousness of the situation," (2) "inadequate " treatment and (3)-abandonment of the patient. The adverse physiological consequences of the dose of thorazine and its causal connection with the suicide are nowhere substantiated by competent medical proof, and thus will not be considered with respect to this motion, since the same would be excluded at the trial (unless the expert's report had been supplemented). After the first argument of this motion counsel were given an opportunity to supply the court with an expert's report prior to the reargument on November 1, 1974, and the above-quoted extracts from plaintiff's expert were the only references to the actions of Dr. Grubin. No affidavits were submitted by either party.

With respect to plaintiff's claim that Dr. Grubin did not adequately assess the situation and should have informed the family of the need for additional treatment and the seriousness of the problem, the deposition of Mrs. Freda is revealing. Where Dr. Grubin has alleged in his interrogatories that he referred the decedent to a competent mental hygiene clinic, it appears that the reference was by means of a written direction which decedent was instructed to bring home to his family, and which they in fact received. The deposition states:

Q. You mentioned earlier when you were trying to convince your brother to seek psychiatric help that you did this on Dr. Grubin's advice.
A. Yes. That was only from the form that he sent to my brother. He wrote on it that my brother needed psychiatric help. He wrote exactly what was wrong, that he was religious orientation and schizophrenia, something about schizophrenia, and something on the bottom he wrote, "needs psychiatric treatment." This is when Dr. Grubin had given this to my brother several days after he saw him. He told him that he would examine, you know, the case to find out just what should be done, and he told my brother to come back and my brother did go back and brought this form home for us.
Q. Do you still have that form?
A. No. That was to be brought to the Mt. Carmel Guild, which my brother did.

The mother, however, gave a different account. She stated:

[Dr. Grubin] just told me what my boy needed and told him to go to Mount Carmel Guild.
Q. In other words, your son had some writing on a slip of paper, is that correct?
A. Yes, written down.
Q. Do you know what George did with the piece of paper?
A. He went to Mt. Carmel Guild with it.

Later she also stated with respect to the Mt. Carmel Guild treatment: "He did went there a few tines." [*sic*]

Thus we see that over a month before decedent's suicide Dr. Grubin had recommended psychiatric care not only directly to decedent, but in the note brought home to decedent's family; also, decedent entered into the recommended relationship with the mental health clinic. It was not until a month later that decedent went to the emergency room at Elizabeth General Hospital for treatment, and was advised to go to the Union County Psychiatric Clinic for further treatment. Two days after that decedent was admitted to the hospital, placed in a medical ward initially, and then in the psychiatric ward just prior to his death. At these latter dates there was no contact with Dr. Grubin. The treatment by the doctor had terminated with respect to this illness when Dr. Grubin informed the patient and family that the decedent needed psychiatric help and referred decedent to a psychiatric clinic. There is no legal authority to support Dr. Vorhaus' opinion that there is a duty (especially in light of the confidential physician-patient relationship) of a physician to contact an adult patient's family with respect to treatment. But here responsibility was in effect placed in the hands of decedent and his family, who were specifically notified of the seriousness of the problem by the note on which was written (according to decedent's sister) "exactly what was wrong," and when the mother was told (according to her) "what my boy needed."

In *Parker* v. *Goldstein,* 78 *N.J.Super*. 472, 479 (App. Div. 1963), certif. den. 40 *N.J*. 225 (1963), the court stated:

> In an action for negligence or malpractice against a physician, the plaintiff ordinarily is required to establish that defendant's treatment or care fell below the standard established and recognized by the medical profession for the indicated condition of the patient, and the standard must be proven by expert medical testimony. [citation omitted]. . . .

There, a hypothetical question posed to an expert postulated an incorrect delivery date of the pregnant decedent. The court commented (at 480): "As will shortly appear, this misleading assumption directly led to the opinion of Dr. Graubard that the defendant deviated from the standard pertaining to [the] claim. . . ." The court therefore did not consider the expert's report as providing a basis for withstanding the argument that plaintiff's claims were unsupported. The seriousness of the situation had been assessed by Dr. Grubin, and procedure similar to that suggested by Dr. Vorhaus was actually followed.

With respect to the treatment that was given, the inadequacy noted in Dr. Vorhaus' report was that Dr. Grubin should have seen that the patient obtained a psychiatric consultation and evaluation before making recommendations and administering the small dose of thorazine. But, applying the principles described above in *Parker,* the facts in our case show that the patient was sent for the very help noted by Dr. Vorhaus—a psychiatric consultation. To require a physician to obtain a consultation from the same source to which he is about to refer his patient would be meaningless. A general practitioner, when faced with a specialized problem, should not be faulted because he referred his patient to a specialist, or in this case a clinic of specialists, in a situation where the patient presumably could not afford private psychiatric help. The duty of the initial doctor ends upon the patient's undergoing the subsequent treatment. (See the following discussion concerning the abandonment issue.)

As noted earlier, no causal connection has been supported by an expert's opinion with respect to the administration of thorazine. Even if Dr. Grubin had been negligent in failing to diagnose depression, and therefore should not have administered or prescribed thorazine, there is no showing that this drug was a factor substantially contributing to the suicide. When this motion was initially argued this court was concerned with whether there could be a causal connection between the administration of thorazine and decedent's death. Consequently, plaintiff's counsel was then given the opportunity to supplement his proof by submitting an expert's report. He was specifically directed to the problem of connecting the thorazine to the death. Since no such connection was supplied by Dr. Vorhaus' report, this court cannot supply this missing medical link in plaintiff's chain of proof. *Parker* v. *Goldstein, supra,* 78 *N.J.Super*. at 480.

It is the third allegation that presents the greatest problem in assessing this case on a motion for summary judgment. The first two points had involved factual references by the expert which were not borne out by the statements of plaintiff's own witnesses in depositions and interrogatories. This third basis, however, involves a sharp conflict as to the facts and an application of legal principles. Of course, this court will accept plaintiff's version of the facts in deciding this motion and assume that Dr. Grubin was repeatedly called for assistance during the days immediately preceding decedent's hospitalization.

The question of proximate cause, given the alleged subsequent negligence of the hospital and supervising doctors, should not be passed upon on this motion for summary judgment. This ought to wait a jury's determination, but only if there were a legal duty of the doctor to give advice to the family and perhaps see that decedent was hospitalized sooner.

The question of abandonment of a patient was considered in detail in *Clark* v. *Wichman,* 72 *N.J.Super.,* 486, 491–492 (App. Div. 1962). In that case plaintiff had been injured in an automobile accident and had been taken to a hospital for treatment of a fractured femur. She developed a traumatic psychosis and was committed by court order to a state mental hospital for approximately 2½ weeks, during which period she was not under the care of her orthopedic surgeon. She argued that the surgeon abandoned her when she was committed to the mental hospital, but the court held that this argument was without merit, particularly when the transfer had been pursuant to an order of the court.

> ... This is not a case of unwarranted forsaking of a patient without notice or without providing a competent substitute physician [citing authorities]. Where a physician under appropriate circumstances ceases to attend a patient, his responsibility ordinarily ceases without any formality [citing cases]. An abandonment consists of "a failure by the physician to continue to provide service to the patient when it is still needed in a case for which the physician has assumed responsibility and from which he has not been *properly* relieved" [citing authorities]. [at 491–492; emphasis in original]

The cases bearing on this point are collected in an Annotation, "Liability of Physician Who Abandons Case," 57 *A.L.R.2d* 432, 439–443. The general statement of the rule concerning a physician's withdrawal from the case is expressed as follows:

> It is the settled rule that one who engages a physician to treat his case impliedly engages him to attend throughout that illness, or until his services are dispensed with. In other words, the relation of physician and patient, once initiated, continues until it is ended by the consent of the parties or revoked by the dismissal of the physician, or until the latter's services are no longer needed. However, the relationship of physician and patient may also be terminated by the physician's withdrawal from the case. *It is well recognized that the physician has a right to withdraw from the case, but only after giving the patient reasonable notice so as to enable him to secure other medical attendance, and such a withdrawal does not constitute abandonment.* [at 439, emphasis supplied]

See also, *Ricks* v. *Budge,* 91 *Utah* 307, 64 *P.2d* 108 (Sup. Ct. 1937); *Mucci* v. *Houghton,* 89 *Iowa* 608, 57 *N.W.* 305 (Sup. Ct. 1894); *Gray* v. *Davidson,* 15 *Wash.2d* 257, 130 *P.2d* 341, 136 *P. 2d* 187 (Sup. Ct. 1942), *Noren* v. *American School of Osteopathy,* 223 *Mo.App.* 278, 2 *S.W.2d* 215 (App. Ct. 1928), cert. quashed 322 *Mo.* 991, 18 *S.W.2d* 487 (Sup. Ct. 1929); *Lawson* v. *Conaway,* 37 *W.Va.* 159, 16 *S.E.* 564 (Sup.Ct. 1892); *Lathrope* v. *Flood,* 6 *Cal.Unrep.* 637, 63 *P.* 1007 (Sup. Ct. 1901) rev'd on other grounds 135 *Cal.* 458, 67 *P.* 683 (Sup. Ct. 1902). *Cf. Sibert* v. *Boger,* 260 *S.W.2d* 569, 571–572 (Mo.Sup.Ct. 1953). In *Sibert* negligence and abandonment of plaintiff were alleged where a doctor had been unable successfully to treat plaintiff and had told her "he could do nothing further for her and suggested that she go to someone else." The Supreme Court of Missouri found that the physician had withdrawn after reasonable notice. The court stated:

> It is true respondent told appellant on February 16, 1944, to go to another physician, but the evidence shows that she was already consulting another physician in the same town during the time she was under the care of respondent. She, therefore, was not abandoned without medical care. Moreover, in a city as large as Sedalia, medical service could have been obtained any day. At least, there is no evidence to the contrary. [at 572]

The editors of the Annotation note further:

> It is a corollary to the physician's right to withdraw from a case upon giving proper notice that he is under a duty to continue his attendance upon the patient until all the conditions for his rightful withdrawal are complied with, and that a breach of this duty may render him liable.
>
> Thus it may be stated as a general rule that a physician who is engaged to attend a patient is liable for any damages caused by his abandoning the patient without due notice to his patient, and without affording the latter an opportunity to procure the attendance of another doctor. Expressed differently, abandonment of a case by a physician without sufficient notice or adequate excuse is a dereliction of duty, and if injury results therefrom, the physician may be held liable in damages. . . . [57 *A.L.R.2d* at 440]

This principle is merely an expansion of the brief statement quoted earlier in *Clark* v. *Wichman* (72 *N.J.Super.* at 492), and is supported in the Annotation and Supplements by cases too numerous to cite.

The foregoing statements of the rule pertain to a physician who has undertaken the general treatment of a patient without an agreement limiting his services. A modified rule pertains, however, to a physician who has been employed only for a specific occasion or service, and such physician "is under no duty to continue his visits or treatment thereafter, and is consequently not liable for abandonment if he ceases treatment of his patient after performance of the specific service." 57 *A.L.R.*2d at 460. The Annotation cites two cases where a physician's services were limited to one call only. "Under such an agreement the physician is not liable for abandonment if he fails or refuses to treat the patient any further." See *Miller* v. *Blackburn,* 170 *Ky*. 263, 185 *S.W.* 864 (Ct. App. 1916); *Brown* v. *Dark,* 196 *Ark*. 724, 119 *S.W.2d* 529 (Sup. Ct. 1938). A similar rule applies if a physician is called for consultation or assistance only. *Shannon* v. *Ramsey,* 288 *Mass*. 543, 193 *N.E.* 235 (Sup. Jud. Ct. 1934); *Tomer* v. *Aiken,* 126 *Iowa* 114, 101 *N.W.* 769 Sup. Ct. 1904), and *Nelson* v. *Farrish,* 143 *Minn*. 368, 173 *N.W.* 715 (Sup. Ct. 1919).

This court is of the opinion that the same rule must apply if a patient is examined by a physician who by reason of his general practice determines that he is unable to provide needed specialized treatment and that the patient must therefore be referred to a specialist. In this case the reference was made to specific clinics where specialized help would be available, and the patient actually underwent care at one of these clinics. The fact that the decedent's mother had briefly utilized defendant's services on an earlier occasion did not render him decedent's physician under any general contract to provide care. The only proofs before the court by way of expert reports, depositions and interrogatory answers show that decedent visited Dr. Grubin for a specific purpose, and after this one visit Dr. Grubin found that he was incapable of providing the requested services. This was explained to decedent, and the subsequent events cannot be legally ascribed to any abandonment by Dr. Grubin. Whatever efforts were made by decedent's family to contact Dr. Grubin are of no legal import since no duty then flowed from Dr. Grubin to decedent.

To summarize, the record has been closely reviewed to determine whether there is a factual and legal basis for plaintiff's claims against Dr. Grubin. In malpractice actions, unlike most other negligence cases, the trial itself may have an adverse effect upon defendant's professional life. Courts should be aware that even allegations of malpractice against physicians and other professionals may have such effect. As noted in this opinion, the application of the principles of negligence law to the facts alleged by plaintiff should not render the defendant liable, and therefore the matter should be terminated at this stage insofar as Dr. Grubin is concerned. A physician who upon an initial examination determines that he is incapable of helping his patient, and who refers the patient to a source of competent medical assistance, should be held liable neither for the actions of subsequent treating professionals nor for his refusal to become further involved with the case.

Defendant Grubin's motion for summary judgment is therefore granted.

LIABILITY OF HOSPITALS OR GOVERNMENT FOR NEGLIGENCE OF PRACTITIONERS

In a bygone era hospitals tended not to be held liable for negligent acts committed on their premises. At that time the two primary owners of hospitals, the government and charitable organizations, were shielded from liability by statutes and common law that provided them with immunity. However, with the decline of the concept of general governmental immunity, the enactment of legislation such as the Federal Torts Claims Act (1946), and the judicial qualifiers that have been placed on what is left of the concept of governmental immunity, the immunity of government hospitals has been greatly, if not entirely, eroded. Similarly, the accountability of charitable institutions has also been on the increase (see for example, *Nicholson* v. *Good Samaritan Hospital,* 145 Fla. 360, 199 So.2d 344 [1940]).

Complementing the general erosion of governmental and charitable immunity, there has been a trend toward assigning greater liability to hospitals based on the greater responsibility hospitals have in managing the care of the patient. Thus in the early case of *Schloendorff* v. *Society of New York Hosp.* 211 N.Y. 125, 105 N.E. 92 (1914), Justice Cardozo opined that hospitals should not be held responsible for the negligent acts of physicians committed on hospital premises, because the hospital was merely providing the facilities for the doctor and not controlling the medical acts. The more enlightened view was expressed in the 1957 decision in *Bing* v. *Thunig,* 2 N.Y.2d 656, 163 N.Y.S.2d 3, 143 N.E.2d 3 (1957), in which Judge Fuld wrote the following: "The conception that the hospital does not undertake to treat the patient, does not undertake to act through its doctors and nurses, but undertakes instead simply to procure them to act upon their own responsibility, no longer reflects the fact."

In fact, hospitals do play a significant role in the care of patients. Hospitals provide medical equipment, supplies, medication, food, and various services to patients. Hospitals adopt internal policies and procedures related to admission of patients, in-hospital care and treatment, and discharge of patients. Hospitals also adopt various policies and procedures related to the granting of staff privileges and the hiring and firing of hospital personnel, and such procedures ultimately impact on patient care. Because of the modern relationship of the doctor to the hospital, the courts have shown a great willingness to assign liability to the hospital under the doctrine of *respondeat superior*. This willingness is reflected in *Adamski* v. *Tacoma General Hospital,* 20 Wash.App. 98, 579 P.2d 970 (1978), in which the court rejected the defense that the negligent physician was an independent contractor. See also the case of *Darling* v. *Charleston Community Memorial Hospital,* 33 Ill.2d 326, 211 N.E.2d 253 (1965), which is an oft-cited example of the application of a theory of corporate liability to hospitals.

In general, actions naming mental hospitals or institutions as defendants or co-defendants most frequently allege that the policies and procedures of the hospital failed to reasonably protect the patient from doing harm to himself or others. At one time the primary duty of such institutions was restraint. However, with the coming of the "open door" policy and the philosophy of treatment holding that freedom of movement and personal responsibility are conducive to rehabilitation, the courts have not held hospitals liable in some instances for harm and injury arising from acts of unsupervised mental patients. Thus, for example, in the 1941 case of *James* v. *Turner,* 201 S.W.2d 691 (1941), the court rejected the plaintiff's argument that the defendants had failed properly to supervise and restrain an institutionalized, suicidal patient who, while out on a walk, darted to a reservoir tower, climbed the ladder, threw himself in, and drowned. The *James* court observed that "the use of ropes or handcuffs or other restraining forces would have retarded his natural progress in regaining his health, both mental and physical."

Of course, reasonable minds may differ as to when the "open door" policy should be invoked and what the limits of such a policy should be. In the California case *Meier* v. *Ross General Hospital,* 445 P.2d 519 (1968), for example, it was claimed that the hospital was negligent in allowing the decedent access to an openable window, through which he jumped head first. One week prior to the suicide, the decedent had attempted to commit suicide by slashing his wrists. The defendant hospital and doctor argued that the policy of the psychiatric wing of the hospital was "open door." The trial court found in favor of the defendants, but the California Supreme Court reversed and issued a remand for a new trial, stating in part that the " 'open door' policy does not necessarily call for an openable window." In *Baker* v. *United States* and *Dinnerstein* v. *United States* pp. 100 and 152, respectively), we find detailed considerations of questions concerning the liability of a psychiatric facility for suicide. Other illustrative cases are as follows: *Benjamin* v. *Havens, Inc.*, 373 P.2d 109; *Carling* v. *State*, 294 N.Y.S.2d 30; *Centeno* v. *City of New York*, 369 N.Y.S.2d 710; *Charouleau* v. *Charity Hospital of New Orleans*, 319 So.2d 464; *Dimitrijevic* v. *Chicago Wesley Memorial Hospital*, 263 N.E.2d 309; *Fatuck* v. *Hillside Hospital*, 356 N.Y.S.2d 105; *Fernandez* v. *State*, 356 N.Y.S.2d 708; *Forde* v. *County of Los Angeles*, 134 Cal.Rptr. 549; *Gregory* v. *Robinson*, 338 S.W.2d 88; *Hebel* v. *Hinsdale Sanatorium and Hospital*, 119 N.E.2d 506; *Hirsh* v. *State*, 202 N.Y.S.2d 296; *Hunt* v. *King Hospital*, 481 P.2d 593; *Johnson* v. *Grant Hospital*, 291 N.E.2d 440; *Mills* v. *Society of N.Y. Hospital*, 1 N.E.2d 346; *Milton* v. *Louisiana*, 293 So.2d 645; *Pietrucha* v. *Grant Hospital*, 447 F.2d 1029; *Vistica* v. *Presbyterian Hospital and Medical Center*, 62 Cal.Rptr. 577, 67 Cal.2d 465; and *White* v. *United States*, 317 F.2d 13.

As we have seen in *Merchants National Bank* (page 164), mental hospitals also have an obligation to exert reasonable care in preventing patients from harming others. Other representative cases in this context are as follows: *Cameron* v. *State*, 322 N.Y.S.2d 562, 282 N.E.2d 118; *Department of Health and Rehabilitative Services* v. *State*, 338 So.2d 220; *Doctors Hospital, Inc.* v. *Kovats*, 494 P.2d 389; *Dunn* v. *State*, 327 N.Y.S.2d 662; *Harris* v. *State of Ohio*, 358 N.E.2d 639; *Hernandez* v. *State*, 360 N.Y.S.2d 314; *Higgins* v. *State*, 265 N.Y.S.2d 254; *Johnson* v. *United States*, 409 F.Supp. 1283; *Logan* v. *St. Luke's Hosp.*, 400 P.2d 296; *Orman* v. *State*, 322 N.Y.S.2d 914; *Semler* v. *Psychiatric Institute of Washington, D.C.*, 538 F.2d 121; *Thall* v. *State*, 329 N.Y.S.2d 837; *Underwood* v. *United States*, 356 F.2d 92.

Adamski v. *Tacoma General Hospital*, 20 Wn.App. 98, 579 P.2d 970 (1978)

REED, A.C.J.—Plaintiff Richard D. Adamski appeals from a Pierce County Superior Court order which granted the motion of defendant Tacoma General Hospital (Tacoma General) for summary judgment and dismissed plaintiff's medical malpractice action against the hospital. We reverse because we find genuine issues of material fact as to (1) whether the emergency room physician who treated plaintiff was Tacoma General's agent, and (2) whether the hospital's emergency room nurses were negligent in their treatment of plaintiff.

On January 9, 1974, plaintiff injured his finger while playing basketball. According to plaintiff the bone had broken and was protruding from a gash on the palmar surface of the finger. Plaintiff, aided by a friend, forced the bone back into position, applied a crude splint, covered the wound with a makeshift bandage and continued the game. Later that evening he presented himself for treatment at the emergency room of Tacoma General. Plaintiff first explained his injury to an emergency room nurse, who had his finger x-rayed, and then to the physician in charge, Dr. Tsoi. The doctor irrigated, debrided and cleansed the wound with saline solution and the cut was closed completely with nylon sutures and bandaged. Plaintiff was told to consult his personal physician in 5 to 6 days for removal of the stitches, or sooner if swelling should occur. Plaintiff was also given a copy of Tacoma General's form which reads as follows:

Tacoma General Hospital Emergency Care

Physician: Date:

Instruction For: *Care for Wounds After Suturing*

All sutures should be removed in your Doctor's office within 5–6 days unless otherwise advised, For your convenience, call the office for an appointment.

If the wound is bandaged, it should be left as it is. Keep it clean and dry, and changed only by your family Doctor. Your Doctor should be notified at once if you notice any redness, pain, swelling, or excessive fresh blood on the dressing.

The Doctors' Exchange, BR 2-3166, may be of help if you cannot locate your Doctor. *If unable to reach him at either his office, home or exchange, feel free to call the EUMERGENCY Department.* MA 7-1181, Ext. 184

[Italics ours.]

That evening plaintiff's hand began to swell and was somewhat tender; the next day the swelling had increased and he experienced severe pain. According to plaintiff, he called Tacoma General's emergency room for advice; plaintiff avers he talked with the nurse on duty, who told him that pain and swelling were not an unusual aftermath of his treatment. The next day, January 11, palintiff avers he again called the hospital and explained to the emergency room nurse that his situation had worsened and that he wished to be seen by the emergency room physician. He claims he was again told his symptoms were not unusual and that he should see his personal physician.

Plaintiff then attempted to contact Dr. R. Marx, an orthopedic specialist with whom he had previously treated. Dr. Marx was not available, however, and his office referred plaintiff to Lakewood General Hospital, where he was examined by its emergency room physician, Dr. North, who tentatively diagnosed a deep infection of the hand and referred him to Dr. Dale Hirz, a private physician. Plaintiff told Dr. Hirz how the injury had been sustained and how he had reduced the fracture so that the bone was not exposed. Based on this history, Dr. Hirz suspected that a staphylococcus infection had entered the joint sheath and determined that immediate treatment was needed to halt the spread of infection. Plaintiff was admitted to Lakewood General Hospital, placed on antibiotics and the next day, because his condition had not improved, Dr. Hirz surgically opened the little finger; the adjacent ring finger and wrist were also opened to permit a thorough flushing of purulent material from the infected area. The wound on the little finger was left open for drainage—it eventually healed naturally without suturing—and plaintiff was placed on specific antibiotics.

Plaintiff brought this action for damages against Dr. Tsoi, Tacoma Emergency Care Physicians, Inc., P.S. (TECP), a group of physicians who had contracted with Tacoma General, and Tacoma General, alleging as to the latter that (1) Dr. Tsoi was negligent in his diagnosis and treatment, (2) Dr. Tsoi was acting as the hospital's agent, and (3) the hospital's nurse-employees were negligent.

Tacoma General moved for summary judgment in its favor, asserting it could not be held liable for Dr. Tsoi's negligence upon the theory of respondeat superior because the doctor was not acting as its agent (employee-servant). Tacoma General argued the doctor was an independent contractor over whose actions it neither had nor exercised any right of control. In support of its motion Tacoma General filed (1) the affidavit of Dr. Tsoi; (2) the affidavit of Bruce Yeats, its assistant administrator; (3) a copy of the contract between Tacoma General and TECP; and (4) excerpts from Dr. Tsoi's deposition. In his affidavit Dr. Tsoi denied negligence and averred that he had treated plaintiff in accordance with the appropriate standard of care. In his deposition the doctor further stated that the TECP physicians exercised complete control over the emergency room facilities and personnel and the diagnosis and treatment of patients therein.

According to the other supporting documents, on January 1, 1973, the hospital contracted with TECP, a group of five licensed physicians, among them Dr. Tsoi, to furnish emergency room physicians on a 24-hour basis. The contract specifically classifies the emergency room doctors as "independent contractors" and not "agents or employees" of the hospital. The agreement further provided *inter alia* that (1) Tacoma General alone is to bill patients for the fees of the physicians, who agree to charge going rates; (2) the hospital undertakes to collect from the patient, by suit if necessary; (3) Tacoma General guarantees TECP $10,000 per month; (4) after certain deductions TECP is to be credited with 85 percent of all doctor fees collected, less the $10,000 guaranty; the hospital retains 15 percent for its collection services; (5) the emergency room doctors must be members of Tacoma General's staff and may *not* carry on a private practice in Pierce County, although they are not prohibited from (a) providing emergency room service to other hospitals, (b) assisting private physicians with surgery upon request, (c) teaching medical subjects and (d) providing medical laboratory consulting services; (6) emergency room physicians are precluded from utilizing the emergency room as a "source of private practice": (7) if TECP desires to furnish a physician other than one of the five named in the contract, Tacoma General's Board must first consent; (8) Tacoma General and TECP will each procure and maintain "professional liability, negligence, errors and omissions, and public liability" policies with limits of $1 million.

On this record, the trial court concluded that Dr. Tsoi was an independent contractor and not an employee of the hospital, and thus refused to hold the hospital liable on a respondeat superior theory. In addition the court found there was no proof Tacoma General's nurses acted negligently. Accordingly, Tacoma General's motion for summary judgment was granted and it was dismissed from the lawsuit.

On appeal we are asked to decide if the trial court should have submitted to the jury (1) the issue of Dr. Tsoi's agency, and (2) the issue of negligence on the part of the nurses. A summary judgment may be granted only when the record before the trial court presents no genuine issues of material fact and entitles the moving party to judgment as a matter of law. *Morris* v. *McNicol,* 83 Wn.2d 491, 519 P.2d 7 (1974). In ruling upon a request for summary judgment the trial court must view the evidence and all reasonable inferences therefrom in the light most favorable to the nonmoving party, *George D. Poe & Co.* v. *Stadium Way Properties,* 7 Wn. App. 46, 498 P.2d 324 (1972). In determining whether the movant has satisfied his burden of excluding any real doubt as to the existence of any genuine issue of material fact, the movant's papers must be closely scrutinized, while those of the nonmovant should be treated with indulgence. Finally, summary judgment will be denied if there appears to be any reasonable hypothesis under which the nonmoving party may be entitled to the relief sought. *Fleming* v. *Smith,* 64 Wn.2d 181, 390 P.2d 990 (1964).

Tacoma General relies upon the law as summarized at Annot., *Hospital—Liability—Neglect of Doctor,* 69 A.L.R.2d 307, 315 (1960):

> The general principle that the employer of an independent contractor is not liable for the torts of such contractor or his servants has frequently been recognized with respect to the liability of a hospital for the negligence or malpractice of a physician or surgeon. In other words, putting aside the difficult question whether, under particular circumstances, a particular medical practitioner was an independent con-

tractor so far as the hospital in which a patient was injured through his carelessness is concerned, the conclusion that, assuming such practitioner was an independent contractor in relation to the hospital, the hospital is not liable for such injury, is supported by many decisions. [Footnote omitted.] *See also* 40 Am. Jur. 2d *Hospitals and Asylums* § 14, at 860 *et seq.* (1968).

We have found no Washington cases addressing the problems inherent in the application of the doctrine of respondeat superior to the hospital-physician relationship. Tacoma General argues that the ordinary rules of agency must be applied and that if this is done, Dr. Tsoi must be held to be an independent contractor for whose negligent acts the hospital is not responsible. We are referred to the case of *Hollingbery* v. *Dunn,* 68 Wn.2d 75, 411 P.2d 431 (1966), which adopts the criteria of the Restatement (Second) of Agency § 220 (1958), and holds that the single most important factor to be considered in determining the status of one who performs services for another is the right of the latter to control the former. Tacoma General points out that nowhere in its contract with TECP does it reserve the right to exercise any control over the actual medical treatment rendered to its emergency room patients. Rather, Tacoma General argues, the only contract requirement is that the doctors must be members of Tacoma General's staff and conform to the usual and accepted professional and ethical standards of conduct.

The experience of the courts has been that application of hornbook rules of agency to the hospital-physician relationship usually leads to unrealistic and unsatisfactory results, at least from the standpoint of the injured patient. Consequently, we have seen a substantial body of special law emerging in this area; the result has been an expansion of hospital liability for negligent medical acts committed on its premises.

For many years the majority of courts followed the rule espoused by Tacoma General and held that physicians, because of their skill and training in a highly technical field, were not subject to control by hospital lay boards and thus could not be servants or employees in the sense required by the doctrine of respondeat superior. Rather, physicians were classified as independent contractors with the result that the hospitals in which they labored could not be held vicariously liable for their medical mistakes. In *Schloendorff* v. *Society of N.Y. Hosp.,* 211 N.Y. 125, 105 N.E. 92 (1914), Justice Cardozo reasoned that hospitals should not be held responsible for the negligent acts of physicians committed on hospital premises because the hospital merely provides the facilities and cannot control the doctors' medical acts. The rationale of *Schloendorff* was followed in many jurisdictions until the decision in *Bing* v. *Thunig,* 2 N.Y.2d 656, 143 N.E.2d 3, 163 N.Y.S.2d 3 (1957). In a masterful opinion by Judge Fuld, the New York court rejected Cardozo's "professional skill" theory of immunity as being out of step with the times.[1] In essence, the *Bing* court reasoned that other highly skilled professionals were not being excluded from application of the rule of respondeat superior and no valid reason existed for excluding

[1]At the time of the decision in *Schloendorff* v. *Society of N.Y. Hosp.,* 211 N.Y. 125, 105 N.E. 92 (1914), New York adhered to the doctrine of "charitable immunity" for hospitals. The case was not decided on that basis, however, and the court in discussing general agency principles, concocted both the "professional skill" theory of immunity and the "administrative act-medical act" dichotomy. As Judge Fuld demonstrates in *Bing* v. *Thunig,* 2 N.Y.2d 656, 143 N.E.2d 3, 163 N.Y.S.2d 3 (1957), the "administrative act-medical act" distinction served only to compound the problem for the courts, *i.e.,* in determining whether an act was medical or administrative. See the cases collected in *Bing* v. *Thunig, supra. See also Cunningham, The Hospital-Physician Relationship: Hospital Responsibility for Malpractice of Physicians,* 50 Wash. L. Rev. 385 (1975).

medical practitioners per se. Judge Fuld stressed that hospitals had become more than just a place for physicians to bring their patients for treatment; that, in fact, the hospital itself renders care and treatment through its facilities and employees. In holding the hospital responsible for the negligence of its nurses, Judge Fuld stated at page 666:

> The conception that the hospital does not undertake to treat the patient, does not undertake to act through its doctors and nurses, but undertakes instead simply to procure them to act upon their own responsibility, no longer reflects the fact. Present-day hospitals, as their manner of operation plainly demonstrates, do far more than furnish facilities for treatment. They regularly employ *on a salary basis* a large staff of physicians, nurses and interns, as well as administrative and manual workers, and they charge patients for medical care and treatment, collecting for such services, if necessary, by legal action. Certainly, the person who avails himself of "hospital facilities" expects that *the hospital will attempt to cure him,* not that its nurses *or other employees* will act on their own responsibility. [Italics ours.]

Once again the majority of courts chose to follow the New York court's lead and embraced the *Bing* concept that, *in certain cases* the doctrine of respondeat superior may serve to render a hospital liable for the negligent acts of the medical personnel who deliver its service to its patients. Since *Bing,* the principal difficulty encountered by the courts has been in determining in which cases to apply the rule of vicarious liability. Application of the traditional right of control test has not solved the problem because the governing body of a hospital never actually exercises, nor can it exercise, much control over a physician's medical decisions and his actual treatment of patients, even when he is clearly an employee of the hospital, such as an intern or resident.

Even before *Schloendorff* and *Bing,* however, the California court, in *Brown* v. *La Societe Francaise de Bienfaisance Mutuelle,* 138 Cal. 475, 71 P. 516 (1903) applied the doctrine of respondeat superior to the hospital-physician relationship because (1) the patient in the case sought treatment primarily from the hospital, and (2) the hospital paid the doctor a salary. It is on the basis of the "*Brown* formula" that many courts now regularly hold hospitals liable for the negligence of their interns and resident physicians.[2]

Conversely, where the patient contacts his personal physician and is by him admitted to a hospital for treatment, and the doctor looks directly to the patient for his fees, the courts uniformly treat the physician as an independent contractor. Such a holding results in a refusal to impose vicarious liability upon the hospital for the physician's medical mistakes even though they may occur on hospital premises.[3]

The *Brown* formula does not, however, cover all the possible variations of the hospital-doctor-patient relationship; the most troublesome situation has been that where the patient, not having contacted his personal physician, presents himself at the hospi-

[2]*See, e.g., Garfield Memorial Hosp.* v. *Marshall,* 204 F.2d 721 (D.C. Cir. 1953); *Bowers* v. Olch, 120 Cal. App. 2d 108, 260 P.2d 997 (1953); *Miami* v. *Oates,* 152 Fla. 21, 10 So. 2d 721 (1942); *Moeller* v. *Hauser,* 237 Minn. 368, 54 N.W.2d 639 (1952); *James* v. *Holder,* 34 App. Div. 2d 632, 309 N.Y.S.2d 385 (1970); *Koubeck* v. *Fairview Park Hosp.,* 17 Ohio Op. 2d 53, 172 N.E.2d 491 (C.P. 1960); *Sepaugh* v. *Methodist Hosp.,* 30 Tenn. App. 25, 202 S.W.2d 985 (1946); *Stuart Circle Hosp. Corp.* v. *Curry,* 173 Va. 136, 3 S.E.2d 153, 124 A.L.R. 176 (1939); *Brant* v. *Sweet Clinic,* 167 Wash. 166, 8 P.2d 972 (1932).

[3]*See, e.g., Mayers* v. *Litow,* 154 Cal. App. 2d 413, 316 P.2d 351 (1957); *Hundt* v. *Proctor Community Hosp.,* 5 Ill. App. 3d 987, 284 N.E.2d 676 (1972); *Lundahl* v. *Rockford Memorial Hosp. Ass'n,* 93 Ill. App. 2d 461, 235 N.E.2d 671 (1968).

tal for treatment and is there provided with or referred to a physician, usually a specialist, who is neither an intern, resident or other salaried employee of the hospital. The courts generally look to all of the facts and circumstances to determine if the hospital and doctor enjoy such a "significant relationship" that the rule of respondeat superior ought to apply. When, in fact, the hospital undertakes to provide medical treatment rather than merely serving as a place for a private physician to administer to his patients, the physician employed to deliver that service for the hospital may be looked upon as an integral part of the total "hospital enterprise."[4] In such cases, it should make no difference that the physician is compensated on some basis other than salary or that he bills his patient directly. These are artificial distinctions, the efficacy of which has long since disappeared and to the perpetuation of which we do not subscribe.

An example of the more enlightened approach is found in *Kober* v. *Stewart,* 148 Mont. 117, 417 P.2d 476 (1966); in that case, doctors comprising the Billings Clinic contracted to provide Billings Deaconess Hospital with a director for its diagnostic x-ray department. An 80-year-old patient was injured when the radiologist tilted the x-ray table, causing the patient to slide downward, so that he sustained serious leg fractures. The Supreme Court of Montana reversed a summary judgment favoring the hospital, finding there was a genuine issue of fact on the question of agency. Stating that the contract may have been merely the means by which the hospital hired a supervisor for its x-ray department, the *Kober* court fastened upon the following facts as relevant to the issue of agency: (1) neither the patient nor his private physician requested Dr. Stewart's services; (2) the three clinic radiologists rotated their periods of service at the hospital; (3) a hospital employee called Dr. Stewart at home and requested him to come to the hospital and read the x-rays; (4) Dr. Stewart was "on call" for the weekend; (5) the hospital's "standard procedure" was to call the radiologist on duty to read films in serious cases; (6) the hospital owned the equipment, operated the department and charged patients for the total service including doctor fees; (7) the clinic received a percentage of gross receipts.

In *Beeck* v. *Tucson Gen. Hosp.,* 18 Ariz. App. 165, 500 P.2d 1153 (1972), a summary judgment in favor of the hospital was reversed, the appellate court finding the relationship between the hospital and the physician in charge of its radiology department was that of employer-employee. Even though the doctor and his partner contracted to staff the department and were compensated by a percentage of revenues rather than by salary, the court found a significant relationship between hospital and doctor and applied the doctrine of respondeat superior. In support of its holding, the Arizona court noted the following pertinent facts: (1) the hospital billed for the radiologist's services; (2) the doctors received no other compensation; (3) the doctors agreed generally not to engage in private practice; (4) the doctors were solely responsible for operation of the department; (5) the doctors provided their own insurance coverage; (6) the doctors were to comply with the policies, rules and regulations of the hospital and the American Osteopathic Association; (7) the contract term was 5 years, terminable upon 120 days' written notice; (8) the hospital owned all the equipment and

[4]The term "significant relationship" is suggested in Cunningham, *The Hospital-Physician Relationship: Hospital Responsibility for Malpractice of Physicians,* 50 Wash. L. Rev. 385 (1975), wherein the author opines that the courts, without saying so, appear to be working toward an "enterprise tort," with the inquiry being addressed solely to whether the tort occurred within the scope of the "hospital enterprise" which is defined as "any service, medical or otherwise, the hospital purports to provide the patient." (50 Wash. L. Rev., *supra* at 418.)

office supplies and provided the supporting technicians; (9) the patient had no choice in selecting a radiologist, the hospital having made that choice for her. The court noted that the hospital could regulate the manner in which the x-ray equipment was used; it had the right to control the standards of the doctors' performance; the doctor was employed for an extended period of time; and he performed a service which was "an inherent function of the hospital, a function without which the hospital could not properly achieve its purpose." *Beeck* v. *Tucson Gen. Hosp., supra* at 170. Finally, the fact that Mrs. Beeck had signed a document acknowledging that all those performing services for her, including the radiologist, were independent contractors, and not employees or agents of the hospital, gave the Arizona court little pause: "unless the radiologist were actually an independent contractor the clause reciting him to be so is of no effect." *Beeck* v. *Tucson Gen. Hosp., supra* at 171.

The *Beeck* court, after reviewing the progress of the law in the hospital-physician field and citing with approval the departure represented by *Bing,* undertook to fashion a statement of policy underlying the extension of liability to a hospital in circumstances such as those before it:

> Having undertaken one of mankind's most critically important and delicate fields of endeavor, concomitantly therewith the hospital must assume the grave responsibility of pursuing this calling with appropriate care. The care and service dispensed through this high trust, however technical, complex and esoteric its character may be, must meet standards of responsibility commensurate with the undertaking to preserve and protect the health and indeed, the very lives of those placed in the hospital's keeping. [*Beeck* v. *Tucson Gen. Hosp., supra* at 169.]

In *Schagrin* v. *Wilmington Medical Center, Inc.,* 304 A.2d 61 (Del. Super. Ct. 1973), defendant hospital contracted with Doctors For Emergency Services (DFES) to staff its emergency facilities. A 9-year-old child died following allegedly negligent treatment in the emergency room. In finding the existence of a genuine issue as to the fact of agency, thus precluding summary judgment for the hospital, the court relied heavily upon *Bing,* stating as follows at page 64:

> While the New York Court was undoubtedly speaking directly of a situation involving medical personnel who were clearly employees of the hospital, *nevertheless, the rationale of the Court would apply equally to independent contractors performing medical services ordinarily performed by the hospital.* This is particularly pertinent in situations where there has been a holding-out or a representation that medical treatment is to be performed or administered in the hospital by medical personnel employed therein. [Italics ours.]

The *Schagrin* court appears to fasten on a nondelegable duty to the public which was assumed by the hospital when it, although not required by law to do so, elected to staff and maintain emergency room services as part of its total hospital enterprise.[5]

[5]Pursuant to RCW 70.41, the Washington State Board of Health has adopted rules and regulations pertaining *inter alia* to the establishment and maintenance of standards for the care and treatment of patients. The regulations are extensive and comprehensive and, as they apply to emergency services, are contained in WAC 248-18-285. The regulations *require* a licensed hospital to provide emergency care services in accordance with the community's needs and the hospital's capabilities. Within this general framework, however, the hospital is also *required* to adopt written policies and procedures specific to emergency care services. One requirement is that there must be a physician responsible for the services, whose functions and responsibilities are subject to the medical direction of the hospital.

It could thus be argued that Washington State has imposed upon hospitals a duty to provide emergency

Turning to the case before us it can readily be seen that the first prong of the *Brown* test is satisfied. Plaintiff went directly to the emergency room of Tacoma General and was there given no choice respecting his physician. In fact, Dr. Tsoi had been chosen for him at the time Tacoma General contracted with TECP for emergency room staffing. It is true vis-à-vis the second prong that Dr. Tsoi does not hold a salaried position; rather, except for the guaranty, his group is dependent upon the charges it makes to patients for professional services. There is, however, substantial evidence that Dr. Tsoi was performing "an inherent function of the hospital, a function without which the hospital could not properly achieve its purpose," *Beeck* v. *Tucson Gen. Hosp., supra* at 170, *i.e.*, he was an integral part of the total hospital function or enterprise. Clearly, when one considers all the facts and circumstances of the relationship between Tacoma General and its emergency room physicians, a substantial and genuine issue arises as to whether that relationship is that of principal and agent. It was error to resolve this issue by summary judgment.

Moreover, where a physician is found not to be the actual agent of the hospital, the latter may still be held responsible for his departures from good medical practice under the so-called "holding out" or "ostensible agent" theory. Restatement (Second) of Agency § 267, at 578 (1958) sets forth the rule as follows:

> One who represents that another is his servant or other agent and thereby causes a third person justifiably to rely upon the care or skill of such apparent agent is subject to liability to the third person for harm caused by the lack of care or skill of the one appearing to be a servant or other agent as if he were such.

In *Seneris* v. *Haas,* 45 Cal. 2d 811, 291 P.2d 915, 53 A.L.R.2d 124 (1955), the court reversed a trial court decision sustaining a challenge to the sufficiency of plaintiff's evidence to establish a cause of action against the hospital for negligence of one of its six anesthesiologists. In so doing, the court reiterated the general rule:

> Unless the evidence is susceptible of but a single inference, the question of agency is one of fact for the jury. . . .
>
> . . .
>
> Plaintiffs here through the questions permitted them showed that defendant West was one of six anesthetists on defendant hospital's panel, or staff; that he gave anesthetics for no other hospital; that all drugs and equipment used by him were supplied by said hospital; that he had regular "on call" duty at said hospital; that a hospital nurse summoned him to give the anesthetic in question. It appears that this evidence is sufficient to establish, prima facie, that defendant West was an agent of defendant hospital. There is nothing in the record to show that plaintiffs should have been on notice that defendant West was not an employee of defendant hospital and it can not be "seriously contended" that she was obliged to inquire whether each person who attended her in said hospital was an employee or an independent contractor. It follows that the trial court erred in taking the issue of agency from the jury. [Citations omitted.] [*Seneris* v. *Haas, supra* at 831-32.]

In finding evidence of ostensible agency, the *Seneris* court utilized the criteria approved in *Stanhope* v. *Los Angeles College of Chiropractic,* 54 Cal. App. 2d 141, 128 P.2d 705, 708 (1942), which are:

---

care services to the public and that they cannot shift the responsibility by contract. This concept was neither developed nor argued at either the trial court level nor in this court on appeal.

> [First] The person dealing with the agent must do so with belief in the agent's authority and this belief must be a reasonable one; [second] such belief must be generated by some act or neglect of the principal sought to be charged; [third] and the third person in relying on the agent's apparent authority must not be guilty of negligence.

In *Howard* v. *Park,* 37 Mich. App. 496, 195 N.W.2d 39 (1972), the defendant clinic referred a little girl patient to an independent doctor for removal of a leg cast using a "vibrating wheel." The patient sustained severe cuts and sought damages from the clinic. The *Howard* court found the clinic liable on ostensible agency grounds. The court noted that (1) treatment took place in the clinic; (2) the clinic chose the physician; and (3) the clinic billed on its stationery for the physician's charges. The court refused to adopt a requirement that the patient must inquire as to the treating doctor's status in order to entertain a reasonable belief he was the hospital's employee.

In *Vanaman* v. *Milford Memorial Hosp., Inc.,* 272 A.2d 718 (Del. Super. Ct. 1970), a private physician substituting for the hospital's regular emergency room doctor, negligently applied a leg cast to a 16-year-old girl. The patient did not inquire as to the doctor's status. After noting the doctor was not paid a salary and was not subject to hospital control, the court found evidence of ostensible agency and reversed a summary judgment for the hospital, stating at page 722:

> [I]f it should be found that the Hospital represented that Dr. Graybeal was its servant or other agent in diagnosing and treating plaintiff in its emergency facility, and if it thereby caused her to justifiably rely upon the care or skill of Dr. Graybeal, then it is liable to her for harm caused by any lack of care or skill by Dr. Graybeal just as if he were the Hospital's servant or agent. Restatement, Agency, 2d § 267.

In *Quintal* v. *Laurel Grove Hosp.,* 62 Cal. 2d 154, 397 P.2d 161, 41 Cal. Rptr. 577 (1964), an anesthesiologist erred during a "routine" eye surgey. The physician was one of a group of specialists who had contracted to staff the hospital's anesthesia department. In holding there was a jury question of ostensible agency, the court stressed that the hospital furnished all equipment and personnel needed to operate the department and that a hospital employee procured from the 6-year-old patient's mother a written "authority to operate."

Finally, in *Schagrin* v. *Wilmington Medical Center, supra,* the court found issues of both actual and ostensible agency even though the hospital had contracted with a group of independent doctors to staff its emergency room facility. As in the case of Mr. Adamski, the patient in *Schagrin* was taken immediately to the emergency room, given no choice of physician, was told to consult her private physician in 5 to 6 days, but nevertheless sought further emergency room treatment.

Tacoma General argues, however, that there can be no "ostensible agency" or agency by estoppel as it is cometimes called, in the absence of proof of an "affirmative misrepresentation" of Dr. Tsoi's status. The hospital relies for this point on *Greene* v. *Rothschild,* 60 Wn.2d 508, 374 P.2d 566 (1962), in which the Yellow Cab Company was held to have created apparent or ostensible agents of its former employees who had been converted to driver-owners. Liability was predicated on the fact the cab company permitted use of its "colors, markings and name" and failed to give adequate notice to the public of the new relationship. If Tacoma General's position is that before liability may be imposed, the hospital must have informed the patient he is being treated by its employee, we do not agree. On the contrary, a "holding out" or representation may arise when the hospital acts or omits to act in some way which leads the patient to a reasonable belief he is being treated by the hospital by one of its employees. *Seneris* v. *Haas, supra; Stanhope* v. *Los Angeles College of Chiropractic, supra; Quintal* v. *Laurel Grove Hosp., supra; Schagrin* v. *Wilmington Medical Center, supra;* Restatement (Second) of Agency § 267.

In the instant case, a jury could find that Tacoma General held itself out as providing emergency care services to the public. A jury could find that plaintiff reasonably believed Dr. Tsoi *was employed by the hospital to deliver that emergency room service.* It appears plaintiff was not advised to the contrary and, in fact, he believed he was being treated by the hospital's agent; in addition, the written instructions provided him after surgery could reasonably be interpreted as an invitation to return for further treatment if plaintiff could not contact his personal physician. The form bearing this instruction also carried the title "Tacoma General Hospital Emergency Care." Clearly, when the facts before the trial court and the fair inferences therefrom are viewed in a light most favorable to plaintiff, a jury could find that the emergency room personnel were "held out" as employees of the hospital. It was error, therefore, not to submit this issue to the jury.

Finally, we think plaintiff's evidence was sufficient to create a genuine issue of negligence on the part of the hospital's emergency room personnel in failing to provide proper follow-up treatment. Plaintiff's affidavit alleges that emergency room nurses told him his symptoms were not unusual, implying that he needed no further treatment. In addition, the affidavits of Doctors McDowell and Hirz support the reasonable inference that plaintiff's symptoms gave notice of a probable infection which needed immediate attention. It is uncontroverted that plaintiff did have to undergo further treatment because of the infection in his hand. Of course it is for the jury to determine what the nurses told plaintiff in response to his inquiries and whether they gave the proper advice. The hospital's position is, however, that plaintiff, in response to the motion for summary judgment, failed to produce medical testimony to establish the appropriate standard of care, its breach, and that plaintiff's damages were a proximate result of the breach. We do not agree. The hospital, as movant, had the burden of producing evidentiary facts to negate the existence of a genuine issue on these matters. *Reed* v. *Streib,* 65 Wn.2d 700, 399 P.2d 338 (1965). Except for the denials contained in its pleadings, the hospital put forward no affidavits, depositions, or other proof which would have required the plaintiff to produce his medical evidence. *Cf. Rossiter* v. *Moore,* 59 Wn.2d 722, 370 P.2d 250 (1962). The decisions in *Swanson* v. *Brigham,* 18 Wn. App. 647, 571 P.2d 217 (1977) and *Shoberg* v. *Kelly,* 1 Wn. App. 673, 463 P.2d 280 (1969), are no support for the hospital's position in this regard because in those cases the movants succeeded in producing evidentiary facts sufficient to force a disclosure of plaintiff's medical evidence.

For this and the other reasons we have outlined, summary judgment was an inappropriate method of disposing of plaintiff's claims.

Reversed and remanded for further proceedings consistent with this opinion.

PETRIE and SOULE, JJ., concur.

REFERENCES FOR CHAPTER III

AMERICAN PSYCHIATRIC ASSOCIATION. The principles of medical ethics, with annotations especially applicable to psychiatry. *American Journal of Psychiatry,* 1973, *130,* 1057-1064.

AMERICAN PSYCHOLOGICAL ASSOCIATION. *Ethical standards of psychologists* (1977 Revision). Washington, D.C.: Author, 1977.

ASNIS, G. M., FINK, M., & SAFERSTEIN, S. ECT in metropolitan New York hospitals: A survey of practice, 1975-1976. *American Journal of Psychiatry,* 1978, *135,* 479-482.

BURT, R. A. *Taking care of strangers: The rule of law in doctor-patient relations.* New York: The Free Press, 1979.

BUTLER, S. Sexual contact between therapists and patients. Unpublished doctoral dissertation, California School of Professional Psychology (Los Angeles), 1975.

BUTLER, S., & ZELEN, S. L. Sexual intimacies between therapists and patients. *Psychotherapy: Theory, Research, and Practice,* 1977, *14,* 139-145.

COHEN, R. J. Socially reinforced obsessing: A reply. *Journal of Consulting and Clinical Psychology,* 1977, *45,* 1166-1171.

COHEN, R. J. The case of Mary and the issue of control. In C. W. McLemore (Chair.), *Religion and psychotherapy.* Symposium presented at the 86th annual convention of the American Psychological Association, Toronto, Ontario, Canada, 1978.

COHEN, R. J. *Malpractice: A guide for mental health professionals.* New York: The Free Press, 1979.

COHEN, R. J., & Smith, F. J. Socially reinforced obsessing: Etiology of a disorder in a Christian Scientist. *Journal of Consulting and Clinical Psychology,* 1976, *44,* 142-144.

COYNE, J. C. The place of informed consent in ethical dilemmas. *Journal of Consulting and Clinical Psychology,* 1976, *44,* 1015-1017.

DAHLBERG, C. Sexual contact between patient and therapist. *Contemporary Psychoanalysis,* 1970, *6,* 107-124.

FEEGEL, J. F. Malpractice and lab tests. *Resident and Staff Physician,* 1974, *20*(4), 47-50.

FREEDMAN, A. M., & Kaplan, H. I. *Comprehensive textbook of psychiatry.* Baltimore: Williams & Wilkins, 1967.

GLASS, E. S. Restructuring informed consent: Legal therapy for the doctor-patient relationship. *Yale Law Journal,* 1970, *79,* 1533-1576.

GOIN, M. K., BURGOYNE, R. W., & GOIN, J. M. Face-lift operation: The patient's secret motivations and reactions to informed consent. *Plastic and Reconstructive Surgery,* 1976, *58,* 273-279.

GORDON, H. L. Fifty shock therapy theories. *Military Surgeon,* 1948, *103,* 397-401.

HALLECK, S. L. Discussion of "Socially Reinforced Obsessing." *Journal of Consulting and Clinical Psychology,* 1976, *44,* 146-147.

HARPER, F. V., & JAMES, F. *The law of torts.* New York: Little, Brown, 1956.

HEALY, W. *The individual delinquent.* Boston: Little, Brown, 1915.

HOCH, P. H. Clinical and biological interrelations between schizophrenia and epilepsy. *American Journal of Psychiatry,* 1943, *99,* 507-511.

HOLROYD, J. C., & BRODSKY, A. M. Psychologists' attitudes and practices regarding erotic and nonerotic physical contact with patients. *American Psychologist,* 1977, *32,* 843-849.

IMPASTATO, D. J. The story of the first electroshock treatment. *American Journal of Psychiatry,* 1960, *116,* 1113-1114.

JAGIM, R. D., WITTMAN, W. D., & NOLL, J. O. Mental health professionals' attitudes toward confidentiality, privilege, and third-party disclosure. *Professional Psychology,* 1978, *9,* 458-466.

KALINOWSKY, L., & HIPPIUS, H. *Pharmacological, convulsive and other somatic treatments in psychiatry.* New York: Grune & Stratton, 1969.

KANNER, L. *Child psychiatry.* 3d ed. Springfield, Ill.: Charles C. Thomas, 1957. (First published, 1935.)

KARDENER, S. H., FULLER, M., & MENSH, I. N. A survey of physicians' attitudes and practices regarding erotic and nonerotic contact with patients. *American Journal of Psychiatry,* 1973, *130,* 1077-1081.

KATZ, J. *Experimentation with human beings.* New York: Russell Sage Foundation, 1972.

LONDON, P. Psychotherapy for religious neuroses? Comments on Cohen & Smith. *Journal of Consulting and Clinical Psychology,* 1976, *44,* 145-147.

MARMOR, J. Some psychodynamic aspects of the seduction of patients in psychotherapy. *The American Journal of Psychoanalysis,* 1976, *36,* 319-323.

MCCARTNEY, J. L. Overt transference. *Journal of Sex Research,* 1966, *2,* 277-237.

McKinney's Consolidated Laws of New York Annotated. St. Paul, Minn.: West Publishing Company, 1962.

MCLEMORE, C. W., & COURT, J. H. Religion and psychotherapy—ethics, civil liberties, and clinical savvy: A critique. *Journal of Consulting and Clinical Psychology,* 1977, *45,* 1172-1175.

MEDUNA, L. J. *Die konvulsions therapie der schizophrenie.* Marhold: Halle, 1936.

PERRY, J. A. Physicians' erotic and nonerotic physical involvement with patients. *American Journal of Psychiatry,* 1965, *122,* 631-638.

RAVITCH, M. M. Informed consent—descent to absurdity. *Resident and Staff Physician,* 1974, *20*(4), 10s-12s; 16s; 20s.

REDLICH, F. C., & FREEDMAN, D. X. *The theory and practice of psychiatry.* New York: Basic Books, 1966.

RICE, N. Informed consent: The illusion of patient choice. *Emory Law Journal,* 1974, *23,* 503-522.

ROBINSON, G. W. JR. Discussion. *American Journal of Psychiatry,* 1962, *118,* 779-780.

SAGALL, E. L., & REED, B. C. The liability of attendings and chiefs. *Resident and Staff Physician,* 1975, *21*(3), 77; 80-81; 85-86; 89; 92.

SERBAN, G., & GIDYNSKI, C. B. Schizophrenic patients in community: Legal misinterpretations of "right to treatment." *New York State Journal of Medicine,* 1974, *74,* 1977-1981.

SHAH, S. A. Privileged communications, confidentiality, and privacy: Privileged communications. *Professional Psychology,* 1969, *1,* 56-59.

SLOVENKO, R. Cited in "Malpsychotherapy" suits may soon beset psychiatrists. *Frontiers of Psychiatry,* March 1, 1978, pp. 1-2.

STOKES, J. B. Comment on "Socially reinforced obsessing: Etiology of a disorder in a Christian Scientist." *Journal of Consulting and Clinical Psychology,* 1977, *45,* 1164-1165.

SWOBODA, J. S., ELWORK, A., SALES, B. D., & LEVINE, D. Knowledge of and compliance with privileged communication and child-abuse-reporting laws. *Professional Psychology,* 1978, *9,* 448–457.

TAYLOR, B. J., & WAGNER, N. N. Sex between therapists and clients: A review and analysis. *Professional Psychology,* 1976, *7,* 593–601.

WAITZKIN, H., & STOECKLE, J. D. The communication of information about illness. *Advances in Psychosomatic Medicine,* 1972, *8,* 196–203.

CHAPTER IV

Other Areas of Professional Liability

As noted in Chapter II, the term "malpractice" is commonly used with reference to a broad range of acts and omissions that extend beyond areas of tortious liability. Included among this wide range of causes of action that may be grounds for professional liability are breach of contract; breach of trust; breach of right to privacy; breach of right to be free from cruel and unusual punishment, undue influence, false imprisonment, and defamation; and breach of right to treatment.

BREACH OF CONTRACT

In the case of *Sard* v. *Hardy,* 281 Md. 432, 379 A.2d 1014 (1977), the court dealt with the issue of whether or not the patient had adequately been informed of the nature of the treatment provided. In that case liability was ultimately premised not on a theory of malpractice but on breach of contract and breach of warranty (see also the discussion of this issue in *Horne* [p. 261], Anclote Manor Foundation [p. 254], and *Nicholson* [p. 256]). In *Guilmet* v. *Campbell*, 385 Mich. 57, 188 N.W.2d 601 (1971), which appears below, we note that the defendant surgeons were assigned liability on a theory of breach of contract and not negligence. The jury in that case construed the surgeon's representations—such as, "After the operation you can throw away your pill box"—as assurances that could be viewed as an express promise to effect a cure or a specific result.

Generally when a health professional undertakes to treat a patient, an implied contract arises. This contract holds that the professional has the requisite training, experience, and skill to render the treatment with at least ordinary care and skill (*Wolfe* v. *Virusky,* 306 F.Supp. 519 [Ga. 1960]). As illustrated by the 1975 Colorado case of *Herrera* v. *Roessing* (cited in Cases Unlimited, Inc., 1976), doctor-patient reassurances do not ordinarily constitute guarantees or warranties. In *Herrera* the defendant physician had told the patient after a tubal ligation "not to worry about the tubes coming undone," that he was sure that she would not become pregnant again, and that she need not take any further precautions against becoming pregnant again. Suit was brought when this woman did in fact become pregnant again. The court found the physician's statements to be opinions and reassurances that did not constitute a guarantee. Further, the court noted that since the patient had not paid any money to the physician for a postsurgical "warranty," she could not recover for a breach of the alleged warranty.

In *Guilmet* (below) we see the line drawn between what constitutes a reassurance and what could be construed as a contract to cure (see also *Rogala* v. *Silva,* 305 N.E.2d 571). Generally, if a doctor guarantees a specific result, then he or she may be held liable for the failure to achieve that result—regardless whether or not ordinary care was used. Thus, for example, in *Stewart* v. *Rudner,* 349 Mich. 459, 84 N.W.2d 816, a physician who told his patient that her baby would be delivered by Cesarean section and who proceeded to deliver the baby by other, usual procedures was found liable under a theory of breach of contract. It is possible that mental health professionals who employ a method of treatment different from what they agree to use initially might be held liable under a theory of breach of contract. Some scholars believe that more breach of contract actions are likely to affect the mental health profession in the future (see "Mal-psychotherapy" suits may soon beset psychiatrists, in *Roche Report Frontiers of Psychiatry,* March 1, 1978, pp. 1-2).

Guilmet v. *Campbell,* 385 Mich. 57, 188 N.W.2d 601 (1971)

Before the Entire Bench.

T. G. KAVANAGH, Justice.

This appeal presents a very simple question but it is fraught with great danger to the public weal.

The question is: Was the trial court in error in refusing to grant defendant's motion for a judgment notwithstanding the jury's verdict for the plaintiffs?

The defendants are skilled surgeons who performed a relatively complicated operation on plaintiff Richard Guilmet, and after such operation the plaintiffs suffered very great damages.

The danger attendant upon decision here is that on one hand if we sanction the award of damages to the plaintiffs we may foster suits which threaten the freedom physicians and surgeons must have in the practice of their vital profession, and on the other hand if we deprive these plaintiffs of their award, we not only may do them an injustice but impair the very process by which we seek to administer justice.

The facts and circumstances giving rise to the suit are as follows:

In the fall of 1963 the plaintiff had suffered near fatal bleeding through a peptic ulcer. at that time he was being treated by Dr. Klewicki and it was Dr. Klewicki who recommended the defendant surgeons. In January of 1964 the plaintiff went to see the surgeon "... curious about an operation, if I should have one or if I shouldn't have one...." It was never indicated to the plaintiff that he *must* have the operation.

Defendant Dr. Campbell testified that prior to the operation the plaintiff was in excellent physical condition and the operation was *not* an emergency.

At the first consultation with the defendant, Dr. Campbell, the following conversation took place according to the plaintiff's testimony:

Q. Now what was the nature of the conversation? Did you state your purpose in being there?
A. Yes, I asked Dr. Campbell—I was curious about an operation, if I should have one or if I shouldn't have one. I told him. He knew of my records. I started to tell him about my records. He said, "I know all about your records." I said, "Fine." He told me, he said, "*Once you have an operation, it takes care of all of your troubles,*" and he said, "*You can eat as you want to, you can drink as you want to, you can go as you please.*"
Q. This type of operation we are talking about then is a stomach or an ulcer operation, is that right?
A. Yes, it is.
Q. Did you talk with him at all about his familiarity with this type of operation or the extent of the operation?
A. Yes, I did.
Q. What was the conversation as you recall it?
A. Well, he explained to me how they do this operation, and at that time he told me that him and his associate, Dr. Arena, were specialists, *and there was nothing to it at all. It was a very simple operation according to them.*
Q. Did he talk at all about whether he had performed these before?
A. Yes, he did.
Q. And what was the conversation along those lines?
A. I asked him how often. He said, "*Very often.*"
Q. Any discussion as to complications or problems that may arise, that may result?
A. I asked him about it, how long I'd be out of work. He said, "Approximately *three to four weeks at the most,*" and I asked him about any complications, anything dangerous. He said, "*No, there is no danger at all in this operation.*"
Q. Was there any discussion as to where it would take place, how long you'd be convalescing in the hospital?
A. He said "Beaumont Hospital." I'd probably be in four to five days and *then I'd be off work maybe another two to three weeks.*
Q. You say he was familiar with your background. Was he aware that you were taking various medications, Maalox and things of this nature?
A. Yes, he was.
Q. You had been taking these pills for a number of months, had you not?
A. Yes, I had.
Q. What was the discussion about the future use of medication?
A. Well, he said, "*after this operation, you can throw your pillbox away, your Maalox you can thow away,*" and then he come up with an example.
Q. Give the example.

A. The example was that "*In twenty years if you could figure out what you spent for Maalox pills and doctors calls, you could buy an awful lot. Weigh it against an operation.*"

Q. Was there any conversation with him as to operations he had performed on other individuals who had treated for a while?

A. Yes. He told me, he never mentioned no names. He just told me of a gentleman that he knows treated for an ulcer thirty years and he went in, had this operation, *and he is altogether a different man at this time.*

Q. Now at the time of the conversation were you back to work?

A. Yes, I was. [Emphasis added]

Following this conversation the plaintiff Richard Guilmet underwent the operation.

The record contains a stark description of the troubles that thereafter befell him.

The record description of the vagotomy reveals activity around and on the esophagus. On March 4, 1964 the day following the operation Dr. Wood—a specialist in thoracic surgery on the staff of Beaumont Hospital examined plaintiff and diagnosed: "Ruptured esophagus due to surgical trauma in doing the vagotomy with bilateral effusion and mediastinal emphysema and mediastinitis." Dr. Wood testified that the symptoms displayed by the patient would cause him concern, that the mortality rate from a ruptured esophagus is 50% to 75%.

After the original operation plaintiff went through three subsequent operations for the insertion of tubes to drain excess fluid from his body; he suffered hepatitis which the defendant Dr. Campbell thought was probably caused by one of the many pints of blood he had been given; due to plaintiff's constant coughing and vomiting when eating, his weight fell from 170 pounds to 88 pounds and he was unrecognizable; he was unable to sleep due to coughing and only a return to the hospital and insertion of a drainage tube enabled him to sleep; and finally, he is scarred badly from the operations; he is unable to hold down two jobs as he once could; he is physically weak and unable to be athletically or socially active, and Dr. Wood testified that it is not unusual for recurrences of one of his infections as long as 20 years later.

The plaintiffs brought suit for their damages in a two count complaint. One count asserted negligence on the part of the defendants in performing the operation, and the other count charged a breach of contract saying:

> 4. That in January of 1964, Plaintiff Richard A. Guilmet, for good and valuable consideration, entered into an agreement with Defendants to perform an operation known as a gastric resection upon Plaintiff and to administer subsequent post-operative care; that thereupon Defendants in furtherance of their contract jointly undertook to examine, diagnose, treat and operate upon and care for Plaintiff so as to cure him of the stomach disorder from which he was then suffering.

At the conclusion of proofs, overruling a defense motion for a directed verdict, the trial court sent the case to the jury and stated in his ruling:

> Turning to the matter of contract, it is true that Plaintiff Richard Guilmet, in his testimony, direct testimony, said that he talked with Dr. Campbell and Dr. Campbell said the operation would take care of all his troubles, and he could do as he pleased afterwards; that it was a simple operation, said that he performed it very often and he would be out of work four weeks and there was no danger.
>
> Now again, this Court would doubt whether those statements were all made, particularly after having listened to the Doctor, and while it is true that the Doctor is

not required to guarantee his work, I suppose there is no reason why a medical doctor can't do that if he wishes, as well as any other person, so there is testimony here from which the Jury might reasonably infer that a contract was made to do these things as Mr. Guilmet testified, and I guess Dr. Campbell would be the first to admit that it was far more than four weeks before this man did go back and there must be a great danger involved as a matter of practical fact, and that apparently the Plaintiff, Mr. Guilmet, has not been able to throw away bis pill box since he recovered.

Well, the record indicates, according to my notes that Plaintiff Richard Guilmet had a conversation with Dr. Campbell prior to the operation, and that Dr. Campbell said that the operation would take care of all troubles and that he could go as he pleased afterwards, and it would be a simple operation; that he had performed many before and that the Plaintiff would not be out of work more than four weeks, there was no danger, and he'd be in the hospital four to five days, and he could throw the pill box away after the operation, and told of other successful operations. . . . *if this be the conversation and if the Jury accepts it, they would be in position to conclude that this Defendant Doctor had assured the plaintiff of the success of his operation, and having failed in that respect, they would be liable for damages.* [Emphasis added]

The jury returned a verdict of "no negligence" on the tort count but awarded the plaintiffs $50,000 on the breach of contract count.

Following this verdict the defendants moved for judgment notwithstanding the verdict, and the trial court denied it.

This decision was affirmed by the Court of Appeals and we granted leave in light of our conviction that it raised questions of the indicated significance to the jurisprudence of this state.

The defendants argue on appeal that "to establish a *special* contract to effect a cure plaintiff must prove a clear and enforceable promise, within the contemplation of the parties, supported by a *special* consideration, followed by reliance." (Emphasis added)

The distracting aspect of casting the question thus is that the plaintiffs never asserted a "special contract".[1] They claim, on the contrary, that the observations and descriptions of the result which the defendant made were promises to achieve that specific end, and were inducements upon which plaintiff, Richard Guilmet, relied in proceeding with the operation. They characterize it as an undertaking to "cure" him of the stomach disorder from which he was then suffering.

This appellation of "cure" may be unfortunate.

The parties when contracting never used the word "cure" and the mere elimination of a troublesome condition may not always be properly so designated. For example, a

[1]In this state, a doctor is free to contract as he sees fit. He may or may not warrant the results of his treatment. He may do so as a term of the contract or as a separate contract subsequent to the original contract. (*Stewart* v. *Rudner*, 349 Mich. 459, 84 N.W.2d 816 [1957]). But in this case the warranties were prior in time to the acceptance and thus did not, as there, present a question of "past" consideration. Inapposite is *Gault* v. *Sideman*, 42 Ill.App.2d 96, 191 N.E.2d 436 (1963) wherein the Illinois court held the complaint did not sound in contract and, observed "Attention has been called by [*sic*] courts to the fact that a promise to cure is not made by a competent and honorable physician and that such a physician knows that he cannot warrant a cure." In addition to the obvious distinction between the cases, the quoted observation (whatever its validity) sheds little light on the question here involved as to whether or not such a promise was made.

It is well settled that a physician or surgeon may bind himself by express contract to perform a cure or obtain specific results by treatment or an operation. 41 Am.Jur., Physicians and Surgeons § 105, p. 220.

headache may be eliminated by decapitation but no one seriously suggests that it is a "cure." Similarly the substitution of a different stomach disorder for a specific one is not properly called a "cure" of the original ailment.

The gravamen of the plaintiffs' breach of contract complaint is that: 1)The following is the gist of what the defendants told him:

> "Once you have an operation it takes care of all your troubles. You can eat as you want to, you can drink as you want to, you can go as you please. Dr. Arena and I are specialists, there is nothing to it at all—it's a very simple operation. You'll be out of work three to four weeks at the most. There is no danger at all in this operation. After the operation you can throw away your pill box. In twenty years if you figure out what you spent for Maalox pills and doctor calls, you could buy an awful lot. Weigh it against an operation."

2) That this amounted to an offer of a contract to achieve by the operation the condition described. 3) That in reliance on the description, the plaintiff accepted the offer, and in breach of the contract the condition described did not result.

In effect by their motion for judgment N.O.V., the defendants ask the court to rule as a matter of law that such statements by defendant *before the parties had contracted for the operation* as to the danger, convalescence, and result can *not* be regarded as a term of a contract between a physician and his patient.

This we will not do for we agree with Mr. Justice Cooley when he said:

. . . where the terms of a negotiation are left to oral proofs the question what the parties said and did, and what they intended should be understood thereby, is single and cannot be separated so as to refer one part to the jury and another part to the judge; but in its entirety the question is one of fact. *Strong* v. *Saunders,* 15 Mich. 339; *Maas* v. *White,* 37 Mich. 126; *Estate of Young,* 39 Mich. 429; *Engle* v. *Campbell,* 42 Mich. 565 [4 N.W. 301]. [*McKenzie* v. *Sykes,* 47 Mich. 294, 295–296, 11 N.W. 164, 165 (1882)].[2]

What we are saying is that under some circumstances the trier of fact might conclude that a doctor so speaking did contract to "cure" his patient.

What was said, and the circumstances under which it was said always determines whether there was a contract at all and if so what it was. These matters are always for the determination of the fact finder. (*Strong* v. *Saunders, et al., supra.*)

Justice Talbot Smith in *Stewart* v. *Rudner,* 349 Mich. 459, 467, 468, 84 N.W.2d 816, 822 (1957) articulated our concern for the sensitivity of this area of engagement, when he said:

> A doctor and his patient, of course, have the same general liberty to contract with respect to their relationship as other parties entering into consenual relationship with one another, and a breach thereof will give rise to a cause of action. It is proper to note, with respect to the contracts of physicians, that certain qualitative differences should be observed, since the doctor's therapeutic reassurance that his patient will be all right, not to worry, must not be converted into a binding promise by the disappointed or quarrelsome.

This sound counsel, however, should not be read to import a different standard to this relationship than to any other. It merely stresses the importance of circumstances in

[2]See also *Beebe* v. *Koshnie,* 55 Mich. 604, 606, 22 N.W. 59, 60 (1885), where in Mr. Justice Cooley stated:

determining the effect of words in establishing a contract. The qualitative difference between the relationship of a physician and his patient and the relationship between a shopkeeper and his customer is a significant circumstance the fact finder must remember in assaying their respective words of undertaking.

In this case the trial judge instructed the jury in part:

> Now, on the other hand, the two doctors take the position first of all, that they did not enter into a contract to effect a cure or a result, but that they only agreed to perform with such degree of care and knowledge and attention as is ordinarily possessed by practitioners of their profession under like circumstances. In other words, *they say that they did not (762) assure to the plaintiffs any cure or specific result, ...*

As in all contract cases for personal services, in order to find for the plaintiffs here the jury must have found from the evidence that the doctors made a specific, clear and express promise to cure or effect a specific result which was in the reasonable contemplation of both themselves and the plaintiff which was relied upon by the plaintiff.

The plaintiffs say they did, the defendants say they did not.

We conclude that under the circumstances disclosed by this record the trial court was correct in sending this case to the jury to determine the offer, acceptance, breach and damages, and refusing to grant judgment notwithstanding their verdict.

As did the Court of Appeals, we affirm.

Plaintiffs may tax costs.

T. M. KAVANAGH, C. J., and SWAINSON, ADAMS and WILLIAMS, JJ., concurred with T. G. KAVANAGH, J.

BRENNAN, Justice (concurring in affirmance).

Plaintiff sued on two counts, one in assumpsit, alleging breach of contract, one in trespass, alleging malpractice.

While it is true that in the contract count, plaintiff alleged that the defendants agreed to cure his ulcer, it is also true that the contract count contained allegations that defendants agreed to perform the operation in a good and workmanlike manner, and contained a number of other specifications of professional negligence, all of which were alleged to have constituted breach of contract by the defendants.

Count I, the contract count, contained the following:

> 4. That in January of 1964, plaintiff, Richard A. Guilmet, for good and valuable consideration, entered into an agreement with Defendants to perform an operation known as a gastric resection upon Plaintiff and to administer subsequent post-operative care; that thereupon Defendants in furtherance of their contract jointly undertook to examine, diagnose, treat and operate upon and care for Plaintiff so as to cure him of the stomach disorder from which he was then suffering.
>
> 5. That Defendants agreed as part of their employment to perform said operation in a good and workmanlike manner; that as specialists in surgery they would cure Plaintiff by said operation and that Plaintiff would be able to leave the hospital in a short time and resume his occupation and normal family life.
>
> 6. That Plaintiff duly performed all the terms and conditions of the agreement to be performed on his part; and thereafter on or about February 27, 1964, at Beaumont Hospital, Royal Oak, Michigan, Defendants, in pursuance of their agreement, placed Plaintiff under anesthetic and undertook to perform the operation herein referred to.

7. That Defendants in the course of said operation and in breach of their contract, in an unworkmanlike, unprofessional and unskilled manner, injured and perforated Plaintiff's esophagus, a heretofore healthy part of his body which required no treatment.

8. That Defendants in further breach of their contract, failed to timely diagnose and ascertain the aforementioned damage and to promptly and properly remedy their unskilled performance by proper operative and post-operative examination and treatment; that Defendants' post-operative procedures, particularly the oral administration of food and liquid which passed through the perforation in Plaintiff's esophagus into his chest cavity thereby causing aggravation and infection, was contrary to Defendants' agreement to exercise care and skill in administering to Plaintiff.

9. That Defendants in further breach of their contract carelessly deposited and left a clamp within Plaintiff's abdomen.

10. That Defendants in further breach of their contract failed to advise Plaintiffs of the risks involved and serious consequences attendant to said operation and failed to achieve satisfactory results.

11. That Defendants wrongfully misrepresented to Plaintiffs and concealed from them the injury to Plaintiff's esophagus and their careless and negligent acts in said operation as well as the extent of the surgery performed and the permanent and serious nature of the injury resulting from their treatment.

The cause was tried and submitted to the jury on both counts. At the conclusion of its deliberations, the jury returned and the following took place:

(The jury, having completed their deliberations, returned to the courtroom.)
Jury roll called.
THE CLERK: Members of the Jury, have ten or more of you agreed upon a verdict? If so, let your Foreman speak.
FOREMAN: Yes, we have.
THE CLERK: What is the verdict of the Jury?
FOREMAN: The verdict of the Jury is that on the Count of Malpractice, not guilty. On breach of contract, guilty.
THE COURT: The word of "guilty" is not used except in criminal matters. Is it your finding that you found no negligence?
FOREMAN: Yes.
THE COURT: The finding of the Jury is no Negligence?
FOREMAN: That's correct.
THE COURT: You find breach of contract?
FOREMAN: That's right. Correct.
THE COURT: What did you assess by way of damages?
FOREMAN: Fifty thousand.
(Jury sworn as to verdict.)
THE COURT: Do either Counsel care to have the Jury polled?
MR. WHITFIELD: Please, your Honor.
(Jury polled by the clerk.)
THE COURT: Ladies and Gentlemen, that concludes the trial of this cause.
(At this time the jurors left the courtroom.)

My Brothers have interpreted this verdict as constituting a finding that, without committing any of the acts of professional negligence alleged, the defendants were nonetheless liable upon a breach of a contract to effect a cure.

I do not so read the verdict of the jury.

While it was proper for the jury to return separate findings upon the two counts—assumpsit and trespass—it was not proper for the jury to return special or separate verdicts on the various specifications of breach of contract.

GCR 514 provides for the submission of a cause to a jury on special issues. In all other cases a jury verdict is a general verdict.

The jury verdict here was a general verdict upon the breach of contract count, and did not, as my Brothers suppose, negate the existence of those acts of negligence which were charged as breach of contract.

The trial court's oral question from the bench,

"The finding of the jury is no negligence?" did not constitute a special verdict under Rule 514. It did not control or limit the general verdict on the contract count.

The trial judge, throughout his instructions, referred to the assumpsit and trespass counts as "contract" and "negligence."

He was attempting to clarify the foreman's report that the verdict was "not guilty" as to malpractice and "guilty" as to breach of contract.

The only proper question the court could have been asking, and, in my opinion, the real purpose of his inquiry was—

"Do you find no cause for action as to the count of negligence?"

Properly considered, the verdict of the jury merely constituted a finding of no cause for action on Count II of the plaintiff's complaint (the trespass or negligence count) and a verdict for the plaintiff upon Count I of the plaintiff's complaint (the assumpsit or contract count).

This result is the more understandable when we consider that the trial judge severely limited the jury's consideration of Count II.

> Now although the plaintiffs in this cause have also claimed that the defendants failed to make timely diagnosis and failed to promptly and properly remedy plaintiff's post-operative complications by proper operative and post-operative examination and treatment, and also claim that the post-operative procedures, particularly the oral administration of food and liquid were careless and negligent and that the defendants carelessly and negligently deposited and left a clamp within the plaintiff's abdomen, and the defendants failed to advise the plaintiffs of the risks involved, and that the defendants failed to use the proper technique in the performance of the operation so as to not injure plaintiff's esophagus, and that the defendants failed to promptly call in consultants, let me say to you that the evidence does not disclose that their performance in these regards was not proper and in accordance with the medical standards of the community. Accordingly I direct that you disregard these claims and that they play no part in your deliberations as to whether or not the defendants were in fact negligent.

The trial judge did not similarly limit its consideration of the jury with respect to the allegations of Count I, and there is no reason here to assume that the jury did not find that the conduct of the defendants was "contrary to Defendants agreement to exercise care and skill in administering to Plaintiff" as alleged in Count I.

In my view, the law should indulge every presumption that a physician's medical assurances do not constitute a contract to cure. The verdict here should be sustained, and can be sustained without encouraging such allegations in the future.

ADAMS and WILLIAMS, JJ., concurred with BRENNAN, J.

BLACK, Justice (dissenting).

First: What is the Specific Nature of Our Divisive Issue?

Plaintiffs, husband and wife, sued the defendant surgeons in separate counts for alleged breach of contract and malpractice, both charged as having arisen out of the same transaction and the same facts. The first count avers that the defendant surgeons for good and valuable consideration contracted with plaintiff Richard A. Guilmet to remove a portion of his stomach by "an operation known as a gastric resection," that defendants performed the agreed operation "in an unworkmanlike, unprofessional and unskilled manner," thereby injuring "plaintiffs esophagus, a heretofore healthy part of his body which required no treatment," and that they were injured thereby to the tune of $365,000.

The second count, for malpractice, charged the defendants similarly excepting only that the breach of contract theory was omitted from that count. Thus the first count was pleaded *ex contractu* upon negligence and the second was pleaded *ex delicto* upon negligence. See full quotation, post at 613–614, of the "breach" paragraphs of count one of plaintiffs' complaint.

The pleaded issues were tried to a jury. The verdict of the jury specifically acquitted the defendants of negligence and found for the plaintiffs under the count *ex contractu,* in the amount of $50,000.

The *verdict* of the jury, and the *verdict* of today's majority with respect to the jury's verdict, expose with precise clarity that which on rehearing has become a simple and quite decisive issue. Here is the jury's verdict:

> FOREMAN: The verdict of the jury is that on the count of malpractice, not guilty. On breach of contract, guilty.
>
> THE COURT: The word "guilty" is not used except in criminal matters. Is it your finding that you found no negligence?
>
> FOREMAN: Yes.
>
> THE COURT: The finding of the jury is no negligence?
>
> FOREMAN: That's correct.
>
> THE COURT: You find breach of contract?
>
> FOREMAN: That's right. Correct.
>
> THE COURT: What did you assess by way of damages?
>
> FOREMAN: Fifty thousand.
>
> (Jury sworn as to verdict [also polled]) . . .
>
> THE COURT: Ladies and Gentlemen, that concludes the trial of this cause.

Here is today's majority verdict, repeated for accentuation.

> The jury's verdict of "no negligence" does not resolve the contract question.
>
> IF THERE WAS A CONTRACT TO EFFECT A CERTAIN RESULT IT DOES NOT MATTER WHETHER THE TREATMENT WAS DONE NEGLIGENTLY OR WITH CONSUMMATE SKILL. IF THE CURE WAS NOT EFFECTED THE CONTRACT WAS BREACHED.[4]

[3]Omitted. "The question, what oral contract parties have made, is not for the court, but for a jury. . . ."

[4](June 21, 1971): Since the foregoing opinion of dissent was submitted to the Justices, this quotation of the

(I have put this last paragraph in full caps, that it may stand forth shamelessly naked before the Courts of other States when they, predictably, are called upon to follow suit.)

As was noted last year, the "unworkmanlike, unprofessional and unskilled" language of count 1 manifestly was taken from, and plaintiffs' contract theory of recovery was planted upon, the most prominent authority cited by them. That authority is *Robins* v. *Finestone* (1955), 308 N.Y. 543, 127 N.E.2d 330, a decision which came to review, not as here after trial and verdict but upon the defendant surgeon's motion to dismiss. His motion assigned New York State's two-year statute of limitations, applicable to non-contract actions, *as the sole basis of dismissal.* The New York Court of Appeals held only that the complaint stated a cause *ex contractu* against the defendant surgeon, thus bringing into play the State's much longer limitational statute. *There was no holding at all that the pleaded cause would hold up without proof and finding of the negligence charged by Mr. Robins' complaint.*

Hence, unlike last year, we are now definitely squared off for and against proposition that the jury's verdict, having absolved the defendants from negligence, wiped out plaintiffs' pleaded and tried theory that the alleged breach was committed by the specific acts of *negligence* that are charged as *breach* in plaintiffs' first count.

Second: May These Plaintiffs Have Judgment Under the First Count, the Defendants Having Been Exonerated of Negligent Conduct as Alleged in that Count?

My then as now negative answer, with reasons based particularly on the reasoning of cases decided in California, Illinois and Montana,[5] appears in the opinion submitted last May. As against this there is no pretense of proffered authority or precedent. My Brothers five just say "This is the law." That they do with an arrantly dixitized vengeance, for all of the skilled research clerks of Lansing, working with no surcease and without food or drink, never could come up with any kind of respectable or even plausible authority holding that a surgeon, said as having contracted to accomplish what none but the Great Maker could perform, may be held to respond in damages for having failed to provide it.

The affirming Brethren attest on their own that no matter the skill with which these unusually competent and experienced specialist surgeons went about a perilously developing and finally successful task; that no matter they managed to save Mr. Guilmet's life by their efforts; that no matter the jury did find them not guilty of negligence, that these same specialists nonetheless "contracted" to provide—yes in "approximately three or four weeks at the most"—a "cure" for Mr. Guilmet's badly diseased and twice dangerously bleeding stomach and, having failed to have him "back at work" at end of that four week period, that they are due for mulct aggregating today more than $63,000.

Such is the announced rule of this case, no more and no less. Let it stand in our books for all to read, wonder and prepare either for more amercement of doctors or more "defensive medicine."

The policy and reasoning declared in the cited California, Illinois and Montana cases is not opposed by *Beebe* v. *Koshnic* (1885), 55 Mich. 604, 22 N.W. 59, which

---

then opinion of affirmance was deleted by means of a new opinion for affirmance. See "ADDENDA," post at 618.

[5] *Wilson* v. *Blair* (1922), 65 Mont. 155, 211 P. 289, 27 A.L.R. 1235; *Marvin* v. *Talbott* (1963), 216 Cal.App.2d 383, 30 Cal.Rptr. 893, 5 A.L.R.3d 908; *Gault* v. *Sideman* (1963), 42 Ill.App.2d 96, 191 N.E.2d 436.

last the Brethren standing for affirmance cite as authority for the proposition that today's issue of contract and breach became one of fact.

Let us examine the *Beebe Case*. There the doctor was the *plaintiff*. His pleaded cause was one of *special* contract, supported by a *special* consideration, to effect a cure on the same basis as in *Hollywood* v. *Reed* (1884), 55 Mich. 308, 21 N.W. 313, that is, "no cure, no pay." In view of our irreconcilably variant views of *Beebe,* hear Chief Justice Cooley tell us in steady—not conveniently expurgated—context what the nature of Dr. Beebe's cause was, and how the issue there came to this Court (pp. 604, 605, 22 N.W. at p. 59):

> COOLEY, C. J. The plaintiff is a physician, and brings suit to recover compensation for services in curing the defendant of a disease of one of the defendant's legs. *It was a part of the plaintiff's case that he performed the services under a special agreement that he was only to be paid in the event of a cure.* He therefore took the burden of showing that a cure had been effected. [emphasis by present writer].

I have read through, again this year, the 778 pages of this trial transcript. It discloses that the plaintiffs made out no submissible case of negligent malpractice under rules often laid down, strikingly applicable here, as in *Lince* v. *Monson* (1961), 363 Mich. 135, 108 N.W.2d 845 and *Skeffington* v. *Bradley* (1962), 366 Mich. 552, 115 N.W.2d 303. It discloses further that the testimony of Mr. Guilmet, taken at its best, failed to make out a submissible case under count one (the "contract" count) of his pleading. The reason is that his testimony did not support any "contract" theory of recovery, *that theory being breach occasioned exclusively by negligence.*

Read now all of the "breach" paragraphs of Mr. Guilmet's complaint:

> 5. That defendants agreed as part of their employment to perform said operation in a good and workmanlike manner; that as specialists in surgery they would cure plaintiff by said operation and that plaintiff would be able to leave the hospital in a short time and resume his occupation and normal family life. . . .
>
> 7. That defendants in the course of said operation and in breach of their contract, in an unworkmanlike, unprofessional and unskilled manner, injured and perforated plaintiff's esophagus, a heretofore healthy part of his body which required no treatment.
>
> 8. That defendants in further breach of their contract, failed to timely diagnose and ascertain the aforementioned damage and to promptly and properly remedy their unskilled performance by proper operative and post-operative examination and treatment; that defendants' post-operative procedures, particularly the oral administration of food and liquid which passed through the perforation in plaintiff's esophagus into his chest cavity thereby causing aggravation and infection, was contrary to defendants' agreement to exercise care and skill in administering to plaintiff.
>
> 9. That defendants in further breach of their contract carelessly deposited and left a clamp within plaintiff's abdomen.
>
> 10. That defendants in further breach of their contract failed to advise plaintiffs of the risks involved and serious consequences attendant to said operation and failed to achieve satisfactory results.
>
> 11. That defendants wrongfully misrepresented to plaintiffs and concealed from them the injury to plaintiff's esophagus and their careless and negligent acts in said operation as well as the extent of the surgery performed and the permanent and serious nature of the injury resulting from their treatment.

Consider the pleaded factual specifics distinguished from the legal conclusions that are set forth in the quoted paragraphs. One is declared by paragraph 7, the other by paragraph 9. Paragraph 7 declares that the defendants "perforated" Mr. Guilmet's healthy esophagus. Paragraph 9 declares that they left a "clamp" in his abdomen.

Take "7" first. Did the defendants "injure and perforate" Mr. Guilmet's esophagus? The claim was based in particular upon an entry in the hospital record made by Dr. Wood, a specialist in thoracic surgery, not abdominal surgery, some five days after the gastric resection was performed. Dr. Wood had been called into consultation by the defendants in view of Mr. Guilmet's then precarious condition. His entry reads:

> History and progress noted. X-ray today shows perforation of the lower esophagus—correction, lower esophageal segment with large pneumothorax on the right and pleural effusion on the left.

Dr. Wood was sworn by plaintiffs as their witness. Unless our standing rules of evidence have changed, plaintiffs vouched for his credibility, which is not to suggest that there was anything incredible or doubtful about his testimony. It developed without shred of dispute, both by Dr. Wood's testimony and that of defendant Arena, that the noun "perforation" was used by customary medical parlance in its broad sense and that the hole in the lower esophagus, discovered some days after the operation as above, is known technically as a "spontaneous fistula." Hear Dr. Wood on this:

> Q. You have indicated a spontaneous fistula. Would you explain to the jury what the mechanics of such a thing might be?
>
> A. It usually occurs in a patient who has some vomiting for any particular reason. Vomiting with a large amount of gas in the stomach can suddenly balloon the esophagus beyond its stretching point and it splits. The esophagus is actually a rather weak structure. It has an inner lining called the mucosa and then a muscular coat but it doesn't have any covering on the outside as the rest of the intestinal tract has, and so it's a structure which does not have a great deal of strength and so it is possible for it to become perforated without a great deal of injury. I mean, a great deal of force let me say. So a patient that suddenly evacuates the contents of the stomach, if it be dilated with gas and fluid, can so perforate the esophagus. This would be called a spontaneous perforation of the esophagus and it is reported and has a syndrome attached to it.

Later, when the trial judge intervened by saying he did not hear a presented question, Dr. Wood responded:

> Q. Actually in reviewing the chart here, my question was going to be is it your opinion that this hole in the esophagus was created during this operation of the gastric resection?
>
> A. I didn't anticipate that question, your Honor. I would be of the opinion that the perforation in the esophagus occurred at some time subsequent to the actual operation. I stated before that if it occurred at the time of operation, the surgeon should see it. It is possible I think that either Levine tube or a situation at the time of surgery precipitated a subsequent perforation, several hours after. I don't know whether the patient vomited after or not, but vomiting or retching could well have produced a perforation some time after surgery, perhaps during the immediate post-operative period, awakening from an anesthesia.
>
> Q. At any rate, it is your opinion that it did not occur during the operation?
>
> A. I think that is what I said.

Q. Is that your opinion?
A. I think that it occurred subsequent to the operation.

It is enough to say that there simply was no proof, or scintilla out of which any permissible inference of actionable practice could be drawn, that the defendants were negligent as charged by quoted paragraph 7, or that they were guilty of "breach" as duplicitously charged in that paragraph. I suggest the Brothers five concede this when they say that the jury's verdict of "no negligence" did not absolve the defendant surgeons of and from the alleged contractual liability. Do they not say that the defendants must respond no matter the "consummate skill" of their surgical doings?

Now for quoted "9." This allegation was actually interred at the trial, when the trial judge considered the requests to charge with counsel. When challenged for proof plaintiffs' counsel admitted that "clip" should have been employed in the place of "clamp." Then this took place, with no objection on the part of plaintiffs' counsel:

MR. CONDIT: I would move to amend the complaint to substitute the word "clip" for the word "clamp."

MR. WHITFIELD: I again suggest there is no evidence in the record that this is not within the standard of care. In fact it was testified to do this. It is intended with clips that they be left in and there is no evidence to the contrary.

THE COURT: I will have to agree with you on that.

A "clip" such as was applied to Mr. Guilmet's vagus nerve, after the latter had been snipped off as a necessary part of the main operation, is of minute size and made of silver. Its *permanent purpose* is to adjust and control—to the radically reduced size and gastric functioning of the remaining part of the stomach—the discharge of gastric juices into that part. There was no showing whatever that this was done other than in accord with regularly accepted medical practice.

Third: A Look at the Consequences of Today's Misfortunate Decision.

From here on the surgeon contemplating a serious operation will undertake knowingly a third and even more menacing risk should he advise affirmatively. The first of course is the ever sobering possibility of sad or untoward results no matter his "consummate skill" and the careful employment thereof. The second is that crescently more perilous exposure to a suit for negligent malpractice should the result turn out funereal or misfortunate. And now comes the third. It is this Court's newly invented and retroactively granted right of suit against a surgeon upon simple allegation that the surgeon contracted to do that which none but the Deity could possibly agree to perform, that is, effect a "cure" or defined result when the scheduled treatment is surgical removal of a substantial part of an anatomical organ; an organ which, to sustain life beyond *extremis,* must continue to perform a daily function.[6]

Does not the complaint before us allege that the defendants entered into an agreement "to perform an operation known as a gastric resection"? Do the Brethren not realize that the recommended operation necessitated the excision of approximately 80% of Mr. Guilmet's stomach, and that the vagotomy of which so much has been made was but a vitally necessary preliminary to the plaintiff-pleaded gastric resection?[7]

.otless the medical profession cannot buy insurance protecting against this new kind of professional ..ility. And even if such insurance were obtainable, what now with *Guilmet* will be the cost thereof, .uperimposed as it must be over the cost of liability insurance against malpractice. See the previously mentioned USNWR article at page 70: "The cost of malpractice insurance for doctors and hospitals has risen astronomically."

[7]Let me again, as done last year, provide an understanding of what a vagotomy is distinguished from a gastric resection. Webster has given it, for at least the last 15 years, as the "Surgical division of the vagus nerve."

One wonders why the minority affirmers of 1970, and now the majority affirmers of 1971, cannot see that their current opinion will not only create an easy new "breach of contract" way to sue physicians and surgeons for untoward or unforeseen results; that it will in addition open the doors of our courts to actions old and new so long as they pass 6-year rather than 2-year muster under M.C.L.A. 600.5807 (M.S.A. 27A.5807). Do the Brethren not perceive that the medics will go even more "defensive" when this latest of our "forward-looking" decisions hits the precedential fan, and that many an operation that might have saved life will not be performed either of professional wariness or, more importantly, inability of the surgeon under new law to prepare his apprehensive patient mentally for the making of an affirmative decision?

It is natural for the sick, and the near kin of the sick, to seek anxiously for more and more medical assurance when the hour for surgical decision arrives. And when that decision is affirmative and the result turns out fatal, disabling or otherwise dismal, it is human to recall the doctor or doctors' preparational encouragement as misrepresentative or even promissory; certainly when money is brought into legal focus. There is the rub as one gazes at testimony that Dr. Campbell, the circumstances being what they were when Mr. Guilmet was suffering the second time from serious internal bleeding,[8] "promised" to have the latter back at work in "approximately three to four weeks at the most."

Another curiosity: What will be contrived out of this case of *Guilmet* when, the presented case being exactly as at bar except only that the patient has died after administration of last rites, the patient's promise-oriented widow sues or attempts to sue as fiduciary under our distinctive wrongful death statute? Is not the tortious linchpin of that statute the exact same as was originally written by Lord Campbell, that is, death "caused by wrongful act, neglect or default"? Has not our unique since-1939 statute provided that "All actions for such death, or injuries resulting in death, shall be brought only under this section." (C.L.S.1961, § 600.2922; M.S.A. 27A.2922)?[9] What will we pronounce to be the measure of damages in such a case of *contracted cure,* when death results?

Still another for meditation is what our presently heady majority will do when an indignant client, having lost his case, insists in court on strength of *Guilmet* that his lawyer *promised* for consideration a damage verdict and judgment for no less than a given amount, or *promised* a decree saving the client's home from an allegedly unjust foreclosure or title-trap, or *promised* a successful action against that life insurer refusing to pay on allegation of medical fraud, or *promised* a successful contest of Grandpa's will, but did not come through. That will be a first class vexer for this Court to grant or deny when the contractual theory of Guilmet is advanced, yes against a lawyer; most certainly when the alleged promisor is a prominent member of the so-called plaintiffs' bar and *he* is nominated for condemnation in damages.[10]

Thus far there appears to the writer still another like bushment the Court should see but does not see, or perhaps is too absorbed to see, dead ahead. But what avails further

[8]To quote plaintiffs' brief: "As to these conversations appellee testified: 'I was in deep thought at that time of bleeding, I am bleeding to death in the woods, on the way home from work, some late night, and then he tells me that "Well if there is any more I can do for you, let me know." Well, I thought about it.' "

[9]The preceding statutory provision, § 2921, really buttons this up: "Actions on claims for injuries which result in death shall not be prosecuted after the death of the injured person except pursuant to the next section."

[10]We have here even now a case which, had Guilmet been handed down a while back, might well have posed for monetary punishment a lawyer who recommended successfully the turndown during trial of an offer to settle for $27,500, only to hear the jury say later "no cause." See *Sifers* v. *Horen,* 22 Mich.App. 351, 177 N.W.2d 189 and our order granting leave to review, 383 Mich. 822.

attempt at persuasion when all caution has been cast aside for the big rush toward more punitive damage awards? In our present exuberance this *Guilmet Case* has become a blind stampede toward another jurisprudential precipice. Hence anyone in the way had best head for the hills of reasoned safety. Even a duty-bound dissenter cannot exhort too long, before stepping aside, lest he be run down or carried over the cliff with the rest.

To Conclude:

Is the above too gloomy? Not at all. Today in America there is a great and critically developing shortage of medical men. They already have too much to do, are stretching their hours the more, and are hardly interested in the assumption of more legal risks than they bear now. You see, Brothers all, no Court may or can force a surgeon to perform an operation he deems risky *both* ways, that is, risky for the patient personally and risky for himself legally. *Guilmet* will simply make him guardedly overcautious in the making of his most serious judgments, and that is not good for the public weal.

The doctor who cannot prepare and condition his patient, both mentally and physically for a *serious* operation, is crippled beforehand. So is the patient, only more so. What is recommended surgically becomes progressive Gethsemane for the patient unless the doctor can provide, as before, that "therapeutic reassurance" which Justice Talbot Smith so wisely preserved inviolate when be wrote our carefully narrowed opinion of *Stewart* v. *Rudner* (1957), 349 Mich. 459, 468, 84 N.W.2d 816. But now with the threatening thrust of *Guilmet* the doctor must so hedge and guard his words (probably from now on with a tape recorder running) as to create more doubt and fear than ever in the patient's mind and, here and there, impel a desperate negative decision by the latter.

All else aside, the stark tragedy of this *Guilmet* precedent is that we Justices will never see or know anything about the hundreds and hundreds of negative decisions today's determination of "contract" liability will force upon the physician-patient relationship, both in the offices of medical consultation and in the hospitals of Michigan. Nor will we ever know about those predictably fewer cases where, more than true to their Hippocratic oath, the specialist in internal medicine and the specialist surgeon will risk despite *Guilmet* their reputations, their property, literally their all upon the sheer need for hopeful assuagement of the patient's misgivings and fears; only to see things go wrong at the hospital through no fault of theirs.

Those cases will be settled, ere they reach us. Not many will defend in court as Dr. Campbell and Dr. Arena have done, only to find themselves at the mercy of a "contract to cure" when they have undertaken to resect in serious part one of the patient's vital organs. I have no doubt, having read the details of Dr. Campbell's enviably proud record in abdominal surgery and of the assiduous skill employed by him and Dr. Arena in bringing Mr. Guilmet finally to that state of health which is reasonably expectable after such an operation, that the ordeal of this trial and of its ensuing appellate history had much to do with his untimely death last year. He and his partner saved Mr. Guilmet's life. He has lost his, after having been acquitted of negligence and yet held in damages for breach of an unbelievable contract.

All of the defensive measures this *Guilmet Case* will breed are not of course foreseeable by one of our profession. Some are, though. Will not the Port Huron or Detroit medic, knowing as he does that equally skilled fellows in medicine are available within 15 minutes across the river, more likely refer that uncertain patient over the international boundary for treatment and surgery; over there where the "law" is a little different? What about Niles to South Bend, or Monroe to Toledo? Withal, words fit for a judicial report are not available with which to characterize properly the reprehensible nature of this war without warning upon a status of mutual trust.

Such is the ominous and wholly uncalled for stuff of which *Guilmet* is made. I consider myself privileged to be here at this time for rude exposure—in our books—of what before both the legal and medical professions will stand forth as incredible judicial folly; folly because we are *not* forced to make such an unreal decision, as occasionally is due when we interpret and apply a statutory or constitutional provision. Here we deal with the common law. Here wisdom is due *from us;* not legislators or electors. That Lady must have departed our midst January 7 last when five gentlemen of the Court announced that they would endorse what by these presents I oppose.

A final word: Have not all thus far directly concerned with this case, counsel, trial judge, three Judges of the Court of Appeals, and now five Justices of this Court and their clerks, given no thought to where lies the really damning error of judgment for these plaintiffs? Is it not likely, had Mr. Guilmet decided against the recommended operation after having been physically and mentally readied for it by the defendants in February of 1964, that he would *not* be alive today? I apprehend that there is some little life-or-death difference between having a major operation when prepared for it with medical care, and undergoing it in desperate emergency after having been brought in by a speeding ambulance with a third attack of internal bleeding.

My vote is cast as before.

Addenda (June 21, 1971):

The foregoing dissent was delivered to the Brethren March 24, 1971. May 3 our majority withdrew the opinion criticized by that dissent and substituted in its place another which, as I understand, the regular plurality stands ready to endorse.

This latest opinion begs literally if unintentionally for more denunciation of its ominous threat, and for further alert to the retroactive extension it is due to make of limitational time within which the disgruntled may think up suits, for *breach of contract,* against members of the medical profession. It should and will be dissected by means of successively contextual quotations, each followed by timid comment.

1. For the first time since this case came to original submission May 5, 1970, the Brethren standing for affirmance have deigned recognition of the fact that their endorsements lockstep over perilously untested legal ground. Let their opinion speak here, for firm inclusion in our annals, lest the following also disappear by amendment or substitution. By the fourth paragraph of this latest opinion five Justices say (ante at 602-603):

> The danger attendant upon decision here is that on one hand if we sanction the award of damages to the plaintiffs we may foster suits which threaten the freedom physicians and surgeons must have in the practice of their vital profession, and on the other hand if we deprive these plaintiffs of their award, we not only may do them an injustice but impair the very process by which we seek to administer justice.[11]

Comment: They go on, nonetheless, to court if not invite the conceded danger by upholding, as due *contractually,* this ''award'' against two blameless surgeons in the

[11]Until now, the writer has assumed that ''justice'' is to be administered ''under law.''

sum of $50,000. Thus the statewide impact of the Court's decision, upon unknown numbers of present and prospective patients and their necessary relationship with the medical profession (saying nothing of the medics themselves), is weighed with, but found wanting against, the claimed right of these plaintiffs whose good fortune it was that the defendant surgeons by their skill succeeded in saving Mr. Guilmet's life. All this, however, is but nothing compared with the Court's sweeping assignment to fact finders of *all* cases that are pleaded and allegedly supported as at bar. See division "4," *post*.

2. On the same page the Court advises, in a one-sentence paragraph:

> Defendant Dr. Campbell testified that prior to the operation the plaintiff was in excellent physical condition and the operation was *not* an emergency. [Italics by my Brothers].

Comment: This is the occasionally deceptive half of the truth. The rest is that when Dr. Campbell was sent for in December of 1963, Mr. Guilmet was in or near *extremis,* suffering from ulcerous internal bleeding which had sent him unconscious to the hospital. There and then at home he had to be nursed slowly to that state of health which would permit the operation recommended by Dr. Campbell. This was done under Dr. Campbell's direction, but not until the doctor was satisfied with Mr. Guilmet's condition vis-à-vis the recommended operation.

It is hardly fair, then, for one to aver upon this record that "the operation was *not* an emergency." To the contrary it turned out to be just that, when the defendant surgeons opened Mr. Guilmet's abdomen and found as they did a stomach so diseased that 80% thereof had to be removed.

True, the operation was not deemed an emergency when it was planned by the patient and his major surgeons. Yet I doubt that anyone here is willing to state from the trial court record—upon *our* record—that it was *not* a critical job, a true emergency that is, when as only may be done with utmost precision the extent of internal disease is brought to surgical vision and palpation. Who indeed is willing to suggest, the two-times critical background of Mr. Guilmet's stomach trouble considered, that he in all probability would be just as alive today had the operation *not* been readied and done when it was?

3. Next comes new reasoning by the Court for sustenance of the award of damages now in scrutiny. Having stated plaintiffs' claim.

(a) That the observations and descriptions of the result which the defendants made were promises to achieve a specific end, and
(b) That they were inducements upon which the plaintiff Richard Guilmet relied in proceeding with the operation, and
(c) That plaintiffs have characterized all this as an undertaking to "cure" Mr. Guilmet of the stomach disorder from which he was then suffering;

our majority proceeds to "cure" this erroneous theory of recovery by *sua sponte* amendment thereof (an amendment not made, pretentiously or otherwise, upon authority of 1963 Court Rule 118.3). Read this (quoted from the majority opinion, *ante* at 606):

> This appellation of "cure" may be unfortunate.
>
> The parties when contracting never used the word "cure" and the mere elimination of a troublesome condition may not always be properly so designated. For

example, a headache may be eliminated by decapitation but no one seriously suggests that it is a "cure." Similarly the substitution of a different stomach disorder for a specific one is not properly called a "cure" of the original ailment.

Then comes what I would suggest is a "gisted" review by the Court, rather than a testimonially quoted presentation, of the facts upon which the Court comes to its judgment and the precedential effect thereof (*ante* at 606):

The following is the gist of what the defendants told him:

"Once you have an operation it takes care of all your troubles. You can eat as you want to, you can drink as you want to, you can go as you please. Dr. Arena and I are specialists, there is nothing to it at all—it's a very simple operation. You'll be out of work three to four weeks at the most. There is no danger at all in this operation. After the operation you can throw away your pill box. In twenty years if you figure out what you spent for Maalox pills and doctor calls, you could buy an awful lot. Weigh it against an operation."

Comment: Compare this "gist" and its preceding quoted counterpart with that which has been deleted from the Court's opinion submitted May 3 last:

The jury's verdict of "no negligence" does not resolve the contract question.

IF THERE WAS A CONTRACT TO EFFECT A CERTAIN RESULT IT DOES NOT MATTER WHETHER THE TREATMENT WAS DONE NEGLIGENTLY OR WITH CONSUMMATE SKILL. IF THE CURE WAS NOT EFFECTED THE CONTRACT WAS BREACHED.[12]

The comparison made, can there be any doubt that a wary Court has decided recently to avoid any precise definition of what it has in mind, as and for some new theory of recovery by plaintiffs? All the profession gets now is "This appellation of 'cure' may be unfortunate."; plus an intimation that defendants may have breached the alleged contract by substituting "a different stomach disorder for a specific one." As against that plaintiffs' pleaded and tried, and briefed and supported on appeal, theory of count one recovery is that defendants contracted "to cure him [plaintiff Richard Guilmet] of the stomach disorder from which he was then suffering."[13]

Come now Brothers, isn't a planned major operation consisting of a "sub-total gastric resection" of one's stomach, 80% in this instance, reasonably expected to result in a somewhat different somach disorder than the infinitely more dangerous "specific" these medics diagnosed, as a basis for their recommendation? What then is the "specific" nature of the contract, and of its breach, upon which the Brethren in majority presently rely? Can we have no answer except that—possibly—the plaintiffs did not intend to plead, or try, an issue of contract of "cure" and breach thereof?

4. Next comes that which, presumably, is designed to soothe a profession already beset by steadily mounting malpractice claims. Plainly it will have an opposite effect.

[12]For quotation of and respects paid this pair of paragraphs, see *ante* at 613.

[13]The quotation is taken from count one of plaintiffs' complaint. It was never amended. The issue of recovery on that basis, plus the effort of plaintiffs to sustain their count for negligent malpractice, were the only issues that were tried below.

Our only question now is whether the plaintiff burden-bearers made out a *prima facie* case of right to recover under contractually ordered count one. A *prima facie* case is defined (*Purity Ice Cream and Dairy Co.* v. *Adams Express Co.* [1922], 217 Mich. 593, 596, 187 N.W. 296, 297):

"A case made out by proper and sufficient testimony; one which is established by sufficient evidence, and can be overthrown only by rebutting evidence adduced on the other side.' 31 Cye. 1172." (Quoted with supporting authority in *People* v. *Licavoli* [1933], 264 Mich. 643, 653, 250 N.W. 520).

Consider Judge Van Valkenburg's recent article, "Can Our Courts Be Saved?" (February 1971 issue of MSBJ, 75, 76, 77, referring to that part headed "Malpractice Cases.") He tells us that which is probably better known to trial lawyers and trial judges throughout Michigan than to appellate Judges:

> Malpractice suits have increased by leaps and bounds in recent years, by about eight to ten percent per year. As every judge knows, they are difficult to try and have a sweeping effect on the medical profession and the public. Doctors become extremely cautious, hospitalize patients for minor matters, order unnecessary tests and X-rays and refuse to handle some cases at all. Further, insurance rates have increased—in one state to $5,000 per year—and inexperienced doctors cannot obtain coverage at all unless connected with a firm.

The Court starts out with observation that "We recognize that what we hold is sometimes made clearer by stating what we do not hold." (*ante* at 606). Then, pursuing such an apparently negative vein, by Brothers proceed to peal out a real alarm rather than an intended "all quiet"; one that is bound to send medics and surgeons posthaste to their lawyers for defensive preparations. To make it doubly clear that this is no overstatement, I repeat from the majority opinion the real "gist" of that which the medical profession is due to face; *nunc pro tunc* six years backward at that (*ante* at 606-607).

> What we are saying is that under some circumstances the trier of fact might conclude that a doctor so speaking did contract to "cure" his patient.
>
> What was said, and the circumstances under which it was said *always* determines whether there was a contract at all and if so what it was. These matters are *always* for the determination of the fact finder. [italics by present writer].

Cited in support of this last is *Strong* v. *Saunders* (1867), 15 Mich. 339. That case is all that is proffered to sustain the quoted and rather remarkable conclusion of law. Now *Strong* was a suit in assumpsit to recover compensation for the use of certain range lights and stakes provided by the plaintiff for the guidance of the defendant's steam tug through the St. Clair Flats, during the navigational season of 1864. The defendant tugboat owner denied obligation to pay on ground that no obligation accrued unless and until the captain of the tug had fixed and certified the amount to be paid, which last had not been done. The Court disposed of the defendant's requests for separate and alternative jury instructions by saying that "There was evidence strongly tending to show an express promise to pay such sum as the defendant's captain should certify to be fair and reasonable; and there also was evidence tending to show an implied promise, or, in other words, a clear duty on the part of the defendant to pay a reasonable compensation, ..."

I have read the *Strong Case* from one end to the other and am unable to find that the Court employed the inclusive word "always," or that it made any commitment such as I oppose, or any commitment remotely like it. Moreover, the case presented no question whatever of right to an instructed verdict of non-liability. It actually went back for retrial on account of an error of jury instruction not pertinent here.

We have a seven-tined forkful of uncommon law here. The point made now, for cases pleaded and tried as at bar, is that the issue of contractual liability or non-liability of the defendant doctor or surgeon is *always* to be one for determination of the jury or, if the issue is tried to the court, *always* for the fact finding determination of the judge. The message will get across. The medical profession and its legal advisers will simply have to ask pardon for taking more defensive measures, as all listen respectfully to the word of the Court.

Now for a few concluding observations:

Throughout a year (plus) of disagreement experienced since this case was initially submitted, one continuantly nagging question persists. It arises out of the jury's reported and accepted verdict of "no negligence," and of "not guilty" (of malpractice). Now most practitioners of law know no way whereby a man may breach a contract another avers he has made excepting (a) by neglect of performance, or (b) by omission or refusal of performance. The latter is not of course charged by these plaintiffs. They do however count upon the former, that is, negligent performance. If any doubt remains on that score, read again the total charging part of count 1 of plaintiffs' complaint (ante at 607–608).

Plaintiffs' charge of negligent ("unworkman-like, unprofessional and unskilled") performance was tried as their count-one issue of contractual liability, along with their count two liability issue of negligent malpractice. The jury found no malpractice and "no negligence." How then, all dixitism aside, can the trial court's judgment stand?

If the doctor cannot win even when the jury says "no negligence," how can he win at all without planning and erecting beforehand his own bar of exposure to what this day is made a newly conceived method of penalizing doctors of medicine and major surgeons for untoward results of the best of treatment, the best of surgery?

The patient who, with fear of his contemplated major operation left not too well assuaged by his consulted but legally forewarned surgeon, cannot be the heartened and trusting patient he should be. The surgeon who must be on legal guard against his patient and the relatives of that patient, simply cannot perform as otherwise he might. Too often he is likely to leave to the patient, by mechanical record, that critical decision of operation or no operation. And when the doctor of medicine or the specialist in surgery learns that he must by law protect himself against suits upon alleged *contracts of cure or result,* suits that are due now to be made expansible timewise from two years to six years, our majority can hardly blame that doctor or surgeon for taking the precautionary advice of his lawyer, rather than what may be intended to be the mollifying word of the Court.

It appears now that the die is cast. We are about to provide for grim ingest by our two most eminent professions the very essence of Michigan's new order of legalistic ultraism. This State, once proud of a national reputation for dependable as well as masterfully written precedents, deserves better than this from a Court which, in the venerable Capitol from which we departed last year, was graced by judges like Cooley in his time, and Fellows in the present century.

As before my vote is cast to reverse and remand for entry of judgment in favor of the defendants.

BREACH OF TRUST AND UNDUE INFLUENCE

The courts have imposed upon physicians—as well as mental health practicioners—a fiduciary duty of care and responsibility. The trust that a patient places in his or her doctor must not be abused, and breaches of that trust and the exertion of undue influence by practitioners will be dealt with by the courts. As recognized by the court in *Collins* v. *Erimann,* 122 Conn. 626, 191

A. 521, "Attending physicians are included among those assumed to have special opportunities for exerting influence." In *Mitchell* v. *Harris,* 268 Ala. 724, 246 So.2d 648 (1971), which appears below, the court is asked to address the legal issues attendant to a physician's purchase of land from a patient one month before the patient died. In this instance the court finds no evidence of undue influence, noting that the doctor had paid the full fair market value for the land.

Mitchell v. *Harris*, 268 Ala. 724, 246 So.2d 648 (1971)

LAWSON, Justice.

Mrs. Mary Cook Mitchell was named in a will executed by Lewis Harris on October 14, 1963, as the devisee of his "house at 1016 Mill Street" in the City of Montgomery. We will refer to the "house at 1016 Mill Street" as the subject property.

On January 18, 1967, Lewis Harris signed a deed which was drafted for the purpose of conveying the subject property to one Allen B. Harris. On January 25, 1967, Lewis Harris signed another deed which was prepared for the purpose of correcting the description in the deed of January 18, 1967. We will refer to those two instruments as the Lewis Harris deed.

Allen Harris and wife, Orleatha, on February 6, 1967, deeded the subject property to Dr. S. Jefferson Underwood.

Lewis Harris died on March 6, 1967. His will, under date of October 14, 1963, was admitted to probate on July 31, 1967.

On August 18, 1967, Mrs. Mary Cook Mitchell filed suit in the Circuit Court of Montgomery County, in Equity, against Allen Harris and wife and against Dr. S. Jefferson Underwood.

Aside from the prayer for process and the prayer for general relief, the bill filed by Mrs. Mitchell prayed:

> . . . And Complainant prays that upon a hearing hereof, the Court will make and enter a Decree declaring the rights and obligations of the parties hereto, and will specifically decree:
>
> a. That said purported Deed from Lewis Harris to Allen B. Harris is null and void and of no effect, and should be cancelled on the records in the Office of the Judge of Probate of Montgomery County, Alabama.
>
> b. That since Allen B. Harris had no title, said deed or purported deed from Allen B. Harris and Orleatha Harris to S. Jefferson Underwood is null and void and should be cancelled on the records in the office of the Judge of Probate of Montgomery County, Alabama.
>
> c. Declaring that any funds obtained by Allen B. Harris from S. Jefferson Underwood were obtained as the result of a conspiracy to defraud and tracing said trust funds and establishing the rights and equities of the Complainant and the Respondent, S. Jefferson Underwood, and requiring said Respondents, Allen B. Harris and Orleatha Harris, to restore the status quo and to return to S. Jefferson Underwood all funds received by them from said Respondent, S. Jefferson Underwood for the deed or purported deed attached hereto as Exhibit One.

In the stating part of the bill, as here pertinent, it was averred that the Lewis Harris deed was null and void and of no effect because Lewis Harris "did not have the mental capacity to understand the effect of his actions'' and because that deed ''was obtained by fraud and undue influence of Allen B. Harris.''

As to the respondent Dr. S. Jefferson Underwood, the stating part of the bill contained the following averment: ''And Complainant avers that the Respondent, S. Jefferson Underwood, knew or should have known of sufficient facts to put him on inquiry as to the mental condition of Lewis Harris and as to the bona fides of Allen B. Harris.''

Neither Allen nor Orleatha Harris made an appearance in the case and a decree pro confesso was rendered against them.

The respondent Dr. S. Jefferson Underwood filed an answer wherein he admitted that he received a deed to the subject property from Allen B. and Orleatha Harris, but denied the averments of the bill to the effect that the Lewis Harris deed was null and void and of no effect.

It was further averred in the answer of the respondent Dr. Underwood as follows:

> A. The Respondent in good faith purchased the real estate described in the Bill of Complaint, for the fair market value of said real estate and without notice of any defects, if there are any defects, in his grantor's ownership of the real estate.
>
> B. The Respondent since his purchase of said real estate, has constructed thereon a four-unit apartment building, the fair market value of which is TWENTY-FIVE THOUSAND DOLLARS ($25,000.00); at the time Respondent purchased said real estate, the fair market value of same was less than FIVE THOUSAND DOLLARS ($5,000.00).

Following a hearing wherein much of the testimony was taken ore tenus, the trial court decreed as follows:

> 1. That the complainant have and recover of the respondents, Allen B. Harris and Orleatha Harris a judgment in the sum of $6,000.00, for which execution may issue.
>
> 2. That the relief sought against respondent Underwood is hereby denied.
>
> 3. That the costs be taxed against respondent Allen B. Harris, for which execution may issue.

From that decree the complainant below, Mrs. Mary Cook Mitchell, appealed to this court.

There are three assignments of error, the first of which reads:

> The Court Below erred in not setting aside and holding as null and void, the purported Deed from Lewis Harris to Allen B. Harris.

As we read the brief filed on behalf of appellant, it is not asserted therein that the trial court erred in not holding the Lewis Harris deed to be and void. Appellant's brief does contain this language: ''We submit that the Court below plainly erred in failing to set aside the deed from Lewis Harris to Allen Harris.'' The only case cited in support of that statement is *Floyd* v. *Green,* 238 Ala. 42, 188 So. 867, which is not authority for the proposition that a deed is null and void and of no effect where it is obtained ''for a grossly inadequate consideration, by unfair advantage taken of great mental weakness, though not amounting to absolute incapacity of the grantor.'' In *Floyd* v. *Green, supra,* it is said:

> . . . In such case, the deed, *being voidable only, and not wholly void,* passes title to the grantee, and the heirs' claim to relief rests not on legal succession to the title,

> but on an equitable right to be invested with such succession. The relief appropriate to be afforded by the courts is by enforcing rescission of the contract of sale, and cancellation of the deed. [Emphasis supplied] [238 Ala. 45, 188 So. 869].

We hold that as to respondent below, Dr. Underwood, the appellee here, Assignment of Error No. 1 is inefficacious.

The two remaining assignments of error read:

> 2. The Court Below erred in not setting aside the Deed from Allen B. Harris to the Respondent Underwood.
>
> 3. The Court Below erred in its Final Decree denying relief against the Respondent Underwood.

It has long been the law of this state that a conveyance executed under duress is not voidable against a purchaser for value and without notice. *Royal* v. *Goss,* 154 Ala. 117, 45 So. 231; *Moog* v. *Strang,* 69 Ala. 98; *Vancleave* v. *Wilson,* 73 Ala. 387; *Pratt Land & Improvement Co.* v. *McClain,* 135 Ala. 452, 33 So. 185; *Gilley* v. *Denman,* 185 Ala. 561, 64 So. 97.

In *Ely* v. *Pace,* 139 Ala. 293, 35 So. 877, it is said:

> The rule as to a *bona fide* purchaser, often repeated in this state is, "that the party pleading it must first make satisfactory proof of purchase and payment. This is affirmative, defensive matter in the nature of confession and avoidance, and the burden of proving it rests on him who asserts it. *Ei incumbit probatio qui dicit.* This done, he need not go further, and prove he made such purchase and payment without notice. The burden here shifts, and if it be desired to avoid the effect of such purchase and payment, it must be met with counter proof that, before the payment, the purchaser had actual or constructive notice of the equity or lien asserted, or of some fact or circumstance sufficient to put him on inquiry, which, if followed up, would discover the equity or incumbrance." *Hodges* v. *Winston,* 94 Ala. [576], 578, 10 So. 535; *Bynum* v. *Gold,* 106 Ala. [427], 434, 17 So. 667. [139 Ala. 298, 35 So. 878.]

To like effect see *Stone* v. *Lacy,* 245 Ala. 521, 17 So.2d 865; *Lightsey* v. *Stone,* 255 Ala. 541, 52 So.2d 376.

Duress has been said to be a species of "fraud proper" and undue influence a species of constructive fraud. *Noel* v. *Noel,* 225 Ala. 302, 143 So. 469. But this distinction usually adverted to in connection with pleading questions does not operate to prevent the rule of the duress cases cited above from being applicable where the conveyance is executed as a result of undue influence.

So the question remains as to whether the evidence was sufficient to support a finding that the respondent, Dr. Underwood, was a purchaser of the subject property for value and without notice, actual or constructive, of facts which would justify a finding that the execution of the Lewis Harris deed resulted from the exercise of undue influence by Allen B. Harris over Lewis Harris.

Dr. Underwood paid Allen B. Harris the sum of $6,000 for the subject property, which the trial court found to be "the fair market value" of that property. Appellant finds no fault with that finding.

The trial court made no express finding as to "notice" by Dr. Underwood, but we think the language of the decree hereinafter quoted is tantamount to a finding that Dr. Underwood at the time he purchased the subject property for a fair and adequate consideration did not have actual or constructive notice of any defect in the title of his grantors. We quote:

> There is nothing in the evidence under all the circumstances to warrant granting the relief sought against respondent Underwood. Where a purchaser pays a fair and adequate consideration for real estate and in return secures a warranty deed, the burden is upon a third party to set the deed aside. *Such a burden requires sufficient evidence and such evidence cannot be found in this case.* . . . [Emphasis supplied]

In view of the clear-cut issues in this case, we repeat that we think the quoted language, particularly that which we have italicized, shows that the trial court entertained the view that Dr. Underwood was an innocent purchaser for value without notice, actual or constructive, of any defect in the title of his grantors. The decree rendered necessitated such a finding and we must presume such finding in the absence of anything to the contrary. *Martin* v. *Cameron,* 203 Ala. 548, 84 So. 270; *Aikin* v. *Murphy,* 282 Ala. 538, 213 So.2d 383.

This court has said that where a finding of facts made by a trial court is based on testimony taken orally before the court, or partly so, such findings will not be disturbed on appeal unless palpably wrong. *Mitchell* v. *Kinney,* 242 Ala. 196, 5 So.2d 788; *Aiken* v. *Barnes,* 247 Ala. 657, 25 So.2d 849; *Ingalls* v. *Ingalls,* 257 Ala. 521, 59 So.2d 898.

We have read the record with care and see no reason to discuss in detail the evidence adduced on the issue of notice. *Rowell* v. *McCollough,* 270 Ala. 576, 120 So.2d 729. The evidence on that issue was in sharp conflict. As above pointed out, the testimony was taken ore tenus and under the applicable law of review, we cannot set aside the finding of fact made by the trial court when testimony is so taken unless we conclude that it is palpably wrong. We cannot so conclude in this case.

The respondent, Dr. Underwood, had treated Lewis Harris approximately six months prior to the time the deeds were executed and in appellant's brief the case of *Collins* v. *Erdmann,* 122 Conn. 626, 191 A. 521, is cited in support of the followig statement: "A physician occupies a confidential relation to a patient." We do not read the *Collins* case, *supra,* as holding that as a matter of law a confidential relationship exists between a physician and his patient. We quote from the *Collins* case: "Attending physicians are included among those assumed to have special opportunities for exerting influence."

In our case of *Black* v. *Campbell,* 217 Ala. 134, 115 So. 19, a conveyance by a patient to her physician was sought to be set aside on the ground that the conveyance resulted from undue influence exercised by the physician over the patient. After relating the circumstances surrounding the execution of the conveyance, we said:

> In these circumstances there is an absence of any of these technical relations from which the relation of trust and confidence is presumed by law to arise, and, if such relation existed, it was one of fact, and the burden of proving it rested upon the complainant, who asserted its existence. *Nelson* v. *Brown* (Brown v. Nelson), 164 Ala. 397, 51 So. 360. . . . [217 Ala. 136, 115 So. 20.]

While we are not certain that we would have evaluated the testimony as did the trial court, we say again that we cannot say that his findings are palpably wrong. It follows, therefore, that the decree of the trial court is due to be affirmed. It is so ordered.

Affirmed.

HEFLIN, C.J., and MERRILL, HARWOOD and MADDOX, JJ., concur.

BREACH OF RIGHT TO PRIVACY

All persons have a right to privacy, a right to be "let alone" (*see Gallela* v. *Onassis,* 353 F.Supp. 196). Wrongful invasion of privacy is a cause of action that may be undertaken for intentional acts (e.g., wiretapping, peeping, doctors' treatment decisions) or unintentional acts (e.g., negligent disclosure of private information to unauthorized sources). In a 1976 case heard by the Supreme Judicial Court of Maine (cited by Ledakowich, 1977) an otolaryngologist/surgeon who had taken photos of a cancer patient at various stages in the patient's illness was sued on the grounds of invasion of privacy. According to the patient's widow, the patient did not consent to the picture-taking and had in fact tried to move from camera range. At one point the patient raised a clenched fist to object to the procedure. The trial court directed a verdict for the defendant doctor, reasoning that "the mere taking of pictures is not an invasion of privacy" and that "medical science must have some information in its effort to track down and search for a cure." However, this ruling was struck down by the higher court, which rejected the argument that such picture-taking over the patient's objections is permissible in the interest of medical science. In ordering a new trial the higher court ruled that the patient's right to be let alone had been violated and that the violation had constituted a tort for which liability could be assessed.

In *Rennie* v. *Klein* (page 208 above) we see an illustration of how the courts have allowed for an involuntary mental patient to refuse medication in the absence of an emergency on the grounds that such unauthorized treatment would constitute an unconstitutional invasion of that patient's right to privacy. In *Schwartz* v. *Thiele,* 242 Cal.App.3d 799, 51 Cal.Rptr. 767 (1966), which appears below, we see an allegation of invasion of privacy against a psychiatrist who, for some undetermined reason, made an examination of a woman in a parking lot. The court in this instance held the psychiatrist immune from liability, presuming that he bad acted in good faith and for probable cause.

Schwartz v. *Thiele*, 242 Cal. App.3d 799, 51 Cal. Rptr. 767 (1966)

FRAMPTON, Justice pro tem.

The appellant, Judith Schwartz, is the plaintiff in an action filed in the Superior Court of Los Angeles County, wherein she seeks damages against the defendant, David A. Thiele, the respondent here, for damages for the alleged invasion of her privacy.

The third amended complaint sets forth the following factual background as the basis of her right to recovery. It is alleged in substance that Thiele was and still is a physician and surgeon duly licensed to practice his profession in the State of California and that he maintains his office for the practice of his profession in Los Angeles County; that Schwartz was, at all times mentioned in the complaint, a resident of Los Angeles County and that her cause of action arose in that county.

The third amended complaint further alleges that the defendant Thiele was and is a stranger to the plaintiff and that at no time, past or present, has the plaintiff ever engaged the defendant or consulted with him in his capacity as a physician and surgeon or in any other capacity or at all and that the plaintiff has never been mentally ill.

The third amended complaint further alleges that at or about the hour of 9:30 o'clock on the morning of September 7, 1962, while the plaintiff and her sister, after having had breakfast at a restaurant in the City of Los Angeles, were walking to her automobile which was parked in a parking area maintained by the restaurant, the defendant, a total stranger to the plaintiff, without cause whatever on the part of plaintiff, and without her consent, purported to make an examination of plaintiff as to her mental illness. That the time consumed in the incident at the parking area did not exceed three minutes in duration, including the time it took the plaintiff to call her attorney by telephone, after which call she obtained the name of the defendant.

The third amended complaint further alleges that on September 7, 1962, without the consent of the plaintiff, the defendant, acting in his capacity as a licensed physician and surgeon and with the intent to gain a profit thereby, wrote a letter, directed to the Psychiatric Department of the Superior Court, stating in substance that he had examined the plaintiff and that in his opinion she was mentally ill and that because of such mental illness she was likely to injure herself or others if not immediately hospitalized or detained. That on or about September 12, 1962, the defendant caused the letter to be delivered to the office of the Counselor in Mental Health of the Psychiatric Department of the Superior Court of Los Angeles County (see §§ 5025 to 5030, Welfare & Institutions Code), which letter became a part of the records of said office.

It further appears from the allegations of the third amended complaint that no verified petition was ever filed wherein it was alleged that the plaintiff was a mentally ill person (see former §§ 5047 to 5049, Welfare and Institutions Code, now 5551-5553), but notwithstanding this, after the filing of said letter in the office of the Counselor in Mental Health and on or about September 12, 1962, a judge of the superior court signed an order, under the provisions of section 1871 of the Code of Civil Procedure,[1] appointing a medical doctor to examine the plaintiff as to her mental health, and that thereafter said medical doctor attempted, through plaintiff's attorney, to arrange an appointment for the purpose of examining the plaintiff as to her mental health. That plaintiff was never examined by the court appointed doctor. However, immediately upon learning of the attempt of the court appointed doctor to examine her as to her mental health and upon learning that the defendant had caused the letter dated September 7, 1962, to be filed in the records of the office of the Counselor in Mental Health, the plaintiff engaged her own medical doctor to and he did examine her and upon such examination he found that she was not a mentally ill person. That her doctor, on September 19, 1962, submitted his written report of his examination and findings to the Counselor in Mental Health and thereupon all of the proceedings against her were dismissed.

Plaintiff alleges that by reason of the foregoing acts the plaintiff's right of privacy has been invaded by the defendant thereby causing her great mental pain and physical suffering, humiliation, annoyance and mortification, and has tended to expose the

[1] "Whenever it shall be made to appear to any court or judge thereof, either before or during the trial of any action or proceeding, civil, criminal, or juvenile court, pending before such court, that expert evidence is, or will be required by the court or any party to such action or proceeding, such court or judge may, on motion of any party, or on motion of such court or judge, appoint one or more experts to investigate and testify at the trial of such action or proceeding relative to the matter or matters as to which such expert evidence is, or will be required, ..."

plaintiff to public ridicule and disgrace and that by reason thereof she has been damaged in the sum of $100,000.

A demurrer to the third amended complaint on the ground that the complaint fails to state a cause of action was sustained without leave to amend, and thereafter the action was dismissed pursuant to the provisions of subdivision 3 of section 581 of the Code of Civil Procedure. Such order of dismissal constitutes a final judgment (Code Civ.Proc., § 581d). The appeal is from this judgment.

Plaintiff based her case in the trial court, as she does here, solely upon the theory that upon the facts pleaded in her third amended complaint she stated a cause of action for the invasion of her right of privacy.

According to the pleadings, the communication caused to be delivered to the office of the Counselor in Mental Health was a letter signed by the defendant in which he expressed the opinion that the plaintiff was mentally ill and by reason of such illness is likely to injure herself or others if not immediately hospitalized or detained. This letter was not in the form of a verified petition, the defendant was not a relative or a friend of the plaintiff nor was he her attending physician, neither was he a physician attached to a public hospital or institution in which the plaintiff was a patient. (Welfare and Institutions Code, former § 5047 no2 § 5551.) Any person, however, may file in the superior court a verified petition alleging that there is in the county a person who is mentally ill and in need of supervision, care of treatment, and asking that examination be made of the mental health of the person, and when no relative, friend or other person can be found in the county who is able and willing to make and file such a petition then any peace officer, probation officer, physician attending the patient, physician attached to a public hospital or institution if the person is a patient therein, or public guardian may make and file the petition. (Welfare and Institutions Code, § 5551.) "... When a petition is filed by any such person, neither the person making or filing the petition, nor his superiors, nor the department, hospital, or institution to which he is attached nor any of its employees, shall be rendered liable thereby either civilly or criminally if there was probable cause for the making and filing of said petition." (Welfare and Institutions Code, § 5551.)

Every counselor, assistant counselor, and deputy counselor in mental health is a peace officer and a probation officer within the meaning of those terms as used in section 5551 of the Welfare and Institutions Code. (Welfare and Institutions Code, §§ 5029, 5030.)

According to the allegations of the third amended complaint, after the letter above referred to was received by the Counselor in Mental Health, he took certain proceedings designed to ascertain the condition of plaintiff's mental health and in connection with such proceedings an order was signed by a judge of the superior court, under the provisions of section 1871 of the Code of Civil Procedure, appointing a medical doctor to examine the plaintiff as to the condition of her mental health.

As heretofore pointed out and according to the pleadings, the letter delivered to the Counselor in Mental Health was not a verified petition as is required under the provisions of section 5551 of the Welfare and Institutions Code and such letter, therefore, did not constitute the commencement of an action or proceeding in the superior court. In the absence of an action or proceeding pending in the superior court such court would have no authority to appoint an expert witness. The court could not appoint an action or proceeding which did not exist. (See § 1871, Code of Civ.Proc.) We can find no authority in the law for the procedure alleged to have been taken by the Counselor in Mental Health after receipt of the letter written by the defendant.

It is not alleged that the act of the defendant in writing the letter and sending it to the office of the Counselor in Mental Health was done without probable cause nor is it alleged that it was done maliciously or that the defendant controlled or aided, assisted and abetted the action of the Counselor in Mental Health in taking the unwarranted procedure adopted by him.

There are no allegations in the pleading before us wherein it is made to appear that the procedure carried out by the Counselor in Mental Health was other than confidential in its nature; and it does not appear that any publicity was attached to it other than to make the plaintiff and her attorney aware of the fact that an examination of the plaintiff as to her mental health was sought. If it can be said that there was any publicity connected with the incident it could be no greater than the publicity which would have attached to the incident had there been a verified petition filed under the provisions of section 5551 of the Welfare and Institutions Code.

If the defendant had filed a verified petition as provided in section 5551 of the Welfare and Institutions Code, not as the plaintiff's attending physician, but as any person may do, and if there was probable cause for the making and filing of such a petition, then the defendant would not be liable therefor either civilly or ciminally. (Welfare and Institutions Code, § 5551.) If the defendant is entitled to immunity in filing a verified petition under the provisions of section 5551 of the Welfare and Institutions Code, where there is probable cause for the filing of such a petition, then he is entitled to the same immunity where his conduct falls short of the filing of a verified petition and amounts only to the making of a complaint to an officer interested in the subject of the complaint and who is authorized to take proper steps to investiage the matter, assuming that there was probable cause to make the complaint. In the absence of allegations in the pleading before us that the defendant acted without probable cause we must assume that there was probable cause for his act. (Code Civ.Proc., § 1963, subd. 1.)

Section 867 of the Restatement of the Law of Torts provides as follows: "A person who unreasonably and seriously interferes with another's interest in not having his affairs known to others or his likeness exhibited to the public is liable to the other." (Rest., Torts, § 867.) The right of privacy is recognized in California as a justifiable right. " 'The right of privacy [has been] defined as the right to live one's life in seclusion, without being subjected to unwarranted and undesired publicity. In short, it is the right to be let alone.' " *Melvin* v. *Reid,* 112 Cal.App. 285, 289, 297 P. 91, 92; see also *Kerby* v. *Hal Roach Studios,* 53 Cal.App.2d 207, 127 P.2d 577.)

Prosser in discussing the right of privacy as it relates to the public disclosure of private facts says: "Some limits of this branch of the right of privacy appear to be fairly well marked out. The disclosure of the private facts must be a public disclosure, and not a private one; there must be, in other words, publicity." (Prosser on Torts, 3rd Ed., § 112, p. 835; see also *Werner* v. *Times Mirror Co.,* 193 Cal.App.2d 111, 120, 14 Cal.Rptr. 208.) "It is pointed out in Prosser on Torts (2nd ed.), § 97 that except in cases of physical intrusion the tort must be accompanied by publicity in the sense of communication to the public in general or to a large number of persons as distinguished from one individual or a few." (*Santiesteban* v. *Goodyear Tire & Rubber Company* [5th Cir.], 306 F.2d 9, 11.) "Tbe gravamen of the tort is ordinarily the unwarranted publication by defendant of intimate details of plaintiff's private life." (*Coverstone* v. *Davies,* 38 Cal.2d 315, 322, 323, 239 P.2d 876, 880.) "The facts concerning the arrest and prosecution of those charged with violation of the law are matters of general public interest. Therefore the publication of details of such official actions cannot, in the absence of defamatory statements, be actionable." (*Coverstone* v. *Davies, supra,* p. 323, 239 P.2d p. 880.) "On the public street, or in any other public place, the plaintiff has no legal right to be alone; and it is no invasion of his privacy to do no more than follow him about and watch him there." (Prosser on Torts, 3rd Ed., § 112, p. 834.)

The restraint and treatment of persons who are mentally ill is a matter of public concern. If a person in good faith and for probable cause makes a written statement to an agency charged with the duty of enforcement of the law, designed to give such agency information upon which it can conduct an investigation, such a communication is not an invasion of the right of privacy of the person who is the subject of the communication.

In the case at bench, so far as it may be determined from the pleading, the defendant had some contact with the plaintiff, the exact nature of which is not disclosed, in a parking lot adjacent to a restaurant which was open to the public. As a result of this contact the defendant made a written communication to the Counselor in Mental Health, a peace officer, in which he stated in substance that the plaintiff was a mentally ill person and was in need of care and treatment. There was probable cause for the making of such communication. The content of the communication was not published as is required in order to give rise to a cause of action for the invasion of privacy. The defendant, having probable cause for the making of such communication, is entitled to immunity from civil damages for the making thereof. The content of the communication not having been published there was no invasion of the plaintiff's right of privacy.

The judgment is affirmed.

SHINN, P.J., and FORD, J., concur.

BREACH OF RIGHT TO BE FREE FROM CRUEL AND UNUSUAL PUNISHMENT

The Eighth Amendment to the Constitution guarantees each citizen the right to be free from cruel and unusual punishment. In *Price* v. *Sheppard* (p. 234), we saw that a hospital's unauthorized administration of electroshock therapy brought forth a claim that the hospital had violated the patient's constitutional right to be free from cruel and unusual punishment as well as the patient's right of privacy. In *Knecht* v. *Gillman,* 488 F.2d 1136 (8th Cir. 1973), below, we see how the court deals with the allegation that the administration of emetic agent to a nonconsenting patient in a mental institution constitutes a violation of the patient's Eighth Amendment rights. Note that a similar situation arose in *Mackey* v. *Procunier,* 477 F.2d 877 (9th Cir. 1973). In that case a prisoner in a California facility was administered a drug that impaired breathing as part of an experiment on how punishment affected behavior. The case was sent back for trial by the Federal Appeals Court, which noted that if the charges were proved true, then "serious constitutional questions respecting cruel and unusual punishment or impermissible tinkering with the mental processes" would be raised.

Knecht v. *Gillman*, 488 F.2d 1136 (8th Cir. 1973)

Before HEANEY, ROSS and STEPHENSON, Circuit Judges.

ROSS, Circuit Judge.

This is an action by Gary Knecht and Ronald Stevenson, both in the custody of the State of Iowa, against officials of that state, under 42 U.S.C. § 1983. Their complaint alleged that they had been subjected to injections of the drug apomorphine at the Iowa Security Medical Facility (ISMF) without their consent and that the use of said drug by the defendants constituted cruel and unusual punishment in violation of the eighth amendment. The trial court dismissed their complaint for injunctive relief. We reverse with directions to enjoin the defendants from further use of the drug except pursuant to specific guidelines hereinafter set forth.

After this case was filed in the district court, an order was entered assigning the case to the United State Magistrate for an evidentiary hearing pursuant to Rule 53 of the Federal Rules of Civil Procedure. This hearing was conducted by the magistrate who later filed his "Report and Recommendation" which included a summary of all of the evidence, findings and recommendations to the trial court. He recommended that the complaint be dismissed but that, if the drug was to be used in the future at ISMF, certain precautionary steps be taken in administering the drug and in employing the help of inmate aides. The trial court then gave the parties ten days within which to file objections to the report and recommendations pursuant to Rule 53(e) (2) of Federal Rules of Civil Procedure. Knecht and Stevenson filed their objections seeking clarification of two factual findings of fact. They objected to the recommendations of the magistrate and again requested that the trial court enjoin the injections of apomorphine into nonconsenting inmates. They also requested that the court incorporate the magistrate's recommendation, regarding the future use of inmate aides, into the court's order. The trial court dismissed the complaint and did not adopt the recommendations of the magistrate concerning the administration of apomorphine in the future.

On this appeal neither party challenges the use of the magistrate as a master pursuant to Rule 53 of the Federal Rules of Civil Procedure, and neither party makes any serious challenge to the factual findings of the magistrate. There is no indication that the reference to the magistrate, as master, was done pursuant to local rule, and we assume it was done because of "some exceptional condition" pursuant to Rule 53(b) Federal Rules of Civil Procedure. Under these circumstances we do not reach the question nor express any opinion on the propriety of referring § 1983 cases to a magistrate pursuant to local rule.[1]

The summary of the evidence contained in the report of the magistrate showed that apomorphine had been administered at ISMF for some time prior to the hearing as

[1]Several courts, tacitly or expressly, condone reference of civil matters to magistrates. *Dewrell* v. *Weinberger*, 478 F.2d 699 (5th Cir. 1973); *Remington Arms Co.* v. *United States*, 461 F.2d 1268 (2d Cir. 1972); *Givens* v. *W. T. Grant Co.*, 457 F.2d 612 (2d Cir. 1972). Other courts have seriously questioned or disapproved of the power of a court to refer matters to magistrates. *Ingram* v. *Richardson*, 471 F.2d 1268 (6th Cir. 1972); *TPO, Inc.* v. *McMillen*, 460 F.2d 348 (7th Cir. 1972). A split of authority also exists on reference of habeas petitions to magistrates. Some courts approve of the procedure, United States ex rel. *Gonzalez* v. *Zelker*, 477 F.2d 797 (2d Cir. 1973); *Johnson* v. *Wainwright*, 456 F.2d 1200 (5th Cir. 1972); *Parnell* v. *Wainwright*, 464 F.2d 735 (5th Cir. 1972), while others have disapproved of the practice, *Wedding* v. *Wingo*, 483 F.2d 1131 (6th Cir. 1973); *Dye* v. *Cowan*, 472 F.2d 1206 (6th Cir. 1972); *Rainha* v. *Cassidy*, 454 F.2d 207 (1st Cir. 1972).

"aversive stimuli" in the treatment of inmates with behavior problems. The drug was administered by intra-muscular injection by a nurse after an inmate had violated the behavior protocol established for him by the staff. Dr. Loeffelholz testified that the drug could be injected for such pieces of behavior as not getting up, for giving cigarettes against orders, for talking, for swearing, or for lying. Other inmates or members of the staff would report on these violations of the protocol and the injection would be given by the nurse without the nurse or any doctor having personally observed the violation and without specific authorization of the doctor.

When it was determined to administer the drug, the inmate was taken to a room near the nurses' station which contained only a water closet and there given the injection. He was then exercised and within about fifteen minutes he began vomiting. The vomiting lasted from fifteen minutes to an hour. There is also a temporary cardiovascular effect which involves some change in blood pressure and "in the heart." This aversion type "therapy" is based on "Pavlovian conditioning."[2]

The record is not clear as to whether or not the drug was always used with the initial consent of the inmate. It has apparently been administered in a few instances in the past without obtaining written consent of the inmate and once the consent is given, withdrawal thereof was not permitted. Apparently, at the time of trial apomorphine was not being used unless the inmate signed an initial consent, but there is no indication that the authorities now permit an inmate to withdraw his consent once it is given. Neither is there any indication in the record that the procedure has been changed to require the prior approval of a physician each time the drug is administered. Likewise there is no indication that there has been any change in the procedure which permits the administration of the drug upon reports of fellow inmates despite a recommendation by the magistrate that this practice should be avoided.

The testimony relating to the medical acceptability of this treatment is not conclusive. Dr. Steven Fox of the University of Iowa testified that behavior modification by aversive stimuli is "highly questionable technique" and that only a 20% to 50% success is claimed. He stated that it is not being used elsewhere to his knowledge and that its use is really punishment worse than a controlled beating since the one administering the drug can't control it after it is administered.

On the other hand, Dr. Loeffelholz of the ISMF staff testified that there had been a 50% to 60% effect in modifying behavior by the use of apomorphine at ISMF. There is no evidence that the drug is used at any other inmate medical facility in any other state.

The Iowa Security Medical Facility is established by Section 223.1, Code of Iowa, 1973. It is an institution for persons displaying evidence of mental illness or psychological disorders and requiring diagnostic services and treatment in a security setting. The patients admitted to the facility may originate from the following sources:

1) residents of any institution under the jurisdiction of the department of social services;
2) commitments by the courts as mentally incompetent to stand trial under Chapter 783 of the Iowa Code;

[2]Pavlovian conditioning is based on the theory that when environmental stimuli or the kinetic stimuli produced by the incipient movements of the punished act are made contiguous with punishment, they take on some of the aversive properties of the punishment itself. The next time the organism begins the act, particularly in the same environment, it produces stimuli which through classical conditioning have become aversive. It is these aversive stimuli which then prevent the set from occurring. Singer, Psychological Studies of Punishment, 58 Calif. L.Rev. 405, 423 (1970).

3) referrals by the court for psychological diagnosis and recommendations as part of the pretrial or presentence procedure or determination of mental competency to stand trial;
4) mentally ill prisoners from county and city jails for diagnosis, evaluation, or treatment.

Section 223.4, Code of Iowa, 1973.

Those transferred from institutions where they were committed pursuant to civil statutes or those who were committed by order of the court prior to conviction, suffer a compromise of their procedural rights in the process of the transfer to ISMF. The constitutional justification of this compromise of procedure is that the purpose of commitment is treatment, not punishment. *Cf. McKeiver* v. *Pennsylvania,* 403 U.S. 528, 552, 91 S.Ct. 1976, 29 L.Ed.2d 647 (White, J., concurring) (1971); *Sas* v. *Maryland,* 334 F.2d 506, 509 (4th Cir. 1964). Beyond this justification for treatment is the clear command of the statutes that the purpose of confinement at ISMF is not penal in nature, but rather one of examination, diagnosis and treatment. Naturally, examination and diagnosis, by their very definition, do not encompass the administration of drugs. Thus, when that course of conduct is taken with respect to any particular patient, he is the recipient of treatment.

The use of apomorphine, then, can be justified, only if it can be said to be treatment. Based upon the testimony adduced at the hearing and the findings made by the magistrate and adopted by the trial court, it is not possible to say that the use of apomorphine is a recognized and acceptable medical practice in institutions such as ISMF. Neither can we say, however, that its use on inmates who knowingly and intelligently consent to the treatment, should be prohibited on a medical or a legal basis. The authorities who testified at the evidentiary hearing indicate that some form of consent is now obtained prior to this treatment. The only question then is whether, under the eighth amendment, its use should be prohibited absent such consent; and if so what procedure must be followed to prevent abuses in the treatment procedures and to make certain the consent is knowingly and intelligently made.

At the outset we note that the mere characterization of an act as "treatment" does not insulate it from eighth amendment scrutiny. In *Trop* v. *Dulles,* 356 U.S. 86, 95, 78 S.Ct. 590, 2 L.Ed. 2d 630 (1958), the Supreme Court stated that the legislative classification of a statute is not conclusive in determining whether there had been a violation of the eighth amendment. Instead, the Court examined the statute by an "inquiry directed to substance," reasoning that "even a clear legislative classification of a statute as 'nonpenal' would not alter the fundamental nature of a plainly penal statute." *Trop* v. *Dulles, supra,* 356 U.S. at 95, 78 S.Ct. at 595.

Other courts have examined nonpenal statutes in the manner suggested by the Supreme Court in *Trop.* The contention that a state's incarceration of runaway juveniles could not violate the eighth amendment because the statute did not authorize any punishment of juveniles was struck down in *Vann* v. *Scott,* 467 F.2d 1235, 1240 (7th Cir. 1972):

> Whatever the State does with the child is done in the name of rehabilitation. Since—the argument runs by definition the treatment is not "punishment," it obviously cannot be "cruel and unusual punishment." But neither the label which a State places on its own conduct, nor even the legitimacy of its motivation, can avoid the applicability of the Federal Constitution. We have no doubt that well intentioned

attempts to rehabilitate a child could, in extreme circumstances, constitute cruel and unusual punishment proscribed by the Eighth Amendment.

The absence of criminal incarceration did not prohibit a federal court from entertaining an eighth amendment claim to test the conditions of confinement in a boys training school:

> The fact that juveniles are *in theory* not punished, but merely confined for rehabilitative purposes, does not preclude operation of the Eighth Amendment. The reality of confinement in Annex B is that it is punishment.

Inmates of the Boys' Training School v. *Affleck,* 346 F.Supp. 1354, 1366 (D.R.I. 1972).

Such findings of cruel and unusual punishment have been sustained with respect to the death penalty,[3] penal incarceration for status,[4] civil commitment for status without treatment,[5] strip-rooms and solitary confinements,[6] tranquilizing drugs,[7] and corporeal punishment for prisoners.[8] However, any such determination rests on the facts of a particular case.

Here we have a situation in which an inmate may be subjected to a morphine base drug which induces vomiting for an extended period of time. Whether it is called ''aversive stimuli'' or punishment, the act of forcing someone to vomit for a fifteen minute period for committing some minor breach of the rules can only be regarded as cruel and unusual unless the treatment is being administered to a patient who knowingly and intelligently has consented to it. To hold otherwise would be to ignore what each of us has learned from sad experience—that vomiting (especially in the presence of others) is a painful and debilitating experience. The use of this unproven drug for this purpose on an involuntary basis, is, in our opinion, cruel and unusual punishment prohibited by the eighth amendment.

We turn then to the question of how best to prevent abuse in the treatment procedures of consenting participants and how to make certain that the consent is knowingly and intelligently given. 42 U.S.C. § 1983 does not specify the scope of judicial relief available in an action successfully sustained under its terms. Yet this fact does not limit the courts in framing appropriate relief. Its counterpart, 42 U.S.C. § 1982, is likewise framed only in declaratory terms, but the Supreme Court has held that a federal court is not thereby precluded from fashioning an effective equitable remedy. *Jones* v. *Alfred H. Mayer Co.,* 392 U.S. 409, 414 n.13, 88 S.Ct. 2186, 20 L.Ed.2d 1189 (1968). The substantive scope of relief available is a matter of the equitable powers of the federal courts. Accordingly, courts have exercised broad remedial power in civil rights actions. See *United States* v. *Ironworkers Local* 86, 443 F.2d 544, 553 (9th Cir.), cert. denied, 404 U.S. 984, 92 S.Ct. 447, 30 L.Ed.2d 367 (1971); *Parham* v. *Southwestern Bell Telephone Co.,* 433 F.2d 421, 428 (8th Cir. 1970) and cases cited therein.

[3] *Furman* v. *Georgia,* 408 U.S. 238, 92 S.Ct. 2726, 33 L.Ed.2d 346 (1972).

[4] *Robinson* v. *California,* 370 U.S. 660, 82 S. Ct. 1417, 8 L.Ed.2d 758 (1962).

[5] *Rouse* v. *Cameron,* 373 F.2d 451 (D.C.Cir. 1966); *New York State Ass'n for Retarded Children* v. *Rockefeller,* 357 F.Supp. 752 (E.D.N.Y.1973); *Martarella* v. *Kelley,* 349 F.Supp. 575 (S.D.N.Y.1972).

[6] *LaReau* v. *MacDougall,* 473 F.2d 974 (2d Cir. 1972), cert. denied, 414 U.S. 878, 94 S. Ct. 49, 38 L.Ed.2d 123 (1973); *Gates* v. *Collier,* 349 F.Supp. 881 (N.D.Miss.1972); *Landman* v. *Royster,* 333 F.Supp. 621 (E.D. Va.1971); *Inmates of Boys' Training School* v. *Affleck,* 346 F.Supp. 1354 (D.R.I.1972).

[7] *Nelson* v. *Heyne,* 355 F.Supp. 451 (N.D. Ind.1972).

[8] *Jackson* v. *Bishop,* 404 F.2d 571 (8th Cir. 1968); *Nelson* v. *Heyne,* 355 F.Supp. 451 (N.D.Ind.1972); *Landman* v. *Royster,* 333 F.Supp.575 (S.D.N.Y.1972).

> Yet although it is generally true that: [w]here all relevant circumstances have properly been evaluated the action of the trial court, whether granting or denying an injunction, ordinarily will be sustained.

Hodgson v. *American Can Co.*, 440 F.2d 916, 920 (8th Cir. 1971), it is not unknown for a federal appellate court to change the scope of an equitable order on appeal. *United States* v. *St. Louis-San Francisco Ry.*, 464 F.2d 301 (8th Cir. 1972), cert. denied, 409 U.S. 1107, 93 S.Ct. 900, 34 L.Ed.2d 687 (1973) (employment discrimination under Title VII); *Carter* v. *Gallagher*, 452 F.2d 315, 324 (8th Cir. 1971), modified en banc, 452 F.2d 327 (8th Cir.), cert. denied, 406 U.S. 950, 92 S.Ct. 2045, 32 L.Ed.2d 338 (1972) (employment discrimination under 42 U.S.C. §§ 1981 and 1983); *Action* v. *Gannon*, 450 F.2d 1227, 1237-1238 (8th Cir. 1971) (civil rights action under 42 U.S.C. §§ 1981, 1982, 1983, 1985).

In this case the trial court should enjoin the use of apomorphine in the treatment of inmates at the ISMF except when the following conditions are complied with:

1. A written consent must be obtained from the inmate specifying the nature of the treatment, a written description of the purpose, risks and effects of treatment, and advising the inmate of his right to terminate the consent at any time. This consent must include a certification by a physician that the patient has read and understands all of the terms of the consent and that the inmate is mentally competent to understand fully all of the provisions thereof and give his consent thereto.
2. The consent may be revoked at any time after it is given and if an inmate orally expresses an intention to revoke it to any member of the staff, a revocation form shall be provided for his signature at once.
3. Each apomorphine injection shall be individually authorized by a doctor and be administered by a doctor, or by a nurse. It shall be authorized in each instance only upon information based on the personal observation of a member of the professional staff. Information from inmates or inmate aides of the observation of behavior in violation of an inmate's protocol shall not be sufficient to warrant such authorization.

The judgment of the district court is reversed with directions to grant the injunction under the terms hereinbefore set forth.

STEPHENSON, Circuit Judge.

I concur with the result.

BREACH OF RIGHT TO AVOID SELF-INCRIMINATION

The Fifth Amendment right to avoid self-incrimination has been held, under certain circumstances, to be a basis for refusing to be examined by a psychiatrist. In *McNeil* v. *Director, Patuxent Institution*, 407 U.S. 245, for example, the plaintiff had been sentenced to five years for assault. When referred to Patuxent Institution for psychiatric examination the plaintiff refused to cooperate with staff who attempted to examine him. The state proposed to keep McNeil at the institution until he cooperated. However, the Supreme Court ruled that after five years had elapsed the state could no longer compel McNeil to cooperate. In a concurring opinion, Justice Douglas pointed out that this constitutional right to refuse to cooperate was grounded in Fifth Amendment privileges.

FALSE IMPRISONMENT

False imprisonment arises from the nonconsensual, improper, or unlawful restraint or confinement of one person by another for any period of time. Mental health professionals who participate in proceedings that result in the involuntary hospitalization or institutionalization of individuals are susceptible to charges of false imprisonment, as in the case below of *Kleber* v. *Stevens,* 39 Misc.2d 712, 241 N.Y.S.2d 497 (Sup.Ct. 1963), as well as related charges such as deprivation of the constitutional right to liberty as in the case below of *O'Connor* v. *Donaldson,* 422 U.S. 563, 45 L.Ed.2d 396, 95 S.Ct. 2486 (1975), and malicious prosecution (see *Daniels* v. *Finney,* 262 S.W.2d 431 [Tex.Civ.App. 1953]). Generally, when the mental health professional participates in such proceedings, she or he is viewed by the court as acting in an official or quasi-official capacity, and as such is accorded witness status and immunities. As stated by the court in *Dunbar* v. *Greenlaw,* 152 Me. 270, 128 A.2d 218, "The role and function of the examining and certifying physician in insanity detention and commitment cases are those of a witness. . . . His relation to the alleged insane person is not *pro hac vice* (for this one occasion), that of a physician with patient." Thus doctors, whether private practitioners or court-appointed, have been granted immunity regardless if their actions were undertaken with malicious intent and in bad faith (see, for example, *Mezullo* v. *Maletz,* 118 N.E.2d 356; *Laing* v. *Mitten,* 70 N.E. 128; *Sheppard* v. *Bryant,* 78 N.E. 394; *Kintz* v. *Harringer,* 124 N.E. 168, 12 A.L.R. 1247). However, this policy has not prevailed across all fact situations (see *Stowers* v. *Wolodzko,* page 244). In *Kleber,* below, we see that a practitioner may be found to be free from liability for the tort of false imprisonment while still being held liable for malpractice—the malpractice deriving from the failure to exercise due care in conducting an examination for commitment.

Kleber v. *Stevens*, 39 Misc.2d 712, 241 N.Y.S.2d 497 (Sup. Ct., 1963)

PAUL J. WIDLITZ, J. The defendants move to set aside a jury verdict awarding the plaintiff the sum of $20,000 as compensatory damages. The complaint alleges three causes of action, the first being false imprisonment by reason of an unlawful emergency commitment to Kings Park State Hospital under the presumed authority of section 75 of the Mental Hygiene Law. More particularly, this portion of the Mental Hygiene Law permits an immediate confinement if "he is dangerous by virtue of his mental condition so as to render it necessary for public safety that he be immediately confined. . . . In such case such mentally ill person shall be received . . . upon a certificate, executed by two examining physicians after examination and upon a petition as provided in section seventy-four."

The second cause of action reiterates those allegations contained in the first cause and adds tbat the certificate submitted to the County Judge, presumably upon authority of section 74 of the Mental Hygiene Law, was falsely, fraudulently and maliciously made by the defendants without ordinary care and prudence and without proper examination into the matter, and that, acting upon such certificate, the County Judge certified plaintiff to the Kings Park State Hospital. This section provides that a person "alleged to be mentally ill . . . may be certified to and confined in any licensed private institution for the care and treatment of the mentally ill, upon an order made by a judge of a court of record . . . upon a certificate made by two examining physicians, accompanied by a petition therefor."

The third cause of action was dismissed during the trial and is not under consideration.

The trial jury returned a verdict in favor of the defendants on the first cause of action asserting false imprisonment, and found the defendants negligent in the second cause of action, awarding the plaintiff compensatory damages under this second cause of action in the amount of $20,000.

The defendants now seek to set aside this verdict as an inconsistent one and not in conformity with the creditable evidence. They argue that the jury's finding of no liability for false imprisonment under the first cause of action precluded the finding of negligence. This on the theory that as mental health officers complying with the law, the defendant doctors could not be charged with breaching any duty owing the plaintiff, i.e., negligence, for there existed no doctor-patient relationship. In *Ayers* v. *Russell* (50 Hun 282, 288, 289) the court stated as follows: "The defendants, the physicians, were such experts as the statute authorizes to make the certificate of the plaintiff's insanity. No allegation is made in the complaint of a defect of a proper request or information, upon which they proceeded to examine the plaintiff and make their certificate, and none can be presumed. The physicians followed the forms of the law. Whether the reasons set forth by them in the certificate for their conclusion, that the plaintiff was insane, were sufficient or not, is immaterial. The presumption is that they set forth such reasons as in their opinion were sufficient, and such as appeared to them to be true in fact. But the complaint charges that the physicians made the certificate 'without proper and ordinary care and prudence, and without due examination, inquiry and proof into the fact whether plaintiff was sane or insane.' We think the physicians owed the plaintiff the duty of making the examination with ordinary care. Their duty must be measured by the trust which the statute reposes in them, and by the consequences flowing from its improper performance. They assumed the duty by accepting the trust. They are not judicial officers, but medical experts. They are not clothed with judicial immunity and are chargeable with that negligence which attaches to a professional expert who does not use the care and skill which his profession, per se, implies that he will bring to his professional work."

Section 70 of the Mental Hygiene Law requires all certificates to contain the facts and circumstances upon which the judgment of the physicians is based and shall show that the condition of the person examined is such as to require care and treatment in an institution for the mentally ill. It was plaintiff's contention throughout the trial that the certificates rendered in compliance to this section were ill-conceived and based on the hearsay of an allegedly vindictive husband rather than good medical practice and examination, and it is conceivable that a doctor examining for purposes of commitment may comply mechanically with the requirements of the law and without malice and yet fail to utilize the minimal skill required to effectuate this process. These motions are accordingly denied.

O'Connor v. *Donaldson*, 422 U.S. 563, 95 S.Ct. 2486, 45 L.Ed.2d 396 (1975)

Mr. Justice STEWART delivered the opinion of the Court.

The respondent, Kenneth Donaldson, was civilly committed to confinement as a mental patient in the Florida State Hospital at Chattahoochee in January 1957. He was kept in custody there against his will for nearly 15 years. The petitioner, Dr. J. B. O'Connor, was the hospital's superintendent during most of this period. Throughout his confinement Donaldson repeatedly, but unsuccessfully, demanded his release, claiming that he was dangerous to no one, that he was not mentally ill, and that, at any rate, the hospital was not providing treatment for his supposed illness. Finally, in February 1971, Donaldson brought this lawsuit under 42 U.S.C. § 1983, in the United States District Court for the Northern District of Florida, alleging that O'Connor, and other members of the hospital staff named as defendants, had intentionally and maliciously deprived him of his constitutional right to liberty.[1] After a four-day trial, the jury returned a verdict assessing both compensatory and punitive damages against O'Connor and a codefendant. The Court of Appeals for the Fifth Circuit affirmed the judgment, 493 F.2d 507. We granted O'Connor's petition for certiorari, 419 U.S. 894, 95 S.Ct. 171, 42 L.Ed.2d 138 because of the important constitutional questions seemingly presented.

I

Donaldson's commitment was initiated by his father, who thought that his son was suffering from "delusions." After hearings before a county judge of Pinellas County, Fla., Donaldson was found to be suffering from "paranoid schizophrenia" and was committed for "care, maintenance, and treatment" pursuant to Florida statutory provisions that have since been repealed.[2] The state law was less than clear in specifying

[1]Donaldson's original complaint was filed as a class action on behalf of himself and all of his fellow patients in an entire department of the Florida State Hospital at Chattahoochee. In addition to a damages claim, Donaldson's complaint also asked for habeas corpus relief ordering his release, as well as the release of all members of the class. Donaldson further sought declaratory and injunctive relief requiring the hospital to provide adequate psychiatric treatment.

After Donaldson's release and after the District Court dismissed the action as a class suit, Donaldson filed an amended complaint, repeating his claim for compensatory and punitive damages. Although the amended complaint retained the prayer for declaratory and injunctive relief, that request was eliminated from the case prior to trial. See 493 F.2d 507, 512–513.

[2]The judicial commitment proceedings were pursuant to § 394.22(11) of the State Public Health Code, which provided:

"Whenever any person who has been adjudged mentally incompetent requires confinement or restraint to prevent self-injury or violence to others, the said judge shall direct that such person be forthwith delivered to a superintendent of a Florida state hospital, for the mentally ill, after admission has been authorized under regulations approved by the board of commissioners of state institutions, for care, maintenance, and treatment, as provided in sections 394.09, 394.24, 394.25, 394.26 and 394.27, or make such other disposition of him as he may be permitted by law. . . ." Fla.Laws 1955–1956 Extra. Sess., c. 31403, § *1*, p. 62.

Donaldson had been adjudged "incompetent" several days earlier under § 394.22(1), which provided for such a finding as to any person who was "incompetent by reason of mental illness, sickness, drunkenness, excessive use of drugs, insanity, or other mental or physical condition, so that he is incapable of caring for

the grounds necessary for commitment, and the record is scanty as to Donaldson's condition at the time of the judicial hearing. These matters are, however, irrelevant, for this case involves no challenge to the initial commitment, but is focused instead, upon the nearly 15 years of confinement that followed.

The evidence at the trial showed that the hospital staff had the power to release a patient, not dangerous to himself or others, even if he remained mentally ill and had been lawfully committed.[3] Despite many requests, O'Connor refused to allow that power to be exercised in Donaldson's case. At the trial, O'Connor indicated that he had believed that Donaldson would have been unable to make a "successful adjustment outside the institution," but could not recall the basis for that conclusion. O'Connor retired as superintendent shortly before this suit was filed. A few months thereafter, and before the trial, Donaldson secured his release and a judicial restoration of competency, with the support of the hospital staff.

The testimony at the trial demonstrated, without contradiction, that Donaldson had posed no danger to others during his long confinement, or indeed at any point in his life. O'Connor himself conceded that he had no personal or secondhand knowledge that Donaldson had ever committed a dangerous act. There was no evidence that Donaldson had ever been suicidal or been thought likely to inflict injury upon himself. One of O'Connor's codefendants acknowledged that Donaldson could have earned his own living outside the hospital. He had done so for some 14 years before his commitment, and immediately upon his release he secured a responsible job in hotel administration.

Furthermore, Donaldson's frequent requests for release had been supported by responsible persons willing to provide him any care he might need on release. In 1963,

---

himself or managing his property, or is likely to dissipate or lose his property or become the victim of designing persons, or inflict harm on himself or others. . . ." Fla.Gen.Laws 1955, c. 29909, § 3, p. 831.

It would appear that § 394.22(11) (a) contemplated that involuntary commitment would be imposed only on those "incompetent" persons who "require[d] confinement or restraint to prevent self-injury or violence to others." But this is not certain, for § 394.22(11) (c) provided that the judge could adjudicate the person a "harmless incompetent" and release him to a guardian upon a finding that he did "not require confinement or restraint to prevent self-injury or violence to others *and* that treatment in the Florida State Hospital is unnecessary or would be without benefit to such person. . . ." Fla.Gen.Laws 1955, c. 29909, § 3, p. 835 (emphasis added). In this regard, it is noteworthy that Donaldson's "Order for Delivery of Mentally Incompetent" to the Florida State Hospital provided that he required "confinement or restraint to prevent self-injury or violence to others, *or* to insure proper treatment." (Emphasis added.) At any rate, the Florida commitment statute provided no judicial procedure whereby one still incompetent could secure his release on the ground that he was no longer dangerous to himself or others.

Whether the Florida statute provided a "right to treatment" for involuntarily committed patients is also open to dispute. Under § 394.22(11) (a), commitment "to prevent self-injury or violence to others" was "for care, maintenance, and treatment." Recently Florida has totally revamped its civil commitment law and now provides a statutory right to receive individual medical treatment. Fla.Stat.Ann. § 394.459 (1973).

[3]The sole *statutory* procedure for release required a judicial reinstatement of a patient's "mental competency." Public Health Code §§ 394.22(15) and (16), Fla.Gen.Laws 1955, c. 29909, § 3, pp. 838-841. But this procedure could be initiated by the hospital staff. Indeed, it was at the staff's initiative that Donaldson was finally restored to competency, and liberty, almost immediately after O'Connor retired from the superintendency.

In addition, witnesses testified that the hospital had always had its own procedure for releasing patients—for "trial visits," "home visits," "furloughs," or "out of state discharges"—even though the patients had not been judicially restored to competency. Those conditional releases often became permanent, and the hospital merely closed its books on the patient. O'Connor did not deny at trial that he had the power to release patients; he conceded that it was his "duty" as superintendent of the hospital "to determine whether that patient having once reached the hospital was in such condition as to request that he be considered for release from the hospital."

for example, a representative of Helping Hands, Inc., a halfway house for mental patients, wrote O'Connor asking him to release Donaldson to its care. The request was accompanied by a supporting letter from the Minneapolis Clinic of Psychiatry and Neurology, which a codefendant conceded was a "good clinic." O'Connor rejected the offer, replying that Donaldson could be released only to his parents. That rule was apparently of O'Connor's own making. At the time, Donaldson was 55 years old, and, as O'Connor knew, Donaldson's parents were too elderly and infirm to take responsibility for him. Moreover, in his continuing correspondence with Donaldson's parents, O'Connor never informed them of the Helping Hands offer. In addition, on four separate occasions between 1964 and 1968, John Lembcke, a college classmate of Donaldson's and a longtime family friend, asked O'Connor to release Donaldson to his care. On each occasion O'Connor refused. The record shows that Lembcke was a serious and responsible person, who was willing and able to assume responsibility for Donaldson's welfare.

The evidence showed that Donaldson's confinement was a simple regime of enforced custodial care, not a program designed to alleviate or cure his supposed illness. Numerous witnesses, including one of O'Connor's codefendants, testified that Donaldson had received nothing but custodial care while at the hospital O'Connor described Donaldson's treatment as "milieu therapy." But witnesses from the hospital staff conceded that, in the context of this case, "milieu therapy" was a euphemism for confinement in the "milieu" of a mental hospital.[4] For substantial periods, Donaldson was simply kept in a large room that housed 60 patients, many of whom were under criminal commitment. Donaldson's requests for ground privileges, occupational training, and an opportunity to discuss his case with O'Connor or other staff members were repeatedly denied.

At the trial, O'Connor's principal defense was that he had acted in good faith and was therefore immune from any liability for monetary damages. His position, in short, was that state law, which he had believed valid had authorized indefinite custodial confinement of the "sick," even if they were not given treatment and their release could harm no one.[5]

The trial judge instructed the members of the jury that they should find that O'Connor had violated Donaldson's constitutional right to liberty if they found that he had

> confined [Donaldson] against his will, knowing that he was not mentally ill or dangerous or knowing that if mentally ill he was not receiving treatment for his alleged mental illness.
>
> . . . .
>
> Now, the purpose of involuntary hospitalization is treatment and not mere custodial care or punishment if a patient is not a danger to himself or others. Without such treatment there is no justification from a constitutional stand-point for continued

[4]There was some evidence that Donaldson, who is a Christian Scientist, on occasion refused to take medication. The trial judge instructed the jury not to award damages for any period of confinement during which Donaldson had declined treatment.

[5]At the close of Donaldson's case in chief, O'Connor moved for a directed verdict on the ground that state law at the time of Donaldson's confinement authorized institutionalization of the mentally ill even if they posed no danger to themselves or others. This motion was denied. At the close of all the evidence, O'Connor asked that the jury be instructed that "if defendants acted pursuant to a statute which was not declared unconstitutional at the time, they cannot be held accountable for such action." The District Court declined to give this requested instruction.

> confinement unless you should also find that [Donaldson] was dangerous to either himself or others.[6]

The trial judge further instructed the jury that O'Connor was immune from damages if he

> reasonably believed in good faith that detention of [Donaldson] was proper for the length of time he was so confined. . . .
>
> However, mere good intentions which do not give rise to a reasonable belief that detention is lawfully required cannot justify [Donaldson's] confinement in the Florida State Hospital.

The jury returned a verdict for Donaldson against O'Connor and a codefendant, and awarded damages of $38,500, including $10,000 in punitive damages.[7]

The Court of Appeals affirmed the judgment of the District Court in a broad opinion dealing with "the far-reaching question whether the Fourteenth Amendment guarantees a right to treatment to persons involuntarily civilly committed to state mental hospitals." 493 F.2d, at 509. The appellate court held that when, as in Donaldson's case, the rationale for confinement is that the patient is in need of treatment, the Constitution requires that minimally adequate treatment in fact be provided. *Id.*, at 521. The court further expressed the view that, regardless of the grounds for involuntary civil commitment, a person confined against his will at a state mental institution has "a constitutional right to receive such individual treatment as will give

[6]The District Court defined treatment as follows: "You are instructed that a person who is involuntarily civilly committed to a mental hospital does have a constitutional right to receive such treatment *as will give him a realistic opportunity to be cured or to improve his mental condition.*" (Emphasis added.) O'Connor argues that this statement suggests that a mental patient has a right to treatment even if confined by reason of dangerousness to himself or others. But this is to take the above paragraph out of context, for it is bracketed by paragraphs making clear the trial judge's theory that treatment is constitutionally required only if mental illness alone, rather than danger to self or others, is the reason for confinement. If O'Connor had thought the instructions ambiguous on this point, he could have objected to them and requested a clarification. He did not do so. We accordingly have no occasion here to decide whether persons committed on grounds of dangerousness enjoy a "right to treatment."

In pertinent part, the instructions read as follows:

"The Plaintiff claims in brief that throughout the period of his hospitalization he was not mentally ill or dangerous to himself or others, and claims further that if he was mentally ill, or if Defendants believed he was mentally ill, Defendants withheld from him the treatment necessary to improve his mental condition.

"The Defendants claim, in brief, that Plaintiff's detention was legal and proper, or if his detention was not legal and proper, it was the result of mistake, without malicious intent.

"In order to prove his claim under the Civil Rights Act, the burden is upon the Plaintiff in this case to establish by a preponderance of the evidence in this case the following facts:

"That the Defendants confined Plaintiff against his will, knowing that he was not mentally ill or dangerous or knowing that if mentally ill he was not receiving treatment for his alleged mental illness.

"[T]hat the Defendants' acts and conduct deprived the Plaintiff of his Federal Constitutional right not to be denied or deprived of his liberty without due process of law as that phrase is defined and explained in these instructions. . . .

. . . .

"You are instructed that a person who is involuntarily civilly committed to a mental hospital does have a constitutional right to receive such treatment as will give him a realistic opportunity to be cured or to improve his mental condition.

"Now, the purpose of involuntary hospitalization is treatment and not mere custodial care or punishment if a patient is not a danger to himself or others. Without such treatment there is no justification from a constitutional stand-point for continued confinement unless you should also find that the Plaintiff was dangerous either to himself or others."

[7]The trial judge had instructed that punitive damages should be awarded only if "the act or omission of the Defendant or Defendants which proximately caused injury to the Plaintiff was maliciously or wantonly or oppressively done."

him a reasonable opportunity to be cured or to improve his mental condition." *Id.*, at 520. Conversely, the court's opinion implied that it is constitutionally permissible for a State to confine a mentally ill person against his will in order to treat his illness, regardless of whether his illness renders him dangerous to himself or others. See *id.*, at 522-527.

II

We have concluded that the difficult issues of constitutional law dealt with by the Court of Appeals are not presented by this case in its present posture. Specifically, there is no reason now to decide whether mentally ill persons dangerous to themselves or to others have a right to treatment upon compulsory confinement by the State, or whether the State may compulsorily confine a nondangerous, mentally ill individual for the purpose of treatment. As we view it, this case raises a single, relatively simple, but nonetheless important question concerning every man's constitutional right to liberty.

The jury found that Donaldson was neither dangerous to himself nor dangerous to others, and also found that, if mentally ill, Donaldson had not received treatment.[8] That verdict, based on abundant evidence, makes the issue before the Court a narrow one. We need not decide whether, when, or by what procedures, a mentally ill person may be confined by the State on any of the grounds which, under contemporary statutes, are generally advanced to justify involuntary confinement of such a person—to prevent injury to the public, to ensure his own survival or safety,[9] or to alleviate or cure his illness. See *Jackson* v. *Indiana,* 406 U.S. 715, 736-737, 92 S.Ct. 1845, 1857-1858, 32 L.Ed. 2d 435; *Humphrey* v. *Cady,* 405 U.S. 504, 509, 92 S.Ct. 1048, 1052, 31 L.Ed.2d 394. For the jury found that none of the above grounds for continued confinement was present in Donaldson's case.[10]

Given the jury's findings, what was left as justification for keeping Donaldson in continued confinement? The fact that state law may have authorized confinement of the harmless mentally ill does not itself establish a constitutionally adequate purpose for the confinement. See *Jackson* v. *Indiana, supra,* 406 U.S., at 720-723, 92 S.Ct., at

[8]Given the jury instructions, see n. 6 *supra,* it is possible that the jury went so far as to find that O'Connor knew not only that Donaldson was harmless to himself and others but also that he was not mentally ill at all. If it so found, the jury was permitted by the instructions to rule against O'Connor regardless of the nature of the "treatment" provided. If we were to construe the jury's verdict in that fashion, there would remain no substantial issue in this case: That a wholly sane and innocent person has a constitutional right not to be physically confined by the State when his freedom will pose a danger neither to himself nor to others cannot be seriously doubted.

[9]The judge's instructions used the phrase "dangerous to himself." Of course, even if there is no foreseeable risk of self-injury or suicide, a person is literally "dangerous to himself" if for physical or other reasons he is helpless to avoid the hazards of freedom either through his own efforts or with the aid of willing family members or friends. While it might be argued that the judge's instructions could have been more detailed on this point, O'Connor raised no objection to them, presumably because the evidence clearly showed that Donaldson was not "dangerous to himself" however broadly that phrase might be defined.

[10]O'Connor argues that, despite the jury's verdict, the Court must assume that Donaldson was receiving treatment sufficient to justify his confinement, because the adequacy of treatment is a "nonjusticiable" question that must be left to the discretion of the psychiatric profession. That argument is unpersuasive. Where "treatment" is the sole asserted ground for depriving a person of liberty, it is plainly unacceptable to suggest that the courts are powerless to determine whether the asserted ground is present. See *Jackson* v. *Indiana*, 406 U.S. 715, 92 S.Ct. 1845, 32 L.Ed.2d 435. Neither party objected to the jury instruction defining treatment. There is, accordingly, no occasion in this case to decide whether the provision of treatment, standing alone, can ever constitutionally justify involuntary confinement or, if it can, how much or what kind of treatment would suffice for that purpose. In its present posture this case involves not involuntary treatment but simply involuntary custodial confinement.

1849–1851; *McNeil* v. *Director, Patuxent Institution*, 407 U.S. 245, 248–250, 92 S.Ct. 2083, 2086–2087, 32 L. Ed.2d 719. Nor is it enough that Donaldson's original confinement was founded upon a constitutionally adequate basis, if in fact it was, because even if his involuntary confinement was initially permissable, it could not constitutionally continue after that basis no longer existed. *Jackson* v. *Indiana, supra*, 406 U.S., at 738, 92 S.Ct., at 1858; *McNeil* v. *Director, Patuxent Institution, supra.*

A finding of "mental illness" alone cannot justify a State's locking a person up against his will and keeping him indefinitely in simple custodial confinement. Assuming that that term can be given a reasonably precise content and that the "mentally ill" can be identified with reasonable accuracy, tbere is still no constitutional basis for confining such persons involuntarily if they are dangerous to no one and can live safely in freedom.

May the State confine the mentally ill merely to ensure them a living standard superior to that they enjoy in the private community? That the State has a proper interest in providing care and assistance to the unfortunate goes without saying. But the mere presence of mental illness does not disqualify a person from preferring his home to the comforts of an institution. Moreover, while the State may arguably confine a person to save him from harm, incarceration is rarely if ever a necessary condition for raising the living standards of those capable of surviving safely in freedom, on their own or with the help of family or friends. See *Shelton* v. *Tucker,* 364 U.S. 479, 488–490, 81 S.Ct. 247, 252–253, 5 L.Ed.2d 231.

May the State fence in the harmless mentally ill solely to save its citizens from exposure to those whose ways are different? One might as well ask if the State, to avoid public unease, could incarcerate all who are physically unattractive or socially eccentric. Mere public intolerance or animosity cannot constitutionally justify the deprivation of a person's physical liberty. See. *e.g., Cohen* v. *California,* 403 U.S. 15, 24–26, 91 S.Ct. 1780, 1787–1789, 29 L.Ed.2d 284; *Coates* v. *City of Cincinnati,* 402 U.S. 611, 615, 91 S.Ct. 1686, 1689, 29 L. Ed.2d 214; *Street* v. *New York,* 394 U.S. 576, 592, 89 S.Ct. 1354, 1365–1366, 22 L.Ed.2d 572; cf. *U.S. Dept of Agriculture* v. *Moreno,* 413 U.S. 528, 534, 93 S.Ct. 2821, 2825–2826, 37 L.Ed.2d 782.

In short, a State cannot constitutionally confine without more a nondangerous individual who is capable of surviving safely in freedom by himself or with the help of willing and responsible family members or friends. Since the jury found, upon ample evidence, that O'Connor, as an agent of the State, knowingly did so confine Donaldson, it properly concluded that O'Connor violated Donaldson's constitutional right to freedom.

III

O'Connor contends that in any event he should not be held personally liable for monetary damages because his decisions were made in "good faith." Specifically, O'Connor argues that he was acting pursuant to state law which, he believed, authorized confinement of the mentally ill even when their release would not compromise their safety or constitute a danger to others, and that he could not reasonably have been expected to know that the state law as he understood it was constitutionally invalid. A proposed instruction to this effect was rejected by the District Court.[11]

[11]See n. 5, *supra.* During his years of confinement, Donaldson unsuccessfully petitioned the state and federal courts for release from the Florida State Hospital on a number of occasions. None of these claims was

The District Court did instruct the jury, without objection, that monetary damages could not be assessed against O'Connor if he had believed reasonably and in good faith that Donaldson's continued confinement was "proper," and that punitive damages could be awarded only if O'Connor had acted "maliciously or wantonly or oppressively." The Court of Appeals approved those instructions. But that court did not consider whether it was error for the trial judge to refuse the additional instruction concerning O'Connor's claimed reliance on state law as authorization for Donaldson's continued confinement. Further, neither the District Court nor the Court of Appeals acted with the benefit of this Court's most recent decision on the scope of the qualified immunity possessed by state officials under 42 U.S.C. § 1983. *Wood* v. *Strickland,* 420 U.S. 308. 95 S.Ct. 992, 43 L.Ed.2d 214.

Under that decision, the relevant question for the jury is whether O'Connor "knew or reasonably should have known that the action he took within his sphere of official responsibility would violate the constitutional rights of [Donaldson], or if he took the action with the malicious intention to cause a deprivation of constitutional rights or other injury to [Donaldson]." *Id.,* at 322, 95 S.Ct. at 1001. See also *Scheuer* v. *Rhodes,* 416 U.S. 232, 247-248, 94 S.Ct. 1683, 1692, 40 L.Ed.2d 90; *Wood* v. *Strickland, supra,* 420 U.S.,at 330, 95 S.Ct., at 1005 (opinion of Powell, J.). For purposes of this question, an official has, of course, no duty to anticipate unforeseeable constitutional developments. *Wood* v. *Strickland, supra,* at 322, 95 S.Ct., at 1004.

Accordingly, we vacate the judgment of the Court of Appeals and remand the case to enable that court to consider, in light of *Wood* v. *Strickland,* whether the District Judge's failure to instruct with regard to the effect of O'Connor's claimed reliance on state law rendered inadequate the instructions as to O'Connor's liability for compensatory and punitive damages.[12]

It is so ordered.

Vacated and remanded.

Mr. Chief Justice BURGER, concurring.

Although I join the Court's opinion and judgment in this case, it seems to me that several factors merit more emphasis than it gives them. I therefore add the following remarks.

I

With respect to the remand to the Court of Appeals on the issue of official immunity from liability for monetary damages,[1] it seems to me not entirely irrelevant that there was substantial evidence that Donaldson consistently refused treatment that was

---

ever resolved on its merits, and no evidentiary hearings were ever held. O'Connor has not contended that he relied on these unsuccessful court actions as an independent intervening reason for continuing Donaldson's confinement, and no instructions on this score were requested.

[12]Upon remand, the Court of Appeals is to consider only the question whether O'Connor is to be held liable for monetary damages for violating Donaldson's constitutional right to liberty. The jury found, on substantial evidence and under adequate instructions, that O'Connor deprived Donaldson, who was dangerous neither to himself nor to others and was provided no treatment, of the constitutional right to liberty. Cf. n. 8, *supra.* That finding needs no further consideration. If the Court of Appeals holds that a remand to the District Court is necessary, the only issue to be determined in that court will be whether O'Connor is immune from liability for monetary damages.

Of necessity our decision vacating the judgment of the Court of Appeals deprives that court's opinion of precedential effect, leaving this court's opinion and judgment as the sole law of the case. See *United States* v. *Munsingwear,* 340 U.S. 36, 71 S.Ct. 104, 95 L.Ed. 36.

[1]I have difficulty understanding how the issue of immunity can be resolved on this record and hence it is very likely a new trial on this issue may be required; if that is the case I would hope these sensitive and important issues would have the benefit of more effective presentation and articulation on behalf of petitioner.

offered to him, claiming that he was not mentally ill and needed no treatment.[2] The Court appropriately takes notice of the uncertainties of psychiatric diagnosis and therapy, and the reported cases are replete with evidence of the divergence of medical opinion in this vexing area. *E.g., Greenwood* v. *United States,* 350 U.S. 366, 375, 76 S.Ct. 410, 415, 100 L.Ed. 412 (1956). See also *Drope* v. *Missouri,* 420 U.S. 162, 95 S.Ct. 896, 43 L.Ed.2d 103 (1975). Nonetheless, one of the few areas of agreement among behavioral specialists is that an uncooperative patient cannot benefit from therapy and that the first step in effective treatment is acknowledgment by the patient that he is suffering from an abnormal condition. See *e.g.,* Katz, The Right to Treatment—An Enchanting Legal Fiction? 36 U.Chi.L.Rev. 755, 768-769 (1969). Donaldson's adamant refusal to do so should be taken into account in considering petitioner's good-faith defense.

Perhaps more important to the issue of immunity is a factor referred to only obliquely in the Court's opinion. On numerous occasions during the period of his confinement Donaldson unsuccessfully sought release in the Florida courts; indeed, the last of these proceedings was terminated only a few months prior to the bringing of this action. See 234 So. 2d 114 (1969), cert. denied, 400 U.S. 869, 91 S.Ct. 104, 27 L.Ed.2d 109 (1970). Whatever the reasons for the state courts' repeated denials of relief, and regardless of whether they correctly resolved the issue tendered to them, petitioner and the other members of the medical staff at Florida State Hospital would surely have been justified in considering each such judicial decision as an approval of continued confinement and an independent intervening reason for continuing Donaldson's custody. Thus, this fact is inescapably related to the issue of immunity and must be considered by the Court of Appeals on remand and, if a new trial on this issue is ordered, by the District Court.[3]

II

As the Court points out, *ante,* at 2491 n. 6, the District Court instructed the jury in part that "a person who is involuntarily civilly committed to a mental hospital does bave a *constitutional* right to receive such treatment *as will give him a realistic opportunity to be cured,*" (emphasis added), and the Court of Appeals unequivocally approved this phrase, standing alone, as a correct statement of the law. 493 F.2d 507, 520 (CA5 1974). The Court's opinion plainly gives no approval to that holding and makes clear that it binds neither the parties to this case nor the courts of the Fifth Circuit. See ante, at 2495 n. 12. Moreover, in light of its importance for future litigation in this area, it should be emphasized that the Court of Appeals' analysis has no basis in the decisions of this Court.

A

There can be no doubt that involuntary commitment to a mental hospital, like involuntary confinement of an individual for any reason, is a deprivation of liberty

[2]The Court's reference to "milieu therapy," *ante,* at 2490 may be construed as disparaging that concept. True, it is capable of being used simply to cloak official indifference, but the reality is that some mental abnormalities respond to no known treatment. Also, some mental patients respond, as do persons suffering from a variety of physiological ailments, to what is loosely called "milieu treatment," *i. e.,* keeping them comfortable, well nourished, and in a protected environment. It is not for us to say in the baffling field of psychiatry that "milieu therapy" is always a pretense.

[3]That petitioner's counsel failed to raise this issue is not a reason why it should not be considered with respect to immunity in light of the Court's holding that the defense was preserved for appellate review.

which the State cannot accomplish without due process of law. *Specht* v. *Patterson,* 386 U.S. 605, 608, 87 S.Ct. 1209, 1211, 18 L.Ed.2d 326 (1967). Cf. *In re Gault,* 387 U.S. 1, 12–13, 87 S.Ct. 1428, 1435–1436, 18 L.Ed.2d 527 (1967). Commitment must be justified on the basis of a legitimate state interest, and the reasons for committing a particular individual must be established in an appropriate proceeding. Equally important, confinement must cease when those reasons no longer exist. See *McNeil* v. *Director, Patuxent Institution,* 407 U.S. 245, 249–250, 92 S.Ct. 2083, 2086–2087, 32 L.Ed.2d 719 (1972); *Jackson* v. *Indiana,* 406 U.S. 715, 738, 92 S.Ct. 1845, 1858, 32 L.Ed.2d 435 (1972).

The Court of Appeals purported to be applying these principles in developing the first of its theories supporting a constitutional right to treatment. It first identified what it perceived to be the traditional bases for civil commitment—physical dangerousness to oneself or others, or a need for treatment—and stated:

> [W]here, as in Donaldson's case, the rationale for confinement is the "*parens patriae*" rationale that the patient is in need of treatment, the due process clause requires that minimally adequate treatment be in fact provided. . . . "To deprive any citizen of his or her liberty upon the altruistic theory that the confinement is for humane therapeutic reasons and then fail to provide adequate treatment violates the very fundamentals of due process." 493 F.2d, at 521.

The Court of Appeals did not explain its conclusion that the rationale for respondent's commitment was that he needed treatment. The Florida statutes in effect during the period of his confinement did not require that a person who had been adjudicated incompetent and ordered committed either be provided with psychiatric treatment or released, and there was no such condition in respondent's order of commitment. Cf. *Rouse* v. *Cameron,* 125 U.S.App.D.C. 366, 373 F.2d 451 (1967). More important, the instructions which the Court of Appeals read as establishing an absolute constitutional right to treatment did not require the jury to make any findings regarding the specific reasons for respondent's confinement or to focus upon any rights he may have had under state law. Thus, the premise of the Court of Appeals' first theory must have been that, at least with respect to persons who are not physically dangerous, a State has no power to confine the mentally ill except for the purpose of providing them with treatment.

That proposition is surely not descriptive of the power traditionally exercised by the States in this area. Historically, and for a considerable period of time, subsidized custodial care in private foster homes or boarding houses was the most benign form of care provided incompetent or mentally ill persons for whom the States assumed responsibility. Until well into the 19th century the vast majority of such persons were simply restrained in poorhouses, almshouses, or jails. See A. Deutsch, The Mentally Ill in America 38–54, 114–131 (2d ed. 1949). The few States that established institutions for the mentally ill during this early period were concerned primarily with providing a more humane place of confinement and only secondarily with "curing" the persons sent there. See *id.,* at 98–113.

As the trend toward state care of the mentally ill expanded, eventually leading to the present statutory schemes for protecting such persons, the dual functions of institutionalization continued to be recognized. While one of the goals of this movement was to provide medical treatment to those who could benefit from it, it was acknowledged that this could not be done in all cases and that there was a large range of mental illness for which no known "cure" existed. In time, providing places for the custodial confinement of the so-called "dependent insane" again emerged as the major goal of the States' programs in this area and remained so well into this century. See *id.*, at 228-271; D. Rothman, The Discovery of the Asylum 264-295 (1971).

In short, the idea that States may not confine the mentally ill except for the purpose of providing them with treatment is of very recent origin,[4] and there is no historical basis for imposing such a limitation on state power. Analysis of the sources of the civil commitment power likewise lends no support to that notion. There can be little doubt that in the exercise of its police power a State may confine individuals solely to protect society from the dangers of significant antisocial acts or communicable disease. Cf. *Minnesota ex rel. Pearson* v. *Probate Court of Ramsey County,* 309 U.S. 270, 60 S.Ct. 523, 84 L.Ed. 744 (1940); *Jacobson* v. *Massachusetts,* 197 U.S. 11, 25-29, 25 S.Ct. 358, 360-362, 49 L.Ed. 643 (1905). Additionally, the States are vested with the historic *parens patriae* power, including the duty to protect "persons under legal disabilities to act for themselves." *Hawaii* v. *Standard Oil Co.*, 405 U.S. 251, 257, 92 S.Ct. 885, 888, 31 L.Ed.2d 184 (1972). See also *Mormon Church* v. *United States,* 136 U.S. 1, 56-58, 10 S.Ct. 792, 807-808, 34 L.Ed. 481 (1890). The classic example of this role is when a State undertakes to act as " 'the general guardian of all infants, idiots, and lunatics.' " *Hawaii* v. *Standard.Oil Co., supra,* 405 U.S., at 257, 92 S.Ct., at 888, quoting 3 W. Blackstone, Commentaries *47.

Of course, an inevitable consequence of exercising the *parens patriae* power is that the ward's personal freedom will be substantially restrained, whether a guardian is appointed to control his property, he is placed in the custody of a private third party, or committed to an institution. Thus, however the power is implemented, due process requires that it not be invoked indiscriminately. At a minimum, a particular scheme for protection of the mentally ill must rest upon a legislative determination that it is compatible with the best interests of the affected class and that its members are unable to act for themselves. Cf. *Mormon Church* v. *United States, supra*. Moreover, the use of alternative forms of protection may be motivated by different considerations, and the justifications for one may not be invoked to rationalize another. Cf. *Jackson* v. *Indiana,* 406 U.S., at 737-738, 92 S.Ct., at 1857-1858. See also American Bar Foundation, The Mentally Disabled and the Law 254-255 (S. Brakel & R. Rock ed. 1971).

However, the existence of some due process limitations on the *parens patriae* power does not justify the further conclusion that it may be exercised to confine a mentally ill person only if the purpose of the confinement is treatment. Despite many recent advances in medical knowledge, it remains a stubborn fact that there are many forms of mental illness which are not understood, some which are untreatable in the sense that no effective therapy has yet been discovered for them, and that rates of "cure" are generally low. See Schwitzgebel, The Right to Effective Mental Treatment, 62 Calif.L.Rev. 936, 941-948 (1974). There can be little responsible debate regarding "the uncertainty of diagnosis in this field and the tentativeness of professional judgment." *Greenwood* v. *United States,* 350 U.S., at 375, 76 S.Ct., at 415. See also Ennis & Litwack, Psychiatry and the Presumption of Expertise: Flipping Coins in the Courtroom, 62 Calif.L.Rev. 693, 697-719 (1974).[5] Similarly, as previously observed, it is universally recognized as fundamental to effective therapy that the patient acknowledge his illness and cooperate with those attempting to give treat-

[4]See Editorial, A New Right, 46 A.B.A.J. 516 (1960).

[5]Indeed, there is considerable debate concerning the threshold questions of what constitutes "mental disease" and "treatment." See Szasz, The Right to Health, 57 Geo.L.J. 734 (1969).

ment; yet the failure of a large proportion of mentally ill persons to do so is a common phenomenon. See Katz, *supra,* 36 U.Chi.L.Rev., at 768-769. It may be that some persons in either of these categories,[6] and there may be others, are unable to function in society and will suffer real harm to themselves unless provided with care in a sheltered environment. See, *e.g., Lake* v. *Cameron,* 124 U.S.App.D.C. 264, 270-271, 364 F.2d 657, 663-664 (1966) (dissenting opinion). At the very least, I am not able to say that a state legislature is powerless to make that kind of judgment. See *Greenwood* v. *United States, supra.*

B

Alternatively, it has been argued that a Fourteenth Amendment right to treatment for involuntarily confined mental patients derives from the fact that many of the safeguards of the criminal process are not present in civil commitment. The Court of Appeals described this theory as follows:

> [A] due process right to treatment is based on the principle that when the three central limitations on the government's power to detain—that detention be in retribution for a specific offense; that it be limited to a fixed term; and that it be permitted after a proceeding where the fundamental procedural safeguards are observed—are absent, there must be a *quid pro quo* extended by the government to justify confinement. And the *quid pro quo* most commonly recognized is the provision of rehabilitative treatment. [493 F.2d, at 522]

To the extent that this theory may be read to permit a State to confine an individual simply because it is willing to provide treatment, regardless of the subject's ability to function in society, it raises the gravest of constitutional problems, and I have no doubt the Court of Appeals would agree on this score. As a justification for a constitutional right to such treatment, the *quid pro quo* theory suffers from equally serious defects.

It is too well established to require extended discussion that due process is not an inflexible concept. Rather, its requirements are determined in particular instances by identifying and accommodating the interests of the individual and society. See, *e.g., Morrissey* v. *Brewer,* 408 U.S. 471, 480-484, 92 S.Ct. 2593, 2599-2602, 33 L.Ed.2d 484 (1972); *McNeil* v. *Director, Patuxent Institution,* 407 U.S., at 249-250, 92 S.Ct., at 2086-2087; *McKeiver* v. *Pennsylvania,* 403 U.S. 528, 545-555, 91 S.Ct. 1976, 1986-1991, 29 L.Ed.2d 647 (1971) (plurality opinion). Where claims that the State is acting in the best interests of an individual are said to justify reduced procedural and substantive safeguards, this Court's decisions require that they be "candidly appraised." *In re Gault,* 387 U.S., at 21, 27-29, 87 S.Ct., at 1440, 1443-1445. However, in so doing judges are not free to read their private notions of public policy or public health into the Constitution. *Olsen* v. *Nebraska ex rel. Western Reference & Bond Ass'n,* 313 U.S. 236, 246-247, 61 S.Ct. 862, 865-866, 85 L.Ed. 1305 (1941).

The *quid pro quo* theory is a sharp departure from, and cannot coexist with, due process principles. As an initial matter, the theory presupposes that essentially the same interests are involved in every situation where a State seeks to confine an indi-

[6]Indeed, respondent may have shared both of these characteristics. His illness, paranoid schizophrenia, is notoriously unsusceptible to treatment, see Livermore. Malmquist. & Meehl, On the Justifications for Civil Commitment, 117 U.Pa.L.Rev. 75. 93. and n. 52 (1968), and the reports of the Florida State Hospital staff which were introduced into evidence expressed the view that he was unwilling to acknowledge his illness and was generally uncooperative.

vidual; that assumption, however, is incorrect. It is elementary that the justification for the criminal process and the unique deprivation of liberty which it can impose requires that it be invoked only for commission of a specific offense prohibited by legislative enactment. See *Powell* v. *Texas,* 392 U.S. 514, 541-544, 88 S.Ct. 2145, 2158-2160, 20 L.Ed.2d 1254 (1968) (opinion of Black, J.)[7] But it would be incongruous, for example, to apply the same limitation when quarantine is imposed by the State to protect the public from a highly communicable disease. See *Jacobson* v. *Massachusetts,* 197 U.S., at 29-30, 25 S.Ct., at 362-363.

A more troublesome feature of the *quid pro quo* theory is that it would elevate a concern for essentially procedural safeguards into a new substantive constitutional right.[8] Rather than inquiring whether strict standards of proof or periodic redetermination of a patient's condition are required in civil confinement, the theory accepts the absence of such safeguards but insists that the State provide benefits which, in the view of a court, are adequate "compensation" for confinement. In light of the wide divergence of medical opinion regarding the diagnosis of and proper therapy for mental abnormalities, that prospect is especially troubling in this area and cannot be squared with the principle that "courts may not substitute for the judgments of legislators their own understanding of the public welfare, but must instead concern themselves with the validity under the Constitution of the methods which the legislature has selected." *In re Gault,* 387 U.S., at 71, 87 S.Ct., at 1466 (Harlan, J., concurring and dissenting). Of course, questions regarding the adequacy of procedure and the power of a State to continue particular confinements are ultimately for the courts, aided by expert opinion to the extent that is found helpful. But I am not persuaded that we should abandon the traditional limitations on the scope of judicial review.

C

In sum, I cannot accept the reasoning of the Court of Appeals and can discern no basis for equating an involuntarily committed mental patient's unquestioned constitutional right not to be confined without due process of law with a constitutional right to *treatment.*[9] Given the present state of medical knowledge regarding abnormal human

[7]This is not to imply that I accept all of the Court of Appeals' conclusions regarding the limitations upon the States' power to detain persons who commit crimes. For example, the notion that confinement must be "for a fixed term" is difficult to square with the widespread practice of indeterminate sentencing, at least where the upper limit is a life sentence.

[8]Even advocates of a right to treatment have criticized the *quid pro quo* theory on this ground. *E. g.,* Developments in the Law—Civil Commitment of the Mentally Ill, 87 Harv.L.Rev. 1190, 1325 n. 39 (1974).

[9]It should be pointed out that several issues which the Court has touched upon in other contexts are not involved here. As the Court's opinion makes plain, this is not a case of a person's seeking release because he has been confined "without ever obtaining a judicial determination that such confinement is warranted." *McNeil* v. *Director, Patuxent Institution,* 407 U.S. 245, 249 92 S.Ct. 2083, 1086, 32 L.Ed.2d 719 (1972). Although respondent's amended complaint alleged that his 1956 hearing before the Pinella County Court was procedurally defective and ignored various factors relating to the necessity for commitment, the persons to whom those allegations applied were either not served with process or dismissed by the District Court prior to trial. Respondent has not sought review of the latter rulings, and this case does not involve the rights of a person in an initial competency or commitment proceeding. Cf. *Jackson* v. *Indiana,* 406 U.S. 715, 738, 92 S.Ct. 1845, 1858, 32 L.Ed.2d 435 (1972); *Specht* v. *Patterson,* 386 U.S. 605, 87 S.Ct. 1209, 18 L.Ed.2d 326 (1967); *Minnesota ex rel. Pearson* v. *Probate Court of Ramsey County,* 309 U.S. 270, 60 S.Ct. 523, 84 L.Ed. 744 (1940).

Further, it was not alleged that respondent was singled out for discriminatory treatment by the staff of Florida State Hospital or that patients at that institution were denied privileges generally available to other persons under commitment in Florida. Thus, the question whether different bases for commitment justify

behavior and its treatment, few things would be more fraught with peril than to irrevocably condition a State's power to protect the mentally ill upon the providing of "such treatment as will give [them] a realistic opportunity to be cured." Nor can I accept the theory that a State may lawfully confine an individual thought to need treatment and justify that deprivation of liberty solely by providing some treatment. Our concepts of due process would not tolerate such a "trade-off." Because the Court of Appeals' analysis could be read as authorizing those results, it should not be followed.

DEFAMATION

Individuals have an interest in protecting their reputation, and the tort of defamation deals with "published" material that would tend to injure the person to whom it refers. The defamatory material may be communicated orally, in writing, by gesture, or by other means (e.g., hanging someone in effigy). When the defamatory material appears in some permanent, physical form such as in writing, in motion pictures, statues, etc., the defamation is said to be "libel." When the defamatory material was "published" (in the broad sense of the word) through a nonpermanent, nonphysical means such as spoken words or through gestures, the defamation is said to be "slander." Patient-plaintiffs have on occasion charged mental health professionals with libel as a result of the diagnosis the professional arrives at after a psychological or psychiatric examination. For example, in *Iverson* v. *Frandsen,* 237 F.2d 898 (10th Cir. 1956), suit was brought against psychologist Arden Frandsen for describing Jo Ann Iverson as "feeble-minded" and "a high-grade moron" in his psychological report. See also *Gasperini* v. *Manginelli,* 196 Misc. 547, 92 N.Y.S.2d 575 (Sup.Ct. 1949), which deals with an allegation of libel resulting from a physician's failure to suffix "Jr." to the name affixed on a medical report.

A defense to defamation is that the defamatory material is true (*Craig* v. *Wright,* 76 P.2d 248), though a minority view holds that material must have been published with justifiable motives (*Hutchins* v. *Page,* 72 A. 689). Another defense to defamation is consent. Another category of defense is that of privileged defamation; included here would be defamatory material that is published in the course of some governmental proceedings and some domestic (family) situations. A related defense is that of qualified privilege, the essential elements of which were defined by Krauskopf and Krauskopf (1965, p. 228):

---

differences in conditions of confinement is not involved in this litigation. Cf. *Jackson* v. *Indiana,* supra 406 U.S., at 723–730, 92 S.Ct., at 1850–1854; *Baxstrom* v. *Herold,* 383 U.S. 107, 86 S.Ct. 760, 15 L.Ed.2d 620 (1966).

Finally, there was no evidence whatever that respondent was abused or mistreated at Florida State Hospital or that the failure to provide him with treatment aggravated his condition. There was testimony regarding the general quality of life at the hospital, but the jury was not asked to consider whether respondent's confinement was in effect "punishment" for being mentally ill. The record provides no basis for concluding, therefore, that respondent was denied rights secured by the Eighth and Fourteenth Amendments. Cf. *Robinson* v. *California,* 370 U.S. 660, 82 S.Ct. 1417, 8 L.Ed.2d 758 (1962).

The essential elements of a qualifiedly privileged communication are (1) good faith by the defendant, (2) a legitimate interest or duty to be furthered by the statement, (3) a statement limited in its scope to that purpose, (4) a proper occasion, and communication in a proper manner and to proper parties only (*Judge* v. *Rockford,* 1958).

Below in *Berry* v. *Moench,* 8 Utah2d 191, 331 P.2d 814 (1958), we see the test of qualified privilege met by the defendant psychiatrist. In another case, *Hammer* v. *Polsky,* 36 Misc.2d 482, 233 N.Y.S.2d 110 (Sup.Ct. 1962), the court found insufficient as a cause of action the complaint that the defendant practitioner, in the course of a custody proceeding, disclosed without consent, and in violation of rules prohibiting such disclosure, information obtained during the course of a professional relationship. The *Hammer* court opined: "Unprofessional conduct does not constitute malpractice, nor the claimed disregard of the rule of evidence embraced in Section 352 of the Civil Practice Act." In general, there has been a lack of judicial consistency with respect to the issue of the appropriateness of revealing confidential doctor-patient communications at custody hearings. In the 1974 South Dakota case of *Schaffer* v. *Spicer,* 215 N.W.2d 135, the court found in favor of the plaintiff who had filed suit against a psychiatrist for divulging confidential information. There was, however, a strong dissenting opinion filed in that case. In *People* v. *Fitzgerald,* 40 Misc.2d 966, 244 N.Y.S.2d 441, the Supreme Court of New York stated:

> [T]he precise question as to whether the court may disregard the patient-physician privilege in a custody proceeding does not appear to have been ruled upon by the courts of this state. There is, of course, ample authority indicative of the court's right to discover the mental condition of a party in a matrimonial matter. . . . The individual rights of infants to invoke the protection of the state in which they reside cannot be ignored.

Thus whether the patient's privilege yields to the rights of the infant or child in a custody proceeding is a matter left to the courts to decide on a case-by-case basis.

Iverson v. *Frandsen,* 237 F.2d 898 (10th Cir., 1956)

Before HUXMAN, MURRAH and PICKETT, Circuit Judges.

MURRAH, Circuit Judge.

The appellant, Jo Ann Iverson, by her mother and guardian ad litem, brought this action against the appellee, Frandsen, in the District Court of Utah, for certain allegedly libellous statements made in a psychological report on the mental level and capacity of the appellant. Federal jurisdiction is based upon requisite diversity of citizenship and amount in controversy.

At the close of the evidence, the trial court directed a verdict in favor of the appellee, from which the appellant appeals. The trial court concluded that the report was qualifiedly privileged without any proof of actual malice; and that requisite publication was lacking.

The appellant takes the position that the trial court usurped the prerogatives of the jury in that the testimony of the guardian ad litem presented a question of fact for the jury as to whether the appellee had gone beyond the bounds of his qualified privilege; and that the language used in the report and evidence of falsity presented a question of fact as to whether the critical words denoted express malice.

Libel, as defined by the statutes of Idaho, is a malicious defamation, expressed either by writing, printing or by signs or pictures, to impeach the honesty, integrity, virtue or reputation; or publish the natural and alleged defects of one who is alive and thereby expose that person to public hatred, contempt or ridicule. § 18-4801, I.C. But generally recognized, public policy exempts certain libellous statements as absolutely privileged, and therefore not actionably defamatory. Absolutely privileged statements or communications are, however, confined to very narrow fields, such as judicial proceedings, statements of executive officers made in the discharge of their duties, and legislative proceedings. *Jones* v. *Kennedy,* 73 App.D.C. 292, 121 F. 2d 40; *Glass* v. *Ickes,* 73 App.D.C. 3, 117 F.2d 273, 132 A.L.R. 1328; *Spalding* v. *Vilas,* 161 U.S. 483, 16 S.Ct. 631, 40 L.Ed. 780. Then there are certain qualified or conditionally privileged communications which, when made in good faith, without malice, to a person having a corresponding interest or duty, are likewise nonactionable. 33 Am.Jur., Libel and Slander, § 126; *White* v. *Nicholls,* 3 How. 266, 11 L.Ed. 591; *Swift & Co.* v. *Gray,* 9 Cir., 101 F.2d 976. A qualifiedly privileged communication rebuts the presumption of malice which attaches to otherwise libellous matter, and it is incumbent upon the complaining party to show express malice from the language itself or by extrinsic evidence. *National Disabled Soldiers' League* v. *Haan,* 55 App.D.C. 243, 4 F.2d 436; *Montgomery Ward & Co.* v. *Watson,* 4 Cir., 55 F.2d 184; *Interstate Transit Lines* v. *Crane,* 10 Cir., 100 F.2d 857. Such is the law in Idaho where this action arose. *Gough* v. *Tribune-Journal Co.,* 75 Idaho 502, 275 P.2d 663.

Since very early childhood, the appellant has admittedly suffered from claustrophobia—a fear of enclosed places. Early in September 1951, the guardian ad litem took her nine-year-old daughter, the appellant, to the State Hospital South, Blackfoot, Idaho, a state institution for the mentally ill, for assistance in overcoming this fear which prevented her child from attending public school. After a short discussion with Dr. Isabella Ralph, a staff psychiatrist, she was advised to return at a later date for a more thorough inquiry. At the subsequent meeting Dr. Ralph directed the mother and daughter to the appellee, Frandsen, an experienced psychologist employed part time at the hospital. It was standard institutional procedure to have all patients examined by psychologist-psychiatrist teams—the psychologist doing the testing and evaluating and the psychiatrist administering the treatment. As a part of his examination Frandsen gave the daughter a Stanford-Benet [*sic*] test—a universally recognized method for determining the intelligence quotient and mental capacity of an individual. He then forwarded to psychiatrist Ralph his report which stated in part that the intelligence quotient of the child classified her as " 'feeble-minded,' at the high-grade moron level of general mental ability." The report further stated that "at the time she is about sixteen, she should have progressed to about the fourth grade level in reading, arithmetic, writing, etc." These two statements are the basis for this libel action. Subsequently, on request of the appellant's school guidance director, and following the practice of the hospital, a copy of Frandsen's report was forwarded to the school officials. It was from this source that embarrassing rumors apparently emanated concerning the mental condition of the appellant. Upon contacting the local school authorities, the mother was shown Frandsen's report and another report made three years later by the school's guidance director which gave her daughter about the same I.Q. rating.

Without taking issue with any of the foregoing facts, the appellant rests her case squarely on the proposition that she went to Dr. Ralph for advice and treatment concerning claustrophobia; that the Stanford-Benet test was beyond the scope of the consultation, wholly unauthorized and therefore not qualifiedly privileged.

There was positive and uncontradicted proof to the effect that the Stanford-Benet test was standard procedure for all patients to ascertain whether such patients had the mental capacity to respond to psycho-therapy and, if so, at what level it must be based; that the report was prepared at the request of Dr. Ralph, in accordance with standard procedures and intended only for hospital officials or professionally interested persons; that Frandsen only saw the appellant on this one occasion; that the report was as accurate as Frandsen could make it; that Frandsen had never seen it since forwarding it to Dr. Ralph; and that he had never been consulted concerning the use of the report by any one other than the hospital officials to whom it was directed. The report was clearly within the duties of Frandsen as a staff psychologist of the state hospital and it contained matter which certainly was of professional interest both to the appellee and Dr. Ralph.

The report is said to be absolutely privileged under the rationale of *Glass* v. *Ickes, supra*. But, we have seen no Idaho decisions indicating a disposition to extend the doctrine of absolute privilege to communications of this kind. See *Dwyer* v. *Libert,* 30 Idaho 576, 167 P. 651, 652, citing *Foster* v. *Scripps,* 39 Mich. 376, 33 Am.Rep. 403, which denied privilege to the communications of an appointed physician in public service "except a bona fide representation made without malice to the proper authority." In the view we take of this case, however, it is unnecessary for us to delineate the field of absolute privilege in Idaho. For, we are convinced that the assailed report, though qualifiedly privileged, was positively free from any actionable malice whatsoever. In the first place, it was incumbent upon the appellant to offer some evidence of an extrinsic character to show actual malice on the part of the appellee. The appellant admittedly consulted a psychiatrist at a public institution for the purpose of receiving psychiatric therapy. And, it is also true that, as a part of the contemplated treatment, she voluntarily submitted herself to an examination by a duly recognized psychologist, and having done so, she cannot prescribe the diagnostic procedure incident to such treatment. To be sure, she is not libeled by the contents of the report. It was a professional report made by a public servant in good faith, representing his best judgment, and therefore could not be maliciously false.

The judgment is affirmed.

Berry v. *Moench,* 8 Utah2d 191, 331 P.2d 814 (1958)

CROCKETT, Justice.

Robert J. Berry appeals from an adverse jury verdict and judgment in a suit against Dr. Louis G. Moench for publishing in a letter allegedly false and derogatory information acquired in connection with treating Mr. Berry as a patient.

Significant portions of the letter are:

Dear Dr. Hellewell:

Since I do not have his authorization, the patient you mentioned in your last letter will remain nameless,

He was treated here in 1949 as an emergency. Our diagnosis was Manic depressive depression in a psychopathic personality. . . .

He had one brother as a manic, and his father committed suicide. . . .

The patient was attempting to go through school on the G.I. bill. . . . Instead of attending class he would spend most of the days and nights playing cards for money.

Because of family circumstances, we treated him for a mere token charge (and I notice even that has never been paid).

During his care here, he purchased a brand new Packard, without even money to buy gasoline.

He was in constant trouble with the authorities during the war, . . . did not do well in school, and never did really support his wife and children.

Since he was here, we have repeated requests for his record indicating repeated trouble. . . .

My suggestion to the infatuated girl would be to run as fast and as far as she possibly could in any direction away from him.

Of course if he doesn't marry her, he will marry someone else and make life hell for that person. The usual story is repeated unsuccessful marriages and a trail of tragedy behind.

The above letter was written September 12, 1956, in respone to one in which Dr. J. S. Hellewell of Evanston, Wyoming had requested information concerning Mr. Berry, asking for "your impression of the man," for the stated purpose of passing it on to a Mr. and Mrs. Williams, parents of Mary Boothe who was then keeping company with Mr. Berry.

The information supplied by Dr. Moench had been obtained seven years earlier in connection with the psychiatric treatment of Mr. Berry. The latter had been having marital difficulties and at the request of his then wife, Ethella Berry, had gone to Dr. Moench. His condition was diagnosed; electric shock treatments recommended and four of them were given. Dr. Moench had not seen plaintiff since that time.

The letter was relayed by Dr. Hellewell to the Williamses and in turn to their daughter, Mary Boothe. Consequently the parents became violently opposed to the marriage. They have since disowned their daughter because she went ahead and married the plaintiff and they are now husband and wife.

In justification of writing the letter, Dr. Moench relied on these defenses: That the statements were true; that he had a reasonable basis for believing them to be true; that he made them under conditional privilege; and that they were not defamatory.

At the pre-trial the court ruled as a matter of law that the doctor had a conditional privilege to make the statements. At the trial the jury was so instructed; and that any finding of malice must be shown by evidence independent of the letter; and also that if the statements were true, or if the doctor had probable cause to believe the statements to be true, that would constitute a defense. These rulings are here assigned as error.

It is recognized that ordinarily the truth is a defense to an action for libel or slander. However, in the instant case there is the special circumstance to reckon with, that a doctor-patient relationship existed between the parties in connection with which Dr. Moench acquired the information upon which he based the letter. That relationship is among those with respect to which it is the policy of the law to encourage confidence. This policy is expressed in Sec. 78-24-8, U.C.A.1953 which provides, inter alia, that a physician cannot be examined as to any information acquired in attending his patient.[1]

[1]Sec. 78-24-8, U.C.A. 1953: Privileged Communications: also prohibits testimony re communications between: husband-wife; attorney-client; priest-confessor; physician-patient.

It is grounded upon the advantage to all concerned in encouraging the full disclosure of all facts which may have a bearing upon diagnosis and treatment of the patient. If the doctor could with impunity publish anything that is true, the patient would be without protection from disclosure of intimacies which might be both embarrassing and harmful to him. This would make him reluctant to tell some things even though they might be important in the treatment of his ills. For this reason it is obligatory upon the doctor not to reveal information obtained in confidence in connection with the diagnosis or treatment of his patient. It is our opinion that if the doctor violates that confidence and publishes derogatory matter concerning his patient, an action would lie for any injury suffered. That of course, presupposes the absence of any privilege, as hereinafter discussed. Compare the obiter dicta statement of the Supreme Court of Washington, "... for so palpable a wrong, the law provides a remedy," which statement was similarly quoted with approval by the Nebraska Supreme Court in *Simonsen* v. *Swenson*.[2] That Dr. Moench himself was aware of his duty not to reveal the secrets of his patient without the latter's consent is shown in the letter, "Since I do not have his authorization, the patient... will remain nameless...."

We do not doubt the correctness of defendant's contention that the responsibility of the doctor to keep confidence may be outweighed by a higher duty to give out information, even though defamatory, if there is a sufficiently important interest to protect. In such event there arises a conditional privilege to make a disclosure reasonably necessary to protect such interest.

The usual situation giving rise to the privilege is where the interest being protected is that of the publisher. Illustrative of this is the case of *Combes* v. *Montgomery Ward & Co.*,[3] relied on by the defendant, wherein we referred with approval to Sec. 594 of the Restatement of Torts. There the statement concerning pilfering of funds was made in the presence of another employee in connection with an investigation of peculations from the cash receipts. It was pointed out that the act was essential to the protection of the interest of the publisher and did not extend beyond the necessity of that purpose. That rule has no application to the instant situation because Dr. Moench had no interest which was being protected by giving out this information.

It should be kept in mind that this is not a situation where a patient had gone to a second doctor for treatment and the latter requested information from the first doctor to assist him in the diagnosis. Conceding that professional custom and comity require that this be permitted in a proper case for the help and protection of both doctors and patients, this is not such a case. Dr. Hellewell had never seen Mr. Berry and had no concern with him as a patient.

We recognize that such a privilege may also extend to the protection of the interests of third persons under proper circumstances. Where life, safety, well-being or other important interest is in jeopardy, one having information which could protect against the hazard, may have a conditional privilege to reveal information for such purpose, even though it be defamatory and may prove to be false.[4] But the privilege is not something which arises automatically and becomes absolute merely because there is an interest to protect. It has its origin in, and it is governed by, the rule of good sense and customary conduct of people motivated by good will and proper consideration for

[2]104 Neb. 224, 177 N.W. 831, 833, 9 A.L.R. 1254; see also, *Munzer* v. *Blaisdell*, 183 Misc. 773, 49 N.Y.S.2d 915.

[3]119 Utah 407, 228 P.2d 272; see (Utah, 1951) 228 P.2d 272.

[4]A.L.I. Restatement of Torts, Sec. 595, et seq.

others. This includes due consideration for the subject being informed about as well as the recipient being protected. The policy of the law concerning this matter is framed in the light of the hazard that defamation can so easily undermine or destroy a most precious possession: a good name and reputation. In ancient writ it is said "A good name is rather to be chosen than great riches."[5] Recognizing that a good name is so hard to acquire and to preserve, yet so vulnerable to being tarnished, the law imposes upon one publishing derogatory information, even for laudatory purposes, the responsibility of exercising due care in what he does and in knowing whereof he speaks.

One purveying such information about one person to protect another is obliged to consider the likelihood and the extent of benefit to the recipient, if the matter is true, as compared with the likelihood of injury and the extent thereof to the subject, if it prove false, or improper to reveal. Whether the privilege exists, depends upon generally accepted standards of decent conduct. Applying that standard, it exists if the recipient has the type of interest in the matter, and the publisher stands in such a relation to him, tbat it would reasonably be considered the duty of the publisher to give the information.[6] If the facts upon which the privilege would rest are not in dispute, whether the privilege exists is a question for the court to determine. If they are in dispute the jury must determine the facts and upon them the court determines the question of privilege.[7]

We are not disposed to disagree with the trial court's ruling that the circumstances here came within the framework of conditional privilege: that is, that Mary Boothe's concern for her well-being and happiness was a sufficient interest to protect, and that it was within the generally accepted standards of decent conduct for the doctor to reveal the information which might have an important bearing thereon. We believe, however, that that is as far as the trial court could go. In submitting the case to the jury on the basis of privilege it was necessary to instruct it as to the limitations upon the manner in which the privilege should be exercised.

We are aware that it is frequently stated that where the situation is privileged there is no liability in the absence of actual malice.[8] However, an examination of the authorities reveals that quite generally, when the matter is actually in issue, they are in accord upon a principle which we consider sound and salutary: that the privilege to pass on derogatory information, which proves false, must have been exercised with at least reasonable discretion, or the publisher will be held responsible therefor. This is well summarized in the Restatement of Torts:

> Even though the occasion is so privileged, a particular person cannot avail himself of the privilege arising therefrom if he abuses the occasion. . . . The occasion may be abused by the publisher's lack of belief or reasonable grounds for belief in the truth of the defamatory matter . . .; by the publication of the defamatory matter for some improper purpose. . . .; by excessive publication . . .; or by the publication of defamatory matter not reasonably believed to be necessary to accomplish the purpose. . . .[9]

It is significant that the privilege we are here concerned with is referred to as a "conditional" or "qualified" privilege. The reason for the limiting adjectives is that it

[5]Proverbs 22.1.

[6]See footnote 4 *supra* Sec. 595.

[7]Ibid, Sec. 619.

[8]53 C.J.S. Libel and Slander § 99, p. 156; 33 Am.Jur. 115.

[9]A.L.I. Restatement of Torts, Sec. 595, comment a; the quoted language adopted and approved in *Sheehan* v. *Tobin*, 326 Mass. 185, 93 N.E.2d 524; *Ward* v. *Ares*, 29 N.M. 418, 223 P. 766.

must be exercised with certain cautions: (a) it must be done in good faith and reasonable care must be exercised as to its truth, (b) likewise, the information must be reported fairly, (c) only such information should be conveyed, and (d) only to such persons as are necessary to the purpose. We comment upon them as applicable to the instant case.

(a) It seems hardly necessary to state that one cannot pass on derogatory information indifferent to its truth, or the consequences thereof, but failure to exercise reasonable care and diligence to ascertain the truth destroys the privilege.[10] Dr. Moench was uncertain as to what information came from what sources: the referring doctor (Dr. Miller), the plaintiff, or plaintiff's then wife, Ethella Berry, or her sister. Experience teaches that an unhappy wife of a blighted marriage is not usually the most impartial source of information as to the conduct and character of a disappointing husband; less so a sister-in-law. Nevertheless, Dr. Moench admitted relying on their statements.

As might be expected, plaintiff sharply disagrees as to facts about him as assumed and reported by Dr. Moench. Illustrative are these:

Dr. Moench: that the plaintiff did not do well in school;

Plaintiff: grade school: I was in the top of my class every year; high school: finished in the top 1% of my class, editor-in-chief of the school paper, on student council and participated in other activities; college: in three years grades were above average, admitted flunking two courses.

Dr. Moench: that he was in constant trouble with the authorities . . .

Plaintiff: this simmered down to about three incidents of minor importance.

Dr. Moench: purchased a new Packard without even money to buy gasoline;

Plaintiff: that he had $200 in the bank and received $4,000 inheritance.

Dr. Moench: that he had not paid his bill.

Plaintiff: that of the charge of $50, all but $5 had long since been paid.

As to the latter item, the doctor relied on a red tab on the card, indicating an unpaid bill. He admitted that checking his record would have revealed the fact that all but $5 had been paid.

(b) Closely related to the duty to use reasonable diligence as to truth is the requirement that the publisher communicate the information fairly. He is not warranted in reporting as undoubted facts information which may have been derived from sources which render its verity questionable. If it is from mere hearsay or there are other circumstances which would render it open to suspicion of unsoundness, fairness requires him to report such circumstances along with the information.[11] This is especially important as to a doctor. His professional status and his duty to keep the confidence of his patient tend to endow information he gives with more than ordinary credibility. In regard to this requirement, plaintiff makes these points: that the doctor was advising about his present condition, based upon skimpy, unverified information obtained seven years earlier, which he assumed to be true and stated as facts, without stating the source; that even if plaintiff had been mentally ill at the prior time, it was wrong to assume that he was still so afflicted; and also for the doctor to fail to make any allowance for the possibility of his getting well, or even that his own treatments had any beneficial effect; particularly so when the doctor on cross examination stated that

[10]As was stated by the Pennsylvania Court in *J. Hartman & Co.* v. *Hyman,* 287 Pa. 78, 134 A. 486, 488, 48 A.L.R. 567: "Want of reasonable care and diligence to ascertain the truth, . . . will destroy the privilege." (Citing cases.)

[11]A.L.I. Restatement of Torts, Sec. 602, comment a.

he had treated about 800 patients with this ailment with such success that most of them were getting along quite well and making a success of their marriages.

(c) Another aspect of the situation to be considered is the requirement, even under a privileged situation, that only such information should be given as is necessary for the purpose for which the privilege exists.[12] E.g., if the fact that the bill had not been paid had any bearing on the situation, which may be open to question, reasonable effort to supply accurate information should be made. The same observation is pertinent to other items set forth above.

(d) There is further question, admittedly more tenuous than the others, as to whether the publication was to more persons than reasonably necessary to afford the protection for which the privilege existed.[13] Neither Mary Boothe nor Mr. Berry were patients of Dr. Moench or Dr. Hellewell, nor had any personal relationship of any character with them. Dr. Hellewell was not acting as a physician to either of them, nor to the Williamses. His only objective was in doing what he regarded as a favor to the Williamses who had been his patients. He can properly be regarded only as an intermediary, who was intended to pass the information on through other intermediaries, the Williamses, to the person directly concerned. The likelihood of the parents being greatly concerned and disposed to talk to others about the matter may be taken into account. Conceding that Mary Boothe had such an interest that Dr. Moench properly thought she should be given the information, it seems to us that reasonable minds might entertain the thought that a more direct method of getting the information to her should have been employed than to relay it through others, even though they had made the inquiry in her interest.

It may well be that Dr. Moench did that which was discreet and proper with respect to the principles discussed under (a), (b), (c) and (d) above. We do not presume to say. It appears to us that the evidence provides a basis upon which reasonable minds might differ as to whether he did so in connection with the passing on of information of the character in question. Thus such issues should have been submitted to the jury. Inasmuch as the manner in which the case was submitted did not permit the jury to pass on these issues it is necessary for us to remand the cause for a new trial. In doing so it is incumbent upon us to comment on certain matters that will be pertinent on the retrial.[14]

Libel may be defined as a false and unprivileged publication in writing which assails the honesty, integrity or virtue of another and thereby exposes him to hatred, contempt, or ridicule, or tends to injure him in his occupation.[15] The letter can be regarded as doing so.

In the law of defamation there is an important difference between the term "malice" when used to denote actual malice, or as it is sometimes called, "malice in fact," as contrasted with implied malice or "malice in law." Actual malice or malice in fact may be found only when it appears that the actor was motivated by spite, hatred or ill will against the subject and it must exist before punitive damages can be awarded. There is a lack of proof of the latter type of malice in this case. Malice in law, which is a necessary prerequisite to recovery for libel, may be implied from the intentional doing of the wrongful act or uttering defamatory matter which is false, or without legal

[12] Ibid, Sec. 595, comment a. and Sec. 605.

[13] Ibid, Sec. 604.

[14] Rule 76(a), U.R.C.P., *Joseph* v. *W. H. Groves Latter Day Saints Hospital*, 7 Utah 2d 39, 318 P.2d 330.

[15] See 33 Am.Jur. 38; 53 C.J.S. Libel and Slander § 1, p. 32.

justification.[16] Whether such malice existed in the utterance is to be determined from all of the facts and circumstances shown by the evidence, including the contents of the letter.[17]

Remanded for a new trial. Costs to appellant.

WADE and WORTHEN, JJ., concur.

MCDONOUGH, C.J., and HENRIOD, J., concur in the result.

BREACH OF RIGHT TO TREATMENT

As illustrated in Justice Burger's concurring opinion in *O'Connor* v. *Donaldson* (page 382 above), patients have a constitutionally ensured right to treatment. This right is extended by the court to minors in *Morales* v. *Turman,* 383 F.Supp. 53 (E.D. Tex. 1974). Below, in *Wyatt* v. *Aderholt,* 503 F.2d 1305 (5th Cir. 1974), we see the court undertake to define the conditions needed for adequate treatment. Following *Wyatt* below, in *State* v. *Harvey,* 162 N.J.Super. 386, 392 A.2d 1248 (1978), the court grapples with treatment issues concerning a convicted sex offender.

Wyatt v. *Aderholt,* 503 F.2d 1305 (5th Cir. 1974)

WISDOM, Circuit Judge:

In this case, we must decide whether federal district courts have the power to order state mental institutions to provide minimum levels of psychiatric care and treatment[1] to persons civilly commiteed to the institutions.

The guardians of patients civilly committed to three Alabama facilities for the mentally handicapped brought this class action on behalf of their wards and other civilly committed patients at those institutions. The Honorable Frank M. Johnson, trial judge, held that mentally ill patients "have a constitutional right to receive such individual treatment as will give each of them a reasonable opportunity to be cured or to improve his or her mental condition". *Wyatt* v. *Stickney,* M.D.Ala.1971, 325 F.Supp. 781, 784. In a later order, Judge Johnson held that the mentally retarded patients have a constitutional right to "such individual habilitation as will give each of them a realistic opportunity to lead a more useful and meaningful life and to return to society." *Wyatt* v. *Stickney,* M.D.Ala.1972, 344 F.Supp. 387, 390. The district court found that conditions at the three facilities deprived the plaintiffs of these constitutional rights, and ordered the defendants-appellants, Alabama officials responsible for the

[16]*Ward* v. *Ares,* 29 N.M. 418, 223 P. 766, 768 citing cases.

[17]Ibid, p. 769.

[1]"Treatment" means care provided by mental health professionals and others that is adequate and appropriate for the needs of the mentally impaired inmate. Treatment also encompasses a humane physical and psychological environment. The term "habilitation," used by the parties and amici in the district court and by the district court in its order of April 13, 1972 (Partlow State School and Hospital) is a term used to describe that treatment which is appropriate to the condition of the mental retardate. For convenience, in this opinion we group "habilitation" and "treatment" under the single term "treatment," and to include those instances where rehabilitation is impossible in which event the requirement is minimally adequate habilitation and care, beyond the subsistence level custodial care that would be provided in a penitentiary. *Donaldson* v. *O'Connor,* 5 Cir., 1974, 493 F.2d 507, 522.

administration of the state's mental health programs, to implement a detailed set of standards designed to ensure the provision of minimally adequate treatment and habilitation at the institutions. From this order, the Alabama Mental Health Board and Alabama's Governor George C. Wallace bring separate appeals.

Together, the Mental Health Board and the Governor advance six major contentions on appeal. They contend (1) that the district court erred in holding that civilly committed mental patients have a constitutional right to treatment; (2) that the court lacked jurisdiction because the suit was in effect a suit against the state proscribed by the eleventh amendment; (3) that the case involves rights and duties not susceptible to determination by judicially ascertainable and manageable standards, and therefore presents a non-justiciable controversy; (4) that the order of the district court invades a province of decision-making exclusively reserved to the state legislature; (5) that the plaintiffs were not entitled to equitable relief because they had adequate remedies at law to protect the rights they asserted; and (6) that the district court erred in awarding plaintiffs a reasonable attorneys' fee.

Neither in the district court nor on appeal to this Court have the defendants challenged the detailed set of standards articulated by the district court. They have conceded that if there is a constitutional right to treatment enforceable by a suit for injunctive relief in federal court, those standards accurately reflect what would be required to ensure the provision of adequate treatment.

I

A. The Proceedings Below

This case began innocuously enough when a cut in the Alabama cigarette tax forced the state to fire 99 professional, subprofessional, and intern employees[2] at the Bryce Hospital, a state-run institution for the mentally ill at Tuscaloosa. The plaintiffs filed their complaint October 23, 1970. The complaint named two classes as plaintiffs. One, represented by Ricky Wyatt and two other named plaintiffs, appellees here, consisted of the patients at Bryce. The other, represented by five of the then recently terminated emloyees, consisted of the employees who had been dismissed for budgetary reasons. The defendants were Stonewall B. Stickney, then Executive Officer of the Alabama State Mental Health Board; Dr. John V. Hottel, his Chief Deputy; the members of the Board; then Governor Albert P. Brewer, both in his capacity as Governor and in his capacity as a member of the Board; and Judge Perry O. Hooper, Probate Judge of Montgomery County, both individually and as a representative of the class consisting of all probate judges in Alabama.

The complaint alleged that the defendants had effected the staff reductions purely for budgetary reasons; that the discharges of the 99 employees had been accomplished without notice and a hearing, and violated the employees' rights under the due process clause; and that as a result of the discharges the patients at Bryce would not receive adequate treatment. The complaint sought injunctive relief requiring the defendants to insure that treatment programs then being administered at Bryce would not be inter-

[2]The 99 employees included 41 who were assigned duties such as food service, maintenance, typing and other mechanical duties not involving direct patient care; 26 persons involved in planning social and other recreational activities for the patients; nine persons from the department of psychology; eleven from the social service department; three registered nurses, two physicians, one dentist, and six dental aides.

rupted or altered, and requiring the defendants to rescind the terminations of the 99 employees.

The original complaint did not allege that treatment levels at Bryce had been inadequate before the terminations. For reasons not entirely clear from the record before us, however, the focus of the litigation soon shifted from the effects of the October 1970 terminations to questions of the overall adequacy of the treatment afforded at the Alabama state mental hospitals. On January 4, 1971, the plaintiffs amended the complaint to add prayers that the defendants be enjoined from operating Bryce "in a manner that does not conform to constitutional standards of delivering adequate mental treatment to its patients"; that the Court order defendants to prepare a "comprehensive constitutionally acceptable plan to provide adequate treatment in any state mental health facility"; and that the court declare that patients confined to a state mental health facility are entitled to "adequate, competent treatment."

On March 12, 1971, the district court ruled on the plaintiffs' motion for a preliminary injunction. 325 F.Supp. 781. The court's opinion reflected the shift in the focus of the case. In its opinion, the court decleared that patients "involuntarily committed through noncriminal procedures and without the constitutional protections that are afforded defendants in criminal proceedings" are "committed for treatment purposes" and so "unquestionably have a constitutional right to receive such individual treatment as will give each of them a realistic opportunity to be cured or to improve his or her mental condition." 325 F.Supp. at 784. The court found that the treatment programs in effect before the institution of a staff reorganization then in progress were "scientifically and medically inadequate," failing to "conform to any known minimums established for providing treatment for the mentally ill." *Id.* The court stated that it was not at that time in a position to determine whether the treatment which would be provided after the reorganization was completed would be adequate. Accordingly, the court allowed the defendants ninety days to report progress made in the reorganization plan, and to file with the Court a "specific plan" for the provision of adequate treatment at Bryce. Also in the March 12 order, the court invited the United States, through the Department of Justice and Health, Education and Welfare, to appear as amicus.

On August 4, 1971, the plaintiffs amended their complaint to allege that the Searcy Hospital at Mount Vernon, Alabama, the one other state hospital for the mentally ill in Alabama, and the Partlow State School and Hospital, Alabama's state facility for the mentally retarded, were being operated in a constitutionally impermissible manner.

On September 13, 1971, six months after the March 12 order, the defendants filed their report on proposed standards of adequate treatment and their implementation. Objections to the report were later filed by the plaintiffs and by the United States, as well as by several interested private organizations which had been granted leave to appear as amici.[3]

The court announced its conclusions upon review of the report and the objections to it in an opinion issued December 10, 1971. 334 F.Supp. 1341. In this opinion, the district court held that there are three "fundamental conditions for adequate and effec-

[3]By order entered August 20, 1971, the district court granted the motion filed by the American Civil Liberties Union, the American Orthopsychiatric Association, and American Psychological Association, and the American Association on Mental Deficiency, for leave to appear as amici. In this Court, these amici have been joined by the National Association for Mental Health, the American Psychiatric Association and the National Association for Retarded Children. The seven have filed a joint brief in this Court.

The district court expressed its gratitude to these organizations for their valuable assistance in this difficult and complex case, 344 F.Supp. 375, 390, and we do so, too.

tive treatment'': a ''humane physical and psychological environment''; qualified staff ''in numbers sufficient to administer adequate treatment''; and individualized treatment plans. The court held that the reports before it showed ''rather conclusively'' that the treatment programs at Bryce did not meet any of these conditions. It also noted that conditions at Searcy and Partlow seemed little better. It concluded that the defendants had failed to ''formulate minimum medical and constitutional standards for the operation of these institutions.'' The court scheduled a formal hearing to take evidence necessary to establish standards, and said that after the hearing it, the court, would itself ''establish standards and in due course order their implementation.''

The court postponed the hearings to give the defendants another opportunity to formulate proposed minimum standards. On January 17, 1972, the parties and *amici* met in Atlanta, Georgia, where they undertook extensive discussions concerning the proper standards of treatment at the Alabama hospitals. Out of these discussions came two Memoranda of Agreement stipulating certain of the standards necessary to define what would constitute minimally adequate mental treatment at a state psychiatric institution. One of the Memoranda covered standards for treatment at the mental hospitals, Searcy and Bryce; the other covered standards to be imposed at the school for the mentally retarded, Partlow. These Memoranda were filed with the district court at the times for the hearings set for determining the proper standards. The hearing concerning Bryce and Searcy was held February 3 and 4, 1972; the hearing concerning Partlow was held February 28–March 2.[4]

The district court announced its orders granting permanent injunctive relief in two opinions issued April 13, 1972. One of the opinions concerned Partlow, the other, Bryce and Searcy. 344 F.Supp. 373 (Bryce-Searcy), 390 (Partlow). In Partlow, Judge Johnson held that ''[b]ecause the only constitutional justification for civilly committing a mental retardate . . . is habilitation, it follows ineluctably'' that civilly committed retardates ''have a constitutional right to receive such individual habilitation as will give each of them a realistic opportunity to lead a more useful and meaningful life and to return to society''. The Bryce-Searcy opinion summarized the court's earlier opinions, noting its holding that the civilly mentally ill have a constitutional right to treatment. Beyond this, the two opinions were substantially identical. Both ordered the defendants (1) to implement an elaborate set of standards of treatment set forth in appendices to the opinions; (2) to establish human rights committees at the institutions to review all research and treatment programs ''to ensure that the dignity and human rights of the residents are preserved''; (3) to prepare and file reports within six months of the orders on the implementation of the standards; and (4) to pay court costs and a reasonable attorneys' fee to the plaintiffs. The Partlow order also required the defendants to hire a qualified administrator for the School within sixty days.[5]

[4]At the conclusion of the Partlow hearing, the district court entered an emergency order requiring the defendants to take certain immediate actions at Partlow. These included the installation of an emergency light system and procedures for emergency evacuation; revision of sanitation measures in the kitchen; revamping of its program for the use of drugs; conducting appropriate immunizations; and employing three hundred additional resident care workers. In its order filed March 2, 1972, the court said it was taking these steps ''to protect the lives and well-being of the residents,'' because it found Partlow to be a ''warehousing institution . . . wholly incapable of furnishing treatment to the mentally retarded and . . . conducive only to the deterioration and debilitation of the residents,'' and because it found conditions at Partlow ''substandard to the point of endangering the health and lives of the residents.''

[5]In both orders, the court refused requests made by plaintiffs and amici to appoint a master and professional advisory committee to oversee implementation of the standards on grounds that ''[f]ederal courts are reluctant to assume control of any organization, but especially one operated by a state.'' 344 F.Supp. at 377,

Governor Wallace and the Mental Health Board filed separate notices of appeal May 12, 1972. On May 22, Governor Wallace filed a motion for modification and for a stay pending appeal. On June 1, the district court issued an opinion fixing the amount due plaintiffs as attorneys' fees at $36,744.62. 344 F. Supp. at 408-411. On June 26, the district court denied the motions for modification and for a stay pending appeal. This Court also denied a motion for a stay pending appeal.

B. The Conditions in the Alabama Hospitals

There has not been any significant dispute, in this Court or in the district court, about the conditions that prevailed in the Alabama hospitals at the time this suit was instituted. The defendants have pitched their defense on their argument that the Constitution does not guarantee a right to treatment; they have virtually conceded that if such a constitutional right exists, the conditions in the hospitals were such that the state's constitutional obligation to provide adequate treatment could not be met. There is therefore little reason for an extended discussion of the conditions that prevailed at the hospitals. Some discussion, however, is essential to understanding this case. We therefore note briefly how far short the hospitals fell of meeting the three "fundamental conditions of adequate and effective treatment" defined by the district court.

First, it is clear that the environment at the hospitals was a far cry from the "humane psychological and physical environment" the district court envisioned as *sine qua non* of rehabilitative treatment. Bryce Hospital was built in the 1850's; it had 5000 inmates of whom 1500 to 1600 were geriatrics, 1000 were mental retardates, and there were allegedly other non-mentally ill persons. Patients in the hospitals were afforded virtually no privacy: the wards were overcrowded; there was no furniture where patients could keep clothing; there were no partitions between commodes in the bathrooms. There were severe health and safety problems: patients with open wounds and inadequately treated skin diseases were in imminent danger of infection because of the unsanitary conditions existing in the wards, such as permitting urine and feces to remain on the floor; there was evidence of insect infestation in the kitchen and dining areas. Malnutrition was a problem: the United States described the food as "com[ing] closer to 'punishment' by starvation" than nutrition. At Bryce, the food distribution and preparation systems were unsanitary, and less than 50 cents per day per patient was spent on food. Dr. Donald L. Clopper, Associate Commissioner for Mental Retardation for the Alabama Department of Mental Health, testified that Partlow was a "step-child" in the State of Alabama; that the physical environment was inadequate for treating inmates; that "we don't have the staff we don't have the facilities, nor do we have the financial resources." According to Dr. Clopper, at least 300 Partlow inmates could be discharged immediately, and about 70 percent of the inmates should never have been committed; yet it was 60 percent over-crowded. Patients at Partlow were forced to perform uncompensated labor. Aides frequently put patients in seclusion or under physical restraints, including straitjackets, without physicians' orders. One resident had been regularly confined in a straitjacket for more than nine years. The Evaluation Report on Partlow by the American Association on Mental Deficiency

---

392-393. The court also, in both orders, reserved ruling on various motions by the plaintiffs to ensure adequate financing for the implementation of the standards. These included a motion that the Mental Health Board be directed to sell or encumber its extensive land holdings, and a motion for an injunction against the expenditure of state funds on any "nonessential" functions until the standards were fully implemented.

stated that nine working residents would feed 54 young boys ground food from one very large bowl with nine plates and nine spoons; "since there were no accommodations to even sit down to eat," it was impossible to tell which residents had been fed and which had not been fed with this system. Seclusion rooms were large enough for one bed and a coffee can, which served as a toilet. The patients suffered brutality, both at the hands of the aides and at the hands of their fellow patients; testimony established that four Partlow residents died due to understaffing, lack of supervision, and brutality.[6]

The hospitals failed to meet the second condition, adequate staffing. The defendants' chief witness on standards maintained that treatment could be delivered with the ratio of one psychiatrist, one graduate level psychologist, and one masters level social worker for every 125 patients, and the district court ultimately adopted this recommendation. The organizations appearing as amici had recommended higher ratios—one psychiatrist, one psychologist, and one social worker for every 30-50 patients. But at the time this suit was instituted there were ratios of only one medical doctor with some psychiatric training for 5,000 patients, one Ph.D. psychologist for every 1,670 patients, and one masters level social worker for every 2,500 patients at Bryce. The parties and amici agreed completely on the minimums necessary for treatment of the mentally retarded. They agreed that adequate treatment could be delivered at Partlow with ratios of one masters level psychologist and one masters level social worker for every sixty patients, and one physician for every two hundred patients. Yet at Partlow there were only one psychologist with masters level training or above for every 1,200 patients; one masters level social worker for every 730 patients; and one physician for every 550 patients. Of the four physicians at Partlow, two were not licensed to practice in Alabama.

A severe shortage of nonprofessional staff paralleled the inadequacies of professional staff. After a tour of Bryce, defendants' own consultants noted that:

> Aide staff is spread very thin, creating extreme stresses for individual aides, who at times must cover one or two or three wards, housing as many as 100 or 200 patients. Obviously, it is impossible under such circumstances to provide anything more than a cursory observation and the hope of avoiding disturbing incidents. An aide under these circumstances is hard pressed to meet even minimum patient needs.

The institutional staff was inadequate not only in sheer numbers but also in training; there was no effective "in-service training" program for, or even any regular supervision over, the nonprofessionals.

Finally, the evidence established that the hospitals failed to meet the third condition, individualized treatment programs. According to one consultant's testimony, care of patients at Partlow was not suited to the needs of particular individuals, but was instead "geared primarily to housekeeping functions—cleaning floors, cleaning beds, cleaning patients—and to a continuation of work assignments." Experts testified that the patient records kept at the hospital were wholly inadequate; that they were written in such a way as to be incomprehensible to the aide level staff that had prime responsibility for patient care; and that they were kept where they were not accessible to the direct care staff particularly in need of them.

[6]One of the four died after a garden hose had been inserted into his rectum for five minutes by a working patient who was cleaning him; one died when a fellow patient hosed him with scalding water; another died when soapy water was forced into his mouth; and a fourth died from a self-administered overdose of drugs which had been inadequately secured.

II.

The appellants' first and principal contention on appeal is that the Constitution does not guarantee persons civilly committed to state mental institutions a right to treatment.[7] This contention is largely foreclosed by our decision, issued since the institution of this appeal, in *Donaldson* v. *O'Connor,* 1974, 493 F.2d 507. In *Donaldson,* we held that civilly committed mental patients have a constitutional right to such individual treatment as will help each of them to be cured or to improve his or her mental condition. We reasoned that the only permissible justifications for civil commitment, and for the massive abridgments of constitutionally protected liberties it entails, were the danger posed by the individual committed to himself or to others, or the individual's need for treatment and care. We held that where the justification for commitment was treatment, it offended the fundamentals of due process if treatment were not in fact provided; and we held that where the justification was the danger to self or to others, then treatment had to be provided as the *quid pro quo* society had to pay as the price of the extra safety it derived from the denial of individuals' liberty.

Our discussion in *Donaldson,* briefly summarized here, answers most of the arguments made by the appellants on this appeal against the recognition of a constitutional right to treatment. Governor Wallace, however, makes one argument not answered by our discussion in *Donaldson,* and it is appropriate that we address that argument here. Governor Wallace challenged the assumption, made by the district court in this case and by this Court in *Donaldson,* that the only permissible justifications for confinement are danger to self or others or need for treatment. Instead, the Governor suggests, the principal justification for commitment lies in the inability of the mentally ill and mentally retarded to care for themselves. The essence of this argument is that the primary function of civil commitment is to relieve the burden imposed upon the families and friends of the mentally disabled. The families and friends of the disabled, the Governor asserts, are the "true clients" of the institutionalization system.[8]

From this premise the Governor proceeds to the conclusion that is the crux of his argument. If "need for care" is a justification for commitment—or is *the* justification—then it follows that the mere provision of custodial care is constitutionally adequate to justify continued confinement. "[T]he providing of custodial care alone is a tremendously important consideration to patients, their families, and the public-at-large," the Governor writes in his brief.

[7]In raising the issue in this Court, the appellants contend that, because there is no constitutional right to treatment, the district court lacked jurisdiction over the suit. In so arguing the issue, the appellants are following, on this point as on the other four of their first five contentions, the decision of the Northern District of Georgia in *Burnham* v. *Department of Public Health,* 1972, 349 F.Supp. 1335, appeal docketed. No. 72-3110, 5 Cir., Oct. 4, 1972. In *Burnham,* the court held that the Constitution does not guarantee a right to treatment. It then held that the consequence of this conclusion was that it was without jurisdiction over the suit, because 28 U.S.C. § 1343(3), the asserted basis of jurisdiction, confers jurisdiction only over "action[s] . . . to redress the deprivation" of a "right, privilege, or immunity" secured by the Constitution or by an Act of Congress providing for equal rights.

[8]Governor Wallace borrows the term "true clients" from the work of Professor Erving Goffman. E. Goffman, Asylums—Essays on the Social Situations of Mental Patients and Other Inmates 384 (1961). Governor Wallace in his brief praises Professor Goffman as a "realistic writer." Be that as it may, it is fairly clear that Professor Goffman's intent, in calling "relatives, police, and judges" the "true clients of the mental hospitals" was critical, indeed harshly so, and that Professor Goffman was insinuating by that statement an embarrassing, though rarely admitted, truth about the institutionalization system in the United States. What Professor Goffman implied was morally unacceptable—that the convenience of relatives and law enforcers justifies stripping away all of the liberties of the civilly committed—we hold today is constitutionally unacceptable.

There are two answers to this line of argument. The first, and more limited, is that even accepting the Governor's premise that "need for care" is a constitutionally adequate justification for confinement, it does not follow that we must accept the conclusion—that *the kind of care that was provided at the Alabama hospitals* is sufficient to make continued confinement constitutional. The assertion that "need for care" justifies confinement implies that the state has an affirmative obligation to provide a certain minimum quality "care," no less than the assertion that "need for treatment" justifies confinement implies that the state has an affirmative obligation to provide a certain minimum quality "treatment." And it is clear that, however that obligation might specifically be defined, it was not being met in the Alabama hospitals. Dr. Gunnar Dybwad, Professor of Human Development at the Graduate School for Advanced Studies in Social Welfare at Brandeis University, and a one time presidential consultant in the field of mental retardation, made essentially this point when he testified about conditions at Alabama's Partlow State School and Hospital:

> The situation which exists and obviously has existed in Partlow for a long time is one of storage, of persons. I am using that word because *I would not use care*, which involves—has a certain qualitative character, and *I would not even use the word, "custodial," because custody, in my term, means safekeeping*. And, as is visible to the visitor at the present time, employees at Partlow are *not in a position to effect safekeeping*, considering the number of people they have to take care of; so I would say it is a storage problem at the moment. [Emphasis supplied.]

Indeed, many of the standards established by the district court in this case—notably those required for what the district court called a "humane psychological and physical environment"—might have to be met for the state to be able legitimately to claim it was providing adequate "care" to its mental patients. At least where the right to a "humane environment" is concerned, then if it is irrelevant whether the right be viewed as a facet of a "right to treatment," or of a "right to care." It is likewise irrelevant for those purposes whether the state interest imputed to the civil commitment system be called the need "to treat" the mentally ill, or the need "to care" for them.

But beyond this, we find it impossible to accept the Governor's underlying premise that the "need to care" for the mentally ill—and to relieve their families, friends, or guardians of the burdens of doing so—can supply a constitutional justification for civil commitment. At stake in the civil commitment context, as we emphasized in *Donaldson*, see 493 F.2d at 520, are "massive curtailments" of individual liberty. Against the sweeping personal interests involved, Governor Wallace would have us weigh the state's interest, and the interests of the friends and families of the mentally handicapped in having private parties relieved of the "burden" of caring for the mentally ill. The state interest thus asserted may be, strictly speaking, a "rational" state interest. But we find it so trivial beside the major personal interests against which it is to be weighed that we cannot possibly accept it as a justification for the deprivations of liberty involved.

The other arguments against recognition of a constitutional right to treatment for civilly committed mental patients advanced by the appellants are, as we noted above, answered by our discussion in *Donaldson*. Following *Donaldson*, we hold that the district court here did not err in finding that civilly committed mental patients have a constitutional right to treatment. Our express holding in *Donaldson* and here rests on the *quid pro quo* concept of "rehabilitative treatment, or, where rehabilitation is impossible, minimally adequate habilitation and care, beyond the subsistence level custodial care that would be provided in a penitentiary.'' 493 F.2d at 522.

III.

The second, third, fourth, and fifth issues raised by the appellants are also substantially affected by our decision in *Donaldson,* and present little difficulty except as to some aspects of remedy which will be discussed in Part IV, *infra.* The argument that this suit is barred by the eleventh amendment is based largely upon *Burnham* v. *Department of Public Health,* N.D.Ga.1972, 349 F.Supp. 1335, appeal docketed, No. 72-3110, 5 Cir., Oct. 4, 1972, a case consolidated for argument on appeal with this case. In *Burnham,* the court held that, because the right to treatment was a right arising only, if at all, under state law, a suit by citizens of the state against state officials to enforce the right was barred by the eleventh amendment. Our holding in *Donaldson,* however, vitiates this argument, of course, for we have now established that the right to treatment arises as a matter of federal constitutional law under the due process clause of the Fourteenth Amendment.

In *Donaldson,* we addressed and rejected the argument that a constitutional right to adequate treatment would present questions not susceptible to ''judicially manageable or ascertainable standards.'' We held that the judiciary was competent to determine, at least in individual cases, whether psychiatric treatment was medically or constitutionally adequate. And we said in dictum that even in cases such as this one, ''when courts are asked to undertake the more difficult task of fashioning institution-wide standards of adequacy,'' 493 F.2d at 526, the courts would be able to formulate workable standards. In *Donaldson,* we took note of the substantial agreement reached in this case among parties and *amici* in developing standards during the course of the proceedings in the lower court. We cited that development as evidence supporting our view that workable standards could be fashioned. We remain mindful of that development here, in reaffirming our belief that the right to treatment can be implemented through judicially manageable standards.

The appellants' fourth contention is that the order of the district court invades a province of decision-making exclusively reserved for the state legislature. Governor Wallace argues that the order will require heavy expenditures of state funds; that these funds will have to come from other state programs; and that the duty of compromising and allocating funds among the many programs competing for them is a duty which must be discharged by the state governor and legislature alone. Governor Wallace concedes in his brief that he is not contending that ''the financial cost of complying with an established constitutional right is a valid reason for failure to comply.'' He ''suggest[s] that before the Court decides to adopt a new constitutional right it should consider all of the consequences of its action, financial and social, and its effect on our federal form of government.'' The Mental Health Board makes the point in a related way, by suggesting that the district court's order here is in effect an order requiring the state to furnish a particular service, and by citing cases establishing the general proposition that ordinarily it is not for the federal courts to say whether or in what amounts a state shall provide any particular government benefit or service. *E.g., Fullington* v. *Shea,* D.Colo.1970, 320 F.Supp. 500, aff'd, 404 U.S. 963, 92 S.Ct. 345, 30 L.Ed.2d 282.

We find these arguments unpersuasive. It goes without saying that state legislatures are ordinarily free to choose among various social services competing for legislative attention and state funds. But that does not mean that a state legislature is free, for budgetary or any other reasons, to provide a social service in a manner which will result in the denial of individuals' constitutional rights. And it is the essence of our holding, here and in *Donaldson,* that the provision of treatment to those the state has involuntarily confined in mental hospitals is necessary to make the state's actions in confining and continuing to confine those individuals constitutional. That being the case, the state may not fail to provide treatment for budgetary reasons alone. "Humane considerations and constitutional requirements are not, in this day, to be measured or limited by dollar considerations." *Jackson* v. *Bishop,* 8 Cir. 1968, 404 F.2d 571, 580 (Blackmun, J.), quoted, *Rozecki* v. *Gaughan,* 1 Cir. 1972, 459 F.2d 6, 8. "Inadequate resources can never be an adequate justification for the state's depriving any person of his constitutional rights." *Hamilton* v. *Love,* E.D.Ark. 1972, 328 F.Supp. 1182, 1194. "[T]he obligation of the Respondents [prison officials] to eliminate unconstitutionalities does not depend upon what the Legislatures may do." *Holt* v. *Sarver,* E.D.Ark.1970, 309 F.Supp. 362, 385, aff'd, 8 Cir. 1971, 442 F.2d 304. See also *Hawkins* v. *Town of Shaw,* 5 Cir. 1971, 437 F.2d 1286, 1292.

This conclusion is not novel. In the context of state penal institutions, the federal courts have repeatedly intervened to assure that the conditions of confinement do not invade the constitutional rights of those confined. *E.g., Cruz* v. *Beto,* 1972, 405 U.S. 319, 92 S.Ct. 1079, 31 L.Ed.2d 263; *Johnson* v. *Avery,* 1968, 393 U.S. 483, 89 S.Ct. 747, 21 L.Ed.2d 718; *Campbell* v. *Beto,* 5 Cir. 1972, 460 F.2d 765; *Landman* v. *Royster,* E.D.Va.1971, 333 F.Supp. 621; *Holt* v. *Sarver,* E.D.Ark.1970, 309 F. Supp. 362, aff'd, 8 Cir. 1971, 442 F. 2d 304. This Court has recognized that "our constitutional duties require that the courts be ever vigilant to assure that the conditions of incarceration do not overstep the bounds of federal constitutional limitations." *Campbell,* 460 F.2d at 767-768. In discharging these duties, the federal courts have in some cases entered decrees requiring substantial restructuring of state prision systems, but the courts have not hesitated to enter such decrees when necessary to safeguard the constitutional rights of prisoners. As the court said in *Holt* v. *Sarver:*

> Let there be no mistake in the matter; the obligation of the Respondents to eliminate existing unconstitutionalities does not depend upon what the Legislature may do, or upon what the Governor may do, or, indeed, upon what Respondents may actually be able to accomplish. If Arkansas is going to operate a Penitentiary System, it is going to have to be a system that is countenanced by the Constitution of the United States.

309 F.Supp. at 385.

Similar developments have occurred in the field of institutions for the detention of juveniles. *Nelson* v. *Heyne,* 7 Cir. 1974, 491 F.2d 352, aff'g, N.D.Ind. 1972, 355 F.Supp. 451; *Martarella* v. *Kelley,* S.D.N.Y.1972, 359 F.Supp. 479, enforcing, 349 F.Supp. 575; *Inmates of Boys' Training School* v. *Affleck,* D.R.I. 1972, 346 F.Supp. 1354; *Morales* v. *Turman,* E.D.Tex.1973, 364 F.Supp. 166.

The appellants' fifth contention, that the plaintiffs had adequate remedies at law, is also unpersuasive. In the *Burnham* case, the court held that the legal remedies of "habeas corpus, medical malpractice, and ordinary tort actions" would supply adequate remedies to mental patients who claimed to have been denied a right to treatment. 349 F.Supp. at 1343. It found the plaintiffs' arguments to the contrary "inconsistent with plaintiffs argument that each individual patient should have his particular therapy or treatment personalized." *Id.* Governor Wallace and the Mental Health Board urge here the argument that damage and habeas corpus actions provide adequate legal remedies to the plaintiffs. They also point to the plaintiffs' argument that treatment must be individualized, and to the tension between that argument and the plaintiffs' insistence that injunctive relief on behalf of the plaintiff class is appropriate in this case.

We are unable to agree that injunctive relief is inappropriate merely because damages or habeas corpus relief may be available to some or all individual plaintiffs. While habeas corpus and tort remedies should play a valuable, indeed essential, role in enforcing he constitutional rights we recognized in *Donaldson,* those remedies are not capable of ensuring what the plaintiffs seek to ensure in this case. In the first place, habeas corpus relief and tort damages are available only after the fact of a failure to provide individual treatment. Here the plaintiffs seek preventive relief, to assure in advance that mental patients will at least have the *chance* to receive adequate treatment by proscribing the maintenance of conditions that foredoom *all* mental patients *inevitably* to inadequate mental treatment. Moreover, there are special reasons why reliance upon individual suits by mental patients would be especially inappropriate. Mental patients are particularly unlikely to be aware of their legal rights. They are likely to have especially limited access to legal assistance. Individual suits may be protracted and expensive, and individual mental patients may therefore be deterred from bringing them. And individual suits may produce distortive therapeutic effects within an institution, since a staff may tend to give especially good—or especially harsh—treatment to patients the staff expects or knows to be litigious.[9]

We see no inconsistency between this conclusion and the position taken by tbe plaintiffs, and by the district court, that treatment must be individualized. The plaintiffs here do not seek to *guarantee* that all patients will receive all the treatment they need or that may be appropriate to them. They seek only to ensure that conditions in the state institutions will be such that the patients confined there will have a *chance* to receive adequate treatment. This requires only the establishment of a program, institution-wide in scope, for developing and formulating individual treatment plans; it of course does not require the formulation, in this suit, of each individual plan. The question of what is necessary to the establishment of such a program is better resolved in a class action brought on behalf of all patients than it would be in a series of individual suits.

IV.

We pretermit decision as to the remedy decreed by the district court to the extent herein stated. As we have held, the legislative power may not be used to deprive appellees of their constitutional right to treatment, but a substantial question is presented as to the scope of judicial power in implementing this right. The ultimate question will be, if all else fails, the method of effecting the financial outlay which will be necessary for the judiciary to give meaning to judicially prescribed minimum constitutional standards for adequate treatment of the mentally ill.

Prior to the entry of the court's orders on April 13, 1972, 344 F.Supp. 373; 344

[9]See 86 Harv.L.Rev. 1282, 1305 (1973).

F.Supp. 387, the parties and amici stipulated to a number of specific conditions they agreed were necessary for a constitutionally acceptable minimum treatment program.[10] Because of these stipulations, we need not and do not reach decision as to whether the standards prescribed by the district court are constitutionally minimum requirements, or whether it is within the province of a federal district court, three-judge or single judge, to prescribe standards as distinguished from enjoining the operation of such institutions while constitutional rights are being violated.

Governor Wallace contends such stipulations are not binding on him or the Alabama legislature. As a party to the stipulations, through counsel, we hold the Governor has for his part agreed that these standards are minimally acceptable under the Constitution. The Alabama legislature presents a different problem. Clearly the Governor is without authority to agree to the expenditure of funds required to implement such a broad spectrum of standards when such a decision under Alabama law is reserved to the legislature. That the legislature was not a party to the stipulations in question or to this law suit reenforces this manifest principle of governmental organization. It is the Governor's role to propose relief to the legislature and, having stipulated the standards, to use his best efforts to accomplish the relief.

With respect to judicial accomplishment of the remedy, profound questions are presented regarding the scope of substantive due process and the role of federal courts in matters affecting the management of state institutions. Here we are concerned with the operation of state mental institutions within the parameters of substantive due process.[11]

The governor argues that the prescribed remedy will entail the expenditure annually of a sum equal to sixty per cent of the state budget excluding school financing, and a capital improvements outlay of $75,000,000. This is contested by appellees. However that may be, we regard as premature any issue as to whether the district court should appoint a Special Master for the purposes of selling or encumbering state lands to finance these standards, or should enjoin certain state officials from authorizing expenditures for nonessential state functions, and thereby alter the state budget, or by other means order a particular mode of financing the implementation of the stipulated standards.

[10]The parties and amici submitted in two Memoranda of Agreement stipulations of standards of adequate care. Virtually all of the specifics of the district court's April 13, 1972 orders were taken from these stipulations. These standards have not been challenged on appeal. Indeed, Governor Wallace's brief to this court begins with the affirmation: "We wish to emphasize at the outset that this appellant, Governor George C. Wallace, is in full and complete agreement with the ultimate achievement of the standards and goals for mental health facilities which are set forth in the District Court's order[s] of April 13, 1972." Brief of Appellant, p. 1.

[11]As noted, *supra,* however rare they may be, federal decrees mandating affirmative action expenditures by state governing authorities to ensure constitutional guarantees are not unprecedented in cases involving equal protection and also cruel and unusual punishment. *E.G., Griffin* v. *County School Bd.*, 1964, 377 U.S. 218, 233, 84 S.Ct. 1226, 12 L.Ed.2d 256, 266; *Swann* v. *Charlotte-Mecklenburg Bd. of Educ.*, N.D.N.C., 1970, 311 F.Supp. 265. 268, vacated and remanded on other grounds, 4 Cir. (en banc), 431 F.2d 138, order reinstated, 1971, 402 U.S. 1, 91 S. Ct. 1267, 28 L.Ed.2d 554; *United States* v. *Plaquemines Parish School Bd.*, E.D.La., 1967, 291 F.Supp. 841, aff'd as modified, 5 Cir., 1969, 415 F.2d 817; *Cruz* v. *Beto*, 1972, 405 U.S. 319. 92 S.Ct. 1079, 31 L.Ed.2d 263; *Holt* v. *Sarver*, 8 Cir., 1971, 442 F.2d 304; *Nelson* v. *Heyne*, 7 (Cir., 1974, 491 F.2d 352; *Gautreaux* v. *Chicago Housing Auth.*, N.D.Ill., 1969. 296 F.Supp. 907, aff'd. 7 Cir., 1970, 436 F.2d 306, cert. denied, 1971, 402 U.S. 922, 91 S.Ct. 1378. 28 L.Ed.2d 661.

See also cases cited Note. Right To Treatment, 1973, 86 Harv.L.Rev. 1282, 1300, nn. 98–104; Developments in the Law. Civil Commitment of the Mentally Ill, 1974, 87 Harv.L.Rev. 1338, n. 96; Comment. Enforcement of Judicial Financing Order; Constitutional Rights in Search of a Remedy, 1970, 59 Geo.L.J. 393.

Such remedial propositions are by the terms of the district court's April 13, 1972 not present orders; they lie in the uncertain future. The district court wrote:

> ... this Court has decided to reserve ruling also upon plaintiff's motion that defendant Mental Health Board be directed to sell or encumber portions of its land holdings in order to raise funds. Similarly, this Court will reserve ruling on plaintiff's motion seeking an injunction against the treasurer and the comptroller of the State authorizing expenditures for nonessential State functions, and on other aspects of plaintiffs' requested relief designed to ameliorate the financial problems incident to the implementation of this order. . . . The responsibility for appropriate funding ultimately must fall, of course, upon the State Legislature and, to a lesser degree, upon the defendant Mental Health Board of Alabama. For the present time, the Court will defer to those bodies in hopes that they will proceed with the realization and understanding that what is involved in this case is not representative of ordinary governmental functions such as paving roads and maintaining buildings. Rather, what is so inextricably intertwined with how the Legislature and Mental Health Board respond to the revelations of this litigation is the very preservation of human life and dignity. . . . In the event, though, that the Legislature fails to satisfy its well-defined constitutional obligation, and the Mental Health Board, because of lack of funding or any other legally insufficient reason, fails to implement fully the standards herein ordered, it will be necessary for the Court to take affirmative steps, including appointing a master, to ensure that proper funding is realized and that adequate treatment is available for the mentally ill in Alabama. [344 F.Supp. at 377–378. See also 344 F.Supp. at 393–394.] [These separate orders cover the three institutions involved.]

To the latter statement, the district court added in a footnote, 344 F.Supp. at 378, n. 8:

> The Court understands and appreciates that the Legislature is not due back in regular session until May, 1973. Nevertheless, special sessions of the Legislature are frequent occurrences in Alabama, and there has never been a time when such a session was more urgently required. If the Legislature does not act promptly to appropriate the necessary funding for mental health, the Court will be compelled to grant plaintiffs' motion to add various State officials and agencies as additional parties to this litigation, and to utilize other avenues of fund raising. [See also 344 F.Supp. at 394, n. 14.]

The district court ordered that defendants file within six months a detailed report on the implementation of the stipulated standards.

The serious constitutional questions presented by federal judicial action ordering the sale of state lands, or altering the state budget, or which may otherwise arise in the problem of financing, in the event the governing authorities fail to move in good faith to ensure what all parties agree are minimal requirements, should not be adjudicated unnecessarily and prematurely. See *Ashwander* v. *Tennessee Valley Authority,* 1936, 297 U.S. 288, 346–348, 56 S.Ct. 466, 80 L.Ed. 688, 710–712 (Brandeis, J., concurring); *cf. Hawkins* v. *Town of Shaw,* 5 Cir. (en banc), 1972, 461 F.2d 1171; *Holt* v. *Sarver,* 8 Cir., 1971, 442 F.2d 304, 309. Since we have now affirmed that part of the district court's orders recognizing the constitutional rights to treatment, determination of good faith efforts by state authorities to ensure these rights should be made in the first instance in the district court.

In any event, as a jurisdictional matter dictated by federal statute, remedies of the type contemplated in the district court order of April 13, 1972 are required to be determined by a district court of three judges. Any federal decree that state lands be sold or legislative appropriations be reallocated or enjoined would involve state laws of statewide significance within the purview of 28 U.S.C.A. § 2281. The federal injunctive decree which might be entered in such circumstances is required to be that of a three-judge district court. *Sands* v. *Wainwright, supra,* 491 F.2d 417. We of course make no prejudgment as to the appropriateness of any such remedial order. Moreover, depending on the improvements made or in progress, such remedies may be unnecessary.

This court views as serious a state's failure to ensure the fulfillment of appellees' constitutional rights, but the interests of all concerned, and the sensitivities of our federal system, will be best served by the parties, amici, and court moving together to meet the constitutional requisites. This is the nature of the remedy ordered by this court in *Hawkins* v. *Town of Shaw, supra,* 461 F.2d at 1174. This appears to be the meaning and intent of the district court's recognition of the function of the Alabama legislature within the Alabama governmental framework, and the court's orders of April 13, 1972 requiring reports on compliance with the stipulated standards.

This approach should hasten the day when the district court can be reasonably assured that appellees' constitutional rights are no longer being violated, and when ultimate control over the institutions in question can be returned to the state. *Cf. Holt* v. *Sarver, supra,* 442 F. 2d at 309.

V.

We reserve decision on the issue presented by the awards of attorneys' fees to plaintiffs pending decision in No. 73-1790, *Gates* v. *Collier;* No. 73-2033, *Newman* v. *State of Alabama;* and *Named Individual Members of the San Antonio Conservation Society* v. *Texas Highway Department,* en banc, argued and submitted on October 2, 1974. See 28 U.S.C.A. § 2106 for the authority to reserve decision.

Affirmed in part; remanded in part for further proceedings not inconsistent herewith; and decision reserved in part.

State v. *Harvey*, 162 N.J.Super. 386, 392 A.2d 1248 (1978)

MCKENZIE, J.S.C.

On April 1, 1977 defendant pled guilty to rape. He was diagnosed as a sex offender under *N.J.S.A.* 2A:164-1 *et seq.* and sentenced to the Adult and Diagnostic Treatment Center (A.D.T.C.) under a 30-year indeterminate sentence.

Defendant was received at A.D.T.C. on April 5, 1977. On April 12, 1977 he committed a sodomy on another resident of the Center. He was thereafter transferred from the sex offender unit to the general prison population of the New Jersey State Prison at Rahway.

On appeal, the matter was remanded to this court for a hearing under *State* v. *Horne,* 56 *N.J.,* 372, 267 A.2d 1 (1970), and to review the inter-institutional transfer of defendant.

After a plenary hearing in which the State was represented by the Office of the Prosecutor of Union County, the court determined that defendant's objection to his classification as a sex offender, not raised at the time of sentencing, was not well founded. The court also ruled that the transfer of defendant from A.D.T.C. was made arbitrarily and without legal authority. Accordingly, this court ordered defendant to be returned to A.D.T.C. Since the Commissioner of the Department of Corrections (Commissioner) was not directly represented at the hearing, the court granted leave to the Commissioner to apply to the court for reconsideration. Such application having been made, the court has heard and considered the evidence adduced by the Commissioner bearing on the transfer of the defendant out of the sex offender unit.

The facts, insofar as is necessary to determine the issues before the court, are not substantially in dispute. The court is satisfied from the evidence that defendant is a violent individual who, within a few days after admission to A.D.T.C., committed an act of sodomy on another resident. Whether a razor was employed by defendant is somewhat in dispute, although he did on one occasion admit to the authorities that he threatened the victim with the same in committing the act, and A.D.T.C. found that he did so. Racial tension within the institution resulted—defendant is black, his victim is white—and a polarization of the residents occurred. White residents reportedly threatened to form a vigilante committee to deal with defendant.

A.D.T.C. does not presently have facilities to segregate residents on a long-term basis. The environment is therapeutic rather than punitive. The principal mode of treatment is group therapy. Under these circumstances it was determined by A.D.T.C. that they did not have the appropriate modality to deal with defendant and meet his needs. Accordingly he was transferred to the New Jersey State Prison at Rahway as a member of the general prison population. No specific program or plan was established by the Commissioner to treat or otherwise deal with defendant thereafter. Simply put, because of his violent nature defendant did not fit in at A.D.T.C., and there is no plan or program to treat him so long as he remains violent.

The case presents both a paradox and an anomaly. Rape by its very nature is a violent crime and specifically "violence" is one of the criteria necessary to find a defendant a proper subject for treatment under the act. *N.J.S.A.* 2A:164-5. Paradoxically, A.D.T.C. is unable and not set up to deal with sex offenders who are *too* violent. Anomalously, one of the purposes of the Sex Offender Act being to afford treatment to a defendant which will protect the public from future assaultive behavior by him, the greater danger he poses to the safety of the public, the less chance there is he will obtain the treatment he needs.

N.J.S.A. 2A:164-7 is relied upon by the Commissioner for the transfer of this defendant and provides as follows:

> The commissioner of the department of institutions and agencies, upon commitment of such person, shall thereupon arrange for his treatment in one of the institutions under the jurisdiction of the department which, in the judgment of the commissioner, is best suited to care for the needs of such person. The commissioner, in his discretion, is hereby authorized and empowered to arrange for the transfer of such person to or from any institution within the jurisdiction of the department for the purpose of providing for the needs and requirements of such person according to the individual circumstances of the case.

The purpose of the act has been construed by our courts to be "cure through treatment of the aberrations which caused the sexually deviant offenses rather than punishment." *State* v. *Clark,* 65 *N.J.* 426, 430, 323 A.2d 470, 472 (1974). See also, *State* v. *Andrews,* 105 N.J.Super. 62, 251 A. 2d 141 (App.Div.1969), remanded on other grounds 56 N.J. 372, 267 A.2d 1 (1970); *State* v. *Mickschutz,* 101 N.J.Super. 315, 244 A.2d 318 (App.Div. 1968).

Our courts have nevertheless recognized the necessity for allowing discretion to the Commissioner to transfer a sex offender to a correctional institution under his jurisdiction, where the circumstances do not permit meaningful treatment of a defendant under the act. See *State* v. *Newton,* 17 N.J. 271, 111 A.2d 272 (1955). *Tully* v. *Tramberg,* 57 *N.J.Super.* 377, 154 A.2d 840 (App.Div.1959), upheld the exercise of discretion by the Commissioner in transferring a violent and disruptive defendant out of the facility to which he was sentenced and to a correctional institution.

The parameters establishing the area of discretion within which the Commissioner may proceed have been set forth thusly:

> When defendants are lawfully committed under the statute, the Department must thereafter conscientiously seek to attain fulfillment of the legislative program. The administrative determinations as to custody and treatment must, of course, rest initially with the departmental officials and courts will generally not disturb their decisions. Nevertheless, there as elsewhere throughout our governmental administration arbitrary or capricious action is impermissible and upon a sufficient showing of such conduct judicial relief will justly be afforded. [*State* v. *Wingler,* 25 *N.J.* 161, 181, 135 A.2d 468, 479 (1957)].

The discretion to transfer conferred upon the Commissioner by *N.J.S.A.* 2A:164-7 is for the express purpose of "providing for the needs and requirements of such person according to the individual circumstances of the case."

Here the only "need" of defendant met by the transfer was the protection of his person from some vague threats of retaliation by other residents. It is clear that such purpose was secondary at best. Primarily, A.D.T.C. had a defendant they could not deal with and who might disrupt their ability to treat other residents. The transfer of defendant to the State Prison system was the solution. Nothing further was done for defendant, nor has any policy been established or implemented which would meet the need of defendant for the treatment which he clearly requires, and which A.D.T.C. recognized when he was classified as a sex offender by that institution. It is perhaps significant that this defendant had stated to the police when first arested and to the authorities at A.D.T.C. that he was sick and needed help.[1]

The Commissioner may not however, as here, simply remove defendant from the institution where he was sentenced to receive treatment under the act and abdicate any further obligation under the act to meet the needs of the defendant.

The court questioned Dr. Mintz, the Superintendent of A.D.T.C., as to the procedures involved in a possible retransfer of defendant if he had in fact while at Rahway become amenable to treatment at A.D.T.C. His response is significant:

> What would happen, if the Institution at Rahway endorsed the idea through the Classification Committee—that's only one psychologist's report,—and by the way, there's another report quite different from that one in the record that it describes Mr. Harvey as very impulsive and volatile and dangerous.
>
> THE COURT: That doesn't mean he's not a sex offender.

[1]At A.D.T.C., when he pleaded for help after the sodomy, he was clearly told that help would be conditioned on his telling the truth. He then admitted putting a razor to the victim's throat. The next day his transfer was recommended.

> DR. MINTZ: I'm saying that. I'm not saying he's not either. What would happen is the psychologist would refer to the Classification Committee and the Committee through the Superintendent would write the recommendation to the Special Classification Committee and all of the records and all materials to date would be considered by the Committee,—that Special Classification Committee. If they endorse the idea, *if there was enough evidence demonstrating self-control and he was no longer a danger, then they would recommend to be returned to A.D.T.C., but that has never occurred.* [Emphasis supplied]

Clearly, a "violent" defendant receives no treatment at A.D.T.C., and once so classified and transferred from A.D.T.C. he apparently receives no further treatment under the program. This court is satisfied that such was not the intent of the Legislature.

The Commissioner has an affirmative duty to treat defendant. It is not conditioned on defendant's ability to fit into a particular modality. If the present operation at A.D.T.C. is unable to meet his needs, the Commissioner has a responsibility to formulate and implement a policy which will.

It is to be noted that as of April 1978 a psychologist at Rahway State Prison reported that defendant should be considered for further therapy, possibly at A.D.T.C. Defendant offered testimony[2] of another psychologist which it was represented would be to the effect that the defendant would now be responsive to the form of treatment provided at A.D.T.C.

Dr. Mintz was unaware of any present amenability to treatment on the part of defendant and explained that numerous procedures by the host institution (Rahway) would be required under present rules and regulations before defendant would be considered for retransfer to A.D.T.C.

Neither *State* v. *Wingler* nor *Tully* v. *Tramburg, supra,* require unconditional affirmance of the Commissioner's action here. In each of those cases (*Wingler* at 172, 135 A.2d 468 and *Tully,* 57 *N.J.Super.* at 381, 154 A.2d 840) the court noted from the record a plan that defendant would receive some form of treatment available at the host institution.

Further, since the decisions in those cases our courts have been more insistent that persons committed involuntarily to our state institutions receive the treatment required. The lack of adequate facilities and staff, accepted as "hard fact" in *State* v. *Newton, supra,* 17 *N.J.* at 275-276, 111 A.2d 272, has more recently been considered as no longer justification for failure to provide the treatment required by persons committed to our institutions. *In re D.D.,* 118 *N.J.Super.* 1, 6, 285 A.2d 283 (App.Div. 1971). See also, *State* v. *Carter,* 64 *N.J.* 382, 316, A.2d 449 (1974); *State* v. *Krol,* 68 *N.J.* 236, 344 A.2d 289 (1975), and *State In Interest of R.G.W.,* 145 *N.J.Super.* 167, 366 A.2d 1375 (*J. & D. R. Ct.* 1976).

Nor can the failure to treat defendant be justified by distinguishing his condition because he has been sentenced for a criminal offense and not been adjudicated insane or mentally incompetent as in the cases cited above. In *State* v. *Clark, supra* our Supreme Court, emphasizing the treatment rather than punishment goal of the Sex Offender Act, set aside consecutive penal sentences imposed on a defendant found to be within the purview of the act, stating:

[2]The court ruled that defendant's charge that A.D.T.C was arbitrary in not admitting defendant at this time was not an issue before the court, and not ripe for determination. The lack of any policy or procedure to affirmatively ascertain and act on such information is however significant in the opinion of the court.

> The scheme of our sex offender act, as previously indicated, is the specialized institutionalization of those sex deviants whose abnormal conduct has resulted in conviction for certain designated sexual crimes, is compulsive and repetitive, and either is accompanied by violence or is imposed upon a victim under 15 years of age. The inherent legislative finding underlying the act is that such persons are suffering from mental and physical illness involuntarily causing their conduct, for which criminal incarceration, whether thought of as punishment or as a deterrent, will accomplish nothing; the same conduct will be repeated after release. [65 *N.J.* at 434, 323 A.2d at 474]

This court therefore holds that the Commissioner here has failed to perform his responsibility to defendant under the Sex Offender Act in transferring him to a penal institution without any plan to furnish necessary treatment to him.

Order accordingly.

REFERENCES FOR CHAPTER IV

CASES UNLIMITED, INC. Must you guarantee a tubal ligation? *Resident and Staff Physician,* 1976, *22*(1), 101.

LEDAKOWICH, A. The right to be left alone. *Resident and Staff Physician,* 1977, *23*(9), 118.

KRAUSKOPF, J. M. & KRAUSKOPF, C. J. Torts and psychologists. *Journal of Counseling Psychology,* 1965, *12,* 227-237.

CHAPTER V

The Countersuit

A RAPID INCREASE in the number of medical malpractice claims was taken note of in a 1973 report published by the Department of Health, Education, and Welfare entitled, *Medical Malpractice Report of the Secretary's Commission on Medical Malpractice*. The trend of increased litigation in this area was similarly taken note of in the 1976 *Report of the Special Advisory Panel on Medical Malpractice* for the State of New York, which in part read as follows:

> Whether the tort system is an effective deterrent to negligent medical care by physicians and hospitals seems hardly susceptible of proof. *What is certain is that whatever its effect, it has not been sufficient to prevent the persistent rise in annual malpractice cases*. A relatively small number of cases, some 2000 in 1974, was large enough to have occasioned a crises in the tort law liability insurance system. The number of cases closed under the program of the Medical Society of the State of New York, the major program for physicians, has risen about 100% from 1966 to 1973 (1127 to 2254). From 1969 to 1974 the number of new cases rose 56% from 1283 to 2003. For the first 6 months of 1975 alone, the number of cases opened was 1324. Furthermore, the frequency of claims is now reported to be 1 case per 10 doctors. These data parallel those reported in other states and across the nation, continuing the trends noted in other studies. (p. 6)

Evidence of similar trends across the nation has come from a variety of sources. The St. Paul Fire and Marine Insurance Company, in its booklet *Preserving a Medical Malpractice Insurance Marketplace* (1975), noted that in 1969 it had one claim pending for every twenty-three of its insured physicians; the ratio had changed to one claim for every ten of its insured physicians by 1974. Of the total 7,100 physicians practicing in Cook County, Illinois, during the period January 1974 to March 1975, 1,010 were sued for malpractice during this fourteen-month period (Kotulak, 1975). In one of their ads, Crum and Forster Insurance Companies pointed out: "In 1975, there were twice as many medical malpractice suits as there were in 1970. . . . And sympathetic juries are making bigger awards. In the last 10 years, the average award has jumped over 6 times."

Included among the astronomical number of suits being filed are claims for damages that have been based on an impressive array of causes of action. Beyond wrongful death, physicians have been sued for wrongful birth (see Eisberg, 1978) and for what might be termed "wrongful life." As an example of what we are referring to as the latter, consider the case cited by Ledakowich (1976) wherein a physician who told his patient that he had between 12 and 18 months to live was sued by the patient when he lived longer than 18 months. The court did not find the doctor to be negligent for expressing an opinion on as complex a matter as the prediction of death. Regardless, the case is illustrative of the extent to which patients are seeking to extend the liability of their physicians. In a medical malpractice case before the Illinois Supreme Court, the question of whether or not a child could sue for alleged pre-conception injuries arose. As discussed by Horsley (1978), the defendants moved to dismiss the complaint in the circuit court claiming that the child was not a person, indeed not even conceived at the time of the alleged infliction of the injury. The Illinois Supreme Court held, in a close, split decision that a child not conceived at the time negligent acts were committed against its mother does have a valid cause of action against the tort-feasors resulting from their conduct.

The rapidly rising number of medical malpractice suits, together with the generally higher dollar amounts for which those suits are settled, has resulted in rapidly escalating insurance premiums for professional liability policyholders. The unprecedented rise in insurance rates has in some instances played havoc with the ability of the individual practitioner to keep insurance costs at a manageable level, and the result has been unprecedented behavior on the part of physicians. Doctors have gone out on strike, moved to other states as a means of coping with disproportionately high insurance premiums, and retired in record numbers. In one attempt to save money on insurance premiums, eleven hospitals and clinics associated with Harvard University set up their own insurance company in the Bahamas. Perhaps a more direct solution to the problem of a medical malpractice litigation crisis has been the increased use of the countersuit as a deterrent to bringing the action in the first place. Although the authors are not aware of any reported countersuit litigation involving mental health professionals, the principles of law we shall be discussing below have equal applicability in such cases.

NATURE OF CAUSES OF ACTION FOR COUNTERSUITS

Countersuits have been filed by physicians against patients and their attorneys who, it is alleged, have brought medical malpractice suits without just cause. Countersuits have been brought claiming abuse of process, malicious prosecution, negligence, barratry, defamation, and intentional infliction of emotional distress. In *Berlin* v. *Nathan,* No. 75 L 16838, 75 M2-542 (Cir. Ct.

Ill., filed June 1, 1976) a theory of "wrongful lawsuit" was asserted on the basis of a clause in the Illinois Constitution that guarantees a remedy for every wrong (see Birnbaum, 1977, pp. 1063–1065). The plaintiff/physician recovered an $8,000 jury verdict, but the decision was reversed by the intermediary appellate court, which held that the constitutional provision that provided "certain remedy" for all injuries and wrongs constituted an expression of a philosophy and not a mandate (see below). The Illinois Supreme Court refused to hear the appeal (*Berlin* v. *Nathan,* No. 51367, Sup. Ct. Ill., filed January 25, 1979).

The basis for another new or novel cause of action for a countersuit was one of the issues before the court in the New York case, *Drago* v. *Buonagurio* (following *Berlin* below). The trial court had determined that Jerome Brownstein, as attorney for Madeline Buonagurio, had had no basis for naming Dr. Eugene Drago as a defendant in a wrongful death action. Still, the court could find no sufficient basis to support a cause of action for abuse of process, malicious prosecution, *prima facie* tort, or negligence, and the complaint was dismissed. On appeal, the order of the trial court was reversed as the complaint was viewed as setting forth a legitimate cause of action; without excuse or justification, a clear, intentional wrong that caused apparent and foreseeable harm to Dr. Drago had taken place. The unique fact pattern before the court compelled it to hold that the "fact that a cause of action is new, novel or nameless should not deprive an injured person of a remedy. . . . It is immaterial and unimportant whether we label the instant cause of action one of prima facie tort or something else." In so doing the court relied on the principle that "the law should never suffer an injury and a damage without a remedy." (62 A.D.2d at 285, 402 N.Y.S.2d at 252). Regardless, the opinion of the Appellate Division was reversed by the Court of Appeals, which agreed with the trial court the the doctor's complaint failed to state a valid cause of action for abuse of process, malicious prosecution, or negligence. The state's highest court went on to hold that Dr. Drago's complaint did not state a cause of action in the nature of a *prima facie* tort because "the courts have not recognized any liability of the lawyer to third parties . . . where the factual situations have not fallen within one of the acknowledged categories of tort or contract liability (46 N.Y.2d at 779, 386 N.E.2d at 822, 413 N.Y.S.2d at 911)."

To litigate a countersuit successfully is difficult, but, as illustrated by the cases (following *Drago* herein) of *Bull* v. *McCuskey* (1980) and *Friedman* v. *Dozorc,* 83 Mich.App.429 (1978), it is by no means impossible. Following the presentation of these cases, we discuss the difficulties attendant to the countersuit (see also *Nelson* v. *Miller,* 607 P.2d 438).

Berlin v. *Nathan,* 64 Ill.App.3d 940, 381 N.E.2d 1367 (1978)

Romiti, Justice:

This case involves another of the many retaliatory actions which physicians in Illinois and other states who have been sued for malpractice are filing against both the original plaintiff and the original attorney. In this case the original plaintiff's husband was sued as well. In accord with the other cases in Illinois and elsewhere, we hold that the complaint which failed to allege either malicious intent or special damages failed to state a cause of action. We also hold that the court correctly dismissed the physician's claim against the husband for barratry.

The pleadings reveal that on October 1, 1973 Harriet Nathan entered the Skokie Valley Community Hospital complaining of an injury to the little finger of her right hand. An x-ray was taken under the supervision of Dr. Berlin, a radiologist on the staff of the hospital. Dr. Berlin read the film as revealing a dislocation of the finger. Dr. Meltzer then applied treatment appropriate for a dislocation. In November, another x-ray was taken. This x-ray disclosed that there had been a chip fracture of that finger.

On September 11, 1975, about two weeks before the statute of limitations would have run, Harriet Nathan, through her attorneys, Benjamin and Shapiro, filed suit against Dr. Berlin, Dr. Meltzer and the hospital alleging various acts of malpractice in the taking of the x-rays and the making of the diagnosis. Dr. Berlin thereupon filed a suit against Mr. Nathan (at whose specific instance and request, he alleged, the malpractice suit was specifically brought), Mrs. Nathan and her attorneys Benjamin and Shapiro. In Count I of that suit he alleged that all four defendants owed him a duty to refrain from willfully and wantonly bringing suit against him without having reasonable cause to believe that he had been guilty of malpractice; that the defendants instead, although having no cause whatsoever to believe he had been guilty of malpractice, had instituted suit with reckless disregard as to the truth or falsity of the allegations. Specifically, Dr. Berlin in Count I complained that Benjamin and Shapiro had acted willfully and wantonly and without probable cause since they had not, before filing suit, obtained an opinion from another physician as to the quality of the x-rays and the correctness of their interpretation thereof; and moreover, that the addamnum ($125,000), which bore no reasonable relationship to the injuries allegedly sustained, was devised to intimidate Dr. Berlin and might affect his ability to procure malpractice insurance at reasonable rates. Dr. Berlin in Count I specifically alleged that Harriet Nathan brought suit willfully and wantonly and without probable cause in that she at no time prior to suit obtained from another physician an opinion as to the quality of the x-rays, the correctness of their interpretation or an opinion whether the condition of which she complained resulted from malpractice by either Dr. Berlin or Dr. Meltzer. Dr. Berlin further alleged that the Nathans had been told by another orthopedic surgeon, prior to the institution of the suit, that no malpractice had occurred but that they willfully and wantonly incited and instituted the suit in retribution for real or imagined discourtesies to them by Dr. Meltzer. Finally, Dr. Berlin complained that as a result of these actions his reputation in his profession had been attacked, he had suffered mental anguish, he had been caused to devote much time to the defense of the malpractice suit and, that because of the institution of the suit, he would be required to pay increased premiums for his malpractice insurance coverage. In Count II, Dr. Berlin claimed that Gilbert Nathan, knowing the malpractice suit to have no merit but intending to extort money either from Dr. Berlin or his malpractice insurance company, wickedly and willfully caused the suit to be brought and caused Harriet Nathan to prosecute said suit, contrary to the Illinois barratry statute. Ill. Rev.Stat.1975, ch. 13, par. 21.

In Count III, Dr. Berlin alleged that the attorneys, Benjamin and Shapiro, had a duty to the plaintiff not to file the malpractice lawsuit without reasonable evidence to support the allegations therein since, as attorneys, they were particularly aware of the time and expense that litigation causes and could foresee the harm an unfounded lawsuit could cause to the reputation and mental well-being of a physician; that by filing the complaint without reasonable cause, the attorneys fell below the standard of care required of attorneys in the performance of their professional duties in good faith and in a legal manner and were negligent towards Dr. Berlin.

Count II was dismissed by the trial court upon Gilbert Nathan's motion before trial. This suit was consolidated with the original suit for discovery and for trial.

On May 27, 1976 the original malpractice suit was voluntarily dismissed, with prejudice, on the motion of Harriet Nathan. The action on the countersuit then proceeded to trial. At the close of the trial the jury was not instructed as to the elements involved in a suit for malicious prosecution but were solely instructed as follows: as to Count I that the plaintiff claimed that the conduct of the defendants was willful and wanton in that a medical malpractice complaint was filed against him when there was no reasonable cause to believe that such a cause of action existed and that the defendant's act was a proximate cause of his damages (all of which the defendants denied); as to Count II (originally Count III) that the plaintiff claimed that he sustained damages while exercising ordinary care and the defendants Benjamin and Shapiro were negligent in filing and prosecuting a lawsuit without taking proper steps to determine that there was reasonable cause to believe any cause of action existed and that this was a proximate cause of his damage (all of which the defendants denied). The jury was also instructed that in filing a lawsuit an attorney must possess and apply the knowledge, skill, care and regard for potential defendants that is ordinarily used and shown by reasonably well-qualified attorneys in the locality. And finally, the jury was instructed that the defendants had a duty before and at the time of the occurrence to refrain from willful and wanton conduct which would endanger the rights of the plaintiff.

The jury found all four defendants guilty of willful and wanton misconduct proximately causing injury to Dr. Berlin and awarded Dr. Berlin $2,000 in compensatory damages and $6,000 in punitive damages.

All the parties have appealed.

I.

The *amicus curiae* has argued that the jury verdict should be upheld since the jury properly found defendant guilty of malicious prosecution. We disagree since we find that the plaintiff's complaint was not sufficient to state a claim for malicious prosecution against any of the defendants, and the instructions to the jury certainly did not submit a claim for malicious prosecution.

A.

Tort litigants, such as the Nathans, may be held liable for malicious prosecution. (25 Illinois Law and Practice *Malicious Prosecution* §§ 1 et seq. [1956].) However, since the law does not look with favor on such suits (*Schwartz* v. *Schwartz* [1937], 336 Ill. 247, 8 N.E.2d 668; *Carlyle* v. *Carlyle* [1960], 28 Ill.App.2d 90, 170 N.E.2d 790; *Lyddon* v. *Shaw* [1978], 56 Ill.App.3d 815, 14 Ill.Dec. 489, 372 N.E.2d 685), there are strict limitations on the availability of such suits. Suits for malicious prosecution cannot be maintained in Illinois unless the plaintiff alleges and proves that the plaintiff in the original tort action acted maliciously and without probable cause (*Hill Co.,* v. *Contractors' Supply Co.* [1911], 249 Ill. 304, 94 N.E. 544; *Lyddon* v. *Shaw* [1978], 56 Ill. App.3d 815, 14 Ill.Dec. 489, 372 N.E.2d 685); that the prior cause terminated in the plaintiff's favor (*Schwartz* v. *Schwartz* [1937], 366 Ill. 247, 8 N.E.2d 688;

Lyddon v. *Shaw* [1978], 56 Ill. App.3d 815, 14 Ill. Dec. 489, 372 N.E.2d 685); and that some special injury not necessarily resulting in any and all suits prosecuted to recover for like causes of action was suffered. (*Schwartz* v. *Schwartz* [1937], 366 Ill. 247, 8 N.E.2d 668; *Lyddon* v. *Shaw* [1978], 56 Ill.App.3d 815, 14 Ill.Dec. 489, 372 N.E.2d 685; *Pantone* v. *Demos* [1978], 59 Ill.App. 3d 328, 16 Ill.Dec. 607, 375 N.E.2d 480.) It is clear that in this case neither of the last two elements was pleaded and, even if we liberally construe the complaint to allege that the suit was brought maliciously and without probable cause by the Nathans, that issue was not submitted to the jury.

B.

Special damages as defined by the Illinois Supreme Court in *Schwartz* v. *Schwartz* are those not necessarily resulting in any and all suits prosecuted to recover for like causes of action. The only damages that Dr. Berlin claimed he suffered are (1) his reputation in his profession has been attacked; (2) he has suffered mental anguish; (3) he has been forced to spend time on the defense; (4) he will be required to pay increased insurance premiums. The first three items of damage claimed are so patently common to all litigation that no discussion is warranted. We agree, moreover, with the Illinois court in *Pantone* that an increase in insurance premiums, while perhaps not a necessary result of the litigation, is, assuming the allegation is anything more than pure speculation, an item necessarily incident to all malpractice cases and not therefore amounting to damages suffered specially by Dr. Berlin as distinct from other physicians who have been defendants in malpractice suits.

The defendant and *amicus curiae* both, however, contend that the requirement of special damages is unreasonable and should be abolished. First of all, we have no authority to overrule the Illinois Supreme Court. (*Chicago Title & Trust Co.* v. *Guarantee Bank* [1978], 59 Ill.App.3d 362, 16 Ill.Dec. 649, 375 N.E.2d 522.) But in any event, we agree with *O'Toole* v. *Franklin* (1977), 279 Or. 513, 569 P.2d 561 and *Ammerman* v. *Newm*an (D.C.App.1978), 384 A.2d 637 which rejected precisely the same argument.As the latter court stated at 384 A.2d 641:

> Appellant effectively concedes that he has suffered no injury that would not normally occur as a consequence of a malpractice suit, and appears to recognize that the authority in this jurisdiction does not support his claim. He seeks to avoid the application of the rule by arguing that it is inequitable in the context of medical malpractice actions. He contends that the fact that such actions are particularly harmful to the reputations and livelihood of physicians calls for a modification of the rule with respect to them. The purpose of the special injury rule, however, is to strike a balance between allowing free access to the courts for the vindication of rights without fear of a resulting suit, and the undue exercise of such right. *Davis* v. *Boyle Bros.*, D.C. Mun.App., 73 A.2d 517, 521 (1950). Appellant's argument, if accepted, would upset that delicate balance. The nature of his profession, given its profound impact on the lives of those with whom he deals, cannot be allowed to insulate him from potential liability. In order to maintain a free access to the courts by persons with grievances who might otherwise be restrained from seeking redress because of their fear of liability should they fail, the special injury rule has consistently been upheld.
>
> The limitation is sound. When disputes reach the litigious stage, usually some

malice is present on both sides. Friendly tort suits are not common. Nor is existence or want of probable cause always easy to determine until the event of the litigation is known. Some margin of safety in asserting rights, though they turn out to be groundless and their assertion accompanied by some degree of ill will, must be maintained. Otherwise litigation would lead, not to an end of disputing, but to its beginning, and rights violated would go unredressed for fear of the danger of asserting them. [*Melvin* v. *Pence*, 76 U.S.App.D.C., 154, 157, 130 F.2d 423, 426 (1942).]

C.

The complaint against the Nathans failed to allege that the malpractice action had been terminated in plaintiff's favor, obviously for the simple reason that it had not been terminated when the complaint was filed, although it was terminated before the counterclaim was actually tried. Nevertheless, if we were to permit such an action under these circumstances, we would create the incongruous situation of permitting the filing of a suit before the cause of action existed or the statute of limitations commenced to run. *Babb* v. *Superior Court* (1971), 3 Cal.3d 841, 92 Cal.Rptr. 179, 479 P.2d 379.

D.

Basically, the complaint against the Nathans merely alleges that their conduct was willful and wanton. Willful and wanton conduct does not amount to malice. (Compare *Myers* v. *Krajeska* [1956], 8 Ill.2d 322, 134 N.E. 277.) However, a suit brought for an improper motive may be malicious (*Carlyle* v. *Carlyle* [1960], 28 Ill. App.2d 90, 170 N.E.2d 790), and Dr. Berlin did allege that the Nathans brought suit solely in retribution for the real or imagined discourtesies of Dr. Meltzer. But, the plaintiff clearly abandoned any attempt at trial to prove a cause of action against the Nathans for malicious prosecution since in the instructions submitted to the jury, the jury was solely instructed as to willful and wanton misconduct and was not instructed as to the elements of a claim for malicious prosecution. The burden was on the plaintiff to submit the issue (35 Illinois Law and Practice *Trial* § 251 [1958]); having failed to do so he cannot contend on appeal that he had a claim for malicious prosecution. And, in all fairness to the plaintiff, he has not made such a claim, only *amicus curiae* has done so.

E.

A suit for malicious prosecution can be brought against an attorney since an attorney cannot always justify himself merely by showing he followed his client's instructions. (*Burnap* v. *Marsh* [1852], 13 Ill. 535.) If an attorney, acknowledging there is no cause of action, and knowing this dishonestly and for some improper purpose files suit, or even if an attorney merely acts knowing that his client has no just claim and that his client is actuated by illegal or malicious motives, the attorney may be held liable for malicious prosecution. *Burnap* v. *Marsh* (1852), 13 Ill. 535; Annot., 27 A.L.R.3d 1113 at 1129–1133 (1969).

However the plaintiff's complaint was totally insufficient to support a claim against the attorneys for malicious prosecution. First, there is no allegation that the attorneys acted maliciously or knew that their client did so. As we noted previously, willful and wanton conduct does not constitute malicious conduct, particularly where, as here, no improper motive of any kind on the part of the attorneys is suggested. Basically, the plaintiff simply complains that the defendants did not get another doctor's opinion before filing suit. But the undisputed facts are that the finger was fractured and that this fracture was not discovered for several weeks. Perhaps more investigation before filing suit would have been prudent, but as the Louisiana court remarked in *Spencer* v. *Burglass* (La.App. 1976), 337 So.2d 596 at 599, 600:

> There are no factual allegations to suggest that when defendant filed his client's suit he knew the allegations were false or that he had a reckless disregard as to whether the allegations were false or not. On the contrary, plaintiff's allegations are to the effect that defendant simply did not know enough about the case at the time he filed it and now in retrospect plaintiff would say this was malice on defendant's part. If that be so many a successful lawsuit would never have been or never would be filed because oftentimes the case comes to the attorney just prior to prescription date and the evidence is not discovered and developed until after the suit is filed. We therefore conclude that the allegation of "frivolously filing suits" cannot be construed as an allegation of malice.
>
> . . . .
>
> Finally, there is the allegation that defendant failed to obtain "competent medical advice," etc. Does this constitute an allegation of malice? It would seem that an affirmative answer to this query would mean that before the attorney brings a malpractice case to trial he must find a medical person who supports the attorney's theory or that of his client, who is willing to testify favorably and who is "competent" by someone's (plaintiff's?) standards. If he finds no such person but he nevertheless, places whatever evidence he can before the court perhaps relying on circumstantial evidence, reasonable inferences and common sense and perhaps realizing that he will probably lose, he runs the risk of having his conduct branded as malicious. When the bald allegation in question is considered in this light it can hardly be construed as one alleging malice. At worst, the allegation is that defendant went to trial with a poor case and got his just desserts, to wit, he lost. If that constitutes malice, the courtrooms are full of malicious attorneys. This we cannot accept.

Furthermore, as we discussed earlier, the complaint was insufficient since no special damages were alleged. And finally, there is no allegation that the malpractice case was terminated favorably to the present plaintiff before the complaint was filed. In fact it is conceded that at the time of filing, the original tort action was still pending. As the court observed in *Lyddon* v. *Shaw* (1978), 56 Ill.App.3d 815, 820, 14 Ill.Dec. 489, 492, 372 N.E.2d 685, 688, to permit the filing of such an action against the attorney prior to the termination of the initial malpractice action "would tend to drive a wedge between the malpractice plaintiff and his attorney; the attorney may be diverted from properly preparing the client's malpractice case by the necessity for readying his own defense to the physician's countersuit, and may, in some cases, even be forced to withdraw from the malpractice action." This we cannot permit.

II.

It is clear, therefore, that Dr. Berlin's complaint is insufficient to allege a cause of action for malicoius prosecution. Indeed, he has not on appeal contended that it is. What he does claim, contrary to the well-established law in Illinois that "a person is not liable for bringing any suit, criminal or civil, . . . , if the court had jurisdiction of the subject-matter and the parties, unless he acts maliciously and without probable cause'' (*Hill Co.* v. *Contractors' Supply Co.* [1911], 249 Ill. 304, at 310, 94 N.E. 544, at 546), is that he should be able to recover against all of the defendants for the willful and wanton filing of a frivolous lawsuit. But *Hill* still represents the state of the law in Illinois. (*Pantone* v. *Demos* [1978], 59 Ill.App.3d 328, 16 Ill.Dec. 607, 375 N.E.2d 480.) Furthermore, since ''it takes a 'special injury' to recover for the *malicious* pursuit of an unfounded civil action, it would be incongruous to base a recovery on mere carelessness without the same requirement.'' (*O'Toole* v. *Franklin* [1977], 279 Or. 513, 569 P.2d 561, at 566.) Likewise, we agree with the court in *Lyddon* v. *Shaw* (1978), 56 Ill.App.3d 815, 14 Ill.Dec. 489, 372 N.E.2d 685 that the failure to plead the outcome of the malpractice action would constitute a fatal defect to Dr. Berlin's complaint, even if he were correct in his contention that malicious prosecution is not the sole course of action available to a party who is put to the expense and vexation of defending a baseless lawsuit. The considerations underlying the requirement that a complaint for malicious prosecution plead the favorable outcome of the prior cause are, in effect, broader than the rule itself. Indeed, we hold that permitting the filing of such a complaint against the attorney before the termination of the original suit would be against public policy since it would tend, as we pointed out earlier, to create a conflict of interest between attorney and client.

A.

Dr. Berlin, however, contends that Article I, Section 12 of the Illinois Constitution requires the creation of a new cause of action. Section 12 reads as follows:

> Every person shall find a certain remedy in the laws for all injuries and wrongs which he receives to his person, privacy, property or reputation. He shall obtain justice by law, freely, completely, and promptly.

It is well established in Illinois that Section 12, like its predecessor Section 19 of Article II of the 1870 Illinois Constitution,[1] is ''an expression of a philosophy and not a mandate that a 'certain remedy' be provided in any specific form or that the nature of the proof necessary to the award of a judgment or degree continue without modification.'' (Sullivan v. *Midlothian Park District* [1972], 51 Ill.2d 274, at 277, 281 N.E.2d 659, at 662). So long as some remedy for the alleged wrong exists, Section 12 does not mandate recognition of any new remedy. (*Pantone* v. *Demos* [1978] 59 Ill. App.3d 328, 16 Ill.Dec. 607, 375 N.E.2d 480.) As recognized by the court in *Lyddon* v. *Shaw* (1978), 56 Ill.App.3d 815, 14 Ill.Dec. 489, 372 N.E.2d 685, in this type of case one may file an action for malicious prosecution, or perhaps for abuse of process, and even if those two remedies are not applicable, he may, if put to the burden of defending allegations made without reasonable cause, recover attorney's fees under section 41 of the Civil Practice Act (Ill.Rev.Stat.1977, ch. 110, par. 41), by motion in the original action. He may also, though we doubt it is much comfort to the plaintiff, in an appropriate case, be instrumental in the institution of disciplinary proceedings against the offending attor-

[1]Section 12 made two changes. One was to add protection against invasion of privacy. The other was the substitution of the word ''shall'' for the words ''ought to.'' However it is clear from the legislative history that the latter change was not ''to create any new rights or to limit any rights.'' 3 Record of Proceedings, Sixth Illinois Constitutional Convention 1491.

ney. Section 12 mandates no additional remedies. (*Pantone* v. *Demos* [1978], 59 Ill.App.3d 328, 16 Ill.Dec. 607, 375 N.E.2d 480.) The mere fact that the relief provided by these remedies is limited (*Cunningham* v. *Brown* (1961), 22 Ill.2d 23, 174 N.E.2d 153), or that the plaintiff is unable to meet the burden of proof required does not dictate the creation of new remedies. The failure to state a cause of action cannot be cured by alleging that the plaintiff should have a remedy as provided in Section 12. CKONSTITUTIONAL RIGHTS ARE NOT INFRINGED WHERE AN INSUFFICIENT COMPLAINT IS DISMISSED. (*Belmar Drive-In Theatre* v. *Illinois State Toll Highway Commission* [1966], 34 Ill.2d 544, 216 N.E.2d 788; *Zamouski* v. *Gerrard* [1971], 1 Ill.App.3d 890, 275 N.E.2d 429.) And as observed in *O'Toole* v. *Franklin* (19773, 279 Or. 513, 569 P.2d 561, at 565 "it would be ironic to derive a looser test of malicious prosecution from a constitutional guarantee of access to the courts."

B.

We are not persuaded by the plaintiff's argument that in light of the recent rise in the volume of malpractice litigation, including the filing of frivolous malpractice suits purely for their settlement value, public policy demands the creation of a cause of action to prtect the courts from their misuse and the physician from the resulting harm.

First of all, we agree with the court in *Pantone* v. *Demos* (1978), 59 Ill.App.3d 328, 16 Ill.Dec. 607, 375 N.E.2d 480 that it is doubtful that the creation of this new remedy would reduce the amount of litigation; it is far more likely that litigation would be increased since each successful defendant would bring suit against the original plaintiff. (See also *Smith* v. *Michigan Buggy Co.* [1898], 175 Ill. 619, 51 N.E. 569.) But even if the creation of this new remedy would reduce congestion in the courts, the price the public would have to pay for the benefit is too great. It is the overriding public policy of Illinois that potential suitors must have free and unfettered access to the courts. (*Pantone* v. *Demos* [1978], 59 Ill.App.3d 328, 16 Ill.Dec. 607, 375 N.E.2d 480; *Lyddon* v. *Shaw* [1978], 56 Ill.App.3d 815, 14 Ill.Dec. 489, 372 N.E.2d 685.) The Illinois courts have consistently adhered to the established policy "that the courts should be open to litigants for settlement of their rights without fear of prosecution for calling upon the courts to determine such rights" (*Franklin* v. *Grossinger Motor Sales, Inc.* [1970], 122 Il.App.2d 391, at 396, 259 N.E.2d 307, at 309, *leave to appeal denied, cert. denied,* 403 U.S. 911, 91 S.Ct. 2207, 29 L.Ed.2d 688 [1971]), and have never deviated from the philosophy expressed in *Smith* v. *Michigan Buggy Co.* (1898), 175 Ill. 619, at 628, 51 N.E. 569, at 571 that:

> [I]t must be remembered that the courts are open to every citizen; and every man has a right to come into a court of justice, and claim what he deems to be his right, without fear os being prosecuted for heavy damages. If such actions are allowed, it might oftentimes happen that an honest suitor would be deterred from ascertaining his legal rights through fear of being obliged to defend a subsequent suit charging him with malicious prosecution.

Thus, our courts have consistently applied, and refused to lessen, the elements necessary in proving a case for malicious prosecution. See *Schwartz* v. *Schwartz* (1937), 366 Ill. 247, 8 N.E.2d 668; *Smith* v. *Michigan Buggy Co.* (1898), 175 Ill. 619, 51 N.E. 569; *Lyddon* v. *Shaw* (1978), 56 Ill. App.2d 815, 14 Ill.Dec. 489, 372

N.E.2d 685; *Pantone* v. *Demos* (1978), 59 Ill.App.3d 328, 16 Ill.Dec. 607, 375 N.E.2d 480; *Westphal* v. *Fridly* (1975), 34 Ill.App.3d 611, 339 N.E.2d 30; *Franklin* v. *Grossinger Motor Sales, Inc.* (1970), 122 Ill.App.2d 391, 259 N.E.2d 307, *leave to appeal denied, cert. denied,* 403 U.S. 911, 91 S.Ct. 2207, 29 L.Ed.2d 688; *Caspers* v. *Chicago Real Estate Board* (1965), 58 Ill.App.2d 113, 206 N.E.2d 787.

While it is true that, as the defendant contends "No man has a constitutional right to maintain vexatious or harassing litigation," (*Guttman* v. *Guttman* [1969], 65 Ill.App.2d 44, at 53, 212 N.E.2d 699, at 704), nevertheless "[s]ome sort of balance has to be struck between the social interests in preventing unconscionable suits and in permitting honest assertion of supposed rights. These interests conflict because a suit which its author thinks honest may look unconscionable to a jury." *Soffos* v. *Eaton* (1945), 80 U.S.App.D.C. 306, at 307, 152 F.2d 682, at 683; *O'Toole* v. *Franklin* (1977), 279 Or. 513, 569 P.2d 561, at 564. Since, as the court in *Lyddon* pointed out, the very purpose of a court of law is to determine whether an action filed by a party has merit, it would be incongruous to hold a party liable in tort for negligently or even wantonly failing to determine in advance that which ultimately only the court can determine.

And as pointed out in *Lyddon* v. *Shaw* at 56 Ill.App.3d 822, 14 Ill.Dec. 494, 372 N.E.2d 690:

> These considerations apply with equal force, not only to a party litigant, but to his counsel, (see *Spencer* v. *Burglass* [1976], La.App., 337 So.2d 596), since a litigant's free access to the courts would frequently be of little value to him if he were denied counsel of his choice by a rule which rendered attorneys fearful of being held liable as insurers of the merits of their client's case, and therefore unwilling to undertake representation in close or difficult matters.

See also *Norton* v. *Hines* (1975), 49 Cal. App.3d 917, 123 Cal.Rptr. 237.

Indeed, we believe it would be contrary to public policy for us to hold that an attorney has a duty to an intended defendant not to file a weak or perhaps "frivolous" lawsuit since we would be creating an insurmountable conflict of interest between the attorney and the client. The attorney owes a duty to his or her client to present the client's case vigorously in a manner as favorable to the client as the rules of law and professional ethics demand. (*Norton* v. *Hines* [1975], 49 Cal.App.3d 917, 123 Cal.Rptr. 237.) When a tort action is brought he has but one intended beneficiary, his client; the adverse party is certainly not an intended beneficiary of the adverse counsel's client. Thus, even in states extending the attorney's responsibility and liability to intended beneficiaries of the client's conduct, such as intended legatees under a will, no liability to the adverse party sued by the client has been found absent malicious prosecution. *Norton* v. *Hines* (1975), 41 Cal.App.3d 917, 123 Cal. Rptr. 237.

C.

Furthermore, we are not convinced by Dr. Berlin's argument that since the defendant attorneys are officers of the court and can be disciplined by the court, they should be held liable in tort for breach of Disciplinary Rule 7-102 and Ethical Consideration 7-10 of the Illinois Code of Professional Responsibility (1970). First of all, the Code is not "designed solely to prevent the risk of the plaintiff's being piqued at being sued. That would be an oversimplication of the ethical complexities which govern the lawyer's conduct to his client, the court and the public." (*Spencer* v. *Burglass* [La.App.1976], 337

So.2d 596 at 601.) Secondly, we see no violation of the Code. The provisions relied on by Dr. Derlin read as follows:

Illinois Code of Professional Responsibility, D.R. 7-102(A)(1) (1970):

> . . . a lawyer shall not: (1) File a suit . . . when he knows or when it is obvious that such action would serve merely to harass or maliciously injure another.

Illinois Code of Professional Responsibility, E.C. 7-10 (1970):

> The duty of a lawyer to represent his client with zeal does not militate against his concurrent obligation to treat with consideration all persons involved in the legal process and to avoid the infliction of needless harm.

As we have already noted, plaintiff in his complaint at no time alleged that the defendant attorneys filed the action knowing it would serve merely to harass or maliciously injure another. All he alleged was that they failed to make the investigation he, Dr. Berlin, felt was proper instead of relying on their client's statement. But, to reiterate, "if that constitutes malice, the courtrooms are full of malicious attorneys." (*Spencer* v. *Burglass* [La.App.1976], 337 So.2d 596 at 600.) And the injunction to avoid infliction of needless harm can hardly be interpreted as an injunction against the filing of weak lawsuits. The attorney is liable if he is guilty of malicious prosecution, that is enough. To create liability only for negligence, for the bringing of a weak case, would be to destroy his efficacy as advocate of his client and his value to the court, since only the rare attorney would have the courage to take other than the "easy" case.

D.

We are aware that, as Dr. Berlin contends, some doctors are being flooded with lawsuits; that all at least suffer the loss of time, fees, and the possibility of an increase in insurance premiums, or even the cancellation of their malpractice policies. We are also aware that the cost of the litigation can be great, whether borne by the doctor himself or by his insurance company. As to this latter problem, we note that the legislature has already responded, to a certain extent, since in 1976 it amended section 41 of the Illinois Civil Practice Act, which subjects a party pleading false allegations to the payment of attorney's fees, by eliminating the former requirement that the allegations be shown to have been made in bad faith, and substituting a requirement for a lesser showing that the allegations were made "without reasonable cause." (Ill.Rev. Stat.1977, ch. 110, par. 41; see *Lyddon* v. *Shaw* [1978], 56 Ill.App.3d 815, 14 Ill.Dec. 489, 372 N.E.2d 685.) While we can sympathize with the physician's predicament, as with that of any person who, confronted with an unwarranted and unfounded lawsuit, must still expend time, money and suffer anxiety, nevertheless we feel, as have the other courts which have considered the problem (see Annot. 84 A.L.R.3d 555, et seq.[2]), that this, unfortunately, is a price which must necessarily be paid to keep

[2]The plaintiff has cited no case where an appellate court has upheld a complaint brought by a treating physician against his former patient or if deceased, the patient's family or the patient's attorneys for the bringing of a tort action against the physician where malicious prosecution has not been shown and this court has found none. Drago *v.* Bounagurio (1978), 61 A.D.2d 282, 402 N.Y.S.2d 250 cited by the plaintiff is not in point. In that case, the court upheld a complaint by a physician who allegedly had never treated the deceased directly or indirectly during the fatal illness and who had been sued simply as a discovery device in order to ascertain where responsibility could be placed. No such flagrant and deliberate abuse of the legal system has been alleged here.

the courts open to the people. It remains a valid truism that "[s]uch ordinary trouble and expense as arise from the ordinary forms of legal controversy should be endured by the law-abiding citizen as one of the inevitable burdens which men must sustain under civil government." (*Smith* v. *Michigan Buggy Co.* [1898], 175 Ill. 619, at 629, 51 N.E. 569, at 572.) The importance of free access to the courts demands that this access be maintained even though occasionally some innocent person must suffer.

III.

While we agree with Mr. Nathan that the claim against him must be dismissed for the same reason it must be dismissed as to the other three defendants, we cannot agree with his contention that he also cannot be held liable because he is not responsible for his wife's conduct. While the Married Women's Act makes it clear that damages for a civil injury committed by a married woman may be recovered from her alone (Ill.Rev.Stat.1975, ch. 68, par. 4), it does not follow that a husband and wife cannot conspire together to commit a tort or jointly commit a tort. 21 Illinois Law and Practice, *Husband & Wife* § 210.

IV.

Dr. Berlin has cross-appealed from the dismissal of Count II against Mr. Nathan for barratry. We agree with Dr. Berlin that under certain circumstances an action in tort might lie against a common barrator. After all, it is clear that at common law an action in tort could be brought against one guilty of maintenance (see for example *Fletcher* v. *Ellis* [Territory of Ark. 1836], 9 Fed.Cas. 266 [No. 4,863a]; *Goodyear* v. *Dental Vulcanite Co.* v. *White* [C.C. S.D.N.Y.1879], 10 Fed.Cas. 752 [No. 5,602]), and we see no reason why the same rules should not apply to common barratry. But we agree with the trial court that no action for common barratry could lie under the situation present in the instant case.

At common law, barratry or common barratry was defined as the offense of frequently exciting or stirring up suits and quarrels between others. Barratry did not consist of a single act but of several acts, and it has been stated that at common law at least three acts of a barratrous nature were necessary to commit the offense. (*Lyddon* v. *Shaw* [1978], 56 Ill.App.3d 823, 14 Ill.Dec. 489, 372 N.E.2d 685; *State* v. *Noell* [1927], 220 Mo.App. 883, 295 S.W. 529; 14 Am.Jur.2d *Champerty and Maintenance* § 19). It is the general practice and not the particular act which constitutes the crime of common barratry. (*Commonwealth* v. *Pray* [1832], 30 Mass. [13 Pick] 359.) Here even if the conduct of Mr. Nathan could be considered to constitute the stirring up of a single suit or quarrel, it alone was insufficient to constitute common barratry.

Furthermore, as pointed out in *Vitaphone Corporation* v. *Hutchinson Amusement Co.* (D.Mass.1939), 28 F.Supp. 526 at 530:

> . . . Blackstone described a barrator in volume 4, p. 125, as "those pests of civil society that are perpetually endeavoring to disturb the repose of their neighbors and are officiously interfering in other men's quarrels. . . ." Assuming barratry still to be an offense in Maine and Massachusetts, where the activities complained of here took place, it would be difficult to suppose that the vexatious person or collection of persons that are called common barrators can be found to exist under the above described circumstances. There was no purpose on the part of either the distributors

> or the Bureau to foment suits in order to oppress persons. *Commonwealth* v. *McCulloch,* 15 Mass. 227. And, surely, the definition in Blackstone cannot fit persons engaged in protecting their legitimate business enterprises.

We do not believe that this definition can apply to a person trying to protect his legitimate domestic enterprise, that is, his family, any more than it can to one protecting a legitimate business enterprise. Compare also *Milk Dealers Bottle Exchange* v. *Schaffer* (1922), 224 Ill.App. 411.

Dr. Berlin, however, argues that the codification of the offense into statutory form has abolished the common law offense. Ill.Rev.Stat.1975, ch. 13, par. 21 reads as follows:

> If any person shall wickedly and wilfully excite and stir up any suits or quarrels between the people of this state, either at law or otherwise, with a view to promote strife and contention, he shall be deemed guilty of the petty offense of common barratry; and if he be an attorney or counselor at law, he shall be suspended from the practice of his profession, for any time not exceeding six months.

Even if we were to agree with the plaintiff that the statute has abolished the common law offense, an issue we do not rule on, we cannot agree with the plaintiff that a single action runs afoul of the statute. If a statute is enacted which covers an area formerly covered by common law, such statute must be construed as adopting common law unless there is clear and specific language showing that change in the common law was intended by the legislature. (*Proud* v. *W. S. Bills & Sons, Inc.* [1970], 119 Ill. App.2d 33, 255 N.E.2d 64, *leave to appeal denied.*) There is no clear and specific language in the statute indicating that it was intended to be more restrictive than common law. While the statute does refer to *any* suits or quarrels, we do not believe that the word "any" clearly indicates that the stirring up of a single suit or quarrel is sufficient since the statute refers to suits or quarrels in the plural. It is still the law in Illinois that the laws against champerty, maintenance and barratry are aimed at the prevention of multitudinous and useless lawsuits and at the prevention of speculation in lawsuits. *Milk Dealers Bottle Exchange* v. *Schaffer* (1922), 224 Ill.App. 411.

Furthermore, we note that the trend in the law has not been toward a more rigorous application of the laws against barratry, champerty and maintenance, but the converse. As the court in *Milk Dealers Bottle Exchange* v. *Schaffer* (1922), 224 Ill.App. 411 pointed out at p. 415:

> While the common-law crime of champerty has not been abolished by statute in this State, the tendency of decisions is to depart from the severity of the old law and at the same time to preserve the principle which tends to defeat the mischief to which the old law was directed, namely, "the traffic of merchandizing in quarrels, of huckstering in litigious discord."

Additionally, it is noted in 14 Am.Jur.2d *Champerty and Maintenance,* § 1, p. 842:

> The doctrines of champerty and maintenance, as known to the common law, arose at an early day in England from causes peculiar to the state of society then existing. Out of the conditions then existing arose the common law rule which prohibited the assignment of choses in action and the sale and transfer of land held adversely. The progress of law, enlightenment, and civilization during the past few hundred years has, however, to a large extent obviated the necessity of the stringent

> rules. In none of the states are the doctrines or laws of champerty and maintenance preserved in their original rigor. In many states they are declared to be obsolete and to have no existence at all; in others they are preserved in a greatly modified form, usually by special statutes. Generally, choses of action are now assignable, and land held adversely may be sold and transferred. Considering the status of society and conditions now prevailing in this country, to transfer a right of action or to maintain the suit of another without having any direct or contingent interest in it will by no means necessarily produce mischief or oppression. Indeed, it may be that such assistance or maintenance will have a tendency to secure rights and promote the ends of justice.

Indeed, we doubt the constitutionality of any statute which could be considered to bar the giving of unsolicited advice by one person to another, without charge, that that person may have a remedy at law and should peruse it, where the first person is not, as was the case in *Ohralik* v. *Ohio State Bar Assn.* (1978), 436 U.S. 447, 98 S.Ct. 1912, 56 L.Ed.2d 444, attempting to obtain remunerative employment for himself as legal counsel. As Mr. Justice Marshall remarked in his concurring opinion in that case, 436 U.S. at 473, 98 S.Ct. at 1928, 56 L.Ed.2d 464:

> The provision of such information about legal rights and remedies is an important function, even where the rights and remedies are of a private and commercial nature involving no constitutional or political overtones. See *United Mine Workers* v. *Illinois State Bar Association,* 389 U.S. 217, 221–223, 88 S.Ct. 353, 19 L.Ed.2d 426 (1967). See also *United Transportation Union* v. *State Bar of Michigan*, 401 U.S. 576, 585, 91 S.Ct. 1076, 28 L.Ed.2d 339 (1971).

And as was pointed out in *In re Primus* (1978), 436 U.S. 412, at 432, 98 S.Ct. 1893, at 1904, 1905, 56 L.Ed.2d 417, at 434:

> The First and Fourteenth Amendments require a measure of protection for ''advocating lawful means of vindicating legal rights.'' *Button,* 371 U.S. at 437, 83 S.Ct. 340, including ''advis[ing] another that his legal rights have been infringed and refer[ing] him to a particular attorney or group of attorneys . . . for assistance'' [*id.*, 436 U.S. at 432, 98 S.Ct. at 1904, 56 L.Ed.2d at 434.]

While it is true that both *Primus* and *NAACP* v. *Button* (1963), 371 U.S. 415, 83 S.Ct. 328, 9 L.Ed.2d 405 were cases involving ''constitutional and political overtones'' and that the court in both distinguished the cases involving private litigation for private gain, serving no public interest, we suspect that the providing of information about legal rights may be on occasion constitutionally protected even where merely private and commercial rights are involved. However, that question is not before us in this case, since, while the defendant, Mr. Nathan, raised the issue in his answer, he has waived it by not raising it on appeal. *Berk* v. *Will County* (1966), 34 Ill.2d 588, 218 N.E.2d 98; Ill.Rev.Stat.1977, ch. 110A, par 341(e)(7).

For the reasons previously discussed in this opinion, the judgment of the trial court in favor of Dr. Berlin is reversed and the case is remanded for the entry of an order dismissing the plaintiff's complaint. The judgment on the cross-appeal is affirmed.

REVERSED IN PART AND REMANDED.

AFFIRMED IN PART.

JOHNSON, P. J., and DIERINGER, J., concur.

Drago v. *Buonagurio*, 61 App.Div.2d 282, 402 N.Y.S.2d 250 (1978)

Opinions of the Court

SWEENEY, J.

The question presented on this appeal is whether the complaint states facts sufficient to constitute a cause of action. Special Term determined it did not and dismissed. We arrive at a contrary conclusion and, therefore, must reverse.

The complaint alleges that plaintiff, a doctor, and others, were sued in an action brought by defendant Madeline Buonagurio, as administratrix of the estate of Francis Buonagurio, deceased, wherein it was alleged that because of certain specified acts of malpractice committed by plaintiff, Francis Buonagurio died and his estate sustained damage in the sum of $1,500,000; that said action was commenced at the direction of the defendant attorney Brownstein; that, in fact, plaintiff never had Francis Buonagurio as a patient during the illness which allegedly caused his death, nor did he treat him directly or indirectly during said illness; that no basis existed for designating plaintiff as a defendant in said action; that it was done indiscriminately and as a discovery device in order to ascertain where responsibility could be placed; that defendant Brownstein's actions were, among other things, malicious, unethical and grossly negligent; and that plaintiff suffered much mental anguish, defamation of character and was otherwise damaged.

As we are concerned solely with the sufficiency of the complaint, the factual allegations are accepted as true (*Kober* v. *Kober,* 16 NY2d 191), and the complaint should not be dismissed merely because it is inartistically drawn (*Foley* v. *D'Agostino,* 21 AD2d 60). Furthermore, the complaint should be liberally construed and if any cause of action can be discerned from the facts alleged, it should not be dismissed (*Torrey Delivery* v. *Chautauqua Truck Sales & Serv.,* 47 AD2d 279).

In order to resolve the controversy it is necessary to analyze the complaint in light of the various possible tort causes of action that might be spelled out from it. Although it contains many of the elements common in traditional theories of tort, it does not fit neatly into any of them. While malice is alleged, the necessary ingredient of interference with plaintiff's person or property required for malicious prosecution is lacking (*Williams* v. *Williams,* 23 NY2d 592, 596). Also lacking is an allegation that the malpractice action against plaintiff terminated in his favor (*Lewis* v. *Village of Deposit,* 40 AD2d 730, affd 33 NY2d 532). Since an attorney in this State is not liable to third parties for negligence in performing services for his client, a cause of action so based on negligence cannot prevail (*Joffe* v. *Rubenstein,* 24 AD2d 752, app dsmd 21 NY2d 721). A careful reading of the complaint requires consideration of a possible cause of action for abuse of process. Here again, a necessary prerequisite is missing. The gist of such a cause of action is the improper use of process after it has been issued, and there must be an unlawful interference with one's person or property under color of process (*Williams* v. *Williams, supra*). The summons in the malpractice action against plaintiff was properly issued to institute the action and there is no allegation of improper use of process thereafter. Finally, the statutory offense of barratry was repealed in 1965 (L 1965, ch 1030).

Must we conclude, therefore, that since the traditional theories of tort do not appear to afford relief to plaintiff, he has no remedy? We think not, for the law should never suffer an injury and a damage without a remedy (*Kujek* v. *Goldman,* 150 NY 176; *Halio* v. *Lurie,* 15 AD2d 62; cf. *Fischer* v. *Maloney,* 43 NY2d 553).

We pass to a consideration of the more innovative theory designated prima facie tort which was first enunciated by Mr. Justice HOLMES in *Aikens* v. *Wisconsin* (195 US 194). Thereafter, it was recognized by many States, including New York (*Opera on Tour* v. *Weber,* 285 NY 348). It has been defined as the intentional infliction of harm, resulting in damage, without excuse or justification, by an act or series of acts which would otherwise be lawful (*Coopers & Lybrand* v. *Levitt,* 52 AD2d 493) and which acts do not fall within the categories of traditional tort (*Knapp Engraving Co.* v. *Keystone Photo Engraving Corp.,* 1 AD2d 170, 172). Factually, the instant case is unique. An action was commenced against plaintiff, a doctor, charging him with malpractice which contributed to the death of a patient. Plaintiff alleges that he, in fact, had no association with the patient, either directly or indirectly. Manifestly, plaintiff could not have been guilty of malpractice under such circumstances. Furthermore, it is alleged that the purpose in designating plaintiff a defendant by attorney Brownstein was to examine plaintiff in order to ascertain where responsibility could be placed. The obvious purpose, therefore, was to benefit the attorney and his client and the natural consequence thereof caused apparent foreseeable harm to plaintiff. The act was not only intentional and wrongful, but under the unusual circumstances alleged, irresponsible and without justification.

The fact that a cause of action is new, novel or nameless should not deprive an injured person of a remedy. The law of torts is not static. The reported cases clearly demonstrate that new and nameless torts are being recognized constantly to cope with society's economic, social and technological changes (Prosser, Torts [4th ed], p. 3). The progress of the common law is marked by many cases of first impression. The instant case has it genesis in the drastic increase in the number of medical malpractice actions during recent years, many of which are considered baseless by members of the medical profession. Considering the complaint in its entirety, and viewing it liberally, as we must (CPLR 3026), and in light of recent case law, we are of the view that it does allege a cause of action which should be cognizable at law (*Board of Educ.* v. *Farmingdale Classroom Teachers Assn., Local 1889, AFT AFL-CIO,* 38 NY2d 397, 405–406; *Morrison* v. *National Broadcasting Co.,* 24 AD2d 284, revd on other grounds 19 NY2d 453; see Birnbaum, "Physicians Counterattack: Liability of Lawyers for Instituting Unjustified Medical Malpractice Actions," 45 Fordham L Rev 1003). It is immaterial and unimportant whether we label the instant cause of action one of prima facie tort or something else.

In summary, we conclude that under the unique facts of this case, a clear intentional wrong, causing apparent and foreseeable harm to plaintiff, without excuse or justification, has been alleged, and we are not persuaded by any argument advanced by defendant to justify denying plaintiff his day in court. Upholding the sufficiency of this complaint does not mean that plaintiff will ultimately succeed on the trial of his allegations, nor should this opinion be read as creating or recognizing a distinctly new cause of action whenever a physician escapes malpractice liability and claims he was wrongfully charged in the first place (cf. *Aquilina* v. *O'Connor,* 59 AD2d 454).

The order should be reversed, on the law, with costs.

MAHONEY, P. J., GREENBLOTT, KANE and HERLIHY, JJ., concur.

Order reversed, on the law, with costs.

Drago v. *Buonagurio*, 46 N.Y.2d 778, 413 N.Y.S.2d 910 (1978)

Opinion of the Court

Memorandum.

The order of the Appellate Division, 61 A.D.2d 282, 402 N.Y.S.2d 250, should be reversed, with costs, and the order of Special Term, 89 Misc.2d 171, 391 N.Y.S.2d 61, granting defendant Brownstein's motion to dismiss the complaint as against him for failure to state a cause of action reinstated.

The allegations of the complaint are described in the opinions at Special Term and in the Appellate Division. We agree with those courts, and for the reasons stated by them, that the complaint does not state a cause of action in negligence, abuse of process or malicious prosecution. Nor does it allege a cause of action for what is sometimes labeled a "prima facie tort," i.e., "the intentional malicious injury to another by otherwise lawful means without economic or social justification, but solely to harm the other" (*Morrison* v. *National Broadcasting Co.*, 24 A.D.2d 284, 287, 266 N.Y.S.2d 406, 409, revd. on other grounds 19 N.Y.2d 453, 280 N.Y.S.2d 641, 227 N.E.2d 572). Whatever may be the constraints imposed by the Code of Professional Responsibility with the associated sanctions of professional discipline when baseless legal proceedings are instituted by a lawyer on behalf of a client, the courts have not recognized any liability of the lawyer to third parties therefor where the factual situations have not fallen within one of the acknowledged categories of tort or contract liability. That there are proposals before the Legislature to create new liabilities in such a circumstance (e.g., Senate Bill No. 8002 and Assembly Bill No. 10586 [1978], to amend Civil Rights Law, § 70) is an additional reason for judicial restraint in response to invitations to recognize what is conceded to be perhaps a "new, novel or nameless" cause of action. We conclude that the complaint fails to state a cognizable cause of action.

BREITEL, C.J., and JASEN, GABRIELLI, JONES, WACHTLER, FUCHSBERG and COOKE, JJ., concur.

Order reversed, with costs, and the order of Special Term reinstated in a memorandum. Question certified answered in the affirmative.

Bull v. *McCuskey*, 615 P.2d 957 (Nev., 1980)

Opinion

THOMPSON, Justice:

Dr. Charles McCuskey commenced this action against attorney Samuel Bull to recover damages for abuse of process. It was his contention that attorney Bull, acting for Catherine Doucette, instituted a malpractice suit against him for the ulterior purpose of coercing a nuisance settlement knowing that there was no basis for the claim of malpractice. A jury returned its verdict for Dr. McCuskey, awarding him $35,000 as compensatory and $50,000 as punitive damages. Bull has appealed from the judgment entered upon jury verdict and from denial of his post-trial motion for judgment n. o. v., or in the alternative, a new trial. The main claim of error is that the evidence does not show an abuse of process. Other errors also are assigned and will be considered.

On May 20, 1974, Catherine Doucette, an 86-year-old woman, was admitted to St. Mary's Hospital following an automobile accident. She had sustained multiple injuries, including fractures of the left wrist, the patellas, and the right femur. Because of her age, she also suffered from an arteriosclerotic heart disease, and was senile. Dr. Charles McCuskey was called to take care of the orthopedic problems, while other doctors managed her other disabilities. The following August, she was transferred from St. Mary's Hospital to the Physicians' Hospital for Extended Care. She was depressed, uncooperative and uncommunicative. While there, she developed bed sores on her hips and heels. Because of this, her nephew, Milan Jeffers, who had been appointed her guardian, dismissed Dr. McCuskey and replaced him with Dr. Jack Sargent. Soon after the substitution, Jeffers inquired of Dr. Sargent whether there had been malpractice by Dr. McCuskey and was told that there was none. Apparently, her bed sores resulted either from her refusal to follow directions, or her inability to do so, and were not traceable to any conduct of the doctor.

In October 1974, Milan Jeffers contacted attorney Bull. An action charging Dr. McCuskey with malpractice, and the Physicians' Hospital with negligence then was filed. The complaint was filed on the basis of Jeffers' statement that the condition of his aunt, Catherine Doucette, had greatly deteriorated, and upon photographs showing bed sores, which photographs were taken by Bull's assistant.

Before filing suit, attorney Bull did not examine nor did he obtain medical records from St. Mary's Hospital or Physicians' Hospital. He did not confer with a doctor. Neither did he submit his client's claim to the Joint Screening Panel, established pursuant to an agreement between the Washoe County Medical Society and the Washoe County Bar Association.[1]

After filing suit, attorney Bull did not secure the deposition of Dr. McCuskey, nor of any doctor. He did not retain an expert for trial, nor attempt to do so.

Shortly before trial, the claim against Physicians' Hospital was settled for $750. Dr. McCuskey refused to authorize his carrier to settle for any amount, although settlement of the claim against him also could have been made for $750.

During trial, attorney Bull called Dr. McCuskey incompetent, a fumble-fingered fellow, a liar, a scoundrel, a damned idiot. He also said, "[i]t will be a cold day in hell when I let that dum-dum take care of my mother." Of the doctor he also stated, "[h]e will lie under oath, steel [sic] an elderly woman's redress, cheat if he can get away with it, and all that is left for him is to make a pact with the devil and murder those who would oppose him."

The jury to whom the medical malpractice action was presented, quickly returned its verdict for Dr. McCuskey. Dr. McCuskey then commenced this action against attorney Bull for abuse of process.

1. The main assignment of error is that the evidence may not be viewed as establishing the elements of the tort of abuse of process. Recently, this court had occasion to consider that tort. *Nevada Credit Rating Bur.* v. *Williams*, 88 Nev. 601, 503 P.2d 9 (1972). We there noted that the two essential elements of abuse of process are an ulterior purpose, and a willful act in the use of the process not proper in the regular

[1]Since April 30, 1975, state statute provides for the joint medical-legal screening panel. See 1975 Nev.Stats. ch. 302.

conduct of the proceeding. The malice and want of probable cause necessary to a claim of malicious prosecution are not essential to recovery for abuse of process. Moreover, we mentioned that abuse of process hinges on the misuse of regularly issued process in contrast to malicious prosecution which rests upon the wrongful issuance of process.

In *Nevada Credit Rating Bur.* we sustained an award of compensatory and punitive damages for abuse of process. In that case, property valued at more than $30,000 was attached to secure an alleged debt of less than $5,000. We deemed that to be a willful misuse of the ancillary remedy of attachment for the ulterior purpose of coercing payment of the sum claimed to be due.

In the case at hand, it is asserted that the process (complaint and summons) charging Dr. McCuskey with malpractice was misused for the ulterior purpose of coercing a nuisance settlement. In considering all evidence presented, it was permissible for the jury to conclude that attorney Bull had utilized an alleged claim of malpractice for the ulterior purpose of coercing a nuisance settlement. His offer to settle the case for the minimal sum of $750 when considered in the light of his failure adequately to investigate before deciding to file suit and the total absence of essential expert evidence, supports such a conclusion by the jury, and we may not set it aside.

2. Next, it is asserted that certain rulings of the trial court in the medical malpractice action preclude recovery by Dr. McCuskey in this case by reason of the doctrine of collateral estoppel. This contention is without substance.

In the malpractice case the district court denied Dr. McCuskey's pre-trial motion for summary judgment, and also his motion for a directed verdict tendered during trial. It is asserted that those rulings conclusively establish that the Doctor's instant action for abuse of process is without merit.

The relitigation of an issue that has been finally resolved in a prior case may be barred by the doctrine of collateral estoppel. *Clark* v. *Clark,* 80 Nev. 52, 389 P.2d 69 (1964). The mentioned rulings in the earlier malpractice action were interlocutory rather than final. The only final determination in that action was a judgment entered upon a jury verdict that Dr. McCuskey was not liable for malpractice. The doctrine of collateral estoppel is not concerned with interlocutory rulings.

3. It is asserted that the evidence simply does not support either the award of $35,000 in compensatory damages or $50,000 in punitive damages.

a. The compensatory damages recoverable in an action for abuse of process are the same as in an action for malicious prosecution. Prosser, Law of Torts at 858 (4th ed. 1971), and include compensation for fears, anxiety, mental and emotional distress. *Spellens* v. *Spellens,* 49 Cal.2d 210, 317 P.2d 613 (Cal.1957). In *Miller* v. *Schnitzer,* 78 Nev. 301, 371 P.2d 824 (1962), a malicious prosecution case, we wrote:

> [T]he plaintiff may recover general money damages to compensate for injury to reputation . . . , humiliation, embarrassment, mental suffering and inconvenience, provided they are shown to have resulted as the proximate consequence of the defendant's act. These elements of damage are wholly subjective. The monetary extent of damage cannot be calculated by reference to an objective standard. The extent of such damage, by its very nature, falls peculiarly within the province of the trier of fact, in this case, a jury (Citations) The only limitation upon the judgment of the jury in this regard is that the damages thus awarded must not have been given under the influence of passion or prejudice. NRCP 59(a)(6).

In the *Miller* case we affirmed a compensatory damage award of $30,000, noting that the record, when read in the light most favorable to plaintiff, contained substantial evidence tending to prove damage to reputation, extreme embarrassment, humiliation, mental suffering and inconvenience as the proximate consequence of the defendant's conduct. That observation applies with equal force to the record now before us. The compensatory damage award of $35,000 is fully supported by the evidence.

b. In an action for the breach of an obligation not arising from contract, punitive damages may be recovered where the defendant has been guilty of oppression, fraud or malice, express or implied. NRS 42.010. It is suggested that malice is not shown, and, in any event, that the award of $50,000 is too high.

Malice may be established by showing that the defendant's conduct was willful, intentional and done in reckless disregard of its possible consequences. *Nevada Credit Rating Bur.* v. *Williams,* 88 Nev. 601, 503 P.2d 9 (1972). It was permissible for the jury to conclude that suit was filed against Dr. McCuskey and an offer to settle made with the intention to force a nuisance payment, and that this occurred intentionally and in reckless disregard of possible consequences. Accordingly, an award of punitive damages was within the province of the jury to allow.

Heretofore, we have recognized the subjective nature of punitive damages, *Caple* v. *Raynel Campers, Inc.,* 90 Nev. 341, 526 P.2d 334 (1974), and the absence of workable standards by which to evaluate the propriety of such an award. Accordingly, we have allowed that determination to rest with the discretion of the trier of the fact, *Midwest Supply, Inc.* v. *Waters,* 89 Nev. 210, 510 P.2d 876 (1973), unless the evidence introduced at trial shows that the amount awarded by the jury would financially destroy or annihilate the defendant, *Miller* v. *Schnitzer, supra,* in which event we would attempt an appropriate adjustment of the award.

In the case at hand, trial evidence as to attorney Bull's net worth was not produced. Therefore, we are unable to conclude that the award was excessive.

4. The denigrating comments of attorney Bull concerning Dr. McCuskey during the trial of the malpractice case (incompetent, a liar, a scoundrel, a damned idiot, etc.) were received in evidence in this case to show malice. A prior motion in limine to preclude such evidence was tendered and denied. This ruling is asserted to be reversible error.

As a general proposition an attorney at law is absolutely privileged to publish defamatory matter concerning another in communications preliminary to a proposed judicial proceeding, or in the institution of or during the course and as a part of, a judicial proceeding in which he participates as counsel, if it has some relation to the proceeding. Restatement (Second) of Torts § 586 (1976); *Richards* v. *Conklin,* 94 Nev. 84, 575 P.2d 588 (1978). The privilege rests upon a public policy of securing to attorneys as officers of the court the utmost freedom in their efforts to obtain justice for their clients.

The malpractice complaint placed in issue Dr. McCuskey's competence as a physician. When Dr. McCuskey testified in that case, he placed in issue his credibility. Attorney Bull's comments may be understood to pertain to either Dr. McCuskey's competence or his credibility, and therefore, are privileged. The motion in limine should have been granted.

It does not follow, however, that the error in admitting such evidence requires this court to set aside the judgment entered upon jury verdict. An error in the reception of evidence which does not affect the substantial rights of the parties must be disregarded as harmless. NRCP 61.

We already have mentioned the evidence that would allow the jury to find malice and award punitive damages. With this in mind, it is evident that the reception of attorney Bull's denigrating comments was not essential to the punitive damage issue and, therefore, may be deemed harmless.

Although the denigrating comments of attorney Bull regarding Dr. McCuskey were privileged, and alone would not supply a basis for liability in damages, it does not follow that an attorney may so conduct himself without fear of discipline. Indeed the oath taken by an attorney licensed to practice in Nevada states in part "that I will abstain from all offensive personalities and advance no fact prejudicial to the honor or reputation of a party or witness, unless required by the justice of the cause with which I am charged . . ." Moreover, SCR 188(4) commands that a lawyer should never be unfair or abusive or inconsiderate to adverse witnesses or opposing litigants. His obligation to present his client's cause vigorously does not contemplate violation of the attorney's oath or of the standards of conduct.

5. We shall not comment upon the remaining assignment of error—that of the impeachment of a witness by reference to his prior felony conviction, when that conviction had been satisfied by an honorable discharge from probation and the witness released from all penalties and disabilities resulting therefrom—since the impeaching evidence already was before the jury through an earlier witness without objection.

Affirmed.

MOWBRAY, C. J., BATJER and MANOUKIAN, JJ., and ZENOFF,[2] Senior Justice, concur.

DIFFICULTIES ATTENDANT TO THE COUNTERSUIT

The law encourages free and open access to the courts without fear of reprisal. If the institution of litigation—medical malpractice or otherwise—automatically precipitated a counterclaim in most instances, one of the immediate adverse consequences would be a vicious cycle of extended litigation; the original plaintiff might then automatically become a defendant, then a plaintiff again, and so forth. Legislation and case law thus seek to balance the public policy of providing free and open access to the courts with remedies for meritless, frivolous litigation by placing restrictions on the situation in which the initiation of one lawsuit can prompt the initiation of a reprisal suit. As we have seen in *Drago* (above), these restrictions are designed to ensure that public policy considerations will remain preeminent. This principle concerning the preeminence of the societal interest over that of the (wrongful) individual was enunciated by the New York Court of Appeals in the case of *Martirano* v. *Frost,* 25 N.Y.2d 505, 307 N.Y.S.2d 425, 255 N.E.2d 693 (1969):

> It may be unfortunate that the plaintiff must suffer an attack on his professional integrity without any means of judicial redress. But the possible harm to him as an individual is far outweighed by the need—reflected in the policy underlying the privilege here involved—to encourage parties to litigation, as well as counsel and witnesses, to speak freely in the course of judicial proceedings.

[2]The Chief Justice designated the Hon. David Zenoff, Senior Justice, to sit in the place of the Hon. E. M. Gunderson, Justice. Nev.Const. art. 6, § 19; SCR 10.

TABLE 1
Essential Elements of Various Causes of Action in New York State

Abuse of Process	• Some civil or criminal process compelling the performance or forbearance of some prescribed act must be regularly issued. • The person activating the process must be moved by a purpose to do harm without that which has been traditionally described as economic or social excuse or justification. • Defendant must be seeking some collateral advantage or corresponding detriment to the plaintiff which is outside the legitimate ends of the process.
Malicious prosecution	• The commencement or continuation of a criminal proceeding or, in a civil action, the interference with person or property by the use of a provisional remedy such as arrest, attachment, or injunction. • The termination of the proceeding in favor of the defendant. • The absence of probable cause. • Actual malice. • Damages.
Prima facie tort	• The infliction of intentional harm without excuse or justification by an act or series of acts which would otherwise be lawful. • The sole motivation for the damaging acts must be malicious intention; where other motives such as economic profit exist there can be no recovery. • Special damages in the form of some specific temporal injury to person, property, or reputation; general damages will be deemed insufficient.

The difficulties attendant to the countersuit can be gleaned by perusal of Table 1 above, which summarizes the essential elements needed to state a cause of action in New York State for abuse of process, malicious prosecution, and *prima facie* tort. In applying the abuse of process theory, it must be proved that some process (e.g., an arrest warrant, a garnishment of wages, etc.) was misapplied. Ordinarily, medical malpractice cases fail to raise the essential elements of abuse of process, as the issuance of a summons to appear in court is not a misuse of process. In New York as well as other jurisdictions the damages suffered as the result of malicious prosecution must be "special damages" (i.e., business losses resulting for example from harm to reputation). See *Drago* v. *Buonagurio*, 89 Misc.2d at 173, 391 N.Y.S.2d at 62 (1977). *Prima facie* tort is a cause of action that arose from the 1904 Supreme Court case of *Aikens* v. *Wisconsin,* 195 U.S. 194. It has been defined as "the intentional malicious injury to another by otherwise lawful means without economic or social justification, but solely to harm the other." *Morrison* v. *National*

Broadcasting Company, 24 App.Div.2d 284, 266 N.Y.S.2d 406 (1965), reversed on other grounds 19 N.Y.2d 453, 227 N.E.2d 572, 280 N.Y.S.2d 641 (1967). In those jurisdictions that accept *prima facie* tort as a viable cause of action, the difficulty in succeeding in a countersuit with this theory lies in the difficulty in proving (1) that the malpractice action was brought without economic or social justification, (2) that special damages were incurred, and (3) that the plaintiff was motivated solely by the desire to harm or injure the physician.

Other theories upon which physicians' countersuits have been based offer little encouragement. Claims that plaintiff's attorney was negligent in failing properly to establish the merits of a particular case may be dismissed on the grounds that plaintiff's attorney owes no duty of care to the defendant physician. As stated in the New York case of *Pulka* v. *Edelman,* 40 N.Y.2d 781, 390 N.Y.S.2d 393, 358 N.E.2d 1019 (1976), "to allege a cause of action in negligence, it must be established that defendant owes a duty to plaintiff. In New York, an attorney owes no duty to third persons for the negligent performance of his obligations to a client, even where such negligence results in damage to third parties" (citations omitted). Claims of defamation may be rejected on the grounds that the defamatory matter, published in the context of a judicial proceeding, was privileged. Claims of barratry, such as that in *Maiel* v. *Sandlin,* 571 S.W.2d 567 (Tex.Civ.App. 1978), have been dismissed on the grounds that the practice of bringing groundless judicial proceedings is a criminal, not a civil offense. As for the claim of infliction of emotional distress, the authors are not aware of any countersuit to date that has sufficiently met the requirements for this cause of action.

ALTERNATIVE MEASURES

For the professional who feels that he or she has been unjustly named as a defendant in a malpractice suit, an alternative to a countersuit is a letter to the American Bar Association. In some cases such a letter may put the machinery in motion to subject the lawyer who brought the suit to disciplinary action. This is so because the bringing of a frivolous suit is in violation of the American Bar Association's Code of Professional Responsibility. However, as Alper (1978) has argued, such a course of action might more likely have a cathartic effect for the letter-writer and not much more.

A preventive measure is the use of malpractice screening panels. Such panels screen prospective malpractice claims and offer opinions as to the merits of the claims. In New York, where Section 148-a of the Judiciary Law (below) makes the use of such panels mandatory before the case will be heard by the supreme court, the panel consists of a supreme court justice, a physician, and an attorney. If all panel members agree as to the defendant physician's liability, a memorandum to that effect may be admitted into evidence at the trial. If the panel members unanimously agree that the case lacks merit, this will give the plaintiff's attorney cause for pause before proceeding—and possibly subjecting himself to a countersuit for malicious prosecution.

New York Judiciary Law § 148–a (McKinney Supp. 1980)

§ 148-a. Medical Malpractice Panel Established

1. Each appellate division of the supreme court shall establish within its judicial department a medical malpractice panel or panels to facilitate the disposition of medical malpractice actions, including malpractice actions where a hospital is a named defendant, in the supreme court. The number and locations of such panels and the rules governing the operation thereof shall be determined by the respective appellate divisions.
   1-a. Each appellate division shall establish separate panels for podiatrists. The members of such separate panels shall be appointed from a list of podiatrists regularly admitted to practice podiatry in the state of New York and shall be prepared by each presiding justice of the appellate division with the assistance of the podiatry society of the state of New York.
2. All hearings shall be before a panel of three consisting of a justice of the supreme court, a physician and an attorney-at-law, both to be designated in accord with the following provisions:
   (a) A list of doctors regularly admitted to practice medicine in the state of New York shall be prepared by each presiding justice of the appellate division with the assistance of the Medical Society of the State of New York, a county medical society and/or the New York Academy of Medicine. Said list shall be divided into lists of doctors according to the particular specialty of each.
   (b) The presiding justice shall prepare a list of attorneys with trial experience, not confined, however, to the field of medical malpractice.
   (c) Names of doctors and attorneys may be added to or taken off the list at any time by the presiding justice in his discretion.
   (d) Any party prior to the date set for the hearing may file a written objection to the designation of a doctor or attorney which objection shall be decided by the justice presiding as a member of the panel.
3. (a) The rules of the appellate division shall provide that prior to the date set for hearing the parties shall submit to the court all written material, including pleadings, bill of particulars, medical and hospital reports (or authorization to obtain the same), said written material to be submitted in triplicate except as to hospital records and X-rays, and that these materials shall be made available to any panel member desiring to see the same in advance of the hearing.
   (b) The rules of the appellate division shall provide that the Medical Society of the State of New York, a county medical society and/or the New York Academy of Medicine shall review the said submitted material and designate the medical specialty involved and notify the court as to such a designation.
4. The hearing shall be informal and without a stenographic record. Except as otherwise provided in this section, no statement or expression of opinion made in the course of the hearing shall be admissible in evidence either as an admission or otherwise in any trial of the action. The justice presiding at the hearing shall not

preside at the trial. No other panel member shall participate in the trial either as counsel or witness except as otherwise provided herein.

5. All parties shall be represented at the hearing by counsel authorized to act for their respective clients. If authority is not conferred, the plaintiff and a representative of the carrier so authorized must attend. Failing an appearance, the justice presiding may order an inquest, strike the case from the calender, or make such direction as justice requires.
6. The panel may request an additional doctor having particular expertise in the specialty involved to assist it in the determination of the claim. Such doctor shall make a report to the panel. The panel shall determine the fee and expenses to be paid to such doctor and the parties to the hearing shall share equally in such fee and expense. The doctor may be called at a subsequent trial as a witness by any of the parties. The party calling such witness shall pay all reasonable fees and expenses of the doctor.
7. Following presentation and discussion between the panel and counsel, if any disposition is arrived at, either as to the whole case or any part thereof, an appropriate order shall be entered. If the justice presiding deems a further hearing necessary or desirable, he shall fix a date for the same. If no disposition is arrived at the case shall be remanded to its regular place on the calendar.
8. If the three members of the panel concur as to the question of liability, a formal written recommendation concerning such question of liability shall be signed by the panel members and forwarded to all parties. In such event, the recommendation shall be admissible in evidence at any subsequent trial upon the request of any party to the action. The recommendation shall not be binding upon the jury or, in a case tried without a jury, upon the trial court, but shall be accorded such weight as the jury or the trial court chooses to ascribe to it.

   If the recommendation is read to the jury or by the trial court, the doctor member or the attorney member of the panel, or both of them, may be called as a witness by any party with reference to the recommendation of the panel only. The party calling such witness or witnesses shall pay their reasonable fees and expenses.

Added L.1974, c. 146, § 1; amended L.1974, c. 657, § 1; L.1974, c. 995, § 1; L.1975, c. 109, §§ 12-16; L.1978, c. 95, § 1.

1978 Amendment. Subd. 1. L. 1978, c. 95, § 1. eff. Apr. 25, 1978, inserted "including malpractice actions where a hospital is a named defendant."

1975 Amendment. Subd. 2, par. (d). L.1975, c. 109, § 12. eff. July 1, 1975, added par. (d).

Subd. 4. L.1975, c. 109, § 13, eff July 1, 1975, substituted "Except as otherwise provided in this section, no statement or" for "No statement nor any," deleted "or hear any application in the case not connected with the hearing itself" following "preside at the trial," and inserted "except as otherwise provided herein" following "counsel or witness."

Subd. 6. L.1975, c. 109, § 15, eff. July 1, 1975, added subd. 6. Former subd. 6, was renumbered 7.

Subd. 7. L.1975, c. 109, § 14, eff. July 1, 1975, renumbered former subd. 6 as 7.

Subd. 8. L.1975, c. 109, § 16, eff. July 1, 1975, added subd. 8.

1974 Amendments. L.1974, c. 657, § 1, eff. Sept. 1, 1974, among other changes, substituted provisions establishing a medical malpractice panel in each appellate division's judicial department in lieu of a malpractice part in each judicial district; omitted former subd. 2 which related to a calendar for pending cases; and renumbered former subds. 3 to 7 as 2 to 6.

Subd. 1-a. L.1974, c. 995, § 1, eff. Sept. 1, 1974, added subd. 1-a.

Effective Date. L.1974, c. 146, § 2, provided that this section shall take effect Sept. 1, 1974.

REFERENCES FOR CHAPTER V

ALPER, P. R. Our irresponsible bar associations. *Private Practice,* April 1974, pp. 31; 34; 36; 41; 42.

BIRNBAUM, S. L. Physician's counterattack: Liability of lawyers for instituting unjustified medical malpractice actions. *Fordham Law Review,* 1977, *45,* 1003-1092.

EISBERG, J. F. Doctor must pay damages, child-rearing expenses for failed vasectomy. *Legal Aspects of Medical Practice,* 1978, *6*(3), 48-49.

HORSLEY, J. E. Here's the nth degree of malpractice liability. *Medical Economics,* April 17, 1978, pp. 149; 153-154; 156; 158.

KOTULAK, R. Malpractice suits: Growing sickness. *Chicago Tribune,* May 11, 1975, p. 1.

LEDAKOWICH, A. An erroneous prediction of death. *Resident and Staff Physician,* 1976, *22*(10), 25.

CHAPTER VI

Malpractice and the Psychotherapist

IN THE PRECEDING CHAPTERS we have reviewed the major legal issues pertinent to practice and malpractice by professionals in the field of mental health. It remains for us to consider in this final chapter the potential liability of the nonprofessional practitioner; the self-proclaimed "psychotherapist" who is unlicensed and who, in fact, may have had little or no formal education and training in the conduct of psychotherapy. To what standard of care will such a practitioner be held? Who may qualify as expert in suits against such psychotherapists who are neither psychologist, nor social worker, nor psychiatrist? What is the applicable statute of limitations with respect to the actions of such unlicensed practitioners? These and related questions beg for answers.

THE STANDARD OF CARE

In general, the law holds unlicensed practitioners to the same standard of care that could be applied to the conduct of a qualified, licensed practitioner. The focus of the court in cases involving unlicensed practitioners has been on the diagnosis made and the care and treatment provided by the unlicensed person, not on the issue of licensure. The test is whether or not the practitioner exercised the requisite skill and care in rendering treatment. The applicable legal principle is enunciated in *Brown* v. *Shyne,* 242 N.Y. 176, 1151 N.E. 197 (1926), in which the court held as follows:

> The defendant in offering to treat the plaintiff held himself out as qualified to give treatment. He must meet the professional standards of skill and care prevailing among those who do offer treatment lawfully. . . . In order to show that the plaintiff has been injured by defendant's breach of the statutory duty, proof must be given that the defendant in such treatment did not exercise the care and skill which would have been

exercised by qualified practitioners within the state, and that such lack of skill and care caused the injury.

It is noteworthy that the defendant in *Brown* was a chiropractor who was being held to the standard of care applied to a medical doctor. In his dissenting opinion, Judge Crane struggles with the question of what the applicable standard should be:

> [T]he judge charged the jury as if this were the ordinary malpractice case, furnishing for the defendant a standard of the legally authorized physician. It is difficult for me personally to follow this reasoning and the logic of the situation. I think this rule all too liberal to the defendant. What he did was prohibited by law. He could not practice medicine without violating the law. The law did not recognize him as a physician. How can the courts treat him as such? Provided his act, in violation of the law, is the direct and proximate cause of injury, in my judgment he is liable, irrespective of negligence. It seems somewhat strange that the courts, one branch of the law, can hold up for such a man the standards of the licensed physician, while the Legislature, another branch of the law, declares that he cannot practice at all as a physician. The courts thus afford the protection which the Legislature denies.

To what standard will the unlicensed psychotherapist be held? to that of a psychiatrist? A psychologist? A social worker? A psychiatric nurse? An occupational therapist? Which, if any, of these standards will apply, and how will the courts decide? Which type of professional will be qualified to testify as an expert in cases involving unlicensed psychotherapists? These questions have, to our knowledge, yet to be dealt with by the courts. However, applying legal principles derived from the case law that impacts on such questions we would predict that specific facts of the case at hand (e.g., how the practitioner represented himself or herself, the nature of the treatment, the nature of the problem, etc.) would then provide the basis for the court to determine the applicable standard.

Below in *Bogust* v. *Iverson,* 10 Wisc.2d 129, 102 N.W.2d 228, Ralph Iverson, a college director of student personnel services who held a Ph.D. in education, was sued for wrongful death by the parents of Jeannie Bogust. Dr. Iverson had psychologically tested and counseled Jeannie through the period of November 11, 1957, to April 15, 1958. On May 27, 1958, Jeannie committed suicide. The plaintiffs brought suit alleging that Dr. Iverson failed to secure proper treatment, failed to advise the parents of Jeannie's condition so that they might obtain proper treatment, and failed to provide proper student guidance. Interestingly, there was no attempt on the part of the plaintiffs to hold Dr. Iverson to the standard required of a psychologist, despite the fact that he regularly administered personality tests to students and counseled students with a variety of emotional and social problems. As stated in the court record:

> Defendant is not a person qualified as a medical doctor or a specialist in mental disorders. It is alleged that he is an "educator by profession," a professor of education with a doctor of philosophy degree. Admitting that a teacher is not an insurer of the health, welfare and safety of his students, *Grosso* v. *Wittemann,* 1954, 266 Wis. 17, 62 N.W.2d 386 plaintiffs argue that he does have the duty to use reasonable care. . . .

It can be seen that both the plaintiffs and the defense in this case were content to view Dr. Iverson as an educator or a teacher as opposed to a psychotherapist or a counselor. Subsequently in the opinion we see what might well have been counseling or therapy session referred to as "meetings," as if between student and teacher.:

> Granting that he had some knowledge of Jeannie's emotional and other difficulties as the result of his meetings with her during a period of five months, as a teacher he cannot be charged with the same degree of care based on such knowledge as a person trained in medicine or psychiatry could exercise.

As seen below, the court rejected as conclusions the allegations made by the plaintiffs. The one question left for judgment was phrased by the court as follows:

> There is no allegation that defendant's counseling caused injury. The only question is whether, at the time he suggested the interviews be terminated, he should reasonably have foreseen, acting as an ordinarily prudent and intelligent person, that as a consequence thereof Jeannie would do harm to herself, i.e., commit suicide.

In *Previn* v. *Tenacre, Inc.*, 70 F.2d 389 (1933) (following *Bogust* below), we see another example of care and treatment of mental and emotional problems being rendered while the practitioners are not held to the same standard as qualified, licensed mental health professionals. Arthur Previn sought treatment for "agitated melancholia of the depressive type" from Tenacre, Inc., an institution that held itself out as offering treatment according to Christian Science methods. The plaintiff alleged that while at that institution he was tied by his hands and feet to his bed and chair, that clamps were applied to his tongue to keep him from shouting, and that physical force was used to make him comply with demands such as taking a ride in a car. The question submitted to the jury was whether or not the treatment Previn received was in accordance with the teaching of Christian Science and whether or not the force and restraints used were reasonable and necessary to properly care for the patient and prevent him from harming himself or the staff.

The two cases below illustrate that the court will look very carefully to the express and implied representations made by the practitioner in determining what the applicable standard of care shall be. Reviewing the law in California, Harris (1973) has noted that the nonprofessional psychotherapist cannot technically be sued for malpractice, as that cause of action is reserved for licensed members of a recognized profession:

> [T]hose persons who are either licensed or members of professions sanctioned by the state, must follow the standards of care of their professions or they may be subject to either liability for negligence, or loss of license, or criminal penalties. Those people who practice outside the law are either quacks or non-professionals not yet under the state's statutory umbrella. Since no standards are established for their reputed professions, someone injured by their "care" will have to rely on tort theories other than malpractice.... (pp. 408–409)

Bogust v. *Iverson*, 10 Wisc.2d 129, 102 N.W.2d 228 (1960)

MARTIN, C. J. Defendant is "an educator by profession." Jeannie Bogust was born May 3, 1939. At the times referred to in the complaint she was a pupil at Stout State College where defendant was employed as a full-time director of student personnel services and professor of education with a Ph.D. degree. It is alleged that in such capacity the defendant was "charged with the maintenance of a counseling and testing center for personal, vocational, educational, scholastic, or other problems, including those students torn by conflicting feelings which cause worry and social ineffectiveness."

The complaint states that commencing in November, 1957, Jeannie, as a student of the college, was under the direct guidance and supervision of the defendant; that defendant administered to her aptitude and personality tests and he was familiar with her personal, social, and educational problems and her conflicting feelings, environment, and social ineffectiveness; that he was well aware of her emotional disturbances, social conflicts, scholastic difficulties, and personal problems during the period of November 11, 1957, through April 15, 1958; and—

> . . . that although said student was constantly in need of professional guidance after April 15, 1958, said defendant suggested termination of future interviews regarding her problems; that as a result of the failure of proper guidance by said defendant as aforesaid, she suffered psychological and emotional injuries and disturbances depriving her of her own volition and resulting in death by her own hand on May 27, 1958.

It is alleged:

> That said defendant negligently and carelessly failed to perform his duties as such director in the following:
>
> (a) That he failed to secure or attempt to secure emergency psychiatric treatment after he was aware or should have been aware of her inability to care for the safety of herself.
>
> (b) That he failed at all times to advise the said parents of Jeannie Bogust or contact them concerning the true mental and emotional state of their said daughter, thus preventing them from securing proper medical care for her.
>
> (c) That he failed to provide proper student guidance.

For the purposes of this decision we can assume the truth of only such allegations as are material statements of fact. Statements which are conclusions are not admitted by demurrer. *Mitchell* v. *Horicon* (1953), 264 Wis. 350, 59 N. W. (2d) 469.

> A demurrer to a complaint admits all the facts therein well pleaded, but it does not admit erroneous conclusions drawn from such facts by the pleader even though the conclusions bear the semblance of statements of fact. [*Northwestern Mut. Life Ins. Co.* v. *State* (1920), 173 Wis. 119, 125, 180 N. W. 138.]

The first question presented on appeal is whether there is a legal duty on the part of the defendant of such nature as will sustain this action. As pointed out by the trial court, before liability can attach there must be found a duty resting upon the person against whom recovery is sought and then a breach of that duty. *Palmer* v. *Janesville*

Improvement Co. (1928), 195 Wis. 607, 219 N. W. 437; *Miller* v. *Welworth Theatres* (1956), 272 Wis. 355, 75 N. W. (2d) 286.

Defendant is not a person qualified as a medical doctor or a specialist in mental disorders. It is alleged that he is an "educator by profession," a professor of education with a Doctor of Philosophy degree. Admitting that a teacher is not an insurer of the health, welfare, and safety of his students, *Grosso* v. *Wittemann* (1954), 266 Wis. 17, 62 N.W. (2d) 386, plaintiffs argue that he does have the duty to use reasonable care, citing the *Grosso Case* and Restatement, 2 Torts, p. 868, sec. 320:

> b. *Helplessness of other*. . . . So too, a child while in school is deprived of the protection of his parents or guardian. Therefore, the actor who takes custody of . . . a child is properly required to give him the protection which the custody or the manner in which it is taken has deprived him. . . .
>
> d. *Duty to anticipate danger*. One who has taken custody of another may not only be required to exercise reasonable care for the other's protection when he knows or has reason to know that the other is in immediate need thereof, but also to make careful preparations to enable him to give effective protection when the need arises, and to exercise reasonable vigilance to ascertain the need of giving it. . . .

The three acts of negligence with which the defendant is charged in the complaint are grounded on the theory that he had such a familiarity with and knowledge of Jeannie's problems and her "emotional disturbances, social conflicts, scholastic difficulties" that in the exercise of reasonable intelligence and judgment he should have realized her need for psychiatric treatment and acted accordingly—in securing such treatment, in advising her parents, and in providing proper guidance.

The trial court held:

> To hold that a teacher who has had no training, education, or experience in medical fields is required to recognize in a student a condition, the diagnosis of which is in a specialized and technical medical field, would require a duty beyond reason.

Plaintiffs allege defendant was charged with the maintenance of a counseling and testing center for various educational, vocational, and personal problems which students of the college might have, but that fact does not qualify him as an expert in the field of medicine or psychiatry. Granting that he had some knowledge of Jeannie's emotional and other difficulties as the result of his meetings with her during a period of five months, as a teacher he cannot be charged with the same degree of care based on such knowledge as a person trained in medicine or psychiatry could exercise.

The first act of negligence alleged is that the defendant failed to secure psychiatric treatment for Jeannie "after he was aware or should have been aware of her inability to care for the safety of herself." This clearly implies that he should have known she had suicidal tendencies. But there is no allegation of fact that would have apprised the defendant, as a reasonably prudent man, that she had such tendencies. The statement is merely a conclusion. The same comment applies to the second act of negligence alleged, that of failing to advise the parents "thus preventing them from securing proper medical care for her." The duty of advising her parents could arise only from facts establishing knowledge on the part of defendant of a mental or emotional state which required medical care; and no such facts are alleged.

The allegation that defendant failed to provide proper student guidance apparently refers to the fact that he "suggested termination of future interviews regarding her problems."

Jeannie was suffering from emotional disturbances and social conflicts before she came under defendant's guidance. Plaintiffs rely on the "further harm" doctrine defined in Restatement, 2 Torts, p. 872, sec. 322, where it is stated, in part, comment *d*:

> The liability which this section recognizes is not imposed as a penalty for the actor's original misconduct, but for a breach of a separate duty to aid and protect the other after his helpless condition caused by the actor's misconduct is or should be known.

There is no allegation that the interviews between the defendant and Jeannie benefited her or that there was a duty on his part to continue them or that their termination caused the injury or placed her in a worse position than she was when they were begun. See Restatement, 2 Torts, p. 873, sec. 323 (2):

> One who gratuitously renders services to another, otherwise than by taking charge of him when helpless, is not subject to liability for discontinuing the services if he does not thereby leave the other in a worse position than he was in when the services were begun.

Jeannie had various problems before the interviews were undertaken, but was she "helpless" in that she was unable to look after her own safety? There is no allegation of such a fact, as pointed out above. Nor is there any allegation that she became so "helpless" during the time the interviews were carried on or that, if she did, she exhibited such manifestations as would charge the defendant with knowledge thereof.

The allegation in point is that although the deceased was in need of professional guidance after April 15, 1958, the defendant suggested termination of the interviews and that:

> . . . as a result of the failure of proper guidance by said defendant as aforesaid, she suffered psychological and emotional injuries and disturbances depriving her of her own volition and resulting in death by her own hand on May 27, 1958.

We may assume the interviews were terminated, although the act complained of is the *suggestion* that they be terminated. There is no allegation that defendant's counseling caused injury. The only question is whether, at the time he suggested the interviews be terminated, he should reasonably have foreseen, acting as an ordinarily prudent and intelligent person, that as a consequence thereof Jeannie would do harm to herself, *i.e.*, commit suicide.

In *Dahlberg* v. *Jones* (1939), 232 Wis. 6, 11, 12, 285 N. W. 841, it was held that where a mental patient was under the care of a doctor in a private hospital, the degree of care owed such patient "should be in proportion to the physical and mental ailments of the patient rendering him unable to look after his own safety." In that case such a patient suffered injuries as the result of escaping from the hospital, and this court held there was no liability on the hospital where there was no evidence to support the conclusion that the doctor or the hospital staff had reasonable grounds to anticipate or to take precautions against suicide or escape. The court referred to language used in applying the same rule in *Breeze* v. *St. Louis & S.F.R. Co.* (1915), 264 Mo. 258, 263, 174 S. W. 409:

> There was no evidence introduced tending to show that the deceased was possessed of suicidal mania, or mania of any kind, for that matter, at most that he was insane at intervals, but no indication whatever, prior to the fatal leap, that he intended to

> do himself or anyone else any personal harm. In the absence of such showing there was no evidence tending to show that the defendant had any reason to anticipate that the deceased contemplated self-destruction.

Paraphrasing the above, in this case we can substitute for evidence or proof the fact that the complaint contains no allegation of a suicidal tendency or mania or any indication that Jeannie showed any disposition to injure herself.

If a hospital for the treatment of mental disorders cannot be held liable for self-injury of a patient where there is no evidence (allegation) that the patient would injure herself if not restrained, certainly the mere allegation of an awareness by a teacher of emotional disturbance and personal problems of a student is insufficient to support an action for death by suicide.

The suicide took place almost six weeks after defendant suggested terminating the interviews. The complaint alleges that Jeannie's loss of volition occurred after the interviews terminated. To hold that the termination was a negligent act, it must be alleged that defendant knew or should have known that Jeannie would commit suicide.

This is an action for wrongful death under sec. 331.03, Stats. The basic theory of plaintiffs' complaint and their argument on appeal is the foreseeability of Jeannie's suicide as the proximate result of defendant's acts and omissions. In a lengthy discussion in 11 A.L.R. (2d), Liability for Suicide, p. 756, sec. 2, it is stated:

> Where an action is brought under a wrongful-death statute the general rule is that suicide constitutes an intervening force which breaks the line of causation from the wrongful act to the death and therefore the wrongful act does not render defendant civilly liable.

The only cases noted where the wrongful act is considered as within and part of the line of causation is where the wrongful act produces a rage or frenzy or uncontrollable impulse, during which state self-destruction takes place. In *Daniels* v. *New York, N. H. & H. R. Co.* (1903), 183 Mass. 393, 67 N. E. 424, 426, 62 L. R. A. 751, decedent had been injured by a blow on the head in a collision of his automobile with the defendant's train and the injury caused him to become insane. Two months later he took his own life. The court held (p. 399);

> . . . we are of opinion that the liability of a defendant for a death by suicide exists only when the death is the result of an uncontrollable impulse, or is accomplished in delirium or frenzy caused by the collision, and without conscious volition to produce death, having knowledge of the physical nature and consequences of the act. An act of suicide resulting from a moderately intelligent power of choice, even though the choice is determined by a disordered mind, should be deemed a new and independent, efficient cause of death that immediately ensues.

Plaintiffs plead that, as the result of defendant's suggestion that the interviews be terminated, Jeannie suffered mental injury depriving her of her own volition and resulting in her death. In the absence of any allegation of fact in that respect, the statement that her self-destruction was the result of loss of her volition is a mere conclusion. It is also significant that the complaint pleads no facts with respect to Jeannie's activities or mental condition during the period from April 15 to May 27, 1958. There are no facts alleged which, if proved, would establish a cause-effect relationship between the alleged nonfeasance of the defendant and the suicide of the deceased.

In *Laidlaw* v. *Sage* (1899), 158 N.Y. 73, 52 N.E. 679, 688, 44 L. R. A. 216, it was said (p. 99):

> A proximate cause is one in which is involved the idea of necessity. . . . A remote cause is one which is inconclusive in reasoning, because from it no certain conclusion can be legitimately drawn. In other words, a remote cause is a cause the connection between which and the effect is uncertain, vague, or indeterminate. . . . The proximate cause being given, the effect must follow. . . . The remote cause being given, the effect may or may not follow.

At page 757, sec. 4 of the annotations referred to above, 11 A.L.R. (2d), it is further stated:

> As a general rule a person will not be relieved of liability by an intervening force which could reasonably have been foreseen, nor by one which is a normal incident of the risk created. However, if such intervening force takes the form of suicide the practically unanimous rule is that such act is a new and independent agency which does not come within and complete a line of causation from the wrongful act to the death and therefore does not render defendant liable for the suicide.

Under sec. 7 of the same annotation, page 763, is cited *Stevens* v. *Steadman* 1913), 140 Ga. 680, 79 S. E. 564, 47 L.R.A. (N.S.) 1009, where demurrer was sustained to a complaint charging the defendant with an act deliberately designed to bring about the suicide of another. The wrongful act was the writing of a letter allegedly composed in such manner as to produce in the recipient a suicidal state of mind. The court said (pp. 685, 687):

> What is termed fact is, after all, in such cases merely a conclusion of the pleader, though it is set forth as fact and put in the place of a fact among other facts joined together in laying the foundation of the plaintiff's case. . . . Mere positiveness of the terms alleging the psychological results which we have set forth above would not prevent the court from holding, upon demurrer, that the results charged could not have been the known and natural results of the acts charged against the accused.

It is pointed out in succeeding pages, in discussing cases involving the duty owed by private hospitals to their patients, that the law does not require of anyone in the exercise of reasonable care to take measures against a danger which a patient's known mental condition does not suggest as likely to happen. The test of actionable negligence in such cases is not what could have been done to prevent a particular accident but whether the hospital had notice of conduct or language evidencing a purpose to inflict self-injury.

The peculiar difficulty encountered in proving causation in a case of this kind is largely due to the nature of the subject matter. The fact that the deceased, before she came under the defendant's counsel, may already have been afflicted with a condition which would account for her suicide further complicates the issue. In discussing the reluctance of courts to extend any doctrine of recovery for mental distress alone to a situation where the defendant is charged with ordinary negligence, it is said in 64 A.L.R. (2d), Emotional Disturbances, p. 113, sec. 6:

> The contention that because of the nature of the evidentiary problems involved, the judicial process is not well adapted to distinguishing valid from fraudulent claims in

this area, has been recognized as probably the most substantial of the reasons advanced for denying recovery for mental distress or its physical consequences.

A further difficulty is present in this case. Defendant is charged with three acts of negligence. Even assuming he had secured psychiatric treatment for Jeannie or that he had advised her parents of her emotional condition or that he had not suggested termination of the interviews—it would require speculation for a jury to conclude that under such circumstances she would not have taken her life.

By the Court.—Order affirmed.

Previn v. *Tenacre, Inc.*, 70 F.2d 389 (1933)

Appeal from the District Court of the United States for the District of New Jersey.

Action by Arthur G. Previn against Tenacre, Incorporated, and others. Judgment for defendants, and plaintiff appeals.

Affirmed.

Arthur G. Previn, of New York City, and Frederic M. P. Pearse, of Newark, N.J., for appellant.

Arthur F. Egner, of Newark, N.J., for appellees.

Before WOOLLEY, DAVIS, and THOMPSON, Circuit Judges.

DAVIS, Circuit Judge.

This was a suit brought by Arthur G. Previn, plaintiff-appellant, to recover damages from the defendants for injuries which he alleges he suffered by reason of his treatment while a patient at the Christian Science institution of Tenacre, at or near Princeton, N.J., and for the return of compensation of $6,000 procured from him by alleged false and fraudulent representations. Judgment was entered for the defendants, and plaintiff appealed.

The plaintiff was afflicted with what was called "agitated melancholia of the depressive type," from which it was frankly conceded that he has fully recovered. Desiring to be treated in accordance with the Christian Science methods, whereby patients "relinquish all reliance on material remedies and depend solely upon spiritual means for healing as taught in Christian Science" institutions, he went to Tenacre. A pamphlet of the institution, which the plaintiff had seen, and which set forth the spirit and purpose of the institution, stated that "every precaution is taken to safeguard this work by conducting it in strict obedience to the teachings of Christian Science."

He alleges that instead of treating him according to the doctrine, teachings, and practice of Christian Science, the respondents tied him by his hands and feet to his bed and chair, terrorized him by threats to apply (and did apply) clamps or surgical forceps to his tongue and by various other threats to stop him from shouting, used physical force to make him take rides in automobiles, etc., assaulted him, failed to give him competent and experienced nursing and attendance as they promised to do, did not provide a resident graduate physician as required by the laws of New Jersey, and filed with the Department of Institutions and Agencies at Trenton a false and libelous diagnosis of his illness upon his admission to Tenacre.

The respondents testified that they treated the plaintiff in good faith according to the teachings of Christian Science and that the force which they used was only such force as was reasonably necessary to restrain him for his own good and to feed him when he refused to eat.

The learned trial judge submitted to the jury the question as to whether or not the treatment which the plaintiff received at the institution was in accordance with the teachings of Christian Science, and whether or not the force and restraints used by the defendants were reasonably necessary and carefully exercised for the plaintiff's good or whether they were done with a "malicious desire and not for his benefit." He charged that if they exercised reasonable care and used only the force necessary to restrain him and prevent him from injuring himself or them, it did not constitute assault or a cause of action. This was a correct statement of the law and the verdict of the jury for the defendants settles the facts.

He further charged the jury that the report of the disease from which plaintiff was suffering, to the Commissioner of the Department of Institutions and Agencies of New Jersey, was a privileged communication and that the contents of the report were not libelous and did not constitute a cause of action unless the information was "wilfully and maliciously and falsely given, or that it was made in reckless disregard as to whether or not the diagnosis there given was correct or false." There was no error in this charge, *King* v. *Patterson,* 49 N. J. Law, 417, 9 A. 705, 60 Am. Rep. 622, and the verdict of the jury also settles this fact.

As to the return of the $6,000 which the plaintiff alleges was fraudulently procured from him by the defendants, upon false representation as to the treatment and teachings practiced at the institution and to be practiced upon him, the court charged the jury that it was its duty to consider all the facts and from them determine whether or not the representations made by the defendants were false and fraudulent; and that if it found from a fair preponderance of the evidence that they were, it was its duty to allow the plaintiff the sum of $6,000. There was no error in that charge and the jury found that the defendants had not made any false and fraudulent representations.

The plaintiff further alleges that the court erred in permitting the defendants to amend their answer and plead justification for the force used and restraints imposed.

The plaintiff said that the amendment did not take him by surprise. The Practice Act of New Jersey permits inconsistent defenses, Rule 24, P.L. 1912, p. 389, S.C.R., rule 38; and, besides, no exception was taken to the allowance. For these reasons the amendment does not furnish a ground for reversal of the judgment.

We have considered all the assignments of error and have carefully read plaintiff's briefs, but do not find that prejudicial error was committed; and so the judgment is affirmed.

THE STATUTE OF LIMITATIONS

What is the applicable statute of limitations in cases involving unlicensed practitioners who falsely represent themselves to be licensed professionals? The answer to this question, at least according to the Court of Appeals of Michigan, below in *Simpson* v. *Hubert,* 35 Mich.App. 523, 193 N.W.2d 68 (1971), is that the unlicensed person is not entitled to receive the benefit of a shorter statute of limitations for licensed professionals, despite the fact that such a person may be held to the same standard of care as the licensed professional. A more extended discussion of this issue appears in Brazener's "Statute of limitations relating to medical malpractice actions as applicable to actions against unlicensed practitioner," 70 A.L.R.3d 114.

Simpson v. *Hubert*, 35 Mich. App. 523, 193 N.W.2d 68 (1971)

Before: LEVIN, P. J., and QUINN and V. J. BRENNAN, JJ.

LEVIN, J. The complaint of plaintiff, James Simpson, alleges that on March 29, 1967, the defendant, Raymond Hubert, contracted to make a set of dentures and to perform other dental services for the plaintiff. It is further alleged that the defendant was not a licensed dentist, that he falsely represented that he was licensed, and that the services were performed inadequately causing injury and expense to the plaintiff. The complaint states a count sounding in tort for misrepresentation and negligence and a count sounding in contract for breach of contract and warranty.

Plaintiff's action was commenced on March 16, 1970, within the three year limitation period generally applicable to actions to recover damages for injuries to persons and property. See RJA § 5805 (7).[1] The defendant moved to dismiss on the ground that the action was for malpractice and it was not commenced within the two-year limitation period for "actions charging malpractice." See RJA § 5805 (3).[2] The trial judge granted the motion and the plaintiff appeals.

In *Kambas* v. *St. Joseph's Mercy Hospital* (1971), 33 Mich App 127, leave to appeal granted 385 Mich 786, we recently had occasion to consider this statutory provision (RJA § 5805[3])[3] providing a shorter limitation period for actions charging malpractice than for personal injury and property damage actions generally. A divided Court held that an action against a hospital for the negligence of a nurse was an action for malpractice because "malpractice" means an action for the professional misconduct of a person who is "a member of a state-licensed profession." I dissented saying that the term "malpractice," as used in RJA § 5805(3), refers only to actions against physicians, surgeons, or dentists.

The issue which divided the panel of our Court that decided the *Kambas* case need not be reconsidered in order to decide this case. We are persuaded that, for the purposes of RJA § 5805(3), whether an "action charging malpractice" means an action against any member of a state-licensed profession or is limited to actions against physicians, surgeons, or dentists, the Legislature did not intend that the short two-year statute of limitation applicable to actions against licensed professionals would limit the time for bringing an action against an unlicensed practitioner who poses as a licensed professional.

The defendant points out that under the provisions of RJA § 2912,[4] a person claiming to have been injured by the failure of an impostor to conform to the standard

[1]MCLA § 600.5805(7) (Stat Ann 1962 Rev § 27A.5805[7]).

[2]MCLA § 600.5805(3) (Stat Ann 1962 Rev § 27A.5805[3]).

[3]"No person may bring or maintain any action to recover damages for injuries to persons or property unless, after the claim first accrued to himself or to someone through whom he claims, he commences the action within the periods of time prescribed by this section. . . .

"(3) The period of limitations is 2 years for actions charging malpractice." MCLA § 600.5805(3) (Stat Ann 1962 Rev § 27A-.5805[3]).

[4]"(1) A civil action for malpractice may be maintained against any person professing or holding himself out to be a member of a state licensed profession. The rules of the common law applicable to actions against members of a state licensed profession, for malpractice, are applicable against any person who holds himself out to be a member of a state licensed profession.

"(2) Malpractice may be given in evidence in defense to any action for services rendered by the member of a state licensed profession, or person holding himself out to be a member of a state licensed profession." MCLA § 600.2912 (Stat Ann 1962 Rev § 27A.2912).

of care of the profession of which he professes to be a member may maintain an action for malpractice against the impostor and hold him to the standard of care of a member of the profession. In establishing in RJA § 2912 a rule which may have obtained at common law,[5] the Legislature did not thereby address itself to the separate question whether an unlicensed practitioner, an impostor, could avail himself of the short two-year statute of limitation.

RJA § 2912 concerns the standard of care to which an impostor may be held. It does not, although the term "malpractice" is used, purport to extend to impostors the benefit of the short statute of limitations set forth in RJA § 5805(3). As the committee note states, § 2912 "does *not* create a new cause of action. Members of state licensed professions are liable for malpractice at common law, *as are unlicensed persons. What this section does* is to hold the unlicensed person to the *standard of care* to which a member of the state licensed profession would be held . . . ."[6] (Emphasis supplied.)

The question of the standard of care to which an impostor should be held and the question of the appropriate statute of limitations in an action against an impostor are separate questions. Different legislative policies are involved. We decline to infer from the codification of the rule concerning the standard of care a legislative purpose to shorten the statute of limitations in actions against impostors from what it was before the Revised Judicature Act was enacted.[7] Relevant is the committee note that "existing time periods have been used."[8]

"In the codification of statutes the general presumption obtains that the codifiers did not intend to change the law; and mere changes of phraseology or punctuation, or the addition or omission of words, or the rearrangement of sections or parts of a statute, or the placing of portions of what formerly was a single section in separate sections, does not operate to change the operation, effect or meaning of the statute unless the changes are of such nature as to manifest clearly and unmistakably a legislative intent to change the former law." *State, ex rel. Johnson* v. *Broderick* (1947), 75 ND 340, 343 (27 NW2d 849, 852).[9]

Construing the two sections (RJA § 2912 and RJA § 5805[3]) together, we hold that the short two-year statute of limitation applies only to action against licensed

[5]See Hawkins, Practice Commentary, MCLA § 600.2912, pp 657, 658, where the following appears:

"Legislative history of the predecessors of RJA § 2912 is carefully analyzed in *Leslie* v. *Mollica* (1926), 236 Mich 610 (211 NW 267). As observed in that opinion, 'Whether this declared more than the common-law rule is questionable.' 236 Mich at 614. That is, notwithstanding the contrary suggestion in the Committee Comment, it is probably the common-law rule, without regard to the statute, that an unlicensed practitioner who holds himself out as belonging to a particular profession or specialty will be judged by the standards he professes, rather than the lower standards of a layman."

The committee note states that "unlicensed persons are held at present" to the standard of care of a layman.

Whether the committee or Professor Hawkins is right about the state of preexisting law, the only question under consideration when § 2912 was drafted was the standard of care. As the committee note itself states, "what this section does" is to hold impostors to the professional standard of care. That is the purpose of § 2912, and no more.

[6]See committee note reprinted as annotation to MCLA § 600.2912 (Stat Ann 1962 Rev § 27A.2912). See discussion of the committee note in fn 5.

[7]Under prior law, the two-year statute applied only to an action for malpractice brought against "physicians, surgeons or dentists." See CL 1948, § 609.13 (Stat Ann § 27.605).

[8]See committee note reprinted as annotation to MCLA § 600.5805 (Stat Ann 1962 Rev § 27A.5805).

[9]Similarly, see *United States* v. *Thompson* (CA2, 1963), 319 F2d 665, 669; *City of Redfield* v. *Wharton* (1962), 79 SD 557, 564 (115 NW2d 329, 332); *Wilson* v. *Miller* (1957), 144 Conn 212 (128 A2d 894); *Austro-Hungarian Consul* v. *Westphal* (1912), 120 Minn 122 (139 NW 300).

professionals.[10] The standard of care, whether the action is against an impostor or a true member of the profession, is the same; both are required to conform to the standard of care of a member of the profession.

Our decision makes it unnecessary to decide whether a person who claims he was injured by an impostor may waive the professional standard of care and sue the impostor for negligence or on some other theory and, if so, what would be the standard of care in such a case. It is also unnecessary to consider whether an action for deceit, separate and apart from a malpractice action, may be maintained against a professional person or an impostor[11] and, if so, whether a different statute of limitations might govern.[12]

Reversed and remanded for trial. Costs to plaintiff.

All concurred.

REFERENCE FOR CHAPTER VI

HARRIS, M. Tort liability of the psychotherapist. *University of San Francisco Law Review,* 1973, *8,* 405–436.

[10]We express no opinion as to the issue decided in *Kambas* v. *St. Joseph's Mercy Hospital* (1971), 33 Mich App 127.

[11]Here, it is alleged that the whole relationship was founded on deceit and tainted by it. But for the defendant's deceit, the plaintiff might never have subjected himself to treatment by the defendant. It would be anomalous to say that in such a case the injured person is limited to the form of action which evolved in cases where the defendants were true members of the profession.

[12]Our Supreme Court has indicated that an action for malpractice may not be the exclusive remedy. See *Johnson* v. *Caldwell* (1963), 371 Mich 368, 380, *et seq.*

In other jurisdictions, courts have held, in cases where a statute of limitations defense was raised, that malpractice is not the exclusive theory. In *McAlpin* v. *Browne* (1958), 15 Misc 2d 255, 257 (181 NYS2d 525, 527), the Court ruled that where "the deceit [or the professional person] is not with respect to the manner of performance of the contract or of any incident thereof, but rather with respect to the stated fact" an action for breach of contract or misrepresentation may be maintained; in so holding the court said that if the breach alleged was for negligent performance, then despite the nomenclature of plaintiff's theory it would constitute an action for malpractice. Similarly, see *Volk* v. *McCormick* (1969), 41 Wis 2d 654 (165 NW2d 185) (physician alleged to have falsely told patient she was not injured by operation he performed for purpose of inducing her to refrain from seeking medical or legal assistance); *Krestich* v. *Stefanez* (1943), 243 Wis 1 (9 NW2d 130) (surgeon knowingly and falsely represented to patient that needles left in her abdomen during surgery had been found and removed). *Contra, Stacey* v. *Pantano* (1964), 177 Neb 694 (131 NW2d 163) (alleged misrepresentation by physician as to nature and cause of postoperative condition). See, also, *Calabrese* v. *Bickley* (1956), 1 App Div 2d 874 (150 NYS2d 542) *modifying* 208 Misc 407 (143 N'S2d 846).

Bibliography

BEHAVIOR MODIFICATION

BALL, T. S. Issues and implications of operant conditioning: The re-establishment of social behavior. *Hospital and Community Psychiatry,* 1968, *19,* 230–232.

BRAGG, R. A., & WAGNER, M. K. Issues and implications of operant conditioning: Can deprivation be justified? *Hospital and Community Psychiatry,* 1968, *19,* 229–230.

CAHOON, D. C. Issues and implications of operant conditioning: Balancing procedures against outcomes. *Hospital and Community Psychiatry,* 1968, *19,* 228–229.

FINKEL, N. J. *Therapy and ethics.* New York: Grune & Stratton, 1980.

LUCERO, R. J., & VAIL, D. J. Authors' response: Public policy and public responsibility. *Hospital and Community Psychiatry,* 1968, *19,* 232–233.

LUCERO, R. J., VAIL, D. J., & SCHERBER, J. Regulating operant conditioning programs. *Hospital and Community Psychiatry,* 1968, *19,* 232–233.

MARTIN, R. *Legal challenges to behavior modification.* Champaign, Ill.: Research Press, 1975.

MIRON, N. B. A final rejoinder. In R. Ulrich, T. Stachnik, & J. Mabry (Eds.), *Control of human behavior* (Vol. 2). Glenview, Ill.: Scott, Foresman & Company, 1970.

MIRON, N. B. The primary ethical consideration, *Hospital and Community Psychiatry,* 1968, *19,* 226–228.

ROGERS, C. R., & SKINNER, B. F. Some issues concerning the control of human behavior: A symposium. *Science,* 1956, *124,* 1057–1066.

WEXLER, D. B. Token and taboo: Behavior modification, token economies and the law. *California Law Review,* 1973, *61,* 81–109.

CONSTITUTIONAL ISSUES

BERNARD, J. L. The significance for psychology of *O'Conner* v. *Donaldson. American Psychologist,* 1977, *32,* 1085–1088.

HANNAH, G. T., CHRISTIAN, W. P., and CLARK, H. B. (Eds.). *Preservation of client rights*. New York: The Free Press, 1981.

KELLEY, V. R., & WESTON, H. B. Civil liberties in mental health facilities. *Social Work,* 1974, *19,* 48-54.

SERBAN, G., & GIDYNSKI, C. B. Schizophrenic patients in community: Legal misinterpretations of "right to treatment." *New York State Journal of Medicine,* 1974, *74,* 1977-1981.

SIEGAL, R. A. The significance for psychology of *O'Conner* v. *Donaldson*: A reply to Bernard. *American Psychologist,* 1978, *33,* 858-861.

WATERMAN, A. S. The civil liberties of the participants in psychological research. *American Psychologist,* 1974, *29,* 470-471.

COUNTERSUITS

BARD, N. Physicians' countersuits—a New York view. *Trial Lawyers Quarterly,* 1978, *12,* 16-28.

BIRNBAUM, S. L. Physicians counterattack: Liability of lawyers for instituting unjustified medical malpractice actions. *Fordham Law Review,* 1977, *45,* 1003-1092.

CAVANAUGH, S. W. Countersuit: A viable alternative for the wrongfully sued physician? *Washburn Law Journal,* 1980, *19,* 450-466.

GREENBAUM, H. Physician countersuits: A cause without action. *Pacific Law Journal,* 1981, *12,* 745-762.

HIGGS, J. G. Physicians countersuits—a solution to the malpractice dilemma? *Drake Law Review,* 1978-1979, *28,* 81-95.

REUTER, S. R. Physician countersuits: A catch-22. *University of San Francisco Law Review,* 1980, *14,* 203-237.

SINGER, A. R., & GIAMPIETRO, W. B. Countersuits. *Litigation,* 1979, *6,* 18-23.

SPENCE, J. B. Closing the courthouse doors: Florida's spurious claims statute. *Stetson Law Review,* 1981, *10,* 397-426.

ELECTROSHOCK THERAPY

ANDREN, H. E. Treatment or mistreatment in psychiatry (observations on electroconvulsive therapy). *Diseases of the Nervous System,* 1976, *37,* 605-609.

ARNOT, R. E. Observations on the effects of electric convulsive treatments in man—psychological. *Diseases of the Nervous System,* 1975, *36,* 499-502.

ASNIS, G. M., FINK, M., & SAFERSTEIN, S. ECT in metropolitan New York hospitals: A survey of practice, 1975-1976. *American Journal of Psychiatry,* 1978, *135,* 479-482.

BERNSTEIN, I. C., BERNSTEIN, D. M., & ADZICK, G. R. Legal aspects of electro-therapy in a catatonic renal transplant patient. *The Journal of Clinical Psychiatry,* 1978, *39,* 252-253.

BUTTERFIELD, W. H. Electric shock—hazards in aversive shock conditioning of humans. *Behavioral Engineering,* 1975, *3,* 1-28.

GORDON, H. L. Fifty shock therapy theories. *Military Surgeon,* 1948, *103,* 397-401.

KROUNER, L. W. Shock therapy and psychiatric malpractice: The legal accommodations to a controversial treatment. *Journal of Forensic Sciences,* 1975, *20,* 404-405.

MOORE, E. Legislative control of shock treatment. *University of San Francisco Law Review,* 1975, *9,* 738-780.

Public opinion, law limit use of ECT as data show efficacy. *Clinical Psychiatry News,* April 1978, pp. 1; 16.

ETHICS

ALPER, P. R. Our irresponsible bar association. *Private Practice,* April 1974, pp. 31; 34; 36; 41; 42.

AMERICAN PSYCHIATRIC ASSOCIATION. The principles of medical ethics with annotations especially applicable to psychiatry. *American Journal of Psychiatry,* 1973, *130,* 1057-1064.

AMERICAN PSYCHOLOGICAL ASSOCIATION. Ethical Standards of Psychologists (1977 Revision). Washington, D.C.: Author, 1977.

BIEBER, I. A discussion of "Homosexuality: The Ethical Challenge." *Journal of Consulting and Clinical Psychology,* 1976, *44,* 163-166.

COHEN, R. J. Comments on the "cattle-prod controversy." *Perceptual and Motor Skills,* 1976, *42,* 146.

COHEN, R. J. Dr. Cohen replies. *American Journal of Psychiatry,* 1976, *133,* 1348-1349.

COHEN, R. J. Is dying being worked to death? *American Journal of Psychiatry,* 1976, *133,* 575-577.

COHEN, R. J. Loyalty or legality in obedience: Note on the Watergate proceedings. *Psychological Reports,* 1973, *33,* 964.

COHEN, R. J. Reich, antipodal legitimacy, and communication in psychology. *American Psychologist,* 1977, *32,* 985-986.

COHEN, R. J. Socially reinforced obsessing: A reply. *Journal of Consulting and Clinical Psychology,* 1977, *45,* 1166-1171.

COHEN, R. J., & SMITH, F. J. Socially reinforced obsessing: Etiology of a disorder in a Christian Scientist. *Journal of Consulting and Clinical Psychology,* 1976, *44,* 142-144.

DAVISON, G. C. Homosexuality: The ethical challenge. *Journal of Consulting and Clinical Psychology,* 1976, *44,* 157-162.

GERGEN, K. F. The codification of research ethics: Views of a doubting Thomas. *American Psychologists,* 1973, *28,* 907-912.

INGELFINGER, F. J. The unethical in medical ethics. *Annals of Internal Medicine,* 1975, *83,* 264-269.

JOHNSON, A. F. Comment on Gergen. *American Psychologist,* 1974, *29,* 470.

LITTLE, R. B., & STRECKER, E. A. Moot questions in psychiatric ethics. *American Journal of Psychiatry,* 1956, *113,* 455-460.

LONDON, P. Psychotherapy for religious neuroses? Comments on Cohen and Smith. *Journal of Consulting and Clinical Psychology,* 1976, *44*, 145-147.

MCLEMORE, C. W., & COURT, J. H. Religion and psychotherapy—ethics, civil liberties, and clinical savvy: A critique. *Journal of Consulting and Clinical Psychology,* 1977, *5,* 1172-1175.

NEWMAN, A. S. Ethical issues in the supervision of psychotherapy. *Professional Psychology,* 1981, *12,* 690-695.

STOKES, J. B. Comment on "Socially reinforced obsessing: Etiology of a disorder in a Christian Scientist." *Journal of Consulting and Clinical Psychology,* 1977, *45,* 1164-1165.

WEST, L. J. Ethical psychiatry and biosocial humanism. *American Journal of Psychiatry,* 1969, *126,* 226-230.

MALPRACTICE INSURANCE

ASHER, J. Confusion reigns in APA malpractice plan. *APA Monitor,* March 1976, *1,* 11.

BECK, L. C., KALOGREDIS, V. J., & CYNWYD, B. Should the solo physician insure his corporation? *Pennsylvania Medicine,* 1977, *80,* (1), 23-24.

"Going bare" becomes popular in South, West. *MLC Commentary,* 1976, *3* (3), 2-3.

Insurance industry cites cultural trends as problem. *MLC Commentary,* 1976, *3* (1), 3-4.

TRENT, C. L., & MUHL, W. P. Professional liability insurance and the American psychiatrist. *American Journal of Psychiatry*, 1975, *132*, 1312-1314.

MALPRACTICE AND THE PSYCHIATRIST

BELLAMY, W. A. Malpractice risks confronting the psychiatrist: A nationwide fifteen-year study of appellate court cases, 1946 to 1961. *American Journal of Psychiatry,* 1962, *118,* 769-779.

CARPENTER, T. Murder on a day pass. *The Village Voice,* February 25, 1980, pp. 1; 23-27.

CASSIDY, P. S. The liability of psychiatrists for malpractice. *University of Pittsburgh Law Review,* 1974, *36,* 108-137.

DAWIDOFF, D. J. *The malpractice of psychiatrists.* Springfield, Ill.: Charles C. Thomas, 1973.

DAWIDOFF, D. J. Some suggestions to psychiatrists for avoiding legal jeopardy. *Archives of General Psychiatry,* 1973, *29,* 699-701.

DAVIDSON, H. A. Legal and ethical aspects of psychiatric research. *American Journal of Psychiatry,* 1969, *126,* 237-240.

FELDMAN, W. S. Who decides admission—Judge or physician? *Legal Aspects of Medical Practice,* March 1978, p. 8.

HAMILTON, J. M. Malpractice from the private practice and institutional psychiatric viewpoint. *Maryland State Medical Journal,* January 1970, *19,* pp. 69-74.

MESSINGER, S. Malpractice suits: The psychiatrist's turn. *The Journal of Legal Medicine,* 1975, *3,* 31-39.

MORSE, H. N. Liability of the psychiatrist. *Syracuse Law Review,* 1967, *18,* 691-727.

ROTHBLATT, H. B., & LEROY, D. H. Avoiding psychiatric malpractice. *California Western Law Review,* 1973, *9,* 260-272.

SADOFF, R. L. New malpractice concerns for the psychiatrist. *Legal Aspects of Medical Practice,* March 1978, pp. 31-35.

SLAWSON, P. F. Psychiatric malpractice: A regional incidence study. *American Journal of Psychiatry,* 1970, *126,* 136-139.

MALPRACTICE AND THE PSYCHOLOGIST

APPLEMAN, J. A. Professional liability of psychologists. *American Psychologist,* 1953, *8,* 686-690.

ATTHOWE, J. M., JR. Legal and ethical accountability in everyday practice. *Behavioral Engineering,* 1975, *3,* 25-38.

BERSOFF, D. N. Professional ethics and legal responsibilities: On the horns of a dilemma. *Journal of School Psychology,* 1975, *13,* 359-376.

CAREY, J. P. Business ethics, employee privacy and the management of insurance information. *Review of Business,* 1981, *3,* 21-24.

JUROW, G. L. & MARIANO, W. E. Law and private practice. In G. D. Goldman & G. Stricker (Eds.), *Practical problems for a private psychotherapy practice.* Springfield, Ill.: Charles C. Thomas, 1972.

KNAPP, S., & VANDECREEK, L. Behavioral medicine: Its malpractice risks for psychologists. *Professional Psychology,* 1981, *12,* 677-683.

KOVACS, A. Implications of the malpractice crisis for training of graduate students. In A. H. Canter (Chair.), *Insurance crisis and psychotherapy.* Symposium presented at the 84th annual convention of the American Psychological Association, Washington, D.C., 1976.

KRAUSKOPF, J. M., & KRAUSKOPF, C. J. Torts and psychologists. *Journal of Counseling Psychology,* 1965, *12,* 227-237.

MCDERMOTT, P. A. Law, liability, and the school psychologist: Systems of law, privileged communication, and access to records. *Journal of School Psychology,* 1972, *10,* 299-305.

Psychologist faces malpractice charges. *APA Monitor,* 1972, *3* (9, 10), 167.

MALPRACTICE AND THE UNLICENSED THERAPIST OR COUNSELOR

GLASS, L. L., KIRSCH, M. A., & PARRIS, F. N. Psychiatric disturbances associated with Erhard Seminars Training: I. A report of cases. *American Journal of Psychiatry,* 1977, *134,* 245-247.

HARRIS, M. Tort liability of the psychotherapist. *University of San Francisco Law Review,* 1973, *8,* 405-436.

JAFFEE, S. J., & SHERL, D. J. Acute psychosis precipitated by T-group experience. *Archives of General Psychiatry,* 1969, *21,* 443-449.

RUBENSTEIN, I. H. Malpractice against Christian Science practitioners. *Medical Trial Technique Quarterly,* 1979, *25,* 372-383.

YALOM, I. D., & LIEBERMAN, M. A. A study of encounter group casualties. *Archives of General Psychiatry,* 1971, *25,* 16-30.

MEDICATION AND MALPRACTICE

APPLETON, W. S. Legal problems in psychiatric drug prescription. *American Journal of Psychiatry,* 1968, *124,* 877-882.

CARSTAIRS, G. M. A land of lotus eaters? *American Journal of Psychiatry,* 1969, *125,* 1576-1580.

DEMARCO, C. T. *Pharmacy and the law.* Germantown, Md.: Aspen Systems Corporation, 1975.

FEEGEL, J. F. Malpractice and lab tests. *Resident and Staff Physician,* April 1974, 47-50.

GREENBLATT, D. J., SHADER, R. I., & KOCH-WEBER, J. Psychotropic drug use in the Boston area. *Archives of General Psychiatry,* 1975, *32,* 518-521.

GOTTLIEB, R. M., NAPPI, T., & STRAIN, J. J. The physician's knowledge of psychotropic drugs: Preliminary results. *American Journal of Psychiatry,* 1978, *135,* 29-32.

Journal of the American Pharmaceutical Association. Pharmacies fall short of legal, professional responsibilities. *Author,* 1977, *17,* (1), 62.

LENNARD, H. J., EPSTEIN, L. J., BERNSTEIN, A., & RANSOM, D. C. Hazards implicit in prescribing psychoactive drugs. *Science,* 1970, *169,* 438-441.

MILLS, D. H. Malpractice and drugs. *Resident and Staff Physician,* April 1974, pp. 35-39; 42; 44.

MULLER, C. The overmedicated society: Forces in the marketplace for medical care. *Science,* 1972, *176,* 488-492.

MYERS, M. J., & FINK, J. L. Liability aspects of drug product selection. *Journal of the American Pharmaceutical Association,* 1977, *NS 17,* 33-35.

Pharmacists fall short of legal, professional responsibilities. *Journal of the American Pharmaceutical Association,* 1977, *NS 17* (1), 62.

PRIVACY, PRIVILEGE, CONFIDENTIALITY, AND CONSENT

ALDRICK, R. *Health records and confidentiality: An annotated bibliography with abstracts.* Washington, D.C.: National Commission on Confidentiality of Health Records, October 1977.

American Psychiatric Association, Task Force on Automation and Data Processing. *Automation and data processing in psychiatry.* Washington, D.C.: Author, 1971.

ANNAS, G. J. Confidentiality and the duty to warn. *The Hastings Center Report,* 1976, *6,* 6.

ANNAS, G. J. Informed consent. *Annual Review of Medicine,* 1978, *29,* 9.

ARLEIGH, R. Could you be sued for invasion of privacy? Suit involving teaching records. *Medical Economist,* April 2, 1973, pp. 77-83.

BERNSTEIN, A. H. Law in brief: Unauthorized disclosure of confidential information. *Hospitals,* 1974, *48* (121), 126.

BERNSTEIN, B. E. The social worker as a courtroom witness, *Social Casework,* 1975, *56,* 521-525.

BUTLER, R. N. Privileged communication and confidentiality in research. *Archives of General Psychiatry,* 1963, *8,* 139.

"Case Notes: *Roe* v. *Doe*: A remedy for disclosure of psychiatric confidence. *Rutgers Law Review,* 1975, *29,* 190-209.

CLARK, K. E. Privacy and behavioral research. *International Journal of Psychiatry,* 1968, *5,* 496-502.

CURRAN, W. J. Confidentiality and the prediction of dangerousness in psychiatry. *New England Journal of Medicine,* 1975, *293* (5), 185-186.

Duty to warn vs. confidentiality is conflict that can be resolved. *Clinical Psychiatry News,* April 1978, pp. 2; 38.

EGER, C. L. Psychotherapists' liability for extrajudicial breaches of confidentiality. *Arizona Law Review,* 1976, *18,* 1061-1094.

FISCHER, C. T. Consent to release of what? *Professional Psychology,* Summer 1970, p. 424.

FOSTER, L. M. Do you want to share your therapy tapes with the court? *Professional Psychology,* 1974, *5,* 369-373.

FOSTER, L. M. Privileged communication: When the psychiatrists envy the clergy. *Journal of Pastoral Care,* 1976, *33,* 116-121.

GINSBERG, F., & CLARKE, B. Patients need privacy—and may sue if they don't get it. *Modern Hospital,* 1972, *118,* (6), 110.

GOBERT, J. J. Accommodating patient rights and computerized mental health systems. *North Carolina Law Review,* 1976, *54,* 153-187.

GORDON, R. E., & BARNARD, G. W. Why a patient should never get a copy of his psychiatric report. *Consultant,* December 1974, pp. 110-111.

GROSSMAN, M. Insurance reports as a threat to confidentiality. *American Journal of Psychiatry,* 1971, *128,* 96-100.

GUREVITZ, H. *Tarasoff*: Protective privilege versus public peril. *American Journal of Psychiatry,* 1977, *134,* 289-292.

HARDY, C. T., JR. Is the wrong person listening? *Hospital Physician,* October 1965, p. 195.

HARE-MUSTIN, R. T., MARECEK, J., KAPLAN, A. G., & LISS-LEVINSON, N. Rights of clients, responsibilities of therapists. *American Psychologist,* 1979, *34,* 3-16.

HOFMANN, A. D. Confidentiality and the health care records of children and youth. *Psychiatric Opinion,* 1975, *12,* 20-28.

KEDWARD, H. B., et al. Computers and psychiatric data recording: Rationale and problems of confidentiality. *Comprehensive Psychiatry,* 1973, *14,* 133-137.

KNERR, C. R. Compulsory disclosure to the courts of research sources and data. Symposium on Privacy, Public Policy ("The Law") and the Practice of Psychology. APA 84th Annual Convention. Washington, D.C., September 7, 1976.

LOUISELL, D. W. The psychologist in today's legal world: Part II; confidential communication. *Minnesota Law Review,* 1957, *41,* 731-750.

MACDONALD, J. B. Confidentiality of patient information: A new basis of physician liability? *Journal of Medical Association of Georgia,* December 1974, pp. 517-529.

MEDINI, G., & ROSENBERG, E. H. Gossip and psychotherapy. *American Journal of Psychotherapy,* 1976, *30,* 473.

MEISEL, A., ROTH, L. H., & LIDZ, C. W. Toward a model of the legal doctrine of informed consent. *American Journal of Psychiatry,* 1977, *134,* 285-289.

MILLER, A. R. The assault on privacy. *Psychiatric Opinion,* January 1975, pp. 6-14.

MORRISON, J. K., FEDERICO, M., & ROSENTHAL, H. J. Contracting confidentiality in group psychotherapy. *Journal of Forensic Psychology,* 1975, *7,* 1-6.

POWLEDGE, F. The therapist as double agent. *Psychology Today.* July 1977, pp. 44-47.

RAVITCH, M. M. Informed consent: Descent to absurdity. *Resident and Staff Physician,* April 1974, pp. 10s-12s; 16s; 20s.

ROTH, L. H., MEISEL, A., & LIDZ, C. W. Tests of competency to consent to treatment. *American Journal of Psychiatry,* 1977, *134,* 279-284.

SADOFF, R. L. The importance of informed consent. *Journal of Legal Medicine,* May/June 1973, pp. 25-27.

SIEGEL, M. Confidentiality. *Clinical Psychologist,* 1976, *30,* 1.

SIMMONS, D. D. Client attitudes toward release of confidential information without consent. *Journal of Clinical Psychology,* 1968, *24,* 364-365.

SINNETT, E. R., & THETFORD, P. E. Protecting clients and assessing malpractice. *Professional Psychology,* 1975, *6,* 117-126.

SPEAKER, F. Informed consent decision offers comfort. *Pennsylvania Medicine,* 1977, *80* (1), 13.

SWAN, P. M. Privacy and record keeping: Remedies for the misuse of accurate information. *North Carolina Law Review,* 1976, *54,* 585-621.

WATSON, A. S. Levels of confidentiality in the psychoanalytic situation. *Journal of the American Psychoanalytic Association,* 1972, *20,* 156-176.

WHITE, T. H. Why the jailing of Farber "terrifies me." *The New York Times Magazine,* November 26, 1978, pp. 27; 70; 72; 74; 76; 78; 82.

WILSON, S. J. *Confidentiality in social work.* New York: The Free Press, 1978.

WISKOFF, M. Ethical standards and divided loyalties. *American Psychologist,* 1960, *15,* 656-660.

PROFESSIONAL LIABILITY: GENERAL ISSUES

ALTON, W. G., JR. *Malpractice: A trial lawyer's advice for physicians.* Boston: Little, Brown, 1977.

BALLIETT, G. 13 ways to protect yourself against malpractice suits. *Resident and Staff Physician,* April 1974, pp. 70-73; 75.

BERNSTEIN, B. E. Legal and social interface in counseling homosexual clients. *Social Casework,* 1977, *58,* 36-40.

BERNSTEIN, B. E. Malpractice: An ogre on the horizon. *Social Work,* 1978, *23,* 106-112.

CLINE, E. J. Viewpoints: The malpractice problem. *Michigan Medicine,* 1973, *72,* 67-68.

COHEN, R. J. *Malpractice: A guide for mental health professionals.* New York: The Free Press, 1979.

CURRAN, W. J. Legal liability in clinical investigations. *The New England Journal of Medicine,* 1978, *298,* 778-779.

CURRAN, W. J. The lawyers' role in medical malpractice claims. *The New England Journal of Medicine,* 1977, *296,* 24-25.

DAWIDOFF, D. J. Insanity, intimacy and infidelity: Trends in psychiatric malpractice. *Trial,* June 1977, pp. 27-30.

EPSTEIN, R. A. Medical malpractice: The case for contract. *American Bar Foundation Research Journal,* 1976, *87,* 96-149.

GREEN, R. K., & COX, G. Social work and malpractice: A converging course. *Social Work,* 1978, *23,* 100-105.

GREENE, P. W. Viewpoints: The malpractice problem. *Michigan Medicine,* 1973, *72,* 67.

HARRIS, M. Tort liability of the psychotherapist. *University of San Francisco Law Review,* 1973, *8,* 405-436.

HERSHEY, N., & MILLER, R. D. *Human experimentation and the law.* Germantown, Md.: Aspen Systems Corporation, 1976.

KENNEDY, C. A. Injuries precipitated by psychotherapy: Liability without fault as a basis for recovery. *South Dakota Law Review,* Spring 1975, *20,* 401-417.

KING, J. H. *The law of medical malpractice.* St. Paul, Minn.: West Publishing Company, 1977.

LEDAKOWICH, A. A case of unreported child abuse. *Resident and Staff Physician,* August 1976, p. 37.

LEDAKOWICH, A. Child abuse decision reversed by Supreme Court of California. *Resident and Staff Physician,* January 1977, p. 112.

LEDAKOWICH, A. An erroneous prediction of death. *Resident and Staff Physician,* October 1976, p. 25.

LEDAKOWICH, A. Malpractice case report. *Resident and Staff Physician,* March 1972, p. 84

LEDAKOWICH, A. Malpractice case report. *Resident and Staff Physician,* April 1972, p. 60.

LEDAKOWICH, A. Malpractice case report. *Resident and Staff Physician,* October 1973, p. 38.

LEDAKOWICH, A. From a malpractice lawyer's casebook (Surgical Rounds). *Resident and Staff Physician,* April 1974, pp. 1s; 2s; 4s; 5s; 9s.

LEDAKOWICH, A. Is fear of the future compensible? *Resident and Staff Physician,* May 1976, p. 18.

MIDDLETON, B. M. The implications of malpractice suits. *Maryland State Medical Journal,* 1970, *19,* 78-79.

MILLER, D., & Burt, R. A. Children's rights on entering therapeutic institutions. *American Journal of Psychiatry,* 1977, *134,* 153-156.

PARKER, D. Some legal implications for personnel officers. *Journal of the National Association of Women Deans and Counselors,* 1961, *24,* 198-202.

PROSSER, W. L. *Law of torts* (4th ed.). St. Paul, Minn.: West Publishing, 1971.

Roche Report Frontiers of Psychiatry. "Mal-psychotherapy" suits may soon beset psychiatrists. *Author,* March 1, 1978, pp. 1-2.

ROSTON, R. A., & SHERRER, C. W. Malpractice: What's new? *Professional Psychology,* August 1973, pp. 270-276.

Six court decisions of current interest. *Resident and Staff Physician,* 1974, *20* (4), 96; 98; 100; 102; 104-105; 119-120.

Six ways to reduce malpractice suits. *Resident and Staff Physician,* 1977, *23* (4), 25s-27s; 30s.

SMITH, F. M. Whose malpractice crisis? *The Journal of the Louisiana State Medical Society,* 1975, *127,* 293-297.

SPADONI, A. J. Legal rights vs. patient needs. *Illinois Medical Journal,* 1977, *151,* 86.

STONE, A. A. Recent mental health litigation: A critical perspective. *American Journal of Psychiatry,* 1977, *134,* 273-279.

TARSHIS, C. B. Liability for psychotherapy. *Faculty of Law Review, University of Toronto,* 1972, *30,* 75-96.

SEXUAL IMPROPRIETIES

BUTLER, S. *Sexual contact between therapists and patients.* Unpublished doctoral dissertation, California School of Professional Psychology (Los Angeles), 1975.

BUTLER, S., & ZELEN, S. L. Sexual intimacies between therapists and patients. *Psychotherapy: Theory, Research, and Practice,* Summer 1977, *14,* 139-145.

DAHLBERG, C. Sexual contact between patient and therapist. *Contemporary Psychoanalysis,* 1970, *6,* 107-124.

DAVIDSON, V. Psychiatry's problem with no name: Therapist-patient sex. *American Journal of Psychoanalysis,* 1977, *37,* 43-50.

DEMAC, D. Masters blasts innumerable patient rapes. *Hospital Tribune,* 1975, *9*(13), 1.

FINNEY, J. C. Therapist and patient after hours. *American Journal of Psychotherapy,* 1975, *29,* 593-602.

FREEMAN, L., & ROY, J. *Betrayal.* New York: Stein & Day, 1976.

HOLROYD, J. C., & BRODSKY, A. M. Psychologists' attitudes and practices regarding erotic and nonerotic physical contact with patients. *American Psychologist,* 1977, *32,* 843-849.

KARDENER, S. H., FULLER, M., & MENSH, I. N. A survey of physicians' attitudes and practices regarding erotic and nonerotic contact with patients. *American Journal of Psychiatry,* 1973, *130,* 1077-1081.

LIEF, H. I. Sexual activity with patients. *Medical Aspects of Human Sexuality,* April 1978, pp. 55; 57.

McCARTNEY, J. L. Overt transference. *Journal of Sex Research,* 1966, *2,* 227-237.

MACKLIN, R. Ethics, sex research and sex therapy. *The Hastings Center Report,* 1976, *6,* 5-7.

MARMOR, J. Sexual acting-out in psychotherapy. *American Journal of Psychoanalysis,* 1972, *32,* 3-8.

MARMOR, J. Some psychodynamic aspects of the seduction of patients in psychotherapy. *The American Journal of Psychoanalysis,* 1976, *36,* 319-323.

PERRY, J. A. Physicians' erotic and nonerotic physical involvement with patients. *American Journal of Psychiatry,* 1976, *133,* 838-840.

SHEPARD, M. The love treatment: *Sexual intimacy between patients and psychotherapists.* New York: Peter H. Wyden, 1971.

SIASSI, I., & THOMAS, M. Physicians and the new sexual freedom. *American Journal of Psychiatry,* 1973, *130,* 1256-1257.

TAYLOR, B. J., & WAGNER, N. N. Sex between therapists and clients: A review and analysis. *Professional Psychology,* 1976, *7,* 593-601.

VOTH, H. M. Love affair between doctor and patient. *American Journal of Psychotherapy,* 1972, *26,* 394-400.

SUICIDE

LESSE, S. Editorial comment. *American Journal of Psychotherapy,* 1965, *19,* 105.

PERR, I. N. Liability of hospital and psychiatrist in suicide. *American Journal of Psychiatry,* 1965, *122,* 631-638.

SCHWARTZ, V. E. Civil liability for causing suicide: A synthesis of law and psychiatry. *Vanderbilt Law Review,* 1971, *24,* 217-256.

SILVING, H. Suicide and law. In N. L. Farberow and E. Shneidman (Eds.), *Clues to suicide.* New York: McGraw-Hill, 1957.

SUPERVISION: LEGAL AND ACADEMIC ISSUES

ALLEN, A. A note on the making of a psychiatrist: The transition from resident to private practitioner. *Psychiatry,* 1971, *34,* 410-418.

ARLOW, J. A. The supervisory situation. *Journal of American Psychoanalysis,* 1963, *11,* 576-594.

ARBUCKLE, D. S. The learning of counseling: Process not product. *Journal of Counseling Psychology,* 1963, *10,* 163-168.

AUSTIN, L. N. Basic principles of supervision. *Social Casework,* 1952, *33,* 411-419.

BARNAT, M. R. Some characteristics of supervisory identification psychotherapy. *Psychotherapy: Theory, Research, and Practice,* 1974, *11,* 189-192.

BARNAT, M. R. Student reactions to the first supervisory year: Relationship and resolutions. *Education for Social Work,* Fall 1973, pp. 3-8.

BARNAT, M. R. Student reactions to supervision: Quests for a contract. *Professional Psychology,* 1973, *4,* 17-12.

BEISER, H. R. Self-listening during supervision of psychotherapy. *Archives of General Psychiatry,* 1966, *15,* 135-139.

BENEDEK, E. P. Training the woman resident to be a psychiatrist. *American Journal of Psychiatry,* 1973, *130,* 1131-1135.

BERGER, D., & GREEBURY, D. R. The acquisition of psychotherapy skills: A learning model and some guidelines for instructors. *Canadian Psychiatric Association Journal,* 1973, *18,* 467-472.

BLATT, S. J. The objective and subjective modes: Some considerations in the teaching of clinical skills. *Journal of Projective Techniques,* 1963, *27,* 151-157.

BOOK, H. E. On maybe becoming a psychotherapist, perhaps. *Canadian Psychiatric Association Journal,* 1973, *18,* 487-493.

BRILL, A. A. *Basic principles of psychoanalysis.* New York: Doubleday, 1949.

BRUGGEN, R., CAESAR, G., FRANK, A., et al. Peer supervision as a method of learning psychotherapy. *Comprehensive Psychiatry,* 1962, *3,* 47-53.

BURGUM, M., DURKIN, H., GONDOR, L. H., et al. The therapeutic implications of supervision. *American Journal of Orthopsychiatry,* 1959, *29,* 357-363.

BURY, J. A., LABRIE, J., & POMERLEAU, G. Apprentissage de la psychotherapie en première année de résidence. Rle de la supervision. *Canadian Psychiatric Association Journal,* 1953, *18,* 481-486.

CHESSICK, R. D. How the resident and the supervisor disappoint each other. *American Journal of Psychotherapy,* 1971, *25,* 272-283.

CHODOFF, P. Supervision of psychotherapy with videotapes: Pros and cons. *American Journal of Psychiatry,* 1972, *128,* 819-823.

COLEMAN, J. V. The teaching of basic psychotherapy. *American Journal of Orthopsychiatry,* 1947, *17,* 622-627.

COHEN, R. J., & DEBETZ, B. Responsive supervision of the psychiatric resident and clinical psychology intern. *American Journal of Psychoanalysis,* 1977, *37,* 51-64.

COTTON, P. G., & PRUETT, K. D. The affective experience of residency training in community psychiatry. *American Journal of Psychiatry,* 1975, *132,* 267-270.

DE BELL, D. E. A critical digest of the literature on psychoanalytic supervision. *Journal of the American Psychoanalytic Association,* 1963, *11,* 564-575.

DE LA TORRE, J., & APPELBAUM, A. Use and misuse of cliches in clinical supervision. *Archives of General Psychiatry,* 1974, *31,* 302-306.

DEROSIS, H. A. Supervision of the first year psychiatric resident: Part 2. *Psychiatric Quarterly,* 1971, *45,* 134-141.

DEUTSCHBERGER, P., MATTHEWS, W. M., POTTHARST, K., & UNDERWOOD, P. Training for professional function in clinical psychology. 3: Supervision in the field of work placement. *American Journal of Orthopsychiatry,* 1951, *21,* 319-324.

EBAUGH, F. G. Graduate teaching of psychiatry through individual supervision. *American Journal of Psychiatry,* 1950, *107,* 274-278.

EKSTEIN, R., & WALLERSTEIN, R. S. *The teaching and learning of psychotherapy.* New York: International Universities Press, 1972.

EMCH, M. The social context of supervision. *International Journal of Psychoanalysis,* 1955, *36,* 298-306.

ESCOLL, P. J., & WOOD, H. P. Perception in residency training: Methods and problems. *American Journal of Psychiatry,* 1967, *124,* 91-96.

FLEMING, J., & BENEDEK, T. *Psychoanalytic supervision.* New York: Grune & Stratton, 1966.

FLIESS, R. Autopsic encumbrance. *International Journal of Psychoanalysis,* 1954, *35,* 8-12.

FORD, E. S. Being and becoming a psychotherapist: The search for identity. *American Journal of Psychotherapy,* 1963, *17,* 472-482.

FRIED, F. E., DOHERTY, E. G., & COYNE, L. Psychiatric residents: A survey of training needs, satisfaction and social attitudes. *American Journal of Psychiatry,* 1973, *130,* 1342-1345.

FRIJLING-SCHREUDER, E. C. On individual supervision. *International Journal of Psychoanalysis,* 1970, *51,* 363-370.

GAONI, B., & NEUMANN, M. Supervision from the point of view of the supervisee. *American Journal of Psychotherapy,* 1974, *31,* 108-114.

GARDNER, G. E. Problems of supervision and training in clinical psychology. Round Table, 1952. 2. The supervision of psychotherapy. *American Journal of Orthopsychiatry,* 1953, *23,* 328-331.

GLAUBER, I. P. A deterrent in the study and practice of medicine. *Psychoanalytic Quarterly,* 1953, *22,* 381-412.

GREBEN, S. E., MARKSON, E. R., & SADAVOY, J. Resident and supervisor: An examination of their relationship. *Canadian Psychiatric Association Journal,* 1973, *18,* 473-479.

GRINBERG, L. The problems of supervision in psychoanalytic supervision. *International Journal of Psychoanalysis,* 1970, *51,* 371-383.

GROTJAHN, M. The role of identification in psychiatric and psychoanalytic training. *Psychiatry,* 1949, *12,* 141-151.

HALLECK, S. L., & WOODS, S. M. Emotional problems of psychiatric residents. *Psychiatry,* 1962, *25,* 339-346.

HAWTHORNE, L. Games supervisors play. *Social Work,* 1975, *20,* 179-183.

HESS, A. K. (Ed.) *Psychotherapy supervision.* New York: Wiley, 1980.

HOLT, R. R. Personality growth in psychiatric residents. *Archives of Neurology and Psychiatry,* 1959, *81,* 203-215.

HORA, T. Contribution to the phenomenology of the supervisory process. *American Journal of Psychotherapy,* 1957, *11,* 769-773.

KADUSHIN, A. Games people play in supervision. *Social Work,* 1968, *13,* 23-32.

KASS, W., & RICHMAN, J. Psychologists' participation in pre-clinical teaching of psychiatry to medical students. *Journal of Nervous and Mental Disease,* 1961, *132,* 109-116.

KELL, B., & MUELLER, W. *Impact and change: A study of counseling relationships.* New York: Appleton-Century-Crofts, 1966.

KUBIE, L. S. Research into the process of supervision in psychoanalysis. *Psychoanalysis Quarterly,* 1958, *27,* 226-236.

LEBOVICI, S. The technical remarks on the supervision of psychoanalytic treatment. *International Journal of Psychoanalysis,* 1970, *51,* 385-392.

LEDAKOWICH, A. Is one specialist on a team responsible for the negligence of another? *Resident and Staff Physician,* June 1976, p. 28s.

LEDAKOWICH, A. Shift the blame onto the surgeon? *Resident and Staff Physician,* June 1976, p. 18.

LEICHTY, M., & SEAGULL, A. A clinical dimension for training psychotherapists. *The Clinical Psychologist,* Winter 1968, pp. 76-80.

LEWIN, K. K. Psychiatric supervision by direct observation. *Journal of Medical Education,* 1966, *4,* 860-864.

LOWER, R. B. Countertransference resistances in the supervisory situation. *American Journal of Psychiatry,* 1972, *129,* 156-160.

MEERLOO, J. A. Some psychological processes in supervision of therapists. *American Journal of Psychotherapy,* 1952, *6,* 467-470.

MODLIN, H. Training to become a psychiatrist. *Journal of Kansas Medical Society,* 1963, *64,* 2-5.

MOLNAR, E. T., KENT, J. T., & HOUSER, A. C. Role playing in preparing junior medical students for psychiatric interviewing. *Small Group Behavior,* 1973, *4,* 157-162.

MOWRER, O. H. Training in psychotherapy. *Journal of Consulting Psychology,* 1951, *15,* 274-277.

NASH, K. B., & MITTLEFEHLDT, V. A. Supervision and the emerging professional. *American Journal of Orthopsychiatry,* 1975, *45,* 93-101.

NEMIAH, J. C. Supervision: Teaching or psychotherapy? *Canada's Mental Health Supplement,* 1971, *66,* 3-6.

NOTMAN, M., & NADELSON, C. Medicine: A career conflict for women. *American Journal of Psychiatry,* 1973, *130,* 1123-1127.

NUNBERG, H. *Practice and theory psychoanalysis.* Nervous and Mental Disease Monographs, 1948.

ORNSTEIN, P. H. The sorcerer's apprentice: The initial phase of training and education in psychiatry. *Comprehensive Psychiatry,* 1968, *9,* 293-315.

PASNAU, R., & BAGLEY, S. Personality changes in the first year of psychiatric residency training. *American Journal of Psychiatry,* 1971, *128,* 78-84.

ROSENBAUM, M. Problems in supervision of psychiatric residents in psychotherapy. *Archives of Neurological Psychiatry,* 1953, *69,* 43-48.

ROSENBLATT, A., & MAYER, J. E. Objectionable supervisory styles: Students' views. *Social Work,* 1975, *20,* 184-189.

RUSSELL, A. T., PASNAU, R. O., & TAINTOR, Z. C. Emotional problems of residents in psychiatry. *American Journal of Psychiatry,* 1975, *132,* 263-267.

RYAN, J. H. Teaching by videotape. *Mental Hospitals,* 1965, *16,* 101-104.

RYAN, J. H., & BUDNER, S. The impact of television: An evaluation of the use of videotapes in psychiatric training. *American Journal of Psychiatry,* 1970, *126,* 1397-1403.

SAGALL, E. L., & REED, B. C. The liability of attendings and chiefs. *Resident and Staff Physician,* March 1975, pp. 77; 80; 81; 85; 86; 89; 92.

SCANLON, J. Physician to student: The crisis of psychiatric residency training. *American Journal of Psychiatry,* 1972, *128,* 1107–1111.

SCHER, M. E., RIPLEY, H. S., & JOHNSON, M. H. Complexities of the clinical psychiatric teaching institution. *Psychiatry,* 1971, *34,* 419–424.

SCHLESSINGER, N. Supervision of psychotherapy. *Archives of General Psychiatry,* 1966, *15,* 129–134.

SCHUSTER, D. B., & FREEMAN, E. N. Supervision of the resident's initial interview. *Archives of General Psychiatry,* 1970, *23,* 516–523.

SEARLES, H. F. The informational value of the supervisor's emotional experiences. *Psychiatry,* 1955, *18,* 135–146.

SHARAF, M. R., & LEVINSON, D. J. The quest for omnipotence. *Psychiatry,* 1964, *27,* 135–149.

SOLNIT, A. J. Learning from psychoanalytic supervision. *International Journal of Psychoanalysis,* 1970, *51,* 359–362.

STEELE, T. E. Psychiatric emergency services: Their relationship to residency training and supervision. *Social Psychiatry,* 1972, *7,* 75–81.

STEIN, S. P., KARASU, T. B., CHARLES, E. S., et al. Supervision of the initial interview. *Archives of General Psychiatry*, 1975, *32*, 265–268.

SZASZ, T. S. Three problems in contemporary psychoanalytic training. *Archives of General Psychiatry*, 1949, *19*, 36–51.

SZUREK, S. A. Remarks on training for psychotherapy. *American Journal of Orthopsychiatry,* 1949, *19,* 36–51.

THOMPSON, C. A study of the emotional climate of psychoanalytic institutes. *Psychiatry,* 1958, *21,* 45–51.

TISCHLER, G. L. The beginning resident and supervision. *Archives of General Psychiatry,* 1968, *19,* 418–422.

TODD, W. E., & PINE, J. Peer supervision of individual psychotherapy. *American Journal of Psychiatry,* 1968, *125,* 780–784.

WAGNER, F. F. Supervision of psychotherapy. *American Journal of Psychotherapy,* 1957, *11,* 759–768.

WEISS, S. S., & FLEMING, J. Evaluation of progress in supervision. *Psychoanalytic Quarterly,* 1975, *44,* 191–205.

WINSEAD, D. K., BONOVITZ, J. S., GALE, M. S., & EVANS, J. W. Resident peer supervision of psychotherapy. *American Journal of Psychiatry*, 1974, *131*, 318–321.

WOLBERG, L. R. Supervision of the psychotherapeutic process. *American Journal of Psychiatry*, 1951, *5*, 147–171.

WORBY, C. M. (Moderator). The first year of psychiatric residence—A normative professional identity crisis. Presented at the 124th Annual Meeting of the American Psychiatric Association, Boston, May 13–17, 1968.

UNGERLEIDER, J. That most difficult year. *American Journal of Psychiatry,* 1971, *128,* 79–84.

General Index

Major legal cases are indexed in full references in **bold** and *italic* typefaces; page numbers in **bold** typeface indicate the pages on which the court cases appear.

Index of Statutes, Regulations, and Other Materials